참 토익
COMPLETE
800+

LC+RC

저자 김진영

이화여자대학교 졸업
SMU–TESOL Certificate
University of Southern Queensland Applied Linguistic 석사 과정

(현) 해커스 인강 토익 LC 강사
(현) YBM Class 인강 LC 강사
(전) YBM e4u 어학원 종합반 1위 토익트레이너 LC 강사
(전) YBM e4u 어학원 대표 강좌 뻔뻔토익 LC 강사
(전) EBS lang 토익 강사

저서 한 권으로 끝내는 모질게 토익 LC + RC
　　　모질게 토익 ECONOMY LC 1000제
　　　모질게 토익 ECONOMY LC 종합서
　　　모질게 토익 기본서 LC

저자 강상진

이화여자대학교대학원 영어교육학 석사

(현) 해커스 인강 토익 RC 강사
(현) 대교 반보 AI 토익 시스템 콘텐츠 제공
(전) 해커스어학원 토익 RC 강사
(전) YBM 어학원 토익 RC 강사

참 토익
COMPLETE
800+ LC+RC

지은이 김진영, 강상진
펴낸이 정규도
펴낸곳 ㈜다락원

초판 1쇄 발행 2024년 6월 17일

편집 홍인표
디자인 김민지, 윤현주
이미지 출처 Shutterstock

다락원 경기도 파주시 문발로 211
내용 문의 (02)736-2031 내선 500
구입 문의 (02)736-2031 내선 250~252
Fax (02)732-2037
출판 등록 1977년 9월 16일 제406-2008-000007호
Copyright © 2024 김진영, 강상진

ISBN 978-89-277-8077-9 13740

www.darakwon.co.kr
다락원 홈페이지를 방문하시면 상세한 출판 정보와 함께 MP3 자료 등의
다양한 어학 정보를 얻으실 수 있습니다.

참 토익
COMPLETE
800⁺
LC+RC

다락원

머리말

교재를 개발하면서 가장 주안점을 둔 것은 이 책 한 권이 토익에서 핵심적인 문제 해결 능력을 향상시키기 위한 완벽한 도구가 될 수 있도록 하는 것이었습니다. 토익에서 목표로 하는 고득점을 얻기 위해서는 문제의 출제 의도를 정확하고 빠르게 파악하는 능력이 필수적입니다. 따라서, 저자들은 학습자들이 이러한 문제 해결 능력을 강화할 수 있도록 그동안 현장에서 쌓아왔던 노하우를 이 교재에 아낌없이 담았습니다.

특히 단기간에 목표 점수가 필요한 수험자들의 경우, 모든 내용을 한꺼번에 공부하려다 많은 부분들을 놓치고 제대로 학습하지 않아서 점수가 정체되는 사례들을 많이 봐 왔습니다. 이 책은 핵심적인 내용들을 모두 담고 있어서, 목표하는 점수를 단기간에 달성할 수 있게 해 주는 전략서입니다.

LC 섹션의 경우 현장 강의에서 수많은 수험자들에게 도움이 되었던 문제 유형 분석 및 풀이법이 제시되어 있으며, 각 유닛마다 실제 시험과 유사한 미니 테스트가 수록되어 있습니다. 교재에서 제시하는 문제 풀이 전략을 따르고 미니 테스트를 통해 실전에 대비한다면, 200~300점대에서 머물러 있는 학습자들도 단기간에 400점대로 진입이 가능할 것입니다. 어려워진 LC로 인해 좌절하고 토익시험 준비에 너무 많은 시간을 쏟느라 지친 수험자들에게 이 책이 LC 고득점의 전략적 길잡이가 되기를 바랍니다.

RC 섹션의 경우 문장 구조 파악과 해석 능력을 충분히 키운 뒤, 이를 바탕으로 문제 풀이 스킬을 익히는 것이 가장 효율적인 학습 방법입니다. 그러나 스킬을 먼저 익히고, 그 후에 해석에 집중하다 보면 점수가 오르지 않는 정체기에 빠지는 경우가 많습니다. 이 교재는 문장 구조 파악 능력과 문맥 이해력을 먼저 기르고, 그 이후에 문제를 효율적으로 해결할 수 있는 방식으로 구성되어 있습니다. LC와 마찬가지로, 유닛마다 실제 시험과 유사한 미니 테스트가 수록되어 있어서, 학습자들이 실제 시험에서 마주하게 될 다양한 유형의 문제에 대비할 수 있도록 했습니다. 또한, 해설에 제시된 문제 해결 방법을 통해 오답을 분석하고 개선한다면 RC에서 고득점을 달성할 수 있을 것입니다.

이 교재는 토익 문제 유형과 대비 방법을 철저히 분석하고 연구한 결과를 반영했습니다. 지금 바로 목표를 설정하고 이 교재를 충실히 활용한다면, 토익 준비에 경험이 있는 학습자는 물론, 토익을 처음 접하는 학습자도 고득점을 이룰 수 있을 것입니다. 여러분의 목표 달성을 진심으로 응원합니다!

김진영, 강상진

목차

Listening Comprehension

Reading Comprehension

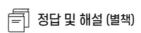 정답 및 해설 (별책)

Listening Comprehension

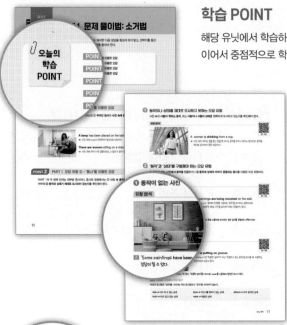

학습 POINT

해당 유닛에서 학습하게 될 파트별 문제 풀이법이 소개되어 있습니다.
이어서 중점적으로 학습하게 될 포인트가 정리되어 있습니다.

유형 분석

각 유닛에서 학습하는 문제 유형, 또는 오답 유형을 분석할 수 있는 '유형 분석' 코너가 구성되어 있습니다. QR 코드를 스캔하여 유형 분석의 음원을 들은 다음, 상세한 설명을 통해 해당 유형을 이해할 수 있습니다.

Daily VOCA

해당 유닛에서 학습한 파트와 관련하여 자주 출제되는 어휘와 예문이 정리되어 있습니다.
수록된 QR 코드를 통해 어휘와 예문을 들으면서 빈출 표현을 학습할 수 있습니다.

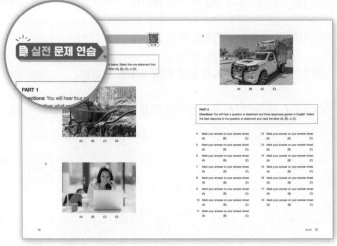

실전 문제 연습

각 유닛이 끝날 때마다 실전과 유사한 LC 미니 테스트가 수록되어 있습니다. 실제 시험의 약 1/3 정도 분량의 LC 미니 테스트를 매일매일 풀어 보면서 실전 감각을 끌어올릴 수 있습니다.

Reading Comprehension

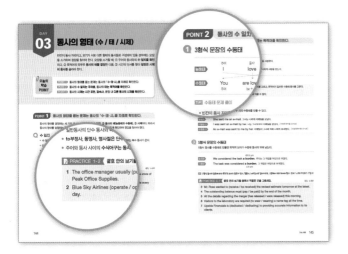

문법 정리

토익에 꼭 필요한 핵심 문법 사항들이 빠짐없이
정리되어 있습니다. 각각의 문법 사항들과 관련하여
꼭 알아야 하는 포인트가 제시되어 있습니다.

PRACTICE TEST

PRACICE TEST를 통해 학습한 문법 사항을 제대로
이해하고 있는지 확인할 수 있습니다.

Daily VOCA

각각의 유닛마다 토익 RC에 자주 출제되는 어휘들이 정리되어 있습니다.
각 어휘들의 사용 예시와 함께 유의어들도 제시되어 있습니다.

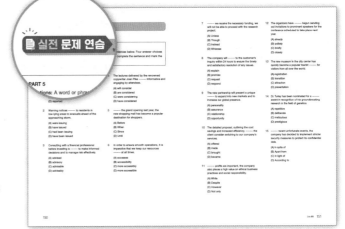

실전 문제 연습

각 유닛이 끝날 때마다 RC 미니 테스트가 수록되어
있습니다. 실전 난이도의 RC 미니 테스트를 풀어 보
면서 고득점을 얻기 위한 충분한 연습을 할 수 있습
니다.

TOEIC은 Test of English for International Communication의 약자로서, 영어를 모국어로 사용하지 않는 사람이 국제 환경에서 생활을 하거나 업무를 수행할 때 필요한 실용 영어 능력을 평가하는 시험입니다. 현재 한국과 일본은 물론 전 세계 약 60개 국가에서 연간 4백만 명 이상의 수험생들이 토익에 응시하고 있으며, 수험 결과는 채용 및 승진, 해외 파견 근무자 선발 등 다양한 목적으로 활용되고 있습니다.

시험 구성

구성	PART	내용		문항 수	시간	배점
Listening Comprehension	1	사진 묘사		6	45분	495점
	2	질의-응답		25		
	3	대화문		39		
	4	담화문		30		
Reading Comprehension	5	단문 공란 채우기		30	75분	495점
	6	장문 공란 채우기		16		
	7	독해	단일 지문	29		
			복수 지문	25		
Total				200문제	120분	990점

출제 분야

토익의 목적은 일상 생활과 업무 수행에 필요한 영어 능력을 평가하는 것이기 때문에 출제 범위도 이를 벗어나지 않습니다. 비즈니스와 관련된 주제를 다루는 경우라도 전문적인 지식을 요구하지는 않으며, 아울러 특정 국가나 문화에 대한 이해도 요구하지 않습니다. 구체적인 출제 범위는 아래와 같습니다.

일반적인 비즈니스 (General Business)	계약, 협상, 마케팅, 영업, 기획, 콘퍼런스 관련
사무 (Office)	회의, 편지, 회람, 전화, 팩스 및 이메일, 사무 기기 및 사무 가구 관련
인사 (Personnel)	구직, 채용, 승진, 퇴직, 급여, 포상 관련
재무 (Finance and Budgeting)	투자, 세금, 회계, 은행 업무 관련
생산 (Manufacturing)	제조, 플랜트 운영, 품질 관리 관련
개발 (Corporate Development)	연구 조사, 실험, 신제품 개발 관련
구매 (Purchasing)	쇼핑, 주문, 선적, 결제 관련
외식 (Dining Out)	오찬, 만찬, 회식, 리셉션 관련
건강 (Health)	병원, 진찰, 의료 보험 관련
여행 (Travel)	교통 수단, 숙박 시설, 터미널 및 공항에서의 안내 사항, 예약 및 취소 관련
엔터테인먼트 (Entertainment)	영화, 연극, 음악, 미술, 전시 관련
주택 / 법인 재산 (Housing / Corporate Property)	건설, 부동산 매매 및 임대, 전기 및 가스 서비스 관련

Listening
Comprehension

DAY 01 PART 1 문제 풀이법: 소거법

PART 1에서는 선택지를 듣고 모두 해석한 다음 정답을 찾으려 하지 말고, 선택지를 들으면서 오답을 하나씩 제거하면서 문제를 풀어야 한다.

오늘의 학습 POINT

> **POINT 1** PART 1 오답 유형 ① - '주어'를 이용한 오답
> **POINT 2** PART 1 오답 유형 ② - '동사'를 이용한 오답
> **POINT 3** PART 1 오답 유형 ③ - '발음'을 이용한 오답
> **POINT 4** PART 1 오답 유형 ④ - '위치'를 이용한 오답
> **POINT 5** PART 1 그 외의 오답 유형

POINT 1 PART 1 오답 유형 ① - '주어'를 이용한 오답

PART 1의 선택지는 모두 명사인 주어로 시작하는데 ① **주어인 명사가 사진 속에 존재하는지**, 그리고 ② **주어의 수 일치가 맞는지** 확인해야 한다.

유형 분석

01-01

A lamp has been placed on the table.
➜ 사진 속에 lamp가 존재하지 않으므로 오답이다.

There are women sitting on a chair.
➜ 사진 속에 여자가 한 명뿐이므로, 수 일치가 맞지 않는 오답이다.

POINT 2 PART 1 오답 유형 ② - '동사'를 이용한 오답

PART 1의 두 번째 단어는 대부분 동사이다. 동사와 관련해서는 ① **사진 속 동작이나 상태를 정확히 묘사하는지** 여부와 ② **동작과 상태가 제대로 묘사되어 있는지**를 확인해야 한다.

① 동작이나 상태를 제대로 묘사하지 못하는 오답 유형

사진 속의 **사람이 취하는 동작**, 또는 **사람이나 사물의 상태**를 정확하게 묘사하고 있는지를 확인해야 한다.

유형 분석

A woman is **drinking** from a cup.

→ 사진 속의 여자는 컵을 들고 있을 뿐 마시는 동작을 취하고 있지는 않으므로, 동작을 제대로 묘사하지 못한 오답이다.

② '동작'과 '상태'를 구별해야 하는 오답 유형

① **동작이 없는 사진에서 동작을 언급**하거나 ② **동작과 상태의 의미가 혼동되는 동사**를 이용한 오답 유형이다.

❶ 동작이 없는 사진

유형 분석

Some paintings **are being mounted** on the wall.

→ 'be being p.p.' 형태의 진행형 수동태는 '동작'을 묘사하는 표현이므로, 걸려 있는 '상태'인 해당 사진을 묘사하기에는 적절하지 않다.

> **cf.** 'Some paintings **have been hung** on the wall.'과 같이 완료 수동태로 묘사하는 경우 상태를 설명하는 표현이 되어 정답이 될 수 있다.

❷ 동작과 상태의 의미가 혼동되는 동사

유형 분석

A man **is putting on** glasses.

→ 'putting on'은 '착용한 상태'가 아닌 '착용하고 있는 동작'을 묘사할 때 사용하는 표현이므로 오답이 된다.

> **cf.** 'A man **is wearing** glasses.'와 같이, '착용한 상태'를 나타내는 wear를 사용해야 알맞은 묘사가 된다.

TIP! 상태를 나타내는 주요 동사

아래의 동사들은 '상태'를 나타내는 주요 동사들로서, '동작'을 의미하지 않는다.

ride → 이미 타고 있는 상태	face → 어딘가를 향하고 있는 상태	attend → 이미 참석한 상태
hold → 이미 잡고 있는 상태	wear → 착용한 상태	

PART 1에서는 「work vs. walk」와 같이 들었을 때 혼동하기 쉬운 단어를 이용한 발음의 오답이 자주 등장한다. 따라서, 단어의 발음을 정확하게 인식할 수 있도록 받아쓰기 연습을 해야 한다.

유형 분석

A man is folding some shirts.

→ hold와 발음이 혼동되는 fold를 이용한 오답이다. 남자는 셔츠를 들고 있을 뿐 접고 있지는 않으므로 오답이 된다.

TIP! 발음이 유사한 단어

아래의 단어들은 자주 출제되는 발음이 유사한 동사들이다.

hold 잡다 – fold 접다	work 일하다 – walk 걷다	sit 앉다 – set 놓다
read 읽다 – lead 안내하다	ramp 경사로 – lamp 램프, 등	file 파일 – tile 타일
copy 복사하다 – coffee 커피	write 쓰다 – ride 타다	globe 지구본 – glove 장갑

사람이 등장하지 않는 사진의 경우, 위치를 잘못 묘사한 오답이 자주 출제된다. PART 1에서 위치를 묘사하는 표현은 항상 문장의 마지막에 전치사구로 등장하기 때문에, 문장을 끝까지 정확하게 듣는 것이 중요하다.

유형 분석

There are some flowers on the table.

→ 테이블이 아니라 주방 조리대 위에 꽃이 놓여있는 모습이므로 'There are some flowers on the counter.'가 정답이 된다.

cf. counter는 우리에게 익숙한 '계산대'라는 표현 이외에도 '주방 조리대'나 '작업대'라는 의미로도 사용된다.

PART 1에서는 위의 4가지 핵심 오답 이외에 아래와 같은 유형의 오답이 출제된다.

▸ 사진 속에 등장하지 않는 사물을 언급하는 경우 (주어 이외의 사물)
▸ 객관적으로 판단할 수 없는 상황을 언급하는 경우 (색깔, 시간 등)

어휘	예문
stroll 걷다, 산책하다 = walk	A woman is **strolling** in the park. 한 여자가 공원을 산책하는 중이다.
bend 굽히다 = lean	A man is **bending** over to pick up the box. 남자가 상자를 들어 올리기 위해 허리를 구부리고 있는 중이다. **cf.** lean은 주로 '기대다'의 의미로 사용되지만, 접촉의 전치사가 아닌 over, forward 등과 쓰이는 경우 '굽히다'의 의미로도 사용된다.
squat 쪼그리고 앉다 = sit, crouch	A woman is **squatting** on the beach. 한 여자가 바닷가에 쪼그리고 앉아 있다.
stare 보다 = look, gaze, glance, view	A man is **staring** at his laptop. 한 남자가 그의 노트북을 보고 있는 중이다.
grasp 잡고 있다 = hold, grip, grab	A man is **grasping** his umbrella. 한 남자가 우산을 잡고 있다.
adjust 조정하다, 조절하다	A woman is **adjusting** her glasses. 한 여자가 안경을 조정하고 있는 중이다.
wheel (바퀴 달린 것을) 밀다 = push, move	A woman is **wheeling** a cart. 한 여자가 카트를 밀고 있는 중이다.
study 보다	A woman is **studying** a menu. 한 여자가 메뉴를 보고 있는 중이다.
greet 인사하다 = shake hands	They're **greeting** each other. 사람들이 서로 인사를 나누고 있는 중이다. **cf.** 인사가 항상 악수하는 것을 의미하는 것은 아니지만, 토익 시험에서 greeting은 주로 악수하는 모습으로 등장한다.
face 향하고 있다	A woman is **facing** the window. 여자가 유리창을 향해 있다. **cf.** face는 '마주보다'라는 의미이지만, PART 1에서는 어딘가를 향하고 있을 때 사용한다.
gather 모여 있다 = form, assemble	Some women have **gathered** around a table. 여자들이 테이블 주변에 모여 있다.
applaud 박수치다 = clap	The audience is **applauding**. 청중들이 박수를 치고 있는 중이다.
paddle 노를 젓다 = row	A woman is **paddling** a boat. 한 여자가 보트를 노 젓고 있는 중이다.
trim 다듬다 = cut	A man is **trimming** the bushes. 한 남자가 덤불을 다듬고 있는 중이다.
place 놓아 두다 = lay	A woman is **placing** a book on the table. 한 여자가 책을 탁자에 놓아 두고 있는 중이다.

PART 1

Directions: You will hear four statements about the picture below. Select the one statement that best describes what you see in the picture and mark the letter (A), (B), (C), or (D).

1

(A)   (B)   (C)   (D)

2

(A)   (B)   (C)   (D)

3

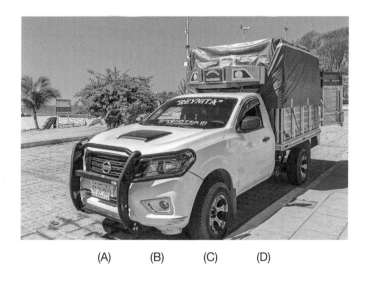

(A)   (B)   (C)   (D)

PART 2

Directions: You will hear a question or statement and three responses spoken in English. Select the best response to the question or statement and mark the letter (A), (B), or (C).

---

4   Mark your answer on your answer sheet.

    (A)   (B)   (C)

5   Mark your answer on your answer sheet.

    (A)   (B)   (C)

6   Mark your answer on your answer sheet.

    (A)   (B)   (C)

7   Mark your answer on your answer sheet.

    (A)   (B)   (C)

8   Mark your answer on your answer sheet.

    (A)   (B)   (C)

9   Mark your answer on your answer sheet.

    (A)   (B)   (C)

10   Mark your answer on your answer sheet.

    (A)   (B)   (C)

11   Mark your answer on your answer sheet.

    (A)   (B)   (C)

12   Mark your answer on your answer sheet.

    (A)   (B)   (C)

13   Mark your answer on your answer sheet.

    (A)   (B)   (C)

14   Mark your answer on your answer sheet.

    (A)   (B)   (C)

15   Mark your answer on your answer sheet.

    (A)   (B)   (C)

16   Mark your answer on your answer sheet.

    (A)   (B)   (C)

17   Mark your answer on your answer sheet.

    (A)   (B)   (C)

18   Mark your answer on your answer sheet.

    (A)   (B)   (C)

Directions: You will hear some conversations between two or more people. You will be asked to answer three questions about what the speakers say in each conversation. Select the best response to each question and mark the letter (A), (B), (C), or (D).

19 Who most likely is the man?

(A) A university student
(B) An architect
(C) A school board member
(D) A technology expert

20 What are the speakers mainly discussing?

(A) A technological upgrade
(B) A science fair
(C) A construction project
(D) An educational program

21 What does Amy Chen inquire about?

(A) Classroom sizes
(B) Internet access
(C) Educational content
(D) Technical requirements

22 What problem is being discussed?

(A) A construction delay
(B) Not enough parking space
(C) A broken security camera
(D) A meeting cancelation

23 What does the man mean when he says, "Tell me about it"?

(A) He is also annoyed.
(B) He wants to know more details.
(C) He thinks it's a great chance.
(D) He hasn't hear the news.

24 What will the woman do on Friday?

(A) Install equipment
(B) Attend a meeting
(C) Go on a business trip
(D) Carry out interviews

25 What did the women do last month?

(A) Visited a factory
(B) Went to a conference
(C) Transferred to another branch
(D) Traveled to another country

26 Why does the man thank Judy?

(A) Because she gave him a list of restaurants
(B) Because she agrees to give him a recommendation
(C) Because she recommended a hotel to him
(D) Because she plans to give him a ride

27 What will the man probably do next?

(A) Attend a conference
(B) Check his e-mail
(C) Make a phone call
(D) Visit a hotel

PART 4

Directions: You will hear some talks given by a single speaker. You will be asked to answer three questions about what the speaker says in each talk. Select the best response to each question and mark the letter (A), (B), (C), or (D).

28   Where most likely is the speaker?

(A) At a café

(B) At an appliance store

(C) At a trade show

(D) At an advertising company

29   What does the speaker say is special about the new machine?

(A) It comes in various designs.

(B) It has a range of drink options.

(C) It is inexpensive.

(D) It is durable.

30   What does the speaker offer the listeners?

(A) Complimentary samples

(B) A coffee maker

(C) Free tickets

(D) A list of products

Bristol Library Construction Project Schedule

April	May	June	July
Book section	Public Computer Areas	Digital Library Center	Periodical Section

31   What will happen this weekend?

(A) A renovation project will begin.

(B) Additional parking spaces will be built.

(C) A building will be completed.

(D) Part of a property will open.

32   Look at the graphic. Which facility can provide computer-based library services?

(A) Book section

(B) Public computer areas

(C) Digital library center

(D) Periodical section

33   What will the listeners hear next?

(A) Music

(B) A weather forecast

(C) A traffic report

(D) A news update

DAY

02 PART 1 고난도 문제 풀이법

토익 응시자들이 PART 1에서 자주 틀리는 고난도의 문제 유형은 ① **사람이 등장하지 않는 사진** ② **진행형 수동태** ③ **고난도의 어휘, 또는 다의어가 등장하는 유형**이다.

오늘의 학습 POINT

POINT 1   PART 1 고난도 유형 ① - 사람이 등장하지 않는 사진
POINT 2   PART 1 고난도 유형 ② - 진행형 수동태
POINT 3   PART 1 고난도 유형 ③ - 고난도의 어휘, 또는 다의어의 등장

POINT 1   PART 1 고난도 유형 ① - 사람이 등장하지 않는 사진

사람 없이 사물만 등장하는 사진의 경우 두 가지를 주의해야 한다. ① **동작이 언급되는 경우에는 오답이 된다.** ② **전치사구에서 언급하는 위치와 사진 속 사물의 위치가 일치하는 않으면 오답이 된다.** 전치사구는 문장의 마지막에 나오기 때문에, 항상 문장을 끝까지 들어야 한다.

유형 분석

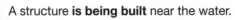

A structure **is being built** near the water.

→ 건물이 이미 건설되어 있으므로 being이 들어간 '동작 묘사'는 오답이 된다. structure 는 '구조물'이라는 의미이지만, 건물, 다리 등에 광범위하게 사용된다.

유형 분석

There are boats **on the beach**.

→ 사진의 배들은 물 위에 떠 있으므로 전치사구 'on the beach'는 위치를 잘못 묘사한 오답이다.

'be + being + p.p.' 형태의 진행형 수동태는 동작을 묘사하는 표현으로서, 이는 'p.p.'에서 언급된 동사가 사진 속에 동작으로 나타나야만 정답이 될 수 있다.

유형 분석

02-03

The floor **has been mopped**.

➜ 바닥을 청소하고 있는 '동작'을 묘사해야 하므로 'The floor is being mopped.'와 같이 진행형 수동태로 표현해야 한다.

TIP! been과 being의 구별

진행형 수동태에서 가장 주의해야 할 것은 완료 수동태인 'been + p.p.'와 구별하는 것이다. 'been'의 경우 약하게 발음되지만, 'being'의 경우 길고 강하게 발음되므로 강세를 통해 구별해야 한다.

유형 분석

02-04

The floor **is being cleaned**.

➜ 사진 속에 청소를 하고 있는 사람은 보이지 않으므로, 'being + p.p.'를 사용해서 '동작' 으로 표현할 수 없다.

TIP! '상태'를 묘사하는 동사

언제나 '상태'만을 묘사하는 동사의 경우 어떤 형태를 취하더라도 '상태'를 의미한다. 아래의 동사들은 진행형 수동태 형태로 '상태'를 묘사 할 때 쓰이는 대표적인 동사들로서, 사람이 등장하지 않는 사진에서도 정답이 될 수 있다.

being displayed 진열된 상태이다	**being cast** (그림자 등이) 드리워진 상태이다
being held 개최된 상태이다	**being ridden** 탑승한 상태이다
being shown 보여지고 있는 상태이다	**being exhibited** 전시된 상태이다

1 고난도 동사

02-05

decorate: 놓여있는 상태를 묘사	**extend: 이어져 있는 모습을 묘사**

A sign **decorates** a building's roof.
간판이 건물의 지붕에 있다.

A hose has been **extended** from a car to a firefighter.
호스가 차에서 소방관에게로 이어져 있다.

span: 가로지르다	**suspend: 단단히 고정되어 있다**

A structure **spans** the waterway.
구조물이 물길을 가로 질러 뻗어 있다.

A light fixture is **suspended** from the ceiling.
조명이 천장에 고정되어 있다.

shade: 그늘지게 하다, 빛을 가리다	**separate / divide: 나누다**

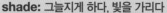

An umbrella is **shading** a table.
파라솔이 테이블을 그늘지게 하고 있다.

The steps are **divided** by railings.
계단이 난간으로 나뉘어 있다.

crouch: 쭈그리다, 쭈그리고 앉다	adjust: 조정하다, 조절하다

The woman is **crouching** down near a tent.
한 여자가 텐트 옆에 쭈그리고 앉아 있다.

A man is **adjusting** his glasses.
한 남자가 안경을 조정하고 있는 중이다.

tack: 압정으로 고정시키다	prune: 나무를 가지치기 하다

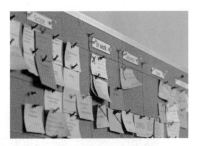 

Some memos have been **tacked** to a board.
메모들이 게시판에 압정으로 고정되어 있다.

cf. pin 핀으로 꽂다, 고정시키다

A man is **pruning** trees.
한 남자가 나무를 가지치기하고 있는 중이다.

undergo: (변화를) 겪다	detach: 떼다, 분리하다

A building is **undergoing** some construction work.
한 건물이 건설 공사 중이다.

A man is **detaching** the cables.
한 남자가 케이블을 분리하고 있는 중이다.

② 다의어

두 가지 이상의 의미를 가지고 있는 동사가 들릴 경우에는 어떤 의미로 사용되었는지 정확하게
파악해야 한다. 동일한 단어가 동사와 명사로 모두 사용되는 경우도 있다.

sit: 앉아 있다 / 놓여 있다

A chair is **sitting** next to the table.
의자가 테이블 옆에 놓여 있다.

The woman is **sitting** on the chair.
여자가 의자에 앉아 있다.

rest: 쉬다 / 놓여 있다, 놓아 두다

The woman is **resting** on the bench.
여자가 벤치에서 쉬고 있다.

A bicycle is **resting** next to the bench.
자전거가 벤치 옆에 놓여 있다.

run: 달리다 / 이어져 있다

Some people are **running** along the
path.
사람들이 길을 따라 달리고 있다.

A road is **running** along the river.
길은 강을 따라 이어져 있다.

lead: 진행하다, 이끌다 / (~로) 나 있다

The man is **leading** a workshop.
남자는 워크샵을 진행 중이다.

The path **leads** to the buildings.
길은 건물쪽으로 나 있다.

pull: 당기다 / (차를) 대다

The woman is **pulling** a suitcase.
여자가 가방을 당기고 있다.

Some cars are **pulled** up near the curb.
차들이 연석 가까이에 세워져 있다.

board: 게시판 / 탑승하다

They are looking at a **board**.
두 사람이 게시판을 바라보고 있는 중이다.

Some passengers are **boarding** an airplane.
몇몇 탑승객들이 비행기에 탑승하고 있는 중이다.

어휘	예문
workstation 작업장; 작업대 = work cubicle	A woman is arranging a **workstation**. 한 여자가 작업 공간을 정리하고 있다.
waterway 수로 = river, stream	The bridge spans the **waterway**. 다리가 수로를 가로지르고 있다.
produce 농작물	Some **produce** is being displayed. 농산물이 진열되어 있다.
light fixture 조명기구	A **light fixture** is hanging above the table. 조명기구가 테이블 위에 달려 있다.
bush 덤불, 관목 = shrub, hedge	There are **bushes** near the house. 집 근처에 덤불이 있다.
rake 갈퀴; 갈퀴질하다	A **rake** is propped against the tree. 갈퀴 하나가 나무에 기대어져 있다.
construction material 건축 자재	**Construction materials** have been stacked. 건축 자재들이 쌓여 있다.
compartment 선반, 보관 장소	Some bags have been stored in the overhead **compartment**. 가방들이 머리 위 선반에 보관되어 있다.
ramp 경사로	A woman is walking down **a ramp**. 한 여자가 경사로를 따라 걸어가고 있는 중이다.
pavement 포장 도로	A cart has been left on the **pavement**. 카트 하나가 포장 도로 위에 남겨져 있다.
performer 공연자	A **performer** is playing a guitar. 공연자가 기타를 연주하고 있는 중이다.
structure 구조물	A **structure** overlooks the river. 구조물이 강을 내려다 보고 있다.
grass 잔디 = lawn	Chairs have been arranged on the **grass**. 잔디에 의자들이 배열되어 있다.
baked goods 제과 제품	**Baked goods** are on display. 제과 제품들이 진열되어 있다.
container 용기, 컨테이너	**Containers** are stacked on the table. 용기들이 테이블에 쌓여 있다.

정답 및 해설 p.008

02-08

PART 1

Directions: You will hear four statements about the picture below. Select the one statement that best describes what you see in the picture and mark the letter (A), (B), (C), or (D).

1

(A)　　　(B)　　　(C)　　　(D)

2

(A)　　　(B)　　　(C)　　　(D)

3

(A)   (B)   (C)   (D)

PART 2

Directions: You will hear a question or statement and three responses spoken in English. Select the best response to the question or statement and mark the letter (A), (B), or (C).

---

4 Mark your answer on your answer sheet.
    (A)   (B)   (C)

5 Mark your answer on your answer sheet.
    (A)   (B)   (C)

6 Mark your answer on your answer sheet.
    (A)   (B)   (C)

7 Mark your answer on your answer sheet.
    (A)   (B)   (C)

8 Mark your answer on your answer sheet.
    (A)   (B)   (C)

9 Mark your answer on your answer sheet.
    (A)   (B)   (C)

10 Mark your answer on your answer sheet.
    (A)   (B)   (C)

11 Mark your answer on your answer sheet.
    (A)   (B)   (C)

12 Mark your answer on your answer sheet.
    (A)   (B)   (C)

13 Mark your answer on your answer sheet.
    (A)   (B)   (C)

14 Mark your answer on your answer sheet.
    (A)   (B)   (C)

15 Mark your answer on your answer sheet.
    (A)   (B)   (C)

16 Mark your answer on your answer sheet.
    (A)   (B)   (C)

17 Mark your answer on your answer sheet.
    (A)   (B)   (C)

18 Mark your answer on your answer sheet.
    (A)   (B)   (C)

PART 3

Directions: You will hear some conversations between two or more people. You will be asked to answer three questions about what the speakers say in each conversation. Select the best response to each question and mark the letter (A), (B), (C), or (D).

19 Where does the man work?

(A) At an automobile repair shop
(B) At an automotive factory
(C) At a construction company
(D) At a car dealership

20 What does the woman ask about?

(A) Whether she should pay a fee
(B) How she can transfer some money
(C) Where she can buy a car
(D) How long a transfer will take

21 Why should the woman visit the Web site?

(A) To calculate fuel efficiency
(B) To figure out an amount of money
(C) To get a driver's license
(D) To find some contact information

22 What has the man volunteered to do today?

(A) Help lead an event
(B) Plan some workshops
(C) Assist with packaging some products
(D) Try out some new products

23 What does the woman ask the man to complete?

(A) An attendance sheet
(B) A specific form
(C) An employee contract
(D) A participant agreement

24 What will the man most likely do next?

(A) Meet some other participants
(B) Complete a form
(C) Review an employee schedule
(D) Take a tour

25 Who most likely are the speakers?

(A) Bakers
(B) Mechanics
(C) Accountants
(D) Florists

26 Look at the graphic. Which building does the man say he likes?

(A) Building 1
(B) Building 2
(C) Building 3
(D) Building 4

27 What does the man suggest doing?

(A) Visiting a realtor
(B) E-mailing a cost estimate
(C) Touring a property together
(D) Finding a parking space

PART 4

Directions: You will hear some talks given by a single speaker. You will be asked to answer three questions about what the speaker says in each talk. Select the best response to each question and mark the letter (A), (B), (C), or (D).

28 What is the main topic of this podcast?

(A) Cooking
(B) Gardening
(C) Sports
(D) Fashion

29 How often does the podcast broadcast?

(A) Once a week
(B) Three times a week
(C) Once a month
(D) Once a day

30 Who does the speaker thank?

(A) The listeners
(B) The guest experts
(C) The donors
(D) The writers

31 What is the topic of the event?

(A) Music
(B) Movies
(C) Books
(D) Paintings

32 What was Harlem known for in the 1920s?

(A) Its beautiful parks
(B) Its distinctive cuisine
(C) Its art and culture
(D) Its unique architecture

33 Why does the speaker say, "We did not anticipate such a large audience today"?

(A) To explain the reason for a problem
(B) To apologize for some technical difficulties
(C) To recommend going to a different event
(D) To introduce the main event

DAY 03 PART 2 문제 풀이법: 소거법

PART 2 문제를 풀 때는 '소거법'을 활용해야 한다. 오답을 하나씩 제거해서 정답을 남기는 소거법을 적용하기 위해서는 오답 유형을 정확히 알고 있어야 한다.

> **오늘의 학습 POINT**
>
> POINT 1 PART 2 오답 유형 ① - '발음'을 이용한 오답
> POINT 2 PART 2 오답 유형 ② - '구조'를 이용한 오답
> POINT 3 그 외의 오답 유형

POINT 1 PART 2 오답 유형 ① - '발음'을 이용한 오답

PART 2의 모든 문제는 음원만 듣고 풀어야 한다. 따라서, **질문과 선택지에 등장하는 단어와 '발음'이 같거나 비슷한 단어를 이용한 오답**이 자주 등장한다.

1 유사 발음 오답

질문의 단어와 발음이 같은 음절을 가지고 있거나 유사 발음 단어를 포함한 선택지는 대부분 오답이다.

유형 분석

Q Who are the main people featured in the **documentary**?

A I didn't review that **document**.

03 - 01

→ documentary와 document는 「documen」까지의 발음이 동일한 대표적인 유사 발음 오답이다.

2 다의어 오답

질문의 단어와 스펠링과 발음이 같지만 의미가 다른 단어를 포함한 선택지는 대부분 오답이다.

유형 분석

Q Did you **book** the flight?

A Oh, I love that **book**.

03 - 02

→ book이라는 단어가 질문에서는 '예약하다'로, 대답에서는 '책'으로 사용된 대표적인 다의어의 오답이다.

③ 동음이의어 오답

질문의 단어와 발음이 같지만 스펠링과 의미가 다른 단어를 포함한 선택지는 대부분 오답이다.

유형 분석

03 - 03

Q The meeting is at 8:00, **right**?

A You have to **write** down the note.

➔ 전혀 다른 단어인 right과 write의 발음이 동일하다는 것을 이용한 동음이의어의 오답 유형이다.

④ 파생어 오답

질문 속의 단어에서 파생된 단어를 포함한 선택지는 대부분 오답이다.

유형 분석

03 - 04

Q Have you ever been to a farmers' **market**?

A The success depends on its **marketing** strategy.

➔ marketing은 market에서 파생된 단어로서, 이는 전형적인 파생어를 이용한 오답 유형이다.

POINT 2 PART 2 오답 유형 ② - '구조'를 이용한 오답

PART 2에서 질문의 핵심은 주로 초반부에 집중되어 있다. 따라서, 질문의 첫 부분에 등장하는 **'시제', '주어'**, 또는 **'의문사'**와 일치하지 않는 「구조적인 오류」가 있는 선택지가 오답으로 자주 등장한다.

① 시제의 불일치

질문과 시제가 일치하지 않는 오답이 출제되는 경우가 많다. 특히, 부가의문문과 제안 의문문의 경우 시제를 잘 들어야 한다.

유형 분석

03 - 05

Q **Have** you **seen** Dr. Joo?

A I **will call** her tomorrow.

➔ 질문의 시제는 현재완료인데 답변의 시제는 미래이므로 정답이 아닐 가능성이 높다.

② 주어의 불일치

질문의 주어와 일치하지 않는 주어를 가지고 있는 선택지가 오답으로 출제되는 경우가 있다. 특히, 부가의문문과 제안 의문문 그리고 일반의문문의 경우 주어를 주의해서 들어야 한다.

유형 분석

Q Will **Shanda** visit tomorrow?

A **You** can visit me.

→ 질문의 주어는 3인칭인데 답변의 주어는 2인칭이므로 정답이 아닐 가능성이 높다.

> **cf.** 최근 난이도가 높은 유형에서는 질문과 주어가 일치하지 않는 응답이 정답으로 출제되는 경우도 있기 때문에, 주어가 일치하지 않는 응답이 항상 오답인 것은 아니다.

③ 의문사의 불일치

의문사 의문문의 경우, 질문 속의 의문사와 의미가 일치하는 정답을 골라야만 한다. 예를 들어, who 의문문의 정답이 되는 선택지는 사람이거나 그 사람을 설명하는 것이어야 한다.

유형 분석

Q **Where** is the meeting going to be held?

A It's on **Friday**.

→ 질문의 의문사는 '장소'를 의미하는 where인데 답변은 '시간'을 의미하므로 정답이 아닐 가능성이 높다.

POINT 3 — 그 외의 오답유형

> ▶ 의문사 의문문과 선택의문문에 대해서는 yes나 no로 대답할 수 없다.
>
> ▶ 명사만으로 답한 응답은 why 의문문, 평서문, 그리고 제안 의문문 문제에 대한 정답이 될 수 없다.
>
> ▶ 제안 의문문은 3인칭 응답을 좋아하지 않는다.
>
> ▶ 평서문은 전치사구 답변을 좋아하지 않는다.

03 - 08

어휘	예문
launch 출시 **lunch** 점심	The company plans to **launch** a new product next month. 회사는 다음 달에 새 제품을 출시할 계획입니다. Let's have **lunch** together at the café down the street. 거리 아래 카페에서 함께 점심을 먹어요.
read 읽다 **lead** 안내하다	I love to **read** books. 저는 책을 읽는 것을 좋아합니다. I find that reading books often **leads** to new ideas. 책을 읽는 것은 종종 새로운 아이디어로 이어진다는 것을 압니다.
copy 복사 **coffee** 커피	Please make a **copy** of this document for me. 이 문서의 복사본을 만들어 주세요. Didn't you buy a new **coffee** machine? 새로운 커피 머신을 사지 않았나요?
letter 편지 **ladder** 사다리	I received a **letter** from my grandmother today. 오늘 저는 할머니로부터 편지를 받았습니다. He climbed up the **ladder** to fix the roof. 그는 지붕을 고치기 위해 사다리를 올라갔습니다.
by ~의 옆에 **buy** 사다	The book is right **by** the window on the shelf. 그 책은 책장 위 창가 바로 옆에 있습니다. I want to **buy** a book. 저는 책을 한 권 사고 싶습니다.
right 오른쪽 **ride** 타다	The conference room is located on the **right** side of the hallway. 회의실은 복도의 오른쪽에 있습니다. I love to **ride** my bike in the park. 저는 공원에서 자전거를 타는 것을 좋아합니다.
live 살다 **leave** 떠나다	She **lives** in a beautiful house by the river. 그녀는 강변의 아름다운 집에 살고 있습니다. She decided to **leave** her job and pursue her passion. 그녀는 자신의 직장을 떠나서 열정을 쫓기로 결정했습니다.
contact 연락하다 **contract** 계약서	Please **contact** me via e-mail for further details. 자세한 내용은 이메일로 연락해 주세요. They signed a **contract** to formalize their business partnership. 그들은 사업 파트너십을 공식화하기 위해 계약서에 서명했습니다.
train 기차 **training** 교육	I'll take the **train** to the city. 저는 도시로 가는 기차에 탈것입니다. I should attend a **training** session this afternoon. 저는 오후에 교육 세션에 참석해야 합니다.

sign 간판 **design** 고안하다 **resign** 사임하다	The **sign** outside the store says "Sale." 가게 밖의 간판에는 "할인"이라고 써 있습니다. He's the one who will **design** the new Web site. 그는 새로운 웹사이트를 고안할 사람입니다. She decided to **resign** from her current job. 그녀는 현재 직장에서 사임하기로 결정했습니다.
annual 연례의 **manual** 매뉴얼	The **annual** report provides a summary of our company's performance. 연례 보고서는 우리 회사의 성과를 요약해 줍니다. The **manual** provides instructions for assembling the furniture. 그 매뉴얼은 가구 조립을 위한 지침을 제공합니다.
bank 은행 **banquet** 연회	I need to go to the **bank** to withdraw some money. 저는 돈을 인출하기 위해 은행에 가야 합니다. They had a grand **banquet** to celebrate their anniversary. 그들은 결혼 기념일을 축하하기 위해 화려한 연회를 열었습니다.
office 사무실 **offer** 제안	I'll be in my **office** all day working on the report. 저는 하루 종일 보고서를 작업하면서 사무실에 있을 것입니다. The company made her an attractive job **offer**. 그 회사가 그녀에게 매력적인 일자리를 제안했습니다.
plant 식물, 공장 **plan** 계획	She loves to **plant** flowers in her garden. 그녀는 정원에 꽃을 심는 것을 좋아합니다. We need to create a detailed **plan** for the project. 우리는 프로젝트를 위해 상세한 계획을 만들어야 합니다.
market 시장 **marketing** 마케팅	The **market** is crowded with shoppers on weekends. 주말에는 시장이 쇼핑객으로 북적입니다. The **marketing** team is developing a new marketing strategy. 마케팅 팀은 새로운 마케팅 전략을 개발하고 있습니다.

PART 1

Directions: You will hear four statements about the picture below. Select the one statement that best describes what you see in the picture and mark the letter (A), (B), (C), or (D).

1

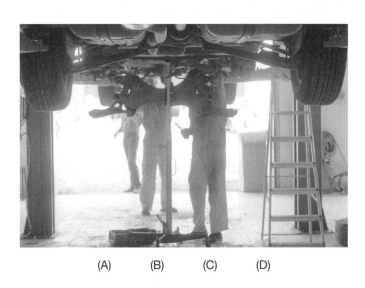

(A)   (B)   (C)   (D)

2

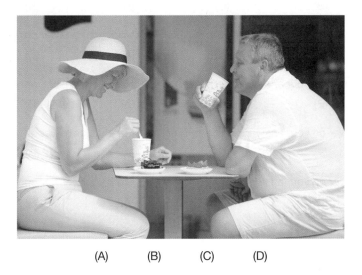

(A)   (B)   (C)   (D)

3

(A)   (B)   (C)   (D)

PART 2

Directions: You will hear a question or statement and three responses spoken in English. Select the best response to the question or statement and mark the letter (A), (B), or (C).

---

4 Mark your answer on your answer sheet.
   (A)   (B)   (C)

5 Mark your answer on your answer sheet.
   (A)   (B)   (C)

6 Mark your answer on your answer sheet.
   (A)   (B)   (C)

7 Mark your answer on your answer sheet.
   (A)   (B)   (C)

8 Mark your answer on your answer sheet.
   (A)   (B)   (C)

9 Mark your answer on your answer sheet.
   (A)   (B)   (C)

10 Mark your answer on your answer sheet.
   (A)   (B)   (C)

11 Mark your answer on your answer sheet.
   (A)   (B)   (C)

12 Mark your answer on your answer sheet.
   (A)   (B)   (C)

13 Mark your answer on your answer sheet.
   (A)   (B)   (C)

14 Mark your answer on your answer sheet.
   (A)   (B)   (C)

15 Mark your answer on your answer sheet.
   (A)   (B)   (C)

16 Mark your answer on your answer sheet.
   (A)   (B)   (C)

17 Mark your answer on your answer sheet.
   (A)   (B)   (C)

18 Mark your answer on your answer sheet.
   (A)   (B)   (C)

Directions: You will hear some conversations between two or more people. You will be asked to answer three questions about what the speakers say in each conversation. Select the best response to each question and mark the letter (A), (B), (C), or (D).

19 What are the speakers talking about?

(A) Some outdated software
(B) A power outage
(C) A computer problem
(D) A broken machine

20 What caused the problem?

(A) A network update
(B) Some renovation work
(C) A delayed shipment
(D) A scheduling conflict

21 What does Steve suggest the woman do?

(A) Update some software
(B) Contact another department
(C) Call a repairperson
(D) Shut down her computer

22 Who most likely is the man?

(A) A conference organizer
(B) A news reporter
(C) A marketing manager
(D) A finance manager

23 Why does the man say, "You've done a lot of presentations before"?

(A) To praise the woman's ability
(B) To point out a mistake
(C) To explain a request
(D) To give an assignment

24 What does the woman recommend?

(A) Making a special request for a room
(B) Recruiting more volunteers
(C) Preregistering for an event
(D) Consulting a colleague

25 Who most likely is the man?

  (A) A train conductor
  (B) A construction worker
  (C) A realtor
  (D) An interior designer

26 What does the woman like the most?

  (A) The price of the rent
  (B) The number of meeting places
  (C) The location of the office
  (D) The size of the place

27 What does the woman want to know?

  (A) The condition of a room.
  (B) The terms of an agreement
  (C) The price of parking
  (D) The location of a facility

28　Where does the talk most likely take place?

(A) At a movie theater

(B) At a restaurant

(C) At a factory

(D) At a museum

29　What is prohibited inside the building?

(A) Taking pictures

(B) Speaking loudly

(C) Carrying bags

(D) Throwing out garbage

30　What does the speaker say the listeners will receive at the end?

(A) A free product

(B) A brochure

(C) A photograph

(D) A discounted coupon

Terry's Gift Card

Special Sale for Our Grand Opening
9:00 A.M. to 5:00 P.M. Tomorrow
20% off All Items!

Hurry! One Day Only Event!

31　Why is the store holding a special event?

(A) It just newly launched an online site.

(B) It will provide free delivery service.

(C) It opened another store.

(D) It has changed its contact information.

32　Look at the graphic. Which information should be updated?

(A) The reason for the sale

(B) The date of the sale

(C) The discount offered on items

(D) The items on sale

33　What will happen tomorrow?

(A) Customers will get a free gift card.

(B) Visitors will receive a discount.

(C) A new branch will open.

(D) The store will stay open for a longer time.

DAY 04 PART 2 유형별 문제 풀이법 I

PART 2에서 의문사가 있는 문제의 경우, 의문사로 정답이 결정되는 경우가 70퍼센트 정도를 차지한다. 하지만, 응시자들이 가장 많이 틀리는 유형은 답변이 의문사와 일치하지 않음에도 정답이 되는 경우이다. 따라서, 오답을 정확하게 파악하여 소거하면서 정답을 찾아야 한다.

오늘의 학습 POINT

POINT 1 의문사 문제 오답 유형 ① - 답변이 의문사와 일치하지 않는 경우
POINT 2 의문사 문제 오답 유형 ② - Yes / No로 대답한 경우
POINT 3 의문사 문제 오답 유형 ③ - How / Why 의문문에 명사로 답한 경우
POINT 4 답변이 의문사와 일치하지 않아도 정답이 되는 경우
POINT 5 그 외의 오답 유형

POINT 1 의문사 문제 오답 유형 ① - 답변이 의문사와 일치하지 않는 경우

의문사로 시작하는 문제의 경우 **의문사에 어울리는 답변**을 찾는 것이 가장 중요하다. 예를 들어 when으로 시작한다면 시간을, where로 시작한다면 장소를 골라야 하는 것처럼, 답변이 의문사의 의미와 일치하는지 여부로 정답을 찾을 수 있는 문제가 70% 정도이다.

유형 분석

Q Where can I find this week's sales figure?

A In two days.

04-01

→ where로 묻는 질문에는 '장소'로 답해야 하지만 '시간'으로 답했으므로 의문사와 일치하지 않는 답변이다.

POINT 2 의문사 문제 오답 유형 ② - Yes / No로 대답한 경우

의문사로 시작하는 질문은 구체적인 정보를 묻는 유형이므로 **yes나 no로는 답할 수 없다.**

유형 분석

Q Who can I speak to about next week's schedule?

A Yes, it's Mr. Lee.

04-02

→ 의문사로 시작하는 질문의 경우 yes / no로 답할 수 없으므로 오답이다.

cf. yes와 no뿐만 아니라 「sure, of course, okay」 등도 정답으로 사용될 수 없다.

POINT 3 의문사 문제 오답 유형 ③ - How / Why 의문문에 명사로 답한 경우

how와 why는 방법과 이유를 묻는 의문사로서, 명사나 명사구만으로는 방법이나 이유를 설명할 수 없다. 따라서, **how와 why로 시작하는 의문사 의문문이 출제되는 경우, 명사나 명사구로 답변하는 선택지는 항상 오답**이다.

유형 분석

04 - 03

Q **Why** are you late for work today?

A **A traffic accident**.

→ 위 답변을 '사고 때문에'라고 오해하기 쉽지만, 답변의 정확한 해석은 '사고'이다. 명사구인 'A traffic accident'만으로는 이유를 설명할 수 없으므로 이는 오답이다.

cf. why의 경우 명사뿐 아니라 「in, on, near」 등과 같이 이유나 목적을 의미하는 것이 아닌 전치사구 또한 오답이 된다.

POINT 4 답변이 의문사와 일치하지 않아도 정답이 되는 경우

의문사로 시작하는 문제 유형이 출제되면 의문사에 어울리지 않는 답변은 오답이 된다. 하지만 **'문장형 답변'의 경우에는 반드시 그 의미를 생각한 다음 오답 여부를 판단**해야 한다. 직접적으로 의문사에 대해 답하지 않고 우회적으로 답변하는 경우가 최근에 자주 출제된다.

유형 분석

04 - 04

Q **Where** is our new printer?

A It won't be here **until this Friday**.

→ 의문사는 장소를 묻는 where이므로, 시간으로 답한 선택지가 오답이라고 생각할 수 있다. 하지만, '새로운 프린터의 위치'를 묻는 질문에 대해 '금요일은 되어야 온다'고 대답한 것은 '지금은 프린터가 없다'고 우회적으로 답한 정답이다. 문장형 선택지의 경우 항상 그 의미를 잘 생각해 보아야 한다.

POINT 5 그 외의 오답 유형

> who나 what으로 시작하는 의문사 의문문의 경우, 전치사구의 답변은 오답일 가능성이 높다.
> what으로 시작하는 질문의 경우, 자주 출제되는 관용어구를 알아야만 문제를 해결할 수 있는 경우가 많으므로, 자주 출제되는 관용어구는 꼭 암기해 두어야 한다.

★ **자주 출제되는 what의 관용적 표현**

- What do you do ~? 직업
- What happened ~? 문제
- What's the weather like? 날씨
- What ~ about/for? 주제/목적
- What do you think of ~? 의견

- What should I do ~? 방법
- What be 사람 like? 성격
- What do 사람 look like? 생김새
- What makes/brings/causes ~? 이유
- What about ~? 제안

어휘	예문
book ① 예약하다 ② 책	Can I **book** a ticket? 제가 티켓을 예약할 수 있을까요? I love her **book**. 저는 그녀의 책을 좋아해요.
order ① 주문 ② 순서	Are you ready to **order**? 주문할 준비가 되셨나요? Put it in numeric **order**. 숫자 순서대로 두세요.
leave ① 놔두다 ② 떠나다	**Leave** them on the desk. 그것들을 책상 위에 두세요. I'm **leaving** tomorrow. 저는 내일 떠나요.
park ① 공원 ② 주차하다	It's a beautiful **park**. 그것은 아름다운 공원이에요. Where should I **park** my car? 어디에 차를 주차해야 하나요?
right ① 오른쪽 ② 옳은	Turn **right** at the intersection. 교차로에서 오른쪽으로 가세요. I think you're **right**. 내 생각에는 당신이 맞는 것 같아요.
left ① 왼쪽 ② leave의 과거	The store is on your **left**. 그 가게는 당신의 왼쪽에 있어요. I **left** the package in your office. 제가 그 소포를 당신의 사무실에 두었어요.
have ① 조동사 ② 가지다	**Have** you ever been to Korea? 한국에 가 보신 적이 있나요? I **have** a pet. 저는 애완동물을 가지고 있어요.
plant ① 공장 ② 식물	I work at a manufacturing **plant**. 저는 제조 공장에서 일하고 있어요. He knows a lot about **plants**. 그는 식물들에 대해 많이 알아요.
show ① 공연물 ② 보여주다	*Friends* is my favorite TV **show**. 프렌즈는 내가 가장 좋아하는 티비 쇼예요. I can **show** you how to use the fax machine. 제가 팩스를 어떻게 사용하는지 보여드릴게요.
change ① 잔돈 ② 변경하다	Keep the **change**. 잔돈은 가지세요. We should **change** our goals. 우리는 목표를 변경해야 해요.
check ① 수표 ② 확인하다	I want to cash my **check**. 저는 수표를 현금으로 바꾸고 싶어요. Let me **check** the list. 제가 목록을 확인해 볼게요.
room ① 방 ② 공간	I reserved a **room** for two nights. 저는 방을 2박 예약했어요. We don't have **room** for the books. 우리는 그 책들을 위한 공간이 없어요..
store ① 가게 ② 보관하다	The **store** will be closing in 30 minutes. 가게는 30분 뒤에 문을 닫아요. You can **store** the baggage under your seat. 좌석 밑에 짐을 보관할 수 있어요.
rest ① 쉬다 ② 나머지	You'd better get some **rest**. 당신은 쉬는 게 좋겠어요. Does anyone want the **rest** of the pizza? 남은 피자를 원하시는 분 있나요?
present ① 선물 ② 발표하다	I want to buy a birthday **present** for my mother. 저는 저희 어머니의 생신 선물을 사고 싶어요. The researcher **presented** his findings. 연구자가 그의 결과를 발표했어요.

PART 1

Directions: You will hear four statements about the picture below. Select the one statement that best describes what you see in the picture and mark the letter (A), (B), (C), or (D).

1

(A)   (B)   (C)   (D)

2

(A)   (B)   (C)   (D)

3

(A)   (B)   (C)   (D)

PART 2

Directions: You will hear a question or statement and three responses spoken in English. Select the best response to the question or statement and mark the letter (A), (B), or (C).

---

4   Mark your answer on your answer sheet.
    (A)   (B)   (C)

5   Mark your answer on your answer sheet.
    (A)   (B)   (C)

6   Mark your answer on your answer sheet.
    (A)   (B)   (C)

7   Mark your answer on your answer sheet.
    (A)   (B)   (C)

8   Mark your answer on your answer sheet.
    (A)   (B)   (C)

9   Mark your answer on your answer sheet.
    (A)   (B)   (C)

10   Mark your answer on your answer sheet.
    (A)   (B)   (C)

11   Mark your answer on your answer sheet.
    (A)   (B)   (C)

12   Mark your answer on your answer sheet.
    (A)   (B)   (C)

13   Mark your answer on your answer sheet.
    (A)   (B)   (C)

14   Mark your answer on your answer sheet.
    (A)   (B)   (C)

15   Mark your answer on your answer sheet.
    (A)   (B)   (C)

16   Mark your answer on your answer sheet.
    (A)   (B)   (C)

17   Mark your answer on your answer sheet.
    (A)   (B)   (C)

18   Mark your answer on your answer sheet.
    (A)   (B)   (C)

Directions: You will hear some conversations between two or more people. You will be asked to answer three questions about what the speakers say in each conversation. Select the best response to each question and mark the letter (A), (B), (C), or (D).

19 Who most likely is the man?

(A) A store owner

(B) A chef

(C) A restaurant server

(D) A food critic

20 What will the woman do next?

(A) Order some food

(B) Look at a menu

(C) Call her friends

(D) Visit a different business

21 What does the woman want to know?

(A) Where to park

(B) What to order

(C) When to arrive

(D) Who to join

22 What does the man want to talk about?

(A) Some renovation plans

(B) Ways to reduce expenses

(C) A job interview

(D) Some travel arrangements

23 What does the woman mean when she says, "I have some time before the meeting"?

(A) She is too busy to take care of a matter.

(B) She wants to have lunch before a meeting.

(C) She should prepare for a meeting.

(D) She has time to set some equipment.

24 What does the woman suggest doing?

(A) Asking employees for ideas

(B) Attending a meeting

(C) Checking equipment every day

(D) Arranging a competition

25 What type of event will be held next month?

(A) A conference
(B) A retirement celebration
(C) A grand opening
(D) A workshop

26 What does the man ask about?

(A) When they will visit a venue
(B) Whether some food can be provided
(C) Whether they can use certain equipment
(D) Who will attend an event

27 What does the man need to do by the end of the week?

(A) Sign a contract
(B) Meet a client
(C) Send an e-mail
(D) Contact a business

Directions: You will hear some talks given by a single speaker. You will be asked to answer three questions about what the speaker says in each talk. Select the best response to each question and mark the letter (A), (B), (C), or (D).

28 What is the topic of the announcement?

(A) A planned local event
(B) An upcoming landscaping project
(C) Damage from a storm
(D) A government policy

29 Who most likely are the listeners?

(A) Construction workers
(B) Dining staff
(C) City officials
(D) Store customers

30 What are the listeners instructed to do?

(A) Keep the windows and front doors closed
(B) Clean up some leaves and twigs
(C) Make safety signs to warn diners
(D) Use a different entrance

Room Layout

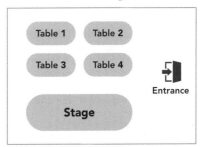

31 What business is the speaker calling from?

(A) A convention center
(B) A catering company
(C) A hotel
(D) A manufacturing factory

32 What event is the speaker's company planning on Friday?

(A) An awards ceremony
(B) A new employee orientation
(C) A retirement party
(D) A product launch

33 Look at the graphic. Where will the recipients be seated?

(A) Table 1
(B) Table 2
(C) Table 3
(D) Table 4

DAY 05 PART 2 유형별 문제 풀이법 II

PART 2에서 의문사가 없는 문제의 경우, 동사의 의미를 정확하게 파악하는 것이 가장 중요하다. 또한, 각각의 질문에서 묻고자 하는 것에 대한 유형별 특징을 기억하는 것이 문제 풀이의 핵심이다.

오늘의 학습 POINT

POINT 1 제안 의문문 / 요청 의문문 해결하기
POINT 2 Yes / No로 답하는 의문문 해결하기
POINT 3 부정의문문 해결하기
POINT 4 부가의문문 해결하기
POINT 5 선택의문문 해결하기

POINT 1 제안 의문문 / 요청 의문문 해결하기 [매달 3-6 문제]

제안 및 요청 의문문의 질문 유형은 허락을 구하거나, 제시하거나, 요청하는 형태이다.

① 질문 유형

- 'Why don't you', 혹은 'Why don't I [we]'로 시작하는 유형
- 조동사(could, would, may, can 등)로 시작하며, 1, 2인칭(I, we, you)으로 묻는 유형
- let 혹은 make sure(be sure to)로 시작하는 평서문 유형
- 명령문 유형
- How about / What about / What if 등의 관용적 표현

② 답변 유형

- 대부분 1, 2인칭으로 답하며, 현재 시제나 미래 시제로 답한다.
- 의견을 명확하게 알 수 있어야 하므로 '단어'나 '구'만으로 답하지 않는다.
- 되묻는 형태, 혹은 다른 제안을 하는 형태가 정답으로 제시된다.
- '시간이 있다', '시간이 없다'로 수락과 거절을 표현한다.
- 'I'll do it.'과 같이 '나'나 '다른 사람'이 할 것이라는 답변이 정답으로 제시된다.

유형 분석

05 - 01

Q **Why don't we** go out for dinner tonight?

A Sorry. I have to finish the budget report.

→ 'Why don't we'로 제안하는 질문에 대해 '오늘 끝낼 보고서가 있으므로 시간이 없다'고 거절하는 전형적인 정답의 유형이다.

1 질문 유형

- 'Do, Will, Have, Be동사'로 시작하는 질문들은 사실 여부를 묻는 질문이므로, 대부분 Yes / No로 답변한다.

- Yes / No로 답변하는 것이 아닌 고난도 문제도 출제되기 때문에, 질문의 내용을 정확하게 해석해야 한다.

2 답변 유형

- 질문 속 동사의 동의어 혹은 반의어가 등장하는 형태

- '잘 모르겠다'고 답하는 유형

- 'Yes, but ~' 혹은 'No, and ~'와 같이 추가 설명이 이어지는 형태

유형 분석

05 - 02

Q **Did you** attend the seminar yesterday?

A **No, but** Sue will fill me in this afternoon.

→ 어제 세미나에 참석한 사실 여부를 묻는 질문에 대해 No로 답한 다음, 'Sue가 오늘 오후에 내용을 알려 줄 것'이라고
추가 설명을 하는 정답 유형이다.

cf. fill in은 무엇인가를 채운다는 의미이지만, 사람을 채운다는 의미로 사용되는 경우, 모르고 있는 내용을 알려준다는 의미로 사용된다.

1 질문 유형

질문을 시작하는 조동사에 'not'을 붙이는 유형으로서, '의외', 또는 '놀람'의 감정을 전달하는 뉘앙스이다.

2 답변 유형

질문에 'not'이 없는 긍정문 형태로 해석한 다음 답한다.

- Do you have any pens? → 상대방이 펜을 가지고 있는지 여부를 묻는 질문

- Don't you have any pens? (I thought you did.)
  → 상대방이 펜을 가지고 있다고 생각했는데, 가지고 있지 않아 이상하다는 뉘앙스의 질문

→ ①과 ② 모두 가지고 있으면 yes, 가지고 있지 않으면 no로 답하면 된다.

유형 분석

05 - 03

Q **Isn't this today's last show**?

A No, there's one more.

→ 이것이 마지막 쇼라고 생각하고 있었는데, '어 이게 마지막이 아니야?', '이게 마지막이지?'라는 뉘앙스의 질문이다.

→ 쇼가 마지막인지 여부에 대해서만 답변하면 되므로, '이게 마지막 쇼인가요? (Is this today's last show?)'라는 긍정문 형태의
질문에 대해 답변하면 된다.

→ '아니요, 하나 더 남았어요'라며 마지막이 아니라고 대답하고 있다.

부가의문문 해결하기 [매달 0-2 문제]

부가의문문이란 평서문 뒤에 짧은 질문을 덧붙여 '그렇지?' '맞지?'와 같이 확인하는 질문 유형이다. 부가의문문에서는 평서문에 묻고자 하는 내용이 있으므로, 평서문의 내용을 파악하는 것이 중요하다. 따라서 다른 유형들에 비해 질문을 듣는 연습을 많이 할 필요가 있다.

유형 분석

Q You bought a new car, **didn't you**?

A Yes, last month.

05 - 04

→ 질문에서 'didn't you' 앞의 평서문인 차를 샀는지 묻는 질문에 대해 '지난달에 샀다'고 답하는 정답이다.

선택의문문 해결하기 [매달 1-2 문제]

① **질문 유형**

질문에 or가 포함되며, 둘 중에서 하나를 선택하라는 의미의 질문 유형이다.

② **답변 유형**

● 직접 한 가지를 선택하는 경우

● 우회적으로 말하며 선택하는 경우

● 두 가지 모두 상관없다고 말하는 경우
 (both, whatever, either, It doesn't matter, up to you 등의 표현이 자주 등장한다.)

● '잘 모르겠다', '둘 다 싫다'와 같이 제 3의 선택을 하는 경우

cf. 선택의문문에서는 질문에서 언급된 '선택지'와 '답변'이 같은 영역인지의 여부를 판단하는 것이 중요하다. 즉, '커피 or 우유?'라고 묻는 경우 '마실 것'을 선택해야 하며, '박물관 or 영화관?'이라고 묻는 경우 '장소'를 선택해야 한다. 문제를 풀 때 자신이 정답이라고 생각하는 '답변'이 질문의 '선택지'와 같은 영역인지를 꼭 염두에 두어야 한다.

유형 분석

Q Should we hire **one or two** photographers for this event?

A We have a limited budget.

05 - 05

→ 한 명이나 두 명 중 몇 명의 사진사를 고용할 것인지를 묻는 질문에 대해 예산이 한정되어 있다고 답하는 것은 '돈이 별로 없다'는 말이므로, 한 명만 고용하자는 것을 우회적으로 말하는 정답의 유형이다.

05 - 06

어휘	예문
billed 청구된 **build** 건설하다	Have you **billed** us for all of the services? 모든 서비스에 대해 청구하셨나요? They plan to **build** a new library in our town. 그들은 우리 마을에 새 도서관을 건설하기로 계획하고 있어요.
right 오른쪽; 옳은 **write** 쓰다	Turn **right** at the corner. 코너에서 우회전하세요. Can you **write** your name on this paper, please? 이 종이에 이름을 작성해 주시겠어요?
fare 비용 **fair** 박람회	Isn't the bus **fare** to the downtown area $3? 시내로 가는 버스 요금은 3달러 아닌가요? Did you have a great time at the county **fair** last weekend? 지난 주말에 카운티 박람회에서 즐거운 시간을 보냈어요?
roll 굴리다 **role** 역할	Let's **roll** the dice and see who goes first. 주사위를 굴려서 먼저 갈 사람을 결정해 봅시다. Did she play the **role** of the queen in the play? 연극에서 그녀는 여왕 역할을 했었죠?
meet 만나다 **meat** 고기	Did you **meet** our new director? 우리 새로운 이사님을 만나셨어요? Some of my colleagues don't eat **meat**. 몇몇 동료들은 고기를 먹지 않아요.
council 의회 **counsel** 조언	The city **council** is discussing the new park project. 시 의회에서는 새로운 공원 프로젝트에 대해 논의하고 있어요. Lisa sought **counsel** about her tasks from her manager. 리사는 자신의 업무에 관해 매니저에게 조언을 구했어요.
weather 날씨 **whether** ~인지 아닌지	The **weather** is nice today with clear skies. 오늘 날씨는 하늘이 맑고 좋아요. I'm not sure **whether** I should go to the party or stay home. 파티에 가야 할지 집에 머물러야 할지 확실하지 않아요.
higher 더 높은 **hire** 고용하다	The mountain peak is even **higher** than I expected. 산봉우리가 제가 기대한 것보다 훨씬 높아요. The company decided to **hire** a new graphic designer. 회사는 새로운 그래픽 디자이너를 고용하기로 결정했어요.

wear 입다 **ware** 물건, 용품	I like to **wear** comfortable shoes when I go for a walk. 산책을 할 때 편안한 신발을 신는 것을 좋아해요. The store sells various kitchen**ware** like pots and pans. 그 상점은 냄비와 프라이팬 같은 다양한 주방 용품을 판매해요.
won (win '이기다'의 과거) **one** 하나	He **won** the race and received a gold medal. 그는 경주에서 우승하고 금메달을 받았어요. Could you pass me that book? I need **one** to read. 그 책 좀 건네 줄래요? 읽을 책이 하나 필요해요.
new 새로운 **knew** (know '알다'의 과거)	My family moved to a **new** house last month. 우리 가족은 지난달에 새집으로 이사했어요. She **knew** the answer to the question. 그녀는 그 질문의 답을 알고 있었어요.
hear 듣다 **here** 여기에	I can't **hear** what you're saying. 당신이 말하는 것이 들리지 않아요. We're meeting **here** at the park. 우리는 여기 공원에서 만날 거예요.
sale 판매 **sail** 돛, 항해	The store is having a big **sale** this weekend. 그 상점은 이번 주말에 큰 할인 행사를 하고 있어요. The ship set **sail** on a journey across the ocean. 그 배는 대양을 건너기 위해 항해를 시작했어요.
wait 기다리다 **weight** 무게	Please **wait** a moment while I find the information for you. 제가 정보를 찾는 동안 잠시만 기다려 주세요. Can you check the **weight** of this box? 이 상자의 무게를 확인해 주실 수 있나요?
our 우리의 **hour** 시간	**Our** family is going on a vacation next week. 우리 가족은 다음 주에 휴가를 갈 거예요. The movie will start in an **hour**. 영화는 1시간 후에 시작될 예정이에요.

PART 1

Directions: You will hear four statements about the picture below. Select the one statement that best describes what you see in the picture and mark the letter (A), (B), (C), or (D).

1

(A)   (B)   (C)   (D)

2

(A)   (B)   (C)   (D)

3

(A)   (B)   (C)   (D)

PART 2

Directions: You will hear a question or statement and three responses spoken in English. Select the best response to the question or statement and mark the letter (A), (B), or (C).

---

4 Mark your answer on your answer sheet.

(A)   (B)   (C)

5 Mark your answer on your answer sheet.

(A)   (B)   (C)

6 Mark your answer on your answer sheet.

(A)   (B)   (C)

7 Mark your answer on your answer sheet.

(A)   (B)   (C)

8 Mark your answer on your answer sheet.

(A)   (B)   (C)

9 Mark your answer on your answer sheet.

(A)   (B)   (C)

10 Mark your answer on your answer sheet.

(A)   (B)   (C)

11 Mark your answer on your answer sheet.

(A)   (B)   (C)

12 Mark your answer on your answer sheet.

(A)   (B)   (C)

13 Mark your answer on your answer sheet.

(A)   (B)   (C)

14 Mark your answer on your answer sheet.

(A)   (B)   (C)

15 Mark your answer on your answer sheet.

(A)   (B)   (C)

16 Mark your answer on your answer sheet.

(A)   (B)   (C)

17 Mark your answer on your answer sheet.

(A)   (B)   (C)

18 Mark your answer on your answer sheet.

(A)   (B)   (C)

PART 3

Directions: You will hear some conversations between two or more people. You will be asked to answer three questions about what the speakers say in each conversation. Select the best response to each question and mark the letter (A), (B), (C), or (D).

19 What problem do the women mention?

(A) They are understaffed.

(B) Office furniture is worn out.

(C) A machine is not functioning.

(D) A corporate event has been canceled.

20 What does the man invite the women to do?

(A) Compare the prices

(B) Check the Web site

(C) Call a business

(D) Attend an event

21 What will happen on the night of the 18th of June?

(A) A reception will be held.

(B) A special lecture will be offered.

(C) International clients will attend it.

(D) A design will be released.

22 Where do the speakers most likely work?

(A) At a laundry service

(B) At a clothing shop

(C) At a cosmetics company

(D) At an alteration shop

23 What does the man suggest the woman do?

(A) Update a Web site

(B) Read customer feedback

(C) Provide free delivery

(D) Pick up some materials

24 What does the woman ask the man to do?

(A) Change a meeting schedule

(B) Send some customer information

(C) Write a report

(D) Call a textile factory

This Month's New Play List

Title	Genre
Father	Drama
Sing	Comedy
Sign	Thriller
Rainbow	Musical

25 Look at the graphic. Which play are the speakers talking about?

(A) *Father*

(B) *Sing*

(C) *Sign*

(D) *Rainbow*

26 Why has the man not seen the play yet?

(A) A theater is under construction.

(B) He could not find anyone to go with him.

(C) Performances have been canceled.

(D) Tickets are unavailable.

27 What does the woman recommend the man do?

(A) Change his seat at the theater

(B) Try calling the theater

(C) Arrive early to avoid waiting in line

(D) Write a review about the play

PART 4

Directions: You will hear some talks given by a single speaker. You will be asked to answer three questions about what the speaker says in each talk. Select the best response to each question and mark the letter (A), (B), (C), or (D).

28 Where does the speaker work?

(A) At a shipping center

(B) At a software company

(C) At a data analytics firm

(D) At a post office

29 Why does the speaker say, "The issue will not be resolved until the end of the day"?

(A) To ask for some help

(B) To complain about a process

(C) To install some new software

(D) To explain a delay

30 What does the speaker want to do?

(A) Change some equipment

(B) Arrange a meeting

(C) Contact a supplier

(D) Revise a design

31 Who are the listeners?

(A) Bus drivers

(B) Shop owners

(C) Tourists

(D) City officials

32 What is mentioned about the tour?

(A) It will take more than 3 hours.

(B) There is no free time.

(C) There are many places to eat.

(D) There is no return bus.

33 What does the speaker remind the listeners to do?

(A) Keep their return tickets

(B) Wear comfortable shoes

(C) Use a city map

(D) Arrive on time

DAY 06 PART 2 고난도 문제 풀이법

PART 2에서 가장 난이도가 높은 유형은 평서문이다. 또한, 일반적인 답변이 아닌 우회적 답변이 출제되는 경우가 많으므로, 이러한 유형에 대한 대비가 필수적이다.

> **오늘의 학습 POINT**
>
> **POINT 1** 평서문 해결하기
>
> **POINT 2** 우회적 답변 해결하기

POINT 1 평서문 해결하기 [매달 3-6 문제]

평서문의 경우, 대화를 마무리하거나 누군가의 질문에 대답하는 것이 아니라, 대부분의 경우 대화를 시작하는 상황이다. 따라서, 평서문에 대한 적절한 답변은 다음 대화를 이어갈 수 있는 유형이다.

① 평서문 유형

- 명령문, 또는 let으로 시작하는 제안의 평서문
- 정보를 제공하는 평서문
- 의견을 제시하는 평서문
- 문제점을 제시하는 평서문

② 답변 유형

- 평서문의 내용에 흥미를 나타내며 되묻는 유형
- 미래의 할 일을 제시하는 유형
- 평서문에 언급된 문제나 의견에 대해 제안을 하는 유형

> **cf.** 평서문은 'Yes, I do'와 같은 단답형 답변, 혹은 'cake'와 같은 명사만으로 답하는 유형의 정답을 좋아하지 않는다.

> **유형 분석**
>
> **Q** I can't start this fax machine.
>
> **A** **Why don't you** call the maintenance office?
>
> → 문제점을 이야기하는 평서문에 대해 제안의 방법으로 해결책을 제시하는 가장 대표적인 정답의 유형이다.

06-01

평서문 문제의 경우 아래의 해법을 통해 문제를 해결한다.

- 질문의 주어와 동사를 정확하게 이해하여, 평서문의 내용을 빠르게 파악한다.
- '명사'나 '단답형'처럼 '대화를 단절시키는 답변'과 '유사 발음 오답'을 제거한다.
- 되묻는 유형, 평서문에서 언급하는 문제나 의견에 대한 의견 제시, 미래에 할 일을 언급하는 형태의 답변이 자주 등장한다는 점을 기억한다.

POINT 2 우회적 답변 해결하기 [매달 10-12문제]

PART 2에서는 정답을 직접적으로 이야기하지 않고 우회적으로 답변하는 유형이 많이 출제는 추세이다.

유형 분석

Q How many people will attend the seminar?

A There is a list on the desk.

→ 일반적으로 생각할 수 있는 질문의 답변은 '사람의 숫자'이지만, 예시 답변과 같이 '책상 위에 리스트가 있다', 즉, '리스트에 원하는 정보가 있다'와 같이 우회적으로 답변하는 경우가 자주 출제된다.

우회적 답변 유형

언제나 우회적인 답변만 출제된다고 생각하게 되면 문제를 풀 때 혼란스러울 수 있으므로, 자주 출제되는 우회적 답변의 유형을 정리해 둘 필요가 있다.

① 직접적으로 정답을 말하지 않고 정보가 있는 위치를 알려주는 유형

「~을 보세요, ~에 있어요, ~는 보았나요?, (메모등)을 받지 않았나요?」 등

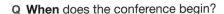

유형 분석

Q Which floor is the movie theater on?

A There is **a building directory** behind you.

→ '영화관의 위치'를 묻는 질문에 대해 '당신 뒤쪽에 건물 안내도가 있다' 즉, '건물 안내도를 보면 알게 될 것이다'라고 원하는 정보가 있는 곳을 우회적으로 알려주고 있다.

Q When does the conference begin?

A Haven't you received **the memo**?

→ 컨퍼런스의 시작 시간을 묻는 질문에 대해 '메모를 받지 못했는지' 되묻는 것은 메모 안에 원하는 정보가 있었음을 의미하는 우회적인 답변의 유형이다.

❷ 제 3자가 알고 있다는 사실을 언급하며, '모른다'는 것을 암시하는 유형

「다른 사람이 할 거예요, 다른 사람이 알 거예요, 다른 사람에게 물어보세요, 다른 사람의 업무예요, 다른 사람의 담당이에요, 다른 사람이 처리했어요, 다른 사람이 참석했어요.」 등

Q What was discussed in this morning meeting?

A Chan attended it.

→ 아침 회의의 내용을 묻는 질문에 대해 'Chan이 참석했다'고 언급하는 것은 'Chan에게 물어봐라' 즉, '자신은 모른다'는 것을 암시하고 있는 전형적인 우회적 답변 유형이다.

❸ 경험, 지식, 또는 시간이 없거나 처음이라고 답하면서 '모른다'는 것을 암시하는 유형

Q What do you think of our new company logo?

A I haven't seen it yet.

→ 로고에 대한 의견을 묻는 질문에 대해 '아직 로고를 보지 못했다'고 대답하는 것은 '나는 의견을 줄 수 없다' 즉, '모른다'는 의미이다.

❹ 언급된 행사의 날짜가 잘못되거나 취소, 또는 변경되는 경우

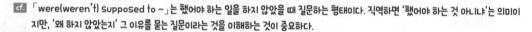

Q Weren't you supposed to attend the seminar at 9:00?

A It's been canceled.

→ '세미나에 가야 하지 않느냐'고 묻는 질문에 대해 '세미나는 취소되었다'고 대답하는 것은 '갈 필요가 없었다'는 것을 암시하는 우회적인 답변이다.

cf. 「were(weren't) supposed to ~」는 했어야 하는 일을 하지 않았을 때 질문하는 형태이다. 직역하면 '했어야 하는 것 아니냐'는 의미이 지만, '왜 하지 않았는지' 그 이유를 묻는 질문이라는 것을 이해하는 것이 중요하다.

❺ actually, I thought, still, already 등으로 시작하는 유형

- **actually, I thought**: 자신이나 상대방이 알고 있는 정보에 오해가 있다는 것을 의미
- **still**: '시간'이나 '돈' 등이 여전히 필요해서 '아직 하지 못했다'는 의미
- **already**: 무엇인가를 제안하는 것에 대해 '이미 종료 되었음'을 알리거나 '이미 해 보았다'는 의미

cf. 이러한 답변들이 항상 정답인 것이 아니므로 다른 선택지들과 비교하면서 정답을 골라야 한다.

Q Why don't you register for the marketing seminar?

A Actually, I attended the same seminar last month.

→ 세미나를 신청하라는 권유에 대해 '이미 참여한 적이 있다'고 답한 것은 신청할 필요가 없음을 우회적으로 언급하는 정답 유형이다. 이와 같이 actually는 질문의 전제가 잘못되었다는 것을 알려줄 때 주로 사용된다.

❻ '모른다'는 의미로 답변하는 유형

어떤 질문에 대해 모른다고 답하는 것은 대부분의 경우 정답이 된다. 다만, 당연히 알아야 하는 일을 모른다고 답할 경우, 이는 오답이 되기도 한다. 예를 들어, 'What's your name?'이라는 질문에 대해 'I don't know'라고 답한다면 이는 정답이 될 수 없다.

TIP! '모른다'는 의미의 표현

- 직접적으로 표현하는 경우
    - I don't know, I'm not sure: 잘 모르겠다

- 간접적으로 표현하는 경우
    - let me check ~, I'll find out ~: 확인해야 한다
    - I can ask ~: 물어보겠다
    - I haven't heard ~: 들은 바가 없다
    - not announced / nothing on the bulletin board: 안내된/게시된 바가 없다
    - haven't decided yet / still deciding: 결정되지 않았다
    - It depends ~: 상황에 따라 다르다

유형 분석

06-08

Q **Who** will be our new president?

A There's **nothing on the bulletin board**.

→ 새로운 사장님이 누구인지 묻는 질문에 대해 '게시판에 아무것도 없다'고 답하는 것은 아직 발표된 것이 없어 알지 못한다는 의미이다.

It hasn't been decided yet. 그것은 아직 결정되지 않았어요.

We're still deciding. 우리는 아직 결정을 내리는 중이에요.

It is still being considered. 그것은 여전히 고려되고 있어요.

It hasn't been announced yet. 아직 발표되지 않았어요.

Let me check. 제가 확인해 볼게요.　　　　　　I'll check it out. 제가 확인해 볼게요.

Let me find out. 제가 알아볼게요.　　　　　　I'll find out. 제가 알아볼게요.

Have you checked the memo? 메모는 확인해 보셨나요?

Have you checked the e-mail? 이메일은 확인해 보셨나요?

Why don't you check the map? 지도를 확인해 보시겠어요?

The information is on our Web site. 그 정보는 저희 웹사이트에 있어요.

Here's the list. 리스트를 보세요.

You should check your e-mail. 이메일을 보세요.

I haven't seen it yet. 저는 아직 보지 못했어요.

I don't have time to read it. 저는 읽을 시간이 없었어요.

There is nothing on the bulletin board. 게시판에는 아무것도 없어요.

I don't have any experience as a manager. 저는 매니저가 처음이에요.

I've only worked here for a week. 저는 이제 일한 지 일주일 되었어요.

I'm a stranger, too. 저도 이 지역은 처음이에요.

Let me ask. 제가 물어볼게요.　　　　　　I'll call to find out. 제가 전화해서 알아볼게요.

It depends on the situation. 그것은 상황에 따라 달라요.

That depends on when it starts. 언제 시작되는 가에 따라 달라요.

Why don't you ask Lucy? 루시에게 물어보시는 게 어떨까요?

Lucy might know. 루시가 알 거예요.

Lucy is in charge of it. 그것은 루시 담당이에요.

Actually, the event is tomorrow. 그 행사는 내일이에요.

The event has been canceled. 그 행사는 취소되었어요.

The clients will be here tomorrow. 고객들은 내일 와요.

The clients have already arrived. 고객들은 이미 도착했어요.

It's for new employees. 그것은 신입 사원들을 위한 거예요.

Only students can attend it. 그것은 학생들만 참여할 수 있어요.

I'll be out all week. 저는 일주일 내내 부재 중이에요.

I have a meeting then. 저는 그때 회의가 있어요.

PART 1

Directions: You will hear four statements about the picture below. Select the one statement that best describes what you see in the picture and mark the letter (A), (B), (C), or (D).

1

(A)   (B)   (C)   (D)

2

(A)   (B)   (C)   (D)

3

(A)   (B)   (C)   (D)

PART 2

Directions: You will hear a question or statement and three responses spoken in English. Select the best response to the question or statement and mark the letter (A), (B), or (C).

---

4   Mark your answer on your answer sheet.
   (A)   (B)   (C)

5   Mark your answer on your answer sheet.
   (A)   (B)   (C)

6   Mark your answer on your answer sheet.
   (A)   (B)   (C)

7   Mark your answer on your answer sheet.
   (A)   (B)   (C)

8   Mark your answer on your answer sheet.
   (A)   (B)   (C)

9   Mark your answer on your answer sheet.
   (A)   (B)   (C)

10   Mark your answer on your answer sheet.
   (A)   (B)   (C)

11   Mark your answer on your answer sheet.
   (A)   (B)   (C)

12   Mark your answer on your answer sheet.
   (A)   (B)   (C)

13   Mark your answer on your answer sheet.
   (A)   (B)   (C)

14   Mark your answer on your answer sheet.
   (A)   (B)   (C)

15   Mark your answer on your answer sheet.
   (A)   (B)   (C)

16   Mark your answer on your answer sheet.
   (A)   (B)   (C)

17   Mark your answer on your answer sheet.
   (A)   (B)   (C)

18   Mark your answer on your answer sheet.
   (A)   (B)   (C)

Directions: You will hear some conversations between two or more people. You will be asked to answer three questions about what the speakers say in each conversation. Select the best response to each question and mark the letter (A), (B), (C), or (D).

19 Who most likely is the woman?

(A) A secretary

(B) A postal worker

(C) A hotel employee

(D) A call center operator

20 What does the woman ask the man about?

(A) How she can arrange appointments

(B) What she should type and prepare

(C) Who supports the other employees

(D) What she is responsible for

21 What will the man most likely do next?

(A) Attend a meeting

(B) Meet a client

(C) Give the woman a tour

(D) Answer the phone

22 Where does the conversation most likely take place?

(A) At a library

(B) In a parking lot

(C) At a bank

(D) At a travel agency

23 What does the woman want to know?

(A) How to use resources

(B) How to sign up for a guided tour

(C) How to reserve a room

(D) How to get a copy

24 What will the woman probably do next?

(A) Head to the information desk

(B) Look for online tutorials

(C) Get a printed guide

(D) Contact another business

Grand Wood Hotel

Wigmore Hall	100-150
Mayo Hall	150-200
Gild Hall	200-250
Jubilee Hall	250-400

25 What event is the man planning?

(A) A retirement party

(B) An awards ceremony

(C) A trade expo

(D) A product launch

26 Look at the graphic. Which hall will the man most likely reserve?

(A) Wigmore Hall

(B) Mayo Hall

(C) Gild Hall

(D) Jubilee Hall

27 What does the woman say she will do?

(A) Send a contract

(B) Call an electrician

(C) E-mail some information

(D) Provide some images

Directions: You will hear some talks given by a single speaker. You will be asked to answer three questions about what the speaker says in each talk. Select the best response to each question and mark the letter (A), (B), (C), or (D).

---

28 What kind of product did the speaker order?

(A) Gloves

(B) Hand cream

(C) A sanitizer

(D) A gift box

29 What problem does the speaker mention?

(A) A product is the wrong kind.

(B) A delivery has been delayed.

(C) A package was not gift-wrapped.

(D) A package is damaged.

30 What does the speaker ask about?

(A) A shipping date

(B) A refund policy

(C) A gift item receipt

(D) A delivery fee

31 Who is the speaker?

(A) A history professor

(B) An artist

(C) A tour guide

(D) A musician

32 Who was Rosy Pisaro?

(A) An architect

(B) A photographer

(C) A curator

(D) A painter

33 Why does the speaker say, "Those objects are fragile"?

(A) To explain why the visitors cannot see some objects

(B) To explain why the visitors are prohibited from touching some objects

(C) To prevent the visitors from visiting a certain place

(D) To ask the visitors to donate some money

DAY 07 PARTS 3·4 문제 분석하기

PARTS 3·4 문제를 풀 때에는 대화나 담화를 듣기 전에 문제를 먼저 읽고 정확하게 분석하는 것이 중요하다. 문제 분석을 통해 정답이 언급되는 위치, 정답을 찾기 위해 집중해야 하는 정보가 무엇인지 미리 파악해야 한다.

> **오늘의 학습 POINT**
>
> **POINT 1** 질문 분석하기 - 정답이 언급되는 위치 파악하기
>
> **POINT 2** 선택지 분석하기 - 선택지 유형에 따라 분석하기

POINT 1 질문 분석하기 - 정답이 언급되는 위치 파악하기

PARTS 3·4의 질문 유형에는 아래와 같은 것들이 있으며, 각 유형에 따라 정답이 언급되는 위치도 다르다. 질문을 읽으면서, ① **문제의 유형을 파악**한 다음, ② **정답의 단서가 언급되는 위치**를 미리 생각해 두고, ③ **질문과 선택지의 키워드를 문제지에 표시**한 다음 대화나 담화를 들어야 한다.

- 주제와 목적을 묻는 질문
- 화자를 묻는 질문
- 대화나 담화의 장소를 묻는 질문
- 세부 사항을 묻는 질문 (키워드를 찾아 풀어야 하는 고난도 유형)
- 제안이나 요청 사항을 묻는 질문
- 다음에 일어날 일을 묻는 질문

cf. 질문의 파악은 각 파트별 디렉션 부분과 문제를 읽어주는 시간을 충분히 활용해서 미리 해 두어야 한다.

유형 분석

Q What are the speakers talking about?

07-01

→ 대화의 주제를 묻는 질문이다.

→ 이러한 유형의 경우 주로 대화의 초반에 정답의 단서가 언급된다.

→ 따라서 대화의 초반에 반복되는 단어들과 동의어에 집중하며 들어야 한다.

유형 분석

Q What will the listeners hear next?

07-02

→ 담화의 청자들이 담화 후 듣게 될 내용을 묻는 질문이다.

→ 이러한 유형의 경우 주로 대화의 마지막 부분에 정답의 단서가 언급된다.

→ 따라서 담화의 마지막 문장에서 언급하는 내용을 집중하며 들어야 한다.

- 질문에 about이 포함된 경우에는 대화나 담화의 전체적인 내용에 집중하며 문제를 풀어야 한다.
- 정답이 paraphrasing되어 제시되는 경우가 대부분이기 때문에 난이도가 높은 문제 유형이다.

cf. 질문에 about이 포함된 대표적인 유형

- What does the woman say about the book?
- What does the speaker mention about the event?

POINT 2 선택지 분석하기 - 선택지 유형에 따라 분석하기

PARTS 3·4 문제에는 4개의 선택지가 있다. 정답의 단서가 선택지 안에 있으므로 음원을 듣기 전에 반드시 선택지를 미리 읽고 근거가 될 부분을 찾아 두어야 한다. 하지만, 무턱대고 모든 선택지를 다 해석하는 것이 아니라 선택지의 유형에 따라 집중해야 하는 부분이 조금씩 다르므로 유형별로 살펴보도록 한다.

유형	분석
선택지가 모두 명사인 경우	선택지의 명사들에 집중하고, 각 명사의 동의어가 언급될 경우 주의하며 듣도록 한다.
선택지가 부정사나 동명사인 경우	부정사나 동명사 뒤의 목적어에 집중한다. 목적어가 언급되는 문장의 앞뒤에서 정답의 근거가 제시되는 경우가 많다.
선택지가 문장인 경우	모든 문장을 해석할 시간이 부족하므로, 문장의 주어와 목적어를 중심으로 최대한 빠르게 해석한다.

유형 분석

Q What will the man give the woman?

(A) A book

(B) A ticket

(C) Proof of purchase

(D) A letter

→ 선택지가 모두 명사이므로 명사에 집중한다.

→ 'I'll give you the receipt'라는 문장이 들렸다고 가정할 경우, give 뒤의 receipt이 정답의 단서이다.

→ 영수증은 '구매의 증거'이므로 동의어로 전환된 (C)가 정답이 될 것이다.

유형 분석

Q What does the man need help with?

(A) Preparing refreshments

(B) Setting up a machine

(C) Writing a report

(D) Accessing a system

→ 선택지가 모두 동명사 형태이므로 동명사의 목적어 부분에 집중한다.

→ 'I have a problem with the projector'라는 문장이 들렸다고 가정할 경우, 문제가 있는 부분인 projector가 정답의 단서이다.

→ projector는 기계이므로 동의어로 전환된 (B)가 정답이 될 것이다.

어휘	동의어	예문
work overtime 초과 근무하다	work after hours, work extra hours	Can you **work extra hours** on this weekend? 이번 주말에 몇 시간 더 일할 수 있나요?
demonstrate 시연하다	show how to	Mr. Miller will **demonstrate** the usage of the new tracking software. 밀러 씨는 우리에게 새로운 추적 프로그램의 사용법을 시연할 거예요.
detour 우회하다	take an alternate route, take a different road	I took a **detour** on my way home. 저는 집에 가는 길에 우회했어요.
locate 찾다	find	I had trouble **locating** your office. 저는 당신의 사무실을 찾는 데 어려움을 겪었어요.
distribute 나눠 주다	hand out, give out, pass out	**Distribute** some information. 정보를 나눠 주세요.
decline 거절하다	reject, turn down	I had to **decline** the invitation to the party. 저는 파티 초대를 거절해야만 했어요.
organize 정리하다; 준비하다	arrange, set up plan, coordinate	She decided to **organize** her bookshelf to make it neater. 그녀는 책꽂이를 더 깨끗하게 하기 위해 정리하기로 결정했어요. I need to **organize** my notes before the presentation tomorrow. 저는 내일 프레젠테이션 전에 저의 노트를 준비해야 해요.
tour 구경하다	show around	I'd like to **tour** the factory. 나는 그 공장을 견학하고 싶어요.
renovate 개조하다, 보수하다	redo, remodel, improve, upgrade	We plan to **renovate** our office. 우리는 우리 사무실을 보수할 계획이에요.
complete 완성하다	fill out	Please **complete** the document. 이 서류를 완성해 주세요.
visit 방문하다	stop by, drop by	I'll **visit** your place on the way to the library. 제가 도서관 가는 길에 당신의 집에 방문할게요.
reach (사람에게) 연락하다	call, contact	I tried to **reach** her, but I couldn't. 저는 그녀에게 연락하려고 시도했으나 할 수 없었어요.
attend 참석하다	make it, be there	She cannot **attend** the event. 그녀는 그 행사에 참여할 수 없어요.
hire 고용하다	employ, staff	The company decided to **hire** a new designer. 그 회사는 새로운 디자이너를 고용하기로 결정했어요.
review 고용하다	go over	Do you have time to **review** this report? 이 보고서를 검토해 줄 시간 있나요?

 실전 문제 연습 정답 및 해설 p.041

07-06

PART 1

Directions: You will hear four statements about the picture below. Select the one statement that best describes what you see in the picture and mark the letter (A), (B), (C), or (D).

1

(A)　　(B)　　(C)　　(D)

2

(A)　　(B)　　(C)　　(D)

3

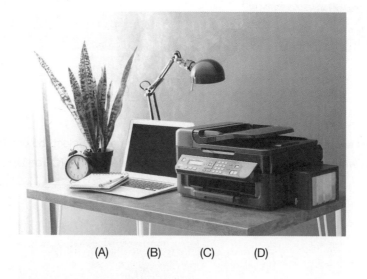

(A)   (B)   (C)   (D)

PART 2

Directions: You will hear a question or statement and three responses spoken in English. Select the best response to the question or statement and mark the letter (A), (B), or (C).

---

4 Mark your answer on your answer sheet.
(A)   (B)   (C)

5 Mark your answer on your answer sheet.
(A)   (B)   (C)

6 Mark your answer on your answer sheet.
(A)   (B)   (C)

7 Mark your answer on your answer sheet.
(A)   (B)   (C)

8 Mark your answer on your answer sheet.
(A)   (B)   (C)

9 Mark your answer on your answer sheet.
(A)   (B)   (C)

10 Mark your answer on your answer sheet.
(A)   (B)   (C)

11 Mark your answer on your answer sheet.
(A)   (B)   (C)

12 Mark your answer on your answer sheet.
(A)   (B)   (C)

13 Mark your answer on your answer sheet.
(A)   (B)   (C)

14 Mark your answer on your answer sheet.
(A)   (B)   (C)

15 Mark your answer on your answer sheet.
(A)   (B)   (C)

16 Mark your answer on your answer sheet.
(A)   (B)   (C)

17 Mark your answer on your answer sheet.
(A)   (B)   (C)

18 Mark your answer on your answer sheet.
(A)   (B)   (C)

Directions: You will hear some conversations between two or more people. You will be asked to answer three questions about what the speakers say in each conversation. Select the best response to each question and mark the letter (A), (B), (C), or (D).

19 Who most likely are the men?

(A) Electricians

(B) Mechanics

(C) Photographers

(D) IT support technicians

20 What caused the problem?

(A) Some staff members are unavailable.

(B) Too many devices were used at the same time.

(C) There are scheduling conflicts.

(D) Some devices have been misplaced.

21 What does Arthur say he can offer for the woman?

(A) A discount

(B) Movie tickets

(C) Antivirus software

(D) A plan upgrade

22 Where does the woman most likely work?

(A) At a clothing company

(B) At a gardening supply store

(C) At a landscaping company

(D) At a sports equipment store

23 Why is the man calling?

(A) He received the wrong size.

(B) He wants to change his order.

(C) There is a mistake in his order.

(D) He is confirming a delivery time.

24 What does the woman offer to do?

(A) Send items free of charge quickly

(B) Give the man a full refund

(C) Send someone to solve the problem

(D) Write a letter of apology to the man

25 Who most likely is the woman?

    (A) The man's assistant

    (B) A shop owner

    (C) An airline employee

    (D) A postal worker

26 What was in the desk drawer?

    (A) A credit card

    (B) A corrected invoice

    (C) A flight schedule

    (D) A delivery notice

27 What does the woman suggest Mr. Kim do?

    (A) Bring a form of identification

    (B) Open an account

    (C) Display a parking permit

    (D) Send some packages by express mail

PART 4

Directions: You will hear some talks given by a single speaker. You will be asked to answer three questions about what the speaker says in each talk. Select the best response to each question and mark the letter (A), (B), (C), or (D).

28 Where do the listeners most likely work?

(A) At a shoe store

(B) At a sporting goods store

(C) At a publishing company

(D) At a restaurant

29 Who is David Wilson?

(A) A famous athlete

(B) A store manager

(C) A chief executive

(D) A journalist

30 What is mentioned about the store?

(A) It will be the biggest store in the area.

(B) It is the most famous store in town.

(C) It is near public transportation.

(D) It has expanded its business.

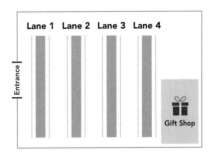

31 Where is the announcement being made?

(A) At a souvenir shop

(B) At a water park

(C) At a shopping mall

(D) At an amusement park

32 Look at the graphic. Which lane is the express pass lane?

(A) Lane 1

(B) Lane 2

(C) Lane 3

(D) Lane 4

33 According to the speaker, what is the most efficient way to report lost items?

(A) Filling out a form online

(B) Receiving assistance from the express lane

(C) Visiting the lost property department

(D) Checking the lost property box near the main entrance

DAY 08 PARTS 3·4 초반부 문제 풀이법

대화나 담화를 듣기 전에 문제를 먼저 읽고 정확하게 분석하는 것이 중요하다. 이때, 문제의 유형에 따라 정답의 단서가 언급되는 부분을 미리 예측한 다음 해당 부분에 집중해야 하는데, 이러한 문제들 중 대화나 담화의 초반부에서 단서가 주어지는 유형들에 대해 알아보자. 참고로, PARTS 3·4의 한 세트에 해당하는 세 문제들 중 첫 번째 문제의 단서는 주로 초반부에서 언급된다.

오늘의 학습 POINT

POINT 1 주제와 목적을 묻는 문제 해결하기
POINT 2 대화나 담화의 장소, 또는 화자를 묻는 문제 해결하기
POINT 3 문제점을 묻는 문제 해결하기

POINT 1 주제와 목적을 묻는 문제 해결하기

주제와 목적을 묻는 문제의 경우, PART 3은 각각의 화자가 첫 번째 언급한 말에서, PART 4는 담화 시작 부분의 세 문장에서 정답의 단서가 언급되는 경우가 95% 정도이다. 이러한 부분에서 ① 질문, ② 화자가 원하거나 필요한 것, ③ 공통적으로 언급되는 단어가 들릴 경우 이는 주제 및 목적과 관련된 정보임을 기억한다.

cf. 전화 통화나 음성 메시지의 경우 'I'm calling to ~', 'because ~'와 같이 전화를 건 목적이 직접적으로 언급되기도 한다.

유형 분석

08-01

M Welcome to your first day at Bright Industries. My name is John, and I'll be guiding today's orientation session. I'd like to start off by expressing how excited we are to have you join our team. While some companies experience frequent employee turnover, we're proud to have a dedicated workforce that has been with us for many years. Now, let's kick things off with an overview of our company's background. Please direct your attention to the presentation on the screen for more information.

Q What is the purpose of the meeting?

(A) To unveil a new marketing campaign
(B) To discuss upcoming company events
(C) To introduce new team members
(D) To present a financial report

→ 목적을 묻는 유형이므로, 시작하는 부분의 세 문장에 집중해서 정답의 단서를 찾는다.
→ 첫 두 문장에서 오리엔테이션을 진행한다고 이야기하면서, 청자들에게 우리 팀에 합류한 것이 기쁘다고 언급했다.
→ 새로운 멤버들을 환영하고 소개하기 위한 것이 회의의 목적임을 알 수 있으므로 정답은 (C)이다.

대화나 담화의 장소, 또는 화자를 묻는 문제는 한 세트의 세 문제들 중 첫 번째나 두 번째 문제인 경우가 대부분이다. 세 번째 문제로 주어지지는 않는다면, 장소나 화자를 묻는 문제의 정답은 시작 부분에서 간접적인 힌트들과 함께 언급된다.

○ 장소 및 화자 관련 빈출 어휘

공항 (airport)	check-in counter, window seat, aisle seat, boarding pass, gate, carousel, baggage claim area, customs office, passport, embarkation card, customs declaration, immigration, flight attendant, captain, transit
호텔 (hotel)	front desk, check in/out, reservation, ocean view, reception, concierge, guest relations office, bellboy, lobby
식당 (restaurant)	cook, chef, order, recipe, appetizer, main course (entrée), dessert, bill (check), waiter/waitress, serve, menu
병원 (hospital)	physician, doctor, surgeon, dentist, patient, medication, fill a prescription, take medicine, symptom, signs, shot, injection, surgery
약국 (pharmacy)	vitamin, OTC drug (over-the-counter medication), bandage, prescription, pharmacist
상점 (store)	return, refund, exchange, warranty, receipt, out of stock, shipment, inventory, store credit, size, color, warehouse
여행사 (travel agency)	trip/travel/tour, catalogue, itinerary, flight ticket, book/reserve, confirm/reconfirm, accommodations
우체국 (post office)	express mail, regular mail, overnight mail, package/parcel, courier service, postage, stamp
은행 (bank)	open an account, account number, balance, bank statement, teller, automatic teller machine (ATM), deposit, withdraw, transfer, cash a check, loan, interest rate, exchange rate, remit, checking account, savings account, personal check, money order, bankbook

08-02

W Good evening! I'm here to start my **stay**.

M Welcome! Could you please provide me with your **reservation** details?

W Sure. My name is Sarah Collins, and I have a **reservation** for a **room** tonight.

M Thank you, Ms. Collins. Let me check you in. Could you also show me some identification, please?

W Of course. Here's my driver's license.

M Perfect. Thank you. You're all set, Ms. Collins. Here's your room key.

Q Where does the conversation most likely take place?

(A) At a department store

(B) At a train station

(C) At a hotel check-in counter

(D) At a restaurant

→ 장소를 묻는 질문이므로 대화 초반에 언급되는 키워드를 잘 들어야 한다.

→ 두 사람의 대화에서 언급된 stay, reservation, 그리고 room이 문제 풀이의 키워드이다.

→ 해당 키워드를 근거로 대화의 장소가 호텔이라는 것을 알 수 있다. 정답은 (C)이다.

POINT 3   문제점을 묻는 문제 해결하기

문제점을 묻는 문제는 주제를 묻는 경우에 많이 사용된다. 따라서, 주제를 묻는 문제와 마찬가지로 정답의 단서가 초반부에 언급된다. 문제점을 묻는 문제는 부정적인 구문인 'but, however, not, actually' 등과 함께 언급된다.

08-03

W Excuse me, but I'm having trouble with this new software installation. It's for the graphic design project. The instructions are quite confusing. Can you spare a moment to assist me?

M I'm in the middle of an important call right now, but I'll be free in about 30 minutes. Can it wait until then?

W Unfortunately, I'm on a tight deadline and need to get this software up and running ASAP.

M In that case, you should reach out to Jake. He's experienced with this type of software and should be able to help you.

Q What does the man ask for help with?

(A) Assembling furniture

(B) Installing software

(C) Writing a research paper

(D) Cleaning his office

→ 문제점을 묻는 유형은 problem, trouble을 사용하여 직접 언급되기도 하지만, 예제와 같이 'need help'나 'ask for help'처럼 도움을 요청하는 유형인 경우도 있다.

→ 해당 유형은 시작 부분에서 부정적인 표현이나 문제점이 직접 언급되는지 집중해서 들어야 한다.

→ 대화 첫 문장의 trouble 뒤에 software installation이 직접 언급되고 있으므로 정답은 (B)이다.

어휘	하위 개념 어휘	예문
feedback 의견; 후기	idea, opinion, suggestion comment, review, testimonial	Can you give me some **feedback** about the budget proposal? 예산 보고서에 대한 의견을 좀 주시겠어요? You can find our customers' **feedback** on our Web site. 우리 웹사이트에서 고객들의 후기를 찾을 수 있습니다.
competition 대회	contest, race, marathon, match, championship, raffle	Thanks for joining us for this year's sports **competition**. 올해 스포츠 대회에 참가해 주셔서 감사합니다.
equipment 장비	모든 종류의 기계: camera, amplifier, projector 등	Can you help me set up some **equipment**? 장비 설치하는 것 좀 도와 주실래요?
change 변화하다	revise, modify, update	Can you **change** my reservation? 제 예약을 좀 바꿔 주시겠어요?
event 모임; 행사	gathering, meeting, function, party, conference, ceremony, festival	Please check the Web site for a full **event** schedule. 행사의 모든 일정표를 보려면 웹사이트를 확인하세요.
ride 수송 수단 = transportation	shuttle, train, bus	Can you give me a **ride** to the airport? 저를 공항에 데려다 주시겠어요?
document 서류, 문서	report, receipt, form	Please hand in all the **documents**. 모든 서류들을 제출해 주세요.
contact 연락하다	call, be in touch with, email, in person	Please **contact** your manager. 매니저에게 연락하세요.
device 장치	tablet, smartphone	I use a fitness tracking **device**. 저는 운동 추적 장치를 사용해요.
vehicle 탈것	car, truck, motorcycle	I plan to buy an electric **vehicle**. 저는 전기 차량을 구매할 계획이에요.
accommodations 숙박	inn, hotel	She lived in rented **accommodations**. 그녀는 임차한 숙소에서 살고 있어요.
place 장소	venue, location	We have to reserve a **place** for the convention. 우리는 컨벤션을 위한 장소를 예약해야 해요.
reading material 읽을 거리	book, journal	She is looking at some **reading materials**. 그녀는 몇몇 읽을 거리를 보고 있는 중이다.
construction work 건설 작업	renovation, building	The **construction work** for the new office building is scheduled to begin next month. 새로운 건물을 위한 건설 작업이 다음달에 시작될 예정입니다.

PART 1

Directions: You will hear four statements about the picture below. Select the one statement that best describes what you see in the picture and mark the letter (A), (B), (C), or (D).

1

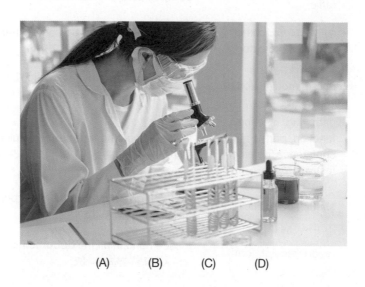

(A)   (B)   (C)   (D)

2

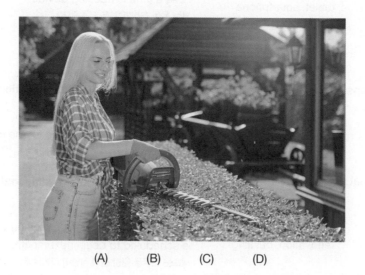

(A)   (B)   (C)   (D)

3

(A)　　　(B)　　　(C)　　　(D)

PART 2

Directions: You will hear a question or statement and three responses spoken in English. Select the best response to the question or statement and mark the letter (A), (B), or (C).

4　Mark your answer on your answer sheet.
　(A)　　　　(B)　　　　(C)

5　Mark your answer on your answer sheet.
　(A)　　　　(B)　　　　(C)

6　Mark your answer on your answer sheet.
　(A)　　　　(B)　　　　(C)

7　Mark your answer on your answer sheet.
　(A)　　　　(B)　　　　(C)

8　Mark your answer on your answer sheet.
　(A)　　　　(B)　　　　(C)

9　Mark your answer on your answer sheet.
　(A)　　　　(B)　　　　(C)

10　Mark your answer on your answer sheet.
　(A)　　　　(B)　　　　(C)

11　Mark your answer on your answer sheet.
　(A)　　　　(B)　　　　(C)

12　Mark your answer on your answer sheet.
　(A)　　　　(B)　　　　(C)

13　Mark your answer on your answer sheet.
　(A)　　　　(B)　　　　(C)

14　Mark your answer on your answer sheet.
　(A)　　　　(B)　　　　(C)

15　Mark your answer on your answer sheet.
　(A)　　　　(B)　　　　(C)

16　Mark your answer on your answer sheet.
　(A)　　　　(B)　　　　(C)

17　Mark your answer on your answer sheet.
　(A)　　　　(B)　　　　(C)

18　Mark your answer on your answer sheet.
　(A)　　　　(B)　　　　(C)

Directions: You will hear some conversations between two or more people. You will be asked to answer three questions about what the speakers say in each conversation. Select the best response to each question and mark the letter (A), (B), (C), or (D).

19   What department do the speakers work in?

(A) The Marketing Department

(B) The Human Resources Department

(C) The Tech Department

(D) The Financial Department

20   Why is the man pleased?

(A) Because some equipment will be upgraded

(B) Because there will be an expansion of the team

(C) Because bonuses will be distributed soon

(D) Because he is being promoted

21   What does the woman say has caused a delay?

(A) Unexpected budget cuts

(B) IT security issues

(C) A problem with the supply

(D) Management restructuring

22   Which department does the man probably work in?

(A) Research & Development

(B) Human Resource Management

(C) Production

(D) Accounting & Finance

23   What is the conversation mainly about?

(A) An employee resignation

(B) Monthly sales data

(C) A vacation request

(D) A product launch

24   What will happen in December?

(A) A tourism exhibition

(B) A birthday party

(C) A business convention

(D) A branch opening

**Silverdale Community Recreation Center
Class Schedule**

Mon	Tue	Wed	Thu	Fri
Yoga	Table Tennis	Tennis	Martial Arts	Badminton

25   Why is the man calling?

(A) To inquire about class supplies

(B) To report an absence

(C) To complain about an instructor

(D) To ask about a course fee

26   Look at the graphic. Which class are the speakers discussing?

(A) Yoga

(B) Table Tennis

(C) Tennis

(D) Badminton

27   Why will the man's class start next week?

(A) Due to the absence of an instructor

(B) Due to low enrollment

(C) Due to a public holiday

(D) Due to a renovation delay

28 What is the purpose of the announcement?

(A) To train some employees

(B) To find a seminar venue

(C) To provide notification of a schedule change

(D) To check the number of participants

29 What does the speaker say about Dr. Phillips?

(A) He will attend the workshop today.

(B) He canceled his seminar.

(C) He is the team leader.

(D) He will distribute training materials.

30 What does the man offer to do?

(A) Set up a venue

(B) Check a list

(C) Attend a training session

(D) Find some materials

31 What is being advertised?

(A) A streaming service

(B) An online magazine

(C) A newspaper subscription

(D) A new movie theater

32 What is mentioned about the business?

(A) It offers a free delivery service.

(B) It includes a subscription plan.

(C) It provides live sports streaming.

(D) It uses an advanced algorithm for recommendations.

33 Why should the listeners sign up through the Web site?

(A) To get a discount coupon

(B) To benefit from a promotional offer

(C) To get a free subscription

(D) To receive a free sample

DAY
09 PARTS 3·4 후반부 문제 풀이법

한 세트의 세 문제 중 마지막 문제로 출제되는 제안 문제의 경우 대화나 담화의 후반부에 정답의 단서가 언급된다. 다음에 할 일을 묻는 문제 또한 정답의 단서가 후반부에 언급된다. 이러한 유형의 문제를 풀 때에는 대화나 담화를 끝까지 들으면서 반전이 있는 내용은 없는지 확인해야 한다.

오늘의 학습 POINT

POINT 1 제안 문제의 정답의 근거 찾기
POINT 2 다음에 할 일 문제의 정답의 근거 찾기

POINT 1 제안 문제의 정답의 근거 찾기

1 질문 유형

제안 문제는 질문에 '제안'을 의미하는 동사가 포함되어 있다.

- What does the man **ask** the woman to do?
- What does the speaker **instruct** the listener to do?
- What is the woman **invited** to do?
- What **should** the listeners do after the event?

○ 제안을 의미하는 동사

suggest	recommend	ask	invite	advise	instruct	should	need to

2 답변 유형

제안 문제에 대한 정답의 단서는 아래의 표현들과 함께 언급된다.

- (please) 명령문 ~
- why don't you ~ / what about ~ / how about ~
- You should ~
- I recommend ~ / I suggest ~ / I ask ~

cf. 질문의 주어와 성별이 동일한 화자의 대화에서 정답의 단서가 언급된다.

- PART 4의 경우, 답변 유형들 중 평서문 유형인 '명령문'과 'you should ~' 형태의 정답이 가장 많이 등장한다.
- 답변에서 'should'는 잘 들리지 않으므로, 자주 듣고 따라 읽는 연습이 필수적이다.

유형 분석

09 - 01

M Excuse me. There are some errors in the database. It's crucial for the meeting with the client tomorrow, and I can't understand the error message. Can you come and fix it?

W I'm installing new software now, but I'll be free in about 20 minutes. Is it okay for you to wait?

M Actually, I need to get this fixed right away.

W If you're in a hurry, you should contact Alex. He's excellent with database issues and might be able to help.

Q What does the woman suggest that the man do?

(A) Wait for her to finish some reports

(B) Talk to a colleague

(C) Contact a software support hotline

(D) Try to figure a problem out on his own

→ suggest가 포함된 질문의 유형이므로 제안 문제임을 알 수 있다.

→ 질문의 주어와 성별이 동일한 화자의 말에서 정답을 찾아야 하므로, 여자의 말에서 정답의 단서를 찾는다.

→ 특히, 제안이나 요청을 하는 표현, 예를 들어 'why don't you', 'you should' 혹은 'please' 등의 표현 뒤에 집중한다.

→ 대화 마지막 부분에서 알렉스(Alex)에게 연락하라고 했으므로 동료에게 말해보라는 내용의 (B)가 정답이 된다.

POINT 2 | 다음에 할 일 문제의 정답의 근거 찾기

1 질문 유형

- What will happen **next**?
- What do the listeners do **after the meeting**?
- What can listeners hear **next**?
- What will the man do **next**?

2 답변 유형

다음에 할 일을 묻는 문제에 대한 정답의 단서는 아래의 표현들과 함께 언급된다. 이와 같은 미래 시제, 앞으로 할 일, 제안 등의 표현과 함께 언급되는 단서를 잘 듣고 정답을 찾을 수 있어야 한다.

- I will ~ / I can ~ / Let me ~
- I'm going to ~
- I need to ~
- Why don't I ~
- Would you like me to ~

cf. 질문에 동사 offer가 포함되어 '내가 무엇을 해 줄지'를 묻는 내용일 경우, 이는 다음에 할 일을 묻는 문제와 동일한 유형이다. 정답의 단서 또한 '다음에 할 일'을 묻는 문제와 동일하게 미래 시제와 함께 언급된다.

TIP! 다음에 할 일 문제 풀이 팁

- 다음에 할 일, 즉 미래에 일어날 일을 묻는 질문 유형의 경우 주로 대화나 담화의 마지막 2~3문장에서 정답의 단서가 언급된다.
- 이미 언급된 정답이 대화나 담화의 마지막 부분에서 반전되기도 하므로 끝까지 집중하며 들어야 한다.
- 선택지 중 두 개의 내용이 들려 혼동된다면, 마지막에 들린 것이 정답일 가능성이 높다.

유형 분석

09 - 02

M Excuse me. Do you have a key to the storage room on the third floor? Someone called me to report that a valuable item is missing, so I need to check on it.

W1 Our security officer should have a key. She's right here. Emma, can you open the storage room?

W2 I'll do that immediately. Just let me know if you need any assistance.

M Thank you. Before I begin the inspection, I need to notify the manager about the situation.

Q What will the man do next?

(A) Begin the inspection
(B) Call the police
(C) Search for the missing item
(D) Notify the manager

→ 다음에 일어날 일을 묻는 질문 유형이므로, 대화의 마지막 부분을 집중해서 들어야 한다.

→ 대화 마지막 부분에서 'I need to'로 시작하는 문장을 듣고, '매니저에게 보고한다'는 내용의 선택지인 (D)를 정답으로 골라야 한다.

09 - 03

어휘	동의어	예문
branch 지점	another office, second office, (지역명) office	Our goal for the next quarter is to open a new **branch**. 우리의 다음 분기의 목표는 지점을 여는 것이다.
schedule 약속; 일정표	appointment, meeting timeline, calendar	I can clear my **schedule** tomorrow. 내일 일정을 비우겠습니다. I'll have to check my **schedule** first. 제 일정표를 먼저 확인해야 하겠네요.
problem 문제	issue, trouble, difficulty	I have a **problem** finding the cheese brand I want. 제가 원하는 치즈 브랜드를 찾기가 어렵네요.
detail 정보, 세부 사항	information, specification	I want to get some **details** about your catering service. 당신의 케이터링 서비스에 관해 정보를 얻고 싶어요.
merger 합병	acquisition, takeover	Did you hear the news about our company **merger**? 우리 회사의 합병 뉴스 들었어요?
coworker 동료	employee, colleague, 사람 이름, 직책	I can ask my **coworker** Andre to attend the meeting instead. 제가 동료인 안드레에게 연락해서 회의에 대신 참석해 달라고 요청할 수 있어요.
bill 청구서, 계산서	invoice	The waiter brought us the **bill**. 웨이터가 우리에게 계산서를 가져다 주었어요.
free 무료의	complimentary, at no charge	We'll provide a **free** shuttle bus to the convention center. 우리는 컨벤션 센터까지 무료 셔틀 버스를 제공할 것입니다.
itinerary 일정표	travel plan, travel schedule	I'll e-mail you the details of your **itinerary**. 여행 일정표의 세부 사항을 이메일로 보내 드릴게요.
size 크기	measurement, dimension	Can you give me the exact **size** of the room? 방의 정확한 크기를 알려 주시겠어요?
online 온라인	internet, Web site	You can find out more information **online**. 온라인에서 더 많은 정보를 찾을 수 있어요.
photo 사진	image, picture	Post your travel **photos** on our social media page. 우리 소셜미디어 페이지에 여행 사진을 올려 주세요.
contract 계약서	agreement	You have to sign the **contract** by the end of the week. 이번 주말까지 계약서에 사인을 해야 합니다.
policy 정책, 방침	rule, regulation, guideline	The company's dress code **policy** requires workers to wear uniforms. 회사의 복장 규정은 직원들이 유니폼을 입는 것입니다.
advertisement 광고	campaign, commercial	I saw the **advertisement** we made for Colson Industry. 저는 우리가 콜슨 사를 위해서 만든 광고를 보았어요.

PART 1

Directions: You will hear four statements about the picture below. Select the one statement that best describes what you see in the picture and mark the letter (A), (B), (C), or (D).

1

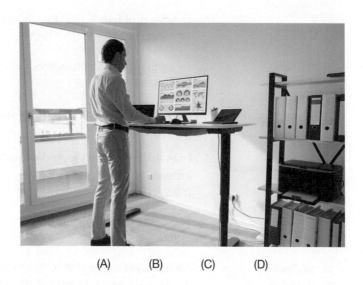

(A)　　(B)　　(C)　　(D)

2

(A)　　(B)　　(C)　　(D)

3

(A)   (B)   (C)   (D)

PART 2

Directions: You will hear a question or statement and three responses spoken in English. Select the best response to the question or statement and mark the letter (A), (B), or (C).

---

4   Mark your answer on your answer sheet.
     (A)   (B)   (C)

5   Mark your answer on your answer sheet.
     (A)   (B)   (C)

6   Mark your answer on your answer sheet.
     (A)   (B)   (C)

7   Mark your answer on your answer sheet.
     (A)   (B)   (C)

8   Mark your answer on your answer sheet.
     (A)   (B)   (C)

9   Mark your answer on your answer sheet.
     (A)   (B)   (C)

10   Mark your answer on your answer sheet.
     (A)   (B)   (C)

11   Mark your answer on your answer sheet.
     (A)   (B)   (C)

12   Mark your answer on your answer sheet.
     (A)   (B)   (C)

13   Mark your answer on your answer sheet.
     (A)   (B)   (C)

14   Mark your answer on your answer sheet.
     (A)   (B)   (C)

15   Mark your answer on your answer sheet.
     (A)   (B)   (C)

16   Mark your answer on your answer sheet.
     (A)   (B)   (C)

17   Mark your answer on your answer sheet.
     (A)   (B)   (C)

18   Mark your answer on your answer sheet.
     (A)   (B)   (C)

PART 3

Directions: You will hear some conversations between two or more people. You will be asked to answer three questions about what the speakers say in each conversation. Select the best response to each question and mark the letter (A), (B), (C), or (D).

19 What is the woman's profession?

(A) Biology teacher
(B) Receptionist
(C) Event coordinator
(D) Tour guide

20 How can the woman organize a field trip?

(A) By calling the garden directly
(B) By completing a document
(C) By paying a fee
(D) By visiting in person

21 What does the man suggest the woman do?

(A) Visit the garden's Web site
(B) Make a reservation
(C) Organize transportation
(D) Submit a lesson plan

22 Why is the man meeting the woman?

(A) To enroll in a program
(B) To evaluate a business
(C) To make some travel arrangements
(D) To conduct a job interview

23 Why did the man decide to make a change?

(A) He is unfamiliar with the area.
(B) His commute is inconvenient.
(C) His job requires too much travel.
(D) He wants to get a raise.

24 What does the woman offer to do?

(A) Give the man time to present his portfolio
(B) Give a tour
(C) Introduce the man to her coworkers
(D) Negotiate a salary

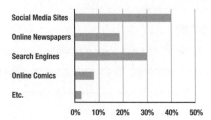

25 Where do the speakers most likely work?

(A) At a fragrance company
(B) At a pharmaceutical company
(C) At an advertising company
(D) At a department store

26 Look at the graphic. Where do the speakers plan to start advertising their product?

(A) Social media sites
(B) Online newspapers
(C) Search engines
(D) Online comics

27 What does the woman say she will do tomorrow?

(A) Carry out some field research
(B) Test a new product
(C) Attend a workshop
(D) Propose a budget adjustment

Directions: You will hear some talks given by a single speaker. You will be asked to answer three questions about what the speaker says in each talk. Select the best response to each question and mark the letter (A), (B), (C), or (D).

28 What does the store sell?

(A) Clothing

(B) Groceries

(C) Glassware

(D) Cosmetics

29 What does the speaker emphasize about the products?

(A) They are fresh.

(B) They are on special offer.

(C) They are not environmentally harmful.

(D) They are almost out of stock.

30 What ends on Friday?

(A) Free paper bags

(B) A sale on fruit

(C) Free delivery

(D) A discount

31 Where is the speaker?

(A) At an amusement park

(B) At a lake

(C) At a zoo

(D) At a park

32 What will happen next month?

(A) A construction project will begin.

(B) A park will open.

(C) A new exhibit will be set up.

(D) A show will take place.

33 Why does the speaker say, "The rules and regulations will be listed at the entry point of the dog park"?

(A) To invite people to use a park

(B) To keep a place clean all the time

(C) To ask people to read a list

(D) To encourage people to donate money

PARTS 3·4 키워드 문제 풀이법

PARTS 3·4 문제의 절반 정도는 '키워드 문제 유형'이다. '키워드 문제 유형'이란 질문에 포함된 키워드인 특정 단어나 구가 언급되는 문장을 듣고 정답을 찾아야 하는 유형이다. 이는 듣기 능력이 매우 중요한 문제 유형이며, 정답이 동일한 단어로 언급되는 경우와 paraphrasing되는 경우의 비율이 거의 동일하다.

오늘의 학습 POINT

POINT 1 질문 속의 주요 키워드
POINT 2 Why나 How 의문사로 시작하는 질문의 키워드
POINT 3 'about + 명사'로 끝나는 질문의 키워드
POINT 4 자주 등장하는 paraphrasing

POINT 1 질문 속의 주요 키워드

키워드 유형이란 질문에 포함된 키워드를 파악한 다음, 대화나 담화에서 해당 키워드인 단어나 구가 언급된 부분에서 정답의 단서를 찾아야 하는 문제 유형이다. 대표적인 키워드 문제는 질문 속에 ① **시간**, ② **숫자**, ③ **장소**, ④ **고유명사(이름, 제품명, 상호 등)** 등이 포함된 유형이다.

> **유형 분석**

Q What will the man do **tomorrow**?
→ 대화나 담화에서 키워드인 tomorrow가 언급된 부분의 앞뒤에 정답의 단서가 있다.
→ 주의할 것은 키워드가 언급된 이후뿐만 아니라, 언급되기 전에 정답의 단서가 먼저 등장하는 비율이 높은 편이다. 이러한 경우에는 문제의 난이도가 더 높다.

10 - 01

> **유형 분석**

Q What does the woman ask **Mark** to do?
→ 대화나 담화에서 키워드인 Mark가 언급된 부분의 앞뒤에 정답의 단서가 있다.
→ PART 3의 경우 다른 성별의 화자가 키워드인 '이름'을 부른 직후에 정답의 단서가 언급되는 경우가 90% 정도이다.

10 - 02

POINT 2 Why나 How 의문사로 시작하는 질문의 키워드

의문사 Why나 How로 시작하는 질문 유형의 경우, 해당 의문사 뒤에 나오는 문장 전체의 내용이 언급되는 부분에 정답의 단서가 있다. 주의해야 할 점은 해당 문장이 그대로 언급되는 것이 아니라, 의미는 같지만 해당 문장과 똑같지 않은 문장이 언급된다는 것이다. 따라서 다른 문제 유형들보다 듣기 능력이 더 중요하게 요구된다.

유형 분석

Q Why **was the woman late for the meeting**?

→ 질문의 키워드는 'the woman late'이다.

→ 여자가 회의에 늦은 이유를 묻는 질문이므로, 남자가 'why are you late?'이라고 묻거나 여자가 'I'm sorry I'm late'와
같이 늦었다고 말하는 부분에서 정답의 단서를 찾아야 한다.

유형 분석

Q How **can the woman find more information**?

→ 질문의 키워드는 'find more information'이다.

→ 여자가 정보를 찾을 수 있는 방법을 묻는 질문이므로 남자의 말에서 정답의 단서를 찾아야 한다.

→ 'to get more details', 'for more information', 혹은 'if you have any questions' 등과 같이 찾는 것과
관련 있는 내용을 언급한 부분을 잘 들어야 한다.

POINT 3   **'about + 명사'로 끝나는 질문의 키워드**

질문이 'about + 명사'로 끝나는 유형으로서, 키워드는 about 뒤의 명사이다. 예를 들면 'What does the man say
about the products?'와 같은 질문의 경우, 키워드는 about뒤에 있는 'the products'이다. 키워드가 언급된 부분
에서 정답의 근거가 등장하는데, 대부분의 경우 paraphrasing되어 언급되기 때문에 대화나 담화의 내용을 정확하
게 이해해야 한다.

유형 분석

Q What does the woman say **about the park**?

→ 질문의 키워드는 the park이므로, the park이 언급되는 부분에서 정답의 단서를 찾도록 한다.

→ 항상 키워드가 언급된 뒤에 정답의 단서가 주어지는 것은 아니며, 키워드가 언급되기 전에 단서가 주어질 수도 있다는
사실에 주의하자.

POINT 4   **자주 등장하는 paraphrasing**

❶ '포괄적 단어'를 사용하는 경우

정답의 단서와 동일한 단어가 아니라, 이를 포함하는 상위 개념의 단어를 사용한 선택지를 정답으로 골라야 하는
유형이다.

문제 What are the speakers talking about?

단서 Please **call** us at 555-1254.

정답 **Contact** the store later

→ 정답의 단서인 call이 상위 개념의 단어인 contact으로 전환되었다.

2 직접적인 동의어를 사용하는 경우

정답의 단서가 되는 단어의 동의어를 이용해서 정답을 주는 경우가 가장 많이 등장하는 유형 중의 하나이다.
이때 중요한 것은 사전적인 동의어가 아니라 문맥상 어울리는 동의어가 사용된다는 것이다.

문제 What can be found on the Web site?

단서 You can find **pictures** on our Web site.

정답 Some **photos**

→ 정답의 단서인 pictures가 동의어인 photos로 전환되었다.

3 단어의 배열 순서를 변경하는 경우

정답의 단서가 되는 단어들의 배열과 품사를 변경한 정답이 자주 등장한다.

문제 What will happen at 4:00 P.M.?

단서 I'll **meet our staff** at 4:00 today.

정답 A **staff meeting**

→ 정답의 단서가 되는 'meet our staff'에서 meet이라는 동사가 명사인 meeting으로 전환되었고, staff와 meet의
순서가 뒤바뀌었다.

4 줄여서 말하는 경우

긴 수식어가 포함된 부분에서 수식어를 빼고 핵심 단어만 남기는 형태 또한 paraphrasing의 한 가지 유형이다.

문제 What will the woman probably do next?

단서 I'll attend **a software developers workshop**.

정답 Attend **a workshop**

→ 정답의 단서는 'a software developers workshop'인데, 수식어 부분인 'software developers'를 제외하고
'a workshop'으로 줄인 형태의 정답이 제시되었다.

TIP! paraphrasing 학습 방법

- paraphrasing의 다른 유형들도 있기는 하지만, 85% 이상의 경우 이와 같은 4가지 유형에 해당한다.
- 문제를 풀 때 대화나 담화에서 언급된 정답의 단서와 선택지를 비교해 보면서, 정답이 어떻게 paraphrasing되었는지를
  파악한다. 그런 다음 본인이 자주 틀리는 유형들을 정리한다.
- 자주 출제되는 '동의어'나 '포괄적 단어'를 정리해서 암기해 두어야 한다.

여행 관련 어휘

passport 여권	I need to obtain a **passport** for this summer vacation. 저는 여름 휴가를 위해 여권을 발급 받아야 합니다.
book 예약하다	He **booked** a plane ticket to Jeju Island. 그는 제주도행 비행기 표를 예약했습니다.
hospitality business 접객업 (ex. 호텔)	The company operates a renowned **hospitality business** known for its high-quality service. 그 회사는 높은 품질의 서비스로 유명한 접객업을 운영하고 있습니다.
excursion (단체로 짧게 하는) 여행	How did you enjoy your **excursion**? 여행은 어땠나요?
transfer 환승하다	I have to **transfer** to another flight to New York from Seoul. 저는 서울에서 뉴욕으로 가는 다른 비행기로 갈아타야 합니다.

구매 관련 어휘

refund 환불	I returned the defective product to the store and received a full **refund**. 저는 결함 있는 상품을 상점에 반품하고 전액 환불을 받았습니다.
invoice 송장, 청구서	I received an **invoice** for the items I ordered online. 저는 온라인으로 주문한 물건에 대한 송장을 받았습니다.
expedite 더 신속히 처리하다	We need to **expedite** the delivery to meet the tight deadline. 우리는 촉박한 마감 기한에 맞추기 위해 배송을 신속히 처리해야 합니다.
inventory 재고	Our **inventory** includes a wide range of electronic gadgets. 우리 재고에는 다양한 전자 장치가 포함되어 있습니다.
in stock 재고가 있는 ↔ out of stock	The popular product is currently **in stock**, so you can order it now. 인기 있는 제품은 현재 재고가 있으므로 지금 주문하실 수 있습니다.

교통 관련 어휘

congested 정체된	The traffic was very **congested**. 교통이 몹시 정체되어 있었습니다.
public transportation 대중교통	Many people prefer using **public transportation** to reduce their carbon footprint. 많은 사람들이 탄소 배출량을 줄이기 위해 대중교통을 이용하는 것을 선호합니다.
transit 교통, 수송	The product is currently in **transit** and is being transported inside a truck. 제품은 현재 배송 중이며, 현재 트럭으로 이동 중입니다.
pave 도로를 포장하다	The road construction team is working diligently every day to **pave** the road. 도로를 포장하기 위해서 도로 건설팀은 매일 부지런히 작업을 하고 있습니다.
fine 벌금; 벌금을 부과하다	The **fine** shall not exceed $300. 벌금은 300달러를 초과하지 못합니다.

PART 1

Directions: You will hear four statements about the picture below. Select the one statement that best describes what you see in the picture and mark the letter (A), (B), (C), or (D).

1

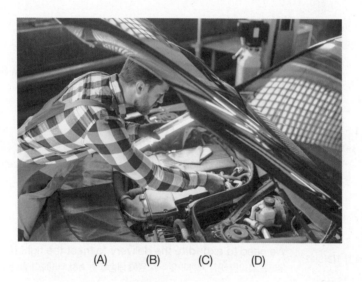

(A)　　　　(B)　　　　(C)　　　　(D)

2

(A)　　　　(B)　　　　(C)　　　　(D)

3

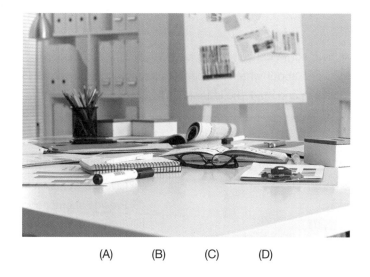

(A)   (B)   (C)   (D)

PART 2

Directions: You will hear a question or statement and three responses spoken in English. Select the best response to the question or statement and mark the letter (A), (B), or (C).

---

4   Mark your answer on your answer sheet.

    (A)   (B)   (C)

5   Mark your answer on your answer sheet.

    (A)   (B)   (C)

6   Mark your answer on your answer sheet.

    (A)   (B)   (C)

7   Mark your answer on your answer sheet.

    (A)   (B)   (C)

8   Mark your answer on your answer sheet.

    (A)   (B)   (C)

9   Mark your answer on your answer sheet.

    (A)   (B)   (C)

10   Mark your answer on your answer sheet.

    (A)   (B)   (C)

11   Mark your answer on your answer sheet.

    (A)   (B)   (C)

12   Mark your answer on your answer sheet.

    (A)   (B)   (C)

13   Mark your answer on your answer sheet.

    (A)   (B)   (C)

14   Mark your answer on your answer sheet.

    (A)   (B)   (C)

15   Mark your answer on your answer sheet.

    (A)   (B)   (C)

16   Mark your answer on your answer sheet.

    (A)   (B)   (C)

17   Mark your answer on your answer sheet.

    (A)   (B)   (C)

18   Mark your answer on your answer sheet.

    (A)   (B)   (C)

PART 3

Directions: You will hear some conversations between two or more people. You will be asked to answer three questions about what the speakers say in each conversation. Select the best response to each question and mark the letter (A), (B), (C), or (D).

19 Where does the conversation take place?

(A) At a corporate party
(B) At a grocery store
(C) On a school campus
(D) At an airport

20 Why is the conversation taking place?

(A) To announce a new company policy
(B) To talk about an advertising campaign
(C) To discuss a job opportunity
(D) To start a new educational program

21 What does the woman offer to do?

(A) Give a tour
(B) Start an interview
(C) Show the state-of-the-art facility
(D) Work on the report

22 Why does the woman need help?

(A) A machine isn't working properly.
(B) She doesn't have time to make copies.
(C) She didn't finish her work on time.
(D) A copy machine is out of paper.

23 What does the woman say she will do?

(A) Call a repairperson
(B) Take a break
(C) Start a machine immediately
(D) Push a red button

24 What is the man asked to do?

(A) Give the woman a manual
(B) Provide another copier
(C) Turn off a machine
(D) Take a break

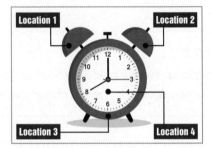

25 What kind of business do the speakers work for?

(A) A manufacturing company
(B) A design company
(C) An employment company
(D) A technology company

26 What problem does the man mention about the product?

(A) Safety
(B) Noise
(C) Price
(D) Size

27 Look at the graphic. Where will the company's logo be placed?

(A) Location 1
(B) Location 2
(C) Location 3
(D) Location 4

Directions: You will hear some talks given by a single speaker. You will be asked to answer three questions about what the speaker says in each talk. Select the best response to each question and mark the letter (A), (B), (C), or (D).

28 Who most likely are the listeners?

(A) Shareholders
(B) Employees
(C) Conference attendees
(D) Competitors

29 What type of company does the speaker work for?

(A) A software development firm
(B) A computer manufacturing company
(C) A cloud service provider
(D) An Internet service provider

30 How can the listeners view project details?

(A) By visiting a Web site
(B) By using some software
(C) By attending a training session
(D) By reviewing a brochure

31 Where most likely does the speaker work?

(A) At a media outlet
(B) At a shopping mall
(C) At a convention center
(D) At a hotel

32 What will happen on Sunday?

(A) A store opening
(B) A live furniture auction
(C) A trade fair
(D) A charity event

33 Why does the speaker say, "The event will last for only one day"?

(A) To ask the listeners for some help
(B) To inform the listeners of a date
(C) To publicize a store
(D) To encourage the listeners to attend an event

DAY
11

PARTS 3·4 시각 정보 문제 풀이법

시각 정보 문제는 PART 3과 PART 4에서 각각 2~3 문제 출제된다. 도표나 그래프 등의 시각 정보가 포함되어 있으며 시각 정보의 내용이 선택지로 주어진다. 선택지의 단어를 그대로 언급하면서 정답의 단서를 주는 것이 아니라, 선택지의 단어 주변의 정보들을 통해서 단서가 주어진다.

오늘의 학습 POINT

POINT 1	시각 정보 문제 풀이의 예시
POINT 2	그래프가 포함된 문제 풀이법
POINT 3	지도나 평면도가 포함된 문제 풀이법
POINT 4	도표가 포함된 문제 풀이법

POINT 1 시각 정보 문제 풀이의 예시

❶ 문제 유형

- 대화나 담화 한 세트에 해당하는 세 문제 중 한 문제가 주어진 이미지를 보고 해결하는 문제 유형으로 등장한다.
- PARTS 3·4 문제 중 매달 4~6문제 출제된다.
- 대부분의 경우 PART 3에서 세 문제, PART 4에서 두 문제 출제된다.
- 시각 정보 문제는 'Look at the graphic.'으로 시작한다.
- 시각 정보의 종류는 도표, 리스트, 그래프, 지도, 평면도, 도면, 쿠폰, 티켓, 영수증 등 다양하다.

❷ 풀이법

❶ 문제를 듣기 전에 시각 정보를 미리 분석해야 한다.

듣기가 시작된 이후에는 시각 정보를 볼 시간이 없다. 따라서, PART 1의 Direction을 읽어 주는 시간에 시각 정보를 미리 분석해 두어야 한다. 이때, 선택지와 일치하는 부분을 시각 정보에서 찾아 표시해 두어야 한다.

Big Festival Sale
UP TO **50%** OFF

A • **25%** Off on Shoes
B • **30%** Off on Sunglasses
C • **45%** Off on Underwear

Q Look at the graphic. How much of a discount does the woman get?

(A) 25%
(B) 30%
(C) 45%
(D) 50%

→ 시각 정보가 주어지면, 선택지와 일치하는 부분을 찾아 (A), (B), (C), (D)로 미리 표시한 다음 듣기를 시작해야 한다.

❷ 선택지가 아닌 시각 정보를 보면서 음원을 들어야 한다.

대화나 담화에서 시각 정보의 내용과 일치하는 정보가 정답의 단서이므로, 시각 정보를 보면서 문제를 풀어야 한다. graph, poster, floor plan 등과 같은 시각 정보의 종류를 언급하면서 대화나 담화가 시작되는 경우가 많다.

❸ 선택지를 직접 언급하는 정답은 주어지지 않는다.

위 유형 분석에서 선택지의 정보는 할인율이지만, 할인율 옆의 정보인 shoes, sunglasses, underwear가 언급되는 부분에서 정답의 단서가 주어진다. 오히려 할인율이 직접 언급되면 함정일 가능성이 높다.

POINT 2 **그래프가 포함된 문제 풀이법**

막대그래프(bar graph)나 선그래프(line graph)가 주어지는 경우 ① **가로축의 각 항목에 해당하는 세로축의 숫자**, ② **증가하거나 감소한 시점**, ③ **가장 낮은 지점과 가장 높은 지점**, ④ **두 번째로 높거나 낮은 지점** 등의 정보에 집중해야 한다.

cf. 최상급을 언급하여 가장 높거나 낮은 지점이 정답으로 주어지는 경우가 많기는 하지만, 최상급 앞에 next나 second를 붙여 두 번째로 높거나 낮은 지점이 정답으로 주어지는 경우도 많다.

○ 반드시 기억해야 하는 증가와 감소의 단어

- **증가하다:** increase, incline, boom, boost, rise, grow, rocket, surge, peak, uplift
- **감소하다:** decrease, fall, decline, plunge, plummet, drop, dive, reduce

Q Look at the graphic. In which month did the company offer a discount?

(A) January

(B) February

(C) March

(D) April

→ 위와 같이 그래프 상에서 '증가', '감소', '최상급' 등을 표시한 다음 음원을 듣도록 한다.

POINT 3 지도나 평면도가 포함된 문제 풀이법

지도나 평면도가 주어지는 경우, ① **오른쪽과 왼쪽 방향을 나타내는 표현**, ② **방향을 알려주는 전치사구**, ③ **'건너편'을 의미하는 표현**, ④ **우회전, 좌회전을 나타내는 표현**, ⑤ **거리를 설명하는 표현** 등에 집중하며 들어야 한다.

○ 반드시 기억해야 하는 표현

- **방향을 알려주는 전치사구**
  next to, by ('옆'을 의미)　　between ('사이'를 의미)　　across ('건너편'을 의미)

- **거리를 설명하는 표현**
  closest to ('가장 가까운 곳'을 의미)　　farthest from ('가장 먼 곳'을 의미)

> **cf.** 지도와 평면도에서 오른쪽과 왼쪽을 구별하기 위한 기준으로 사용할 수 있는 것은 elevator와 entrance가 가장 대표적이다.

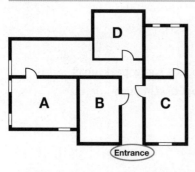

Q Look at the graphic. Which office will the man use?

(A) A

(B) B

(C) C

(D) D

→ 방향을 구별하는 것은 지문을 듣는 동안에는 혼동될 수 있으므로, 항상 기준점이 되는 단어에 표시해 두어야 한다.

→ 위의 시각 정보에서 (C)가 정답일 경우 'right side of the entrance', 'corner office' 등의 표현이 정답의 단서가 된다.

POINT 4   도표가 포함된 문제 풀이법

도표가 주어지는 경우, 선택지의 정보가 작성된 열이 아닌 다른 열의 정보를 듣고 정답을 찾아야 한다. 열이 2개인 경우가 대부분이지만, 열이 3개인 문제도 출제되는 추세이다.

유형 분석

Service Plan

Service	Price	Number of People
Sunflower	$100	30
Marigold	$200	50
Rose	$300	70
Lily	$400	100

Q Look at the graphic. Which service will the woman choose?

(A) Sunflower
(B) Marigold
(C) Rose
(D) Lily

→ 위 도표에서 선택지에 있는 서비스명이 직접적으로 언급되지는 않는다.

→ 가격이나 사람의 수가 언급되면, 이를 듣고 해당되는 서비스를 정답으로 골라야 한다.

TIP! 순서를 의미하는 표현

• 시각 정보 문제의 경우 첫 번째인지 마지막인지 등의 순서를 묻는 문제 유형이 출제될 수 있다. 그러므로 대화나 담화에서 '서수'와 같은 순서를 의미하는 표현이 언급될 경우 잘 들어야 한다.

대중매체 관련 어휘

autobiography 자서전	His **autobiography** will be published soon. 그의 자서전이 곧 출판될 것입니다.
press conference 기자회견	The company has scheduled a **press conference** for tomorrow. 그 회사는 내일 기자회견을 계획했습니다.
periodical 정기 간행물	I subscribe to several **periodicals** to stay updated on the latest developments. 저는 최신 동향을 계속해서 알기 위해 몇 권의 정기 간행물을 구독 중입니다.
copyright 판권, 저작권	The author retained the **copyright** to her novel. 그 작가는 자신의 소설에 대한 저작권을 유지했습니다.
subscribe to ~을 구독하다	I **subscribe to** a weekly magazine to keep up with the latest news and trends. 저는 최신 뉴스와 트렌드를 따라가기 위해 주간 잡지를 구독합니다.

환경 관련 어휘

pollutant 오염 물질	The government has implemented strict regulations to control water **pollutants**. 정부는 수질 오염 물질을 관리하기 위해 강력한 규제를 실행하고 있습니다.
eco-friendly 환경친화적인	Many people are adopting **eco-friendly** lifestyles. 많은 사람들이 친환경적인 삶의 방식을 적용하고 있습니다.
preserve 보호하다	National parks are established to **preserve** natural beauty. 국립 공원은 자연의 아름다움을 보존하기 위해 설립됩니다.
sustainable (환경 파괴 없이) 지속 가능한	The fashion industry is increasingly focusing on **sustainable** fashion. 패션 산업은 지속 가능한 패션에 더욱 관심을 기울이고 있습니다.
recycle 재활용하다	It's important to **recycle** paper, glass, and plastic to reduce waste. 쓰레기를 줄이기 위해 종이, 유리, 그리고 플라스틱을 재활용하는 것이 중요합니다.

산업 관련 어휘

cooperation 협력 = collaboration	The successful project was the result of excellent **cooperation** among team members. 성공한 프로젝트는 팀 구성원들 간의 훌륭한 협력의 결과였습니다.
ensure 보증하다 = guarantee	Wearing a seatbelt helps **ensure** your safety while driving. 안전벨트를 착용하는 것은 운전 중 안전을 확보하는 데 도움이 됩니다.
transaction 거래	The bank provides a detailed statement of every **transaction**. 은행은 모든 거래에 대한 상세한 명세서를 제공합니다.
utility company 공공 서비스 회사	The **utility company** is responsible for supplying electricity and water to our city. 공공 서비스 회사는 우리 도시에 전기와 물을 공급하는 역할을 담당합니다.
apparel 의복 = clothing	The fashion store offers a wide range of **apparel**, including dresses, jeans, and shirts. 이 패션 매장은 드레스, 청바지, 셔츠를 포함한 다양한 의류를 제공합니다.

 실전 문제 연습

정답 및 해설 p.068

PART 1

Directions: You will hear four statements about the picture below. Select the one statement that best describes what you see in the picture and mark the letter (A), (B), (C), or (D).

1

(A) (B) (C) (D)

2

(A) (B) (C) (D)

3

     (A)   (B)   (C)   (D)

PART 2

Directions: You will hear a question or statement and three responses spoken in English. Select the best response to the question or statement and mark the letter (A), (B), or (C).

---

4   Mark your answer on your answer sheet.
    (A)   (B)   (C)

5   Mark your answer on your answer sheet.
    (A)   (B)   (C)

6   Mark your answer on your answer sheet.
    (A)   (B)   (C)

7   Mark your answer on your answer sheet.
    (A)   (B)   (C)

8   Mark your answer on your answer sheet.
    (A)   (B)   (C)

9   Mark your answer on your answer sheet.
    (A)   (B)   (C)

10 Mark your answer on your answer sheet.
    (A)   (B)   (C)

11 Mark your answer on your answer sheet.
    (A)   (B)   (C)

12 Mark your answer on your answer sheet.
    (A)   (B)   (C)

13 Mark your answer on your answer sheet.
    (A)   (B)   (C)

14 Mark your answer on your answer sheet.
    (A)   (B)   (C)

15 Mark your answer on your answer sheet.
    (A)   (B)   (C)

16 Mark your answer on your answer sheet.
    (A)   (B)   (C)

17 Mark your answer on your answer sheet.
    (A)   (B)   (C)

18 Mark your answer on your answer sheet.
    (A)   (B)   (C)

Directions: You will hear some conversations between two or more people. You will be asked to answer three questions about what the speakers say in each conversation. Select the best response to each question and mark the letter (A), (B), (C), or (D).

19 What most likely is the man's occupation?

(A) Photographer
(B) Wedding planner
(C) Dancer
(D) Interior designer

20 What does the woman want to do?

(A) Schedule an event
(B) Provide feedback for a project
(C) Receive a free gift
(D) Get an extra service

21 What does the man say he will do?

(A) Take some pictures
(B) Provide free shipping
(C) Drop by a studio
(D) Select a frame

22 What are the speakers talking about?

(A) Relocating a business
(B) Opening a new branch
(C) Painting a new house
(D) Training for a race

23 What does the woman want to buy?

(A) Paint
(B) Furniture
(C) Office supplies
(D) Fitness equipment

24 Why does the woman say, "I checked the account balance half an hour ago"?

(A) To provide reassurance
(B) To stress the urgency of a situation
(C) To express surprise
(D) To offer an excuse

25 Who is Jane Parker?

(A) A technical support staff member

(B) A Human Resources manager

(C) A maintenance worker

(D) A new recruit

26 Why does the man need an access code?

(A) To retrieve personal information

(B) To sign in to the computer system

(C) To set up some new software

(D) To enter work hours into the system

27 What will the man most likely do next?

(A) Walk around the company

(B) Wait for the technical support team

(C) Set up a computer system

(D) Go to his desk

Directions: You will hear some talks given by a single speaker. You will be asked to answer three questions about what the speaker says in each talk. Select the best response to each question and mark the letter (A), (B), (C), or (D).

28 What are the instructions about?

(A) How to set up a bike

(B) How to assemble a desk

(C) How to install a bookshelf

(D) How to plant a garden

29 How can the listeners get the necessary tools?

(A) They can visit a store nearby.

(B) They can buy them at any supermarket.

(C) They can buy them online.

(D) They can find them in a package.

30 Which activity might require help?

(A) Adjusting the height

(B) Aligning a part

(C) Attaching a cable

(D) Placing a frame

Order Form

Food Item	Quantity
Chocolate Fudge	5
Cheese Scone	10
Bagel	30
Blueberry Muffin	20

31 Where does the speaker most likely work?

(A) At a bakery

(B) At a restaurant

(C) At a cafeteria

(D) At a café

32 Look at the graphic. Which number does the speaker want to change?

(A) 5

(B) 10

(C) 30

(D) 20

33 Why does the speaker ask the woman to call him?

(A) To make an order for next week

(B) To apologize in person

(C) To clarify another order

(D) To ask for new food items

DAY 12 PARTS 3·4 의도 파악 문제 풀이법

PARTS 3·4에서는 PART 3에서 2~3 문제, 그리고 PART 4에서 2~3문제의 의도 파악 문제가 출제된다. 이 유형의 문제들은 주어진 문장만으로는 해결할 수 없으므로, 해당 문장의 앞과 뒤따라 오는 문장들을 모두 이해해야만 정답을 찾을 수 있다.

오늘의 학습 POINT

POINT 1 의도 파악 문제 풀이법
POINT 2 자주 등장하는 기억할 표현과 내포된 의미

POINT 1 의도 파악 문제 풀이법

의도 파악 문제는 PARTS 3·4 문제들 중 매달 4~6문항이 출제되는데, 대부분의 경우 PART 3에서 2문제, PART 4에서 3문제가 출제된다.

1 질문 형태

- 질문에 "문장"이 포함된 형태이다.
- What does the man mean "문장", Why does the man say "문장", What does the woman imply "문장"과 같은 형태이다.
- 질문에 포함된 "문장"의 의미는 두 가지 이상인 경우가 대부분이며, 선택지에는 이 "문장"이 가지고 있는 의미가 모두 등장한다.

2 풀이법

- 의도 파악 문제의 경우 질문에 주어진 "문장"만으로는 정답을 유추할 수 없다.
- 주어진 "문장" 앞의 두 문장과 "문장" 뒤의 한 문장을 정확하게 이해해야 문제를 풀 수 있다.
- 질문에 주어진 "문장"이 가지는 정반대의 의미가 선택지에 모두 포함되어 있을 경우, 두 선택지 중 하나가 정답일 가능성은 80퍼센트 이상이다.
- 의도 파악 문제의 경우 선택지의 내용을 이해해야만 문제를 해결할 수 있으므로, 지문을 듣기 전에 선택지의 내용을 완벽하게 이해해야 한다.
- 대화나 담화의 내용 또한 완벽하게 이해해야 정답을 찾을 수 있으므로, 듣기에 집중하는 것이 핵심이다.

12-01

Q Why does the man say, "I'm a new member here"?

(A) He is worried about finishing a task.

(B) He needs some help.

→ 질문에 주어진 "문장"은 "나는 새로 온 사람이다"라는 뜻으로서 "경험이 없다"는 의미인데, "경험이 없다"는 것은 "업무를 담당하는 데 걱정이 된다", 또는 "도움이 필요하다"는 의미를 모두 가지고 있다.

→ 위 예시 문제와 선택지에서 볼 수 있는 것처럼, 주어진 문장이 가지고 있는 여러 가지 의미가 선택지에 제시될 수 있다.

POINT 2 자주 등장하는 기억할 표현과 내포된 의미

의도 파악 문제 유형은 LC에서 가장 난이도가 높은 유형이다. 의도 파악 문제 유형에 자주 등장하는 표현들이 있으므로, 이를 정리해 둔다면 정답을 찾는 데 도움이 된다.

표현	예시	의미
시간이 있다	I'm free this afternoon. I have some time now.	제안에 대한 수락, 또는 도움을 제공하겠다는 의미
시간이 없다	I have another meeting. I'm busy right now.	제안에 대한 거절, 또는 도움을 요청하는 의미
경험이 있다	I've worked here for 20 years. I attended the seminar last year.	업무를 담당하는 데 적절한 사람이라는 의미 업무에 대해 잘 알고 있음을 의미
경험이 없다	I started working here last week. I've never done it before.	업무를 담당하는 데 적절하지 않은 사람이라는 의미 업무에 대해 잘 모르고 있음을 의미 업무에 대한 도움이 필요함을 의미
할 수 있다	You can't miss it. It's easy to follow. It's easy to find.	길을 찾거나, 어떤 과정을 해 나가는 것이 쉽다는 의미
맞는 말이다	Tell me about it.	맞장구를 치거나 동의한다는 의미

12-02

M Olivia, do you know how to use this new fabric cutting machine? I need to use it, but I can't find the manual.

W Oh, I've never used the machine before. Why don't you ask Kathy? I saw her using it yesterday.

M Thanks. I'll give her a call now.

Q What does the woman mean when she says, "I've never used the machine before"?

(A) She doesn't want to do a task.

(B) She wants to learn how to use a machine.

(C) She cannot help the man.

(D) She wants to change machines.

→ 질문의 "문장"은 "나는 한 번도 기계를 사용해 본 적이 없다"는 의미이다.

→ "경험이 없다"는 표현은 자신이 업무를 담당하는 데 적절하지 않다는 의미를 내포하고 있다. 따라서, 문제를 먼저 읽고 이와 같은 의미의 답변을 예상해 볼 수 있다.

→ "문장" 앞에서 남자가 여자에게 도움을 요청하고 있고, 여자는 경험이 없다고 말하고 있다.

→ 따라서, 남자가 물어본 일에 도움을 줄 수 없음을 의미한다는 것을 알 수 있다. 그러므로, (C)가 정답이 된다.

12-03

M Hey, Sue. Why don't you join us for John's retirement party tomorrow?

W Is it tomorrow? Oh, I'll be heading to New York then.

M Are you attending a meeting with a client?

W No, there's a major convention.

Q Why does the woman say, "I'll be heading to New York then"?

(A) To change a reservation

(B) To correct a mistake

(C) To turn down an invitation

(D) To get some advice

→ 질문의 "문장"은 "내가 내일 뉴욕을 가야한다"는 뜻으로, "내일은 시간이 없다"는 의미이다.

→ "시간이 없다"는 표현은 "요청에 대한 거절", 혹은 "도움을 요청"하는 의미를 내포하고 있다. 따라서, 문제를 먼저 읽고 이와 같은 의미의 답변을 예상해 볼 수 있다.

→ 대화의 시작 부분에서 남자가 은퇴 기념 행사에 초대하는 질문에 대해 "내일은 시간이 없다"고 답하고 있으므로, 초대에 대한 거절이라는 것을 알 수 있다. 그러므로, 정답은 (C)이다.

금융 관련 어휘	
balance 잔고, 잔액	I checked my bank **balance** online. 나는 온라인으로 은행의 잔고를 확인했다.
allot 할당하다	The manager decided to **allot** more resources to the Marketing Department. 매니저는 마케팅 부서에 더 많은 자원을 할당하기로 결정했다.
fiscal 재정의	The **fiscal** year for the company ends in December. 회사의 회계 연도는 12월에 끝난다.
appraise 감정하다	The real estate agent will **appraise** the value of the house. 부동산 중개업자는 그 가치를 감정할 것이다.
withdraw 인출하다	You can **withdraw** cash from the ATM located in the bank's lobby. 은행 로비에 위치한 현금인출기에서 현금을 인출할 수 있습니다.

건강 관련 어휘	
physical checkup 건강검진	I schedule a **physical checkup** with my doctor every year. 나는 매년 의사와 건강검진 일정을 잡는다.
prescription 처방전	The doctor wrote a **prescription** for antibiotics to treat my bacterial infection. 의사는 내 박테리아 감염을 치료하기 위해 항생제 처방전을 썼다.
diagnose 진단하다	The medical team worked together to **diagnose** the patient's rare medical condition. 의료 팀은 환자의 희귀한 의료 상태를 진단하기 위해 협력했다.
transmit 전염시키다	The virus can be **transmitted** through respiratory droplets. 바이러스는 호흡기 분비물을 통해 전염될 수 있다.
relieve 완화하다	Taking over-the-counter pain relievers can help **relieve** mild headaches. 일반적인 진통제 복용은 경미한 두통을 완화하는 데 도움이 될 수 있다.

회의 관련 어휘	
dispute 논쟁하다 = contest	The two coworkers had a **dispute** over the project's approach. 두 동료는 프로젝트 접근 방식에 대한 논쟁을 했다.
oppose 반대하다 = counteract	Some members of the committee **oppose** the new policy. 위원회의 일부 멤버는 새로운 정책에 반대한다.
postpone 연기하다 = put off, push back	The outdoor event had to be **postponed** until next weekend. 야외 행사는 다음 주말로 연기되어야 했다.
confidential 비밀의, 기밀의	The **confidential** company documents are stored in a secure locked cabinet. 기밀 회사 문서는 안전하게 잠긴 캐비닛에 보관됩니다.
consent 동의하다; 동의서	Before conducting the medical procedure, the patient must provide informed **consent**. 의료 절차를 진행하기 전에 환자는 사전 동의서를 제공해야 한다.

PART 1

Directions: You will hear four statements about the picture below. Select the one statement that best describes what you see in the picture and mark the letter (A), (B), (C), or (D).

1

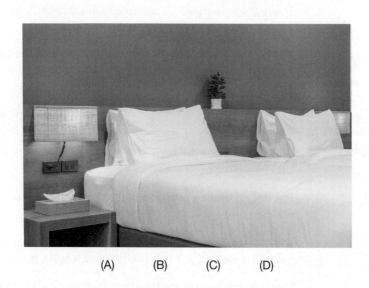

(A)   (B)   (C)   (D)

2

(A)   (B)   (C)   (D)

3

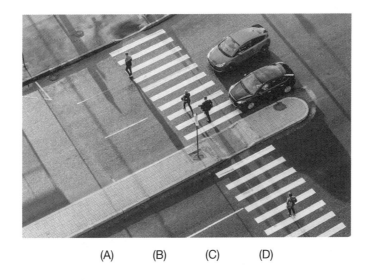

(A)   (B)   (C)   (D)

PART 2

Directions: You will hear a question or statement and three responses spoken in English. Select the best response to the question or statement and mark the letter (A), (B), or (C).

---

4 Mark your answer on your answer sheet.
  (A)   (B)   (C)

5 Mark your answer on your answer sheet.
  (A)   (B)   (C)

6 Mark your answer on your answer sheet.
  (A)   (B)   (C)

7 Mark your answer on your answer sheet.
  (A)   (B)   (C)

8 Mark your answer on your answer sheet.
  (A)   (B)   (C)

9 Mark your answer on your answer sheet.
  (A)   (B)   (C)

10 Mark your answer on your answer sheet.
  (A)   (B)   (C)

11 Mark your answer on your answer sheet.
  (A)   (B)   (C)

12 Mark your answer on your answer sheet.
  (A)   (B)   (C)

13 Mark your answer on your answer sheet.
  (A)   (B)   (C)

14 Mark your answer on your answer sheet.
  (A)   (B)   (C)

15 Mark your answer on your answer sheet.
  (A)   (B)   (C)

16 Mark your answer on your answer sheet.
  (A)   (B)   (C)

17 Mark your answer on your answer sheet.
  (A)   (B)   (C)

18 Mark your answer on your answer sheet.
  (A)   (B)   (C)

PART 3

Directions: You will hear some conversations between two or more people. You will be asked to answer three questions about what the speakers say in each conversation. Select the best response to each question and mark the letter (A), (B), (C), or (D).

19 What is the man preparing?

(A) A video manual
(B) A machine delivery
(C) A new movie
(D) A television show

20 Why does the man say "You're the most experienced supervisor"?

(A) To correct a mistake
(B) To ask for help
(C) To give a promotion
(D) To support the woman's opinion

21 What does the man ask the woman to do tomorrow?

(A) Give her opinion
(B) Write a new manual
(C) Return a call
(D) Visit the man's office

22 What is the topic of the conversation?

(A) A lunch menu
(B) A new editor
(C) A newspaper article
(D) A famous writer

23 What kind of business do the speakers work for?

(A) A restaurant
(B) A grocery store
(C) A newspaper company
(D) A library

24 According to the man, what will probably happen today?

(A) More chairs will be ordered.
(B) There will be more customers than usual.
(C) There will be exciting news for the restaurant.
(D) There will be a celebration.

25 Why is the woman calling?

(A) To reschedule an appointment

(B) To check a timeline

(C) To submit a request

(D) To provide directions

26 Look at the graphic. Which business is the woman calling from?

(A) ABC Market

(B) Beau Salon

(C) Basil Garden

(D) Tim's Coffee

27 When will the work begin?

(A) At 9:30 A.M.

(B) At 9:00 A.M.

(C) At 5:00 P.M.

(D) At 7:00 P.M.

PART 4

Directions: You will hear some talks given by a single speaker. You will be asked to answer three questions about what the speaker says in each talk. Select the best response to each question and mark the letter (A), (B), (C), or (D).

28 What is the speaker discussing?

(A) A newly renovated building

(B) A new director

(C) A new city plan

(D) New research results

29 What does the speaker imply when she says, "Now there are over 100 species in the center"?

(A) A system was outdated.

(B) An office needs more staff.

(C) A space was not big enough.

(D) A budget has to be increased.

30 According to the speaker, what will be offered on Friday?

(A) A banquet

(B) Free guided tours

(C) Computer workshops

(D) Free concert tickets

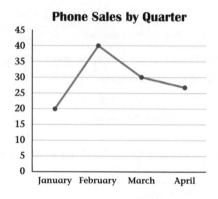

Phone Sales by Quarter

31 What happened last week?

(A) A business offered a discount.

(B) A business gave away free gifts.

(C) A business launched a new cellular phone.

(D) A business conducted a survey.

32 Look at the graphic. When was the promotion held?

(A) January

(B) February

(C) March

(D) April

33 What will the listeners discuss next?

(A) A project timeline

(B) A marketing plan

(C) A product design

(D) A customer survey

Reading
Comprehension

01 동사와 문장의 구조

동사는 문장의 구조를 파악하는 단서가 되는 가장 중요한 문장의 구성 성분이다.
동사의 종류에 따른 문장의 구조를 파악할 수 있다면 정답을 쉽게 찾을 수 있다.

오늘의 학습 POINT

POINT 1 한 문장의 동사의 개수 = 「1 + 접속사의 수」
POINT 2 동사의 종류에 따라 문장에서 목적어나 보어의 유무가 결정된다.
POINT 3 타동사는 전치사 없이 목적어를 취하는 반면, **완전자동사** 뒤에 명사를 연결하려면 **전치사**가 필요하다.

POINT 1 한 문장의 동사의 개수 = 「1 + 접속사의 수」

Q 동사의 개수

- 동사는 문장의 가장 기본적인 성분이며, 하나의 문장(절)에는 하나의 동사가 존재한다.
- 한 문장의 동사의 개수는 「1 + 접속사의 수」이다. 동사가 추가되려면 절과 절을 연결하는 접속사가 필요하다.

cf. 등위접속사는 절과 절을 연결하는 것뿐만 아니라 단어와 단어, 구와 구를 연결할 수도 있다. 그러므로 등위접속사가 포함된 문장에는 동사가 두 개 이상이 아닐 수도 있다. → DAY 09 참고

PRACTICE 1-2 아래 문장에서 동사에는 ○ 표시를, 접속사에는 △ 표시를 하세요. 정답 p.082

1 My new computer is very expensive, but its performance is great.
2 There is a high demand for electric cars nowadays because the price of gas has been increasing continuously.

POINT 2 동사의 종류에 따라 문장에서 목적어나 보어의 유무가 결정된다.

Q 동사와 문장의 구조

문장의 형식	문장의 구성			
1형식	주어	완전자동사		
2형식	주어	불완전자동사	주격 보어	
3형식	주어	완전타동사	목적어	
4형식	주어	완전타동사	간접목적어	직접목적어
5형식	주어	불완전타동사	목적어	목적격 보어

3 Our hotel is currently hiring receptionists.

4 This coupon includes free access to the salad bar.

5 Ms. Grey found the revised financial report considerably more detailed.

❶ 꼭 알아 두어야 하는 완전자동사

완전자동사는 1형식 문장에 사용되며 목적어나 보어를 취하지 않는다.

단어	의미	예
arrive, depart, commute	오다, 가다	**arrived** at the airport 공항에 도착했다 **depart** from the station 그 역에서 출발한다 **commute** to work 통근하다
rise, increase, fall, decrease	오르다, 떨어지다	The sun **rises**. 해가 뜬다. The population **is increasing**. 인구가 증가하는 중이다. Profits **have fallen**. 이윤이 떨어졌다. The number **has decreased**. 수가 감소했다.
speak, talk, comment, remark	말하다, 언급하다	I had to **speak** to the manager. 나는 담당자에게 말해야 했다. I will **talk** to him about the itinerary. 나는 그에게 일정표에 대해 말할 것이다. He **commented** on the company's decision. 그가 회사의 결정에 대해 언급했다. **cf.** speak은 '말하다'의 의미로는 자동사이지만, '(특정한 언어를) 구사하다'의 의미로는 타동사이다. She can **speak** several languages. 그녀는 몇 가지 언어를 구사한다.
occur, happen, take place	발생하다, 열리다	The incident **occurred**. 사건이 발생했다. **happen** in the park 공원에서 열리다 **take place** in March 3월에 열리다
register, enroll, apply	등록하다, 신청하다	**register for** the class 그 수업에 등록하다 **enroll in** the course 그 강좌에 등록하다 **apply for** the position 그 직책에 지원하다
work expire proceed complain collaborate specialize subscribe	일하다 만료되다 진행하다 불평하다 협력하다 전문으로 하다 구독하다	**work** from home 재택근무를 하다 The license **has expired**. 면허증이 만료되었다. **proceed with** the project 프로젝트를 진행하다 **complain about** the service 서비스에 대해서 불평하다 **collaborate with** other teams 다른 팀들과 협력하다 **specialize in** computer security 컴퓨터 보안을 전문으로 하다 **subscribe to** the publication 출판물을 구독하다

❷ 꼭 알아 두어야 하는 불완전자동사

불완전자동사는 2형식 문장에 사용되며 주격 보어를 취한다.

단어	의미	예
be become	~이다, ~이 되다	He **is** a manager at the store. 그는 상점의 매니저이다. It **became** cloudy. 날씨가 흐려졌다.
keep, remain, stay	유지하다	We **kept** quiet for a moment. 우리는 잠시 조용히 했다. You need to **stay** calm. 침착해야 한다.
look, seem, sound	보이다, 들리다	She **looks** pleased. 그녀는 즐거워 보인다. That **sounds** perfect. 그것은 완벽한 것 같다.

cf.1 주격 보어가 명사인 경우 주어와 주격 보어는 동일하다.

She **is** a new employee. 그녀는 신입 사원이다. [She = a new employee]

cf.2 주격 보어가 형용사인 경우 형용사는 주어의 상태를 설명한다.

The problem **has remained** unsolved. 그 문제는 해결되지 않은 상태이다.

📝 PRACTICE 6-7 ◀ 괄호 안의 보기들 중에서 적절한 것을 고르세요.
정답 p.082

6 The stock price of KMC Insurance has (risen / raised) steadily.

7 Mr. Klein will be a valuable (position / addition) to the management team.

❸ 꼭 알아 두어야 하는 완전타동사

완전타동사는 대부분 3형식 문장에 사용되며 하나의 목적어를 취한다.

단어	의미	예
raise, increase reduce, lower, decrease	올리다, 높이다 줄이다, 낮추다	**raise** public awareness 대중의 인식을 높이다 **reduce** traffic congestion 교통 혼잡을 줄이다
say, mention explain, describe	말하다 설명하다	**mention** the issue 그 문제를 언급하다 **describe** your experience 경험을 묘사하다
monitor, observe examine, inspect	관찰하다, 주시하다 조사하다, 검사하다	**monitor** the progress 진행 상황을 주시하다 **examine** the benefits 혜택을 살펴보다
suggest, propose recommend	제안하다 추천하다	**suggest** minor changes 사소한 변경을 제안하다 **recommend** a good place 좋은 곳을 추천하다
access, approach	접근하다	**access** the website 그 웹사이트에 접속하다
affect, influence	영향을 미치다	**affect** their decision 그들의 결정에 영향을 미치다
call, contact	전화하다, 연락하다	**Call** us today! 우리에게 오늘 연락하세요!

타동사는 전치사 없이 목적어를 취하는 반면, 완전자동사 뒤에 명사를 연결하려면 전치사가 필요하다.

🔍 자동사와 타동사 비교

완전자동사	완전타동사	의미
account for a situation	**explain** a situation	상황을 **설명하다**
appeal to the young	**attract** the young	젊은이들을 **끌다**
arrive at the airport	**reach** the airport	공항에 **도착하다**
conform to the rules **comply with** the rules **abide by** the rules	**observe** the rules	규칙을 **따르다**
confer about the issue **talk about** the issue	**discuss** the issue	그 문제에 대해서 **논의하다**
consent to the plan **agree on** the plan	**approve** the plan	그 계획에 **동의하다, 승인하다**
deal with a problem	**handle** a problem **address** a problem	문제를 **처리하다**
consist of many islands	**comprise** many islands	많은 섬들로 **구성되어 있다**
dispose of old books	**discard** old books	낡은 책들을 **버리다**
enroll at the college	**join** the college	대학에 **등록하다**
interfere with a business	**interrupt** a business	사업을 **방해하다**
look for a job	**seek** a job	일자리를 **찾다**
object to the opinion	**oppose** the opinion	그 의견에 **반대하다**
participate in a discussion	**attend** a discussion	논의에 **참여하다(참석하다)**
respond to the questions	**answer** the questions	질문에 **응답하다**
refer to a manual	**consult** a manual	설명서를 **참고하다**

📝 PRACTICE 8-9 　 괄호 안의 보기들 중에서 적절한 것을 고르세요.　　정답 p.082

8　Engineers are expected to (deal / address) the malfunctions.

9　If you (enroll / join) the membership club today, you will receive a 10% discount.

● 「-en, -ise, -ize, -fy, -ate」 등으로 끝나는 단어는 대부분 동사이다. 예시를 통해 각 동사의 뒤에 어떤 성분이 오는지 알아두자.

accelerate 가속화하다 accelerate a process 진행을 가속화하다	**contribute** 기여하다 contribute to economic growth 경제 성장에 기여하다
achieve 달성하다, 성취하다 🔁 accomplish 성취하다, 해내다 achieve a goal 목표를 달성하다	**deliberate** 심사숙고하다 deliberate on the plan 그 계획에 대해서 심사숙고하다
acknowledge 알리다, 인정하다 acknowledge receipt of a document 서류의 수령을 알리다	**demonstrate** 시연하다, 설명하다 demonstrate how it works 어떻게 작동하는지 보여주다
advocate 지지하다, 옹호하다 advocate their stances 그들의 입장을 옹호하다	**designate** 지정하다, 지명하다 🔁 nominate 후보로 지명하다, 추천하다 designate a new CEO to take over the role 그 역할을 이어받을 새로운 CEO를 지정하다
arrange 준비하다 arrange an appointment 약속을 잡다 arrange for a special event 특별 행사를 준비하다	**determine** 알아내다, 밝히다 🔁 identify 밝히다, 알아내다 determine the cause of a malfunction 오작동의 원인을 알아내다
assign 할당하다 🔁 allocate 할당하다 assign a project to him 그에게 프로젝트를 할당하다	**diagnose** 진단하다 diagnose a variety of diseases 다양한 질병들을 진단하다
attempt 시도하다 attempt to attract people 사람들을 모으려고 시도하다	**discontinue** 중지하다 🔁 suspend 중지하다, 연기하다 discontinue subscribing to a journal 잡지의 구독을 중지하다
authorize 인가하다, 권한을 부여하다 🔁 approve 승인하다 authorize the use 사용을 승인하다	**enhance** 강화하다 🔁 reinforce 강화하다, 보충하다 enhance a reputation 평판을 강화하다
benefit 유익하다, ~에서 득을 보다 benefit from the merger 합병으로 득을 보다	**exceed** 초과하다 exceed a speed limit 제한 속도를 초과하다
categorize 분류하다 🔁 classify 분류하다 categorize data and information 자료와 정보를 분류하다	**extend** 연장하다; 베풀다; (초대장을) 보내다 cf. expand 확장하다, 넓히다 extend an invitation to them 그들에게 초대장을 보내다
clarify 명확하게 하다 clarify the terms of a contract 계약서의 조건을 명확히 하다.	**evaluate** 평가하다 🔁 assess 평가하다, 사정하다 evaluate the effectiveness of the system 그 시스템의 효과를 평가하다
compensate 보상하다 compensate for a loss 손실에 대해 보상하다	**emphasize** 강조하다 🔁 stress 강조하다 emphasize the importance 중요성을 강조하다
confirm 사실임을 보여주다, 확인해주다 confirm your acceptance of the offer 제안에 대한 수락 여부를 확인해주다	**encounter** 맞닥뜨리다, 부딪히다 🔁 face 직면하다 encounter a technical difficulty 기술적 문제에 부딪히다
contain 담고 있다, 함유되어 있다 🔁 include 포함하다 contain enough nutrition 충분한 영양을 함유하다.	**feature** 특색으로 삼다, 특집으로 하다 The software features a user-friendly interface. 그 소프트웨어는 사용자 친화적인 인터페이스를 특징으로 한다.
assure 장담하다, 확인하다 **vs. ensure** 보장하다 • assure: 누군가에게 확신을 주는 의미 • ensure: 무엇인가를 확실히 해 둔다는 의미	**support** 지지하다, 응원하다 **vs. supply** 공급하다 • support: 비물질적인 지원이나 원조를 의미 • supply: 물리적이거나 유형의 물건을 제공하는 것을 의미

PART 5

Directions: A word or phrase is missing in each of the sentences below. Four answer choices are given below each sentence. Select the best answer to complete the sentence and mark the letter (A), (B), (C), or (D).

1   ------- should have valid identification when entering the lecture hall.

(A) Attending
(B) Attendees
(C) Attends
(D) Attended

2   Effectively ------- consumer complaints is critical to the success of our business.

(A) address
(B) addresses
(C) addressing
(D) addressed

3   The appointment of the new marketing director ------- in the company newsletter last Monday.

(A) was announced
(B) having announced
(C) to be announced
(D) announcement

4   Beginning next week, the new security card must be used by everyone ------- access to the research laboratory.

(A) has gained
(B) to gain
(C) was gained
(D) is gaining

5   Any employee ------- to join the weekly on-the-job training sessions must submit an application to the Human Resources manager.

(A) is wishing
(B) wishing
(C) has wished
(D) wishes

6   ------- the Barton Research Center, the survey is expected to be concluded by the end of the month.

(A) In case of
(B) As far as
(C) Prior to
(D) According to

7   The company is carrying out an aggressive marketing campaign ------- its market presence.

   (A) reinforcement
   (B) is reinforcing
   (C) has reinforced
   (D) to reinforce

8   Director Clay Brown has requested that we ------- the release date of the movie until the end of the year.

   (A) postpone
   (B) to postpone
   (C) were postponing
   (D) have postponed

9   Staff members must submit original receipts for such ------- as accommodations and transportation after returning from their business trips.

   (A) assignments
   (B) expenses
   (C) estimates
   (D) bookings

10 Alvino Stores, Inc. plans to ------- its growth strategy by investing in expanding its market reach.

   (A) alleviate
   (B) accelerate
   (C) anticipate
   (D) accumulate

11 The new regulations are designed to address the ------- complex challenges of the global financial market.

   (A) precisely
   (B) assertively
   (C) particularly
   (D) immediately

12 Finance Director Brian Cross has ------- the training session on the automated payroll system for next Monday.

   (A) invited
   (B) presented
   (C) scheduled
   (D) delivered

13 The instructions for operating the machine were so complicated that even ------- technicians had difficulty understanding them.

   (A) considerate
   (B) demanding
   (C) preventable
   (D) experienced

14 Adam Lines will ------- the proper use of the new equipment during tomorrow's training session.

   (A) supervise
   (B) customize
   (C) accomplish
   (D) demonstrate

15 Profits have been soaring for ten months in a row, ------- the company is now considering expanding into overseas markets.

   (A) so
   (B) of which
   (C) therefore
   (D) whereas

PART 6

Directions: Read the text below. A word, phrase, or sentence is missing in parts of the text. Four answer choices for each question are given below the text. Select the best answer to complete the text and mark the letter (A), (B), (C), or (D).

Questions 16-19 refer to the follow memo.

Dear employees,

This notice is to inform you that effective -------, all requests for expenses or purchases made on
16.

behalf of the company must be approved by a supervisor or manager. -------. Please note that any
17.

expenses or purchases made ------- prior approval will not be reimbursed by the company.
18.

Thank you for your cooperation in ------- that all expenditures are properly authorized.
19.

Sincerely,

Laya Gavin

Accounting Manager

16 (A) markedly
(B) potentially
(C) immediately
(D) substantially

17 (A) The company policy needs to be
changed.
(B) Only authorized expenses will be
reimbursed.
(C) The reimbursement you requested will
be processed.
(D) Our expenses have increased
significantly this year.

18 (A) during
(B) in order
(C) besides
(D) without

19 (A) pointing
(B) imposing
(C) ensuring
(D) agreeing

Questions 20-23 refer to the following announcement.

Currently, the Sunburst Hotel ------- a very special opportunity exclusively to our staff members.
      20.

Each employee can now book a room at a 50% discounted rate simply by making a reservation

at least two weeks in advance. -------. This means that the room cannot be booked for someone
         21.

else. We take pride in providing this ------- to our hardworking employees as a token of our
               22.

appreciation. ------- it is for business or leisure, we are always looking for the best ways to reward
        23.

our employees and to show our gratitude.

---

20 (A) to offer
   (B) is offering
   (C) was offering
   (D) being offered

21 (A) Call us now and find a way to save even more.
   (B) We are now offering our guests discounted rates.
   (C) As a result, many workers have taken advantage of it.
   (D) The employees must stay in the room they have reserved.

22 (A) salary
   (B) vision
   (C) benefit
   (D) location

23 (A) Either
   (B) Whenever
   (C) Though
   (D) Whether

Directions: In this part you will read a selection of texts. The text or set of texts is followed by several questions. Select the best answer for each question and mark the letter (A), (B), (C), or (D).

Questions 24-25 refer to the following notice.

NOTICE

Effective today, passengers will be unable to purchase unreserved tickets at the ticket vending machines in Bedford Station. The machines are currently undergoing upgrades to provide faster and more convenient service. We anticipate the work to be completed by Friday, March 21. In the meantime, passengers are kindly requested to book their train tickets online or to purchase them at the ticket counters located within the station. We apologize for any inconvenience this may cause. We would like to remind passengers that they can save 5% and avoid waiting in line by purchasing their tickets online at www.easytrip.com

24 Why can the ticket vending machines not be used?

(A) They have been removed from the station.

(B) They are being improved to provide better service.

(C) They are out of service due to a power outage.

(D) They became outdated and require replacement.

25 How can passengers buy discounted tickets?

(A) By visiting the ticket counter in the station

(B) By getting an online membership

(C) By purchasing monthly passes

(D) By booking tickets online

November 10

Gina Kent
51 Sunset Blvd.
Baltimore 21202

Dear Ms. Kent,

We want to take this opportunity to thank you for your loyalty to Lehman Apparel. We also appreciate your recent purchase of jeans and sweaters from our store. To further enhance our customers' shopping experiences, we are conducting a brief survey and kindly ask for your participation. For your convenience, we have enclosed a prepaid and addressed envelope. Please use this envelope to return the survey to us.

As a sign of our appreciation, customers who submit a completed survey before November 21 will receive a limited-edition scarf specially designed by renowned artist Lala Colbert. Those who submit it after this date will be offered a voucher for 5% off their next purchase.

We appreciate your time and feedback, which will help us continue improving our products and services. Thank you for being a valued customer of Lehman Apparel.

Sincerely,

Angela Weaver
Customer Service Manager

Lehman Apparel

Your participation in our survey will help us provide the best possible shopping experience for our customers.

Name	*Gina Kent*
Date	*November 27*

A. How often do you purchase clothing?
☐ Once a week   ☑ Once a month   ☐ Every few months   ☐ Once a year or less

B. How do you typically hear about new clothing brands or products?
☑ Social media   ☐ Friends/family   ☐ Advertising (TV, print, online)   ☐ In-store displays
☐ Other (please specify): _____

C. How do you typically acquire our products?
☑ In-store at one of our Lehman Apparel locations   ☑ Online through our Web site
Please specify more details: *I prefer to visit one of your Lehman Apparel locations near me to view your products in person before making a purchase online.*

D. During your most recent visit to Lehman Apparel, did you find the ideal item you were looking for?   ☐ Yes   ☑ No
Please specify more details: *I was impressed with the variety of items, particularly the sweaters, but I was unable to find the exact color that I wanted. However, the salesperson was very helpful and offered to ship the desired item directly from the warehouse.*

26 What is the purpose of Ms. Weaver's letter?

(A) To inform Ms. Kent about survey findings

(B) To ask Ms. Kent to fill out a form for a refund

(C) To address a complaint raised by Ms. Kent

(D) To request feedback from Ms. Kent

27 In the letter, the word "enhance" in paragraph 1, line 3, is closest in meaning to

(A) undergo

(B) evaluate

(C) improve

(D) motivate

28 What can be inferred about Ms. Kent?

(A) She usually browses online stores to buy clothes.

(B) She obtains product information from her friends.

(C) She makes a monthly visit to Lehman Apparel.

(D) She has made some recent clothing purchases.

29 What will Ms. Kent most likely receive from Lehman Apparel?

(A) A specially designed scarf

(B) A coupon providing a discount

(C) A painting by a famous artist

(D) A sweater she was looking for

30 What does Ms. Kent mention about Lehman Apparel?

(A) It effectively uses social media.

(B) Its salespeople are not friendly.

(C) It has a diverse range of products.

(D) It often experiences product shortages.

02 동사의 종류

자동사와 타동사를 구분하고 **동사의 종류에 따라 필요한 성분을 구분**할 수 있어야 한다. 이를 통해 빈칸에 들어갈 정답을 빠르게 고를 수 있을 뿐 아니라 문장을 해석하는 데에도 큰 도움이 된다.

오늘의 학습 POINT

POINT 1 대부분의 타동사는 3형식 동사이므로 **4형식과 5형식 동사를 외워 두자.**

POINT 2 **목적격 보어의 성분에 따라 5형식 동사를 구분하여 외워 두자.**

POINT 1 | 대부분의 타동사는 3형식 동사이므로 4형식과 5형식 동사를 외워 두자.

1 목적어가 두 개인 4형식 동사

「4형식 동사 + 간접목적어(~에게) + 직접목적어(~을)」의 형태이다.

❶ 대표적인 4형식 동사

동사	의미	예
give, offer, award, bring, assign	주다, 수여하다	**offer** employees special benefits 직원들에게 특별한 혜택을 제공하다 **award** them compensation 그들에게 보상금을 지급하다 **assign** him suitable work 그에게 적절한 일감을 배정하다
send, mail	보내다	**send** them the package by air freight 그들에게 물건을 항공 화물로 보내다 **mail** attendees details about the conference 참석자들에게 컨퍼런스에 관한 상세 사항을 메일로 보내다
tell, show, buy, make, cook	~해주다	**tell** me the reason 저에게 이유를 말해주세요 **show** them the evidence 그들에게 증거를 보여주다 He will **cook** us dinner. 그가 우리에게 저녁을 해줄 것이다.
ask	묻다	**ask** him the next question 그에게 다음 질문을 하다

❷ 4형식 문장을 3형식 문장으로 변환

직접목적어를 간접목적어 앞에 위치시켜 3형식 문장으로 변환할 수 있다. 이때 간접목적어 앞에는 전치사가 오며, 동사에 따라 사용되는 전치사가 달라진다.

동사	전치사	예
give, offer, award, bring, send, mail, tell, show	to	**offer** special benefits **to** the employees 직원들에게 특별한 혜택을 제공하다
buy, make, cook	for	He will **cook** dinner **for** us. 그가 우리에게 저녁을 해줄 것이다.
ask	of	**ask** a favor **of** him 그에게 부탁하다

📝 **PRACTICE 1-2** 괄호 안의 보기들 중에서 적절한 것을 고르세요. 정답 p.086

1 Please (arrange / show) me the documented evidence to support your claims.

2 Parrot Airline is now (offering / suggesting) passengers a choice of vegan in-flight meals on all its flights.

② 목적어가 간접목적어인 3형식 동사

일반적인 3형식 동사의 목적어는 ~을/를로 해석되는 **직접목적어**이다. 하지만 아래 표에 정리된 3형식 동사의 목적어는 ~에게로 해석되는 **간접목적어**이므로 정리해 두어야 한다. 이러한 동사가 명사 역할을 하는 that절과 함께 쓰일 경우에는 4형식 동사로 볼 수 있다.

동사	의미	예
inform, notify, advise, remind	알리다, 상기시키다	inform, remind, notify, advise + 대상(~에게) + of + 명사 Please **inform me of** any changes in the itinerary. 여행 일정에 변경 사항이 있으면 저에게 알려주세요. This e-mail is to **remind you of** the upcoming seminar. 이 이메일은 귀하에게 다가오는 세미나에 대해 상기시키기 위한 것입니다. We will **advise everyone of** the final decision. 우리는 모두에게 최종 결정에 대해 공지할 것이다. inform, remind, notify, advise + 대상(~에게) + that절 Please **notify them that** the clients will visit the office tomorrow. 내일 의뢰인들이 사무실에 올 것임을 그들에게 알려주세요.
persuade, convince, assure	설득하다, 납득시키다, 보장하다	persuade, convince, assure + 대상(~에게) + of + 명사 He managed to **convince the board members of** the need for expansion. 그는 확장의 필요성을 이사들에게 가까스로 납득시켰다. persuade, convince, assure + 대상(~에게) + that절 I can **assure you that** your order will arrive within a week. 주문하신 상품이 1주일 내에 도착할 것임을 당신에게 보장할 수 있습니다.

📝 **PRACTICE 3-4** 괄호 안의 보기들 중에서 적절한 것을 고르세요. 정답 p.086

3 Please (inform / deliver) Ms. Reeds that she is required to prepare a presentation on the recent shifts in consumer interests within the film industry.

4 We would like to (assure / ensure) you that every effort will be made to address your concerns and to resolve the issue promptly.

목적격 보어의 성분에 따라 5형식 동사를 구분하여 외워 두자.

① 명사와 형용사를 목적격 보어로 취하는 5형식 동사

❶ 명사를 보어로 취하는 동사

동사	의미	예
call, appoint, name, elect, consider, make	부르다, 임명하다, 선출하다, 여기다	'목적어'를 '무엇(명사)'으로 부르다 / 임명하다 / 선출하다 / 여기다 They **call** him **Captain**. 그들은 그를 캡틴으로 부른다. **appoint** him (as) **the manager** of the department 그를 그 부서의 관리자로 임명하다 **elect** him **chairperson** of the city council 그를 시의회의 의장으로 선출하다 **consider** this **our top priority** 이것을 우리의 최우선으로 여기다

❷ 형용사를 보어로 취하는 동사

동사	의미	예
keep, find, consider, make	유지하다, 알게되다, 여기다, 만들다	'목적어'를 '어떠한 상태(형용사)'로 유지하다 / 알게되다 / 여기다 / 만들다 **keep** our customers **satisfied** 우리 고객이 만족을 느끼도록 하다 **find** it **impossible** to convince them 그들을 납득시키는 것이 불가능하다는 것을 알게 되다 **consider** the project **successful** 그 프로젝트를 성공적이라고 여기다

☑ Further Point! 다양한 문장 구조를 만드는 동사들

make	He will **make** an excellent chef. [2형식] 그는 뛰어난 요리사가 될 것이다. (= become) I have to **make** a brief report. [3형식] 나는 간략한 보고서를 만들어야 한다. Chris **made** me a beautiful fabric bag. [4형식] 크리스가 나에게 예쁜 천 가방을 만들어 주었다. She **made** it a big issue. [5형식 (명사 목적격 보어)] 그녀는 그것을 큰 문제로 만들었다. Paul always **makes** people happy. [5형식 (형용사 목적격 보어)] 폴은 항상 사람들을 행복하게 한다. The teacher **made** the students recite the poem in front of the class. [5형식 (동사원형 목적격 보어)] 선생님은 학생들이 교실 앞에서 시를 암송하도록 했다.
find	They finally **found** a suitable location for their new office. [3형식] 그들은 마침내 새 사무실에 적합한 장소를 찾았다. The survey results revealed that the majority of participants **find** the new product highly satisfactory. [5형식 (형용사 목적격 보어)] 설문 조사 결과에 따르면 대다수의 참가자들은 신제품이 매우 만족스럽다고 생각하는 것으로 나타났다.
consider	Please **consider** my suggestion for the project. [3형식] 프로젝트에 대한 저의 제안을 고려해 주세요. Many people **consider** him a leader due to his exceptional vision. [5형식 (명사 목적격 보어)] 많은 사람들은 그의 뛰어난 비전 때문에 그를 지도자로 여긴다. When working on a team, **consider** it crucial to communicate effectively. [5형식 (형용사 목적격 보어)] 팀에서 일할 때, 효과적으로 의사소통하는 것이 중요하다고 생각하세요.

❷ to부정사와 동사원형을 목적격 보어로 취하는 5형식 동사

❶ to부정사를 보어로 취하는 동사

동사	의미	예
ask, require, invite, encourage, advise, allow, enable	요청하다, 권장하다, 허락하다	'목적어'에게 'to부정사'하라고 요청하다 / 권장하다 / 허락하다 **require** job applicants **to submit** their résumé 지원자들에게 이력서를 제출하라고 요청하다 **encourage** staff members **to make** suggestions 직원들에게 제안을 하도록 권장하다 **allow** the company **to reduce** expense 회사가 비용을 줄이도록 해주다

❷ 동사원형을 보어로 취하는 동사

동사	의미	예
사역동사 「make, have, let」	시키다, 만들다	'목적어'가 '동사원형'하도록 시키다 / 만들다 Please **let** us **know** if you need help. 도움이 필요하시면 저희에게 알려주세요. **have** the customers **get** discounts 고객들에게 할인을 받도록 하다
지각동사 「see, watch, feel, hear」	보다, 듣다, 느끼다	'목적어'가 '동사원형'하는 것을 보다 / 듣다 / 느끼다 **watch** our guests **enjoy** the event 고객들이 행사를 즐기는 것을 보다

☑ Further Point! 준사역 동사

- **help + 목적어 + 동사원형 / to부정사:** help us (to) conserve energy 에너지를 아끼도록 돕다

- **get + 목적어 + to부정사:** get people to use public transportation 사람들이 대중교통을 이용하도록 하다

📝 PRACTICE 5-7 괄호 안의 보기들 중에서 적절한 것을 고르세요. 정답 p.086

5 The manager (offers / allows) his employees to take a 30-minute break after 3:00 P.M.

6 According to environmental experts, the favorable weather this spring will help crops (flourish / will flourish).

7 Small business owners represent a diverse group that plays a vital role in (keeping / helping) the local economy productive.

⊙ 「-en, -ise, -ize, -fy, -ate」 등으로 끝나는 단어는 대부분 동사이다. 예시를 통해 각 동사의 뒤에 어떤 성분이 따라 오는지 알아보자.

finalize 완성하다, 마무리 짓다
🔁 complete 완성하다, 완료하다
finalize a contract 계약을 완료하다

postpone 연기하다, 미루다
postpone the meeting until next Monday
다음 주 월요일까지 회의를 연기하다

forward 보내다, 전달하다 🔁 send 보내다, 전하다
Your order has been forwarded. 주문이 전달되다

preserve 지키다, 보존하다 🔁 conserve 아끼다, 보존하다
preserve endangered species 멸종 위기의 종들을 보호하다

fulfill (의무, 약속 등을) 이행하다
fulfill a request 요청을 이행하다

prolong 연장하다, 늘리다 🔁 extend 연장하다
prolong a procedure 절차가 길어지다

guarantee 보장하다
guarantee excellent service 훌륭한 서비스를 보장하다

recommend 추천하다 🔁 endorse 지지하다
recommend her for employment 그녀를 고용할 것을 추천하다

hesitate 주저하다
Please do not hesitate to call me.
저에게 전화하시는 것을 주저하지 마세요.

recruit 모집하다
recruit employees at a job fair
직업 박람회에서 직원들을 모집하다

implement 실행하다
implement new guidelines 새로운 지침을 실행하다

renew 갱신하다
renew a contract 계약을 갱신하다

intend ~할 작정이다
intend to increase prices 가격을 올리고자 하다

replace 교환하다, 교체하다 🔁 substitute 교체하다
replace the chairs with new ones 의자들을 새것들로 교체하다

institute (제도, 정책 등을) 도입하다 🔁 establish 수립하다
institute a new policy 새로운 정책을 도입하다

restore 회복시키다, 복구하다
restore an old facility 낡은 시설을 복구하다

instruct 지시하다, 가르치다 🔁 order 지시하다
instruct employees to prepare for an event
직원들에게 행사를 준비하라고 지시하다

reveal 드러내다, 폭로하다 🔁 disclose 밝히다, 드러내다
reveal the details of an acquisition
인수의 세부사항을 밝히다

last 지속하다
The meeting will last half an hour.
회의가 30분간 지속될 것이다.

settle 해결하다; 정착하다
settle a dispute 분쟁을 해결하다
settle down in the town 그 마을에 정착하다

negotiate 협상하다; 성사시키다
negotiate with a contractor 건설사와 협상을 하다
negotiate a deal 거래를 성사시키다

specify (구체적으로) 명시하다
specify an exact date and venue
정확한 날짜와 장소를 명시하다

operate 운영하다
manage to operate a business 그럭저럭 사업을 운영하다

submit 제출하다 🔁 present 제시하다
submit the final proposal on time 최종안을 제때 제출하다

permit 허용하다
Parking in the area is not permitted.
그 지역에 주차하는 것은 허가되지 않는다.

terminate 끝내다, 종결시키다
terminate the original plan 원래의 계획을 중단하다

persist 고집하다 🔁 insist 주장하다
persist with the measures 그 조치를 고수하다

undergo 겪다 🔁 experience 경험하다
undergo regular inspections 정기 검사를 받다

sustain 지탱하게 하다 vs. **maintain** 유지하다
• sustain: 지속시키거나 성장시키는 데 중점을 둠
• maintain: 특정한 상태로 유지, 보존하는 것을 뜻함

obtain 얻다, 획득하다 vs. **retain** 유지하다, 보유하다
• obtain: 가지고 있지 않은 무엇인가를 획득하는 행위
• retain: 이미 가지고 있는 것을 유지하거나 지키는 행위

PART 5

Directions: A word or phrase is missing in each of the sentences below. Four answer choices are given below each sentence. Select the best answer to complete the sentence and mark the letter (A), (B), (C), or (D).

---

1 The board ------- all cost estimates submitted over the last month and will make a final decision next Monday.

(A) examining
(B) will be examined
(C) to examine
(D) has examined

2 In order to ------- his flight scheduled for Sunday at 2:00 P.M., Mr. Lenz placed a call to Pacific Airlines.

(A) consent
(B) remind
(C) confirm
(D) proceed

3 It is crucial to thoroughly review the terms of the contract to ensure that they comply ------- standard business practices.

(A) with
(B) to
(C) at
(D) from

4 The publicity manager ------- Mr. Graff his position before deciding to depart from Bole Investment.

(A) requested
(B) invited
(C) recruited
(D) offered

5 The company's management team ------- delayed the product launch to coincide with a major industry event.

(A) intentionally
(B) intentional
(C) intention
(D) intend

6 The board of directors found the financial report Mr. Kent made ------- and well structured.

(A) comprehends
(B) comprehending
(C) comprehension
(D) comprehensive

7 Acosta Finance ------- clients to seek the guidance of a financial planner when making significant purchases.

   (A) demands
   (B) advises
   (C) indicates
   (D) mentions

8 Thomas Supermarket offers a ------- variety of fresh produce, including fruits, vegetables, and herbs.

   (A) many
   (B) wide
   (C) heavy
   (D) quick

9 ------- postponing the meeting, we should make every effort to ensure that it takes place as scheduled.

   (A) Except for
   (B) So as
   (C) Instead of
   (D) Even if

10 We are committed to ------- our obligations to shareholders and ensuring sustainable growth in the long term.

   (A) altering
   (B) settling
   (C) fulfilling
   (D) obtaining

11 The company's premium membership plan includes many benefits, such as free shipping and an extended ------- on all purchases.

   (A) operation
   (B) warranty
   (C) expense
   (D) inventory

12 The IT Department is implementing new security measures to ensure that sensitive company information remains -------.

   (A) recent
   (B) critical
   (C) main
   (D) secure

13 You can be ------- that our product undergoes rigorous quality control measures to meet the highest standards of performance.

   (A) insisted
   (B) assured
   (C) checked
   (D) expressed

14 ------- the new restaurant has received mixed reviews, it continues to attract a steady stream of customers every day.

   (A) In spite of
   (B) However
   (C) Although
   (D) Apart from

15 Professor Allen Kim ------- to his students that his passion for developing renewable energy intensified after working at an environmental organization.

   (A) informed
   (B) allowed
   (C) convinced
   (D) explained

Directions: Read the text below. A word, phrase, or sentence is missing in parts of the text. Four answer choices for each question are given below the text. Select the best answer to complete the text and mark the letter (A), (B), (C), or (D).

Questions 16-19 refer to the following article.

Westcott Financials' Commitment to Address Concerns and to Rebuild Trust

Westcott Financials is ------- immediate action to address concerns and to regain stakeholder
16.
confidence. Through transparency and accountability, the company is committed to resolving the
issue and rebuilding trust. A dedicated task force investigates ------- and implements effective
17.
solutions. -------. It is expected to provide them with accurate and timely information. The company
18.
views this situation as a chance for growth and improvement and ------- to prevent future incidents
19.
by addressing concerns promptly and transparently.

16 (A) using
(B) taking
(C) calling
(D) failing

17 (A) incidentally
(B) previously
(C) creatively
(D) thoroughly

18 (A) We all appreciate your continued
dedication.
(B) Stakeholders can receive regular updates
as well.
(C) After extensive research, we finally found
them.
(D) Inquiries about the new product have
been received.

19 (A) has aimed
(B) is aimed
(C) will aim
(D) aiming

To: nelsen@webconstructor.com

From: beth_rider@mycutecloset.com

Date: September 19

Subject: Request for assistance

Dear Mr. Nelsen,

I recently made some changes to the product pages on my Web site. -------. Despite my best
                                                                          20.
efforts, I was unable to recover the missing content. I was wondering if you could assist me in

retrieving the deleted photos and ------- them to my Web site. -------, I would greatly appreciate
                                     21.   **22.**
your guidance on how to make basic edits to my Web site myself. I am eager to learn and prefer

not to ------- someone else every time I need to make a simple update.
       23.

Thank you for your time and assistance.

Best regards,

Beth Rider

20 (A) In the process, I accidentally deleted
        some photographs.
    (B) However, I don't have any problems with
        this project.
    (C) In my opinion, the circumstances have
        gotten better.
    (D) I made a few adjustments to see how
        they would work.

21 (A) restored
    (B) to restore
    (C) restoring
    (D) will restore

22 (A) Unfortunately
    (B) Specifically
    (C) Additionally
    (D) Consequently

23 (A) account for
    (B) carry out
    (C) subscribe to
    (D) depend on

Directions: In this part you will read a selection of texts. The text or set of texts is followed by several questions. Select the best answer for each question and mark the letter (A), (B), (C), or (D).

Questions 24-26 refer to the following notice.

Flint Technology is currently seeking to fill the position of Public Relations (PR) director as Mr. Scott Bryant is set to retire after serving the company for approximately ten years. His last day at work will be April 30. – [1] –.

As the head of the Flint Technology's Public Relations Department, the PR director will report directly to the vice president and be responsible for developing and implementing a wide range of promotional strategies that support the company's goals. – [2] –. The role also requires the ability to manage the company's public relations effort, including media relations, crisis communications, and reputation management.

Vice President Logan Hall emphasizes that the position entails significant responsibilities. "We seek candidates with extensive experience in developing and maintaining brand identities and messaging across all communications channels for companies or organizations," he stated. – [3] –.

The company has scheduled interviews for the PR director position to begin in early February. – [4] –. The goal is to appoint a new PR director by the end of March.

---

24 What is required for the PR director position?

(A) Experience in creating brand images
(B) Expertise in personnel management
(C) An advanced degree in marketing
(D) Fluency in multiple languages

25 What is suggested about Mr. Bryant?

(A) He will interview the candidates.
(B) His supervisor is Mr. Hall.
(C) He was the PR director for a decade.
(D) He will be promoted to vice president.

26 In which of the positions marked [1], [2], [3], and [4] does the following sentence best belong?

"Applications submitted after February 5 will not be considered."

(A) [1]
(B) [2]
(C) [3]
(D) [4]

Exciting News!

I'm thrilled to share fantastic news with our dedicated team. *Savory Spoon Magazine* will feature our restaurant in an upcoming article highlighting San Francisco's top dining spots! It will showcase our signature dish, clam chowder, as the city's best. The magazine is also eager to capture our warm, welcoming atmosphere created by our friendly staff. A person will be taking photos of our team serving valued customers and group shots of the entire staff.

A photoshoot is scheduled for Friday, June 8, at 9:30 A.M. All employees will be in the group photos, so please arrive slightly earlier on Friday morning and wear your uniforms.

When I launched this restaurant just last year, I couldn't have predicted our incredible success. This achievement is thanks to each of you, and you should all take pride in this well-deserved recognition.

E-Mail Message	
To:	Brenda Oliveria <chefbrenda@seaharvestkitchen.com>
From:	Mark Johnson <mark77@savoryspoon.com>
Subject:	Friday Appointment
Date:	Thursday, June 7

Dear Mr. Oliveria,

I'm writing to confirm our scheduled photography session tomorrow at 9:30 A.M. as we discussed during our phone conversation. The photo shoot will take place at your restaurant, where I'll be capturing images of your dishes and staff.

To start, I'll be photographing one of your most renowned dishes, the clam chowder, so it would be greatly appreciated if you could have it prepared for the session. Following that, I'll be photographing your staff as they gather in the main dining area. You mentioned that your staff will need to be ready by 10:30 A.M., which should not pose any issues. The group photo session is expected to conclude by 10:00 A.M. Additionally, after the photo shoot, our reporter Kathy Wall will conduct a brief interview with you and some of your customers.

If you have any questions or concerns regarding the schedule, please don't hesitate to reach out. Otherwise, I look forward to meeting with you tomorrow.

Best regards,

Mark Johnson
Savory Spoon Magazine

Sea Harvest Kitchen

The popular Sea Harvest Kitchen draws early crowds with diners arriving up to 30 minutes before opening to secure their spots by noting their precise arrival times on a chalkboard. This bustling waitlist underscores the appeal of its fresh and delightfully uncomplicated cuisine, including its classic, mild, and creamy chowder served with a side of sourdough.

Despite opening just last year, this restaurant has swiftly risen to local fame, known for its menu of traditional Irish dishes crafted by owner and chef Brenda Oliveria. Oliveria emphasizes, "We select ingredients at the peak of each season and reflect them in our menu."

During a recent Friday afternoon visit, Carol Reen, a loyal patron, shared her enthusiasm, "In addition to the famous clam chowder in a bread bowl, don't forget to leave room for dessert; the sourdough apple pie is a must!"

Beyond its delectable fare, Sea Harvest Kitchen's charm lies in its warm and accommodating staff, creating an inviting atmosphere that contributes to its widespread popularity.

By Kathy Wall
Photography by Mark Johnson

---

27 Who most likely posted the notice?

(A) Mark Johnson
(B) Kathy Wall
(C) Brenda Oliveria
(D) Carol Reen

28 What are employees asked to do on June 8?

(A) Arrive earlier than usual
(B) Attend an awards ceremony
(C) Be interviewed for a newspaper article
(D) Photograph their new menus

29 What is NOT indicated about Ms. Oliveria?

(A) She has several restaurants in San Francisco.
(B) She is a chef at Sea Harvest Kitchen.
(C) She opened a restaurant last year.
(D) She talked with Mr. Johnson before the photo shoot.

30 What is true about Sea Harvest Kitchen?

(A) It is open for lunch every day.
(B) It recently relocated.
(C) It was not that popular last year.
(D) It updates its menu seasonally.

31 What can be inferred about Ms. Reen?

(A) She is impressed with the restaurant's atmosphere.
(B) She had lunch at Sea Harvest Kitchen on June 8.
(C) She had not visited the restaurant before the interview.
(D) She didn't think the restaurant would be very popular.

빈칸이 동사 자리이고, 보기가 서로 다른 형태의 동사들로 구성되어 있을 경우에는 오답을 소거하여 정답을 찾아야 한다. 오답을 소거할 때, ① 주어와 동사와의 **수 일치를 확인**하고, ② 목적어의 유무로 **동사의 태를 결정**한 다음, ③ 시간의 단서를 찾아 **알맞은 시제의 동사**를 골라야 한다.

오늘의 학습 POINT

POINT 1 동사의 형태를 묻는 문제는 동사의 「**수·태·시**」를 차례로 확인한다.

POINT 2 동사의 **수 일치**는 주어를, 동사의 **태**는 목적어를 확인한다.

POINT 3 동사의 **시제**는 시간 표현, 접속사, 문장 내 **다른 동사의 시제를 확인**한다.

POINT 1   동사의 형태를 묻는 문제는 동사의 「수·태·시」를 차례로 확인한다.

동사의 형태를 결정하는 세 가지 요소는 주어와의 ① **수 일치**, ② **동사의 태(능동태와 수동태)**, ③ **시제**이다. 따라서 동사의 형태를 결정하는 문제는 「**수일치 → 태 → 시제**」를 순서대로 빠르게 확인하며 정답을 찾아야 한다.

수 일치

- 수 일치는 **주어와 동사와의 관계**이다. 즉, 단수 주어 뒤에는 단수 동사가, 복수 주어 뒤에는 복수 동사가 온다.
- 단수 동사는 동사의 기본형에 '-(e)s'를 붙이고, 복수 동사는 동사의 기본형을 그대로 쓴다.
- 일반동사의 단수 동사와 복수 동사의 구별은 **현재형일 때만 해당**된다.
- **to부정사, 동명사, 명사절은 단수**로 취급한다.
- 주어와 동사 사이의 **수식어구**는 동사의 수일치에 영향을 주지 않는다.

PRACTICE 1-2   괄호 안의 보기들 중에서 적절한 것을 고르세요.

정답 p.091

1 The office manager usually (purchase / purchases) supplies through the online store of Peak Office Supplies.

2 Blue Sky Airlines (operate / operates) four airplanes on its northeast Asia route every day.

① 3형식 문장의 수동태

주어　　　　　동사　　　　　목적어

능동태 I　　　　love　　　　you. 나는 당신을 사랑한다.

수동태 You　　　are loved　　by me. 당신은 나에게 사랑을 받는다.
주어　　　be + p.p.　　by + 명사(목적격)

TIP! 수동태 문제 풀이

- 빈칸이 동사 자리일 때, 빈칸 뒤에 목적어가 있으면 능동태 동사를 고르고, 목적어가 없으면 수동태 동사를 고른다. (목적어의 성분은 명사, 명사구, 명사절이다.)
- 자동사는 목적어를 취하지 않으므로, 원칙적으로 수동태로 바꿀 수 없다.

② 4형식 문장의 수동태

4형식 문장은 목적어가 두 개이므로, 두 개의 수동태를 만들 수 있다.

능동태 She sent me an e-mail. 그녀는 나에게 이메일을 보냈다.

수동태 ① I was sent an e-mail by her. 나는 그녀로부터 이메일을 받았다. [간접목적어를 주어로]

수동태 ② An e-mail was sent to me by her. 이메일이 그녀에 의해 나에게 보내졌다. [직접목적어를 주어로]

③ 5형식 문장의 수동태

5형식 동사를 수동태로 만들면 목적격 보어가 수동태 동사의 뒤에 남는다.

목적격 보어

능동태 We considered the task **a burden**. 우리는 그 작업을 부담으로 여겼다.

수동태 The task was considered **a burden**. 그 작업은 부담으로 여겨졌다.
주격 보어

cf. 5형식 동사의 종류에 따라 목적격 보어의 종류가 명사, 형용사, to부정사로 달라지므로, 구분해서 외워 두어야 한다. (DAY 07의 POINT 2 참고)

📝 PRACTICE 3-7 괄호 안의 보기들 중에서 적절한 것을 고르세요.　　　　정답 p.091

3 Mr. Ross wanted to (receive / be received) the revised estimate tomorrow at the latest.

4 The outstanding balance must (pay / be paid) by the end of the month.

5 All the details regarding the merger (has released / were released) this morning.

6 Visitors to the laboratory are required (to wear / wearing) a name tag all the time.

7 Upside Financials is (dedicated / dedicating) to providing accurate information to its clients.

1 현재 시제

1 시간·조건 부사절

when, while, before, after, until 등이 연결하는 시간 부사절이나 if, unless, as long as 등이 연결하는 조건 부사절에서는 내용이 미래일지라도 현재 시제를 사용한다. 다만, 주절의 시제는 그대로 미래 시제를 사용한다.

<u>After</u> the break **ends**, the presentation will start. 휴식이 끝난 후에, 발표가 시작될 것이다.

2 왕래발착동사

go, come, start, begin, return, arrive, leave, depart 등의 '왕래발착동사'의 현재 시제는 tomorrow, soon, next week 등의 미래 표현과 함께 사용할 수 있다. 또한, 시간표, 규칙, 계약서의 내용 등과 같이 이미 정해진 일을 말할 경우에도 현재 시제로 미래를 표현할 수 있다.

Dr. Grace's speech **starts** <u>soon</u>. 그레이스 박사의 연설이 곧 시작할 것이다.

3 현재진행 시제

일반 동사의 현재진행 시제는 미래 시제를 대신하여 사용될 수 있다. 특히 '왕래발착동사'의 경우 현재진행 시제가 미래 시제를 대신하는 경우가 많다.

The items I ordered **are arriving** <u>tomorrow</u>. 내가 주문한 물품들이 내일 도착할 것이다.

> **PRACTICE 8-9** 괄호 안의 보기들 중에서 적절한 것을 고르세요.   정답 p.091
>
> **8** Once Ms. Benson (goes / will go) to Singapore next week, she will visit the factory.
>
> **9** (Because / As long as) Mr. Cave approves our proposal, we will be able to proceed with the project next month.

2 과거 시제 vs. 현재완료 시제

1 단순 과거 시제: 특정 과거 시점 표현과 함께 사용

ago, last night, yesterday, at that time 등의 특정 과거 시점 표현과 함께 사용된다.

The board **approved** next year's budget <u>yesterday</u>. 이사회는 어제 내년도 예산안을 승인했다.

2 현재완료 시제 (계속): 과거부터 현재까지 계속

기간을 나타내는 for, over, since, 또는 this month, this year 등의 표현과 함께 사용된다.

The price of oil **has increased** <u>for</u> three months. 유가가 3개월 동안 상승해왔다.

cf. 현재완료 시제는 특정 과거 시점 표현과 함께 사용되지 않는다.

The board **has approved** next year's budget <u>yesterday</u>. (×)

③ 현재완료 시제 (경험): 과거부터 현재까지의 경험

횟수를 의미하는 once, twice, three times, multiple times 등의 표현이나, 경험한 때를 의미하는 before, never, seldom, often, sometimes 등의 표현과 함께 사용된다.

Mr. Robinson **has** <u>never</u> **been** to Moscow. 로빈슨 씨는 모스크바에 가 본 적이 없다.

cf. 기타 현재완료 시제와 함께 자주 사용되는 표현

already	yet	lately	recently	in the recent years	these days 등

* already, recently는 과거 시제와, these days는 현재 시제와도 함께 자주 사용된다.

📝 PRACTICE 10-12   괄호 안의 보기들 중에서 적절한 것을 고르세요.   정답 p.092

10 It has been only two months since he (joined / has joined) KLM Realty, but he is already performing noticeably.

11 The copy machine has not been working properly (until / since) this morning.

12 *Prime Daily News* recently (has added / add) several new features to its Web site.

③ 과거완료 시제

① 과거완료 시제 (계속): 대과거부터 과거까지 계속

They **had lived** in the city for 10 years <u>before they decided</u> to move.
그들이 이사하기로 결정하기 전까지 그들은 10년 동안 그 도시에 살았다.

② 과거완료 시제 (완료): 특정 과거 시점에 완료

<u>By the time the storm arrived</u>, we **had** already **secured** our belongings.
폭풍이 도달했을 때쯤에, 우리는 이미 물품들을 고정시켰다.

cf. 과거완료 시제와 함께 사용되는 표현

- **by the time** + 주어 + 과거 시제 동사, 주어 + **had p.p.**
- **before** + 주어 + 과거 시제 동사, 주어 + **had p.p.**
- **after** + 주어 + **had p.p.**, 주어 + 과거 시제 동사

TIP! 과거완료 문제 풀이 팁

- 시제 문제에서 과거완료가 정답이 되려면 문장 내에 특정 과거 시점이 언급되어 있어야 한다.
- PART 6의 경우에는 빈칸이 포함된 문장이나 혹은 다른 문장에서 내용상 특정 과거 시점이 언급되어 있다면 과거완료 시제가 정답이 될 수 있다.

📝 PRACTICE 13   괄호 안의 보기들 중에서 적절한 것을 고르세요.   정답 p.092

13 Ms. Ellis had been studying marketing for about three years when she (applied / has applied) for the internship.

④ 미래 시제 vs. 미래완료 시제

① 단순 미래 시제: 특정 미래 시점 표현과 함께 사용

tomorrow, next week, at the end of the year, soon 등의 특정 미래 시점 표현과 함께 사용된다.

We **will complete** the project <u>at the end of the month</u>. 우리는 이달 말에 프로젝트를 완료할 것이다.

② 미래완료 시제: 과거부터 현재까지 계속

「will have p.p.」의 형태로서, 특정 미래 시점까지 계속되거나 특정 미래 시점에 완료되는 일을 표현한다.

<u>By the time you arrive</u>, we **will have finished** setting up for the event.
당신이 도착할 때쯤이면, 우리는 행사 준비를 모두 마쳤을 것이다.

cf. 미래완료 시제와 함께 사용되는 표현

- by the time + 주어 + 현재 시제 동사, 주어 + **will have p.p.**

📝 **PRACTICE 14** 괄호 안의 보기들 중에서 적절한 것을 고르세요. 정답 p.092

14 By the time the project has finished, they (work / will have worked) on it for almost three years.

148

⚙ 구동사는 「동사 + 전치사」, 또는 「동사 + 부사」의 형태로서, 동사의 원래 의미와는 다른 의미를 만들어 낸다.

attend to ~을 처리하다; 돌보다; 주의하다
attend to the details 세부 사항에 주의하다

call off 취소하다 ⊕ cancel 취소하다
The event was called off due to rain.
행사가 비 때문에 취소되었다.

call for (공식적으로) 요구하다; 소집하다
An urgent meeting has been called for.
긴급 회의가 소집되었다.

carry on 계속하다
carry on a conversation 대화를 이어가다

carry out 실행하다, 수행하다 ⊕ conduct 실행하다
carry out the plan 계획을 실행하다

come up with 생각해내다
come up with new ideas 새로운 아이디어를 생각해내다

cut town on 줄이다 ⊕ reduce 줄이다
cut down on the amount of paperwork
서류 작업의 양을 줄이다

drop by 잠시 들르다 ⊕ stop by 잠시 들르다
drop by the office 사무실에 들르다

figure out 이해하다; 생각해내다
figure out the cause of malfunction
오작동의 원인을 알아내다

fill in for 대신하다
fill in for his role 그의 역할을 대신하다

fill out 작성하다 ⊕ complete 작성하다
fill out the immigration form 출입국 신고서를 작성하다

find out 알아내다, 찾아내다
find out if they offer the service
그들이 그 서비스를 제공하는지 알아보다

follow up on 후속 조치를 취하다
the message to follow up on this morning's meeting
오늘 아침 회의의 후속 조치에 대한 메시지

get along with ~와 잘 지내다
get along with my classmates 반 친구들과 잘 지내다

give up 포기하다
give up the chance to work abroad
해외에서 일할 기회를 포기하다

go through 경험하다
go through the drastic changes 많은 변화를 겪다

lay off 해고하다 ⊕ fire 해고하다
Over 100 workers were laid off.
100명 이상의 직원들이 해고되었다

look into 조사하다 ⊕ investigate 조사하다
look into the matter 그 문제를 조사하다

make up for 보상하다; 만회하다
trying to make up for the deficit 적자를 만회하려 노력하다

put aside 제쳐두다
put aside their views 그들의 의견을 제쳐두다

put off 연기하다, 미루다 ⊕ postpone 연기하다, 미루다
The meeting was put off for weeks.
회의가 몇 주 연기됐었다.

put together 조립하다; 준비하다
put together a presentation for tomorrow's meeting
내일 회의를 위해 발표를 준비하다

run out (공급품이) 다 떨어지다
We have run out of paper. 우리는 용지가 고갈되었다.

set up 설치하다; 설립하다
⊕ install 설치하다, establish 설립하다
set up a business 사업을 시작하다

show up 나타나다
Many people showed up at the book-signing event.
책 사인회에 많은 사람들이 왔다.

sign up for 등록하다 ⊕ register 등록하다
sign up for a training session 교육 과정을 등록하다

sort out 분류하다; 문제를 해결하다
⊕ classify, categorize 분류하다
sort out a matter 문제를 해결하다

take over 인수하다
take over the smaller local companies
더 작은 지역 회사들을 인수하다

take part in ~에 참가하다
⊕ participate in ~에 참여하다
take part in the competition 대회에 참가하다

turn in 제출하다 ⊕ hand in, submit 제출하다
Turn in your report by next week
다음주까지 보고서를 제출하세요.

PART 5

Directions: A word or phrase is missing in each of the sentences below. Four answer choices are given below each sentence. Select the best answer to complete the sentence and mark the letter (A), (B), (C), or (D).

1. Ron Zuber, the president of Weichart Retail, is expected ------- a significant profit growth this year.

   (A) report
   (B) to report
   (C) reporting
   (D) reported

2. Warning notices ------- to residents in low-lying areas to evacuate ahead of the approaching storm.

   (A) were issuing
   (B) have issued
   (C) had been issuing
   (D) have been issued

3. Consulting with a financial professional before investing is ------- to make informed decisions and to manage risk effectively.

   (A) advised
   (B) advisory
   (C) advisable
   (D) advisably

4. The lectures delivered by the renowned copywriter Joan Pike ------- informative and engaging by attendees.

   (A) will consider
   (B) are considered
   (C) were considering
   (D) have considered

5. ------- the grand opening last year, the new shopping mall has become a popular destination for shoppers.

   (A) Before
   (B) When
   (C) Since
   (D) Until

6. In order to ensure smooth operations, it is imperative that we keep our resources ------- at all times.

   (A) accesses
   (B) accessibility
   (C) more accessibly
   (D) more accessible

7 ------- we receive the necessary funding, we will not be able to proceed with the research project.

(A) Unless
(B) Though
(C) Instead
(D) Whereas

8 The company will ------- to the customer's inquiry within 24 hours to ensure the timely and satisfactory resolution of any issues.

(A) explain
(B) promise
(C) request
(D) respond

9 The new partnership will present a unique ------- to expand into new markets and to increase our global presence.

(A) personality
(B) assurance
(C) relationship
(D) opportunity

10 The detailed proposal, outlining the cost savings and increased efficiency, ------- the client consider switching to our company's services.

(A) offered
(B) made
(C) brought
(D) became

11 ------- profits are important, the company also places a high value on ethical business practices and social responsibility.

(A) While
(B) Despite
(C) However
(D) Not only

12 The organizers have ------- begun sending out invitations to prominent speakers for the conference scheduled to take place next year.

(A) already
(B) politely
(C) briefly
(D) closely

13 The new museum in the city center has quickly become a popular tourist ------- for visitors from all over the world.

(A) registration
(B) transition
(C) attraction
(D) presentation

14 Dr. Turley has been nominated for a ------- award in recognition of his groundbreaking research in the field of genetics.

(A) repetitive
(B) deliberate
(C) meticulous
(D) prestigious

15 ------- recent unfortunate events, the company has decided to implement stricter security measures to protect its confidential data.

(A) In spite of
(B) Apart from
(C) In light of
(D) According to

PART 6

Directions: Read the text below. A word, phrase, or sentence is missing in parts of the text. Four answer choices for each question are given below the text. Select the best answer to complete the text and mark the letter (A), (B), (C), or (D).

Questions 16-19 refer to the following brochure.

Would you like to unlock your creative potential? The Sarasota University Extension Program is offering a diverse range of programs to our community members wanting to improve ------- writing **16.** skills. Our team of experts specialize in various mediums, ------- poetry, fiction, literary translation, **17.** and screenwriting.

With our program, you'll have the opportunity not only to develop your writing skills but also to showcase your work. Selected pieces ------- on our Web site, giving you the chance to gain **18.** recognition for your hard work. Registration for classes is available on our Web site at www.stetsonextension.org. -------. **19.**

16 (A) oneself
    (B) yours
    (C) their
    (D) which

17 (A) includes
    (B) inclusive
    (C) included
    (D) including

18 (A) have featured
    (B) will be featured
    (C) had been featured
    (D) could have featured

19 (A) Many have shown interest in the book-signing event.
    (B) A detailed schedule of programs is also available online.
    (C) At the end of the course, your writing will be published.
    (D) Curriculums must be submitted by the end of the month.

Questions 20-23 refer to the following memo.

To: Sales Team at Crossed Palms Housing

From: Karl Tunberg, Sales Manager

Date: Wednesday, April 13

Subject: Scheduled Tours for Camelback Condominiums

We are thrilled to see the immense interest in Camelback Condominiums, our ongoing housing development project, -------- potential buyers. It's great to inform you that all available times for **20.** home tours throughout this weekend are now filled. --------. However, the responsibility to close the **21.** deal lies with you. Since we -------- only three display homes, you need to help prospective buyers **22.** visualize living at Camelback Condominiums. As visitors will tour these model homes, you should -------- the development's close proximity to upscale shops, restaurants, and convenient public **23.** transportation options.

20 (A) within
    (B) among
    (C) through
    (D) about

21 (A) Only those with an invitation can visit the model homes.
    (B) Directions to the model homes can be found on our Web site.
    (C) We are currently negotiating a contract with a customer.
    (D) This confirms that people are eager to own a home here.

22 (A) will be completed
    (B) have completed
    (C) should complete
    (D) had been completed

23 (A) emphasize
    (B) accelerate
    (C) accompany
    (D) encounter

PART 7

Directions: In this part you will read a selection of texts. The text or set of texts is followed by several questions. Select the best answer for each question and mark the letter (A), (B), (C), or (D).

Questions 24-26 refer to the following form.

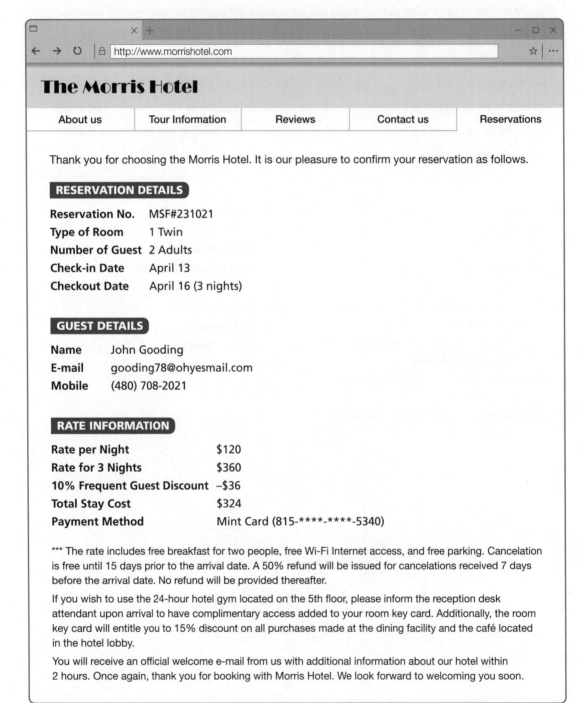

The Morris Hotel

| About us | Tour Information | Reviews | Contact us | Reservations |

Thank you for choosing the Morris Hotel. It is our pleasure to confirm your reservation as follows.

RESERVATION DETAILS

Reservation No.	MSF#231021
Type of Room	1 Twin
Number of Guest	2 Adults
Check-in Date	April 13
Checkout Date	April 16 (3 nights)

GUEST DETAILS

Name	John Gooding
E-mail	gooding78@ohyesmail.com
Mobile	(480) 708-2021

RATE INFORMATION

Rate per Night	$120
Rate for 3 Nights	$360
10% Frequent Guest Discount	–$36
Total Stay Cost	$324
Payment Method	Mint Card (815-****-****-5340)

*** The rate includes free breakfast for two people, free Wi-Fi Internet access, and free parking. Cancelation is free until 15 days prior to the arrival date. A 50% refund will be issued for cancelations received 7 days before the arrival date. No refund will be provided thereafter.

If you wish to use the 24-hour hotel gym located on the 5th floor, please inform the reception desk attendant upon arrival to have complimentary access added to your room key card. Additionally, the room key card will entitle you to 15% discount on all purchases made at the dining facility and the café located in the hotel lobby.

You will receive an official welcome e-mail from us with additional information about our hotel within 2 hours. Once again, thank you for booking with Morris Hotel. We look forward to welcoming you soon.

24 What is NOT included in Mr. Gooding's reservation?

(A) Internet access

(B) Fitness center usage

(C) Free shuttle bus service

(D) A complimentary breakfast

25 What can be implied about Mr. Gooding?

(A) He has booked two rooms under his name.

(B) He will be able to make a free cancelation any time.

(C) He will pay for the accommodations in cash.

(D) He has previously stayed at the hotel.

26 What should be presented to get a discount at the hotel restaurant?

(A) A confirmation letter

(B) A meal coupon

(C) A room key card

(D) A form of identification

Zelkova, Inc.

September 15 - With a strong foundation established over 50 years, Zelkova, Inc. offers comprehensive engineering, technology, logistics, and management services. We have built an exceptional team of individuals and partners and consistently provide exemplary performance while serving our customers.

Currently, we are expanding our business to include not only commercial clients but also governmental organizations. As a result, we are seeking talented individuals who share our passion for providing excellent service and value to our customers.

We currently have openings in the following areas:

Entry-Level Positions:	Management Positions:
• Data Entry	• Engineering
• Production Line Operating	• Marketing
Recruiter: Tamie Cohen	Recruiter: Susan Travers
E-mail: tamie@zelkova.com	E-mail: susan@zelkova.com
Entry-Level Positions:	Management Positions:
• Customer Service	• Accounting
• Sales	• Computer Programming
Recruiter: Jeff Fields	Recruiter: Russ Lyon
E-mail: jeff@zelkova.com	E-mail: russ@zelkova.com

Interested candidates for any of the listed positions are required to submit their applications, along with three references, via e-mail to the recruiters in their desired department. Applications received after September 20 will not be considered. Only selected candidates will be contacted via e-mail for interviews with notifications sent no later than September 30. For further information, please reach out to any of the recruiters listed above.

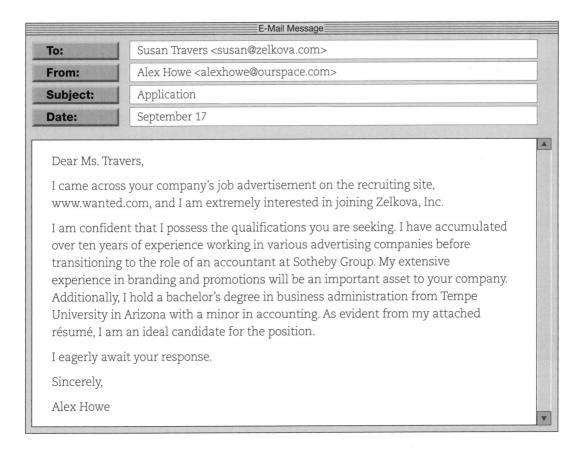

E-Mail Message

To:	Susan Travers <susan@zelkova.com>
From:	Alex Howe <alexhowe@ourspace.com>
Subject:	Application
Date:	September 17

Dear Ms. Travers,

I came across your company's job advertisement on the recruiting site, www.wanted.com, and I am extremely interested in joining Zelkova, Inc.

I am confident that I possess the qualifications you are seeking. I have accumulated over ten years of experience working in various advertising companies before transitioning to the role of an accountant at Sotheby Group. My extensive experience in branding and promotions will be an important asset to your company. Additionally, I hold a bachelor's degree in business administration from Tempe University in Arizona with a minor in accounting. As evident from my attached résumé, I am an ideal candidate for the position.

I eagerly await your response.

Sincerely,

Alex Howe

---

27 By when should applications be submitted to be considered?

(A) September 15
(B) September 17
(C) September 20
(D) September 30

28 How will Ms. Travers most likely contact Mr. Howe?

(A) By calling him
(B) By mailing a document to him
(C) By posting an announcement on a Web site
(D) By sending him an e-mail

29 In the email, the word "accumulated" in paragraph 2, line 1, is closest in meaning to

(A) conducted
(B) remained
(C) extended
(D) gained

30 What qualification does Mr. Howe NOT indicate in the e-mail?

(A) He has experience supervising sales staff.
(B) He has worked at advertising companies before.
(C) He majored in business administration.
(D) He has more than 10 years of experience.

31 What department is Mr. Howe most likely applying to?

(A) Customer Service
(B) Marketing
(C) Accounting
(D) Computer Programming

04 명사

명사는 **주어, 목적어, 보어 자리**에 오는 품사이다. 출제 빈도가 높기 때문에 문장에서 명사의 자리를 잘 파악해 두어야 한다. 그리고 **가산 명사와 불가산 명사를 구분**해 두어야 수 일치, 한정사, 지시형용사, 수량형용사 등의 수식어 관련 문제에 대비할 수 있다.

오늘의 학습 POINT

POINT 1 명사는 주어, 목적어, 보어 자리에 오는 품사이다.
POINT 2 단수 가산 명사에는 한정사가 꼭 붙는다.
POINT 3 명사는 형용사의 수식을 받고, 동명사는 부사의 수식을 받는다.

POINT 1   명사는 주어, 목적어, 보어 자리에 오는 품사이다.

- 명사의 자리는 동사 앞 **주어** 자리, 타동사 뒤 **목적어** 자리, **주격 보어**나 **목적격 보어** 자리이다.
- **전치사, 관사, 소유격, 한정사, 형용사 뒤** 자리가 명사 자리이다.

📝 PRACTICE 1-10 ◀ 문장의 주어에는 ○, 목적어에는 □, 보어에는 △ 표시를 하세요. 정답 p.097

1 The company's profits have increased by 20% compared to last year.

2 The conference will be held at the Garwood Hotel on Friday, October 12.

3 Our new product line has received positive feedback from customers.

4 The shipment of goods has been delayed due to unforeseen circumstances.

5 Please submit your résumé and cover letter to the HR Department by the end of the week.

6 The members of the sales team achieved their monthly targets ahead of schedule.

7 The company is considering expanding its operations to international markets.

8 As a responsible employer, we always consider the work-life balance of our employees our highest priority.

9 The training session will take place in the conference room on the second floor.

10 The deadline for submitting the monthly sales report is next Monday.

① 가산 명사와 불가산 명사

명사의 종류	특징
단수 가산 명사	• '하나'임을 표현하는 부정관사 'a/an'이 붙는다. • 부정관사 없이 쓰이는 경우, 정관사(the)나 소유격(my, your, Kate's 등), 그 외의 한정사 (this, that, another 등)가 꼭 붙어야 한다. **e.g.** a pen, the pen, my pen, this pen (○) / pen (×)
복수 가산 명사	• 보통 뒤에 '–s/es'가 붙지만 불규칙 변화형도 존재한다. • 앞에 부정관사를 제외한 한정사(정관사, 소유격 등)가 붙을 수 있지만, 한정사가 꼭 필요한 것은 아니다. **e.g.** pens, the pens, my pens, these pens (○) / a pens (×)
불가산 명사	• 고유 명사, 추상 명사는 보통 불가산 명사이다. • 부정관사 'a/an'이나 '–s/es'를 붙일 수 없다. • 정관사(the)와 this, that등의 한정사는 붙을 수 있지만 한정사가 꼭 필요한 것은 아니다. **e.g.** water, the water, this water (○) / a water, waters, these water (×)

cf. 가산 명사와 불가산 명사는 주로 수 일치 문제로 출제된다.

• 동사를 보고 주어 자리의 빈칸을 채우는 문제
• 명사 앞의 수식어나 한정사를 고르는 문제

> **✎ PRACTICE 11-12** 괄호 안의 보기들 중에서 적절한 것을 고르세요. 　　　정답 p.097

11 The new manufacturing (facility / facilities) has significantly increased production capacity.

12 This fierce (competition / competitions) in the market requires us constantly to adapt and to improve our strategies.

① 대부분의 명사는 가산 명사이므로 불가산 명사를 위주로 외워 두자.

불가산 명사 (집합적 물질 명사)	가산 명사
information 정보	details, clarifications, descriptions, specifics 등
furniture 가구	desks, chairs, shelves, tables, couches 등
money 돈, cash 현금, change 잔돈	bills, coins, expenses, budgets, fares, fees, prices, costs, profits 등
equipment 장비	devices, cameras, computers, videos, copiers 등
transportation 교통 수단	trains, flights, buses, cabs 등
luggage, baggage 짐	bags, suitcases, boxes, crates 등
mail 우편물	letters, messages, cards 등
staff, personnel 직원	employees, clerks, assistants, members, directors 등

cf. 총체적 의미의 집합적 물질 명사들은 불가산 명사이며, 여기에 포함되는 하위 개념의 명사들은 가산 명사이다.

• furniture는 총체적 의미의 '가구'를 의미하는 불가산 명사, 하위 개념의 명사들은 모두 가산 명사
• money는 총체적 의미의 '돈'을 의미하는 불가산 명사, 하위 개념의 명사들은 가산 명사

② 사람 명사는 대부분 가산 명사이다.

사람 명사	추상 명사	사람 명사	추상 명사
a competitor 경쟁자	competition 경쟁	a manager 관리자	management 관리
an advisor 조언자	advice 조언	a critic 비평가	criticism 비평
an analyst 분석가	analysis 분석	a photographer 사진작가	photography 사진술
a donator 기부자	donation 기부	a resident 거주자	residence 거주, 상주
a rival 경쟁자	rivalry 경쟁	a performer 연주자	performance 연주
a guide 안내자	guidance 안내	a distributor 배급업자	distribution 배급

③ 의미가 비슷해서 혼동하기 쉬운 가산 명사와 불가산 명사

가산 명사	불가산 명사	가산 명사	불가산 명사
a permit 허가(증)	permission 허가	a suggestion 제안	advice 조언
a document 서류, 문서	documentation 서류 작업	an approach 접근법	access 접근
a certificate 증명(서)	certification 증명	a survey 설문, 조사	research 연구
a product 상품	merchandise 상품	a decision 결정	approval 승인

④ 단수 명사일 때와 복수 명사일 때 의미가 달라지는 명사

단수	복수	단수	복수
manner 방법, 방식	manners 풍습, 예절	feature 특징	features 용모
custom 습관	customs 세관, 관세	authority 권위	authorities 당국
purchase 구매	purchases 구입한 것	saving 절약	savings 저축
content 만족	contents 내용	writing 쓰기	writings 저작, 작품

📝 PRACTICE 13-14 괄호 안의 보기들 중에서 적절한 것을 고르세요. 정답 p.097

13 (Purchase / Purchases) made at one store cannot be refunded at another store even if both stores are owned by the same parent company.

14 The violinist received a standing ovation for his (performer / performance) of *Partita No. 1*.

② 명사를 수식하는 형용사

형용사의 종류	수식 받는 명사의 종류	예
this, that	단수 가산 명사 불가산 명사	**this** survey **this** research
every, each	단수 가산 명사	**each** product
these, those, (a) few, many, several, multiple, a number of, a variety of	복수 명사	**those** people **a variety of** items
(a) little, much, an amount of	불가산 명사	**little** doubt

cf. a lot of와 lots of는 가산 명사와 불가산 명사를 모두 수식한다.

정답 p.097

> 📝 **PRACTICE 15-16** 괄호 안의 보기들 중에서 적절한 것을 고르세요.

15 We conducted a (research / survey) to find out how many hours teenagers spend on the Internet each day.

16 To keep customers satisfied, every customer (complaint / complaints) should be handled promptly.

POINT **3** 명사는 형용사의 수식을 받지만, 동명사는 부사의 수식을 받는다.

❶ 명사와 동명사의 차이

명사	동명사
명사 앞에는 한정사가 붙을 수 있다. (한정사: a, an, the, this, that, each, every 등)	동명사 앞에는 한정사가 붙지 않는다. **cf.** 동명사가 의미상의 주어로 사용될 경우 앞에 소유격이 붙는다. **e.g.** your joining us (당신이 우리에게 합류 하는 것)
명사와 명사를 연결하려면 전치사가 필요하다. **e.g.** attendance at the seminar	(타동사에서 파생된) 동명사 뒤에는 목적어인 명사가 존재한다. **e.g.** attending the seminar
명사는 형용사가 수식한다. **e.g.** heavy rain	동명사는 부사가 수식한다. **e.g.** heavily raining

정답 p.097

> 📝 **PRACTICE 17-18** 괄호 안의 보기들 중에서 적절한 것을 고르세요.

17 These issues should be taken into (consideration / considering) before making a final decision.

18 The board of directors made a unanimous decision after (careful / carefully) reviewing the submission.

❷ 주의할 -ing형 명사

가산 명사	불가산 명사	가산 명사	불가산 명사
a seat 좌석	seating 좌석 배치	a process 과정	processing 처리
a fund 자금	funding 기금 조성	an account 계좌	accounting 회계
a ticket 표	ticketing 발권	a market 시장	marketing 마케팅
a house 집	housing 주거	a width 폭	widening 확장
a price 가격	pricing 가격 책정	an advertisement 광고	advertising 광고 행위
a plan 계획	planning 기획	a speed 속도	speeding 과속

cf. 대부분의 -ing형 명사는 불가산 명사이지만 opening(공석)이나 offering(선물, 팔 것)과 같은 가산 명사도 존재한다.

정답 p.097

> 📝 **PRACTICE 19-20** 괄호 안의 보기들 중에서 적절한 것을 고르세요.

19 Thanks to exceptional (plan / planning), the construction firm completed the shopping center earlier than expected.

20 Katherine is highly interested in an (opening / open) in the Public Relations Department at Star Bank.

❂ 「-tion / -sion / -ment / -ness / -ity / -nce」 등으로 끝나는 단어는 대부분 명사이다. 「-al, -ive」 등의 형용사형 어미로 끝나는 명사에도 주의하자.

---

acceptance 수락
Please confirm your acceptance of the offer.
제안에 대한 수락을 확답해 주세요.

access 접근, 접근권
access to information 정보에 대한 접근(권)

acquisition 습득, 구입한 것, 인수 **cf.** merger 합병
an increasing number of mergers and acquisitions in this industry 이 산업에서 증가하고 있는 인수 합병의 수치

affiliation 소속; 제휴
affiliations with diverse businesses 다양한 사업자들과의 제휴

anniversary 기념일
celebrate its first anniversary 창립 1주년을 축하하다

application 지원(서), 신청(서)
complete an application form 신청서를 작성하다

appointment 약속; 임명
the appointment of the new managers
신임 관리자들의 임명

appraisal 평가, 판단
the annual staff appraisal 연례 직원 평가

approval 승인, 찬성
We will need the approval of the board.
우리는 이사회의 승인이 필요할 것이다.

assistance 도움, 지원 **cf.** assistant 조수
provide advice and assistance in finding jobs
일자리를 구하는 데 조언과 도움을 제공하다

attendance 출석; 참석자 수 **cf.** attendee 참석자
Attendance at the event was considerably high.
그 행사의 참석자 수는 상당히 많았다.

benefit 혜택; 복리 후생 **cf.** beneficiary 수혜자
review the personnel policies and company benefits
인사 정책과 복리 후생 제도를 검토하다

category 범주
They have a couple of items within the price category.
그들은 그 가격 범주 안에 몇 가지 품목들을 가지고 있다.

commitment 약속; 전념, 헌신
our commitment to providing quality customer service 양질의 고객 서비스를 제공하기 위한 우리의 노력

price 가격, 값 **vs.** **cost** 비용
• price: 생산자(판매자)가 제시한 가치로서의 가격
• cost: 소비자가 구매할 때 들어가는 가격(비용)

---

competition 경쟁
Competition in the food delivery service has been increasing. 음식 배달 서비스의 경쟁이 증가하고 있다.

completion 완료, 완성
completion of a training course 훈련 과정의 수료

contribution 기여, 기부금; 기고문
his valuable contribution to the research
그 연구에 대한 그의 귀중한 공헌

disruption 혼란; 중단
the disruption to production 생산 중단

distribution 분배, 분포, 배급
digital distribution via online market
온라인 시장을 통한 디지털(방식의) 배급

division (조직의) 분과(부)
the promotional campaign division 판촉 부서

employment 직장; 고용, 취업
seeking employment through online job sites
온라인 취업 사이트를 통한 구직

estimate 추정; 견적서 **⑤** quotation 견적
the estimate for the repairs 수리 견적서

evaluation 평가, 감정
an employee performance evaluation 직원 성과 평가

expense 비용, 경비 **⑤** budget 예산
The actual expense was higher than expected.
실제 비용은 예상보다 높았다.

extension (영향력 등의) 확대; (기간의) 연장
an extension of the contract 계약의 연장

facility 시설; 기능, 재능
a facility for languages 언어에 대한 재능

feasibility 실현 가능성
conduct a feasibility study 실현 가능성 연구를 실행하다

flexibility 융통성, 유연성
provide flexibility to increase employee productivity
직원 생산성 향상을 위한 유연성을 제공하다

fare 교통 요금 **vs.** **fee** 수수료, 입장료
• fare: 교통 요금에 한정
• fee: 가입, 등록, 입장 요금, 서비스 수수료 등을 의미

PART 5

Directions: A word or phrase is missing in each of the sentences below. Four answer choices are given below each sentence. Select the best answer to complete the sentence and mark the letter (A), (B), (C), or (D).

1   Pantheon Investment offers excellent ------- in order to retain its valued employees effectively.

(A) benefitting
(B) beneficial
(C) benefitted
(D) benefits

2   By conducting monthly employee training sessions, Aurora Electronics ensures that its sales staff remains ------- of product developments.

(A) informs
(B) informed
(C) information
(D) have informed

3   Please direct all ------- to order equipment and supplies for the new location to Mr. Noble in the support services division.

(A) request
(B) requests
(C) requested
(D) requesting

4   While we have various options for generating cash, ------- another series of corporate bonds appears to be the most prudent course.

(A) issues
(B) issued
(C) issuing
(D) issuer

5   For detailed ------- and additional product information, kindly visit our Web site at www.bellappliance.com.

(A) faculties
(B) descriptions
(C) resolutions
(D) installments

6   Once the realtor ------- a new tenant, the landlord will be able to return your deposit.

(A) found
(B) founding
(C) finds
(D) would find

7 Seymour Construction has submitted its proposal ------- how it plans to overcome the budget constraints on the remodeling project.

(A) outline
(B) outlines
(C) outlining
(D) outlined

8 Due to increasing competition in the market, Sherman Insurance has been suffering revenue ------- this year.

(A) costs
(B) losses
(C) expenses
(D) budgets

9 In an effort to ------- interaction between departments, management has decided to hold a general staff meeting every Monday.

(A) facilitate
(B) indicate
(C) appraise
(D) dominate

10 Sun City Publication aims to provide readers with convenient access to all the contents it publishes based on digital -------.

(A) distribution
(B) distributing
(C) distributors
(D) distributes

11 We encourage all staff members to take the ------- to share their creative ideas on the sales promotion campaign for our new cosmetics line.

(A) appraisal
(B) precaution
(C) initiative
(D) directory

12 Swan Realty offers a reasonable ------- for those seeking environmentally conscious residential construction.

(A) alternation
(B) alternating
(C) alternative
(D) alternatively

13 As a healthcare provider, we only produce the highest quality nutritional supplements that show our ------- to wellness.

(A) commitment
(B) measurement
(C) employment
(D) arrangement

14 The objective of the Web site is to provide consumers with ------- tips aimed at lowering their living expenses.

(A) practical
(B) repetitive
(C) comparable
(D) knowledgeable

15 Starting next month, ------- member of the sales team will be required to submit a weekly progress report.

(A) one another
(B) every
(C) other
(D) most

PART 6

Directions: Read the text below. A word, phrase, or sentence is missing in parts of the text. Four answer choices for each question are given below the text. Select the best answer to complete the text and mark the letter (A), (B), (C), or (D).

Questions 16-19 refer to the follow notice.

The tenth annual Fresno County Readers is set to take place on September 10. Due to ------- **16.** immense popularity, the reading festival will be held in a new location, the historical Fresco Theater. This venue is expected to accommodate up to 500 attendees. The larger ------- will allow **17.** more members of the community to participate. This year's featured author is George Laughton, ------- is a prominent environmentalist from this region. He will sign copies of his latest book, **18.** *The Silent Signal*. People interested are encouraged to bring a copy of Mr. Laughton's work for this occasion. -------. For more information on the festival and a list of upcoming events, please **19.** visit www.fresnos.com.

16 (A) its
    (B) ours
    (C) his
    (D) theirs

17 (A) amount
    (B) facility
    (C) situation
    (D) program

18 (A) as to
    (B) who
    (C) in order
    (D) among

19 (A) This year's event was also very successful.
    (B) He is now planning his new book in the series.
    (C) The festival will be held in the park this year.
    (D) It is now available at several local bookstores.

Renowned chef Donna Holmes's lifelong dream of opening an authentic southern-style restaurant in Brooklyn has finally come true ------- almost 20 years of being a chef in restaurants at five-star hotels. Join us at Donna's Table, ------- at 1343 Utica Ave., Brooklyn, on Friday, May 15, from **20.** **21.** 10:00 A.M. to 9:00 P.M., as we celebrate our grand opening. -------. Esteemed community leaders **22.** have been invited to participate in this ceremony. Indulge in our classic southern dishes and savor Chef Holmes's culinary passion. ------- will have the opportunity to enjoy exclusive discounts and **23.** coupons. For more information, visit donnastable.com or call (212) 310-2525.

20 (A) while
(B) prior to
(C) after
(D) only if

21 (A) located
(B) locations
(C) locating
(D) to locate

22 (A) A larger crowd than anticipated assembled at the event.
(B) It marks the opening of the second branch in the town.
(C) The restaurant remains closed every Sunday and Monday.
(D) The ribbon-cutting ceremony will commence at 11:00 A.M.

23 (A) Attending
(B) Attendance
(C) Attendees
(D) Attendants

Directions: In this part you will read a selection of texts. The text or set of texts is followed by several questions. Select the best answer for each question and mark the letter (A), (B), (C), or (D).

Questions 24-25 refer to the following text message chain.

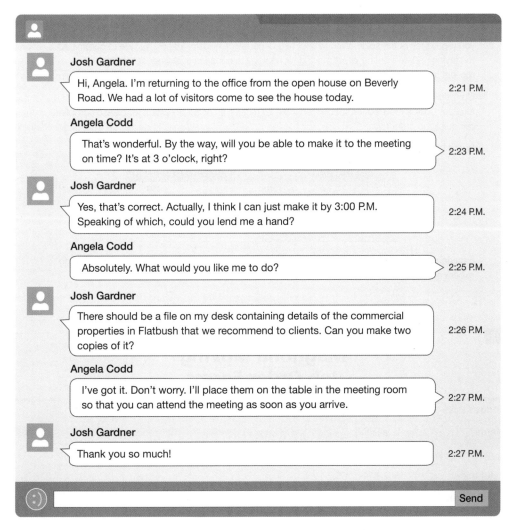

Josh Gardner

Hi, Angela. I'm returning to the office from the open house on Beverly Road. We had a lot of visitors come to see the house today.

2:21 P.M.

Angela Codd

That's wonderful. By the way, will you be able to make it to the meeting on time? It's at 3 o'clock, right?

2:23 P.M.

Josh Gardner

Yes, that's correct. Actually, I think I can just make it by 3:00 P.M. Speaking of which, could you lend me a hand?

2:24 P.M.

Angela Codd

Absolutely. What would you like me to do?

2:25 P.M.

Josh Gardner

There should be a file on my desk containing details of the commercial properties in Flatbush that we recommend to clients. Can you make two copies of it?

2:26 P.M.

Angela Codd

I've got it. Don't worry. I'll place them on the table in the meeting room so that you can attend the meeting as soon as you arrive.

2:27 P.M.

Josh Gardner

Thank you so much!

2:27 P.M.

Send

24 At 2:25 P.M., what does Ms. Codd mean when she writes, "Absolutely"?

(A) Mr. Gardner's contact has brought her pleasure.

(B) She is ready to offer assistance to Mr. Gardner.

(C) She has confidence in Mr. Gardner's success.

(D) She is currently on her way to attend the meeting.

25 For what type of business does Mr. Gardner most likely work?

(A) A landscaping company

(B) A publishing company

(C) An advertising company

(D) A real estate company

Discover Magnolia Moving: Your Complete Moving Solution

Magnolia Moving offers an array of customizable moving services to cater to your needs. Whether it's a local relocation or a cross-country move, our experienced team is ready to assist you regardless of the scale. With almost two decades of industry leadership, we're committed to staying updated on the latest moving technology to enhance customer satisfaction. Our movers are efficient, courteous, and attentive to detail, ensuring the safety of your belongings.

Our pricing is simple: $50 per hour for each mover. Additional charges may apply if a truck or a furniture dolly is required for specialized jobs. To receive an accurate estimate, please complete our quick job order form.

Listed below are our standard rates.

MOVERS	PRICE PER HOUR
1	$50
2	$100
3	$150
4+	$200 - $300

Experience the convenience of Magnolia Moving as we guide you through a seamless moving experience. Your belongings are in capable hands.

Magnolia Moving
Job Order Forms

Today's Date	Thursday, October 28
Name	Lala Smith
E-mail address	lalasmith@worldnet.com
Telephone	602-811-1165
Moving from	6993 Camelback Rd, D300, Scottsdale, AZ, 85552
Moving to	8773 Pecos Rd, Suite 355, Mesa, AZ, 85212
Move date	November 20
Items to be moved	12 wooden shelves: five of them are 3.5 feet wide by 6 feet long, three of them are 3 feet wide by 5 feet long, and rest of them are 2 feet wide by 5 feet long.
Comments	I require assistance in transporting 12 wooden shelves from the manufacturer to my upcoming shoe store. The store is situated on the third floor of the Mesa Shopping Center. A colleague of mine, who had a comparable volume of items moved last month and highly recommended your services, mentioned that moving the items I've described would likely require at least two individuals. I've indicated November 20 as the preferred moving date, but I am open to any other day within the same week if November 20 is unavailable.

To:	Lala Smith <lalasmith@worldnet.com>
From:	Branden Johnson <branden77@magnoliamoving.com>
Subject:	Estimate
Date:	October 28
Attachment:	Quote_R1028_M1120.pdf

Thank you for choosing Magnolia Moving for your delivery needs. In our experience, due to the items' sizes and the third-floor location, we recommend a crew of three professional movers. We've provided an estimate attached, which covers the service along with a fully equipped truck, complete with ramps and protective covers. Please be aware that assembly is not included. Unfortunately, we're unavailable on November 20, but the next day works for delivery. Should you have inquiries or wish to confirm details, feel free to contact us at 480-225-2757 or via e-mail at the provided address.

Sincerely,

Branden Johnson
Magnolia Moving

26 In the Web page, the phrase "cater to" in paragraph 1, line 1, is closest in meaning to

(A) reconstruct
(B) accommodate
(C) transform
(D) strengthen

27 What does Ms. Smith mention about her move?

(A) It will include items of different sizes.
(B) It is already far behind schedule.
(C) It will require special equipment.
(D) It will involve moves between states.

28 What is the standard hourly payment Ms. Smith will most likely pay if she uses Magnolia Moving?

(A) $100
(B) $150
(C) $200
(D) $300

29 What is suggested about Ms. Smith?

(A) She used the service from Magnolia Moving last month.
(B) She is planning to close her shoe store in November.
(C) She contacted a business recommended by her friend.
(D) She is running a furniture manufacturing plant.

30 According to Mr. Johnson, what can his company do?

(A) Offer the most affordable price in town
(B) Provide references from former customers
(C) Assemble the furniture for free upon delivery
(D) Make the move later than suggested

대명사는 크게 **지시대명사, 인칭대명사, 부정대명사**로 분류되며, 각각의 특징을 구분하여 정리해 두어야 한다. 특히 인칭대명사 중 '**소유격 대명사**'와 '**재귀대명사**', '**지시대명사 that과 those**' 등은 자주 출제되므로, 출제 패턴을 잘 익혀 두자.

오늘의 학습 POINT

POINT 1 명사 앞에는 소유격 대명사가 오며, 소유 대명사는 올 수 없다.

POINT 2 재귀대명사는 목적어나 부사 자리에 위치한다.

POINT 3 those who는 "~하는 사람들"로 통째로 외워 두자.

POINT 4 many는 복수 가산 명사를, much는 불가산 명사를 대신할 수 있다.

POINT 1 명사 앞에는 소유격 대명사가 오며, 소유 대명사는 올 수 없다.

Q 인칭대명사

종류	특징
주격 대명사	**I, you, we, he, she, it, they**: 동사 앞에 위치 **We** have just sent the items so that **you** can receive them before this weekend. 당신이 이번 주말 이전에 그것들을 받으실 수 있도록 우리는 그 물품들을 지금 막 보냈다.
목적격 대명사	**me, you, us, him, her, it, them**: 타동사와 전치사 뒤에 위치 We have just sent the items so that you can receive **them** before this weekend. 당신이 이번 주말 이전에 그것들을 받을 수 있도록 우리는 그 물품들을 방금 보냈다.
소유격 대명사	**my, your, our, his, her, its, their**: 명사 앞에서 한정사 역할 **Your** room has been booked successfully. 당신의 객실은 성공적으로 예약되었다.
소유 대명사	**mine, yours, ours, his, hers, theirs**: 모든 명사 자리에 위치 A colleague of **mine** will visit the site today. 내 동료 한 명이 오늘 여기에 방문할 것이다.

- 소유격 대명사는 명사 앞에서 한정사 역할을 하므로, 명사 없이 혼자 사용될 수 없다.

- 소유 대명사는 "**소유격 대명사 + 명사**"의 역할을 하며, 그 자체가 명사이므로 명사 앞에 위치할 수 없다.
  [my family = mine, your idea = yours, his note = his]

📝 PRACTICE 1-3 괄호 안의 보기들 중에서 적절한 것을 고르세요. 정답 p.102

1 Mr. Tiller's proposal closely resembles (your / yours.)

2 While Heffern's profits have increased by 17% compared to last year's, (we / ours) have been continuously decreasing.

3 The economic forecast predicted that the majority of companies would be cutting down on (their / theirs) labor expenses.

재귀대명사

재귀대명사에는 myself, yourself, ourselves, himself, herself, itself, themselves 등이 있으며, 재귀 용법 (목적어)과 강조 용법(부사)으로 사용된다.

❶ 재귀 용법: 주어와 목적어가 동일할 때 목적어로 사용됨

Jeff Hill described **himself** as a young entrepreneur. 제프 힐은 스스로를 젊은 사업가라고 설명했다.

cf. 목적격 대명사는 주어와 목적어가 서로 다른 경우에 사용한다.

❷ 강조 용법: 강조하고자 하는 명사 및 대명사 뒤, 또는 완전한 절의 끝에 위치

The artwork is a masterpiece **itself**. 그 작품은 그 자체로 걸작이다.

❸ 관용 표현

by oneself 혼자서 (= on one's own)	for oneself 혼자의 힘으로	of oneself 스스로, 저절로
to oneself 혼자서만	in itself 본래	of itself 저절로

Everything will be clear **of itself**. 모든 것이 저절로 명확해질 것이다.

> **PRACTICE 4-6** 괄호 안의 보기들 중에서 적절한 것을 고르세요.   정답 p.102

4 The students organized the event (their own / themselves), showcasing their initiative and leadership.

5 While Mr. Peck was in a meeting with a client, Ms. Glenn worked on the project by (her / herself).

6 Mr. Robin has proven (him / himself) to be a valuable asset to the company through his exceptional performance.

❶ 지시대명사

종류	출제 포인트
it	• **3인칭 단수 대명사**: 앞에서 언급된 단어, 구, 절을 대신한다. • **비인칭 주어**: 시간, 날짜, 날씨 등을 표현할 때 주어로 사용된다. **e.g.** It is 2:30 P.M. • **가주어**: to부정사, 동명사, 명사절이 주어로 사용되어 너무 길어지면 그 자리에 it을 대신 쓴다. 이 때, 진주어인 to부정사, 동명사, 명사절은 뒤로 이동시킨다. **It** is necessary for all the employees to learn about the updated system. 모든 직원들이 업데이트된 시스템에 대해 배울 필요가 있다.
this, that these, those	• 지시 대명사 this와 that은 **단수명사**를, these와 those는 **복수명사**를 대신한다. • 지시 형용사 this와 that은 **단수명사**를, these와 those는 **복수명사**를 수식한다. **These** two teams survived to the finals. 이 두 팀이 결승전까지 살아 남았다.

that, those	• **those who ~**: those가 관계절인 who절의 수식을 받아 "~하는 사람들"이라는 의미로 사용된다. **cf.** 'these who~'와 같은 표현은 없다. The ocean view rooms go to **those who** book the earliest. 오션뷰 객실은 가장 먼저 예약한 고객에게 배정된다. • **those + 수식어구**: those는 those 뒤에서 "who + be동사"가 생략되어, 분사(-ing / p.p.)나 전명구와 같은 수식어구 바로 앞에 위치하기도 한다. The ocean view rooms go to **those booking** the earliest. • **의미하는 것은 다르지만 동일한 명사가 반복될 때**: 앞에서 언급된 명사의 반복을 피하기 위해 that이나 those가 사용된다. 주로 비교급에 많이 등장한다. Mr. Powell's sales figures exceeded **those** of anyone else in the department. 파월 씨의 판매 수치는 부서의 어떤 직원의 것보다 높았다. **cf.** 위 예문에서 those는 앞에서 언급된 sales figures를 의미하지만, 앞에 언급된 sales figures는 Powell 씨의 판매 수치인 반면, those는 부서의 다른 사람들의 판매 수치를 대신한다.

PRACTICE 7-10 괄호 안의 보기들 중에서 적절한 것을 고르세요. 정답 p.102

7 (These / Those) who demonstrate exceptional dedication are more likely to succeed in their endeavors.

8 Only (these / those) with approval from the departmental manager can apply for the open position at the main headquarters.

9 (It / That) is expected that employees who attend the training sessions will experience increased productivity.

10 Despite the increased costs of materials, our prices remain much lower than (that / those) of our competitors.

❷ 부정대명사

❶ 부정대명사 one

• 불특정한 사람이나 사물을 가리키는 대명사이다. it은 특정한 사물을 지칭하지만, one은 같은 종류 중 막연한 하나를 지칭한다. **e.g.** I like the current system. It is faster than old **one**.

• 명사처럼 형용사의 수식을 받을 수 있다. **e.g.** I can make a **better one** than this.

cf. 일반적으로 대명사는 형용사나 관계대명사의 수식을 받을 수 없다.

• 소유격 뒤에는 사용하지 않는다. **e.g.** my **one** (×)

• 복수형은 ones이다. **e.g.** I can make **better ones** than these.

❷ 부정대명사의 구별

전체가 둘일 때	• 둘 중 하나: one / 나머지 하나: the other **One** of the foreign students was from France, and **the other** was from Japan. 외국인 학생들 중 한 명은 프랑스에서 왔고, 다른 한 명은 일본에서 왔다.
전체가 셋일 때	• 셋 중 하나: one / 나머지 전부: the others • 셋 중 하나: one / 또 다른 하나: another / 나머지 하나: the other **One** student chose to study engineering, and **another** pursued a degree in literature while **the other** opted for a business program. 한 학생은 공학을 공부하기로 결정했고, 다른 한 명은 문학 학위를 계속했으며, 나머지 한 명은 경영학 과정을 선택했다.
전체가 다수일 때	• 다수 중 하나: one / 나머지 전부: the others • 다수 중 하나: one / 또 다른 하나: another / 나머지 전부: the others • 다수 중 일부(몇): some / 나머지 전부: the others • 다수 중 일부(몇): some / 다른 일부(몇): others **Some students** prefer studying alone while **others** thrive in group settings. 몇몇 학생들은 혼자서 공부하는 것을 선호하는 반면, 다른 몇몇 학생들은 그룹 환경에서 잘한다.

cf. other(다른)는 한정사로 명사 앞에만 사용하며, 대명사로 사용할 수 없다.

❸ each other와 one another

- **each other** (둘 사이) 서로, **one another** (셋 이상 사이) 서로
- 부사로 착각하기 쉬우나 목적어로 사용되는 대명사이다.
- 주어로 사용하지 않는다는 점을 주의하자.

The team members helped and depended on **each other** to reach their goals.
그 팀의 구성원들은 그들의 목표를 달성하기 위해서 서로 돕고 의지했다.

❹ 품사 구별

종류	대명사	형용사
one, another, the other, each	O	O
others, the others	O	×
other, every	×	O

cf. each는 대명사와 형용사로 모두 사용할 수 있지만, every는 대명사로 사용할 수 없다.

✎ PRACTICE 11-13 ‹ 괄호 안의 보기들 중에서 적절한 것을 고르세요. 정답 p.102

11 One candidate was highly experienced while (other / the other) possessed exceptional problem-solving skills.

12 The new employees finished one training session and are currently participating in (another / it).

13 Some employees prefer to work on teams while (ones / others) excel at individual tasks.

❶ 부분대명사

all, most, some	• 복수 명사와 불가산 명사를 모두 대신할 수 있다. • all, most, some은 대명사와 형용사로 모두 사용 가능하다.
some, any	• some은 긍정 평서문에서 사용한다. • any는 부정문, 의문문, 조건문 등에 사용된다. If you have **any** further questions, please don't hesitate to ask. 문의 사항이 더 있으면, 망설이지 말고 문의하세요.

> **cf.** all은 대명사와 형용사 외에도 부사로도 사용 가능하다. [Jason painted the wall all in blue.]

❷ 수량형용사

수량형용사는 대명사로 사용할 수 있다.

few, both, several, many	• 복수 명사를 대신할 수 있다. • 주어로 사용될 때 복수 동사가 붙는다. **Many** of them **were** impressed by the new technology's efficiency. 그들의 다수는 신기술의 효율성에 감명을 받았다.
little, much	• 불가산 명사를 대신할 수 있다. • 주어로 사용될 때 단수 동사가 붙는다. **Much** of the success **is** attributed to the team's hard work. 성공의 많은 부분이 그 팀의 노고 덕분이다.
few, little	• 전체 문장을 부정문으로 만든다. **Little is known** about the origins of the ancient artifact. 고대 유물의 기원에 대해서는 거의 알려져 있지 않다.

PRACTICE 14-15 괄호 안의 보기들 중에서 적절한 것을 고르세요. 정답 p.102

14 (Many / Much) of the information provided in the report was outdated and no longer relevant.

15 Most participants in the study (has / have) expressed a strong preference for the new product over its competitors.

❋ 「-tion / -sion / -ment / -ness / -ity / -nce」 등으로 끝나는 단어는 대부분 명사이다. 「-al, -ive」 등의 형용사형 어미로 끝나는 명사에 주의하자.

fluctuation 변동
the fluctuation in interest rates 금리의 변동

initiative 계획; 진취성; 주도(권)
take the initiative in establishing new regulations
새로운 규정을 제정하는 데 주도적으로 참여하다

inspection 점검, 검사
Regular inspections should be carried out.
정기적인 검사가 수행되어야 한다.

itinerary 여행 일정표
The itinerary is subject to change. 여행 일정이 변경될 수 있다.

measure 조치, 정책 cf. measurement 측정, 측량
safety / security measures 안전 / 보안 조치

necessity 필요(성); 필수품
the necessity of accurate information 정확한 정보의 필요성

objective 목적 cf. objection 이의, 반대
the objective of this meeting 이 회의의 목적

obligation 의무
the obligation to provide education 교육을 제공할 의무

opportunity 기회
an opportunity to work abroad 해외에서 근무할 기회

performance 공연; 실적, 성과
the recent performance of the company 회사의 최근 실적

persistence 인내력; 지속
the persistence of the recession 경기 침체의 지속

preference 선호(도)
a preference for organic food 유기농 식품에 대한 선호

priority 우선 사항, 우선권
Customer satisfaction is our top priority.
고객 만족이 우리의 최우선 사항이다.

promotion 승진; 홍보(활동)
He is due for a promotion soon. 그는 곧 승진될 것이다.

procedure 절차(방법) vs. **progress** 진전, 진척
• procedure: 시스템이나 행위의 절차를 의미
• progress: 일이나 상태가 더 나은 쪽으로 진행될 때 사용
the procedure for applying for a credit card
신용 카드 신청 절차
Progress has been made in the negotiations.
그 협상에 진전이 있었다.

property 재산, 부동산, 건물
It is the company's property. 그것은 그 회사의 재산이다.

proportion 부분; 비율
a large proportion of the labor force 노동력의 많은 비율

proximity 가까움, 근접
close proximity to shops and restaurants
상점들과 식당에 근접함

qualification 자격, 자질
necessary qualifications for a job 일자리에 필요한 자격

receipt 영수증; 수령 cf. recipient 받는 사람, 수령인
acknowledge receipt of an order 주문의 수령을 알리다

reliability 신뢰할 수 있음, 신빙성
reliability of the survey results 조사 결과의 신뢰성

representative 대표, 대리인
sales representatives 판매 직원들

resident 거주자, 주민 cf. residence 주택, 거주지
We provide every resident with free Internet access.
우리는 모든 주민에게 무료 인터넷 접속을 제공한다.

standard 수준, 기준
The quality meets the standard. 그 품질은 기준에 맞는다.

surplus 과잉; 흑자
a growing trade surplus 상승하는 무역 흑자

transition 이동; 변화 cf. transaction 거래, 매매
during the transition to the new system
새로운 시스템으로 전환되는 동안

vacancy 결원, 공석; 빈 방 ⓢ opening 공석, 결원
job vacancies 결원인 일자리들

venture 사업; 모험
create a joint venture to sell a service
그 서비스를 판매하기 위한 합작 사업을 만들다

vicinity 부근, 인근
shops in the vicinity of the station 그 역 주변의 상점들

observation 관찰 vs. **observance** 준수
cf. observe가 '관찰하다'와 '준수하다'를 의미하여 두 개의 명사가
파생됨
The patient is under observation. 그 환자는 관찰 중이다.
a strict observance of the rules 엄격한 규칙 준수

PART 5

Directions: A word or phrase is missing in each of the sentences below. Four answer choices are given below each sentence. Select the best answer to complete the sentence and mark the letter (A), (B), (C), or (D).

1   Marketing Director Chris Harvey will be stepping down from that position soon in order to venture into ------- own business.

(A) he
(B) his
(C) him
(D) himself

2   Mr. Pratt shared that he has already encountered several exciting ------- to deal with in his new position in the Cummings Group.

(A) challenge
(B) challenges
(C) challenging
(D) challenged

3   Audrey Shaw, a renowned novelist, has gained notoriety for being one of ------- authors who possess a demanding demeanor.

(A) that
(B) those
(C) which
(D) whose

4   Altman Architecture has ensured that the finalized plans for the shopping center in the Market District will ------- by the end of the week.

(A) delivers
(B) delivered
(C) be delivered
(D) delivering

5   Due to the lack of better-informed team members, Mr. Torres completed the sales report ------- in order to meet the tight deadline.

(A) he
(B) him
(C) himself
(D) his

6   We have compiled a list of ------- food suppliers that provide the ingredients for our new vegetarian dishes.

(A) acceptable
(B) accepting
(C) being accepted
(D) accepts

7 ------- of the major donors are sent a booklet detailing how the donated funds are allocated along with a letter of appreciation every year.

(A) Much
(B) All
(C) Every
(D) Each

8 The construction project took longer to finish because of unexpected weather, and it ended up costing the firm more than it -------.

(A) are planned
(B) planning
(C) has planned
(D) had planned

9 The prices of Holt Electronics' new smartphones are comparatively higher than ------- of the products offered by its primary competitors.

(A) it
(B) that
(C) them
(D) those

10 In close ------- to the city center, this newly constructed commercial complex offers a prime location for businesses to establish their presence.

(A) proximity
(B) durability
(C) alignment
(D) designation

11 Kwartler Advertising, a globally renowned advertising company, has received multiple awards for its ------- achievements.

(A) considerate
(B) compatible
(C) experienced
(D) outstanding

12 Jeff Hill and Lisa Bradley will be collaborating on the project, and they are expected to provide mutual assistance to -------.

(A) anyone
(B) them
(C) each other
(D) others

13 The company aims to integrate various departments to ------- operations and to improve overall efficiency.

(A) identify
(B) distribute
(C) cooperate
(D) streamline

14 The company's premium membership plan includes many benefits, such as free shipping and an extended ------- on all purchases.

(A) advantage
(B) warranty
(C) expense
(D) inventory

15 Brooke Footwear was filled with customers on its opening day, but ------- of them actually made any purchases.

(A) whoever
(B) few
(C) little
(D) those

Directions: Read the text below. A word, phrase, or sentence is missing in parts of the text. Four answer choices for each question are given below the text. Select the best answer to complete the text and mark the letter (A), (B), (C), or (D).

Questions 16-19 refer to the following notice.

Dear All Employees,

We would like to remind you that on June 30, Zelko Retailing will be conducting a --------
16.
emergency procedure testing. This is a routine test of our equipment and procedures, as required by law, to ensure your safety in case of an emergency.

At the sound of the alarm, please turn off your equipment immediately and leave the office in an

-------- manner. Proceed to the designated outdoor meeting location and remain there until you
17.
receive further instructions. --------.
18.

We appreciate your cooperation and participation in this trial to ensure that our emergency

procedures are effective and up to date. As always, your safety is our top --------.
19.

16 (A) unexpected
(B) industrious
(C) prolonged
(D) mandatory

17 (A) orderly
(B) ordering
(C) ordered
(D) order

18 (A) The event is scheduled to be held at the location.
(B) We will inform you when to return to your stations.
(C) The meeting has been postponed until next week.
(D) Please carefully read the instructions in the manual.

19 (A) posting
(B) request
(C) priority
(D) ranking

Questions 20-23 refer to the following e-mail.

From: customersupport@petswellness.com

To: Kevinweil@globalnet.com

Date: November 3

Re: Subscription

Congratulations on becoming a valued subscriber to *Pets Wellness* monthly magazine. Your chosen subscription plan entitles you to unlimited access to our online content. ------- If you **20.** would like to make any adjustments to your subscription preferences, please don't hesitate to contact our dedicated customer service team at 515-323-2800. Alternatively, subscribers have the convenience of updating their account details ------- on our Web site at www.petswellness.com. **21.**

We are pleased to inform you that you will receive our November issue free of charge ------- of **22.** subscribing during our promotional period. Therefore, starting from December, your subscription fee will be charged -------. **23.**

We greatly appreciate your business and continued support.

20 (A) Your subscription needs to be renewed this month.
    (B) You will also receive a printed copy each month.
    (C) You can reduce the time you spend online every day.
    (D) Our readership spans over 10 countries worldwide.

21 (A) their
    (B) them
    (C) theirs
    (D) themselves

22 (A) as a result
    (B) in advance
    (C) in charge
    (D) on behalf

23 (A) whenever
    (B) similarly
    (C) accordingly
    (D) otherwise

PART 7

Directions: In this part you will read a selection of texts. The text or set of texts is followed by several questions. Select the best answer for each question and mark the letter (A), (B), (C), or (D).

Questions 24-27 refer to the following e-mail.

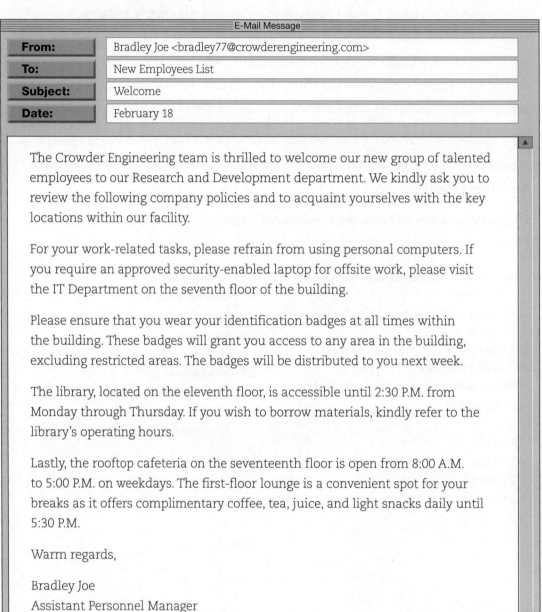

E-Mail Message
From:	Bradley Joe <bradley77@crowderengineering.com>
To:	New Employees List
Subject:	Welcome
Date:	February 18

The Crowder Engineering team is thrilled to welcome our new group of talented employees to our Research and Development department. We kindly ask you to review the following company policies and to acquaint yourselves with the key locations within our facility.

For your work-related tasks, please refrain from using personal computers. If you require an approved security-enabled laptop for offsite work, please visit the IT Department on the seventh floor of the building.

Please ensure that you wear your identification badges at all times within the building. These badges will grant you access to any area in the building, excluding restricted areas. The badges will be distributed to you next week.

The library, located on the eleventh floor, is accessible until 2:30 P.M. from Monday through Thursday. If you wish to borrow materials, kindly refer to the library's operating hours.

Lastly, the rooftop cafeteria on the seventeenth floor is open from 8:00 A.M. to 5:00 P.M. on weekdays. The first-floor lounge is a convenient spot for your breaks as it offers complimentary coffee, tea, juice, and light snacks daily until 5:30 P.M.

Warm regards,

Bradley Joe
Assistant Personnel Manager

24 What is the purpose of the e-mail?

(A) To provide details to newly hired workers

(B) To explain a company benefits package

(C) To offer guidance for a facility tour

(D) To assign workspaces to employees

25 What is suggested about the new employees?

(A) They will be issued their security badges next week.

(B) They will work in the Personnel Department.

(C) They will be able to access restricted areas.

(D) They will be able to use the library every day.

26 Where can new employees get a security-enabled laptop?

(A) On the first floor

(B) On the seventh floor

(C) On the eleventh floor

(D) On the seventeenth floor

27 According to the e-mail, what is provided to all employees?

(A) A mailbox

(B) An approved laptop

(C) Snacks and beverages

(D) A library card

Questions 28-32 refer to the following e-mails.

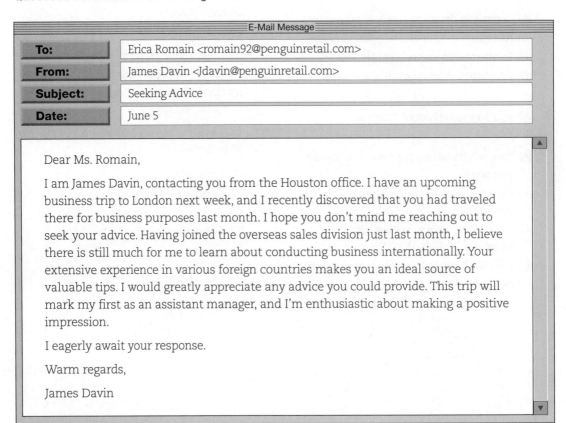

E-Mail Message

To:	Erica Romain <romain92@penguinretail.com>
From:	James Davin <Jdavin@penguinretail.com>
Subject:	Seeking Advice
Date:	June 5

Dear Ms. Romain,

I am James Davin, contacting you from the Houston office. I have an upcoming business trip to London next week, and I recently discovered that you had traveled there for business purposes last month. I hope you don't mind me reaching out to seek your advice. Having joined the overseas sales division just last month, I believe there is still much for me to learn about conducting business internationally. Your extensive experience in various foreign countries makes you an ideal source of valuable tips. I would greatly appreciate any advice you could provide. This trip will mark my first as an assistant manager, and I'm enthusiastic about making a positive impression.

I eagerly await your response.

Warm regards,

James Davin

To:	James Davin <jdavin@penguinretail.com>
From:	Erica Romain <romain92@penguinretail.com>
Date:	June 6
Subject:	Re: Tips
Attachment:	The list

Dear Mr. Davin,

I'll be glad to assist you in any way I can. I can gather some information about London that you can refer to before your departure. While it would be nice to visit landmarks like Tower Bridge and the National Gallery, I suggest exploring local cafés and shops once you arrive. I also recommend trying restaurants run by renowned chefs as they can provide interesting conversation topics with potential clients. I have attached a list of these establishments.

Additionally, make sure to allow sufficient time for reaching your meetings or appointments. Traffic, especially in the mornings, can be quite heavy and may cause longer travel times than anticipated. If you have any further questions, please let me know. I am planning to visit your office for a meeting next month and hope to see you then.

Have a safe trip and enjoy yourself.

Erica Romain

28 Why did Mr. Davin send the e-mail?

(A) To request information about the overseas sales division

(B) To seek assistance with the preparation of a presentation

(C) To inquire about popular attractions to visit in London

(D) To solicit advice regarding an upcoming business trip

29 What is suggested about Mr. Davin?

(A) He will be relocated to London in the near future.

(B) He recently began to work in a new position.

(C) He went on a business trip to London last month.

(D) He frequently travels overseas for business purposes.

30 What is NOT mentioned about London?

(A) It boasts several celebrated attractions worth visiting.

(B) It experiences significant morning traffic congestion.

(C) It serves as the central business hub of the nation.

(D) It has some restaurants owned by well-known chefs.

31 What is most likely true about Ms. Romain?

(A) She has been working in London for many years.

(B) She has prior experience in the overseas sales division.

(C) She has run her own business in a foreign country.

(D) She has plans to travel to Houston in the coming month.

32 What is NOT one of Ms. Romain's suggestions?

(A) Discovering local stores and coffee shops

(B) Ensuring punctuality for meetings

(C) Arranging a meeting at a restaurant

(D) Creating discussion topics in advance

형용사와 부사 문제의 경우, 보기에 항상 형용사와 부사가 함께 등장하므로 둘의 자리를 확실하게 구분해 두어야 한다. 또한 **의미상 혼동하기 쉬운 형용사와 부사 어휘 문제**가 출제되므로, 빈출 형용사와 부사의 의미를 확실하게 정리해 두어야 한다.

오늘의 학습 POINT

POINT 1 형용사의 자리는 **명사 앞**과 **be동사 뒤**이다.

POINT 2 부사는 **동사, 형용사, 준동사, 문장 전체**를 수식한다.

POINT 1 형용사의 자리는 명사 앞과 be동사 뒤이다.

1 형용사의 자리

용법	자리	예
한정적 용법	한정사 + 형용사 + 명사	형용사 앞에는 한정사를 쓸 수 없다. **its** nice weather (○) [nice its weather (×)]
	부사 + 형용사	형용사를 수식하는 부사는 형용사 앞에 온다. its **incredibly nice** weather
	타동사 + 형용사 + 명사 전치사 + 형용사 + 명사	형용사는 명사 앞에 위치한다.
서술적 용법	주격 보어 자리	2형식 동사인 be, become, remain, stay, keep 등의 주격 보어 자리 The contents of the contract **remain undisclosed** throughout its validity. 계약 내용은 유효 기간 동안 비밀로 유지된다.
	목적격 보어 자리	5형식 동사인 keep, find, consider, make 등의 목적격 보어 자리 I **find** it **interesting** how different cultures celebrate holidays. 나는 다양한 문화들이 어떻게 휴일을 축하하는지 흥미롭게 생각한다.

☑ Further Point! 주의해야 할 형용사의 자리

- 「**형용사 + 전치사구**」가 의미상으로 연결될 때에는 수식하는 **명사 뒤**에 위치한다.
  A **handbook useful to the attendees** should be made. 참석자들에게 유용한 핸드북이 제작되어야 한다.

- 「**-thing, -body, -one**」으로 끝나는 **명사**를 수식할 때에는 형용사가 **명사 뒤**에 위치한다.
  His new movie contained **something intriguing**. 그의 새 영화에는 흥미로운 내용이 포함되어 있다.

- 「**a-**」로 시작하는 형용사와 「**liable, worth, ready**」 등의 형용사는 **서술적 용법**으로만 사용한다.
  The book **is worth** reading. 그 책은 읽을 가치가 있다. [the worth book (×)]

- be동사 뒤의 전명구가 보어 역할을 하면 그 사이에 부사가 올 수 있다.
  Many shops and restaurants in the town **are currently in transition**.
  도시의 많은 상점과 식당들이 현재 과도기에 있다.

1 John's excellent communication abilities have made him (ideal / idealism) for the leadership position.

2 Mr. Long was not (aware / known) of the new policy until his colleague informed him this morning.

② 주의해야 할 형용사

① 수량 형용사

형용사	역할	예
one, another, every, each	단수 가산명사 수식	every employee (○) / every employees (×) **cf.** every가 "매 ~마다"의 뜻으로 기간이나 거리 등을 수식할 때는 복수명사를 수식할 수 있다. [every three months]
(a) few, both, several, multiple, many, a number of, various, a variety of, one of, each of	복수 가산명사 수식	a few people, several issues, a variety of items, one of my colleagues, each of the buildings
(a) little, much, a great deal of	불가산명사 수식	much information
all, most, some, other, a lot of, lots of, plenty of, a wide range of	복수 가산명사 수식 불가산명사 수식	No other details are released yet. No other information is available at this moment.

② 사람 형용사 vs. 사물 형용사

사람을 주어로 하거나 사람을 수식	사물을 주어로 하거나 사물을 수식
argumentative 따지기 좋아하는	arguable 논쟁의 여지가 있는
considerate 사려 깊은, 배려하는	considerable 상당한, 중요한
understanding 이해심이 많은	understandable 이해할 수 있는
respectable 존경받을 만한 respectful 공손한	respective 각각의

③ 빈출 분사형 형용사

현재 분사 형태	appealing 매력적인 existing 현존하는 ongoing 진행 중인 pending 미결의	challenging 힘든 following 다음의 opposing 반대편의 promising 유망한	demanding 까다로운 increasing, rising, mounting 증가하는 overwhelming 압도적인 remaining 남은	deteriorating 악화하는 outstanding 뛰어난 surrounding 인근의
과거 분사 형태	accomplished 뛰어난 damaged 파손된 distinguished 유명한 estimated 어림잡아 ~인 skilled 숙련된	celebrated 인기있는 designated 지정된 established 탄탄한 limited 제한된 sophisticated 정교한	complicated 복잡한 detailed 상세한 experienced 경험이 있는 preferred 우선의 specialized 전문적인	committed 전념하는 dedicated 헌신하는 qualified 실력이 있는 talented 유능한

PRACTICE 3-5 괄호 안의 보기들 중 적절한 것을 고르세요.

3 I would appreciate any (another / other) information you can provide on the subject.

4 Please be (considerate / considering) of others and keep the noise level down in the library.

5 The hotel offers stunning views of the (surrounding / surrounded) area.

POINT 2 부사는 동사, 형용사, 준동사, 문장 전체를 수식한다.

❶ 부사의 자리

역할	위치	예
동사 수식	주어 + 부사 + 동사 주어 + 동사 + 목적어 + 부사 조동사 + 부사 + 동사	We should **promptly** respond to their complaints. He finished the work **quickly**. The flight had **already** left before we arrived.
형용사 수식	한정사 + 부사 + 형용사 + 명사 be동사 + 부사 + 형용사	a **highly** productive system They were **obviously** exhausted.
(다른) 부사 수식	부사 + 부사	The issue should be reviewed **especially** carefully.
문장 전체 수식	부사, + 완전한 문장 완전한 문장 + 부사	**However**, no one really knows. The policy will be implemented **immediately**.
분사 수식	be동사 + 부사 + 과거분사 be동사 + 부사 + 현재분사	It is **clearly** mentioned in the contract. The presentation was **particularly** interesting.

cf.1 완전한 문장 앞에 쉼표가 있고, 그 앞에 빈칸이 있다면 정답은 부사이다.

cf.2 분사는 동사에서 파생되었으므로 동사를 수식하는 부사가 분사도 수식한다.

❷ 주의해야 할 부사

형용사와 형태가 같은 부사	early ⑱이른 ⑭일찍 right ⑱옳은 ⑭정확히 near ⑱가까운 ⑭가까이	hard ⑱열심인 ⑭어려운; 열심히 high ⑱높은 ⑭높게 close ⑱가까운 ⑭가까이에	late ⑱늦은 ⑭늦게 fast ⑱빠른 ⑭빠르게 enough ⑱충분한 ⑭충분히
의미가 다른 유사한 형태의 부사	late 늦게 – lately 최근에 close 가까이 – closely 면밀히 right 정확히 – rightly 정당하게 most 가장 – mostly 대부분	hard 열심히 – hardly 거의 ~ 아닌 near 가까이 – nearly 거의 high 높게 – highly 매우 fair 공정하게 – fairly 상당히, 꽤	

cf. enough는 형용사로서 수식하는 명사 앞에 위치하지만, 부사로는 수식하는 형용사 뒤에 위치한다.

enough money (충분한 돈) / good **enough** (충분히 좋은)

PRACTICE 6-7 괄호 안의 보기들 중에서 적절한 것을 고르세요.

6 It is (convenient / conveniently) located near public transportation.

7 The security team will (close / closely) monitor the premises to ensure the safety of all occupants.

③ 자주 출제되는 부사

'증가/감소하다'라는 의미의 동사를 수식하는 부사	• 상당히 considerably, substantially, significantly, greatly • 꾸준히 slowly, steadily, gradually • 눈에 띄게 remarkably, markedly, noticeably • 급격히 sharply, dramatically, drastically, rapidly

시제 부사	• **already** 이미, 벌써 [과거 동사나 현재완료 동사와 자주 사용]
	• **yet** 아직 [현재완료 부정문에서 부정어 뒤에 자주 사용]
	  cf. 관용 표현인 'have yet to do(아직 ~하지 못했다)'가 시험에 자주 출제됨
	• **still** 여전히 [be동사와 조동사 뒤, 일반 동사 앞에 위치, 긍정문과 부정문에 모두 사용]
	  cf. 부정문에서 부정어 앞에 위치하므로, 'not yet, still not'으로 외워둔다.
	• **once** 한때 / **previously, formerly** 예전에 / **ago** ~ 전에 [과거 시제와 주로 사용]
	  cf. once는 '~하자마자'를 뜻하는 시간/조건 부사절 접속사로도 사용됨
	• **before** 이전에 [과거나 현재완료 시제와 자주 쓰이며, 문장 맨 뒤에 위치]
	• **since** 그 이래로 [과거부터 현재까지 지속된다는 의미로 현재완료 시제와 사용]
	  cf. since는 '~이래로'를 뜻하는 시간/조건 부사절 접속사로도 사용됨

빈도부사	① 횟수 once, twice, three times ② 반복 always, frequently, often, sometimes, regularly, monthly, annually **cf.** 빈도부사는 단순 시제와 자주 사용됨
수량표현을 수식하는 부사	• 거의 almost, nearly • 대략 approximately, roughly, about, around • ~보다 많은 over, more than • 겨우 just, only, barely • 최대 up to, as much as • 최소 at least
비교급을 강조하는 부사	• 훨씬 a lot, much, far, even, still, considerably • 약간 a little
최상급을 강조하는 부사	• 한정사(관사, 소유격) 앞 quite, by far • 최상급 앞 single, very • 문장 끝 possible, ever
접속부사	• 게다가 moreover, additionally, in addition, besides, furthermore, also • 하지만, 그럼에도 불구하고 however, nevertheless, nonetheless • 그러므로 therefore, thus, as a result, consequently • 그 후에 afterwards, subsequently • 사실 in fact, actually • 그렇지 않으면 otherwise • 그런데 by the way • 그 목적을 달성하기 위하여 to that end **cf.** 접속부사는 접속사와 유사한 의미를 가질 뿐, 절과 절을 연결하는 접속사의 역할은 할 수 없다.

복합 명사

★ 복합 명사는 둘 이상의 명사가 모여 하나의 명사처럼 쓰인다. 복합 명사에서 앞에 오는 명사는 형용사 역할을 하여 뒤에 오는 명사의 종류나 성격 등을 설명해 준다. 또한 뒤에 오는 명사는 가산, 불가산, 단수, 복수 여부를 결정한다.

account number 계좌번호 the account number on the checks 수표에 있는 계좌번호	**office supplies** 사무 용품 order office supplies 사무 용품을 주문하다
application form 지원서, 신청서 complete an application form 지원서를 작성하다	**pay increase** 급여 인상 offer a huge pay increase 대폭적인 급여 인상을 제공하다
assembly line 조립라인 simplify an assembly line 조립 공정을 단순화하다	**profit margin** 이윤 cf. net profit 순이익 increasing turnover and profit margin 증가하는 매출액과 이윤
attendance record 출석 기록 maintain a perfect attendance record 완벽한 출석 기록을 유지하다	**registration process** 등록 절차 The registration process is underway. 등록 절차가 진행 중이다.
baggage allowance 수화물 중량 제한 provide a generous baggage allowance 넉넉한 수화물 허용량을 제공하다	**safety regulation** 안전 규칙 유 safety standard 안전 기준 comply with safety regulations 안전 규칙을 따르다
customer satisfaction 고객 만족 try to improve customer satisfaction 고객 만족을 향상시키기 위해 노력하다	**tourist attraction** 관광 명소 the town's most popular tourist attraction 그 마을에서 가장 인기 있는 관광 명소
entrance fee 입장료 cf. enrollment fee 등록비 the entrance fee to the exhibition 전시회 입장료	**vacation policy** 휴가 정책 cf. return policy 반품 정책 Our vacation policy is specified in the employee manual. 우리의 휴가 정책은 직원 매뉴얼에 명시되어 있습니다.
expiration date 만기일, 유효 기간 cf. delivery date 배송일 the expiration date on your passport 여권의 만기일	**workplace safety** 작업장 안전 need strong regulations on workplace safety 작업장 안전에 대한 강력한 규제가 필요하다
identification card 신분증 issue a temporary identification card 임시 신분증을 발급하다	**awards ceremony** 시상식 an awards ceremony held every year 매년 열리는 시상식
information distribution 정보 분배 develop a new form of information distribution 정보 분배의 새로운 형식을 개발하다	**earnings growth** 소득 증가 3 consecutive years of earnings growth 3년 연속 수익 증가
installment payment 할부금 accept an installment payment 할부금을 받다	**electronics company** 전자 회사 run a major electronics company 큰 전자 회사를 운영하다
insurance coverage 보험 적용 범위 expand insurance coverage 보험 적용 범위를 확장하다	**customs clearance** 세관 수속 customs clearance of imported goods 수입품의 통관
job opening 공석, (직장의) 빈자리 a job opening in the Technology Department 기술 부서의 공석	**customs declaration** 세관 신고 fill out a customs declaration form 세관 신고서를 작성하다
job performance 직무 수행 properly evaluate a job performance 직무 수행을 적절하게 평가하다	**sales figure** 판매 수치 The sales figure is below analysts' forecasts. 판매 수치가 분석가들의 예상치를 밑돌고 있다.
maintenance work 정비 작업 routine maintenance work on the bridge 교각의 정기 정비 작업	**savings account** 보통 예금 계좌 open a savings account 예금 계좌를 개설하다

PART 5

Directions: A word or phrase is missing in each of the sentences below. Four answer choices are given below each sentence. Select the best answer to complete the sentence and mark the letter (A), (B), (C), or (D).

---

1   Sams Organic Food offers a ------- range of convenient and healthy prepared meals suited for customers who don't have time to cook.

(A) widen
(B) width
(C) wide
(D) widely

2   In a diverse group of people, some enjoy outdoor activities like hiking while ------- find pleasure in indoor pursuits like playing online games.

(A) ones
(B) others
(C) the other
(D) those

3   The research team concluded that the population of the endangered species had decreased by ------- 30% over the past decade.

(A) approximate
(B) approximately
(C) approximated
(D) approximates

4   The sales ------- demonstrated exemplary professionalism and expertise throughout the client engagement.

(A) representative
(B) representatively
(C) representation
(D) representing

5   Eric Adams received the prestigious journalist of the year award from the Press Club of Long Island in recognition of his ------- contributions.

(A) impress
(B) impressive
(C) impressively
(D) impressed

6   The limited-edition sneakers designed by notable artist Fred Wester are available ------- at the ACE Gear located on Ironwood Avenue.

(A) exclusive
(B) exclusively
(C) exclusion
(D) exclude

7   Despite Struss Funding's claims that it has become ------- following government assistance, its investors are still experiencing losses.

(A) profits
(B) profited
(C) profitable
(D) profitably

8   The ------- date of the contract with Clarfield Retail is set to be October 31, at which point it will no longer be valid.

(A) expiration
(B) appointment
(C) specification
(D) requirement

9   In addition to the printed T-shirts, the event organizers also distributed ------- promotional items to the attendees.

(A) other
(B) another
(C) the others
(D) every

10 Before installing the upgraded Quick Tax Pro, please check which software packages are ------- with it and be well informed of their features.

(A) compatible
(B) qualified
(C) supportive
(D) comparable

11 The adoption of renewable energy sources has ------- reduced the carbon footprint of the industrial sector of the city.

(A) markedly
(B) normally
(C) formerly
(D) elaborately

12 Pelle Sports has ------- implemented new marketing strategies for its ambitious launch of a new line of biking gear.

(A) conveniently
(B) recently
(C) extremely
(D) securely

13 Doria Cosmetics consistently performs ------- safety testing on all our products prior to their release on the market.

(A) extensive
(B) competitive
(C) respective
(D) tentative

14 Due to favorable economic conditions, the housing market has been on an ------- trend with home prices steadily increasing.

(A) beyond
(B) upward
(C) pending
(D) reverse

15 The new gaming console of Play Joy, despite its recent release, is ------- popular among enthusiastic gamers worldwide.

(A) already
(B) enough
(C) seldom
(D) elsewhere

PART 6

Directions: Read the text below. A word, phrase, or sentence is missing in parts of the text. Four answer choices for each question are given below the text. Select the best answer to complete the text and mark the letter (A), (B), (C), or (D).

Questions 16-19 refer to the following information.

Welcome to the Powell Hotel, where dogs and cats are warmly welcomed! We take pride in offering a wide selection of pet-friendly rooms at ------- every Powell Hotel nationwide. We are pleased to
16.
offer pet-friendly rooms for an extra fee of $10 per night, allowing your beloved pets to join you during your stay.

-------, if you are accompanied by a guide dog, it is welcome to stay with you in your room at no
17.
additional cost. -------. To ensure we can accommodate your furry companion properly, please
18.
contact us ------- making a reservation on our Web site or through our application.
19.
We look forward to providing you and your four-legged friend with a delightful experience at the Powell Hotel!

16 (A) audibly
    (B) already
    (C) around
    (D) almost

17 (A) In spite of
    (B) Whereas
    (C) However
    (D) Afterward

18 (A) In this case, we kindly request supporting documents.
    (B) An additional charge was applied for the early check-in.
    (C) The hotel swimming pool is located on the 17th floor.
    (D) Staying with a dog or cat helps with mental wellbeing.

19 (A) in order to
    (B) on account of
    (C) prior to
    (D) aside from

Questions 20-23 refer to the following article.

Today, the mayor's office of Oklahoma City made an announcement stating that over $35 million
------- for the long-anticipated Historic Bridge Construction Project. -------. According to Mayor
20.   **21.**
David Holt, "Unfortunately, numerous bridges in Oklahoma City are in desperate need of repair."

He further added, "We are ------- to supplying vital funding to modernize the city's infrastructure
22.
for future generations." Many residents of Oklahoma City are warmly welcoming this, ------- it as a
23.
much-needed source of financial support to rebuild the city's old physical infrastructure.

20 (A) has been designated
   (B) was designating
   (C) will have designated
   (D) had been designating

21 (A) The city's oldest bridge will no longer be
       accessible to motorists.
   (B) Officials have confirmed that construction
       has been postponed.
   (C) The new bridge in the city is expected to
       open next month.
   (D) These funds will be utilized to restore old
       bridges.

22 (A) considering
   (B) impossible
   (C) decisive
   (D) committed

23 (A) recognizing
   (B) acquiring
   (C) speculating
   (D) transforming

Directions: In this part you will read a selection of texts. The text or set of texts is followed by several questions. Select the best answer for each question and mark the letter (A), (B), (C), or (D).

Questions 24-27 refer to the following article.

David Lillo Takes a Daring Step
By Erika Demma, *Owl Dispatch*

San Jose (21 February) – Promising composer David Lillo, known for his exceptional musical contributions to some recent films, including the critically acclaimed *A Rainy Day in Seattle*, which earned him the prestigious American Movie Award for Best Original Music, has recently ventured into the realm of Internet gaming. Lillo has lent his remarkable composing skills to Hero and Victory, an online game developed by Game Empire, a seasoned creator of interactive entertainment for the past eight years.

The collaboration between David Lillo and Game Empire began when he was introduced to Ken Morgan, the art director of Game Empire, at a social event hosted by Alex Forward, who previously collaborated with Mr. Lillo on composing several film scores. It was during this event that Mr. Morgan invited him to create the music for Hero and Victory.

During an interview, Lillo expressed his deep admiration for the captivating graphics and animation featured in Hero and Victory. He likened the experience of playing the game to watching a movie, which immediately led him to readily accept the collaboration. Lillo also mentioned that the process of composing music for an Internet game closely resembled his work on film scores. "All I had to do was create music that aligns with the atmosphere of the various scenes depicted in the game," Lillo added.

In the same interview, Mr. Morgan confidently stated that Hero and Victory had already received an impressive 50,000 pre-orders. With the game's official release scheduled for May 10, he firmly believes that the company's latest product is destined for success.

24 Who most likely is Mr. Forward?

(A) The host of a TV show
(B) A developer of Internet games
(C) A director of movies
(D) A composer of music

25 What is suggested about Mr. Morgan?

(A) He recently became the art director at Game Empire.
(B) He participated in organizing some social events.
(C) He collaborated with Mr. Lillo in the past.
(D) He recently had a conversation with Ms. Demma.

26 What is implied about Hero and Victory?

(A) It took years to develop until its release.
(B) It will be available exclusively to 50,000 users.
(C) It is expected to be released in May.
(D) It was inspired by the film *A Rainy Day in Seattle*.

27 What is NOT mentioned about Mr. Lillo?

(A) He has been honored with an award for his exceptional work.
(B) He was previously invited to an event hosted by Mr. Forward.
(C) He enjoys playing Internet games in his leisure time.
(D) He has been involved in music production for several films.

From:	Craig Nelson <customerservice@bryanthotels.com>
To:	Jennifer Gilson <gilson77@networld.com>
Date:	October 12
Attachment:	Bryant_Hotels_Membership_Program

Dear Ms. Gilson,

Based on our records, your membership in the Bryant Hotels Membership Program is set to expire on November 30 of this year. We kindly request that you renew your membership prior to the expiration date to ensure uninterrupted access to the array of benefits we offer, as you have enjoyed for the past three years. As an additional incentive, if you renew by October 31, you will receive a 15-percent discount on your annual membership fee.

Furthermore, we would like to bring to your attention that we have made updates to our membership programs. These new programs will come into effect at the beginning of the upcoming year and encompass various advantageous policies, including extended checkout times, complimentary room upgrades, and expedited points accumulation. For further details, please refer to the attached file accompanying this e-mail.

Warm regards,

Craig Nelson
Bryant Hotels Customer Service

New Bryant Hotels Membership Policy Update

Commencing on January 1, we are pleased to introduce enhanced benefits for our esteemed Bryant Hotel members. The following additional privileges will be available:

✔ **Extended Checkout Time**: For Diamond Prestige members, the checkout time will be extended to 3:30 P.M. while Ruby Elite members can enjoy a checkout time of 2:30 P.M., both surpassing the regular 11:00 A.M. checkout time. Crystal Tier members will be eligible for a checkout time of 1:30 P.M.

✔ **Complimentary Room Upgrades**: Diamond Prestige and Ruby Elite members will receive complimentary room upgrades when they stay for more than 2 consecutive nights at the hotel. To qualify for this perk, rooms must be reserved under the member's name.

✔ **Bonus Points**: Diamond Prestige members will earn points equivalent to 20 percent of every dollar they spend at the hotel. Additionally, Diamond Prestige members will be awarded an extra 1,000 bonus points for each stay. Ruby Elite and Crystal Tier members can earn 500 and 300 bonus points, respectively, for every stay.

We are excited to provide these added advantages to our valued members and look forward to continually enhancing your experience at Bryant Hotels.

Best regards,

Bryant Hotels Membership Services

Bryant Hotels Membership Program Renewal Form

Date of Application: November 8

MEMBER NAME	Jennifer Gilson
PHONE	(510) 913-8582
E-MAIL ADDRESS	gilson77@networld.com
RESIDENTIAL ADDRESS	1688 Van Ness AVE, San Francisco, CA, 94103
MEMBERSHIP TYPE	Ruby Elite
CREDIT CARD NUMBER	1001 5382 2021 1819

☑ I hereby confirm my acceptance of the revised membership program terms.

☐ Would you like to consider upgrading your membership? If you are interested, one of our customer service associates will reach out to you within 24 hours.

SUBMIT

28 What is mentioned in the e-mail?

(A) Bryant Hotels is currently offering discounted rates.

(B) The upgraded membership program will take effect immediately.

(C) Ms. Gilson has been a member for the last few years.

(D) Ms. Gilson will lose her accumulated points in December.

29 What is the purpose of the notice?

(A) To invite hotel guests to renew their memberships

(B) To inform members of an adjustment in room rates

(C) To provide details of vacation policies to hotel staff members

(D) To communicate updates made to a membership policy

30 What is suggested about Ms. Gilson?

(A) She is interested in upgrading her membership.

(B) She renewed her membership after it had already expired.

(C) She was unable to get a 15% discount on the annual fee.

(D) Her membership was scheduled to expire in October.

31 When is the latest time Ms. Gilson will be able to check out of the hotel?

(A) 11:00 A.M.

(B) 1:30 P.M.

(C) 2:30 P.M.

(D) 3:30 P.M.

32 What is indicated in the online form?

(A) A customer service team will get in touch with Ms. Gilson.

(B) Ms. Gilson's membership is set to expire on November 8.

(C) The membership fee is lower compared to the previous year.

(D) There will be no alteration to Ms. Gilson's membership type.

07 준동사 I (to부정사와 동명사)

준동사에는 **to부정사, 동명사, 분사**가 있다. **준동사**는 문장에서 동사 역할을 할 수 없으며, **명사, 형용사, 부사 역할**을 한다. 동사는 아니지만 동사에서 파생되었기 때문에 **동사의 성격을 유지**한다는 특징이 있다.

> **오늘의 학습 POINT**
>
> **POINT 1** to부정사는 동사의 역할을 할 수 없다.
> **POINT 2** to부정사를 목적어와 목적격 보어로 취하는 동사를 구분하자.
> **POINT 3** 동명사도 동사의 역할을 할 수 없지만, 목적어를 취할 수 있다.

POINT 1 to부정사는 동사의 역할을 할 수 없다.

1 to부정사의 용법

❶ 명사적 용법

명사의 역할, 즉 **주어, 목적어, 보어로 사용**된다. '~하는 것'으로 해석된다.

To meet the deadline is our priority now. 마감일을 맞추는 것이 지금 우리의 최우선 과제이다.

❷ 형용사적 용법

형용사 역할을 하며 **명사를 뒤에서 수식**한다. '~할, ~하기 위한, ~해야 할'로 해석된다.

We have the ability **to distribute your products** worldwide. 우리는 당신의 제품을 전 세계에 유통할 능력이 있다.

TIP! 「명사 + to부정사」 구조로 쓰이는 명사

ability to do ~하는 능력	attempt to do ~하려는 시도	authority to do ~할 권한
right to do ~할 권리	opportunity to do ~할 기회	chance to do ~할 기회
way to do ~할 방법	effort to do ~하기 위한 노력	time to do ~할 시간
plan to do ~할 계획	decision to do ~할 결정	need to do ~할 필요

cf. to부정사는 아직 일어나지 않은 미래의 일을 표현할 때 주로 사용된다.

❸ 부사적 용법

부사적 용법의 to부정사는 보통 **완전한 절 앞이나 뒤, 형용사 뒤**에 온다. '~하기 위해서, ~하게 되어서'로 해석된다.

Your total commitment is needed **to achieve our goal**. 목표를 달성하기 위해 당신의 완전한 헌신이 필요하다.

TIP! 부사적 용법을 강조하는 관용 표현

in order to V, so as to V ~하기 위해서	in an effort to V ~해보려는 노력으로

cf. 'in order to V', 'so as to V'가 to부정사의 부사적 용법으로 자주 출제된다.

He woke up early **so as to catch** the first train to the city. 그는 도시로 가는 첫 기차를 타려고 일찍 일어났다.

📝 PRACTICE 1-2　괄호 안의 보기들 중에서 적절한 것을 고르세요.　정답 p.113

1 She studied diligently in an effort (to improve / improving) her chances of getting a scholarship.

2 I was thrilled to have the opportunity (to travel / traveling) abroad and to experience different cultures.

② to부정사의 특징

- **의미상 주어**: to부정사 앞에 「for + 명사」로 표현

I prepared a detailed guide **for them** to follow during their trip.
그들이 여행하는 동안 따라올 수 있도록 상세한 가이드를 준비했다. ['그들(for them)'이 '따라가는(to follow)' 행동을 함]

- **to부정사의 수동태**: to부정사와 주어의 관계가 수동인 경우에는 「to be p.p.」로 표현

The meeting time and location need **to be arranged**. 회의 시간과 장소가 정해질 필요가 있다.

- **부정사의 완료형**: 본동사보다 to부정사의 시제가 앞설 때 「to have p.p.」로 표현

He seems **to have been** a doctor. 그는 의사였던 것 같다. ['그가 의사였던 것'이 'seems'보다 이전 시제]

📝 PRACTICE 3-4　괄호 안의 보기들 중에서 적절한 것을 고르세요.　정답 p.113

3 (In terms of / In order for) them to achieve their goals, they must remain focused and dedicated to their work.

4 (To be / To have) considered for the scholarship, applicants must meet the eligibility criteria.

POINT 2　to부정사를 목적어와 목적격 보어로 취하는 동사를 구분하자.

① 동사와 to부정사

❶ to부정사를 목적어로 취하는 동사 (동사 + to부정사)

agree 동의하다	afford ~할 여유가 있다	choose 선택하다	decide 결정하다
fail 실패하다	hope 희망하다	wish 바라다	manage 가까스로 해내다
plan 계획하다	promise 약속하다	propose 제안하다	refuse 거절하다

❷ to부정사를 목적격 보어로 취하는 동사 (동사 + 목적어 + to부정사)

allow 허락하다	permit 허락하다	enable ~을 가능하게 하다	encourage 장려하다	advise 조언하다
ask 요청하다	invite 권유하다	require 요구하다	force 강요하다	urge 촉구하다
remind 상기하다	persuade 설득하다	convince 설득하다	cause 야기하다	

❸ to부정사를 목적어와 목적격 보어로 모두 취하는 동사

want 원하다	need 필요하다	expect 예상하다

📝 PRACTICE 5　괄호 안의 보기들 중에서 적절한 것을 고르세요.　정답 p.113

5 She couldn't (afford / enable) to miss another day of work, so she went to the office despite feeling unwell.

② 형용사와 to부정사

be able to do ~할 수 있다	be eager to do ~하기를 간절히 원하다
be eligible to do ~할 자격이 있다	be entitled to do ~할 자격이 있다
be liable to do ~할 책임이 있다	be likely to do ~할 것 같다
be willing to do 기꺼이 ~하다	be reluctant to do ~하기를 꺼리다
be ready to do ~할 준비가 되다	be pleased to do ~하게 되어 기쁘다

③ be + p.p. + to부정사

be advised to do ~하라고 조언받다	be encouraged to do ~할 것을 장려받다
be invited to do ~하라고 권유받다	be allowed to do ~하도록 허락받다
be asked to do ~하라고 요청받다	be required to do ~하라고 요구받다
be forced to do ~하라고 강요받다	be expected to do ~할 것으로 예상되다
be scheduled to do ~하기로 예정되어 있다	be supposed to do ~하기로 되어 있다

📝 **PRACTICE 6-7** 괄호 안의 보기들 중에서 적절한 것을 고르세요. 정답 p.113

6 The new product launch is (likely / perhaps) to generate significant interest and drive sales.

7 The meeting is (scheduling / scheduled) to take place in the conference room at 2:00 P.M. tomorrow.

POINT 3 동명사도 동사의 역할을 할 수 없지만, 목적어를 취할 수 있다.

① 동명사의 역할

- **주어 역할**: 동명사가 주어 역할을 할 때 **단수 취급**을 하여 **단수 동사**를 취한다.
- **보어 역할**: 동명사가 보어 역할을 할 때 **동명사와 주어는 동일**하고, **to부정사로 대체 가능**하다.
- **목적어 역할**: 동명사는 **타동사나 전치사의 목적어 역할**을 한다.

② 동명사의 특징

- **동명사의 목적어**: 타동사에서 파생된 동명사 뒤에는 동명사의 목적어가 존재함

Her procrastination in **completing** the form led to a delay in **processing** her request.
그녀가 양식을 작성하는 것을 미루어서 그녀의 요청을 처리하는 것이 지연되었다.

- **의미상의 주어**: 동명사의 의미상 주어는 「소유격 + 동명사」로 표현

His visiting the office caused quite a stir among the staff.
그의 사무실 방문은 직원들 사이에서 상당한 소동을 일으켰다.

- **동명사의 수동태**: 동명사와 주어의 관계가 수동일 경우에는 「being p.p.」로 표현

Because of **being prepared** meticulously, the gourmet meal is ready to be served to the guests.
철저하게 준비되어 있어서, 그 고급 요리는 손님들에게 제공될 준비가 되어 있다.

- **동명사의 완료형**: 본동사보다 동명사의 시제가 앞설 경우 「having p.p.」로 표현

He received recognition from his colleagues for **having implemented** an innovative solution.
혁신적인 해결책을 시행했기 때문에 그는 동료들에게 인정받았다.

③ 동명사를 목적어로 취하는 동사 / 동명사 관용 표현

① 동명사를 목적어로 취하는 동사

admit 인정하다	avoid 피하다	consider 고려하다	enjoy 즐기다	mind 꺼리다
delay 미루다	postpone 연기하다	put off 연기하다	suggest 제안하다	recommend 추천하다
give up 포기하다	finish 끝내다	quit 그만두다	stop 멈추다	discontinue 중단하다

② 동명사의 관용 표현

be busy -ing ~하느라 바쁘다	worth -ing ~할 가치가 있다
have difficulty/trouble -ing ~하는 데 어려움이 있다	cannot help -ing ~하지 않을 수 없다
it is no use -ing ~해도 아무 소용 없다	spend + 시간/돈 + -ing ~하는 데 시간/돈을 소비하다

☑ Further Point! 명사 vs. 동명사

명사	동명사
명사 앞에는 한정사가 올 수 있다.	동명사 앞에는 한정사가 올 수 없다.
cf. 한정사: a, an, the, this, that, each, every 등	**cf.** 동명사의 의미상의 주어에 사용되는 소유격은 예외
명사와 명사를 연결하려면 전치사가 필요하다.	(타동사에서 파생된) 동명사 뒤에는 목적어인 명사가 존재한다.
e.g. attendance at the seminar	**e.g.** attending the seminar
명사는 형용사가 수식한다.	동명사는 부사가 수식한다.
e.g. heavy rain	**e.g.** heavily raining

📝 PRACTICE 8-9 ◀ 괄호 안의 보기들 중에서 적절한 것을 고르세요.　　　정답 p.113

8　Attracting young customers (make / makes) its products and services trendier and more relevant in the market.

9　The designers spent more than a month (to improve / improving) the new product design.

④ to부정사와 동명사 비교

① 전치사 to + 명사/동명사

be used to -ing / be accustomed to -ing ~에 익숙하다	look forward to -ing ~하기를 고대하다
be opposed to -ing / object to -ing ~에 반대하다	be subject to -ing ~하기 쉽다
be committed to -ing / be dedicated to -ing ~에 헌신하다	be devoted to -ing ~에 몰두하다, 헌신하다

② to부정사와 동명사를 모두 목적어로 취하는 동사

동사	to부정사 목적어 (미래적 의미)	동명사 목적어 (과거와 연결된 의미)
remember	앞으로 ~할 것을 기억하다	예전에 ~했던 것을 기억하다
forget	앞으로 ~할 것을 잊다	예전에 ~했던 것을 잊다
regret	~하게 되어 유감이다	과거에 ~했던 것을 후회하다

● 「–able, –ible, –ive, –ful, –ous, –ory, –ic, –al, –ant」 등으로 끝나는 단어는 대부분 형용사이다.

accessible 접근 가능한, 이용 가능한 The stadium is easily accessible. 경기장은 쉽게 갈 수 있다.	**inevitable** 불가피한, 필연적인 🔁 unavoidable 불가피한 Changes are inevitable. 변화가 불가피하다.
accountable 책임이 있는 🔁 responsible 책임이 있는 Hold yourself accountable for your actions. 자신의 행동에 책임을 지세요.	**integral** 필수적인 Communication is integral to a successful relationship. 대화는 성공적인 관계에 필수적이다.
adequate 적합한 🔁 proper 적절한 give an adequate response 적절한 대응을 하다	**meticulous** 꼼꼼한, 세심한 He is attentive and meticulous. 그는 세심하고 꼼꼼하다.
affordable 감당할 수 있는 🔁 reasonable 합리적인 affordable health insurance 저렴한 의료 보험	**necessary** 필수적인 Advance booking is necessary. 사전 예약이 필요하다.
apparent 분명한 🔁 obvious 분명한 no apparent errors in the data 데이터에 명백한 오류가 없음	**optimistic** 낙관적인 🔄 pessimistic 비관적인 She is optimistic about the outcome. 그녀는 결과에 대해 낙관적이다.
appropriate 적절한 🔁 suitable 적합한 appropriate compensation 적절한 보상	**previous** 이전의 🔁 former 예전의, 이전의 Previous experience is necessary. 이전의 경험이 필요하다.
available 이용할 수 있는, 구할 수 있는, 시간이 있는 The book is available at any bookstore. 그 책은 어느 서점에서나 구할 수 있다.	**significant** 중요한, 커다란 🔁 substantial 상당한 a significant increase in sales 의미 있는 매출 증가
beneficial 이득이 되는 a mutually beneficial agreement 상호간에 이로운 합의	**spacious** 넓은 a spacious lounge 넓은 라운지
conscious 의식하고 있는 health-conscious consumers 건강을 염려하는 소비자들	**sufficient** 충분한 Allow sufficient time to get there. 그곳에 가기에 충분한 시간을 감안하세요.
consistent 일관된 provide our customers with a consistent supply 고객에게 꾸준한 공급을 제공하다	**thorough** 빈틈없는, 철두철미한 a thorough investigation 빈틈없는 수사
credible 믿을 만한 🔁 reliable 믿을 만한 reliable and credible data 신뢰할 만하고 믿을 만한 자료	**uncertain** 불명확한, 분명치 않은 uncertain of the test results 시험 결과에 확신이 없는
enthusiastic 열성적인 🔁 passionate 열정적인 They are enthusiastic about the upcoming event. 그들은 다가오는 행사에 열광하고 있다.	**upcoming** 다가오는, 곧 있을 🔁 following 다음의 We are looking forward to the upcoming release. 우리는 다가오는 출시를 기대하고 있다.
essential 필수적인 🔁 vital 아주 중요한 an essential precondition 필수적인 전제 조건	**valued** 귀중한, 값진 🔁 valuable 소중한, 귀중한 We appreciate our valued customers' loyalty. 우리는 우리의 소중한 고객들의 충성심에 감사하고 있습니다.
equivalent 동등한, 상응하는 His success is equivalent to his hard work. 그의 성공은 그의 노력에 상응한다.	**vulnerable** 상처 입기 쉬운 vulnerable to infections 감염에 취약한
tentative 잠정적인 vs. **temporary** 일시의 • tentative: 정해지지 않아 이후에 바뀔 수 있는 것을 의미 • temporary: 영속적이지 않고 일시적임을 의미	**favorable** 호의적인, 유리한 vs. **favorite** 마음에 드는 • favorable: 상황이나 상태가 좋거나 그에 대한 사람의 감정이 호의적임을 의미 • favorite: 누군가가 무엇인가를 가장 좋아한다는 의미

PART 5

Directions: A word or phrase is missing in each of the sentences below. Four answer choices are given below each sentence. Select the best answer to complete the sentence and mark the letter (A), (B), (C), or (D).

1   Employees ------- to attend a mandatory safety training session before starting their new job.

   (A) have required
   (B) were requiring
   (C) are required
   (D) requirement

2   The McHale Medical Center had to postpone ------- new beds and other nontechnical equipment due to budget constraints.

   (A) purchase
   (B) purchases
   (C) purchasing
   (D) to purchase

3   Although our company has made significant progress in the market, we are continuously striving to improve our services to exceed ------- of our competitors.

   (A) others
   (B) them
   (C) these
   (D) those

4   The research team has ------- to conclude their investigation and publish their findings in a peer-reviewed journal.

   (A) finally
   (B) by far
   (C) yet
   (D) so as

5   Despite the challenging circumstances, the team ------- to deliver the project on time and within budget, showcasing their dedication.

   (A) regulated
   (B) managed
   (C) achieved
   (D) undertook

6   The organization is devoted to ------- positive changes in local communities through education and empowerment initiatives.

   (A) facilitate
   (B) facilitating
   (C) facilitation
   (D) facilitates

7 Following the ------- of his latest proposal, Mr. Rankin had to put the other project that he was in charge of on hold.

(A) capacity
(B) approval
(C) allowance
(D) flexibility

8 ------- participant is requested to complete the pre-event survey to ensure a tailored and meaningful experience during the conference.

(A) Several
(B) Each
(C) Single
(D) All

9 Our company has achieved record-breaking sales for the fifth ------- year, which demonstrates our consistent growth.

(A) repetitive
(B) thorough
(C) consecutive
(D) profitable

10 ------- her outstanding achievements, she has exceptional leadership skills, making her an ideal candidate for the position.

(A) In which
(B) Whom
(C) In order to
(D) Along with

11 The role requires a high level of expertise and a strong work ethic to meet the ------- expectations of our clients.

(A) demanding
(B) accountable
(C) longtime
(D) collective

12 The facility will be ------- closed until further notice as we work diligently to address the necessary repairs.

(A) temporarily
(B) recently
(C) uncertainly
(D) substantially

13 The workshop will provide a comprehensive guide on ------- to effectively utilize the new software system to enhance productivity.

(A) what
(B) who
(C) why
(D) how

14 The company has set goals to expand its market share by 25% ------- the next three years through targeted marketing campaigns.

(A) above
(B) behind
(C) about
(D) within

15 Please refer to the attached document for ------- information regarding the project timeline and a breakdown of the budget.

(A) arbitrary
(B) supplemental
(C) superfluous
(D) potential

Directions: Read the text below. A word, phrase, or sentence is missing in parts of the text. Four answer choices for each question are given below the text. Select the best answer to complete the text and mark the letter (A), (B), (C), or (D).

Questions 16-19 refer to the following e-mail.

Dear Mr. Chan,

We regret to inform you that your flight ticket purchase to Miami through Freethy Trip has been canceled for the ------- reasons. The coupon you used for this purchase was specifically issued to
16.
Blooming cardholders for transactions made ------- their Blooming card. However, it has come to
17.
our attention that this coupon was mistakenly distributed to non-Blooming cardholders, resulting in its improper usage for purchases made with cards other than Blooming cards. -------, the terms
18.
and conditions of the coupon also include additional restrictions. -------. For your reference, we
19.
have attached a copy of the coupon you used.

We apologize for any inconvenience caused.

Sincerely,

Customer Service

Freethy Trip

16 (A) following
(B) equivalent
(C) specialized
(D) favorable

17 (A) it
(B) from
(C) where
(D) with

18 (A) Therefore
(B) Furthermore
(C) To that end
(D) Nevertheless

19 (A) We greatly appreciate your using our Blooming card.
(B) We hope your journey to Miami was comfortable.
(C) Using more than one coupon per account is prohibited.
(D) Please read the enclosed leaflet before using the card.

We are delighted that you --·--- the position of regional sales manager at Camas Retail
20.
Springdale. Jim Fisher from Human Resources will be your trainer. --·----. As we discussed
21.
previously, you will receive your paycheck every two weeks, following the company's payroll policy.
--·----, performance-based compensation will be granted annually along with comprehensive
22.
medical insurance coverage. If you have any further questions or concerns, please reach out to
Nick Randall at randall84@camas.com. We are --·--- to work with you.
23.

20 (A) are accepting
    (B) should accept
    (C) have accepted
    (D) were accepted

21 (A) Please obtain permission from your
        supervisor.
    (B) He will provide details on your
        responsibilities.
    (C) You need to submit three references.
    (D) A cash bonus will be given as a reward.

22 (A) Additionally
    (B) Consequently
    (C) In other words
    (D) Otherwise

23 (A) used
    (B) reliable
    (C) valued
    (D) eager

PART 7

Directions: In this part you will read a selection of texts. The text or set of texts is followed by several questions. Select the best answer for each question and mark the letter (A), (B), (C), or (D).

Questions 24-27 refer to the following report.

Nordstorm Fashions
Weekly Progress Report for June 6-12
Prepared by Todd Wiley, Project Manager

Accomplishments for this week:
- Initiated contact with three manufacturing companies in Guangzhou, China, that possess expertise in swimsuit production. Shared our new swimsuit design specifications with them and inquired about minimum order quantity, production and shipping costs, and turnaround time. —[1]—.
- After evaluating the initial response, it seems that Chiya Industries is the most appropriate manufacturer for meeting our requirements. —[2]—. Moreover, Allen Fung, an overseas sales manager, promptly reached out to me and demonstrated professionalism and cordiality. He provided clear and candid responses to all of my inquiries. —[3]—. I anticipate the possibility of cultivating a mutually beneficial business association with him.
- The remaining two companies contacted were either unable to accommodate our schedule or did not meet our pricing criteria. —[4]—. Consequently, they have been excluded from further consideration.

Planned activities for the week of June 13-19:
- Continue ongoing discussions with Chiya Industries regarding project requirements and payment terms.
- Instruct the design team to document final measurements, fabrics, and colors as well as outline the production process steps. Subsequently, submit this information to Chiya Industries to facilitate the creation of a sample.

---

24 What can be inferred about Nordstorm Fashions?

(A) It is considering a move to Guangzhou, China.

(B) It is currently recruiting an overseas sales manager.

(C) It is engaged in the development of a new product.

(D) It is involved in a merger with another company.

25 According to the report, what did Mr. Wiley do during the week of June 6?

(A) He developed shipping schedules.

(B) He obtained construction permits.

(C) He provided training to factory employees.

(D) He assessed potential business partners.

26 What information is provided about Mr. Fung?

(A) He talked with Mr. Wiley in person.

(B) He is working in the design division.

(C) He received several inquiries about the project.

(D) He was being proficient and cooperative.

27 In which of the positions [1],[2],[3], and [4] does the following sentence best belong?

"Although it is relatively smaller than the other two, it is ready to increase its workforce in order to meet our order requirements."

(A) [1]

(B) [2]

(C) [3]

(D) [4]

Questions 28-32 refer to the following e-mail and voucher.

To:	Bruno Baldini <baldini80@bigcircle.net>
From:	Mary Fenton <maryfenton@citylight.com>
Date:	August 3
Attached:	Voucher

Dear Mr. Baldini,

I regret to hear about the recent issue you encountered during your stay at the City Light Hotel Vancouver on July 23. It has come to my attention that despite having a confirmed reservation, the specific room you had booked was unavailable. Nevertheless, I am pleased that our dedicated front desk staff managed to arrange alternative accommodations for you.

After conducting an investigation, we have discovered that a malfunction in our computer program led to certain rooms being falsely listed as available despite their already being reserved. Unfortunately, your visit to Vancouver coincided with an international conference in the vicinity of our hotel, resulting in an unexpectedly high number of guests. This unintentionally led to overbooking.

I sincerely apologize for the inconvenience caused on behalf of the City Light Hotel. As a gesture of goodwill, I would like to offer you a complimentary one-night stay at any of our City Light Hotel locations (Vancouver, Toronto, Montreal, or Calgary). Please refer to the attached voucher for further information.

Best regards,

Mary Fenton
Director of Customer Service
City Light Hotel

City Light Hotel Voucher

#A003023

This voucher entitles you to a free one-night stay in a standard room at any of the following City Light Hotel locations: the Guest Suites City Light Vancouver, the Oceanview City Light Montreal, the High Square City Light Toronto, or the Forest City Light Calgary.

Please note that the room reservation must be made in advance. Meals are not included.

GUEST SIGNATURE: _____

DATE: _____

If you have any inquiries, please reach out to our customer services team:

Via e-mail: customerservices@citylight.com
Via phone: 604-665-5111
Via mail: 53 Water St, Toronto, ON M6B 2A5, Canada

28 Why did Ms. Fenton send the e-mail?

(A) To confirm Mr. Baldini's reservation

(B) To address Mr. Baldini's complaint

(C) To help Mr. Baldini with a booking

(D) To ask about Mr. Baldini's itinerary

29 What does Ms. Fenton indicate happened on July 23?

(A) The hotel staff members resolved an issue.

(B) The hotel implemented a new reservation system.

(C) Mr. Baldini received a voucher for a free stay.

(D) An international convention was held at the hotel.

30 What is suggested about Mr. Baldini?

(A) He traveled to Vancouver to attend a conference.

(B) He made a room change request upon arrival.

(C) He had made a prior reservation for a room.

(D) He regularly stayed at the City Light Hotel.

31 What does Mr. Baldini need to do to use the voucher?

(A) Enroll in the hotel membership program

(B) Make a reservation beforehand

(C) Contact the customer service center

(D) Provide proof of his previous stay

32 Where most likely is Ms. Fenton's office located?

(A) Vancouver

(B) Toronto

(C) Montreal

(D) Calgary

08 준동사 II (분사)

분사는 명사를 수식하거나 보어로 사용되는 **형용사 역할**을 한다. 반면에 **분사구문**은 부사절 접속사 뒤에 오거나 문장을 수식하는 **부사 역할**을 하기 때문에 둘을 잘 구분해야 한다. 또한 감정 분사와 분사형 형용사 등 난이도가 높은 문제가 출제된다.

오늘의 학습 POINT

POINT 1 분사는 명사의 앞이나 뒤에서 명사를 수식한다.
POINT 2 자동사의 분사형이 명사를 수식하는 경우에는 항상 현재분사(-ing)이다.
POINT 3 '감정분사'의 경우 사람은 과거분사, 사물은 현재분사로 수식한다.
POINT 4 부사절 접속사와 주어가 생략되면 동사는 분사구문이 된다.

POINT 1 분사는 명사의 앞이나 뒤에서 명사를 수식한다.

① 분사의 역할

• 분사는 형용사 역할로 **명사를 수식**한다.

Those working tirelessly on the project were rewarded with well-deserved promotions.
→ 분사인 working이 대명사인 those를 수식
프로젝트에 끊임없이 노력한 사람들은 충분한 자격이 있는 승진을 받았다.

• 명사가 **능동적인 의미로 분사의 주어 역할**을 하면 **현재분사(~하는)**가 수식한다.

a facility meeting the needs of the residents → 주민들의 요구를 충족하는 시설

• 명사가 **수동적인 의미로 분사의 목적어 역할**을 하면 **과거분사(~된, ~당하는)**가 수식한다.

a report prepared by the marketing team → 마케팅 팀에 의해 작성된 보고서

② 분사의 성질

관계대명사절에서 「**주격관계대명사 + be동사**」는 **생략이 가능**하다. 이때 주격관계대명사가 생략되면 분사만 남아 있게 된다.

「주절 + 주격관계대명사 + be동사 + 분사」 → 「주절 + 분사」

I saw children **who were digging** a hole in the garden.
→ I saw children **digging** a hole in the garden. 나는 정원에 구덩이를 파는 아이들을 보았다.

📝 PRACTICE 1-3 괄호 안의 보기들 중에서 적절한 것을 고르세요. 정답 p.118

1 The guest (staying / stayed) in room 302 reported a minor issue with the air conditioning.

2 The (revising / revised) article received positive feedback from the editor.

3 The new system, (which / which is) designed to streamline operations, has been successfully implemented.

자동사의 분사형이 명사를 수식하는 경우에는 항상 현재분사(-ing)이다.

1 현재분사와 과거분사

❶ 「명사 + _____ + 명사」형태의 문제에서 빈칸에는 현재분사가 온다.

타동사에서 파생된 현재분사 앞에는 의미상의 주어로서 수식을 받는 명사가 오고, 뒤에는 의미상 목적어인 명사가 온다.

Anyone **buying** more than five items will receive a special discount.
5개 이상의 제품을 구매하는 사람은 특별 할인을 받을 것이다. [anyone = 의미상 주어 / more than five items = 의미상 목적어]

❷ 「한정사 + _____ + 명사」형태의 문제는 현재분사보다 과거분사가 정답인 경우가 훨씬 많다.

과거분사는 수동의 의미로 뒤에 목적어가 올 수 없고, 앞이나 뒤에 수식을 받는 명사만 존재한다.

The **reduced** budgets forced the city council to prioritize essential infrastructure projects over non-urgent developments.
줄어든 예산으로 인해 시의회는 긴급하지 않은 개발보다 필수적인 기반시설 프로젝트를 우선시해야 했다.

❸ 자동사의 분사형이 명사를 수식하는 경우에는 항상 현재분사이다.

자동사는 목적어를 취하지 않기 때문에 수동형이 될 수 없으며, 항상 현재분사로 명사를 수식한다.

The company is expanding its production capacity to meet the **growing** needs of its customers.
회사는 증가하는 고객의 요구를 충족시키기 위해 생산 능력을 확장하고 있다.

> **PRACTICE 4-5** 괄호 안의 보기들 중에서 적절한 것을 고르세요. 정답 p.118
>
> 4 Professional development workshops provide valuable resources for those (working / worked) in the education sector.
> 5 The HR Department provides guidance to employees (seeking / are seeking) reimbursement for eligible expenses.

2 분사형 형용사

❶ 명사 앞에서 항상 현재분사 형태인 형용사

the challenging task 어려운 임무	the missing item 잃어버린 물건
the closing shift 마감 근무조	the mounting debt 늘어나는 빚
the coming year 다가오는 해	the opening ceremony 개회식
the demanding customer 까다로운 고객	the opposing direction 반대 방향
the existing equipment 기존의 장비	the outstanding performance 뛰어난 성과
the emerging technology 떠오르는 기술	the presiding officer 진행자
the following week 그 다음 주	the promising employee 유망한 직원
the growing needs 증가하는 요구	the rising cost 증가하는 비용
the inviting display 매력적인 전시	the remaining food 남은 음식
the lasting impression 지속되는 인상	the rewarding work 보람 있는 일
the leading company 앞서가는 기업	the surrounding area 주변 지역
the living author 살아있는 작가	the welcoming atmosphere 환영하는 분위기

❷ 명사 앞에서 항상 과거분사 형태인 형용사

the accomplished musician 뛰어난 음악가	the established company 탄탄한 회사
the celebrated place 인기있는 장소	the guided tour 안내되는 여행
the complicated system 복잡한 시스템	the limited time 제한된 시간
the customized item 주문 제작 상품	the preferred date 선호되는 날짜
the damaged product 파손된 상품	the qualified candidate 적격의 후보자
the designated seat 지정석	the revised edition 개정판
the dedicated team 헌신적인 팀	the seasoned actor 노련한 배우
the detailed analysis 상세한 분석	the sophisticated technology 정교한 기술
the distinguished author 저명한 작가	the skilled worker 노련한 근로자
the experienced staff 경험이 풍부한 직원	the talented student 재능 있는 학생
the enclosed coupon 동봉된 쿠폰	the written permission 서면 허가증

❸ 동명사와 현재분사의 구분

'-ing'의 위치에 따라 동명사와 현재분사를 구분할 수 있다.

형태	구분	설명
전치사 + -ing + 한정사 + 명사	동명사	분사는 형용사 역할을 하므로 한정사 앞에 올 수 없다.
한정사 + -ing + 명사	현재분사	한정사와 명사 사이는 형용사 자리이므로 현재분사이다.
명사 + -ing + 명사	현재분사	앞의 명사가 '-ing'의 수식을 받으므로 현재분사이다.
전치사 + -ing + 명사	대부분 동명사	자동사에서 파생된 경우 현재분사일 수도 있다.

✐ PRACTICE 6 ◀ 괄호 안의 보기들 중에서 적절한 것을 고르세요. 정답 p.118

6 The preliminary results of the study show (promising / promised) outcomes, indicating potential advancements in the field.

POINT 3 '감정분사'의 경우 사람은 과거분사, 사물은 현재분사로 수식한다.

◎ 감정분사

❶ 감정동사는 의미상 사람만을 목적어로 취한다.

alarm 불안하게 만들다	disappoint 실망시키다	interest ~의 관심을 끌다
amuse 즐겁게 하다	distract 산만하게 하다	overwhelm 압도하다
annoy 짜증나게 하다	embarrass 당황스럽게 만들다	please 기쁘게 하다
astonish 깜짝 놀라게 하다	encourage 용기를 북돋우다	satisfy 만족시키다
bore 지루하게 만들다	excite 들뜨게 만들다	shock 깜짝 놀라게 하다
confuse 혼란스럽게 만들다	fascinate 마음을 사로잡다	surprise 놀라게 하다

The comment can **confuse** the readers. 그 논평은 독자들을 혼란스럽게 할 수 있다.

② 감정동사에서 파생된 분사는 사람은 과거분사, 사물은 현재분사를 쓴다.

alarming rate 무서운 속도	encouraging response 고무적인 회신
alarmed officials 불안해하는 관료들	encouraged staff 고무된 직원들
amusing story 재미있는 이야기	exciting opening 신나는 도입부
amused spectators 즐거워하는 구경꾼들	excited crowd of people 들뜬 군중
annoying noise 짜증스러운 소음	fascinating history 흥미로운 역사
annoyed presenter 짜증이 난 진행자	fascinated travelers 매료된 여행객들
astonishing success 정말 놀라운 성공	interesting idea 흥미로운 아이디어
astonished audience 깜짝 놀란 관중	interested buyer 관심있는 구매자
boring conversation 재미없는 대화	overwhelming support 압도적인 지지
bored listeners 지루해 하는 청자들	overwhelmed readers 압도된 독자들
confusing numbers 혼동되는 숫자들	pleasing painting 기분 좋은 그림
confused people 혼란스러워 하는 사람들	pleased parents 기쁜 부모들
disappointing movie 실망스러운 영화	satisfying result 만족스러운 결과
disappointed fans 실망한 팬들	satisfied guests 만족한 고객들
distracting gesture 마음을 산란케 하는 행동	shocking news 충격적인 소식
distracted kids (정신이) 산만해진 아이들	shocked shareholders 충격 받은 주주들
embarrassing situation 당혹스러운 상황	surprising answer 놀라운 답변
embarrassed performer 당황한 연주가	surprised interviewer 놀란 면접관

cf. 감정동사에서 파생된 현재분사는 목적어 없이 단독으로 형용사로 사용할 수 있다.

📝 PRACTICE 7 괄호 안의 보기들 중에서 적절한 것을 고르세요. 정답 p.118

7 Our company strives to provide excellent service to keep our customers (satisfying / satisfied) and loyal.

POINT 4 부사절 접속사와 주어가 생략되면 동사는 분사구문이 된다.

🔵 분사구문

- 부사절 접속사 뒤 주어가 생략되면, 그 뒤의 동사는 분사가 된다.
- 분사구문 앞 접속사는 생략할 수 있다.

After we carefully reviewed the report, we decided to proceed with the proposed plan.
→ **After carefully reviewing** the report, we decided to proceed with the proposed plan.
→ **Carefully reviewing** the report, we decided to proceed with the proposed plan.
　보고서를 신중히 검토한 후, 우리는 제안된 계획대로 진행하기로 결정했다.

- 주절의 주어와 분사와의 관계가 능동이면 현재분사구문, 수동이면 과거분사구문이 온다.
- 뒤에 목적어가 있으면 현재분사구문, 목적어가 없으면 과거분사구문을 선택한다. 단, 자동사에서 파생된 분사구문은 항상 현재분사구문이다.

Visiting the town, **he** immersed himself in its rich history and culture. [he와 visiting은 능동 관계]
마을에 방문했을 때, 그는 그곳의 역사와 문화에 몰두했다.

Chosen by the readers, **she** graciously accepted the literary award. [she와 chosen은 수동 관계]
독자들에게 선택받아서, 그녀는 품위있게 문학상을 수락했다.

⊙ 「-able, -ible, -ive, -ful, -ous, -ory, -ic, -al, -ant」 등으로 끝나는 단어는 대부분 형용사이다.

considerable 상당한, 중요한
considerable expertise 상당한 전문 지식

extended 연장된
an extended period of recession 장기화된 경기 불황

considerate 사려 깊은 ⊜ thoughtful 사려 깊은
Please be considerate to others. 다른 사람들을 배려해 주세요.

extensive 광범위한 ⊜ immense 엄청난, 어마어마한
extensive repair work 대대적인 수리 작업

sensitive 민감한, 예민한
sensitive to criticism 비판에 민감한

comparable 비교할 만한
The two cars are comparable in performance.
저 두 대의 차는 성능에 있어 비교할 만하다.

sensible 분별 있는, 현명한
a very sensible decision 매우 분별 있는 결정

compatible 호환되는
compatible with existing equipment 기존의 장비와 호환되는

economic 경제의
forecast an economic recovery 경제 회복을 예측하다

reliant 의존하는 ⊜ dependent 의존하는
become reliant on computers 컴퓨터에 의존하게 되다

economical 알뜰한, 절약하는
Bulk purchases are economical. 대량 구매가 경제적이다.

reliable 신뢰할 수 있는 ⊜ dependable 믿을 만한
He is reliable and punctual. 그는 믿을 만하고 시간도 엄수한다.

respective 각각의, 각자의
return to their respective teams 각자의 팀으로 돌아가다

comprehensive 포괄적인
a comprehensive listing 모두 포함된 리스트

respectful 공손한, 예의 바른
cf. respectable 존경할만한
a respectful relationship 존중하는 관계

comprehensible 이해할 수 있는
⊜ understandable 이해하기 쉬운
The manual is easily comprehensible.
사용 설명서가 이해하기 쉽다.

industrial 산업의, 공업의
industrial workers 산업 근로자들

satisfied 만족스러워 하는
satisfied customers 만족스러워 하는 고객들

industrious 근면한, 부지런한
industrious workers 부지런한 근로자들

satisfactory 만족스러운; 충분한
a satisfactory arrangement 만족스러운 조치

successful 성공한
the successful candidate 합격자

responsible 책임지고 있는 ⊜ accountable 책임이 있는
She is responsible for recruiting. 그녀는 모집을 책임지고 있다.

successive 연속적인 ⊜ consecutive 연이은
for three successive weeks 3주 연속으로

responsive 즉각 반응하는
responsive to consumer demand
소비자 요구에 즉각 대응하는

impressive 인상깊은
His career is very impressive. 그의 경력은 매우 인상적이다.

informative 유용한 정보를 주는, 유익한
The lecture was informative. 그 수업은 유익했다.

impressed 감명받은
We were impressed by her presentation.
그녀의 발표에 깊은 인상을 받았다.

informed 잘 아는, 정보통인 ⊜ knowledgeable 많이 아는
Keep me informed of any updates.
새로운 소식 있으면 저에게 알려주세요.

various 다양한 vs. **variable** 변동이 심한
• various: 다양성과 많음을 의미
• variable: 양이나 정도의 변형과 변화, 혹은 차이를 의미
various goods 다양한 상품들
The weather is variable. 날씨가 변덕이 심하다.

required 필수적인 vs. **obligated** 의무가 있는
• required: 어떤 일에 필요한 요청 사항이나 조건
• obligated: 법률적, 도덕적으로 지켜야 할 의무
Teamwork is required for this job.
이 일을 위해 팀워크가 필요하다.
You are obligated to pay tax. 당신은 세금을 낼 의무가 있다.

PART 5

Directions: A word or phrase is missing in each of the sentences below. Four answer choices are given below each sentence. Select the best answer to complete the sentence and mark the letter (A), (B), (C), or (D).

1 The sales staff ------- to actively engage with customers and to provide personalized assistance to enhance the shopping experience.

(A) is encouraging
(B) was encouraged
(C) has encouraged
(D) being encouraged

2 The success of the marketing campaign is ------- on effective targeting and engaging content.

(A) relied
(B) relies
(C) reliable
(D) reliant

3 The laboratory technician ------- various chemicals should be well trained in handling them safely and efficiently.

(A) manages
(B) managing
(C) manageable
(D) managed

4 ------- with experience in project management are often sought for leadership roles within the organization.

(A) That
(B) Each
(C) Those
(D) Another

5 The newly ------- chairperson is eager to implement fresh strategies and to lead the organization to greater heights.

(A) appointment
(B) appointing
(C) appointed
(D) to appoint

6 Those ------- to attend the conference are advised to register early enough to secure their spots.

(A) planning
(B) which plan
(C) planned
(D) are planning

7   The Hewitt Legal Company received numerous applications from many ------- lawyers eager to join its esteemed team.

(A) challenging
(B) promising
(C) rewarding
(D) experiencing

8   To minimize ------- to nearby businesses, event organizers holding events in Union Square are required to hire traffic control workers.

(A) movement
(B) convenience
(C) infection
(D) disruption

9   The availability of certain resources for the project has been limited, ------- delays in its completion.

(A) has caused
(B) caused
(C) will cause
(D) causing

10 The timeline of the construction project has been updated to reflect the changes as ------- during the team meeting.

(A) discussion
(B) discuss
(C) discussed
(D) discussing

11 ------- the main course, the restaurant also offers a variety of appetizers and desserts to enhance the dining experience.

(A) Among
(B) Apart from
(C) Owing to
(D) On account of

12 Customers who fail to return the equipment within the specified timeframe will ------- additional charges as outlined in the rental agreement.

(A) alternate
(B) coincide
(C) incur
(D) inspire

13 The company's profits have steadily increased over the past year ------- its market share has remained relatively stagnant.

(A) themselves
(B) whenever
(C) elsewhere
(D) whereas

14 The CEO expressed his gratitude to the team, ------- highlighting their exceptional dedication throughout the project.

(A) originally
(B) shortly
(C) particularly
(D) ambiguously

15 We conducted an extensive market analysis, gathering data and insights about ------- company would be the best partner for our expansion.

(A) only
(B) which
(C) latest
(D) that

PART 6

Directions: Read the text below. A word, phrase, or sentence is missing in parts of the text. Four answer choices for each question are given below the text. Select the best answer to complete the text and mark the letter (A), (B), (C), or (D).

Questions 16-19 refer to the following article.

On June 15, Janice Lee, the marketing director of Bonnie Premium Food, made an announcement ------- the company's plan to invest three million dollars in expanding and relocating its operations
16.
from Burbank to Willowbrook, IL. This strategic move aims to support the company's growth.
-------. The new location, ------- on 75th St. in Willowbrook, is projected to become operational
17.   **18.**
by the end of August. Since its establishment in Chicago in 1969, the company has consistently
grown its portfolio of restaurants and established a premium food service customer distribution
network, which includes more than five warehouses ------- fifteen states.
19.

16 (A) with all
   (B) according to
   (C) in order that
   (D) regarding

17 (A) They have offered outstanding relocation
      services.
   (B) It will also cater to increasing demand.
   (C) There has been notable growth in the
      food industry.
   (D) The site of a new factory is under
      consideration.

18 (A) situating
   (B) is situated
   (C) situated
   (D) has situated

19 (A) serving
   (B) remaining
   (C) holding
   (D) following

The Queen Bee Steakhouse is currently seeking leaders who will ------- responsibility for
20.
overseeing the overall management of our restaurant alongside a team of dedicated individuals.
Successful candidates should possess a genuine passion for the restaurant industry. Our
performance-driven environment will prepare you to build a ------- career in this field.
21.

As a newly hired manager, your primary focus will be on enhancing both guest and employee
satisfaction. This will involve leading the development and training of teams to drive improved
outcomes. -------. For further details about this position, please visit our Web site at
22.
queenbee.com. ------- competitive compensation, we offer benefits such as paid vacation and a
23.
comprehensive medical plan.

20 (A) assume
    (B) withstand
    (C) cooperate
    (D) maintain

21 (A) rewards
    (B) rewarded
    (C) rewarding
    (D) reward

22 (A) Therefore, there is potential for career
       growth.
    (B) To that end, they will collaborate with the
       sales staff.
    (C) All of our kitchen managers possess
       culinary expertise.
    (D) Moreover, it entails upholding our high
       standards.

23 (A) In addition to
    (B) By means of
    (C) In an effort to
    (D) In advance of

Directions: In this part you will read a selection of texts. The text or set of texts is followed by several questions. Select the best answer for each question and mark the letter (A), (B), (C), or (D).

Questions 24-26 refer to the following document.

Welcome to the Goldenrod Hotel Orlando!

Whether you're in Orlando for business or leisure, we invite you to indulge in our exceptional amenities and top-tier service. At the Goldenrod Hotel, we present our guests with spacious and inviting rooms and suites that provide breathtaking views of the Orlando skyline.

Should you require Internet access or a productive workspace, our second-floor business center, known as the Office in Goldenrod, is at your service. Furnished with computers, printers, a fax machine, and other essential equipment, it's the perfect spot for your research and document needs. Located next to the Office in Goldenrod is the Cozy Lounge, where you can treat yourself to reasonably priced refreshments and snacks as you take a moment to unwind.

If maintaining your fitness routine is a priority during your business trip or vacation, we have you covered. The Fitness Studio, our recently revamped fitness center on the seventh floor, awaits your visit. Equipped with state-of-the-art gym facilities, it also boasts a heated indoor pool for your enjoyment.

After a bustling day exploring the sights of Orlando, satisfy your appetite with ease. For an array of delectable options, consult the room service menu located in the dining section starting on page 20 of the directory. Alternatively, immerse yourself in the culinary delights of the acclaimed Holiday in Orlando restaurant. Indulge in thoughtfully curated local wines and innovative small plates and savor traditional regional dishes. The restaurant welcomes guests for breakfast, lunch, and dinner.

Thank you for selecting the Goldenrod Hotel for your Orlando experience. We trust you'll have a remarkable stay filled with comfort and delight.

24 What is stated about the hotel?

(A) It is located near a large park.

(B) It offers a variety of services for guests.

(C) It is popular with business travelers.

(D) It provides discounts to frequent guests.

25 What is indicated about the Cozy Lounge?

(A) It is equipped with computers.

(B) It was recently renovated.

(C) It offers free coffee and snacks.

(D) It is located on the second floor.

26 What is NOT mentioned as a feature of the hotel?

(A) An exercise center

(B) A renowned dining establishment

(C) A spacious parking lot

(D) A business center

Azure Sky Tours
New York

In celebration of the new year, Azure Sky Tours has introduced exclusive packages that offer a 15-percent discount compared to last year's rates. This special offer is applicable to bookings made before January 15. Our Australia tours are available every week, but we recommend securing your spot early to ensure you don't miss out. Below, you'll find a preview of a selection of our standard package choices:

Brisbane & Gold Coast Getaway: Urban Adventures and Coastal Charms
This 7-day tour starts in Queensland's sunny capital, Brisbane, where you can enjoy outdoor dining, riverside picnics, and visit nearby coastal islands. Then, continue to the exquisite leisure destination of the Gold Coast. Explore its golden beaches and vast national parks.

Sydney Splendors: Explore the Best of Australia's Harbour City!
Discover the magic of Sydney, where famous places like the Sydney Opera House and the Sydney Harbour Bridge create a stunning view. During our 5- or 7-day tours, experience the lively culture, the beautiful beaches, and the delicious food that will keep you fascinated and wanting to experience more.

Perth Unveiled: Discover the Treasures of Australia's West Coast
Get ready for an adventure in Perth, where beautiful beaches meet exciting city life. The clear waters of Scarborough Beach are great for relaxing and having fun. You can watch dolphins play at the Dolphin Discovery Centre and learn about the city's history by the sea. This 7-day tour will offer an amazing trip for everyone to enjoy and remember.

*** We can create tailored tours for specific groups by adjusting the tour duration and the types of attractions included.

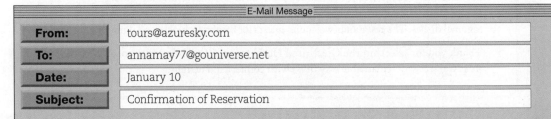

E-Mail Message

From:	tours@azuresky.com
To:	annamay77@gouniverse.net
Date:	January 10
Subject:	Confirmation of Reservation

Dear Ms. May,

Thank you for choosing Azure Sky Tours. We're pleased to confirm your booking for two passengers.

Tour Title: Perth Unveiled: Discover the Treasures of Australia's West Coast
Departure from New York: Saturday, March 10, 9:30 A.M.
Return to New York: Sunday, March 18, 8:00 P.M.
Total Amount Charged to Your Card: $3,600.00

Feel free to contact our customer relations coordinator if you have any questions before your travel date. For inquiries, please send an e-mail to tours@azuresky.com or call (212) 245-9090.

> **Q** http://www.azuresky.com/reviews

Feedback from Travelers
★★★★☆

After coming across Azure Sky Tours' promotion, we made the exciting choice to journey to Australia in honor of our 10th wedding anniversary. This company truly understands how to provide exceptional customer experiences, and we're eagerly looking forward to more adventures with it. Our guide, Marcus Donovan, impressed us with his enthusiasm and wealth of knowledge. Being a local of the city we explored, he shared captivating insights into its traditions and culture.

Shared by: Anna May

27 What is suggested about Azure Sky Tours?

(A) Its headquarters is located in Australia.
(B) It offers discounted packages every year.
(C) It has developed new tours to meet demand.
(D) It arranges its tours multiple times a month.

28 According to the advertisement, what can Azure Sky Tours offer clients?

(A) Free admission to famous performances
(B) Reduced prices for loyal clientele
(C) Customized tours for special groups
(D) Group discounts based on a specific number

29 What is mentioned about Sydney Splendors?

(A) It offers complimentary theater tickets.
(B) It provides the option to choose a duration.
(C) It offers an opportunity to observe wildlife.
(D) It includes a boat trip to nearby islands.

30 What is NOT true about Ms. May's tour?

(A) It will last for a week.
(B) It was acquired at a discounted price.
(C) It includes visits to national parks.
(D) It will offer a chance to learn about history.

31 What is indicated about Mr. Donovan?

(A) He is a resident of Perth.
(B) He hopes to be back for more trips.
(C) He traveled to celebrate an anniversary.
(D) He teaches history at a university.

전치사는 명사 앞에 위치하며 접속사는 절과 절을 연결한다. (등위접속사는 절과 절 뿐만 아니라, 단어와 단어, 구와 구를 연결할 수 있다.) 접속사는 종류에 따라 문장 내 위치와 역할이 달라지므로, 전치사와 접속사의 구분뿐만이 아니라 접속사의 종류를 구분할 수 있어야 한다. 또한, 전치사의 의미와 역할을 묻는 어려운 문제들이 출제되므로 이에 대비하자.

오늘의 학습 POINT

POINT 1 명사 상당어구 앞에는 전치사가, 절 앞에는 접속사가 정답이다.

POINT 2 각각의 전치사마다 어떤 종류의 명사를 연결하는지를 알아두자.

POINT 1 명사 상당어구 앞에는 전치사가, 절 앞에는 접속사가 정답이다.

① 전치사와 접속사의 위치

① 빈칸 뒤에 명사 상당어구(명사, 대명사, 명사구, 명사절)가 있으면 전치사가 정답이다

She arrived **at** the airport just in time to catch her flight. 그녀는 비행기 탑승 시간에 정확히 맞게 공항에 도착했다.

② 빈칸 뒤에 절(주어 + 동사)이 있으면 접속사가 정답이다.

The book **that** I'm reading is quite engaging. 내가 읽고 있는 책은 꽤 흥미롭다.

② 유사한 의미의 전치사와 접속사

의미		전치사 (명사 상당어구 앞)	접속사 (절 앞)
시간	~ 동안	during, for	while
	~ 전에	before, prior to	before
	~ 후에	after, following	after
	~할 때	at, on, upon	when, once
	~까지	until, by	until, by the time
이유	~ 때문에	because of, due to, owing to, on account of	because, as, since, now that
양보	~에도 불구하고, ~일지라도	despite, in spite of, notwithstanding	though, although, even though, even if
조건, 가정	~이 아니라면	barring, without	unless
	~ 경우를 대비하여	in case of	in case (that)

cf. before, after, until은 전치사와 접속사로 모두 사용될 수 있다.

정답 p.124

PRACTICE 1-2 괄호 안의 보기들 중에서 적절한 것을 고르세요.

1 (Despite / Although) it was cold, the event was held outdoors.

2 (While / During) she studied for her exam, he watched TV in the same room.

3 전치사구와 접속사절의 역할

❶ 전치사구(전치사 + 명사)는 형용사나 부사 역할을 한다.

They decided to dine at a restaurant **near the lake** to celebrate their anniversary.
그들은 기념일을 축하하기 위해서 호수 근처의 식당에서 식사하기로 결정했다. [near the lake가 a restaurant를 수식]

❷ 접속사절(접속사 + 절)은 접속사의 종류에 따라 명사, 형용사, 부사 등의 역할을 한다.

- **명사절 접속사**: 문장에서 주어, 목적어, 보어 역할을 한다. 명사절 접속사에는 that과 if/whether가 있으며, 의문사도 명사절 접속사로 사용될 수 있다.

She needed more time to decide **whether** she should accept the job offer.
그녀는 입사 제안을 받아들여야 할지 여부를 결정하기 위해 더 많은 시간이 필요했다. [whether 절이 decide의 목적어]

- **형용사절 접속사**: 관계대명사절과 관계부사절로서 형용사의 역할을 한다.

The museum, **which** recently underwent renovations, is now a stunning cultural hub in the city.
최근 개보수를 한 박물관은 이제 도시의 멋진 문화 중심지이다. [관계대명사절이 the museum을 수식]

- **부사절 접속사**: 부사절은 완전한 절을 수식한다. 부사절 접속사 뒤에는 완전한 절이나 분사구문이 온다.

시간	when, while, before, after, until, once	이유	because, as, since, now that
조건	if, unless	양보	(even) though, although, even if

Although we were tired, we worked overtime to meet the deadline.
우리는 피곤했지만, 마감일을 맞추기 위해 야근했다. [부사절이 완전한 절을 수식]

- **등위접속사**: 'and, but, or, so, yet' 등이 있으며, 단어와 단어, 구와 구, 절과 절을 모두 연결할 수 있다. 단, 연결되는 성분의 종류는 같아야 한다.

The company opened a flagship store **and** an online store to reach customers worldwide.
회사는 전 세계 고객에게 접근하기 위해 체험 판매장과 온라인 매장을 열었다. [명사구와 명사구를 연결]

cf. So는 절과 절만을 연결할 수 있다.

- **상관접속사**: 둘 이상의 단어로 이루어져 있으며 항상 함께 사용된다.

not A but B A가 아닌 B	not only A but (also) B A뿐 아니라 B도	both A and B A와 B 둘 다
either A or B A나 B 둘 중 하나	neither A nor B A도 B도 아닌	

cf. 'both A and B'는 복수로 취급하며, 나머지는 모두 B에 동사를 일치시킨다.

For assistance, you can **either** visit the store **or** contact our customer relations team.
도움을 위해, 당신은 상점에 방문하거나 고객서비스부서에 연락할 수 있다.

PRACTICE 3-4 괄호 안의 보기들 중에서 적절한 것을 고르세요.

정답 p.124

3 We don't know (whether / because) they will arrive on time for the meeting.

4 She couldn't decide whether to spend her vacation at the beach (either / or) in the mountains.

각각의 전치사마다 어떤 종류의 명사를 연결하는지를 알아두자.

❶ 전치사의 종류와 의미

❶ in / at / on + 시간 / 장소

전치사	특징	예
in ~에	• 장소: 도시, 나라 등의 큰 장소 • 시간: 연도, 월, 계절 등의 긴 시간	• **in** the city, **in** Seoul, **in** the country, **in** Korea • **in** winter, **in** 1945, **in** March
at ~에	• 장소: 정확한 지점 • 시간: 시각 등의 정확한 시간	• **at** the desk, **at** the corner, **at** the bus stop • **at** noon, **at** 10:30, **at** 3 o'clock, **at** night
on ~에	• 장소: 바닥, 벽, 테이블 위 등의 표면 • 시간: 날짜나 요일 등 하루 개념의 시간	• **on** the floor, **on** the ceiling, **on** the road • **on** Friday, **on** April 3, **on** the anniversary

cf. in은 이 외에 '~ 안에'를 의미하는 장소 전치사로도 사용된다. **e.g.** in the box

❷ for / during / throughout / within + 기간

전치사	특징	예
for ~ 동안에	특정 기간 동안 계속 일어나고 있는 일이나 상태를 표현	He talked about it **for** a long time. It has been raining **for** three hours.
during ~ 동안에	특정 기간 명사 앞에 쓰이며, 특정 기간 전체, 또는 특정 기간 내에 일어난 일을 표현	I saw him once **during** my stay in London.
throughout ~ 동안 내내	특정 기간 내내 일어난 일을 표현	He will be out of town **throughout** the summer.
within ~ 이내에	일반적으로 숫자로 표현된 기간 앞에 쓰이며, 그 기간 내에 일어나거나 완료된 일을 표현	You will be sent a draft of the estimate **within** a week.

❸ through / throughout / within / along / toward / under + 장소 / 범위 / 위치

전치사	특징	예
through ~을 통과하여	(어떤 장소를) 통과하여, 가로질러	**through** the park 공원을 가로질러 **through** the pipe 파이프를 통과하여
throughout ~ 여기저기에	(어떤 장소나 공간) 여기 저기에	**throughout** the city 도시 전역에 **throughout** the building 건물 여기저기에
within ~ 이내에	(특정 거리나 범위) 이내에	**within** walking distance 걸어서 갈만한 거리에 **within** ten miles 10마일 이내에
along ~을 따라서	(길게 뻗은 장소)를 따라서	**along** the river 강을 따라 **along** the street 길을 따라
toward ~을 향해	(방향을) 향해, (목표를) 향해	**toward** the door 문을 향해 **toward** the goals 목표를 향해
under ~ 아래에, ~ 하에	(특정 위치) 아래에, (어떤 상태나 조건) 하에	**under** the desk 책상 아래에 **under** no circumstance 어떤 경우라도

④ by / until / since / before / prior to / after / following + 시점

전치사	특징	예
by ~까지	특정 시점까지 행위나 일이 완료될 때	It will be completed **by** next Monday.
until ~까지	특정 시점까지 행위나 일이 지속될 때	The store will be closed **until** noon.
since ~ 이래로	과거의 특정한 시점 이래로 현재까지	I haven't seen her **since** last weekend.
before, prior to ~ 전에	특정한 시점을 기준으로 그 이전	Please send me the file **before** lunch. Turn it off **prior to** your departure.
after, following ~ 후에	특정한 시점을 기준으로 그 이후	Brush your teeth right **after** every meal. Its stock price soared **following** the merger.

⑤ by / with / through / via + 수단 / 도구

전치사	특징	예
by ~로	교통·통신·지불 수단 등을 의미하는 명사 앞에 사용 **cf.** 이때, 명사 앞에는 관사를 쓰지 않는다.	**by** bus, **by** phone, **by** credit card, **by** hand, **by** plane
with ~로	구체적인 도구나 수단을 의미하는 명사 앞에 사용	**with** this pen, **with** a hammer, **with** glue, **with** a brush
through ~을 통해서	매개나 경로를 의미하는 명사 앞에 사용 (수단, 경험, 인터넷 등)	**through** his experience, **through** the Internet
via ~을 통하여	특정한 사람이나 시스템을 의미하는 명사 앞에 사용	**via** satellite, **via** courier, **via** express mail

---

📝 PRACTICE 5-6 ◢ 괄호 안의 보기들 중에서 적절한 것을 고르세요.　　　정답 p.124

5　The company achieved its market expansion (through / along) a meticulously planned strategy.

6　The project was completed successfully (within / under) the guidance of a seasoned project manager.

② 혼동하기 쉬운 전치사

① for / during + 기간

전치사	특징	예
for ~ 동안에	수사 앞에 쓰이며, 그 기간 동안 상황이 지속됨을 의미	They had to wait **for** two hours to get a table.
during ~ 동안에	특정 기간을 의미하는 명사 앞에 쓰이며, 그 기간 동안 발생한 일, 상황을 의미	**During** the thunderstorm, the power went out.

② by / until + 시점

전치사	특징	예
by ~까지	특정 시점까지 완료되는 동작을 의미 **cf.** finish, complete, submit, receive 등의 동사와 사용	I need to finish this project **by** the end of the month. [이달 말까지 프로젝트가 완료됨]
until ~까지	특정 시점까지 계속되는 동작을 의미 **cf.** stay, remain, wait, continue 등의 동사와 사용	The sale will continue **until** the end of the month. [이달 말까지 할인이 지속됨]

❸ in / within + 기간

전치사	특징	예
in ~ 후에, ~만에	in이 특정 기간을 의미하는 명사 앞에 쓰이면 '그 기간이 지난 시점'을 의미	I have a dental appointment scheduled **in** <u>two weeks</u>. [2주가 지난 시점에 치과 예약]
within ~ 이내에	within이 특정 기간를 의미하는 명사 앞에 쓰이면, '그 기간 이내'를 의미	You can expect to receive your package **within** <u>two weeks</u>. [2주일 이내로 수령]

❹ among / between

전치사	특징	예
among ~ 중에	셋 이상의 불특정 다수를 나타낼 때 사용 (복수 명사 앞에 쓰임)	The painting stood out as the most impressive **among** all the artworks in the gallery.
between ~ 사이에	둘 사이의 관계를 나타낼 때 사용 ('수 명사'나 'A and B' 앞에 쓰임)	The meeting is scheduled to take place **between** 2:00 and 3:00 in the afternoon.

❺ across / opposite

전치사	특징	예
across ~을 건너, ~을 지나	'across the street'처럼 건너거나 지나 가는 장소 명사 앞에 쓰임	She walked **across** <u>the bridge</u> to get to the other side of the river. [다리를 걸어서 건넘]
opposite ~의 맞은편에	'opposite the café'와 같이 맞은편에 있는 장소 명사 앞에 사용	The park is located **opposite** <u>the movie</u> <u>theater</u>. [공원이 극장 맞은편에 있음]

> **cf.** across는 '~ 전체에 걸쳐서', 또는 '~ 전체에'를 의미하는 장소 전치사로도 사용된다.

The store has branches **across** <u>the country</u>, making it easily accessible to customers.
그 상점은 전국에 지점을 두고 있어서, 고객들이 쉽게 접근할 수 있다.

> **📝 PRACTICE 7-8** ❮ 괄호 안의 보기들 중에서 적절한 것을 고르세요. 　　정답 p.124
>
> **7** (Until / By) the end of the year, we aim to have completed the renovation of our office
> space.
> **8** The restaurant is located (across / opposite) City Hall, making it a convenient meeting spot.

❸ 주의해야 할 기타 전치사

❶ −ing형 전치사

regarding ~에 관하여	concerning ~에 관하여	pertaining to ~에 관계된	following ~ 후에
barring ~을 제외하고, ~이 없다면		including ~을 포함하여	notwithstanding ~에도 불구하고

❷ 두 단어 이상으로 구성된 전치사

in addition to ~에 더하여	according to ~에 따르면	regardless of ~에 상관없이	ahead of ~보다 빨리
out of ~로부터	except for ~을 제외하고	apart from ~외에는, ~을 제외하고	

absolutely 전적으로, 절대적으로
absolutely true 완전히 사실인

accordingly 따라서, 그에 맞춰
Check the weather and make an itinerary accordingly. 날씨를 확인하고 그에 맞춰 여행 일정을 잡으세요.

actually 실제로
The movie was actually quite fun.
그 영화는 사실 (예상과 달리) 꽤 재미있었다.

adequately 적절하게
adequately rewarded 적절하게 보상된

adversely 불리하게
The competition adequately affected its business.
경쟁이 사업에 나쁜 영향을 주었다.

altogether 완전히 ⊕ completely 완전히
altogether different 완전히 다른

apparently 듣자하니, 보아하니 ⊕ seemingly 보아하니
Apparently, he will be late. 보아하니, 그는 늦겠다.

approximately 대략 ⊕ roughly 대략, 거의
take approximately 2 hours 대략 두 시간이 걸리다

appropriately 적당하게, 알맞게
appropriately respond 적절히 대응하다

arguably 거의 틀림없이
arguably the most important 단연코 가장 중요한

attentively 조심스럽게 ⊕ cautiously 조심스럽게
listen attentively 주의 깊게 듣다

broadly 널리, 폭넓게 ⊕ widely 널리, 폭넓게
broadly cover various topics 다양한 주제를 폭넓게 다루다

collectively 집단으로, 총체적으로
collectively work 다 함께 일하다

consequently 그 결과, 따라서
She missed the train, and consequently, she was late for the meeting. 그녀는 기차를 놓쳤고, 그 결과 회의에 늦었다.

consistently 지속적으로 vs. **constantly** 끊임없이
• consistently: 행동이나 상태가 변함없이 지속되는 경우
• constantly: 수시로 반복되어 발생하는 경우
a consistently strong performance 지속적으로 강력한 성능
constantly complain 끊임없이 불평하다

conveniently 편리하게
conveniently located 편리한 위치에 있는

conventionally 관습적으로, 통상적으로
Various materials are conventionally used.
통상적으로 다양한 재료가 사용된다.

definitely 확실히, 분명히 ⊕ certainly 틀림없이, 분명히
has not been definitely decided yet
아직 확실히 결정되지 않았다

directly 곧장, 직접적으로
directly after the show 공연이 끝난 직후에

dramatically 극적으로 ⊕ drastically 대폭, 과감하게
improve dramatically 극적으로 개선되다

eagerly 간절히, 열심히
an eagerly awaited movie 간절히 기다렸던 영화

efficiently 효율적으로
utilize space more efficiently 공간을 더 효율적으로 활용하다

entirely 전적으로, 완전히, 전부 ⊕ fully 완전히
entirely unexpected 완전히 예기치 못한

especially 특히 ⊕ specifically 특별히, 구체적으로
love music, especially classical 음악, 특히 클래식을 좋아하다

exclusively 오로지, 독점적으로 ⊕ solely 오로지, 단지
The event is exclusively for invited guests.
그 행사는 초대된 손님들만을 위한 것이다.

immediately 즉시
evacuate the office immediately 즉시 사무실을 떠나다

incidentally 부수적으로, 우연히
incidentally discovered 우연히 발견된

increasingly 점점 더, 갈수록 더
become increasingly popular 점점 더 인기가 있다

initially 처음에 ⊕ at first 처음에
Initially, I was hesitant to try the new restaurant.
처음에 나는 새로운 식당을 시도하는 것을 망설였다.

primarily 주로 vs. **largely** 주로
• primarily: 주된 원인과 중심적인 측면을 강조
• largely: 대부분을 차지하고 영향을 미치는 것을 강조
The success is primarily due to the innovative product design. 성공은 주로 혁신적인 제품 디자인 덕이다.
Her contribution was largely acknowledged.
그녀의 기여가 대체로 인정받았다.

PART 5

Directions: A word or phrase is missing in each of the sentences below. Four answer choices are given below each sentence. Select the best answer to complete the sentence and mark the letter (A), (B), (C), or (D).

1   Ms. Walsh wants to know ------- the availability of seats and the price of airfare to Los Angeles on Friday morning.

   (A) both
   (B) whether
   (C) never
   (D) either

2   Thorough market research is ------- in order for Dunlap Motors to formulate a well-informed international expansion strategy.

   (A) necessity
   (B) necessary
   (C) necessarily
   (D) necessitate

3   Once completed, the new highway will significantly reduce commuting time and ------- traffic congestion in the city.

   (A) alleviate
   (B) alleviating
   (C) alleviation
   (D) alleviated

4   ------- interns demonstrated exceptional dedication and proficiency throughout the project and contributed to its successful completion.

   (A) Now
   (B) Every
   (C) Once
   (D) Those

5   ------- the competition was fierce, our team still managed to secure the top position in the industry.

   (A) Nevertheless
   (B) Even though
   (C) Whether
   (D) So that

6   The Art Welch Foundation wishes to extend our deepest appreciation to the volunteers for their ------- to the preparations for this fundraising event.

   (A) professions
   (B) instructions
   (C) contributions
   (D) occupations

7 ------- Prime Burger's delivery service is efficient and quick, its pricing surpasses that of other local eateries.

(A) Despite
(B) In spite
(C) While
(D) However

8 The company's revenue ------- increased by 15% in the last quarter, according to the recently published financial statements.

(A) conventionally
(B) domestically
(C) thoughtfully
(D) reportedly

9 The artist created a masterpiece ------- discarded materials, proving his exceptional creativity and resourcefulness.

(A) out
(B) onto
(C) from
(D) up

10 It was rather surprising ------- the proposal was put forward by Mr. Harry, who recently became a member of the team.

(A) while
(B) however
(C) that
(D) whether

11 The requested documents must be reviewed and a response provided ------- two weeks of their receipt.

(A) by
(B) throughout
(C) about
(D) within

12 All team members were present for the meeting ------- Mr. Larsen, who had a prior engagement with clients.

(A) whereas
(B) likewise
(C) except for
(D) along with

13 Based on the current market trends, the company's profits will ------- experience a positive upturn in the coming quarter.

(A) originally
(B) likely
(C) tightly
(D) haltingly

14 ------- the challenges posed by the global recession, the company successfully launched a new product line and maintained its market share.

(A) Nevertheless
(B) As though
(C) Notwithstanding
(D) Aside from

15 After completing his studies at the university, Eckert decided to pursue his career opportunities -------, ultimately relocating to New York City.

(A) marginally
(B) beyond
(C) evidently
(D) elsewhere

PART 6

Directions: Read the text below. A word, phrase, or sentence is missing in parts of the text. Four answer choices for each question are given below the text. Select the best answer to complete the text and mark the letter (A), (B), (C), or (D).

Questions 16-19 refer to the following the article.

Art Exhibition Inspires Environmental Awareness

In recent decades, artists have ------- used their work to highlight the urgency of addressing the
16.
climate crisis. This year, exhibitions ------- Europe continue to show how art can center around
17.
climate change and the environment.

Among the environmentally conscious exhibitions is a significant one called "Back to Earth." -------.
18.
Running from May 10 to June 13, this event gathers leading contemporary artists to explore how
humans connect with nature and tackle the challenges we encounter.

Stacey Krolak, Montrose Gallery's curator, shares, "Join us to rethink how art and environmentalism
-------."
19.

16 (A) increasingly
    (B) sequentially
    (C) expectedly
    (D) regrettably

17 (A) apart from
    (B) among
    (C) across
    (D) along

18 (A) The loss of natural environments is the biggest threat to us.
    (B) The gallery welcomes everyone to experience art.
    (C) This is currently taking place at London's Montrose Gallery.
    (D) We have plenty of interesting cultural events going on.

19 (A) collaborating
    (B) to collaborate
    (C) collaborate
    (D) collaboratively

228

Questions 20-23 refer to the following letter.

Shena Korn

1880 Camelback Road

Suite 310, Scottsdale, AZ

84522

Dear Ms. Korn,

Thank you for purchasing your new four-door refrigerator from Smart Way's online store. ------- **20.** Smart Way, we are fully dedicated to ensuring customer satisfaction, which is why we provide all our customers with a ------- **21.** product warranty. We are confident that our warranty offers coverage far superior to what is provided by any ------- **22.** appliance shops. -------. **23.** During this time, you are eligible to receive free repair services. If you have any questions, please don't hesitate to contact our customer support team at 202-555-2323.

Kind regards,

Jason Button

Customer Support

---

20 (A) With
　　(B) At
　　(C) Under
　　(D) On

21 (A) subsequent
　　(B) comprehensive
　　(C) incompatible
　　(D) successive

22 (A) each
　　(B) their
　　(C) these
　　(D) other

23 (A) You will receive your refrigerator within five business days.
　　(B) Please have your warranty card and unit number ready.
　　(C) We will send the brochure of our new products upon request.
　　(D) The warranty expires two years after the date of purchase.

PART 7

Directions: In this part you will read a selection of texts. The text or set of texts is followed by several questions. Select the best answer for each question and mark the letter (A), (B), (C), or (D).

Questions 24-27 refer to the following online chat discussion.

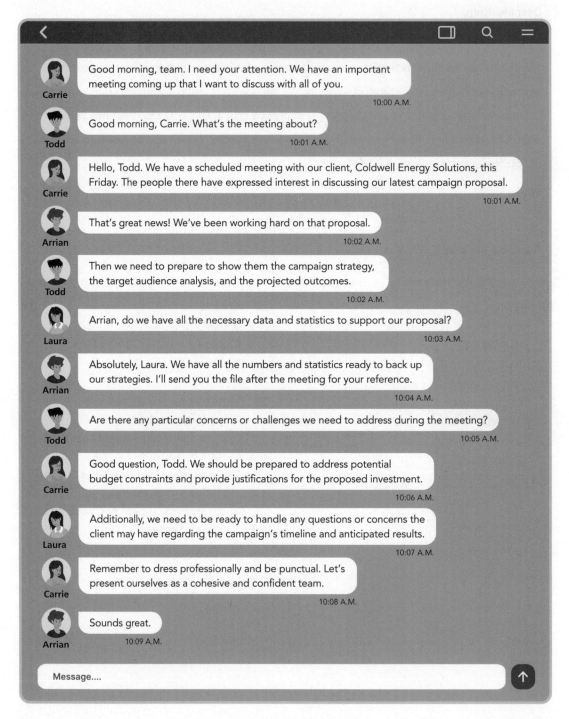

Carrie Good morning, team. I need your attention. We have an important meeting coming up that I want to discuss with all of you.
10:00 A.M.

Todd Good morning, Carrie. What's the meeting about?
10:01 A.M.

Carrie Hello, Todd. We have a scheduled meeting with our client, Coldwell Energy Solutions, this Friday. The people there have expressed interest in discussing our latest campaign proposal.
10:01 A.M.

Arrian That's great news! We've been working hard on that proposal.
10:02 A.M.

Todd Then we need to prepare to show them the campaign strategy, the target audience analysis, and the projected outcomes.
10:02 A.M.

Laura Arrian, do we have all the necessary data and statistics to support our proposal?
10:03 A.M.

Arrian Absolutely, Laura. We have all the numbers and statistics ready to back up our strategies. I'll send you the file after the meeting for your reference.
10:04 A.M.

Todd Are there any particular concerns or challenges we need to address during the meeting?
10:05 A.M.

Carrie Good question, Todd. We should be prepared to address potential budget constraints and provide justifications for the proposed investment.
10:06 A.M.

Laura Additionally, we need to be ready to handle any questions or concerns the client may have regarding the campaign's timeline and anticipated results.
10:07 A.M.

Carrie Remember to dress professionally and be punctual. Let's present ourselves as a cohesive and confident team.
10:08 A.M.

Arrian Sounds great.
10:09 A.M.

Message....

24 At what kind of company does Carrie most likely work?

(A) A Web design company

(B) An advertising agency

(C) An accounting firm

(D) An investment company

25 What do the writers have to do by Friday?

(A) They have to produce an advertisement.

(B) They have to decide where to invest.

(C) They have to tackle budget limitations.

(D) They have to revise the original strategies.

26 What did Carrie NOT ask her team to do?

(A) Wear appropriate clothing

(B) Demonstrate confidence to a customer

(C) Forward her some documents

(D) Be on time for a meeting

27 At 10:06 A.M., what does Carrie mean when she writes, "Good question, Todd"?

(A) She wants to discuss potential difficulties.

(B) She wants to respond to customer complaints.

(C) She wants Todd to lead the Friday meeting.

(D) She wants to review the outcome of the advertisement.

Job Openings

Applebee Steakhouse, 22906 Bothell Everett Hwy, Bothell, WA 98021

Applebee Steakhouse, recognized as *Gourmet Road* Magazine's Choice Restaurant of the Year, understands that it is our employees who truly make a difference. We are seeking enthusiastic and hardworking individuals to join our team.

Host
This position is ideal for someone with excellent communication skills and an outgoing personality. The successful candidate will oversee restaurant reservations, greet and accompany guests to their tables, and monitor the flow of seating. This role involves evening shifts from Fridays through Sundays.

Server
The chosen applicant will be responsible for serving food and beverages as well as ensuring guest satisfaction by continuously attending to their needs. Previous experience is preferred but not required. The availability required for this position is Wednesday through Saturday from 10:00 A.M. to 5:00 P.M.

Cashier
The selected individual will handle payment transactions, issue receipts, verify the accuracy of guest checks, and calculate the restaurant's revenue at the end of each night. This position is available on Fridays and Saturdays from 5:00 P.M. to 9:00 P.M.

Cook Helper
In this role, our culinary team focuses on combining modern techniques with seasonal ingredients sourced from various regions. Basic knowledge of food preparation is necessary for this position. The working hours are 25 per week from Mondays to Thursdays.

Applebee Steakhouse offers competitive compensation to acknowledge our staff's hard work. In addition to a high hourly wage, our employees are eligible for quarterly performance bonuses. Staff members also receive a 30-percent discount on all menu items. If you are interested, please contact Susan Reynolds, the restaurant manager, at susanreynolds@applebees.com no later than March 31.

To:	Susan Reynolds <susanreynolds@applebees.com>
From:	Allen Gray <allen89@worldnet.com>
Date:	March 17
Subject:	Application
Attachment:	résumé

Dear Ms. Reynolds,

I am writing to express my interest in joining your restaurant as either a host or a server. I have relevant experience in both roles and believe that I can bring value to your establishment. I have attached my résumé for your reference.

I wanted to inform you that I am currently attending classes from Monday through Wednesday, but I am available to dedicate my time to the restaurant outside of those hours. Furthermore, I would appreciate it if you could provide information regarding the hourly wages for both positions. Thank you for considering my application. I look forward to hearing from you soon.

Best regards,

Allen Gray

28 What can be inferred about the advertised jobs?

(A) They require working at multiple branches.
(B) They have a wide range of working hours.
(C) They demand relevant experience in the field.
(D) They need expertise of food preparation.

29 According to the advertisement, what is NOT indicated as a role of a cashier?

(A) Handling payment transactions
(B) Examining the validity of checks
(C) Checking the restaurant's revenue
(D) Managing seating arrangements

30 What benefit is mentioned in the advertisement for successful candidates?

(A) Medical insurance coverage
(B) Performance incentives
(C) Free meals during shifts
(D) Paid vacation days

31 In which position is Mr. Gray most likely to be employed?

(A) Host
(B) Server
(C) Cashier
(D) Cook helper

32 In the e-mail, what does Mr. Gray inquire about?

(A) The opening and closing hours of the restaurant
(B) When she can be contacted for interviews
(C) Whether training sessions are provided or not
(D) How much the salary would be for two jobs

10 명사절과 형용사절

명사절은 문장에서 **주어, 목적어, 보어** 역할을 하며, 형용사절은 **명사 뒤에서 명사를 수식**한다. 이들이 포함된 문장은 구조가 복잡하고 길어질 수 있으므로, 각각의 문법적 특징을 잘 알아 두어야 한다.

> **오늘의 학습 POINT**
>
> **POINT 1** 의문사와 that은 **명사절 접속사와 형용사절 접속사** 역할을 한다.
> **POINT 2** 다양하게 사용되는 접속사 that의 용법을 정리해 두어야 한다.
> **POINT 3** **관계대명사**는 앞의 명사를 수식하는 **형용사절**을 이끈다.

POINT 1 의문사와 that은 명사절 접속사와 형용사절 접속사 역할을 한다.

❶ 명사절과 형용사절의 역할

❶ **명사절 접속사**: 문장에서 주어, 목적어, 보어 등 명사 역할을 하는 절 앞에 쓰인다.

She <u>asked</u> **where the nearest grocery store is located**.
그녀는 가장 가까운 식료품점이 어디에 있는지 물었다. [where가 이끄는 절이 ask의 목적어 역할]

❷ **형용사절 접속사**: 명사 뒤에서 그 명사를 수식하는 절을 이끈다.

The park **where we had our picnic last weekend** is a beautiful place with a serene lake.
지난 주말에 소풍을 갔던 공원은 고요한 호수가 있는 아름다운 곳이다. [where가 이끄는 절이 the park를 수식]

> **📝 PRACTICE 1-2** 아래 문장에서 명사절 접속사에는 ○, 형용사절 접속사에는 △표시를 하세요.　정답 p.129
>
> **1** That he was able to complete the marathon despite the challenging weather conditions was truly impressive.
> **2** The job that she applied for required extensive experience in project management.

❷ 명사절 접속사의 종류

❶ **that**: 완전한 절 앞에 쓰이며, 주로 확실한 사실을 설명하는 절을 이끈다.

Everyone knows **that** the sun rises in the east and sets in the west.
해가 동쪽에서 떠서 서쪽으로 진다는 사실을 모두 알고 있다.

❷ **if / whether**: 완전한 절 앞에 쓰이며, 주로 결정되지 않은 일을 의미하는 절을 이끈다.

Nobody knows **if** the concert will be canceled due to the thunderstorm.
폭풍우 때문에 콘서트가 취소될 여부는 아무도 모른다.

cf. whether 뒤에는 or not이 올 수 있지만, if 뒤에는 or not이 올 수 없다.

③ what, which, who, whom: 불완전한 절 앞에 쓰이며, 문장에서 주어, 목적어, 보어 역할을 한다.

As she looked at the gift on her doorstep, she couldn't help wondering **who** had left it there.
그녀는 문 앞에 있는 선물을 보며, 거기에 누가 놓아 둔 것인지 궁금해 하지 않을 수 없었다.

④ when, where, why: 완전한 절 앞에 쓰인다.

Waiting at the café, she was constantly wondering **when** he would show up.
카페에서 기다리면서, 그녀는 그가 언제 나타날지 계속 궁금해 했다.

⑤ how: '어떻게'라는 의미로 '방법'과 관련된 의미 앞에 쓰이면 「주어 + 동사 + 목적어/보어」 형태의 완전한 절을 이끈다. 반면에, '얼마나'라는 의미인 경우에는 how 뒤에 형용사나 부사가 붙어서, 「how + 형용사/부사 + 주어 + 동사」와 같은 형태의 절이 된다.

The manual provided clear instructions on **how** it should be operated. [how = 어떻게]
매뉴얼은 그것이 어떻게 작동해야 하는지 명확한 지침을 제공했다.

Before attempting the challenging hike, she wasn't sure **how** hard it would be. [how = 얼마나]
도전적인 하이킹을 시도하기 전에, 그녀는 그것이 얼마나 어려울지 확신하지 못했다.

📝 PRACTICE 3-5 ▶ 괄호 안의 보기들 중에서 적절한 것을 고르세요. 정답 p.129

3 She asked (if / whether) or not the meeting had been rescheduled due to the heavy rain.

4 John needed to decide (what / when) he would schedule his job interview.

5 Seeing the finished artwork, she couldn't help but admire (how / why) impressive his talent was.

POINT 2 다양하게 사용되는 접속사 that의 용법을 정리해 두어야 한다.

관계사	특징
명사절 접속사 that	that절이 문장에서 주어, 목적어, 보어 역할을 한다. The important thing to remember <u>is</u> **that** consistency is key to achieving your fitness goals. 기억해야 할 중요한 점은 피트니스 목표를 달성하는 데 일관성이 중요하다는 것이다. 가주어 진주어 구문에서 that절이 진주어 역할을 한다. <u>It</u> is essential **that** you follow the safety guidelines when operating heavy machinery to prevent accidents. 중장비를 운전할 때는 사고 예방을 위해 안전수칙을 지키는 것이 중요하다. that절은 앞의 명사와 동격을 이룬다. I know <u>the fact</u> **that** he's been working diligently on this project for months. 나는 그가 이 프로젝트에 몇 달 동안 열심히 노력해왔다는 사실을 알고 있다. **e.g.** the news that (~라는 소식), the subject that (~라는 주제), the idea that (~라는 생각)
형용사절 접속사 that	that이 명사 뒤에 위치하여 관계대명사로 쓰일 경우, 이는 형용사 역할을 한다. The <u>place</u> **that** we visited last summer had stunning beaches and crystal-clear waters. 지난 여름 우리가 방문했던 곳은 멋진 해변들과 수정같이 맑은 바다가 있었다. **cf.** 명사절 접속사로 쓰일 때와 달리, 관계대명사 that 뒤에는 불완전한 절이 온다.

① 형용사절 접속사

관계사	특징
관계대명사	관계대명사 = 접속사 + 대명사 역할 This house is for sale, **and it** has four bedrooms. → This house **which** has four bedrooms is for sale. **cf.** 관계대명사절 앞에는 수식을 받는 명사가 오며, 이를 선행사라고 한다.
관계부사	관계부사 = 접속사 + 부사 역할 The park has a beautiful lake, **and** we will throw a party **there**. → The park **where** we will throw a party has a beautiful lake. **cf.** 관계부사절은 부사가 가리키는 명사 뒤에 오며, 이를 선행사라고 한다.
관계형용사	관계형용사 = 접속사 + 뒤에 오는 명사를 수식하는 형용사 역할 He has asked **which** restaurant is reserved for the company banquet.

① 관계대명사

종류	사람	사물	사람, 사물
주격	who	which	that
목적격	whom, who	which	that
소유격	whose	whose, of which	×

● **주격 관계대명사**: 선행사 + who / which / that + 동사 + 목적어/보어
관계대명사 절의 주어 역할을 하므로 뒤에 동사가 온다.

She wanted to talk with a manager **who** is in charge of customer complaints.
그녀는 고객 불만 사항을 담당하는 관리자와 이야기하고 싶었다.

● **목적격 관계대명사**: 선행사 + whom / who / which / that + 주어 + 타동사(혹은 자동사 + 전치사)
관계대명사절의 목적어를 대신하므로 뒤에 목적어가 생략된 불완전한 절이 온다.

I spoke to the person **whom** you recommended for the job.
나는 당신이 그 직무에 추천한 사람과 이야기를 나누었다.

● **소유격 관계대명사**: 선행사 + whose / of which + 완전한 절
관계대명사절에서 소유격 대명사의 역할을 할 뿐이므로 뒤에 완전한 절이 온다.

She is the student **whose** project impressed the entire class.
그녀는 학급 전체에 깊은 인상을 준 프로젝트를 진행한 학생이다.

cf. 소유격 관계대명사 뒤에 오는 명사가 주어인 경우 명사 앞에 관사가 오지 않는다.

📝 PRACTICE 6-7 괄호 안의 보기들 중에서 적절한 것을 고르세요. 정답 p.129

6 The house, (whose / which) windows were shattered by the storm, needed extensive repairs.

7 I visited the city (that / where) never sleeps last summer, and it was an unforgettable experience.

❷ 관계부사

선행사	관계부사	전치사 + 관계대명사
시간 (day, month, time, summer 등)	when	at / on / in which
장소 (place, house, room, city 등)	where	at / on / in / to which
이유 (reason)	why	for which
방법 (way)	how	in which

- 선행사 + 관계부사 + 완전한 절 = 선행사 + 전치사 + 관계대명사 + 불완전한 절

The town **where** she lives is by the river. 그녀가 살고 있는 도시는 강변에 있다.
→ The town **in which** she lives is by the river. (= The town **which** she lives **in** is by the river.)

cf. 관계부사는 관계부사절에서 부사를 대신할 뿐이므로, 뒤에 완전한 절이 온다.

❸ 관계형용사: 관계대명사가 명사 앞에서 명사를 수식하는 형용사 역할과 접속사 역할을 같이 한다.

Tom and Katie can't decide **what** color they should choose for the corporate office's interior.
톰과 케이티는 회사 사무실 내부에 어떤 색상을 선택해야 할지 결정하지 못한다.

❹ 관계대명사의 생략

- **주격 관계대명사의 생략**: 관계대명사가 생략되면 뒤의 동사가 분사로 바뀐다.

Any employee **who requests** time off should follow the formal procedure.
→ Any employee **requesting** time off should follow the formal procedure.
휴가를 신청하는 전 직원은 공식 절차를 따라야 한다.

- **목적격 관계대명사의 생략**: 목적격 관계대명사는 생략이 가능하다. (단, 목적격 관계대명사 앞에 전치사가 있으면 생략할 수 없다.)

He found the book **which** he had been searching for on the top shelf.
→ He found **the book he had been searching for** on the top shelf.
그는 찾고 있던 책을 맨 위 선반에서 찾았다.

❷ 복합관계사

❶ 복합관계대명사: 「관계대명사 + ever」 형태로서, 명사절과 부사절을 이끈다.

Whoever arrives first at the meeting should set up the presentation equipment.
회의에 먼저 도착한 사람이 프레젠테이션 장비를 설치해야 한다. [whoever + 절 = 주어 역할]

The award will go to **whomever the committee deems the most deserving**.
상은 위원회가 가장 자격이 있다고 여기는 사람에게 주어질 것이다. [whomever + 절 = 전치사의 목적어 역할]

Whosever job it is to clean the breakroom, please ensure it's done by the end of the day.
휴게실 청소 일을 맡은 사람은, 오늘까지 일을 마쳐 주세요. [whosever + 완전한 절 = 부사 역할]

❷ 복합관계부사: 「관계부사 + ever」 형태로서, 부사절을 이끈다.

Kate is always welcome to visit us **wherever she travels**.
케이트가 어디를 여행하든 우리를 방문하는 것을 환영한다. [wherever + 완전한 절]

However hard he tried, he couldn't lift the crate.
그가 아무리 노력해도, 그는 상자를 들지 못했다. [however + 형용사/부사 + 주어 + 동사]

literally 말그대로, 문자 그대로
There were literally thousands of people at the concert. 콘서트에는 말그대로 수천 명의 사람들이 있었다.

moderately 중간 정도로, 적당히
🔄 reasonably 꽤, 합리적으로
moderately successful marketing 어느 정도 성공적인 마케팅

mutually 상호간에
a mutually beneficial relationship 서로 득이 되는 관계

necessarily 어쩔 수 없이, 필연적으로
Studying longer doesn't necessarily lead to higher grades. 더 오래 공부하는 것이 꼭 더 높은 성적을 내는 것은 아니다.

occasionally 때때로, 가끔
occasionally visit the place 때때로 그 장소를 방문하다

otherwise 그렇지 않으면; (~와는) 다르게, 달리
The weather was pleasant; otherwise, we would have canceled the picnic.
날씨가 좋지 않았다면, 소풍을 취소했을 것이다.

particularly 특히, 특별히 🔄 especially 특별히
Traffic was heavy, particularly in the city center.
특히 도심에서의 교통이 혼잡했다.

periodically 주기적으로 🔄 regularly 정기적으로
a list updated periodically 주기적으로 업데이트되는 목록

precisely 바로, 꼭, 정확히 🔄 exactly 정확히
arrived precisely on time 정확히 제시간에 도착하다

practically 사실상, 거의
The shop is practically empty. 그 상점은 사실상 텅 비었다.

previously 이전에
The building was previously used as a theater.
그 건물은 이전에는 극장으로 사용되었다.

probably 아마
He told me that he probably wouldn't come.
그는 아마 오지 않을 것 같다고 나에게 말했다.

promptly 지체없이
promptly at ten o'clock 10시 정각에

properly 제대로, 적절히
properly handled and cooked 적절히 처리되고 조리된

markedly 현저하게 vs. **prominently** 눈에 띄게
Sales have risen markedly. 매출이 현저히 올랐다.
The painting is prominently displayed.
그림이 눈에 띄게 전시되었다.

rarely 드물게
She rarely misses her morning yoga routine.
그녀는 아침 요가 루틴을 거의 놓치지 않는다.

readily 손쉽게, 순조롭게
The ingredients are readily available.
그 재료들은 쉽게 구할 수 있다.

relatively 상대적으로, 비교적
relatively easy to understand 이해하기 비교적 쉬운

remarkably 현저하게, 몹시 🔄 noticeably 눈에 띄게
remarkably good condition 몹시 좋은 상태

repeatedly 되풀이하여, 여러 차례
practice it repeatedly 반복적으로 연습하다

separately 따로, 개별적으로
pay for each item separately
각 항목에 대해 개별적으로 지불하다

significantly 상당히, 크게, 중요하게
Profits have increased significantly this year.
올해는 이익이 크게 늘었다.

simultaneously 동시에
We have multiple projects going on simultaneously.
우리는 동시에 진행되고 있는 여러 프로젝트가 있다.

somewhat 어느 정도, 약간, 다소
somewhat remote from reality 다소 현실과 동떨어진

specifically 명확하게, 특별히
specifically designed for children
어린이를 위해 특별히 고안된

subsequently 그 뒤에, 나중에
After the rain stopped, the sun came out subsequently. 비가 그친 뒤, 뒤이어 해가 나왔다.

temporarily 임시로, 일시적으로
temporarily out of stock 일시 품절된

thoroughly 철저히, 대단히
read the instructions thoroughly 설명서를 정독하다

typically 보통, 일반적으로, 전형적으로
He typically wakes up at 7:00. 그는 보통 7시에 일어난다.

unanimously 만장일치로 vs. **anonymously** 익명으로
unanimously agree 만장일치로 동의하다
make comments anonymously 익명으로 견해를 밝히다

PART 5

Directions: A word or phrase is missing in each of the sentences below. Four answer choices are given below each sentence. Select the best answer to complete the sentence and mark the letter (A), (B), (C), or (D).

1 Architects at George Green Construction are known for skillfully ------- modern architectural trends into old-style buildings.

(A) incorporates
(B) incorporated
(C) incorporation
(D) incorporating

2 The tenth New Orleans Jazz Festival will feature many ------- musicians from across the nation.

(A) accomplish
(B) accomplishing
(C) accomplished
(D) accomplishment

3 Payton Engineering's management is undecided as to ------- or not to invest more resources in research and development currently.

(A) either
(B) whether
(C) what
(D) that

4 It is Inaba Bank's policy ------- all vacation requests should be approved with a minimum of two weeks' advance notice.

(A) might
(B) that
(C) along with
(D) to

5 All the guest speakers ------- the Ernest Future Energy Foundation invites will be offered flights to San Diego and accommodations for two nights.

(A) while
(B) whom
(C) whose
(D) when

6 Those ------- in our products can obtain more detailed information on our Web site at www.baldinijewelry.com.

(A) are interested
(B) interested
(C) who interested
(D) be interesting

7 When asked ------- Mitch Rice is considering selling his company, he declined to comment to reporters.

(A) for

(B) if

(C) about

(D) what

8 The new compact electric car from Miller Motors won this year's design innovation prize for its ------- design.

(A) uneasy

(B) rigorous

(C) temporary

(D) unique

9 Now, Keden Furniture products can be shipped ------- from the warehouse to customers for faster delivery.

(A) thoroughly

(B) directly

(C) evidently

(D) rarely

10 Charman Logistics has recently ------- innovative approaches to dominate a niche market.

(A) estimated

(B) compromised

(C) presided

(D) implemented

11 Employees ------- sales records show an increase of more than fifteen percent compared to the previous month are eligible to receive a bonus.

(A) who

(B) whom

(C) whose

(D) that

12 Her performance at the piano recital was truly outstanding, and everyone in the audience couldn't help but comment on how ------- her skills were.

(A) impressive

(B) impressed

(C) impressively

(D) impression

13 He couldn't decide ------- to take his vacation as there were so many exciting and affordable travel options to consider.

(A) what

(B) through

(C) if

(D) when

14 Victoria Kitchenware plans to open at least five additional retail ------- in Washington and Oregon by the end of the year.

(A) appliances

(B) vacancies

(C) locations

(D) designs

15 The cost of arranging next Friday's company function will be approximately $8,500 ------- a catering charge of $3,500.

(A) whatever

(B) in addition

(C) plus

(D) how much

PART 6

Directions: Read the text below. A word, phrase, or sentence is missing in parts of the text. Four answer choices for each question are given below the text. Select the best answer to complete the text and mark the letter (A), (B), (C), or (D).

Questions 16-19 refer to the following letter.

Dear Ms. McLean,

I want to express my sincere gratitude for extending a job offer that ------- at the Union Job Fair
16.
last Thursday. After careful consideration, I regret to inform you that I must decline your generous

offer. ------- you explained about the role of the position and the benefits your company is offering
17.
was very impressive. -------. The job aligns more closely with my career aspirations by focusing on
18.
customer service management rather than the technical aspects.

It was a genuine pleasure meeting you, and I hope our paths cross again ------- different
19.
circumstances. I wish you continued success in your endeavors.

Best regards,

Daniel Flores

16 (A) makes
    (B) have made
    (C) was made
    (D) are making

17 (A) That
    (B) What
    (C) When
    (D) So that

18 (A) I require additional information regarding the job.
    (B) Please kindly review the résumé attached to this e-mail.
    (C) However, I have decided to pursue another opportunity.
    (D) The medical and dental benefits are exceptionally appealing.

19 (A) under
    (B) by far
    (C) except
    (D) wherever

Questions 20-23 refer to the following letter.

Dear Valued Customers,

------- Friday, April 27, the Murphy Furniture Maker Wisconsin branch will be relocating to a
  20.

spacious new facility within the Stevens Point Building at 2725 Church St, Stevens Point, WI,

54481. Please take note of our new telephone number: (715) 555-7500.

------- to mark this exciting relocation, we are delighted to offer exclusive discounts on our
  21.

entire product range. -------. You can find more details about our exquisite offerings in the
      22.

enclosed brochure. -------, for a comprehensive view of our products and to explore our ongoing
     23.

promotions, please visit our Web site at www.murphyfurniture.com.

We sincerely appreciate your continued support, and we look forward to serving you better in our

new location.

---

20 (A) For
   (B) As of
   (C) When
   (D) Prior

21 (A) Whether
   (B) How
   (C) So that
   (D) In order

22 (A) We are pleased to offer you a discounted
     shipping rate.
   (B) You can find the brochures displayed at
     the front desk.
   (C) We extend an invitation to join us at the
     grand opening.
   (D) This special offer is valid until the end of
     the month.

23 (A) Subsequently
   (B) Accordingly
   (C) Additionally
   (D) In other words

Directions: In this part you will read a selection of texts. The text or set of texts is followed by several questions. Select the best answer for each question and mark the letter (A), (B), (C), or (D).

Questions 24-26 refer to the following advertisement.

Shrewsbury Well-Being Center (SWBC)

Conveniently located just a 15-minute drive from downtown Bristol with a picturesque view of Lake Buckeye, the SWBC has become a popular destination in the community for people interested in leisure, exercise, and relaxation. Our center offers a diverse range of rejuvenating experiences, such as yoga, meditation, fitness, and cycling classes, and indulgent massages at our modern spa.

We understand the demands of our busy lives, where work and family commitments often leave little time for self-care. That's why the SWBC is here to help. It's the perfect place for you to prioritize your wellbeing and to regain the energy needed to move forward. Our dedicated coordinators are available to assist you in creating a personalized plan tailored to your needs. Additionally, we offer an optional bath accessory package for an extra charge.

To reach our membership coordinator, please call us at (480) 543-7070 or send an e-mail to org.customerservice@swbc.org. For further information, please visit our Web site at www.swbc.org.

24 What is indicated about the SWBC?

(A) It is situated in the heart of downtown Bristol.

(B) Meditation classes are available as part of its offerings.

(C) It offers space for hosting gatherings and events.

(D) A cafeteria is conveniently located in its building.

25 What is available for an additional charge?

(A) A set of yoga classes

(B) Dining at a restaurant

(C) Access to the exercise facility

(D) Bathroom supplies

26 According to the advertisement, what service do the coordinators offer?

(A) Assisting in creating plans

(B) Providing relaxation techniques

(C) Organizing private parties

(D) Verifying room availability

Questions 27-31 refer to the following advertisement, Web page, and form.

The Brown Institute of Online Business Training

Make next year the year you finally start or grow your business by investing in yourself. At the Brown Institute of Online Business Training, we offer a range of online training sessions tailored to busy entrepreneurs, business owners, and those contemplating starting their own businesses. Join our online seminars and sessions, led by distinguished business experts, from the comfort of your home, office, or workspace. Our upcoming training sessions are designed to propel your business toward success! Secure your spot by registering online now as each seminar is limited to just 100 participants. For more information about our training sessions, please visit us at www.browninstitute.org or contact Nick Cooper at (415) 940-2911.

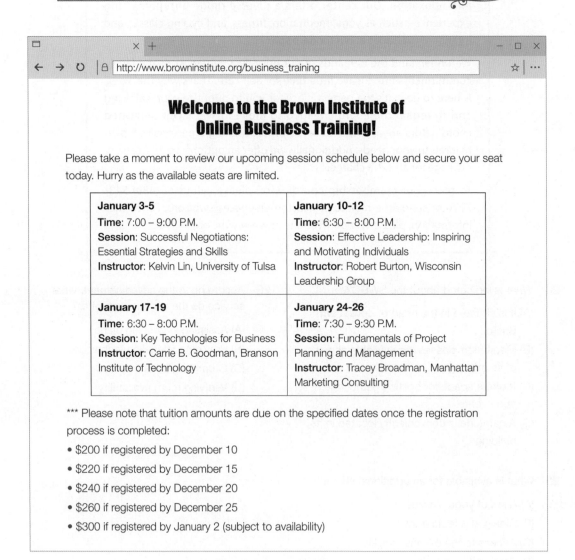

http://www.browninstitute.org/business_training

Welcome to the Brown Institute of Online Business Training!

Please take a moment to review our upcoming session schedule below and secure your seat today. Hurry as the available seats are limited.

January 3-5 **Time**: 7:00 – 9:00 P.M. **Session**: Successful Negotiations: Essential Strategies and Skills **Instructor**: Kelvin Lin, University of Tulsa	**January 10-12** **Time**: 6:30 – 8:00 P.M. **Session**: Effective Leadership: Inspiring and Motivating Individuals **Instructor**: Robert Burton, Wisconsin Leadership Group
January 17-19 **Time**: 6:30 – 8:00 P.M. **Session**: Key Technologies for Business **Instructor**: Carrie B. Goodman, Branson Institute of Technology	**January 24-26** **Time**: 7:30 – 9:30 P.M. **Session**: Fundamentals of Project Planning and Management **Instructor**: Tracey Broadman, Manhattan Marketing Consulting

*** Please note that tuition amounts are due on the specified dates once the registration process is completed:

- $200 if registered by December 10
- $220 if registered by December 15
- $240 if registered by December 20
- $260 if registered by December 25
- $300 if registered by January 2 (subject to availability)

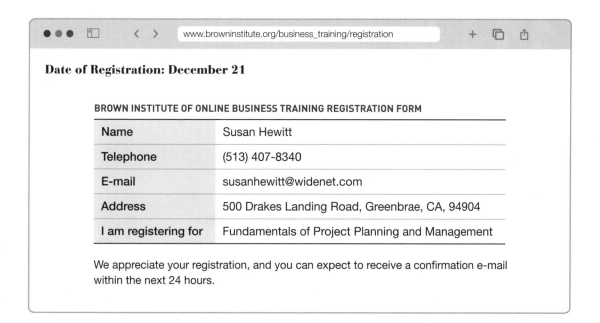

Date of Registration: December 21

BROWN INSTITUTE OF ONLINE BUSINESS TRAINING REGISTRATION FORM

Name	Susan Hewitt
Telephone	(513) 407-8340
E-mail	susanhewitt@widenet.com
Address	500 Drakes Landing Road, Greenbrae, CA, 94904
I am registering for	Fundamentals of Project Planning and Management

We appreciate your registration, and you can expect to receive a confirmation e-mail within the next 24 hours.

27 Who most likely is the advertisement for?

(A) Computer engineers
(B) University professors
(C) Language instructors
(D) Business owners

28 What is NOT suggested about the sessions?

(A) They will begin in December.
(B) They are led by well-known figures.
(C) They have limited seating capacity.
(D) They will all be held online.

29 When will the effective way to lead a team be addressed?

(A) January 3
(B) January 12
(C) January 18
(D) January 24

30 How much will Ms. Hewitt pay for the seminar?

(A) $220
(B) $240
(C) $260
(D) $300

31 Whose session is Ms. Hewitt registering for?

(A) Kelvin Lin
(B) Robert Burton
(C) Carrie B. Goodman
(D) Tracey Broadman

부사절은 주절의 앞이나 뒤에서 **주절을 수식**한다. 부사절을 이끄는 종속접속사는 그 의미가 다양하며, 접속사들을 비교하는 해석 문제, 유사한 의미의 전치사나 접속부사와 비교하는 문법 문제 등의 형태로 다양하게 출제된다.

오늘의 학습 POINT

POINT 1 부사절이 생략되어도 주절에는 영향을 주지 않는다.
POINT 2 시간의 부사절에서는 will을 사용하지 않는다.
POINT 3 접속부사는 접속사가 아닌 부사이다.

POINT 1 부사절이 생략되어도 주절에는 영향을 주지 않는다.

1 부사절의 역할과 특징

- 부사절은 수식하는 주절의 앞이나 뒤에 위치한다.

Although she had studied all night, she still felt unprepared for the exam. [부사절이 주절 앞에 오면 쉼표로 구분]
그녀는 밤새 공부했지만, 시험을 준비하지 못한 느낌이 들었다.

She has been working as a software engineer **since she graduated**.
그녀는 졸업한 이후로 소프트웨어 엔지니어로 근무하고 있다.

- 부사절을 이끄는 종속접속사 뒤에는 완전한 절이 온다.

Because they shared similar interests, they quickly became close friends. [Because 뒤에 완전한 절]
서로 비슷한 관심사를 공유했기 때문에, 그들은 빠르게 친한 친구가 되었다.

- 부사절은 주절을 수식할 뿐이므로 생략해도 주절에 아무런 영향을 주지 않는다.

(Since I moved to the city,) I've been exploring new restaurants every weekend.
(내가 이 도시로 이사한 이후로,) 나는 매주 새로운 식당을 찾아다니고 있다.

2 부사절을 이끄는 종속접속사의 종류

시간	when ~할 때	while ~하는 동안에	before ~하기 전에	after ~한 후에
	since ~이래로	as ~할 때, ~하면서	until ~할 때까지	once 일단 ~하면
	as soon as 하자마자	by the time ~할 때쯤이면		
조건	if, provided (that), providing (that) 만약 ~라면		unless ~하지 않는 한, ~이 아닌 한	
	as long as ~하는 한	given that ~을 고려하면	assuming (that) ~이라 가정하면	
	only if ~해야만	in case (that) ~한 경우에		
이유	because, since, as, now that ~이기 때문에			
양보	although, though, even though 비록 ~일지라도		even if ~라고 할지라도	
	while ~일지라도, 반면에	whereas ~한 반면에	whether or not ~인지 아닌지, ~이든 아니든	

1 (Although / Despite) it was raining heavily, they decided to go for a hike in the mountains.

2 (Because / Though) the restaurant was fully booked, we had to find an alternative place to eat.

POINT 2 시간의 부사절에서는 will을 사용하지 않는다.

1 주의해야 할 접속사

❶ **시간 부사절의 시제**: 시간의 부사절에서는 현재 시제가 미래 시제를 대신한다.

Once the contract **is signed**, the deal **will** be official. 계약이 체결되면 거래는 공식화될 것이다.

☑ **Further Point! 시간 부사절의 시제에 따른 주절의 시제**

시간 부사절의 시제	주절의 시제
현재 시제	현재 시제, 또는 미래 시제
과거 시제	과거 시제, 또는 과거완료 시제
과거완료 시제	과거 시제

> cf. Since (~ 이래로) 뒤에는 기준이 되는 과거 시점(과거 시제)이 오고, 주절에는 보통 완료 시제가 온다.

• 접속사 since + 과거 시제, 완료 시제

• 전치사 since + 과거 시점을 의미하는 명사, 완료 시제

Since I **passed** my driving test, **I have been driving** to work every day.
나는 운전 시험에 합격한 이후로 매일 운전해서 출근하고 있다.

❷ **before, after, until, since는 접속사와 전치사로 모두 사용할 수 있다.**

Before the sun rises, the city streets are calm and quiet, awaiting the bustle of another day.
해가 뜨기 전에, 도시의 거리는 고요하고 조용하여 또 다른 날의 분주함을 기다리고 있다. [접속사로 사용]

Before the invention of the Internet, people relied on libraries and encyclopedias for information.
인터넷의 발명 이전에, 사람들은 정보를 찾기 위해 도서관이나 백과사전에 의존했다. [전치사로 사용]

> cf.1 since가 '~이래로'라는 의미일 때는 접속사와 전치사로 모두 사용할 수 있다. 하지만 '~ 때문에'라는 의미일 때는 접속사로만 사용할 수 있다.

Since last summer, he has lost a lot of weight. 작년 여름 이후로, 그는 살이 많이 빠졌다. [전치사]

Since they finished their work early, they have time to relax. [접속사]
그들은 일을 일찍 마쳤기 때문에, 쉴 시간이 있다.

> cf.2 as가 접속사로 쓰이면 '~ 때문에', '~할 때', '~대로', '~하면' 등의 의미이며, 전치사로 쓰이면 '~로서'의 의미이다.

As a doctor, he was well respected for his expertise by the medical community. [전치사]
의사로서, 그는 그의 전문성으로 의료계에서 좋은 평가를 받았다.

As you receive the contract, please review it carefully. [접속사]
계약서를 받으면, 주의 깊게 검토해 주세요.

PRACTICE 3-4 괄호 안의 보기들 중에서 적절한 것을 고르세요.　　　정답 p.134

3 (Since / Because of) the heavy traffic, we arrived at the party much later than expected.

4 Ever since she started working from home, her productivity (increases / has increased).

❸ whether or not

whether는 명사절과 부사절을 모두 이끌 수 있다. 명사절의 경우 'or not'을 생략할 수 있지만, 부사절의 경우 'or not'을 생략할 수 없다.

- **명사절**: I'm not sure **whether** I should attend the meeting (or not). 나는 회의에 참석할지 말지 확실하지 않다.

- **부사절**: I'll support your decision **whether** it aligns with my own beliefs **or not**.
　　　　　내 의견과 일치하든 아니든, 나는 당신의 결정을 지지할 것이다.

PRACTICE 5-6 괄호 안의 보기들 중에서 적절한 것을 고르세요.　　　정답 p.134

5 Once you (will complete / complete) the registration process, you'll have access to all the features.

6 She decided to take the job offer (whether / although) it meant relocating to a new city.

❷ 부사절 접속사 + 분사구문

부사절 접속사 뒤의 주어가 생략되면 그 뒤의 동사는 분사가 된다.

Before you make a decision, it's important to weigh the pros and cons of your options.
→ **Before making a decision**, it's important to weigh the pros and cons of your options.
결정을 내리기 전에, 당신의 선택지의 장단점을 따져 보는 것이 중요하다.

❸ 현재분사 vs. 과거분사

주절의 주어와 분사와의 관계가 능동이면 현재분사구문, 수동이면 과거분사구문이 된다. 뒤에 목적어가 있으면 현재분사구문, 목적어가 없으면 과거분사구문을 선택한다. 단, 자동사에서 파생된 분사구문은 항상 현재분사구문이다.

The thunderstorm began just before sunset, **creating** a dramatic and eerie atmosphere.
일몰 직전에 천둥번개가 시작되어, 극적이고 으스스한 분위기를 만들었다. [thunderstorm과 creating이 능동 관계]

☑ **Further Point!** 부사절 접속사 뒤에 '주어 + be동사'가 생략되어 '형용사'나 '전치사 + 명사'가 올 수도 있다.

The police officer remained vigilant and alert **while** on duty, ensuring the safety of the neighborhood.
경찰관은 근무 중에 경계심을 유지하며, 지역의 안전을 확보했다. [while과 on duty 사이에 the police officer is가 생략]

PRACTICE 7-8 괄호 안의 보기들 중에서 적절한 것을 고르세요.　　　정답 p.134

7 Once (completing / completed), the new highway will significantly reduce travel times between the two cities.

8 (During / When) responsible for managing the project, she ensured that all tasks were completed within the budget.

① 접속부사의 특징

접속부사는 부사이기 때문에 문장의 앞, 중간, 끝 어디에든 위치할 수 있지만, 절과 절을 연결하는 역할을 할 수는 없다. 따라서, 접속부사는 비슷한 의미의 접속사와 비교되는 경우가 많다.

She studied diligently for the exam. **However**, she still found it quite challenging.
그녀는 시험을 위해 열심히 공부했다. 하지만, 여전히 상당히 어려웠다. [접속부사 however는 절과 절을 연결할 수 없음]
She still found it quite challenging **although** she studied diligently for the exam.
그녀는 시험을 위해 열심히 공부했지만, 여전히 상당히 어려웠다. [접속사 although는 절과 절을 연결할 수 있음]

② 접속부사의 종류

그럼에도 불구하고, 그러나	however, nevertheless, nonetheless, still	반대로, 반면에	contrarily, in contrast, on the contrary
따라서, 결과적으로	therefore, thus, consequently, accordingly, as a result, hence	사실상	in fact, indeed, actually
더욱이, 게다가	besides, furthermore, moreover, in addition	그 다음에, 그 후에	then, afterward(s), thereafter
그런데	in the meantime, meanwhile, by the way	예를 들어	for example, for instance
기타	otherwise 그렇지 않으면　　likewise 이와 같이　　on the other hand 한편 in other words 다시 말해서　　to that end 그 목적을 달성하기 위해서		

It was raining heavily. **Therefore**, they decided to postpone the outdoor event.
비가 많이 내렸다. 그래서, 그들은 야외 행사를 연기하기로 결정했다.

Please turn off the lights when you leave a room. **Otherwise**, it's a waste of energy.
방을 나갈 때 불을 끄세요. 그렇지 않으면, 에너지 낭비입니다.

PRACTICE 9-10　괄호 안의 보기들 중에서 적절한 것을 고르세요.　정답 p.134

9　He had to complete the assignment by the deadline. (Otherwise / Unless) he would face a penalty for a late submission.

10　The road was closed due to construction work, (so / therefore) we had to take a detour to reach our destination.

above all 무엇보다도 ⓤ noticeably 눈에 띄게
Above all, prioritize your health. 무엇보다도 건강을 우선시해라.

get along with ~와 잘 지내다 cf. along with ~와 함께
get along with my coworkers 동료들과 사이좋게 지내다

as a result of ~의 결과로서
As a result of his hard work, he received a promotion.
열심히 일한 결과, 그는 승진했다.

go into effect 효력을 발휘하다
The new policy will go into effect starting next
month. 새 정책은 다음달부터 시행된다.

aside from ~외에도 ⓤ apart from ~외에도
Aside from the main course, we have many delicious
appetizers. 메인 코스 외에도, 맛있는 전채 요리가 많다.

in accordance with ~에 따라서
complete the task in accordance with the guidelines
지침에 따라 임무를 완수하다

at most 기껏해야 cf. at least 적어도
the repairs to take two hours at most
기껏해야 두 시간 정도 걸리는 수리

in addition to ~뿐만 아니라
In addition to studying science, she also enjoys art
classes. 과학을 공부하는 것 외에도, 그녀는 미술 수업도 즐긴다.

at no cost 무료로
The event is open to the public at no cost.
이 행사는 대중에게 무료로 공개된다.

in advance of ~보다 앞서 cf. in advance 미리
submit your report in advance of the deadline
마감 기한 전에 보고서를 제출하다

at one's convenience ~가 편리한 때에
Please schedule the meeting at your convenience.
당신이 편리한 시간에 회의 일정을 잡으세요.

in business 영업 중인 cf. on business 업무 차, 업무로
He has been in business for over 20 years.
그는 20년 넘게 사업을 하고 있다.

at the latest 늦어도
The report must be submitted by Friday at the
latest. 보고서는 늦어도 금요일까지 제출되어야 한다.

in case of ~의 경우에
In case of an emergency, please dial 911.
비상시에는 911로 전화해 주세요.

be subject to ~하기 쉽다
The price may be subject to change. 가격은 변동될 수 있다.

in conjunction with ~와 협력해서
in conjunction with other departments 다른 부서와 협력하여

by means of ~에 의해서
We communicated by means of e-mail.
우리는 이메일을 통해서 연락했다.

in charge of ~을 담당하는
She is in charge of the Marketing Department.
그녀는 마케팅 부서를 책임지고 있다.

come up with 생각해내다
come up with a solution to this problem
이 문제의 해결 방안을 생각해내다

in compliance with ~에 따라서
in compliance with all relevant laws and regulations
모든 관련 법규를 준수하여

comparable with ~와 비교할 만한
Her skills are comparable with those of
professionals. 그녀의 기술은 전문가들의 기술에 필적할 만하다.

in comparison with ~와 비교하여
In comparison with last year, our sales have
increased. 작년과 비교하며, 우리의 매출이 늘었다.

compatible with ~와 호환되는
This software is compatible with the current system.
이 소프트웨어는 현재 시스템과 호환된다.

in conclusion 결론적으로
In conclusion, I believe this is the best.
결론적으로, 나는 이것이 최고라고 생각한다.

equivalent to ~에 맞먹는
This task is equivalent to the one you completed
last month. 이 작업은 당신이 지난달에 완료한 것과 동일하다.

in contrast to ~와 대조되는
In contrast to the sunny morning, the afternoon
turned cloudy. 화창한 아침과 달리, 오후는 흐려졌다.

for free 무료로
You can download the app for free.
앱을 무료로 다운로드할 수 있습니다.

in favor of ~을 찬성하여
The majority voted in favor of the new policy.
대다수가 새 정책에 찬성했다.

for the purpose of ~을 목적으로
We are meeting for the purpose of discussing the
project. 우리는 프로젝트에 대해 논의하기 위해서 만나는 것이다.

in general 일반적으로
In general, people tend to prefer warm weather.
일반적으로, 사람들은 따뜻한 날씨를 선호하는 경향이 있다.

PART 5

Directions: A word or phrase is missing in each of the sentences below. Four answer choices are given below each sentence. Select the best answer to complete the sentence and mark the letter (A), (B), (C), or (D).

1   The contents of this ------- may not necessarily align with the views or policies of Finance Today.

   (A) publishing
   (B) publication
   (C) publisher
   (D) publish

2   Langford Investment's employee training manual is ------- designed to place employee growth at the core of its mission.

   (A) deliberating
   (B) deliberation
   (C) deliberate
   (D) deliberately

3   Please contact your college, student organizations, and other campus programs ------- about additional scholarship opportunities.

   (A) have inquired
   (B) inquiring
   (C) to inquire
   (D) inquires

4   At the board meeting, discussions on ------- to focus on in order to maximize productivity are currently in progress.

   (A) how
   (B) what
   (C) when
   (D) where

5   Paul Warrin's three-month probationary period concludes at the end of this month, and he will work ------- a permanent employee starting next month.

   (A) as
   (B) since
   (C) once
   (D) of

6   ------- this year's classic concert in Swetland Park will be entirely free, we would greatly appreciate any contributions.

   (A) Equally
   (B) While
   (C) Except
   (D) Despite

7 ------- the new bridge has opened, traffic on Montano Bridge will flow much more smoothly than it does currently.

(A) Instead

(B) Once

(C) Especially

(D) As though

8 ------- airlines typically provide flights between major European cities at an average cost of $180.

(A) Sensitive

(B) Expense

(C) Pending

(D) Budget

9 ------- her acting career, world-famous star Paula Rose has ventured into music, with her debut single set to be released next week.

(A) By the time

(B) In addition to

(C) As far as

(D) In the event of

10 We kindly request that you present your health card when ------- in for each appointment, so please ensure it is valid and has not expired.

(A) checking

(B) check

(C) checks

(D) to check

11 If you receive ------- calls or messages, you can block the caller or sender's number by using your phone's built-in call rejection features.

(A) interested

(B) outstanding

(C) unwelcome

(D) interactive

12 Ernie Martin was able to meet last quarter's sales goal ------- recording, analyzing data, and revising customer service procedures.

(A) by

(B) under

(C) within

(D) toward

13 Due to budget constraints, Penn had to request modifications to the ------- marketing campaign plans from the project manager.

(A) inevitable

(B) occasional

(C) upcoming

(D) original

14 Mitch Rice, the executive chef of Savoria Bistro, is ------- responsible for overseeing and directing kitchen operations.

(A) gradually

(B) admiringly

(C) primarily

(D) hastily

15 ------- the unexpected budget cuts, the board of directors has decided to evaluate our financial priorities for the upcoming fiscal year.

(A) In spite of

(B) In lieu of

(C) In light of

(D) Just as

PART 6

Directions: Read the text below. A word, phrase, or sentence is missing in parts of the text. Four answer choices for each question are given below the text. Select the best answer to complete the text and mark the letter (A), (B), (C), or (D).

Questions 16-19 refer to the following letter.

Dear Ms. Baldini,

I'd like to express our heartfelt gratitude -------- Westbrook Furniture for the exceptional Web site
              16.
design you've created. The transformation of our Web site has exceeded our expectations, and the

positive response from our customers has been overwhelming. --------.
                         17.

We are thoroughly impressed with your work and would like to extend a request for your expertise

in designing our other family sites, -------- Westbrook Interiors and Westbrook Kitchen. To further
                       18.
discuss this matter, I would like to arrange a meeting at your convenience, preferably at your office.

Please let me know your -------- time for this meeting. You can reach me at 512-5800.
               19.

Thank you and best regards,

Michael Young

Westbrook Furniture

---

16 (A) in case of
    (B) in regard to
    (C) on behalf of
    (D) as a result of

17 (A) One of my colleagues highly praised your
        services.
    (B) It has also attracted many new clients to
        our business.
    (C) It is imperative that we change our office
        interior.
    (D) Our previous design received great
        acclaim from the public.

18 (A) urgently
    (B) recklessly
    (C) specifically
    (D) periodically

19 (A) preferring
    (B) prefer
    (C) preference
    (D) preferred

Concrete work is currently underway at Franklin Hall and North Merrick Hall and is ------- to
20.
continue throughout the spring. These buildings will serve the College of Engineering and Elmont
Polytechnic Institute, providing facilities for design studios, instructional areas, collaboration
spaces, and administrative offices. -------.
21.

Please anticipate increased truck activity in the ------- of Westbury Street and Uniondale Avenue
22.
due to ongoing construction, which will extend into the summer months. Consequently, we urge
pedestrians, cyclists, and motorists to ------- caution in the area and to adhere to all posted
23.
signage. For inquiries, kindly contact Matt Fuller, the project manager, at mattfuller@elmont.edu.

20 (A) schedule
(B) schedules
(C) scheduled
(D) scheduling

22 (A) vicinity
(B) duration
(C) fraction
(D) aspect

21 (A) Enhancing instructional spaces is
imperative.
(B) The administrative office is relocating to
Meridian Hall.
(C) The new offices are currently in the
construction phase.
(D) Moreover, they will serve as new campus
gateways.

23 (A) estimate
(B) exercise
(C) preside
(D) describe

PART 7

Directions: In this part you will read a selection of texts. The text or set of texts is followed by several questions. Select the best answer for each question and mark the letter (A), (B), (C), or (D).

Questions 24-26 refer to the following memo.

Retirement Announcement - Chief Curator of Collections Patrick Adams

We have some bittersweet news to share. After an incredible 40-year journey with the Nashville Natural History Museum (NNHM), our esteemed chief curator of collections, Patrick Adams, will be retiring. From his early days as an intern to his remarkable six-year role as chief curator, Mr. Adams has been dedicated to preserving Nashville's history in every way possible. He played a pivotal role in shaping the NNHM by developing exhibits, preserving valuable objects, and educating students and visitors through tours and lectures. His recently published book, *Nashville Filled with History*, is a testament to his four decades of research.

In recognition of his remarkable career, the NNHM board of directors has decided to present Mr. Adams with a lifetime achievement award. We'll be honoring him with a commemorative plaque at our year-end party this Friday. We invite all NNHM staff to stay for the reception following the ceremony to celebrate Mr. Adams and his contributions. If you'd like to leave a farewell message, please stop by Terry Watson's office to sign a photo album for him.

Mr. Adams' retirement signifies the end of an era, and while we bid him farewell, we also celebrate his legacy. His passion, knowledge, and dedication will be missed, but they will continue to inspire us.

Thank you, Patrick, for your outstanding service. We wish you a well-deserved and joyful retirement.

24 In what field does Mr. Adams work?

(A) Corporate education
(B) Historical archiving
(C) Wildlife conservation
(D) Urban development

25 What is true about Mr. Adams?

(A) He joined the NNHM six years ago.
(B) He teaches students at the university.
(C) He has written several books about history.
(D) He has cataloged numerous artifacts.

26 What will NOT be given to honor Mr. Adams?

(A) A plaque
(B) An award
(C) A biography
(D) A photo album

Questions 27-31 refer to the following Web page and e-mail.

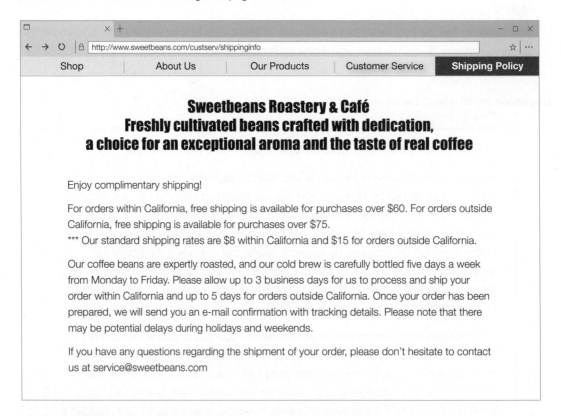

http://www.sweetbeans.com/custserv/shippinginfo

| Shop | About Us | Our Products | Customer Service | **Shipping Policy** |

Sweetbeans Roastery & Café
Freshly cultivated beans crafted with dedication,
a choice for an exceptional aroma and the taste of real coffee

Enjoy complimentary shipping!

For orders within California, free shipping is available for purchases over $60. For orders outside California, free shipping is available for purchases over $75.
*** Our standard shipping rates are $8 within California and $15 for orders outside California.

Our coffee beans are expertly roasted, and our cold brew is carefully bottled five days a week from Monday to Friday. Please allow up to 3 business days for us to process and ship your order within California and up to 5 days for orders outside California. Once your order has been prepared, we will send you an e-mail confirmation with tracking details. Please note that there may be potential delays during holidays and weekends.

If you have any questions regarding the shipment of your order, please don't hesitate to contact us at service@sweetbeans.com

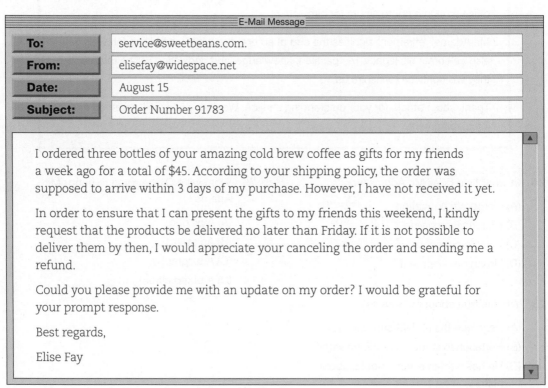

E-Mail Message

To:	service@sweetbeans.com.
From:	elisefay@widespace.net
Date:	August 15
Subject:	Order Number 91783

I ordered three bottles of your amazing cold brew coffee as gifts for my friends a week ago for a total of $45. According to your shipping policy, the order was supposed to arrive within 3 days of my purchase. However, I have not received it yet.

In order to ensure that I can present the gifts to my friends this weekend, I kindly request that the products be delivered no later than Friday. If it is not possible to deliver them by then, I would appreciate your canceling the order and sending me a refund.

Could you please provide me with an update on my order? I would be grateful for your prompt response.

Best regards,

Elise Fay

27 In the Web page, what is indicated about Sweetbeans Roastery & Café?

(A) It is open seven days a week.

(B) It offers a wide range of shipping rates.

(C) It has multiple locations across the country.

(D) It recently opened a store in California.

28 In the Web page, the word "process" in paragraph 2, line 2, is closest in meaning to

(A) handle

(B) develop

(C) expedite

(D) consult

29 What is the purpose of the e-mail?

(A) To place an order for a purchase

(B) To inquire about the types of coffee beans

(C) To report receiving the wrong product

(D) To check the current status of an order

30 What is the shipping fee for Ms. Fay's order?

(A) $0

(B) $8

(C) $15

(D) $45

31 In the e-mail, what is implied about Ms. Fay?

(A) She is a regular customer at the café.

(B) She is going to meet her friends this Friday.

(C) She has an inquiry regarding the shipping fee.

(D) She wants to receive a refund if necessary.

가정법은 출제 빈도가 낮은 편이지만 오답률이 높기 때문에 정확히 알아 두어야 한다. 비교급과 최상급 문제는 문장의 구조를 분석하고 자주 출제되는 유형을 공부해 둔다면 비교적 쉽게 정답을 고를 수 있다.

오늘의 학습 POINT

POINT 1 가정법의 시제를 확실하게 이해하고 암기해 두어야 한다.
POINT 2 평서문의 맨 앞에 should가 있으면, 「if + 주어 + should ~」로 해석한다.
POINT 3 that절의 동사가 「(should) 동사 원형」 형태로 쓰이는 경우를 알아 두자.
POINT 4 비교급 문제는 ① **형용사/부사 자리** ② **동반되는 수식어구**를 확인한다.

POINT 1 가정법의 시제를 확실하게 이해하고 암기해 두어야 한다.

1 가정법 미래

'만약 ~한다면, ~할 수 있을 것이다'라는 의미로, 미래에 대한 강한 의혹이나 가정을 나타낸다.

> If + 주어 + should + 동사 원형, 주어 + [will / can / should / would] + 동사 원형
> If + 주어 + should + 동사 원형, (please) 명령문

If you **should leave** Seoul tomorrow, I **will** at least **buy** you dinner tonight.
당신이 내일 서울을 떠나야 한다면, 적어도 오늘 저녁은 내가 사 주겠다.

2 가정법 현재

현재나 미래를 단순히 추측하고 기대하는 경우로, 현실 가능성이 있는 일에 주로 사용된다.

> If + 주어 + 현재 동사, 주어 + [will / can / may] + 동사 원형

If it **rains** tomorrow, we **will have to cancel** our picnic. 내일 비가 오면 소풍을 취소해야 할 것 같다.

cf. 시간/조건 부사절에서는 will을 사용하지 않으므로 if절에서는 보통 현재 시제가 미래 시제를 대신하여 사용된다.

3 가정법 과거

현재 상황과 반대되는 일이나 일어날 수 없는 상황을 가정할 때 쓰인다.

> If + 주어 + 과거 동사, 주어 + [would / should / could / might] + 동사 원형

If I **were** a professional singer, I **would perform** on stage every night.
내가 만약 프로 가수라면, 매일 밤 무대에 섰을 것이다.

→ 내가 현재 프로 가수가 아니라서, 무대에 서지 않는다는 의미.

cf. 가정법 과거 문장에서 be동사의 과거는 주어와 상관없이 were를 사용한다.

4 가정법 과거완료

과거의 일이라서 바꿀 수 없는 일을 반대로 가정할 때 사용된다.

> If + 주어 + 과거완료 동사, 주어 + [would / should / could / might] + have p.p.

If he **had visited** the museum last week, he **would have seen** some incredible art exhibits.
만약 그가 지난주에 박물관을 방문했더라면, 그는 놀라운 예술 전시회들을 보았을 것이다.
→ 그가 지난주에 박물관을 방문하지 않았기 때문에, 그는 놀라운 예술 전시회를 보지 못했다는 의미

5 혼합 가정법

if절은 과거 사실의 반대를, 주절은 현재 사실의 반대를 나타낼 때 사용된다.

> If + 주어 + 과거완료 동사, 주어 + [would / should / could / might] + 동사 원형

If I **had worked** on my time management skills, I **wouldn't be** so stressed right now.
내가 시간 관리에 힘썼다면, 지금 당장 스트레스를 많이 받지는 않을 것이다.
→ 과거에 시간 관리에 힘쓰지 않아서, 현재 스트레스를 많이 받고 있다는 의미

📝 PRACTICE 1-2 괄호 안의 보기들 중에서 적절한 것을 고르세요. 정답 p.139

1 If she (were / is) more confident in her abilities, she could achieve even greater success in her career.

2 If I had arrived at the airport earlier, I would (catch / have caught) my flight last night.

POINT 2 평서문의 맨 앞에 should가 있으면, 「if + 주어 + should ~」로 해석한다.

1 도치 문장의 형태

❶ 주어 + be동사 + 나머지 문장성분 → be동사 + 주어 + 나머지 문장성분

Hardly was the ink dry on the contract when they began discussing their future plans together.
계약서에 잉크가 마를 새도 없이 그들은 함께 미래의 계획에 대해 논의하기 시작했다.

❷ 주어 + 조동사 + 동사 원형 → 조동사 + 주어 + 동사 원형

Hardly can he resist the temptation of chocolate when it's right in front of him.
초콜릿이 그의 눈앞에 있을 때 그는 초콜릿의 유혹을 거의 참을 수 없을 정도였다.

❸ 주어 + 일반동사 + 나머지 문장성분 → do/does/did + 주어 + 동사 원형 + 나머지 문장성분

Hardly did she begin her presentation when the fire alarm went off, causing an evacuation of the building. 그녀가 발표를 시작한 직후에 화재 경보가 울려, 건물 대피 상황이 발생했다.

② 도치가 일어나는 문장

❶ 부정어가 문장의 맨 앞에 위치할 때, 뒤의 주어와 동사의 위치가 바뀐다.

Never <u>does she leave</u> for work without first enjoying a cup of her favorite coffee.
그녀는 자신이 좋아하는 커피를 꼭 마시고 출근한다.

> **cf.** 부정어의 예: not, never, few, little, seldom, rarely, hardly, not until, not only 등

❷ if가 생략되면 주어와 동사의 위치가 바뀐다.

가정법 미래	if + 주어 + should 동사 원형 → Should + 주어 + 동사 원형
가정법 과거	if + 주어 + were/과거 동사 → Were/Did + 주어
가정법 과거완료	if + 주어 + had p.p. → Had + 주어 + p.p.

If you should encounter any difficulties, call our 24/7 customer support hotline for assistance.
→ **Should you encounter** any difficulties, call our 24/7 customer support hotline for assistance.
어려움이 있을 경우 지원을 받으려면 24/7 고객 지원 핫라인으로 연락하세요. [가정법 미래]

If I were near your office, I would have dinner with you.
→ **Were I** near your office, I would have dinner with you.
내가 당신의 사무실 근처에 있다면, 당신과 저녁 식사를 할 텐데. [가정법 과거]

If you had known about the event earlier, you could have made arrangements to attend.
→ **Had you known** about the event earlier, you could have made arrangements to attend.
행사에 대해 미리 알고 있었더라면, 당신이 참석할 수 있도록 준비했을 것이다. [가정법 과거완료]

> **✏ PRACTICE 3-4** ◀ **괄호 안의 보기들 중에서 적절한 것을 고르세요.** 정답 p.139
>
> **3** (Would / Should) you have any questions or concerns, please feel free to contact our customer support team for assistance.
>
> **4** Had she asked for directions earlier, she wouldn't (get / have gotten) lost in an unfamiliar city.

POINT 3 ⟩ that절의 동사가 「(should) 동사 원형」 형태로 쓰이는 경우를 알아 두자.

❶ 요구/주장/제안의 동사 + that + 주어 + (should) 동사 원형

「요구, 주장, 제안의 동사」인 ask, require, request, suggest, recommend, demand, insist 뒤의 that절의 동사는 주어의 수에 상관없이 「(should) + 동사 원형」 형태가 된다.

We **suggested** that he <u>consider</u> taking a different approach to solve the problem.
우리는 그가 문제를 해결하기 위해 다른 접근 방식을 고려해 보는 것이 좋겠다고 제안했다.

② 형용사 "중요한, 필수적인, 의무적인" + that + 주어 + (should) 동사 원형

「중요한, 필수적인, 의무적인 등의 의미를 가진 형용사」인 important, essential, necessary, imperative, mandatory, compulsory 뒤의 that절의 동사는 주어의 수에 상관없이 「(should) + 동사 원형」 형태가 된다.

It is **imperative** that everyone <u>complete</u> the safety training before starting their new job.
모든 사람이 새로운 직무를 시작하기 전에 안전 교육을 이수하는 것은 필수적이다.

> **📝 PRACTICE 5-6** 괄호 안의 보기들 중에서 적절한 것을 고르세요. 정답 p.139
>
> **5** I strongly recommended that he (try / tries) the new restaurant downtown; the food is amazing.
>
> **6** It is mandatory that every employee (attend / attends) the annual safety training course.

POINT 4 · 비교급 문제는 ① 형용사/부사 자리 ② 동반되는 수식어구를 확인한다.

① 원급 비교

❶ 불완전한 문장 + as 형용사 as + 비교대상

Staying hydrated during hot weather is **as important as** wearing sunscreen to protect your skin.
날씨가 더울 때 수분을 섭취하는 것은 피부를 보호하기 위해 선크림을 바르는 것만큼 중요하다.

❷ 완전한 문장 + as 부사 as + 비교 대상

The new software system allows us to manage our inventory **as effectively as** the old one.
새로운 소프트웨어 시스템을 통해 우리는 이전 시스템만큼 효율적으로 재고를 관리할 수 있다.

② 비교급

- 형용사와 부사의 비교급은 뒤에 '-er', '-ier'을 붙이거나 앞에 more을 붙여 만들며, 주로 than과 함께 사용된다.
- more은 many/much의 비교급, better는 good/well의 비교급, less는 little의 비교급이다.
- less는 음절과 상관없이 형용사나 부사 앞에 위치하여 '덜'이라는 의미로 사용된다.

Learning to use this new software is **less complicated than** I initially thought.
이 신규 소프트웨어를 사용하는 것은 처음에 생각했던 것보다 덜 복잡하다.

- 비교급을 강조하는 부사는 a lot, much, far, even, still, 혹은 '상당히'라는 뜻의 significantly, markedly 등이 있다.

> **cf.** very, so, too, just, quite 등은 원급의 형용사나 부사를 강조하며 수식한다.

After the recent price reduction, the sales of the product increased **markedly more than** in the previous quarter. 최근 가격 인하 이후에, 제품의 판매량이 이전 분기보다 상당히 증가했다.

- 「the 비교급 + (주어 + 동사), the 비교급 + (주어 + 동사)」는 '~할수록 ~하다'라는 의미이다.

The more you practice playing the piano, **the better** your skills will become.
피아노 연습을 하면 할수록, 실력이 향상된다.

③ 최상급

- 「the + 최상급 + of/among(~ 중에서) + 집단, 범위 등」

Of the new employees, he showed **the most dedication** and quickly played a key role on the team.
새로 온 직원들 중에서, 그는 가장 헌신적이고 빠르게 팀에서 주요 역할을 수행하는 모습을 보였다.

- 「the + 최상급 + in(~에서, ~ 안에서) + 장소, 분야 등」

She received **the most** votes **in the election**, making her the new mayor of the city.
그녀는 선거에서 가장 많은 표를 받아서 새로운 시장이 되었다.

- 「the + 최상급 + 주어 + have (ever) p.p.」

The sunset over the ocean last night was **the most breathtaking sight I have ever seen**.
어젯밤에 바다 위로 내려다본 일몰은 내가 본 가장 숨막히는 광경이었다.

> **cf.** 최상급 앞에는 정관사 the나 소유격이 오지만, 동사를 꾸며주는 역할을 하는 부사의 최상급 앞에서는 the를 생략할 수 있다.

Among all the team members, Sarah consistently **works hardest** to exceed expectations.
모든 팀원들 중에서, 새라는 항상 기대치를 넘어 가장 열심히 일하는 편이다.

📝 PRACTICE 7 〈 괄호 안의 보기들 중에서 적절한 것을 고르세요. 정답 p.139

7 The new smartphone offers (necessarily / significantly) more storage space compared to its predecessor.

in honor of ~을 기념하여
a ceremony in honor of his retirement 은퇴를 기념하여

in light of ~의 측면에서
in light of recent events 최근의 사건들을 고려할 때

in line with ~와 일치하여
His actions were in line with company policies.
그의 행동은 회사 정책과 일치했다.

in observance of ~을 준수하여
close the office in observance of the national holiday
국경일을 준수하여 사무실을 닫다

in reference to ~에 관하여
In reference to your question, here are the details.
당신의 질문과 관련하여, 자세한 내용은 여기 있습니다.

in regard to ~에 관하여
In regard to your complaint, we are taking it seriously.
당신의 불만에 관해서, 우리는 심각하게 받아들이고 있습니다.

in response to ~에 대한 응답으로
in response to the customer's complaint
고객의 불만사항에 대한 응답으로

in spite of ~에도 불구하고
in spite of the bad weather 궂은 날씨에도 불구하고

in terms of ~라는 점에서
In terms of qualifications, she is the most suitable candidate. 자격에 있어서는, 그녀가 가장 적합한 후보.

in the event of 만일 ~하는 경우에
In the event of a fire, please use the nearest exit.
화재 시에는 가까운 출구를 이용해 주시기 바랍니다.

in writing 서면으로
The agreement was documented in writing.
그 합의는 서면으로 기록되었다.

keep track of ~을 추적하다
It's important to keep track of your expenses.
지출 내역을 파악하는 것이 중요하다.

look forward to ~하기를 고대하다
look forward to meeting you 만나 뵙기를 고대합니다

on account of ~ 때문에
The game was canceled on account of heavy rain.
그 경기는 폭우로 취소되었다.

on behalf of ~을 대신하여, ~을 대표하여
on behalf of our team 우리 팀을 대표해서

on purpose 고의로
He broke the vase on purpose. 그는 일부러 꽃병을 깨뜨렸다.

on sale 할인 중 **cf** for sale 판매 중
The products are on sale for a limited time.
그 제품들은 기간 한정으로 할인하고 있다.

on the basis of ~에 근거하여
His decision was made on the basis of the available data. 그의 결정은 이용 가능한 데이터에 근거하여 내려졌다.

out of date 구식인
This document is out of date and needs to be updated. 이 문서는 최신 버전이 아니므로 업데이트해야 한다.

out of order 고장 난
The elevator is out of order. 엘리베이터가 고장 났다.

out of print 절판된
That book is out of print. 그 책은 절판되었다.

relevant to ~에 관계된
Your comments are relevant to our discussion.
당신의 의견은 우리의 논의와 관련이 있습니다.

run short of ~가 부족하다
run short of supplies 물자가 부족하다

suitable for ~에 적합한 **유** ideal for ~에 이상적인
This dress is suitable for formal occasions.
이 옷은 격식을 차리기에 적합하다.

take advantage of ~을 이용하다
You should take advantage of this opportunity.
당신은 이 기회를 이용해야 합니다.

under no circumstance 어떤 상황에서도
Under no circumstance should you share your password. 어떤 경우에도 비밀번호를 공유해서는 안 된다.

under pressure 압박을 받는
He made a decision under pressure.
그는 압박감 속에 결정을 내렸다.

upon request 요청시에
provide a copy of a report upon request
요청시 보고서의 사본을 제공하다

with caution 조심스럽게
When handling chemicals, it's essential to proceed with caution. 화학물질을 취급할 때, 주의해서 처리해야 한다.

without a doubt 의심의 여지없이
without a doubt, the best candidate
의심의 여지없이, 최고의 후보자

PART 5

Directions: A word or phrase is missing in each of the sentences below. Four answer choices are given below each sentence. Select the best answer to complete the sentence and mark the letter (A), (B), (C), or (D).

1   Todd Wiley ------- multiple awards for his innovative artistry over the past ten years since his professional debut.

(A) earn
(B) earns
(C) earned
(D) has earned

2   When Mr. Shaw ------- next week's conference in Vancouver, he will be staying at the Fairview Hotel, where the event is being held.

(A) attending
(B) to attend
(C) attends
(D) will attend

3   The offer for the property in Newberg made by Cohen Development seems to be ------- more reasonable than other offers.

(A) ever
(B) too
(C) soon
(D) even

4   The Watts Group has decided to produce camping gear after seeing how ------- those of its competitors were this season.

(A) popular
(B) popularize
(C) popularity
(D) popularly

5   If one of the team members ------- how to operate the new machine, hiring an external engineer would be unnecessary.

(A) knew
(B) has known
(C) had known
(D) will know

6   Maintaining a robust online presence is an effective strategy for connecting with ------- clients, especially young professionals.

(A) potential
(B) artificial
(C) partial
(D) optional

7   Spinella Technology has ------- implemented significant changes to its employee benefits package, aiming to enhance the working environment.

    (A) soon
    (B) shortly
    (C) recently
    (D) currently

8   If Mr. Balog had known that he was going to receive another job offer, he ------- the offer from Core Values Investment last week.

    (A) will not accept
    (B) is not accepting
    (C) would not accept
    (D) would not have accepted

9   This year's charity auction raised ------- money as it did the last time, and the proceeds will be donated to local foundations.

    (A) so much
    (B) as most
    (C) as much
    (D) as many

10 Should the guests from the Prosperity Capital Group come late, the conference ------- for two or three hours.

    (A) had been postponing
    (B) would have postponed
    (C) have been postponed
    (D) will be postponed

11 ------- the latest survey, Naturally Fresh Market's premium organic products attracted twice as many shoppers compared to last year.

    (A) In addition to
    (B) According to
    (C) To that end
    (D) Provided that

12 Unexpected weather conditions delayed the construction project and ------- resulted in the exceeding of the firm's budget.

    (A) urgently
    (B) densely
    (C) eventually
    (D) occasionally

13 To ensure efficient loading onto trailers, ------- shipping containers are required, providing a uniform and compatible solution.

    (A) standardizing
    (B) standards
    (C) standardize
    (D) standardized

14 The ------- the number of commuters to Elizabeth City, the heavier the smog that fills the air in the city becomes.

    (A) high
    (B) higher
    (C) highest
    (D) highly

15 EcoPower Innovations installed solar panels on its office building to promote energy-saving measures and hopes other businesses will do -------.

    (A) apparently
    (B) furthermore
    (C) likewise
    (D) consistently

PART 6

Directions: Read the text below. A word, phrase, or sentence is missing in parts of the text. Four answer choices for each question are given below the text. Select the best answer to complete the text and mark the letter (A), (B), (C), or (D).

Questions 16-19 refer to the following notice.

Tranquil Serenity Spa - Temporarily Closed

On Wednesday, July 13, we made the difficult decision to temporarily close Tranquil Serenity Spa due to damage caused by a recent severe storm. -------, this temporary closure presents an
16.
opportunity for us not only to restore the facilities but also to upgrade and replace some aging equipment. We believe this ------- an even better-equipped and rejuvenated spa experience.
17.

Your satisfaction has always been our top priority, and we deeply care about each one of you. We appreciate your understanding ------- this decision. -------. During this period, we'll keep you
18. **19.**
updated on our progress and plans. We look forward to welcoming you back to an even more revitalized Tranquil Serenity Spa in the near future.

16 (A) Otherwise
    (B) For instance
    (C) However
    (D) In other words

17 (A) creates
    (B) creating
    (C) created
    (D) will create

18 (A) regarding
    (B) despite
    (C) instead of
    (D) up to

19 (A) Building a new facility cost us a lot more than expected.
    (B) We are committed to reopening as soon as possible.
    (C) Please attend the opening ceremony of our new branch.
    (D) We are currently looking for a place to relocate to.

Lisa Halman

5700 Gilbert Ave.

Western Springs, IL

60438

Dear Ms. Halman,

For over two decades, the Cummings Research Center has been one of the ------- research
20.

foundations in Chicago. In celebration of our twentieth anniversary, we are delighted to extend

an invitation to you for an appreciation banquet to be held at the Clarendon Hotel on December

15, starting at 7:00 P.M. The event is dedicated to honoring our generous sponsors and donors,

including you. -------.
21.

We are acutely aware of the significant contributions you ------- to our continued success, and we
22.

are eager to express our gratitude for your steadfast support throughout the years. To confirm your

attendance, kindly reach out to us at 535-1311 or send an e-mail to mikecave@cummingsresearch.org

at your earliest -------. We earnestly look forward to welcoming you to the banquet.
23.

With warm regards,

Mike Cave

Public Relations Manager

Cummings Research Center

20 (A) innovatively
   (B) more innovative
   (C) more innovatively
   (D) most innovative

21 (A) The new medicine is a result of a lengthy
       effort.
   (B) Your dedication to that research was
       remarkable.
   (C) Thank you for your help in organizing this
       event.
   (D) Your presence would be an exceptional
       pleasure.

22 (A) will be making
   (B) to be made
   (C) should have made
   (D) have made

23 (A) attention
   (B) possibility
   (C) convenience
   (D) feasibility

Directions: In this part you will read a selection of texts. The text or set of texts is followed by several questions. Select the best answer for each question and mark the letter (A), (B), (C), or (D).

Questions 24-27 refer to the following letter.

Wordsmith Publishers

350 1st Ave., New York, NY 10019
Web site: www.wordsmithpublishers.com

Harper Singh
599 Battery St.
Seattle, WA 95213

September 13

Dear Ms. Singh

We at Wordsmith Publishers are thrilled to continue our collaboration on the updated edition of your book, *Living with Style: A Guide to Crafting Your Ideal Lifestyle.* –[1]–. In response to evolving industry trends, we've chosen electronic distribution to enhance accessibility and to make your valuable content easily available to a wide audience.

As we discussed during our previous meeting at our New York office, all prior contract terms will remain unchanged except for a modest adjustment to your royalty fees. –[2]–. If you have not yet returned the author information form, which my assistant previously sent, please include it along with the signed contract. –[3]–.

We deeply appreciate your contributions to Wordsmith Publishers. If you approve of the proposed terms, kindly return the signed contract by September 25. –[4]–. We are honored to continue licensing and publishing your work in various formats.

Should you have any questions or concerns, please do not hesitate to reach out to me at your convenience.

Sincerely,

Frank Nolan
Chief Editor, Wordsmith Publishers

24 Why did Mr. Nolan send the letter to Ms. Singh?

(A) To request that she review a book

(B) To arrange a schedule for an interview

(C) To ask her to attend a book-signing event

(D) To explain a modification to an agreement

25 The word "easily" in paragraph 1, line 4, is closest in meaning to

(A) readily

(B) willingly

(C) briefly

(D) clearly

26 What is suggested about Ms. Singh?

(A) She is currently residing in New York.

(B) She has met Mr. Nolan in person.

(C) She recently wrote a book with Mr. Nolan.

(D) Her first book is soon to be published.

27 In which of the positions marked [1], [2], [3], and [4] does the following sentence best belong?

"Enclosed, you will find the updated contract for your review and signature."

(A) [1]

(B) [2]

(C) [3]

(D) [4]

Laura Bryant Honored with Award for Documentary Excellence

The Documentary Film Association is thrilled to announce the upcoming presentation of its prestigious award for the year's best documentary to Laura Bryant. This well-deserved recognition will take place on December 21, commemorating her remarkable achievement in making *Dreams in the Crossfire: Children and Civil Wars*. Through this extraordinary film, Ms. Bryant has passionately advocated the cause of children in crisis, raising awareness for charitable endeavors nationwide. Since its release, the film has sparked an incredible surge in donations—by over 10%—to support homeless children and orphanages suffering from the devastating effects of civil wars worldwide.

Laura Bryant has always been dedicated to revealing the challenges that children face when they grow up in areas affected by conflict. In her earlier documentary, *Silenced Voices*, she showed the difficult lives of these young children. Ms. Bryant also highlighted nonprofit groups that help kids affected by war. This led to almost double the funding for these organizations, allowing them to provide more important help and to rescue kids from dangerous areas.

For those eager to be a part of this momentous occasion, tickets for the award ceremony are now available for purchase on the Documentary Film Association's official Web site at www.dfa.org/awards. The entirety of the event's proceeds will be allocated to charities in accordance with Ms. Bryant's heartfelt request.

Join us in celebrating the remarkable work of Laura Bryant, *Dreams in the Crossfire: Children and Civil Wars*, on December 21.

---

http://www.sunsethaven.com/events

Exciting December Specials Await You!

December 1-15: Elevate your stay by indulging in the luxury of our elegant suites! Book two or more consecutive nights, and you'll enjoy an exclusive 25% discount. Your delightful package includes two nights of accommodations and scrumptious breakfasts at our ground floor Italian restaurant. This offer is an exclusive treat for our cherished Sunset Haven Hotel Loyalty members.

December 19-23: Join us in celebrating the prestigious award ceremony hosted by the nearby Metropolitan Arts Plaza for the esteemed Documentary Film Association (DFA). As our guest attending this remarkable event, you'll receive a generous 30% discount on your stay. Plus, enjoy a complimentary breakfast buffet voucher at our five-star restaurant. What's more, this fantastic offer extends to two days before and two days after the event, ensuring that you make the most of your visit.

To claim your discounted rate, simply present your DFA event ticket at our front desk during check-in, and we'll adjust your rate accordingly. Please note that this special rate is applicable for the five specified days, and any additional days during your stay will be charged at the standard rate unless otherwise specified. Don't miss out on these incredible December deals!

```
***********************************************

Sunset Haven Hotel

3606 Balboa Blvd., Los Angeles, CA 90022
(310) 725-5000
_____

Guest Name: Robert Stuart
Address: 1085 59th St. Apt. 10, Oakland, CA 94508
Check-in Date: December 20
Checkout Date: December 22
Room Number: 1008 (deluxe queen room with two queen beds)
Room Rate: $150 (breakfast included) / 2 nights
_____

Total: $210 (Adjusted: Discount Applied)
Payment Credit Card Number: 3002-XXXX-XXXX-0815

***********************************************
```

28 What is mentioned about Ms. Bryant?

(A) She recently made her debut as a film director.

(B) She works at a nonprofit organization.

(C) She supports charities for children.

(D) She has received awards for her films many times.

29 In the article, the word "proceeds" in paragraph 3, line 6, is closest in meaning to

(A) advances

(B) profits

(C) initiatives

(D) predictions

30 In the Web page, what is indicated about the special offers?

(A) They are offered throughout the month of December.

(B) They are only for Sunset Haven Hotel Loyalty members.

(C) They include free breakfasts at hotel restaurants.

(D) They will be applied only for stays of three nights or longer.

31 What was Mr. Stuart qualified to receive during the hotel stay?

(A) One night of free accommodations

(B) Qualification for a hotel membership

(C) A 30% discount on his hotel stay

(D) A ticket for the awards ceremony

32 What is suggested about Mr. Stuart?

(A) He is a Sunset Haven Hotel Loyalty member.

(B) He paid for his room with cash.

(C) He stayed at the hotel with his family.

(D) He showed proof of event attendance.

미니 테스트만으로 끝내는 **토익 실전서**

참 토익
COMPLETE
800+

김진영 · 강상진 공저

LC+RC

정답 및 해설

다락원

참 토익
COMPLETE
800+
LC+RC

정답 및 해설

다락원

Listening
Comprehension

DAY 01 **PART 1**
문제 풀이법: 소거법

실전 문제 연습
p.014

🎧 01-08

1	(A)	**2**	(C)	**3**	(B)	**4**	(C)
5	(C)	**6**	(B)	**7**	(A)	**8**	(B)
9	(C)	**10**	(C)	**11**	(C)	**12**	(B)
13	(C)	**14**	(B)	**15**	(C)	**16**	(C)
17	(B)	**18**	(A)	**19**	(C)	**20**	(C)
21	(D)	**22**	(B)	**23**	(A)	**24**	(D)
25	(A)	**26**	(B)	**27**	(B)	**28**	(C)
29	(B)	**30**	(A)	**31**	(D)	**32**	(C)
33	(C)						

PART 1

1

(A) A wheelbarrow has been left unattended.
(B) A wheelbarrow is being pushed.
(C) A woman is planting some flowers.
(D) A woman is putting on a jacket.

(A) 손수레가 방치되어 있다.
(B) 손수레가 밀리고 있다.
(C) 여자가 꽃을 심고 있다.
(D) 여자가 재킷을 입고 있다.

어휘 wheelbarrow 손수레 unattended 방치된

해설 손수레가 사람이 없는 채 방치되어 있는 모습이므로 (A)가 정답이다. being pushed의 경우 현재 밀고 있는 동작이 보여야 하는데 그렇지 않으므로 (B) 역시 오답이다. 사람이 보이지 않으므로 여자가 언급된 (C)와 (D)는 오답이 된다.

2

(A) The woman is sipping from a mug.
(B) The woman is writing something in a notebook.
(C) **The woman is using a laptop.**
(D) The woman is arranging a chair.

(A) 여자가 머그잔을 홀짝이고 있는 중이다.
(B) 여자가 노트에 무엇인가를 작성하는 중이다.
(C) 여자가 노트북을 사용하고 있는 중이다.
(D) 여자가 의자를 배열하고 있는 중이다.

어휘 sip 홀짝이다, 조금씩 마시다

해설 머그잔이 노트북 옆에 있기는 하지만 마시고 있지 않으므로 (A)는 오답이며, 노트에 무엇인가를 쓰고 있거나 노트가 보이지 않으므로 (B) 역시 오답이다. 노트북을 사용하는 모습이 맞으므로 (C)는 정답이 된다. 의자를 배열하고 있는 동작이 보이지 않으므로 (D)도 정답이 될 수 없다.

3

(A) Some vehicles have stopped at the crosswalk.
(B) **A vehicle has been parked near the curb.**
(C) Some flowers are being arranged.
(D) There is a sign next to the car.

(A) 몇몇 차들이 횡단보도에 멈춰 서 있다.
(B) 차량이 연석 근처에 주차되어 있다.
(C) 꽃들이 배치되고 있는 중이다.
(D) 차 옆에 표지판이 있다.

어휘 curb 연석

해설 횡단보도는 보이지 않고 차량도 한 대이므로 (A)는 오답이다. 자동차 한 대가 연석 근처에 세워져 있는 모습을 묘사한 (B)가 정답이다. 건너편에 식물이 있기는 하지만, 꽃을 배치하는 동작을 묘사한 (C)는 정답이 될 수 없다. 차 옆에 표지판은 없으므로 (D) 역시 오답이다.

PART 2

4

Don't you need to print some materials today?
(A) The copier is also broken.
(B) I'll be there tomorrow.
(C) **The seminar has been canceled.**

오늘 자료를 출력해야 하지 않나요?
(A) 복사기도 고장 났어요.
(B) 저는 내일 그곳에 갈 거예요.
(C) 세미나가 취소되었어요.

해설 자료를 출력해야 하는지 묻는 질문에 대해, 세미나가 취소 되었으므로 할 필요가 없다는 의미로 대답한 (C)가 정답이 된다. 질문의 print에서 연상되는 copier가 사용된 (A)와, today에서 연상되는 tomorrow로 답한 (B)는 오답이다.

5

How did you finish the report on time?
(A) I didn't report it either.
(B) Maria was late for the event.
(C) **I worked late at night.**

어떻게 보고서를 제시간에 끝냈어요?
(A) 저도 역시 보고하지 않았어요.
(B) 마리아는 행사에 늦었어요.
(C) 저는 초과 근무를 했어요.

해설 제시간에 보고서를 끝낸 방법을 묻는 질문에 대해 초과 근무를 해서 끝냈다고 답한 (C) 정답이다. (A)의 report는 '보고하다'라는 의미의 동사이며, 마리아가 행사에 늦은 것은 보고서와는 상관 없는 대답이므로 (A)와 (B)는 오답이다.

6

Do you have the request form, or should I print it?
(A) I don't have a printer.
(B) I have some on the desk.
(C) Formal attire.

신청서를 가지고 계신가요, 아니면 제가 출력해야 하나요?
(A) 프린터가 없어요.
(B) 책상 위에 몇 부 있어요.
(C) 정장 차림이에요.

어휘 attire 의복

해설 신청서가 있는지 출력이 필요한지를 묻는 질문에 대해 책상 위에 있으므로 출력을 하지 않아도 된다는 의미로 답한 (B)가 정답이다. print와 발음이 유사한 printer를 사용한 (A)는 전형적인 오답 유형이다. form과 발음이 유사한 formal을 사용한 (C)역시 오답이다.

7

Why did you move your office?
(A) Didn't you get the memo?
(B) No, I don't like that movie.
(C) I got a job offer.

왜 사무실을 옮겼어요?
(A) 메모를 받지 못했나요?
(B) 아니요, 저는 그 영화를 좋아하지 않아요.
(C) 저는 일자리를 제안 받았어요.

해설 사무실을 옮긴 이유를 묻는 질문에 대해 메모를 받지 못했는지 반문하는 것은 메모에 이유가 적혀 있었음을 암시하는 정답 패턴이다. 따라서, 정답은 (A)이다. move와 발음이 유사한 movie를 이용한 (B)와 office와 발음이 유사한 offer를 이용한 (C)는 모두 오답이다.

8

When can you give me the list of participants?
(A) A party of six.
(B) We are still accepting registrations.
(C) Via Internet.

언제 참석자 명단을 주실 수 있나요?
(A) 6명요.
(B) 우리는 아직 등록을 받고 있어요.
(C) 인터넷을 통해서요.

해설 참석자 명단을 줄 수 있는 때를 묻는 질문에 대해 '아직 등록을 받고 있으므로 언제 줄 수 있을지 모른다'는 의미로 답한 (B)가 정답이다. (A)는 how many로 묻는 질문에 적절한 대답이며, (C)는 방법을 묻는 질문에 어울리는 대답이다.

9

Is there a pharmacy near the office?
(A) I need a prescription.
(B) Yes, there is a big farm.
(C) There's one at 112 Main Street.

회사 근처에 약국이 있나요?
(A) 처방전이 필요해요.
(B) 네, 큰 농장이 있어요.
(C) 메인 가 112번지에 하나 있어요.

해설 회사 근처에 약국이 있는지를 묻는 질문에 대해 특정 주소를 알려주는 (C)가 적절한 대답이다. pharmacy(약국)에서 연상되는 처방전(prescription)을 이용한 (A)는 오답이며, (B)는 pharmacy의 유사 발음 오답인 farm이 사용되었다.

10

I want you to review some documents.
(A) I have an interview tomorrow.
(B) Summer is my favorite season.
(C) Okay. I'll check them later.

당신이 몇 가지 서류를 검토해 주셨으면 해요.
(A) 저는 내일 면접이 있어요.
(B) 여름은 제가 가장 좋아하는 계절이에요.
(C) 알았어요. 나중에 확인해 볼게요.

해설 서류 검토를 부탁하는 질문에 대해 나중에 검토하겠다고 대답한 (C)가 정답이다. (A)는 review와 발음이 유사한 interview를, (B)는 some과 발음이 유사한 summer를 활용한 오답이다.

11

Are you planning to dine in or get takeout?
(A) I want to buy a dining table.
(B) With my coworkers.
(C) I'll take the food with me, please.

식사는 안에서 하실 건가요 포장하실 건가요?
(A) 식탁을 사고 싶어요.
(B) 동료들과 함께요.
(C) 음식을 가지고 갈게요.

해설 실내와 실외 중 어디에서 음식을 먹을 것인지를 묻는 질문에 대해 포장해 가겠다고 이야기한 (C)가 정답이다. (A)는 dine에서 파생된 단어인 dining을 이용한 오답이다. (B)는 함께 식사할 사람이 누구인지를 묻는 질문에 어울리는 대답이다.

12

Will this couch fit in your house?
(A) Yes, he is my coach.
(B) I should measure the exact size.
(C) The fitness club near my place.

이 소파가 당신의 집에 맞을까요?
(A) 네, 그는 제 코치예요.

(B) 정확한 사이즈를 측정해봐야 할 것 같아요.

(C) 우리 집 근처에 있는 피트니스 클럽요.

해설 소파의 크기가 집에 맞을지 묻는 질문에 대해 정확한 사이즈를 측정해야 알 수 있다는 의미로 답한 (B)가 정답이 된다. couch와 발음이 유사한 coach를 사용한 (A)와 fit과 발음이 유사한 fitness를 사용한 (C) 모두 오답이다.

13

We have to check the inventory once a week, right?

(A) That's a fantastic invention.

(B) On your left side.

(C) No, the policy has been changed.

우리는 일주일에 한 번씩 재고 확인을 해야 해요, 그렇죠?

(A) 그것은 환상적인 발명품이에요.

(B) 왼쪽에요.

(C) 아니요, 정책이 변경되었어요.

어휘 inventory 재고

해설 일주일에 한 번씩 재고를 확인해야 하는지 묻는 질문에 대해 정책이 바뀌었다고 답한 (C)가 정답이다. (A)는 inventory와 발음이 유사한 invention을, (B)는 right에서 연상되는 left를 활용한 오답이다.

14

I need to know when the workshop registration is due.

(A) I plan to walk there.

(B) Not until Friday.

(C) The registration form.

워크숍 등록 마감일이 언제인지 알고 싶어요.

(A) 저는 걸어서 갈 계획이에요.

(B) 금요일까지는 안 돼요.

(C) 등록 양식이에요.

해설 시간을 묻는 질문에 대해 금요일은 되어야 한다고 시간을 언급한 (B)가 정답이 된다. (A)는 walk와 work의 발음이 비슷한 점을 활용한 오답이며, (C)는 registration을 반복한 오답이다.

15

I'd like to order some paper clips.

(A) In numerical order.

(B) We're out of paper.

(C) Have you checked the storage room?

종이 클립을 주문하고 싶어요.

(A) 번호순으로요.

(B) 종이가 다 떨어졌어요.

(C) 창고는 확인해 보셨어요?

어휘 numerical 번호의

해설 종이 클립을 주문하고 싶다는 말에 대해 창고에 있는지를 확인해 보았는지 묻는 (C)가 정답이다. 질문의 order는 '주문하다'라는 의미의 동사이지만 (A)의 order는 '순서'라는 뜻의 명사이다. paper를 반복한 (B) 역시 오답이다.

16

What is this sweater made of?

(A) The shirts and sweaters.

(B) I want the one made of cotton.

(C) There is a label in the pocket.

이 스웨터는 무엇으로 만들어졌나요?

(A) 셔츠와 스웨터요.

(B) 저는 면으로 만든 것을 원해요.

(C) 주머니에 라벨이 있어요.

어휘 cotton 면

해설 스웨터의 소재를 묻는 질문에 대해 주머니 안의 라벨을 확인해 보라고 간접적으로 답하는 (C)가 정답이 된다. sweater를 반복한 (A)는 전형적인 오답이다. (B)는 cotton이라는 재료가 언급되어 정답일 것 같지만, 무엇을 구매할 것인지를 묻는 질문이 아니므로 오답이다.

17

Shouldn't you have sent the samples to the store?

(A) Could you sample some desserts?

(B) I've been in a meeting all day.

(C) I stored them in the closet.

매장으로 샘플을 보냈어야 하지 않아요?

(A) 디저트를 시식해 주실 수 있나요?

(B) 저는 하루 종일 회의를 하고 있어요.

(C) 저는 그것을 옷장에 보관해 두었어요.

해설 매장으로 샘플을 보냈어야 하는 것이 아닌지를 묻는 질문에 대해 하루 종일 회의하느라 보내지 못했다고 변명한 (B)가 정답이다. 'should have p.p.'는 해야 할 일을 하지 않았다는 의미로, 질문에 사용되면 '해야 할 일을 왜 하지 않았는지' 묻는 의미이다. (A)의 sample은 '맛을 보다'라는 의미이며, (C)의 store는 '저장하다'라는 의미이다.

18

How far along are you on the grant proposal?

(A) It's almost finished.

(B) About 20 miles.

(C) Yes, I proposed the plan.

지원금 제안서는 얼마나 진행되었나요?

(A) 거의 다 끝났어요.

(B) 20마일 정도요.

(C) 네, 저는 그 계획을 제안했어요.

어휘 how far along are you on ~ ~는 얼마나 진행이 되었나요?

해설 'how far along ~'은 얼마나 진행되었는지를 묻는 질문으로서 난이도가 높은 문제이다. 제안서가 얼마나 진행되었는지를 묻는 질문에 대해 거의 끝났다고 답한 (A)가 정답이 된다. 'how far'만 듣고 거리를 묻는 질문으로 잘못 이해할 경우 (B)를 고르는 실수를 하게 된다. 의문사 의문문에 yes나 no로 답할 수 없으므로 (C)도 오답이다.

PART 3

[19-21]

W1	Hi, Dr. Bennett. 20) **Thank you for meeting us today to discuss the new school library my company is designing for your district.**
M	19) **On behalf of the school board**, we're thrilled about this new addition to our educational facilities.
W1	Wonderful. As the library will have an extensive digital section, I've brought our IT specialist, Amy Chen, to join our talk.
W2	It's a pleasure to meet you, Dr. Bennett. With the digital focus, 21) **have you considered the necessary tech support and equipment?**
M	Yes, we are aware of these needs and are prepared to fund these aspects.
W1	안녕하세요, 베넷 박사님. 당신의 구역에 설계하는 새로운 학교 도서관에 대해 논의하기 위해 만나 주셔서 감사합니다.
M	학교 이사회를 대신해서, 우리는 우리의 교육 시설에 이 새로운 건물을 추가하게 되어 매우 기쁩니다.
W1	멋지네요. 도서관에는 방대한 디지털 섹션이 갖춰질 예정이어서, 저희 IT 전문가인 에이미 첸을 논의에 참여시켰습니다.
W2	반갑습니다, 베넷 박사님. 디지털 기술에 초점을 맞추고 있는데, 필요한 기술적인 지원과 설비에 대해 고려해 보셨어요?
M	네, 우리는 이러한 필요성을 인식하고 있고 이 부분들에 자금을 지원할 준비가 되어 있습니다.

어휘 on behalf of ~ ~을 대신해서   thrilled 매우 기쁜, 흥분한   extensive 광범위한, 폭넓은   be aware of 인지하고 있다

19
남자는 누구인 것 같은가?
(A) 대학생
(B) 건축가
(C) 학교 이사회 구성원
(D) 기술 전문가

해설 남자가 'On behalf of the school board'라고 한 것으로 보아 그는 학교 이사회의 구성원임을 알 수 있다. 정답은 (C)이다.

20
화자들은 주로 무엇을 논의하고 있는가?
(A) 기술적인 업그레이드
(B) 과학 박람회
(C) 건설 프로젝트
(D) 교육 프로그램

해설 대화의 첫 부분에서 여자가 언급한 'Thanks for meeting us today to discuss the new school library my company is designing for your district.'에서 여자의 회사가 설계하고 있는 새로운 학교의 도서관에 대한 대화라는 것을 알 수 있다. 따라서 정답은 (C)이다.

21
에이미 첸은 무엇에 관해 질문하고 있는가?
(A) 교실의 크기
(B) 인터넷 접속
(C) 교육 컨텐츠
(D) 기술적인 요구 사항

해설 첫 번째 여자가 두 번째 여자를 소개하면서 '에이미 첸'이라고 이름을 불렀고, 이어서 그녀가 'have you considered the necessary tech support and equipment?'라고 했다. 따라서 에이미 첸이 질문한 것은 기술적인 지원과 장비, 즉, 기술적인 요구 사항이라는 것을 알 수 있다. 정답은 (D)이다.

[22-24]

W	22) **I can't believe it took over 30 minutes to find a parking space.** When will the renovation work be finished? It's getting annoying.
M	23) **Tell me about it. I take the subway these days due to the parking problem.**
W	I think we have to discuss the problem in the staff meeting this Friday.
M	That's a good idea.
W	Yes. But as you know, 24) **I won't be attending the meeting since I'm in charge of conducting interviews on Friday.** So would you bring it up at the meeting?
M	No problem. I'll be there to demand a solution to the parking issue.
W	주차 공간을 찾는 데 30분도 넘게 걸렸다는 것을 믿을 수가 없네요. 언제 보수 공사가 끝나나요? 점점 짜증나기 시작하네요.
M	말도 마세요. 저는 주차 문제 때문에 요즘 지하철을 타요.
W	이번 금요일 직원 회의에서 이 문제를 논의해야 해요.
M	좋은 생각이네요.
W	네. 그런데 아시다시피, 제가 금요일에 면접을 진행해야 해서 회의에 참석할 수 없어요. 당신이 이 문제를 언급해 줄래요?
M	문제 없어요. 제가 참석해서 주차 문제에 대한 해결책을 요구할게요.

어휘 tell me about it 말도 마세요 (동감의 의미)   bring ~ up ~을 언급하다   issue 문제

22
어떤 문제가 언급되는가?
(A) 건설 연기
(B) 불충분한 주차 공간
(C) 망가진 보안 카메라
(D) 회의 취소

해설 주제를 묻는 문제의 단서는 주로 대화 초반에 언급된다. 대화 초반 'I can't believe it took over 30 minutes to find a parking space.'에서 주차하느라 30분이나 걸렸다고 이야기하고 있으므로 주차에 대한 문제를 언급하고 있음을 알 수 있다. 따라서, 정답은 (B)이다.

23

남자가 "말도 마세요"라고 말할 때 그가 의미하는 것은 무엇인가?

(A) 그도 역시 짜증이 난다.
(B) 그는 더 많은 정보를 원한다.
(C) 그는 그것이 좋은 기회라고 생각한다.
(D) 그는 그 뉴스를 듣지 못했다.

해설 'tell me about it'을 직역하면 '그것에 대해 나에게 말해봐'라는 의미가 되지만, 동의의 표현으로 '말도 마세요'라는 의미이다. 인용된 문장 뒤의 'I take the subway these days due to the parking problem.'에서 남자는 주차 문제 때문에 지하철을 타고 다닌다고 이야기하고 있으므로, 앞에서 언급된 여자의 말에 동의하고 있음을 알 수 있다. 정답은 (A)이다.

24

여자는 금요일에 무엇을 할 것인가?

(A) 장비 설치하기
(B) 회의에 참석하기
(C) 출장 가기
(D) 면접 진행하기

해설 'I won't be attending the meeting since I'm in charge of conducting interviews on Friday.'에서 여자는 금요일에 인터뷰를 한다고 말했으므로 정답은 (D)이다.

[25-27]

> M   Judy, I am attending a conference in San Francisco next week. **25-1) You went there on a business trip last month, didn't you?**
>
> W1   Yes, I did. Actually, **25-2) Sarah and I made a visit to our manufacturing plant there.**
>
> W2   We stayed there for two weeks, so we are very familiar with the area.
>
> M   Then you guys can definitely recommend some good sights I can visit during my stay.
>
> W1   Tell me where you will be staying so that **26-1) I can recommend some beautiful attractions close by.**
>
> M   **26-2) Thanks, Judy.** **27) Let me check the confirmation e-mail for the address of the hotel.**

> M   쥬디, 저는 다음 주에 샌프란시스코의 컨퍼런스에 참여해요. 지난달에 당신이 그곳으로 출장을 갔었군요, 그렇지 않아요?
>
> W1   네, 다녀왔어요. 사라와 제가 그곳에 있는 제조 공장에 갔었죠.
>
> W2   우리는 그곳에 2주 동안 있었기 때문에, 그 지역을 잘 알아요.
>
> M   그러면 여러분은 분명히 제가 그곳에 머무는 동안 방문할 좋은 곳들을 추천해 줄 수 있겠군요.
>
> W1   어디에서 머물 것인지 이야기해주시면 제가 근처에 있는 아름다운 명소들을 추천해 드릴 수 있어요.
>
> M   고마워요 쥬디. 제가 확정 이메일을 확인해서 호텔 주소를 찾아 볼게요.

어휘 manufacturing plant 제조 공장   be familiar with 익숙하다, 알다   attraction 명소   confirmation 확인, 확정

25

여자들은 지난달에 무엇을 했는가?

(A) 공장을 방문했다.
(B) 회의에 참석했다.
(C) 다른 지점으로 전근했다.
(D) 다른 나라를 여행했다.

해설 시간과 관련된 문제의 단서는 시간이 언급된 부분에서 찾을 수 있다. 'You went there on a business trip last month, didn't you?'에서 '지난달'이 언급된 이후 여자는 'Sarah and I made a visit to our manufacturing plant there.'라고 했다. 따라서 공장을 방문했다는 내용의 (A)가 정답이다.

26

남자는 왜 쥬디에게 고마워하는가?

(A) 그녀가 그에게 식당 리스트를 주었기 때문에
(B) 그녀가 그에게 추천하는 것에 동의하기 때문에
(C) 그녀가 그에게 호텔을 추천해 주었기 때문에
(D) 그녀가 그를 태워 줄 것이기 때문에

해설 대화 마지막에서 여자가 'I can recommend some beautiful attractions close by.'라고 말하며 명소를 추천해 주겠다고 했는데, 이에 대해 남자가 'Thanks, Judy'라고 말했다. 따라서 정답은 (B)이다.

27

남자는 아마도 다음에 무엇을 할 것인가?

(A) 회의에 참석하기
(B) 이메일을 확인하기
(C) 전화를 걸기
(D) 호텔을 방문하기

해설 대화 마지막의 'Let me check the confirmation e-mail for the address of the hotel.'에서 남자는 이메일을 확인해 보겠다고 했으므로 정답은 (B)이다.

PART 4

[28-30]

> M   **28) Thank you for visiting our booth here at the household appliances trade show.** We're very excited to show you our latest coffee maker, which was released only last month. Our coffee makers are especially popular with office workers because all of them are designed for brewing large pots of delicious coffee conveniently. Moreover, **29) our latest coffee maker is capable of brewing up everything from a latte to cold brew quickly and easily, giving you that barista experience. 30) We are giving away**

free samples of freshly made coffee brewed by our coffee maker. I can say with confidence that once you taste the coffee, you will fall in love with our coffee maker.

M 가전제품 무역 박람회의 저희 부스를 방문해 주셔서 감사합니다. 지난달에 막 출시된 당사의 최신 커피 메이커를 보여드리게 되어 매우 기쁩니다. 저희 커피 메이커는 많은 양의 맛있는 커피를 편리하게 내릴 수 있도록 설계되었기 때문에 특히 직장인들에게 인기가 많습니다. 게다가, 저희 최신 커피 메이커는 라떼부터 콜드브루까지 모든 것을 빠르고 쉽게 만들 수 있어서, 여러분들이 쉽게 바리스타를 경험할 수 있게 해줍니다. 저희의 커피 메이커로 만든 커피 샘플을 무료로 드리고 있습니다. 일단 커피를 맛보시면 저희 커피 메이커에 반하실 거라고 자신 있게 말씀드릴 수 있습니다.

어휘 give away 무료로 주다　household appliance 가전제품　release 출시하다　brew (커피나 차를) 끓이다

28
화자는 어디에 있는 것 같은가?
(A) 카페에
(B) 가전제품점에
(C) 무역 박람회에
(D) 광고 회사에

해설 담화의 장소를 묻는 문제의 단서는 주로 담화의 초반부에서 찾을 수 있다. 담화 초반의 'Thank you for visiting our booth here at the household appliances trade show.'에서 무역 박람회의 우리 부스에 방문해 주셔서 감사하다고 했으므로 정답은 (C)이다.

29
화자가 말한 새로운 기계의 특별한 점은 무엇인가?
(A) 다양한 디자인이 있다.
(B) 다양한 음료의 옵션을 가지고 있다.
(C) 저렴하다.
(D) 내구성이 좋다.

해설 담화 중반의 'our latest coffee maker is capable of brewing up everything from a latte to cold brew quickly and easily, giving you that barista experience.'라는 부분에서 새로운 기계는 라떼부터 콜드브루까지 모든 것을 만들 수 있다고 했으므로, 다양한 음료의 옵션을 가지고 있다는 내용의 (B)가 정답이다.

30
화자는 청자들에게 무엇을 제공하는가?
(A) 무료 샘플
(B) 커피 메이커
(C) 무료 티켓
(D) 상품 리스트

해설 화자가 제공하는 것을 묻는 문제는 청자들이 받는 것으로 전환되어 단서가 제시되기도 한다. 담화 마지막의 'We are giving away free samples of freshly made coffee brewed by our coffee maker.'에서 갓 만든 무료 샘플을 제공하고 있다고 했으므로 정답은 (A)이다.

[31-33]

W Good morning. This is Sherry Anderson, and you are listening to Bristol Local Radio. Let me give you an update on the Bristol Library Construction Project. It began last month in April. Work started with the renovating of the book sections. **31) The mayor of Bristol, Tony Jackson, announced last week that the library will be partially opening this Saturday**, and the good news is that you will be able to borrow some books. However, the seating area is not finished, so you can only check out books to take home. The other sections of the library will be opening one at a time. **32) If you are waiting for computer-based library services, they will be accessible to the public next month in June.** After that, work will be done on the periodical section on the second floor. **33) Next up, Paul will update you on the latest traffic conditions and road closures.**

W 좋은 아침입니다. 저는 셰리 앤더슨이며, 여러분은 브리스톨 지역 라디오를 듣고 계십니다. 브리스톨 도서관 건설 프로젝트에 대한 최신 정보를 알려 드리겠습니다. 이는 지난달인 4월에 시작되었습니다. 작업은 도서 섹션들을 전면 개보수하는 것으로 시작했습니다. 지난주에 브리스톨 시장 토니 잭슨은 도서관이 이번 주 토요일에 부분적으로 개관할 것이라고 발표했고, 좋은 소식은 책을 대출할 수 있다는 것입니다. 하지만, 좌석 구역이 마무리되지 않아서, 여러분은 집에 가져갈 책들만 대출할 수 있습니다. 도서관의 다른 구역들은 하나씩 개방될 예정입니다. 컴퓨터 기반 도서관 서비스를 기다리신다면, 다음 달인 6월에 대중들이 이용할 수 있습니다. 그 후, 2층의 정기 간행물 섹션의 작업이 완료될 것입니다. 다음으로, 폴이 여러분께 최신 교통 상황과 도로 폐쇄에 대해 알려드릴 것입니다.

어휘 renovate 개보수하다　one at a time 차례로, 하나씩　accessible 접근할 수 있는　periodical 정기 간행물　public 대중　periodical 정기 간행물

31
이번 주말에 무슨 일이 있을 것인가?
(A) 개보수 공사가 시작된다.
(B) 추가 주차 공간이 건설될 것이다.
(C) 건물이 완성이 된다.
(D) 건물의 일부가 개방을 한다.

해설 시간이 언급된 문제는 시간 주변에서 정답의 단서가 주어진다. 담화 초반의 'The mayor of Bristol, Tony Jackson, announced last week that the library will be partially opening this Saturday.'에서 토요일에 도서관의 일부가 개관될 것이라고 언급되어 있으므로 정답은 (D)가 된다.

7

4월	**5월**	**6월**	**7월**
도서 섹션	공용 컴퓨터 구역	디지털 도서관 센터	정기 간행물 섹션

브리스톨 도서관 건설 프로젝트 일정

32

시각 정보를 보시오. 어떤 시설에서 컴퓨터 기반 도서관 서비스를 제공하는가?
(A) 도서 섹션
(B) 공용 컴퓨터 구역
(C) 디지털 도서관 센터
(D) 정기 간행물 섹션

해설 시각 정보 문제의 경우 선택지의 단어 주변에서 단서를 찾아야 한다. 'If you are waiting for computer-based library services, they will be accessible to the public next month in June.'이라고 언급되어 있으므로, 6월에 오픈하는 곳인 (C)가 정답이 된다.

33

청자들은 다음에 무엇을 듣게 될 것인가?
(A) 음악
(B) 날씨
(C) 교통방송
(D) 뉴스

해설 담화 마지막 부분의 'Next up, Paul will update you on the latest traffic conditions and road closures.'에서 교통 상황을 알려준다고 말하고 있으므로 정답은 (C)이다.

DAY 02 PART 1
고난도 문제 풀이법

📑 실전 문제 연습 p.025

🎧 02-08

1 (A)	2 (D)	3 (D)	4 (B)
5 (C)	6 (C)	7 (C)	8 (A)
9 (B)	10 (B)	11 (C)	12 (C)
13 (C)	14 (A)	15 (B)	16 (B)
17 (A)	18 (C)	19 (D)	20 (A)
21 (B)	22 (D)	23 (B)	24 (A)
25 (D)	26 (B)	27 (C)	28 (B)
29 (A)	30 (C)	31 (B)	32 (C)
33 (A)			

PART 1

1
(A) The woman is walking a dog.
(B) The woman is wearing a backpack.
(C) The woman is resting on the lawn.
(D) The woman is gathering rocks.

(A) 여자가 개를 산책시키고 있다.
(B) 여자가 배낭을 메고 있다.
(C) 여자가 잔디밭에서 쉬고 있는 중이다.
(D) 여자가 돌을 모으고 있는 중이다.

해설 여자가 개를 데리고 걷고 있는 모습이므로 개를 산책시킨다는 의미를 가진 (A)가 정답이 된다. 배낭이 보이지 않으므로 (B)는 오답이 되며 잔디에서 쉬는 모습이 아니므로 (C)도 소거한다. 여자는 돌을 모으고 있지 않으므로 (D)도 오답이다.

2
(A) A rug is being placed under the table.
(B) Some cushions are placed on the chair.
(C) A picture is being hung on the wall.
(D) An armchair is facing the window.

(A) 깔개가 테이블 아래에 놓이고 있는 중이다.
(B) 의자에 쿠션 몇 개가 놓여 있다.
(C) 벽에 그림이 걸리고 있는 중이다.
(D) 팔걸이 의자가 창문 쪽을 향해 있다.

해설 동작이나 사람이 보이지 않으므로 「being + p.p.」 표현으로 움직임을 묘사한 (A)와 (C)는 오답이다. 의자 위에 쿠션이 없으므로 (B)도 오답이다. 의자가 창문을 향해 있는 모습을 묘사한 (D)가 정답이다.

3
(A) They are picking some flowers.
(B) Some bicycles are propped against a tree.
(C) A man is riding a bicycle.
(D) Some people are seated near the river.

(A) 그들은 꽃을 따고 있는 중이다.
(B) 자전거들이 나무에 기대어 있다.
(C) 한 남자가 자전거를 타고 있는 중이다.
(D) 몇몇 사람들이 강 근처에 앉아 있다.

어휘 prop 받치다

해설 두 사람이 강가에 앉아서 쉬고 있는 모습이므로 (D)가 정답이다. 꽃을 따는 동작이 보이지 않으므로 (A)는 오답이며, 자전거들이 세워져 있지만 나무에 기대어 있지 않으므로 (B)도 오답이다. 자전거를 타는 남자의 모습 역시 보이지 않으므로 (C)도 소거한다.

PART 2

4
Where will the delivered groceries be stored?
(A) A delivery service.
(B) In the cabinet next to the back door.
(C) I don't have time to try it.

배달된 식료품은 어디에 보관되나요?

(A) 배달 서비스예요.
(B) 뒷문 옆에 있는 수납장에요.
(C) 저는 그것을 먹어 볼 시간이 없어요.

해설 식료품을 둘 위치를 묻는 질문에 대해 뒷문 옆의 수납장이라고 답한 (B)가 정답이 된다. cabinet은 여러 종류의 수납장을 통칭하기도 한다. (A)는 deliver에서 파생된 delivery를 사용한 오답이고, groceries와 의미상 연관성이 있는 '먹어볼 시간이 없다'고 답한 (C) 역시 오답이다.

5
When's the last day to submit the application?
(A) To apply for the marketing manager position.
(B) It will last about four hours.
(C) This weekend.

신청서 제출의 마지막 날은 언제인가요?
(A) 마케팅 매니저 직책에 지원하기 위해서요.
(B) 그것은 약 4시간 동안 지속될 거예요.
(C) 이번 주말요.

해설 신청서 제출하는 마지막 날을 묻는 질문에 이번 주말이라고 요일을 언급한 (C)가 정답이다. day는 요일, date는 날짜로 답해야 한다. application의 유사한 발음을 이용한 (A)는 오답인데, 파트 2에서 to부정사는 주로 why 의문문에 대한 정답으로 사용된다. four hours는 기간을 이야기하는 'how long'에 대한 정답이므로 (B) 역시 소거한다.

6
Did someone reserve a hotel room?
(A) Reservations are required.
(B) Tammy already checked out.
(C) I thought you did.

누군가 호텔 예약을 했나요?
(A) 예약은 필수예요.
(B) 태미는 이미 체크 아웃했어요.
(C) 저는 당신이 했을 줄 알았는데요.

해설 호텔을 예약을 한 사람이 있는지를 묻는 질문인데, '당신이 한 줄 알았다'고 답하며 잘못 알고 있는 사실을 언급한 (C)가 정답이다. reserve에서 파생된 reservation을 이용한 (A)는 오답이며, '호텔'에서 연상할 수 있는 check out과, someone에서 연상되는 '사람의 이름'을 이용한 (B)역시 오답이다.

7
When does the workshop begin?
(A) Yes, I often shop there.
(B) In the conference room.
(C) We can still grab a cup of coffee.

워크샵 언제 시작하나요?
(A) 네, 저는 그곳에서 자주 쇼핑해요.
(B) 회의실에서요.
(C) 아직 커피 한 잔은 마실 수 있어요.

어휘 grab 집다; 간단히 먹다

해설 의문사 질문에 yes로 답한 (A)와 when에 대해 장소로 답한 (B) 둘 다 정답이 될 수 없다. 워크샵이 시작하는 시간을 묻는 질문에 대해 아직 커피 한 잔을 마실 수 있다는 내용의 (C)는 관계 없는 답변처럼 보이지만, 커피를 한 잔 하려던 상황에서 워크샵 시작 시간을 묻는 다면 이는 자연스러운 대답이 된다.

8
Why were you late for the staff meeting?
(A) My alarm clock didn't go off.
(B) They offer a corporate rate.
(C) I'll meet you at 7:00.

직원 회의에 왜 늦었나요?
(A) 제 자명종 시계가 울리지 않았어요.
(B) 그들은 법인 요금을 제공해요.
(C) 7시에 만나요.

어휘 go off 울리다

해설 좋지 않은 상황에 대한 이유를 묻는 질문의 정답은 대부분 부정적인 형태이다. 이 문제에서도 자명종이 울리지 않아서 늦었다며 늦잠을 잤다는 의미의 (A)가 정답이다. late과 rate의 유사 발음을 이용한 (B)는 오답이며, (C)는 meet이라는 단어를 반복한 오답 유형이다.

9
Where is the nearest bank?
(A) I have to deposit some money.
(B) It's next to Granville Station.
(C) In an hour.

가장 가까운 은행은 어디인가요?
(A) 저는 돈을 좀 입금해야 해요.
(B) 그랜빌역 옆에 있어요.
(C) 한 시간 후에요.

해설 은행의 위치를 묻는 질문에 대해 역 옆에 있다고 답한 (B)가 정답이다. '은행'에서 연상되는 '입금'을 언급한 (A)는 대표적인 오답 유형이다. 장소를 묻는 질문에 시간으로 답한 (C) 또한 오답이다.

10
Would you take the meeting minutes?
(A) Two seconds.
(B) I cannot attend the meeting today.
(C) It only takes fifteen minutes.

회의록 좀 작성해 주시겠어요?
(A) 2초요.
(B) 저는 오늘 회의에 참석할 수 없어요.
(C) 그것은 15분밖에 안 걸려요.

어휘 minutes 의사록, 회의록

해설 회의록 작성을 부탁하는 질문에 대해 오늘 회의에 참석하지 못하므로 불가능하다고 거절하는 (B)가 정답이다. minute에서 연상되는 second를 이용한 (A)는 오답이며, 회의록이라는 의미로 쓰인 minute을 '분'이라는 의미의 minute을 이용한 (C)는 전형적인 다의어 오답이다.

11

Who designed the poster?

(A) He resigned his position.

(B) Yes, I already posted a memo.

(C) A friend of mine.

누가 포스터를 디자인했나요?

(A) 그는 자신의 직책을 사임했어요.

(B) 네, 저는 이미 메모를 올렸어요.

(C) 제 친구요.

해설 포스터를 디자인한 사람을 묻는 질문에 자신의 친구라고 답한 (C)가 정답이다. who 의문문의 답변으로 어울리는 he로 답하면서, design과 발음이 유사한 resign을 이용하여 혼동을 유발한 (A)는 오답이다. 의문사 의문문의 경우 yes와 no로 답할 수 없으므로 (B) 역시 소거한다.

12

Can you help me with this customer survey?

(A) That's not what I meant.

(B) Yes, he's a regular customer.

(C) I'm free all afternoon.

이 고객 설문 조사 좀 도와 주시겠어요?

(A) 제 말은 그런 뜻이 아니었어요.

(B) 네, 그는 우리의 단골 고객이에요.

(C) 저는 오후 내내 한가해요.

해설 도움을 요청하는 질문에 대해 시간이 있다고 답한 (C)가 정답이 된다. 의도를 묻는 질문이 아니므로 (A)는 정답이 될 수 없다. 지칭하는 사람이 불명확한 he가 주어인 (B) 또한 오답이다.

13

The appliance store has relocated to 4th Avenue, hasn't it?

(A) Yes, I applied for that position.

(B) My office is on 5th Avenue.

(C) I heard it needed more space for its products.

가전제품 매장이 4번가로 이전했어요, 그렇지 않나요?

(A) 네, 저는 그 직책에 지원했어요.

(B) 제 사무실은 5번가에 있어요.

(C) 제품을 위한 공간이 더 필요하다고 들었어요.

해설 매장의 이전 여부를 묻는 질문에 대해 더 많은 공간이 필요하다고 들었다고 답하면서 이전의 이유를 설명한 (C)가 가장 적절한 대답이다. 질문의 4번가에서 연상되는 5번가를 언급한 (B)와 application과 유사 발음 단어인 apply를 이용한 (A)는 오답이다.

14

That car is expensive, isn't it?

(A) Yes, it certainly is.

(B) A shopping cart.

(C) No, I prefer public transportation.

그 차는 비싸요, 그렇지 않나요?

(A) 네, 정말로 비싸요.

(B) 쇼핑 카트요.

(C) 아니요, 저는 대중 교통을 선호해요.

해설 차의 가격이 비싸지 않느냐는 질문에 대해 정말로 그렇다고 답한 (A)가 정답이다. car와 유사한 발음의 cart를 이용한 (B)는 오답이며, 자동차에서 연상할 수 있는 대중 교통이 언급된 (C)도 오답이다.

15

How do you operate the new coffee machine?

(A) Two cups, please.

(B) There's a manual next to it.

(C) It's a great addition to the kitchen.

새로운 커피 머신은 어떻게 작동하나요?

(A) 두 잔요.

(B) 기계 옆에 매뉴얼이 있어요.

(C) 주방에 좋은 보탬이 되겠네요.

해설 기계의 작동법을 묻는 질문에 대해 '매뉴얼이 있다'고 해결 방법을 간접적으로 알려주는 (B)가 정답이다. coffee에서 연상되는 cup을 이용한 (A)는 오답이며, '방법'에 대해 '자신의 생각'을 언급한 (C) 역시 오답이다.

16

We should upgrade the computer software.

(A) It's a new mouse.

(B) Yes, I think that's necessary.

(C) I'm wearing a sweater.

컴퓨터 소프트웨어를 업그레이드해야 해요.

(A) 새로운 마우스예요.

(B) 네, 그게 필요하다고 생각해요.

(C) 저는 스웨터를 입고 있어요.

해설 소프트웨어 업데이트의 필요성을 언급한 평서문에 대해 필요하다고 동의한 (B)가 정답이다. 컴퓨터에서 연상되는 마우스를 언급한 (A), software에서 ware와 발음이 같은 wear를 이용한 (C)는 오답이다.

17

Will you be attending the meeting with the clients?

(A) I have a conflicting appointment.

(B) The Italian restaurant nearby.

(C) I met her yesterday.

고객과의 회의에 참석하시겠어요?

(A) 저는 다른 약속이 있어요.

(B) 근처의 이탈리아 식당이에요.

(C) 저는 어제 그녀를 만났어요.

해설 회의 참석 여부를 묻는 질문에 대해서 다른 약속이 있다고 답한 (A)가 정답이다. conflict는 '상충되는'이라는 의미지만, 시간과 관련해서 사용될 때에는 같은 시간에 두가지 일을 해야 하는 상황을 의미한다. 참석 여부를 묻는 질문에 장소로 대답한 (B)는 오답이며, (C)의 경우 질문의 clients는 복수인데, 답변의 her는 단수이므로 정답이 될 수 없다.

18

The password you entered is incorrect.
(A) I have it written down.
(B) Follow the path.
(C) Let me check it.

당신이 입력한 비밀번호가 잘못되었어요.
(A) 제가 받아 적었어요.
(B) 그 길을 따라가세요.
(C) 제가 확인해 볼게요.

해설 당신이 입력한 비밀번호가 잘못되었다는 문제점에 대한 해결책으로 '내가 확인해 보겠다'고 답한 (C)가 정답이다. 비밀번호를 받아 적었다고 이야기하는 (A)는 문맥상 어색하며, pass와 path의 유사 발음을 이용한 (B)역시 오답이다.

PART 3

[19-21]

> W   19) **I've decided to buy this car. How do I transfer the title to myself?**
>
> M   Just go to the Department of Motor Vehicles Web site. When you and the seller both fill out and sign a change of ownership form and sign the certificate of title, the ownership will be transferred.
>
> W   20) **Will I have to pay any fees?**
>
> M   All of the transfer fees are the responsibility of the buyer. You must take care of this before anything else. 21) **If you go to the DMV's Web site, you can easily find a special formula to calculate the fees.**
>
> W   저는 이 차를 구매하기로 결정했어요. 어떻게 이 차의 소유권을 이전할 수 있나요?
>
> M   차량관리부서의 웹사이트로 가시기만 하면 됩니다. 당신과 판매자 둘 다 소유권 이전 양식을 작성해서 서명하고 차량 권리증에 서명하시면, 소유권이 이전됩니다.
>
> W   제가 수수료를 지불해야 하나요?
>
> M   모든 이전 수수료는 구매자의 책임입니다. 다른 것보다 먼저 그것을 처리해야 합니다. 차량관리부서의 웹사이트에 가시면, 수수료를 계산할 수 있는 특별 공식을 쉽게 찾을 수 있습니다.

어휘 ownership 소유권   certificate of title 권리 증서, 차량 권리증   DMV (Department of Motor Vehicle) 차량관리부서

19

남자는 어디에서 일하는가?
(A) 자동차 수리점에서
(B) 자동차 공장에서
(C) 건설 회사에서
(D) 자동차 판매회사에서

해설 대화 초반부의 'I've decided to buy this car. How do I transfer the title to myself?'에서 여자가 이 차를 사기로 결정 했다고 말했으므로 남자는 자동차 판매 회사에 근무하고 있을 것이다. 정답은 (D)이다.

20

여자는 무엇을 질문하는가?
(A) 그녀가 수수료를 내야하는지
(B) 어떻게 돈을 이체하는지
(C) 어디에서 차를 구입할 수 있는지
(D) 이전이 얼마나 오래 걸리는지

해설 여자가 질문하는 것을 묻는 문제의 경우 여자의 질문에서 정답의 단서를 찾아야 한다. 'Will I have to pay any fees?'에서 수수료를 내야 하는지를 묻고 있으므로 정답은 (A)이다.

21

왜 여자는 웹사이트를 방문해야 하는가?
(A) 연비를 계산하기 위해
(B) 금액을 확인하기 위해
(C) 운전 면허증을 받기 위해
(D) 연락처를 찾기 위해

해설 why 의문문의 경우, 질문의 내용이 언급된 부분 주변이 정답의 근거가 된다. 대화 마지막 부분의 'If you go to the DMV's Web site, you can easily find a special formula to calculate the fees.'에서 웹사이트에 계산 공식이 있다고 했으므로 정답은 (B)이다.

[22-24]

> W   22) **Thank you for volunteering to taste our new chocolates today, Mr. Patterson.**
>
> M   There's nothing more exciting than eating different chocolates for free!
>
> W   Well, I'm glad you think so. But after trying more than ten different flavors, you might think differently. 23) **The first thing you need to do is fill out this allergy awareness form and sign it at the bottom.** For example, you must tell us if you have any peanut allergies because all of our chocolates—those that contain nuts and those that don't—are made on the same manufacturing line.
>
> M   Here you are.
>
> W   Perfect. Now, 24) **please follow me to room 10. There are ten other participants who will be participating in today's chocolate testing.**
>
> W   오늘 새로운 초콜릿 시식에 자원해 주셔서 감사합니다, 패터슨 씨.
>
> M   각양각색의 초콜릿을 무료로 먹는 것만큼 신나는 것은 없어요!

W 음, 그렇게 생각하시니 기쁘네요. 하지만 10가지 이상의 다른 맛을 드신 후라면, 아마도 생각이 달라지실 수도 있어요. 가장 먼저 해야 할 일은 이 알레르기 인식 양식을 작성하고 하단에 서명하시면 됩니다. 예를 들어, 땅콩 알레르기가 있는지 알려주셔야 하는데, 견과류가 들어 있는 초콜릿과 들어 있지 않은 초콜릿은 모두 동일한 제조 라인에서 제조되기 때문입니다.

M 여기 있어요.

W 좋습니다. 자, 이제 저를 따라 10번 방으로 오세요. 오늘 초콜릿 테스트에 참여할 다른 10명의 참가자가 있습니다.

22

남자는 오늘 무엇을 하는 것을 자원했는가?
(A) 행사를 담당하는 것을 돕기
(B) 워크샵 계획하기
(C) 상품 포장 돕기
(D) 몇몇 새로운 상품 맛보기

해설 남자가 오늘 자원한 일을 찾는 문제이므로 '날짜'와 '자원하다'라는 표현을 듣고 정답을 찾아야 한다. 'Thank you for volunteering to taste our new chocolates today, Mr. Patterson.'이라는 부분에서 새로운 초콜릿을 맛보는 것에 자원해 주어서 감사하다고 했으므로, 신제품의 맛을 보기 위해 왔다는 내용의 (D)가 정답이다.

23

여자는 남자에게 무엇을 작성할 것을 요청하는가?
(A) 출석표
(B) 특정 양식
(C) 직원 계약서
(D) 참여 동의서

해설 여자가 'The first thing you need to do is fill out this allergy awareness form and sign it at the bottom.'에서 알레르기 인식 양식을 작성하라고 했으므로 정답은 (B)이다.

24

남자는 다음에 무엇을 할 것인가?
(A) 몇몇 다른 지원자들 만나기
(B) 양식 작성하기
(C) 직원의 일정 확인하기
(D) 관광하기

해설 대화 마지막 부분의 'please follow me to room 10. There are ten other participants who will be participating in today's chocolate testing.'에서 여자는 다른 지원자들이 있는 곳으로 남자를 안내하고 있으므로 정답은 (A)이다.

[25-27]

M Sandra, did you get the e-mail I sent you this morning? 25) **I attached a map of the neighborhood I'm considering opening our flower shop in.**

W Yes, I got your e-mail. I especially like the fact that there is a park right in the middle of the district.

M I'm glad you like the district, but that's the problem. I am having a hard time deciding where to open our shop.

W Well, if you ask me, 26-1) **I think the place closest to the department store would be best because there will be a lot of potential customers walking by.**

M That's a good point. However, 26-2) **I strongly believe having sufficient parking is a big advantage, too.** We actually have a competitor in the neighborhood.

W Let me have another look at the map. 26-3) **How about the store across from the Cotton Dessert Shop on 113th Street?**

M Good! 27) **I would like to go and see the store now before somebody else takes it. Do you have time now?**

M 산드라, 제가 오늘 아침에 보낸 이메일 받았어요? 우리의 꽃집을 열기 위해 고민 중인 지역의 지도를 첨부했어요.

W 네, 이메일 받았어요. 저는 특히 그 지역의 중심부에 공원이 있다는 사실이 좋았어요.

M 그 지역이 마음에 든다니 다행이지만, 바로 그게 문제예요. 저는 점포 개업 위치 결정에 어려움을 겪고 있거든요.

W 음, 저한테 물어보신다면, 잠재 고객들이 많이 지나다니기 때문에 백화점에서 가장 가까운 곳이 제일 좋아 보여요.

M 좋은 지적이군요. 하지만 저는 충분한 주차 공간 또한 아주 큰 장점이라고 생각해요. 그리고 사실 그 지역에는 경쟁해야 하는 가게도 있거든요.

W 지도를 다시 한 번 보죠. 코튼 디저트 샵에서 113번로 건너편에 있는 상점은 어떤가요?

M 좋네요! 다른 사람들이 차지하기 전에 상점에 가서 한 번 봐야겠어요. 지금 시간 되세요?

25

화자들은 누구인 것 같은가?
(A) 제빵사들
(B) 기계공들
(C) 회계사들
(D) 플로리스트들

해설 화자들의 직업을 묻는 문제의 경우 주로 대화 초반에 단서가 등장한다. 'I attached a map of the neighborhood I'm considering opening our flower shop in.'에서 우리의 꽃집을 개업하기 위한 지역을 고민하고 있다고 했으므로 화자들이 플로리스트라는 것을 알 수 있다.

26

시각 정보를 보시오. 남자가 마음에 든다고 말한 건물은 어느 것인가?

(A) 건물 1
(B) 건물 2
(C) 건물 3
(D) 건물 4

해설 여자가 'I think the one closest to the department store would be best because there will be a lot of potential customers walking by.'라고 하며 백화점에서 가장 가까운 가게를 추천했는데, 남자는 'I strongly believe having sufficient parking is a big advantage, too.'라고 하며 넉넉한 주차 공간을 강조하면서 다른 의견을 제시하고 있다. 이어서 언급된 여자의 말에서 'How about the store across from the Cotton Dessert Shop on 113th Street?'이라고 말했고 남자가 이에 동의했으므로 정답은 (B)이다.

27

남자는 무엇을 하자고 제안하는가?

(A) 부동산을 방문하는 것
(B) 가격 견적을 이메일로 보내는 것
(C) 건물을 함께 보러 가는 것
(D) 주차 공간을 찾는 것

해설 대화 마지막 부분의 'I would like to go and see the store now before somebody else takes it. Do you have time now?'에서 상점을 같이 보러 가자고 했으므로 정답은 (C)이다.

PART 4

[28-30]

> M You're tuned in to *The Green Thumb*, 28) 29) **a weekly podcast about gardening and plant care**. In this episode, we're diving into the best techniques for indoor plant maintenance. Today, unlike usual, instead of answering your gardening questions at the end, I'll address them right at the start. These questions are related to some key topics we'll explore with my expert guest today. But before we get into that, 30) **I want to express my gratitude to everyone who has contributed to our podcast through monthly donations**. Your support means a lot.

> M 여러분은 원예와 식물 관리에 관한 주간 팟캐스트인 *그린 섬*을 듣고 계십니다. 이번 에피소드에서는, 실내 식물 관리를 위한 가장 좋은 기술들을 자세히 알아보도록 하겠습니다. 오늘은, 평소와 다르게, 질문에 대한 답변을 마지막에 하는 것이 아니라, 시작 부분에서 바로 다루도록 하겠습니다. 이 질문들은 오늘 우리가 객원 전문가와 함께 다룰 주요 주제들과 관련이 있습니다. 하지만 시작하기에 앞서, 저는 매달 기부를 통해 우리 팟캐스트에 기여해 주시는 모든 분들께 감사를 표하고 싶습니다. 여러분의 지원은 정말 큰 의미가 됩니다.

어휘 dive 빠져들다 (어떤 주제 등에 깊이 들어가다) address 다루다 gratitude 감사 contribute 기여하다 donation 기부

28

팟캐스트의 주요 주제는 무엇인가?

(A) 요리
(B) 원예
(C) 스포츠
(D) 패션

해설 대화의 시작 부분 'a weekly podcast about gardening and plant care'에서 팟캐스트의 주제를 언급하고 있다. 주제는 원예와 식물 관리이므로 정답은 (B)이다.

29

팟캐스트는 얼마나 자주 방송하는가?

(A) 일주일에 한 번
(B) 일주일에 세 번
(C) 한 달에 한 번
(D) 하루에 한 번

해설 이 문제는 난이도가 높은 문제인데, 대화의 주제를 언급하는 부분인 'a weekly podcast about gardening and plant care'에서 weekly라는 단어를 놓치면 문제의 힌트가 더 이상 언급되지 않기 때문이다. weekly를 놓치지 않고 들었다면 (A)가 정답임을 알 수 있다.

30

화자는 누구에게 감사하는가?

(A) 청취자들
(B) 객원 전문가들
(C) 기부자들
(D) 작가들

해설 gratitude라는 단어를 모른다면 이 문제를 틀릴 가능성이 높다. '감사'라는 의미의 단어인 gratitude가 언급된 부분인 'I want to express my gratitude to everyone who has contributed to our podcast through monthly donations'에서 화자는 매달 기부를 해주는 사람들에게 감사를 표하고 싶다고 했다. 따라서 (C)가 정답이 된다.

[31-33]

> W 31) **Welcome to the first event of our park's summer outdoor film series!** We are so excited to start the event with a movie directed by our very own local director,

Nanya Lange. We'll be playing Ms. Lange's latest release, *Family Tree*, which is a 32) **historic movie set in the 1920s in Harlem, New York. It covers the city's vibrant art scene during the Harlem Renaissance, which was known as the birthplace of the cultural revival of African-American art and music.** Before we start the movie, 33) **we'd like to apologize for the lack of seating space. We did not anticipate such a large audience today.** For future events, we'll make sure to prepare enough chairs.

W 저희 공원의 여름 실외 영화 시리즈의 첫 행사에 오신 것을 환영합니다! 바로 우리 지역 출신 감독인 난야 랑쥬가 연출한 영화로 행사를 시작하게 되어 너무 기대됩니다. 우리는 랑쥬 씨의 최신작 패밀리 트리를 상영할 예정인데, 이는 1920년대 뉴욕의 할렘 지역을 배경으로 합니다. 이 영화는 할렘 르네상스 시기 동안 도시의 활기찬 예술 현장을 다루고 있는데, 이곳은 아프리카계 미국인들의 미술과 음악의 문화 부흥의 발상지로 알려졌습니다. 영화를 시작하기 전에, 우리는 좌석이 부족한 것에 대해 사과하고 싶습니다. 우리는 오늘 이렇게 많은 관객을 예상하지 못했습니다. 앞으로 있을 행사를 위해, 의자를 충분히 준비하도록 하겠습니다.

어휘 release 출시 vibrant 활기찬 cover 다루다 revival 부활, 부흥 anticipate 예상하다

31
행사의 주제는 무엇인가?
(A) 음악
(B) 영화
(C) 책
(D) 그림

해설 담화의 첫 문장 'Welcome to our first event of our park's summer outdoor film series!'에서 정답이 (B)임을 알 수 있다.

32
할렘은 1920년대에 무엇으로 유명했는가?
(A) 그곳의 아름다운 공원들
(B) 그곳의 특별한 요리들
(C) 그곳의 예술과 문화
(D) 그곳의 독특한 건축

해설 문제에 언급된 시간과 장소인 'in the 1920s'와 'Harlem'에 집중하며 단서를 찾아야 한다. 담화 중반 'historic movie set in the 1920s in Harlem, New York. It covers the city's vibrant art scene during the Harlem Renaissance, which was known as the birthplace of the cultural revival of African-American art and music.'에서 1920년대 할렘이 아프리카계 미국인들의 예술과 음악의 발상지라고 했으므로 정답은 (C)이다.

33
화자는 왜 "우리는 오늘 이렇게 많은 관객을 예상하지 못했습니다"라고 말하는가?
(A) 문제의 원인을 설명하기 위해
(B) 기술적인 문제에 대해 사과하기 위해
(C) 다른 행사에 갈 것을 추천하기 위해
(D) 중요 행사를 소개하기 위해

해설 의도 파악 문제의 경우 해당 문장 주변의 내용을 듣고 문제를 풀어야 한다. 'we'd like to apologize for the lack of seating space. We did not anticipate such a large audience today.'에서 부족한 좌석에 대해 사과한 후, 청중이 예상보다 많았다고 말했다. 즉, 좌석이 부족한 문제가 발생한 이유를 설명하고 있으므로 정답은 (A)이다.

DAY 03 PART 2 문제 풀이법: 소거법

실전 문제 연습 p.035

🎧 03-09

1 (C)	2 (B)	3 (A)	4 (A)
5 (C)	6 (A)	7 (A)	8 (A)
9 (C)	10 (A)	11 (C)	12 (A)
13 (B)	14 (B)	15 (A)	16 (A)
17 (B)	18 (C)	19 (C)	20 (A)
21 (B)	22 (C)	23 (A)	24 (A)
25 (C)	26 (B)	27 (D)	28 (C)
29 (A)	30 (A)	31 (C)	32 (C)
33 (B)			

PART 1

1
(A) A wheel of a bicycle is being changed.
(B) A car is leaving a garage.
(C) The car has been lifted up in the air.
(D) A man is working on a motorcycle.

(A) 자전거의 바퀴 하나가 교환되고 있는 중이다.
(B) 차 한 대가 차고를 떠나는 중이다.
(C) 차는 공중에 들어올려진 상태이다.
(D) 남자는 오토바이의 작업 중이다.

어휘 wheel 바퀴 motorcycle 오토바이(= motorbike) garage 차고 lift 들어올리다 work on ～의 작업을 하다; 수리하다 up in the air 공중에 떠 있는

해설 「has/have been p.p.」는 상태를, 「be being p.p.」는 진행 중인 상황을 설명할 때 쓰인다. 차가 이미 들어올려져 있는 상태를 적절하게 묘사한 (C)가 정답이 된다. 수리하는 모습에만 집중해서 (A)를 고르

거나, 작업 중인 대상이 오토바이라고 잘못 표현된 (D)를 고르지 않도록 주의해야 한다. (D)의 work on은 '작업을 하다'라는 의미도 있지만 '수리 하다'의 의미도 있다.

2

(A) A woman is leaning against the wall.
(B) Two people are seated opposite each other.
(C) They are both wearing hats.
(D) A woman is pouring water into a cup.

(A) 여자는 벽에 기대어 있다.
(B) 두 사람은 서로 반대편에 앉아 있다.
(C) 그들은 모두 모자를 쓰고 있다.
(D) 여자가 컵에 물을 붓고 있는 중이다.

어휘 be seated 앉은 상태이다 opposite each other 서로 반대 편에

해설 (B)의 be seated라는 표현은 앉아 있는 상태를 묘사하는 것으로, be sitting과 같은 의미를 가진 정답이다. (C)의 경우 여자만 모자를 쓰고 있으므로 오답이다. (D)와 같이 pour라는 동사가 나오면 사진에서 물을 붓는 동작이 있어야 한다. 파트 1에서는 both, each와 같이 함께 일어나는 일을 파악해야 하는 문제들이 출제된다.

3

(A) The cups are being filled.
(B) Some people are drinking coffee.
(C) The cups are being washed.
(D) The cups are being arranged on the counter.

(A) 컵들이 채워지고 있다.
(B) 사람들이 커피를 마시고 있다.
(C) 컵들이 씻어지고 있다.
(D) 컵들이 카운터 위에 정리되고 있다.

어휘 arrange 정리하다

해설 「be being p.p.」 형태의 진행형 수동태에서는 동작의 일치를 확인하는 것이 포인트이다. 네 개의 동작 중 사진과 일치하는 것은 "채워 지다"라는 의미를 가진 (A)뿐이다. 사진 속에 사람이 등장하지 않으므로 사람이 언급된 (B)는 전형적인 오답이다.

PART 2

4

Didn't you hire a new secretary?
(A) Yes, she started working last week.
(B) Hang it a bit lower.
(C) I'd better use the old one.

새로운 비서를 고용하지 않았나요?
(A) 네, 그녀는 지난주에 일을 시작했어요.
(B) 조금만 더 낮게 걸어주세요.
(C) 저는 예전 것을 사용하는 것이 낫겠어요.

해설 비서의 고용 여부를 묻는 질문에 대해 지난주부터 일을 시작했다고 말하며 간접적으로 고용했다는 사실을 알려주는 (A)가 정답이 된다.

hire와 발음이 같은 higher에서 연상되는 lower를 사용한 (B)는 오답이다. new의 반대말인 old를 포함하고 있는 (C)도 오답이다.

5

Have you sampled our new ice cream flavor?
(A) I can give you some samples.
(B) Because it's my favorite.
(C) I got back from my vacation yesterday.

새로 나온 아이스크림 맛을 시식해 보셨어요?
(A) 제가 샘플을 드릴 수 있어요.
(B) 그것은 제가 제일 좋아하는 것이니까요.
(C) 저는 어제 휴가에서 돌아왔어요.

어휘 sample 맛보다; 샘플 flavor 맛

해설 새로 나온 아이스크림의 맛을 시식해 봤는지를 묻는 질문에 대해 휴가에서 막 돌아와서 맛볼 수 없었음을 우회적으로 답한 (C)가 정답이 된다. sample이 가지고 있는 다른 의미를 이용한 (A)는 소거한다. favor 와 favorite은 음절이 겹치는 유사 발음 단어인데, 이것을 활용한 (B)도 오답이다.

6

Where can I find the list of participants?
(A) We're still accepting registrations.
(B) I agree with you.
(C) I'm fine. Thank you.

참가자 명단은 어디에서 확인할 수 있나요?
(A) 등록은 아직 받고 있어요.
(B) 당신의 말에 동의해요.
(C) 저는 괜찮아요. 감사해요.

해설 참가자 명단의 위치를 묻는 질문에 대해 아직 등록을 받고 있으므로 명단이 완성되지 않았다는 의미의 간접 답변인 (A)가 정답이 된다. 의문사 의문문의 경우 맞장구나 동의하는 패턴은 정답이 될 수 없으므로 (B)는 오답이다. find와 fine의 유사 발음을 이용한 (C)도 소거한다.

7

When should I finish the budget report?
(A) By the end of this week.
(B) Yes, the reporter is coming tomorrow.
(C) To acquire more funds for the coming year.

예산 보고서는 언제 끝내야 하나요?
(A) 이번 주말까지요.
(B) 네, 내일 그 기자가 올 거예요.
(C) 내년도 자금을 더 많이 확보하기 위해서요.

어휘 acquire 획득하다

해설 예산 보고서의 마감 기한을 묻는 질문에 대해 이번 주말까지 끝내 라는 기한을 언급한 (A)가 정답이다. 의문사 의문문에 yes/no로 답할 수 없으므로 (B)는 소거한다. to부정사의 경우 목적을 의미하는 답변으로서 주로 why 의문문의 정답으로 사용되므로 (C)도 오답이다.

8

Would you like to make a reservation?
(A) Yes, a party of four, please.
(B) I already made the bed.
(C) I really like the view.

예약하시겠어요?
(A) 네, 4명 일행 부탁해요.
(B) 저는 이미 침구를 정리했어요.
(C) 저는 이 경치가 정말 좋아요.

어휘 make the bed 침구를 정리하다

해설 예약을 원하는지 묻는 질문에 4명의 일행을 예약해달라고 대답하는 (A)가 정답이다. make라는 단어를 반복하고, reservation을 통해 연상되는 호텔과 관련된 단어인 bed가 활용된 (B)는 오답이다. 유사 발음인 would like와 like를 이용한 (C)도 오답이다.

9

Do you know who I can get the network password from?
(A) There will be a networking event after the seminar.
(B) We didn't pass the inspection.
(C) You can ask the receptionist at the front desk.

네트워크 비밀번호를 누구에게 받을 수 있는지 아시나요?
(A) 세미나가 끝난 후 네트워킹 행사가 있을 예정이에요.
(B) 우리는 검사에 통과하지 못했어요.
(C) 프런트에 있는 접수 담당자에게 물어보세요.

어휘 networking event 네트워킹 행사(인맥을 만드는 행사)

해설 인터넷의 비밀번호를 알려줄 사람을 찾는 질문에 대해 프런트 데스크의 접수 담당자에서 물어보라고 답하는 (C)가 정답이 된다. 일부 발음이 겹치는 password와 pass의 유사 발음을 활용한 오답인 (B)는 소거한다. network가 반복된 (A) 역시 오답이다.

10

Isn't my office too small for the meeting?
(A) There is a conference room on the 3rd floor.
(B) There are two people in the meeting.
(C) At the end of the month.

회의하기에 제 사무실이 너무 좁지 않나요?
(A) 3층에 회의실이 있어요.
(B) 회의에 두 사람이 있어요.
(C) 월말에요.

해설 회의 공간의 넓이가 적절한지를 묻고 있다. 이에 대해 3층에 회의실이 있다고 언급한 (A)는 장소를 옮기자는 간접적인 대답이다. 인원을 묻는 것이 아니므로 인원수를 이야기하면서 meeting을 반복한 (B)는 오답이다. 시간을 묻는 질문이 아니므로 (C) 역시 오답이다.

11

Have you sent the invitation to the office party yet?
(A) I'll get the offer.

(B) Okay, I'll invite you to the party.
(C) I will do it later today.

회사 파티 초대장 벌써 보냈어요?
(A) 제가 그 제안을 받을게요.
(B) 좋아요, 제가 당신을 파티에 초대할게요.
(C) 제가 오늘 오후에 할게요.

해설 초대장을 보냈는지 묻는 질문에 대해 오후에 보내겠다고 대답하며 아직 보내지 않았음을 언급한 (C)가 정답이다. (A)의 offer는 office와 함께 자주 등장하는 유사 발음이다. invite의 파생어인 invitation을 활용한 (B) 역시 오답이다.

12

What is the best way to get to the airport?
(A) Take the airport shuttle.
(B) No, I'm on my way there.
(C) My plane has been delayed.

공항까지 어떻게 가는 것이 가장 좋을까요?
(A) 공항 셔틀을 타고요.
(B) 아니요, 지금 가는 중이에요.
(C) 제 비행기가 연착되었어요.

어휘 delayed 연착된   on one's way 가는 중인

해설 공항으로 가는 가장 좋은 방법을 묻는 질문에 대해 공항 셔틀을 타고 가라고 알려주는 (A)가 가장 적절한 답변이다. 의문사의 경우 yes/no가 들어간 선택지는 오답이 되므로 (B)는 소거한다. 공항에서 연상되는 단어인 plane을 활용한 (C) 역시 오답이다.

13

I'm having trouble finding some pictures to decorate our office with.
(A) We'll get a photo of our employee badge.
(B) Kelvin knows some emerging artists.
(C) Louis is a good architect.

사무실을 장식할 그림을 찾기가 힘들군요.
(A) 우리는 직원 배지의 사진을 찍을 거예요.
(B) 켈빈이 떠오르는 아티스트들을 알고 있어요.
(C) 루이스는 좋은 건축가예요.

어휘 emerging 떠오르는, 신흥의

해설 사무실을 장식할 만한 그림을 찾는 것에 어려움을 겪고 있다는 내용의 평서문에 대해, 캘빈이 떠오르는 아티스트들을 알고 있다고 답하며 그가 좋은 그림을 소개할 수 있을 것임을 간접적으로 답한 (B)가 정답이다. picture에서 연상되는 photo를 이용한 (A)는 오답이며, 건축에 대한 질문이 아니므로 건축가를 언급한 (C) 역시 오답이다.

14

Why has production been delayed?
(A) No, he didn't get the promotion.
(B) Didn't you get an e-mail?
(C) Yes, she is a famous producer.

왜 생산이 지연되고 있나요?
(A) 아니요, 그는 승진하지 못했어요.
(B) 이메일 받지 못했나요?
(C) 네, 그녀는 유명한 프로듀서예요.

[해설] 생산이 지연된 이유를 묻는 질문에 대해 이메일을 받지 못했는지를 묻는 것은 이메일에 설명이 있다는 의미이므로 (B)가 정답이다. 의문사 의문문에 대해 yes/no로 답할 수 없으므로 (A)와 (C)는 모두 오답이다. (C)는 production과 발음이 유사한 producer를 활용하였다.

15

How should I fix the broken fax machine?
(A) You should call maintenance.
(B) I need to take a break.
(C) We have to pay tax.

고장 난 팩스 기기를 어떻게 고쳐야 하나요?
(A) 유지보수팀에 전화하시는 것이 좋겠어요.
(B) 저는 조금 쉬어야겠어요.
(C) 우리는 세금을 내야 해요.

[해설] 고장 난 기계를 고치는 방법을 묻는 질문에 대해 유지보수팀에 전화해 보라고 말하는 (A)가 정답이다. break에는 '고장 나다'라는 의미와 '쉬다'라는 의미가 있는데, 이와 같이 다의어를 이용한 (B)는 전형적인 오답이다. (C)의 경우 fax와 tax역시 자주 등장하는 유사 발음 오답이다.

16

Would you like me to install the software for you?
(A) My assistant Tom has done it before.
(B) You can pay it in installments.
(C) It's not that soft.

제가 당신을 위해 소프트웨어를 설치해 드릴까요?
(A) 저의 조수인 톰이 전에 해 본 적이 있어요.
(B) 할부로 지불하시면 돼요.
(C) 그렇게 부드럽지는 않아요.

[어휘] pay in installments 할부로 지불하다

[해설] 소프트웨어 설치를 원하는지 묻는 질문에 대해 비서가 전에 해 본 적이 있다고 이야기함으로써, 자신의 비서가 해 줄 것임을 암시하는 (A)가 정답이다. install의 파생어인 installments를 사용한 (B)는 오답이다. 질문의 software에서 soft만 반복한 유사 발음 오답인 (C) 역시 소거한다.

17

Where should I put the table, on the third floor or the fourth floor?
(A) We don't need a new table.
(B) Just put it in the main conference room.
(C) I need new floor tiles.

3층과 4층 중 어디에 테이블을 놓을까요?
(A) 우리는 새 테이블이 필요 없어요.
(B) 그냥 주 회의실에 놔두세요.
(C) 새 바닥 타일이 필요해요.

[해설] 어느 곳에 두는 것이 좋은지를 선택하도록 하는 선택의문문이다. 주 회의실에 두라고 말하며 장소를 지정해 주고 있는 (B)가 정답이다. table을 반복한 (A)는 동일한 발음을 활용한 오답이며, floor를 반복한 (C) 역시 오답이다.

18

The seminar was well attended, wasn't it?
(A) It went well.
(B) I didn't attend the meeting.
(C) Yes, the SNS marketing surely worked.

세미나 참석자가 정말 많았죠, 그렇지 않나요?
(A) 그것은 잘 되었어요.
(B) 저는 그 회의에 참석하지 않았어요.
(C) 네, SNS 마케팅은 확실히 효과가 있었어요.

[어휘] well attended 참석자가 많은

[해설] 세미나 참석자가 많았다는 이야기에 대해 마케팅이 효과가 있었다고 답한 (C)가 정답이다. well을 반복한 (A)는 발음의 오답인데, 간혹 '사람이 많았죠?', '정말 잘 되었어요.'라고 우리말로 잘못 해석하는 경우가 있다. 'it went well'은 뭔가 어떻게 되었는지를 묻는 질문에 대해 상황을 설명하는 표현일 뿐이며 동의하는 의미로 쓰이는 것이 아니라는 것을 기억한다. 대화의 주제는 seminar인데 회의의 참석 여부를 말한 (B) 역시 오답이다.

PART 3

[19-21]

M1	Hello, Angela and Steve. How's it going? **19) Is your computer working this morning?**
W	Well, I have some problems logging in. I keep getting an error message.
M2	Didn't you see the notice? **20) There is a notice in the breakroom about the network update this morning.**
M1	Oh, I didn't see it.
W	Steve, do you know when it will be finished? I have a webinar at 11:00 this morning.
M2	I'm not sure. **21) Why don't you call tech support?**

M1	안녕하세요, 앤젤라와 스티브. 어떻게 지내세요? 당신의 컴퓨터는 오늘 아침에 작동이 잘 되던가요?
W	음, 로그인하는 데 문제가 좀 있어요. 계속 오류 메시지가 떠요.
M2	공지 못 보셨어요? 오늘 아침에 네트워크 업데이트에 대한 공지가 휴게실에 있었어요.
M1	아, 저는 못봤어요.
W	스티브, 언제 업데이트가 끝나는지 아세요? 저는 아침 11시에 웹 상에서 진행하는 세미나가 있는데요.
M2	저도 확실하지 않아요. 기술 지원부에 전화해 보는 게 어떨까요?

[어휘] work 작동하다; 사용하다 webinar 웹 상에서 하는 세미나 log in 로그인하다 tech support 기술지원부

19

화자들은 무엇에 대해 이야기하고 있는가?

(A) 구형 소프트웨어

(B) 정전

(C) 컴퓨터의 문제점

(D) 고장 난 기계

해설 대화 초반에 두 사람이 컴퓨터와 로그인의 문제점에 대해 이야기하고 있으므로, 정답은 (C)이다. update를 듣고 outdated가 포함된 (A)를 정답으로 고르는 실수를 할 수도 있으므로 주의한다.

20

무엇이 문제를 발생시켰는가?

(A) 네트워크 업데이트

(B) 개조 공사

(C) 배송 지연

(D) 일정 충돌

해설 대화 초반부에서 두 사람이 컴퓨터에 대해 문제점을 언급했고, 이어서 등장하는 첫번째 남자의 말 'There is a notice in the breakroom about the network update this morning.'에서 네트워크 업데이트가 있다고 언급했다. 그러므로, 정답은 (A)이다.

21

스티브는 여자에게 무엇을 하라고 제안하는가?

(A) 소프트웨어 업데이트하기

(B) 다른 부서에 연락하기

(C) 수리 기사에게 전화하기

(D) 그녀의 컴퓨터를 종료하기

해설 질문에서 사람의 이름이 언급되는 경우, 그 사람의 이름을 듣는 것이 문제를 푸는 가장 큰 힌트가 된다. 마지막 여자의 말에서 여자가 스티브의 이름을 부르고 있는데, 다음에 이어지는 남자의 말속에 포함된 제안의 표현인 'Why don't you call tech support?'에서 정답을 찾아야 한다. 남자가 기술지원부에 전화해보라고 말하고 있으므로, 정답은 다른 부서에 연락해 보라는 의미인 (B)이다.

[22-24]

M Hi. This is Peter. 22) **As you know, the marketing symposium is coming up in less than a week. I was wondering if you have some time to review the presentation handouts that I prepared to give during the symposium for other managers. 23) I know you're quite busy with other projects, but you've done a lot of presentations before.** So I really want your feedback on my materials.

W Oh, is this the presentation about the analytics project? Sorry. I forgot to reply to your e-mail, but actually, I did take a look at the presentation material and thought you were spot on. I especially liked that you

included some illustrative outcomes so that the audience can get a better idea of the expected outcomes.

M Right. I thought that the audience might be more engaged if they can see some realistic figures.

W 24) **The only tip I'd give is that you may want to let the conference committee know that you'll need a projector to show your slides.** Otherwise, they may just give you a regular meeting room without a screen.

M 안녕하세요. 저는 피터예요. 당신도 알다시피, 마케팅 심포지엄이 앞으로 일주일도 안 남았어요. 제가 다른 관리자들을 위한 심포지엄에서 하기로 되어 있는 발표 자료를 당신이 봐줄 시간이 있는지 궁금해서요. 당신이 다른 일들로 바쁜 것을 알지만, 당신은 이전에 많은 프레젠테이션 경험이 있잖아요. 저는 정말 저의 자료에 대한 당신의 피드백을 원해요.

W 오, 분석학 프로젝트에 관한 그 발표인가요? 미안해요. 잊어버리고 당신의 이메일에 회신하지 않았지만, 사실, 저는 발표 자료를 살펴 보았고, 당신이 정확하다고 생각했어요. 청중들이 예측되는 결과를 더 잘 이해할 수 있도록 분명한 결과들을 포함시킨 한 점이 특별히 좋았어요.

M 맞아요. 청중들이 실제 수치를 볼 수 있다면 참여도가 더 집중할 것이라고 생각했어요.

W 저의 유일한 제안은 당신이 슬라이드들을 보여 주기 위해 컨퍼런스 위원회에 프로젝터가 필요하다고 알려주어야 한다는 것이에요. 그렇게 하지 않으면, 그들은 당신에게 스크린이 없는 일반 회의실을 줄 수도 있거든요.

어휘 analytics 분석학, 해석론   spot on 딱 맞는, 정확한   illustrative 실제적 예가 되는, 분명히 보여주는

22

남자는 아마도 누구일 것 같은가?

(A) 컨퍼런스 준비 위원

(B) 뉴스 리포터

(C) 마케팅 관리자

(D) 재무 관리자

해설 대화 초반에 남자가 마케팅 심포지엄을 준비한다고(the marketing symposium is coming up in less than a week) 했으므로 남자는 마케팅 부서에서 일하고 있다는 것을 알 수 있다. 이어서 언급되는 'I was wondering if you have some time to review the presentation handouts that I prepared to give during the symposium for other managers.'에서 다른 관리자들을 위한 심포지엄이라고 했으므로 남자 역시 관리자라는 것을 알 수 있다. 따라서, 정답은 (C)가 된다. other, another, the other와 같은 표현은 '동일한 것'이 있을 때에만 사용할 수 있는 표현이라는 것을 기억한다.

23

남자는 왜 "당신은 전에 많은 프레젠테이션을 해봤잖아요"라고 하는가?

(A) 여자의 능력을 칭찬하기 위해서

(B) 실수를 지적하기 위해서

(C) 요청한 이유를 설명하기 위해서

(D) 할 일을 주기 위해서

해설 의도 파악 문제의 경우, 해당 문장의 바로 앞뒤에 단서가 주어지지만, 문장 자체가 가지고 있는 의미 역시 간과해서는 안 된다. 누군가의 경험에 대해 강조하는 표현의 경우, 대부분 대화하고 있는 내용에 대해 잘 알고 있음을 의미한다. 따라서, 여자가 인용구 앞에서 남자에게 피드백을 부탁하고 나서 'you've done a lot of presentations before'라고 말한 것은, 여자의 경험을 강조하면서 그녀가 잘 알 것이라고 말하는 것인데, 이는 남자가 왜 여자에게 부탁했는지를 설명하려는 의도이다. 따라서 정답은 (C)이다. explain 뒤에 명사가 나오는 선택지의 경우, '해당 명사의 이유를 설명하다'라는 의미로 이해하면 된다. 따라서, (C)의 선택지는 '요청한 이유를 설명하다'라는 의미이다.

24

여자는 무엇을 제안하는가?

(A) 방에 대해 특별 요청을 하는 것

(B) 지원자들을 더 모집하는 것

(C) 행사에 예비 등록하는 것

(D) 동료에게 상담하는 것

해설 여자의 제안을 묻는 문제이므로 제안의 표현을 찾아야 한다. 여자의 마지막 말에 'you may want to'라는 제안의 표현이 있는데, 여자는 'you may want to let the conference committee know that you'll need a projector to show your slides'라고 하며 프로젝터가 필요하다고 요청하라고 말했다. 따라서 정답은 (A)이다.

[25-27]

M	Well, Ms. Lee, 25) **this is the only available office near the subway station. How do you like it?**
W	I like the size of the office and the location, 26) **but what I like the most is the number of meeting rooms it has.** However, I'm a bit worried about the wood flooring. It certainly makes noise and is hard to clean.
M	I understand. I'll check if we can change the flooring or install new carpeting.
W	Good! 27) **And is there a parking lot?**
M	There's one right across the street.
M	음, 이 선생님, 이곳이 지하철 근처에 있는 유일한 이용 가능한 사무실입니다. 어때요?
W	사무실의 크기와 위치가 마음에 들어요. 그런데, 가장 마음에 드는 것은 회의실의 수예요. 하지만, 나무 바닥인 것이 조금 걱정되네요. 분명히 소음을 일으키고, 청소하기 힘들거든요.
M	무슨 말씀인지 알겠습니다. 혹시 바닥을 바꾸거나 카페트를 깔아도 되는지 확인해 볼게요.
W	좋아요! 주차장은 있나요?
M	길 바로 건너에 하나 있어요.

어휘 available 이용 가능한 flooring 바닥재 install 설치하다 carpeting 카페트류

25

남자는 아마도 누구일 것 같은가?

(A) 기차 차장

(B) 건설 직원

(C) 부동산 중개인

(D) 인테리어 디자이너

해설 대화 초반에서 남자는 'This is the only available office near the subway station. How do you like it?'이라고 말하며 이용 가능한 사무실에 대해 설명하고 있다. 따라서, 남자의 직업은 부동산 중개인일 것이므로 정답은 (C)이다.

26

여자가 가장 좋아하는 것은 무엇인가?

(A) 임차료

(B) 회의 장소의 수

(C) 사무실의 위치

(D) 장소의 크기

해설 최상급이 아닌 단순히 좋아하는 것들에 대해 듣다 보면, (C)와 (D) 때문에 혼동하기 쉽다. 'but what I like the most is the number of meeting rooms it has'라는 부분에서 최상급 표현을 사용하여 '회의실의 수가 마음에 든다'고 했으므로 정답은 (B)이다.

27

여자는 무엇을 알고 싶어 하는가?

(A) 방의 상태

(B) 계약 조건

(C) 주차 비용

(D) 시설의 위치

해설 여자가 주차장의 위치를 묻고 있으므로 주차장을 facility로 바꾸어 표현한 (D)를 정답으로 고른다. parking이라는 단어가 직접 들어가 있는 (C)를 고르는 실수를 하지 않도록 주의한다.

PART 4

[28-30]

M	28) **Welcome to Sarah's Ice Cream Factory.** In just a few minutes, we'll begin the factory tour, where you can see all the steps it takes to make the delicious ice cream that you all love. 29) **Please remember that there is one rule: You are not allowed to take any pictures inside the factory.** This is to ensure that none of our confidential information is leaked outside the company. 30) **At the end of the tour, you'll get the chance to taste our newest flavor of ice cream for free!** The tour will begin in about five minutes, so if you need to use the restroom or take a short break, please feel free to do so. We'll meet again in the lobby at 8:00 A.M. sharp and start the tour by watching a short film about the history of our company.

M 세라의 아이스크림 공장에 오신 것을 환영합니다. 몇 분 후에, 우리는 공장 견학을 시작할 것이며, 여러분은 여기에서 모두가 좋아하는 맛있는 아이스크림이 어떻게 만들어지는지 모든 단계를 볼 수 있습니다. 한 가지 규칙이 있음을 꼭 기억하세요: 공장 내부에서는 사진을 한 장도 촬영할 수 없습니다. 이것은 기밀 정보가 회사 밖으로 유출되는 것을 방지하기 위한 것입니다. 견학이 끝날 때쯤, 새로운 맛의 아이크림을 무료로 맛 볼 수 있는 기회를 얻을 것입니다! 견학은 약 5분쯤 후에 시작하므로, 화장실을 이용하시거나 휴식을 원하는 분들은 마음껏 다녀오세요. 우리는 오전 8시에 로비에서 다시 만나서 회사의 역사에 관한 짧은 영상을 보면서 견학을 시작할 것입니다.

어휘 confidential 기밀의　leak 새다, 유출하다　flavor 맛, 풍미

28

담화는 어디에서 일어날 것 같은가?

(A) 영화관에서
(B) 식당에서
(C) 공장에서
(D) 박물관에서

해설 담화 첫 문장에서 'Welcome to Sarah's Ice Cream Factory'라고 언급하고 있으므로 정답은 (C)이다.

29

건물 안에서는 무엇이 금지되는가?

(A) 사진을 찍는 것
(B) 크게 말하는 것
(C) 가방을 들고 다니는 것
(D) 쓰레기를 버리는 것

해설 금지되는 것을 묻는 질문의 경우, 정답의 근거는 not allow 혹은 don't에서 찾아야 한다. 대화 중반에 'you are not allowed to take any pictures inside the factory'라는 부분에서 사진 촬영을 'not allow'한다고 말했으므로 정답은 (A)이다.

30

화자는 마지막에 청자들이 무엇을 받게 될 것이라고 말하는가?

(A) 무료 제품
(B) 안내 책자
(C) 사진
(D) 할인 쿠폰

해설 중간 부분에서 'At the end of the tour, you'll get the chance to taste our newest flavor of ice cream for free!'라고 하면서 무료로 아이스크림 맛을 볼 수 있다고 했으므로 정답은 (A)가 된다.

[31-33]

W Terry's gift card store will make your holiday shopping easy. A one-stop shopping destination, Terry's is convenient and offers various kinds of gift cards, including ones for dining, clothing, movies, and even appliances. Terry's allows you to choose the perfect items for your friends, family, and colleagues for special events. And this month, we opened a new branch on Berry Street! 31) 32) 33) **We will hold a 10% discount promotion from 9:00 A.M. to 5:00 P.M. tomorrow to celebrate the opening of the Berry Street store, so come and visit our new store and take advantage of some great deals!**

W 테리스 선물 카드 매장은 휴일 쇼핑을 쉽게 만들어 줄 것입니다. 원스톱 쇼핑 장소인 테리스는 편리하고 식사, 의류, 영화, 심지어 가전제품까지 포함하는 다양한 선물 카드를 한 곳에서 제공합니다. 테리스는 당신이 친구, 가족 그리고 동료의 특별한 행사를 위한 완벽한 아이템을 고를 수 있도록 합니다. 그리고 이번 달에, 저희는 베리 가에 새로운 지점을 오픈했습니다. 베리 가의 오픈을 축하하기 위해서 내일 오전 9시에서 오후 5시까지 10% 할인 행사를 개최하오니, 새로운 매장에 오셔서 이 할인 행사를 활용하세요.

어휘 appliances 가전제품　promotion 판촉 행사
take advantage of ~의 이득을 보다　deal 거래

31

왜 그들은 특별 행사를 여는가?

(A) 온라인 사이트를 막 런칭했다.
(B) 무료 배달 서비스를 시작할 것이다.
(C) 또 다른 매장을 열었다.
(D) 연락처를 변경했다.

해설 대부분의 경우 첫번째 문제는 초반에서 정답이 주로 등장하지만, 이 담화의 경우 모든 문제의 정답이 후반에 몰려 있어서 정답을 찾기 힘든 유형이다. 담화 후반부의 'We will hold a 10% discount promotion from 9:00 A.M. to 5:00 P.M. tomorrow to celebrate the opening of the Berry Street store'에서 베리 가에 문을 여는 새로운 매장의 오픈을 축하하기 위해 할인을 한다고 했다. 따라서, 행사를 개최하는 이유는 새로운 매장의 오픈 때문이므로 정답은 (C)이다.

테리스 상품권

개업을 위한 특별 세일
내일 오전 9시 에서 오후 5시까지
전 품목에 대해 20% 할인

서두르세요! 단 하루 행사입니다!

32

시각 정보를 보시오. 어떤 정보가 수정되어야 하는가?

(A) 할인의 이유
(B) 할인 일자
(C) 상품의 할인율
(D) 할인 품목

해설 담화 마지막 부분의 'We will hold a 10% discount promotion from 9:00 A.M. to 5:00 P.M. tomorrow to celebrate the opening of the Berry Street store.'에서 10%의 할인을 한다고 말했는데, 시각 정보에는 할인율이 20%로 되어 있다. 그러므로 잘못된 정보는 상품의 할인율이라는 것을 알 수 있다. 정답은 (C)가 된다.

33

내일 어떤 일이 일어날 것인가?
(A) 손님들은 무료 선물 카드를 받게 될 것이다.
(B) 방문객들은 할인을 받게 될 것이다.
(C) 새로운 지점이 문을 열 것이다.
(D) 상점이 더 긴 시간 동안 영업할 것이다.

해설 'We will hold a 10% discount promotion from 9:00 A.M. to 5:00 P.M. tomorrow to celebrate the opening of the Berry Street store, so come and visit our new store and take advantage of some great deals!'에서 내일 오픈 축하 세일을 한다고 했으므로, 방문객들은 할인을 받게 된다는 것을 알 수 있다. 정답은 (B)이다.

PART 2
유형별 문제 풀이법 I

📝 실전 문제 연습   p.043

🎧 04-06

1 (B)	2 (B)	3 (C)	4 (A)
5 (B)	6 (B)	7 (A)	8 (A)
9 (B)	10 (C)	11 (B)	12 (B)
13 (A)	14 (A)	15 (A)	16 (C)
17 (A)	18 (B)	19 (C)	20 (B)
21 (A)	22 (B)	23 (D)	24 (A)
25 (D)	26 (B)	27 (A)	28 (B)
29 (B)	30 (C)	31 (B)	32 (A)
33 (C)			

PART 1

1
(A) A woman is hanging up the phone.
(B) Work cubicles are divided by some partitions.
(C) A jacket has been put on a desk.
(D) A man is walking in the office.

(A) 여자는 전화를 끊고 있는 중이다.
(B) 작업 공간들은 칸막이로 나뉘어 있다.
(C) 자켓 하나가 책상 위에 놓여진 상태이다.
(D) 남자가 사무실 안을 걸어 다니는 중이다.

어휘 work cubicle 작업 공간, 작업 구역   partition 칸막이

해설 여자가 전화를 걸거나 끊고 있지 않으므로 (A)는 오답이다. '일하는 공간'은 workstation이나 work cubicle로 묘사할 수 있는데, 작업 공간이 칸막이들로 나뉘어 있으므로 (B)가 정답이다. 눈에 보이지 않는 자켓을 언급한 (C), work와 walk의 유사 발음을 이용한 (D)는 오답이다.

2
(A) Some tracks are being worked on.
(B) Trains have pulled in to the station.
(C) Commuters are waiting to board the train.
(D) A train is moving into the station.

(A) 선로에 작업이 진행되고 있다.
(B) 기차들이 역에 정차해있다.
(C) 통근자들이 기차에 탑승하기 위해 기다리고 있다.
(D) 기차가 역 안으로 움직이고 있다.

어휘 tracks 선로   commuter 통근자

해설 pull에는 move의 의미가 있으므로, 기차가 이미 역 안에 들어와 있는 상태를 has pulled in으로 표현한 (B)가 정답이다. 선로에서 작업을 하거나 기차에 탑승하려는 사람이 보이지 않으므로 (A)와 (C)는 모두 정답이 될 수 없다. 기차는 이미 역 안에 있고, 움직이고 있지도 않으므로 (D) 역시 오답이다.

3
(A) She is buying some shoes.
(B) She's putting flowers on the shoes.
(C) Some shoes have been organized along the wall.
(D) A woman is standing near the chair.

(A) 그녀는 신발을 사고 있다.
(B) 그녀는 신발에 꽃을 달고 있다.
(C) 신발들이 벽을 따라 정렬되어 있다.
(D) 한 여자가 의자 근처에 서 있다.

어휘 organize 정리하다, 정렬하다 (= arrange)

해설 여자가 신발을 구매하고 있다고 생각하기 쉽지만, (A)가 정답이 되려면 현금이나 카드 등으로 지불하는 동작이 사진 속에 있어야 한다. 여자가 신발에 꽃을 달고 있거나 서 있지 않기 때문에 (B)와 (D) 역시 오답이다. 벽을 따라 신발들이 놓여있는 모습을 묘사한 (C)가 정답이다.

PART 2

4
Where can I find the sales report from last week?
(A) It's available on the shared drive.
(B) There was a network outage.
(C) No, he's attending a meeting.

지난주의 판매 보고서는 어디에서 찾을 수 있나요?
(A) 공유 드라이브에 있어요.
(B) 네트워크 장애가 있었어요.
(C) 아니요, 그는 회의에 참석 중이에요.

어휘 outage 정전; 사용 불능

해설 판매 보고서의 위치를 묻는 질문에 대해 공유 드라이브에 있다고 설명한 (A)가 가장 적절한 대답이다. 네트워크 장애가 있다고 말한 (B)는 매력적인 오답인데, 장애가 있어서 찾지 못한다고 생각하기 쉽지만, 단순히 장애를 언급할 뿐 파생되는 효과에 대해서는 설명하고 있지 않다. 의문사 의문문에 대해 no로 답한 (C) 또한 오답이다.

5

How do you recommend getting to the library?
(A) There are many resources.
(B) By taking a bus.
(C) Let's ask the librarian.

도서관에 어떻게 가는 것을 추천하나요?
(A) 많은 자료가 있어요.
(B) 버스를 타고요.
(C) 사서에게 물어보죠.

해설 'get to + 장소'는 '해당 장소로 가다'라는 의미로서, 교통 수단을 물어보는 질문이다. (A)는 library에서 연상되는 resource를 이용한 오답이며, library와 유사한 발음의 librarian을 이용한 (C) 역시 오답이다. 교통 수단을 묻는 질문에 대해 버스라고 답한 (B)가 정답이다.

6

When will the new product launch take place?
(A) At headquarters.
(B) It's scheduled for next month.
(C) I prefer working independently.

신제품의 출시는 언제 이루어질 건가요?
(A) 본사에서요.
(B) 다음 달에 예정되어 있어요.
(C) 저는 독립적으로 일하는 것을 선호해요.

어휘 launch 출시 be scheduled for 예정되어 있다

해설 신제품의 출시 시기를 묻는 질문이므로 시간과 관련된 답변을 정답으로 고른다. 장소로 대답한 (A)는 오답이며, 혼자 일하는 것이 좋다는 내용의 (C) 역시 시간에 대한 대답으로 적절하지 않다. 다음 달에 예정되어 있다며 시기를 언급한 (B)가 정답이다. for는 '~ 동안에'라는 기간의 의미로 사용되는 경우가 많지만, 'be scheduled for'의 형태로 '예정되어 있다'라는 의미로 사용된다.

7

I can help you set up the conference call.
(A) That meeting has been delayed.
(B) Okay, I'll call you back then.
(C) The setting isn't complicated.

제가 컨퍼런스 콜을 준비하는 것을 도와드릴 수 있어요.
(A) 그 회의는 연기됐어요.
(B) 좋아요, 제가 그때 회신 전화를 할게요.
(C) 그 세팅은 복잡하지 않아요.

해설 회의 준비를 돕겠다는 제안에 대해 연기됐다고 답하는 것은 준비가 필요 없다는 의미이므로 정답은 (A)이다. call만 반복되었을 뿐 회의

준비와 상관없는 내용의 (B)와, set에서 파생된 setting을 이용한 (C)는 모두 오답이다.

8

Are you familiar with the latest industry regulations?
(A) Yes, I attended a training session last week.
(B) No, I'm not late today.
(C) This document is confidential.

당신은 최신 업계 규정을 잘 알고 있나요?
(A) 네, 저는 지난주에 교육에 참가했어요.
(B) 아니요, 저는 오늘 늦지 않았어요.
(C) 이 문서는 기밀이에요.

해설 규정을 잘 알고 있는지를 묻는 질문에 대해 교육에 참여 했다고 답한 (A)가 정답인데, 이는 교육을 받아 잘 알고 있다는 의미이다. (B)는 latest와 발음이 유사한 late을 이용한 오답이다.

9

Who will be accompanying the CEO on the business trip?
(A) No, it's not that urgent.
(B) Let me check the travel arrangements.
(C) In the company meeting room.

출장에서 CEO와 동행할 사람은 누구인가요?
(A) 아니요, 그렇게 급한 일은 아니에요.
(B) 제가 출장 일정을 확인해 볼게요.
(C) 회사 회의실에서요.

어휘 travel arrangement 여행 준비 (여행에 필요한 비행기, 호텔 등의 예약)

해설 출장에서 CEO와 동행할 사람을 묻는 질문에 대해 출장 일정을 확인해 본다고 대답한 (B)가 정답이다. 이는 출장 일정을 통해 동행자를 알아보겠다는 간접적인 답변이다. 의문사 의문문은 yes/no로 답할 수 없으므로 (A)는 오답이며, accompany와 유사 발음인 company를 이용한 (C)는 전형적인 오답이다.

10

Do you prefer a wired or wireless headset for the conference call?
(A) Near the printer.
(B) Yes, we need some more wires.
(C) Wireless would be more convenient.

컨퍼런스 콜을 위해 유선과 무선 헤드셋 중 어느 것을 선호하세요?
(A) 프린터 근처에요.
(B) 네, 전선이 조금 더 필요해요.
(C) 무선이 더 편리할 것 같아요.

해설 무선과 유선 중에서 선택하라는 선택 의문문에서 무선이 더 편리할 것 같다고 답한 (C)가 정답이다. 선호하는 헤드셋의 종류를 묻는 질문에 대해 '프린터 근처'라며 장소로 대답한 (A)는 오답이다. 질문의 wired와 발음이 유사한 wire를 이용한 (B) 역시 오답이다.

11

Shall I assist you in preparing the presentation slides?

(A) It's a lovely present.

(B) Oh, I got Jonathan's help.

(C) Will that be cash or credit?

프레젠테이션 슬라이드를 준비하는 데 도움을 드릴까요?
(A) 그건 사랑스러운 선물이에요.
(B) 아, 저는 조나단의 도움을 받았어요.
(C) 현금이나 신용카드 중 어느 것으로 결제하시겠어요?

해설 슬라이드 준비를 도와줄지 묻는 질문에 대해 조나단의 도움을 받았으므로 필요 없다고 간접적으로 대답한 (B)가 정답이다. presentation과 발음이 유사한 present를 이용한 (A)는 오답이다. 도움을 묻는 질문에 지불 수단을 언급하고 있는 (C) 역시 오답이다.

12

Why don't we get some noodles delivered?

(A) I visited there before.

(B) There is a great place on Main Street.

(C) It takes about 15 minutes to deliver.

국수를 시켜 먹는 게 어때요?
(A) 저는 이전에 그곳에 가봤어요.
(B) 메인 가에 좋은 데가 있어요.
(C) 배달하는 데 15분 정도 걸려요.

해설 국수를 시키자는 질문에 대해 괜찮은 곳을 알려주는 (B)가 정답이다. 과거에 방문해 봤다는 (A)는 시제와 의미 모두 질문에 대한 답으로 적절하지 않다. (C)는 deliver를 반복한 오답인데, '국수를 시키자'는 질문에 대해 '배달에 15분 걸린다'라는 대답이 주문에 동의하는 것 같지만, 이는 주문 시간이 얼마나 걸리는지 묻는 질문에 적절한 대답이다.

13

I can't access the project files at the moment.

(A) There is a temporary system error.

(B) A new update will be released soon.

(C) I need a projector.

현재 프로젝트 파일에 접근할 수 없어요.
(A) 일시적인 시스템 오류예요.
(B) 곧 새로운 업데이트가 출시될 예정이에요.
(C) 저는 프로젝터가 필요해요.

해설 파일에 접근할 수 없는 문제점을 언급했는데, 이에 대해 일시적인 시스템 오류가 있다며 문제의 원인을 알려주는 (A)가 정답이다. 파일에 접근할 수 없는 문제와 새로운 업데이트 여부는 관련이 없으므로 (B)는 오답이다. project의 파생어인 projector을 이용한 (C) 역시 오답이다.

14

Will you be available to join us tomorrow afternoon?

(A) I have a doctor's appointment.

(B) Enjoy your trip.

(C) This bag is currently out of stock.

내일 오후에 참석할 수 있나요?
(A) 병원 예약이 있어요.
(B) 즐거운 여행 되세요.
(C) 이 가방은 현재 품절이에요.

해설 내일 시간이 있는지 묻는 질문에 대해 병원 예약이 있다고 답하며 간접적으로 시간이 없다는 표현을 한 (A)가 정답이다. join과 enjoy는 자주 등장하는 유사 발음 오답이므로 (B)는 소거한다. (C)는 available의 다른 의미를 이용한 오답인데, available이 사람과 함께 쓰이는 경우 시간이 있다는 의미이지만, 물건과 사용되면 재고가 있다는 의미이다.

15

Who should I contact for network errors?

(A) You can call tech support.

(B) Yes, we signed the new contract.

(C) There will be a networking event.

네트워크 오류에 대해 누구에게 연락해야 하나요?
(A) 기술 지원부에 연락하시면 돼요.
(B) 네, 우리는 새로운 계약서에 서명했어요.
(C) 교류 행사가 있을 예정이에요.

어휘 networking 인적 교류

해설 문제를 해결해 줄 수 있는 사람을 묻는 질문에 대해 부서로 답한 (A)가 정답이다. (B)의 contract는 contact의 유사 발음 오답이다. network과 발음이 유사한 networking을 이용한 (C)역시 오답이다.

16

Why don't we hold the training session next week?

(A) I'll arrange transportation for everyone.

(B) No, the train will depart in 30 minutes.

(C) Some team members will be on vacation.

다음 주에 교육 세션을 진행하는 것이 어떨까요?
(A) 모두를 위한 교통 수단을 준비할게요.
(B) 아니요, 기차는 30분 뒤에 출발할 거예요.
(C) 일부 팀원들이 휴가를 가요.

해설 교육을 하자는 제안에 대해 일부 팀원들이 휴가를 간다고 답하며, 교육을 진행할 수 없다고 간접적으로 답변하는 (C)가 정답이다. (B)는 training과 발음이 유사한 train을 이용한 오답이다. train에서 연상되는 transportation을 이용한 (A) 역시 질문과 상관없는 답변이다.

17

Where is the nearest post office located?

(A) Just across the street.

(B) I'll be out of the office tomorrow.

(C) No, I don't need any stamps.

가장 가까운 우체국은 어디에 있나요?
(A) 길 건너편에 있어요.
(B) 저는 내일 사무실에 없을 거예요.
(C) 아니요, 우표는 필요하지 않아요.

해설 우체국을 묻는 질문에 대해 길 건너에 있다고 답한 (A)가 정답이다. post office에서 office만 반복한 (B)는 발음을 이용한 오답이다. 의문사는 yes/no로 답할 수 없으므로 (C) 역시 오답이다.

18

Why don't we share a taxi to the convention center?
(A) In the main meeting room.
(B) Sure, I'm leaving in 15 minutes.
(C) Because I didn't take the train.

컨벤션 센터까지 택시를 같이 타는 게 어떨까요?
(A) 주 회의실에서요.
(B) 네, 저는 15분 후에 출발할 거예요.
(C) 기차를 타지 않았기 때문이에요.

해설 택시를 함께 타자는 제안에 대해 좋다고 답하며, 출발 시간을 언급한 (B)가 가장 적절한 대답이다. (A)는 컨벤션 센터에서 연상되는 회의실을 언급한 오답이다. (C)의 경우 원인을 묻는 질문이 아니므로 because로 답할 수 없다. 또한, 질문의 taxi에서 연상되는 다른 교통수단을 언급한 오답이기도 하다.

PART 3
[19-21]

> M 19) **Welcome to Gloria's Dining. How many are in your party?**
>
> W Three. Two more people will be joining me.
>
> M Okay. We have one last table. Please follow me. Here's the menu. Today's specials are spaghetti Bolognese and pumpkin soup. Do you want to order something to drink first, or do you need more time?
>
> W 20) **I will take a look at the menu** while waiting for my friends.
>
> M Okay. I'll be back then.
>
> W Oh, by the way, 21) **is there a parking lot?** My friends will probably drive here.
>
> M There is street parking in front of the store.
>
> M 글로리아 다이닝에 오신 걸 환영합니다. 일행이 몇 분이세요?
>
> W 세 명이에요. 두 명이 더 합류할 것이고요.
>
> M 네. 마지막 테이블이 하나 남았군요. 저를 따라 오세요. 여기 메뉴판이 있습니다. 오늘의 특선 요리는 스파게티 볼로네즈와 호박 수프입니다. 음료 먼저 주문하시겠어요, 아니면 시간이 더 필요하신가요?
>
> W 친구들을 기다리는 동안 메뉴판을 보고 있을게요.
>
> M 네. 그때 다시 오겠습니다.
>
> W 아, 그런데, 주차장이 있나요? 제 친구들이 아마 여기로 운전해서 올 거예요.
>
> M 가게 앞에 노상 주차장이 있어요.

어휘 specials 특선요리 take a look at ~을 보다 parking lot 주차장

19

남자는 누구인 것 같은가?
(A) 가게 주인
(B) 요리사
(C) 레스토랑 서버
(D) 음식 비평가

해설 'Welcome to Gloria's Dining. A table for two?'에서 남자는 식당에서 자리를 안내하고 있으므로 정답은 (C)이다.

20

여자는 다음에 무엇을 할 것인가?
(A) 음식 주문하기
(B) 메뉴 보기
(C) 친구들에게 전화하기
(D) 다른 업체에 방문하기

해설 여자가 'I will take a look at the menu'라고 했으므로 정답은 (B)이다.

21

여자는 무엇을 알고 싶어 하는가?
(A) 어디에 주차할 것인지
(B) 무엇을 주문할 것인지
(C) 언제 도착할 것인지
(D) 누가 합류할 것인지

해설 대화의 마지막 부분에서 여자는 'is there a parking lot?'이라고 하며 주차장이 있는지 묻고 있으므로 정답은 (A)이다.

[22-24]

> M Liz, 22) **is there any way to cut down on expenses in the office? Any ideas?**
>
> W How about reducing paper consumption to start with? That way, we can benefit both the company budget and the global environment. I heard the company is starting a green initiative. 23) **It's easy to set the printers to determine which ones are used the most and which users print the most documents. I have some time before the meeting.**
>
> M Great. The most important thing is to encourage a "think before you print" mentality with our employees. We need to notify everyone about current levels of paper consumption. Another thing is to design logos and to develop slogans and place them in the printing area. For example, a tree character could ask, "Do you really need this hard copy?"

W **24) Why don't we ask the employees if they have any creative ideas on the subject?** We could even create competition between departments and offer rewards.

M 리즈, 사무실에서 경비를 줄일 방법이 있을까요? 좋은 생각 있어요?

W 우선 종이 소비를 줄이는 것부터 시작하는 것은 어떨까요? 그렇게 하면, 회사 예산과 글로벌 환경 모두에 이익이 될 수 있어요. 회사에서 그린 이니셔티브를 시작한다고 들었어요. 어떤 프린터가 가장 많이 사용되고 어떤 사용자가 문서를 가장 많이 인쇄하는지 확인하도록 세팅하는 것은 어렵지 않아요. 회의 전에 시간이 조금 있어요.

M 좋아요. 가장 중요한 것은 우리 직원들 내부적으로 "인쇄하기 전에 생각하라"는 사고방식을 장려하는 것이에요. 우리는 현재의 종이 소비량에 대해 모두에게 알릴 필요가 있어요. 또 다른 방법은 로고를 디자인하고 슬로건을 개발해서 인쇄 영역에 배치하는 거예요. 예를 들어, 나무 캐릭터가 "이 하드 카피는 정말로 필요한가요?"라고 묻는 것처럼요.

W 직원들에게 그 주제에 대한 창의적인 아이디어가 있는지 물어볼까요? 부서 간에 경쟁을 유발하고 보상도 할 수 있어요.

어휘 expense 경비 consumption 소비 initiative 계획 mentality 사고방식 notify 알리다

22
남자는 무엇에 대해 이야기하고 싶어 하는가?
(A) 보수 공사 계획
(B) 경비를 절감하는 방법
(C) 면접
(D) 여행 준비

해설 대화의 첫 부분에서 남자는 'is there any way to cut down on expenses in the office? Any ideas?'라고 하며 사무실 경비를 줄이는 방법에 대한 아이디어가 있는지 묻고 있다. 따라서 정답은 (B)이다.

23
여자가 "회의 전에 시간이 있어요"라고 말할 때 무엇을 의미하는가?
(A) 그녀는 그 문제를 처리하기에 너무 바쁘다.
(B) 그녀는 회의 전에 점심을 먹기를 원한다.
(C) 그녀는 회의를 준비해야 한다.
(D) 그녀는 장비를 세팅할 시간이 있다.

해설 의도 파악 문제의 경우 해당 문장이 아닌 주변의 문장들을 파악해야 한다. 뿐만 아니라, 해당 문장의 기본적인 의미도 잘 파악해야 한다. '시간이 있다'는 것은 '어떤 일을 할 수 있다', 혹은 '부탁을 수락한다'는 의미인데, 'It's easy to set the printers to determine which ones are used the most and which users print the most documents. I have some time before the meeting.'라고 하며 프린터를 세팅하는 것이 어렵지 않다고 했다. 따라서 회의를 가기 전에 프린터의 세팅을 할 수 있다는 의미이므로 정답은 (D)이다.

24
여자는 무엇을 하자고 제안하는가?
(A) 직원들에게 아이디어를 묻는 것
(B) 회의에 참석하는 것
(C) 장비를 매일 확인하는 것
(D) 대회를 준비하는 것

해설 대화의 마지막 부분에서 여자는 'Why don't we ask the employees if they have t creative ideas on the subject?'라고 하며 동료들에게 아이디어를 물어보자고 제안하고 있으므로 (A)가 정답이다.

[25-27]

W I need your approval on the proposed contract I received from the Cynn Center this morning.

M **25) Is it for our employee training workshop next month?**

W Yes, that's right. Please take a close look at it since this is our first time holding a workshop at the Cynn Center.

M Okay. 26) **Did you check whether it can provide lunch for the event attendees?**

W I received a positive response from the person I spoke with.

M Okay. Just leave the contract on my desk. I will take a look at it after I come back from the meeting.

W Thanks. 27) **You need to sign the agreement by the end of the week**.

W 오늘 아침에 신 센터로부터 받은 계약서에 대한 승인이 필요합니다.

M 다음 달에 열릴 워크숍을 위한 것인가요?

W 네, 맞습니다. 신 센터에서 처음으로 워크숍을 개최하는 것이니 꼼꼼히 검토해 주세요.

M 알겠습니다. 행사 참가자들에게 점심을 제공할 수 있는지 여부는 확인했나요?

W 논의했던 사람으로부터 긍정적인 답변을 받았습니다.

M 좋습니다. 책상 위에 계약서를 두고 가세요. 회의에서 돌아와서 검토할게요.

W 감사합니다. 이번 주말까지 계약서에 서명하시면 됩니다.

어휘 approval 승인 contract (= agreement) 계약서 attendee 참석자 positive 긍정적인

25
다음 달에 어떤 종류의 행사가 열릴 것인가?
(A) 컨퍼런스
(B) 퇴임 축하
(C) 개업
(D) 워크숍

해설 문제에 시간이 언급되어 있으면, 그 시간이 언급된 부분에서 정답을 찾아야 한다. 대화 초반의 'Is it for our employee training workshop next month.'에서 다음 달(next month)에 직원 교육 워크숍이 있다고 했으므로 정답은 (D)이다.

26

남자는 무엇에 대해 질문하는가?
(A) 언제 행사 장소를 방문하는지
(B) 음식이 제공되는지
(C) 그들이 특정 장비를 사용할 수 있는지
(D) 누가 행사에 참여할 것인지

해설 대화 중반부의 'Did you check whether it can provide lunch for the event attendees?'에서 남자는 참석자들에게 점심을 제공할 수 있는지를 묻고 있으므로 정답은 (B)이다.

27

남자는 이번 주말까지 무엇을 해야 하는가?
(A) 계약서에 서명하기
(B) 고객을 만나기
(C) 이메일 보내기
(D) 사업체에 연락하기

해설 대화 마지막의 'You need to sign the agreement by the end of the week.'에서 계약서에 서명해야 한다고 했으므로 정답은 (A)이다.

PART 4

[28-30]

M　Good morning, staff. 28) **Just a quick reminder that contractors will be trimming and pruning trees on Wellesley Street for the next two weeks**. The work will include the removal of branches and dead wood. I am assuming that the work is going to create a lot of noise and that there will be a mess of leaves and fallen branches everywhere. 29) **They will be working on the trees in front of our restaurant all day today**, so we need to exercise extra caution while traveling in this area and keep an eye out for workers until the completion of this work. A city official assured me the sidewalks will remain open. 30) **Let's put up a sign near the entrance to alert our diners**. Now, let's go over the opening checklist before we open for service.

M　직원 여러분, 좋은 아침입니다. 계약업체들이 앞으로 2주 동안 웰즐리 가에서 나무를 다듬고 가지치기할 것임을 알려드립니다. 이 작업에는 가지와 죽은 나무를 제거하는 것이 포함될 것입니다. 이 작업 때문에 발생하는 많은 소음과 낙엽 및 떨어진 나뭇가지들로 인해 곳곳이 지저분해질 것으로 예상됩니다. 오늘은 하루 종일 저희 식당 앞 나무 위에서 작업을 할 예정이어서, 이 지역을 돌아다닐 때 각별히 주의하고 이 작업이 끝날

때까지 작업자들을 잘 지켜봐야 합니다. 시의 공무원은 인도가 계속 개방될 것이라고 확실히 말했습니다. 우리 식당 손님들에게 경고하기 위해 입구 근처에 안전 표지판을 설치합시다. 이제, 영업을 시작하기 전에 오프닝 체크리스트를 확인해 봅시다.

어휘 trim 다듬다, 잘라 내다 prune 가지치기 removal 제거 assume 추정하다 exercise 발휘하다 keep an eye out 지켜보다, 살펴보다

28

공지의 주제는 무엇인가?
(A) 계획된 지역 행사
(B) 곧 있을 조경 작업
(C) 폭풍에 의한 재해
(D) 정부의 정책

해설 담화 초반부의 'Just a quick reminder that contractors will be trimming and pruning trees on Wellesley Street for the next two weeks.'에서 다음 2주간 나무를 다듬고 가지치기를 한다고 했으므로, 조경 작업이 있을 것이라는 사실을 알 수 있다. 정답은 (B)이다.

29

청자들은 누구일 것 같은가?
(A) 건설업자들
(B) 식당의 직원들
(C) 시의 공무원들
(D) 상점의 고객들

해설 담화 중반부의 'They will be working on the trees in front of our restaurant all day today,'라는 부분에서 '우리 레스토랑 앞에서' 작업을 한다고 했으므로 청자들은 레스토랑의 직원일 것이다. 정답은 (B)이다.

30

청자들은 무엇을 하라는 제안을 받는가?
(A) 유리창과 앞문을 닫아 둘 것
(B) 나뭇가지와 잎을 치울 것
(C) 식당의 고객들에게 경고하기 위한 안전 표지판을 만들 것
(D) 다른 입구를 이용할 것

해설 청자들이 제안을 받은 것은 화자가 요청한 것을 찾으라는 것과 같다. 마지막 부분에서 화자는 'Let's put up a sign near the entrance to alert our diners'라고 하며 식사 고객들을 위한 안전 표지판을 설치하자고 했으므로 정답은 (C)이다.

[31-33]

W　Hello, Mr. Evans. 31) **This is Margaret Jung from Happy Helpers Catering.** 32) **I'm calling you about your company's employee awards ceremony scheduled for this Friday** at the Georgia Convention Center. Looking at the meeting room layout,

I think it will be best to set up the buffet table near the entrance at the back of the room in the corner to avoid any distractions. **33) In addition, the award recipients are seated at the table in front of the stage farthest from the entrance.** I've e-mailed you the catering agreement form again as you requested. Please read it carefully and have it signed and sent to us by tomorrow at the latest. If you have any questions, please don't hesitate to contact me. Thank you for being our valued customer. We are so grateful for the pleasure of serving you, and we will do our best to meet your expectations.

W 안녕하세요, 에반스 씨. 해피 헬퍼즈 케이터링의 마가렛 정입니다. 이번 주 금요일에 조지아 컨벤션 센터에서 열릴 예정인 귀사의 직원 시상식 때문에 전화드립니다. 회의실 배치도를 보니, 방해를 받지 않도록 뒤쪽 구석의 입구 근처에 뷔페 테이블을 배치하는 게 좋을 것 같습니다. 또한, 수상자들은 입구에서 가장 먼 곳에 있는 무대 앞 테이블에 배정했습니다. 요청하신 대로 케이터링 계약서를 다시 메일로 보내드렸습니다. 주의 깊게 읽어보시고 서명하여 늦어도 내일까지 보내주시기 바랍니다. 궁금하신 점이 있으면 언제든지 연락해주세요. 우리의 소중한 고객이 되어 주셔서 감사합니다. 귀하를 모실 수 있는 기쁨에 감사드리며, 기대에 부응할 수 있도록 최선을 다하겠습니다.

어휘 layout 배치도 distraction 방해 hesitate 망설이다
valued 소중한 expectation 기대

31
화자는 어떤 회사로부터 전화를 걸고 있는가?
(A) 컨벤션 센터
(B) 출장 연회 서비스
(C) 호텔
(D) 제조 공장

해설 담화 초반부의 'This is Margaret Jung from Happy Helpers Catering.'에서 화자는 케이터링 업체에서 전화하고 있다고 밝히고 있으므로 정답은 (B)이다.

32
화자의 회사는 금요일에 어떤 행사를 준비하는가?
(A) 시상식
(B) 신입 직원 오리엔테이션
(C) 퇴임 파티
(D) 신상품 출시

해설 문제에 있는 '금요일'이 언급된 부분을 잘 들어야 한다. 담화 초반의 'I'm calling you about your company's employee awards ceremony scheduled for this Friday'에서 시상식이 계획되어 있다고 했으므로 정답은 (A)이다.

회의실 배치도

테이블 1   테이블 2
테이블 3   테이블 4
입구
무대

33
시각 정보를 보시오. 수상자들은 어디에 앉을 것인가?
(A) 테이블 1
(B) 테이블 2
(C) 테이블 3
(D) 테이블 4

해설 담화 중반의 'In addition, the award recipients are seated at the table in front of the stage farthest from the entrance.'에서 수상자들은 입구에서 가장 먼 곳의 무대 앞 테이블에 앉을 것이라고 했으므로 정답은 (C)이다.

DAY 05 **PART 2 유형별 문제 풀이법 II**

실전 문제 연습 p.053

🎧 05-07

1 (A)	2 (C)	3 (B)	4 (A)
5 (C)	6 (C)	7 (B)	8 (A)
9 (C)	10 (A)	11 (B)	12 (A)
13 (C)	14 (C)	15 (C)	16 (A)
17 (B)	18 (B)	19 (B)	20 (D)
21 (B)	22 (B)	23 (B)	24 (C)
25 (B)	26 (D)	27 (B)	28 (A)
29 (D)	30 (B)	31 (C)	32 (C)
33 (A)			

PART 1

1
(A) A woman is taking a picture.
(B) A woman is baking some cookies.
(C) A woman is putting bread into the oven.
(D) Some baked goods are being set on the table.

(A) 한 여자가 사진을 찍고 있는 중이다.
(B) 한 여자가 과자를 굽고 있는 중이다.

(C) 한 여자가 빵을 오븐에 넣고 있는 중이다.

(D) 제과류들이 테이블에 놓이고 있는 중이다.

어휘 baked goods 제과류

해설 여자가 제과류의 사진을 찍고 있는 모습이므로 정답은 (A)이다. 쿠키들이 있기는 하지만 여자가 굽고 있지 않으므로 (B)는 오답이다. 오븐이 보이지 않으므로 (C) 역시 오답이다. (D)의 경우 놓여 있는 상태를 묘사하는 'have been set'이었다면 정답이 될 수 있지만, 'are being set'으로 동작을 묘사하고 있으므로 오답이다. being과 been의 경우 발음이 혼동되므로 잘 구분해야 한다.

2

(A) The man is operating a machine.

(B) The man is putting on a helmet.

(C) The man is wearing gloves.

(D) The man is opening the door.

(A) 남자가 기계를 작동시키는 중이다.

(B) 남자가 헬멧을 쓰는 중이다.

(C) 남자가 장갑을 끼고 있는 상태이다.

(D) 남자는 문을 여는 중이다.

어휘 put on 입다 (동작) wear 입다 (상태) operate 작동하다

해설 put on과 wear를 구분하는 문제이다. (B)의 put on은 무엇인가를 착용하는 '동작'을 묘사하는 동사이고 (C)의 wear는 착용하고 있는 '상태'를 묘사하는 동사이다. 남자는 헬멧과 장갑을 모두 착용한 상태이므로 정답은 (C)이다. 기계를 만지고 있지만 작동시키는 모습은 아니므로 (A)는 오답이며, 사진에서 문은 보이지 않으므로 (D)역시 오답이다.

3

(A) A woman is riding a bicycle.

(B) A bench has been placed near a path.

(C) A woman is sitting on the grass.

(D) Some trees are being planted near the water.

(A) 한 여자가 자전거를 타고 있다.

(B) 벤치 하나가 길 옆에 자리하고 있다.

(C) 한 여자가 풀밭에 앉아 있다.

(D) 나무들이 물가에 심어지고 있는 중이다.

해설 자전거가 보이기는 하지만, 타고 있는 모습은 아니므로 (A)는 소거한다. 참고로 자전거가 기대어 있는 모습을 'A bicycle has been propped against the bench.'나 'A bicycle is leaning against the bench.'와 같이 묘사하는 정답으로 자주 출제되므로 해당 표현들을 기억해 두자. 여자는 풀밭이 아닌 벤치에 앉아 있으므로 (C)역시 오답이다. 나무들이 있기는 하지만 심어지고 있지는 않으므로 (D)도 오답인데, 이는 동작과 상태의 혼동을 유발한 오답 유형이다. 길 옆에 벤치가 놓여 있는 모습을 묘사한 (B)가 정답이다.

PART 2

4

What did you do for your mother's birthday?

(A) I bought some flowers for her.

(B) Yes, I had a great time.

어머니 생일 파티 때 무엇을 하셨어요?

(A) 꽃을 사 드렸어요.

(B) 네, 즐거운 시간을 보냈어요.

(C) A party of four.

어머니 생일 파티 때 무엇을 하셨어요?

(A) 꽃을 사 드렸어요.

(B) 네, 즐거운 시간을 보냈어요.

(C) 네 명의 그룹이에요.

어휘 party 파티(행사); 그룹; 정당

해설 생일 파티에서 무엇을 했는지 묻고 있으므로 '행동'으로 답해야 한다. 즐거운 시간을 보냈다고 대답하는 (B)를 정답으로 생각할 수 있지만, 의문사로 묻는 질문에 yes나 no로 답할 수 없으므로 소거해야 한다. (C)의 party는 행사를 의미하는 것이 아닌 그룹이라는 의미이므로 (C) 역시 오답이 된다. 따라서, 꽃을 사 드렸다는 행동으로 대답한 (A)가 정답이다.

5

Who will attend the staff meeting tomorrow?

(A) Yes, I will.

(B) In the main meeting room.

(C) Everyone in this room.

내일 직원 회의에 누가 참석하나요?

(A) 네, 저는 참여할 거예요.

(B) 주 회의실에서요.

(C) 이 방에 있는 모두요.

해설 회의에 참석할 사람이 누구인지 묻는 질문이다. 누가 참여할 것인지 묻는 질문에 대해 '나'라고 답하는 (A)를 정답으로 고르는 실수를 하기 쉽다. 의문사의 문제에 yes와 no가 등장하는 순간, 바로 소거한다. 장소로 답한 (B)는 오답임을 쉽게 알 수 있다. 정답은 '이 방의 모든 사람들'이라고 답한 (C)이다.

6

Why do we have to put on a helmet?

(A) No, I didn't put it there.

(B) Some gloves and masks, too.

(C) Because of the safety policy.

우리는 왜 헬멧을 써야 하나요?

(A) 아니요, 저는 그것을 거기에 두지 않았어요.

(B) 장갑과 마스크도요.

(C) 안전 정책 때문에요.

해설 의문사 의문문에 yes나 no로 답할 수 없으므로 (A)는 오답이다. why 의문문은 구체적인 설명을 필요로 하기 때문에 단어만으로 답변할 수는 없다. 따라서, 장갑과 마스크라는 단어를 나열한 (B)역시 오답이다. 이유를 나타내는 전치사인 because of를 사용한 (C)가 정답이다.

7

When will you place an order for printing paper?

(A) Sure, I'll do it right away.

(B) We have plenty in our storeroom.

(C) Where should I visit?

프린터 용지를 언제 주문하실 건가요?

(A) 물론이죠, 제가 바로 할게요.

(B) 우리 창고에 충분히 있어요.

(C) 제가 어디를 방문해야 하나요?

어휘 plenty 충분한 양

해설 (A)의 경우 언제 주문할 것인지 묻는 질문에 대해 지금(right now)이라고 답했으므로 정답이라고 생각하기 쉽지만, 의문사 의문문에 sure로 대답할 수 없다. 장소로 되묻는 (C)는 시간을 묻는 질문에 어울리지 않는다. 용지를 언제 주문할 것이냐는 질문에 대해 창고에 충분히 있다고 답하며 주문할 필요가 없음을 우회적으로 말한 (B)가 정답이다.

8

Can I borrow your pen?

(A) That's the only one I have.

(B) A pencil might be good.

(C) No, I don't need one.

펜 좀 빌릴 수 있을까요?

(A) 저도 이거 하나밖에 없어요.

(B) 연필이 좋을 것 같아요.

(C) 아니요, 저는 필요하지 않아요.

해설 펜을 빌릴 수 있는지를 묻는 질문에 대해 펜이 하나밖에 없다고 답하며 우회적으로 거절한 (A)가 정답이다. pen과 유사한 발음의 pencil을 이용한 (B)는 오답이다. (C)의 경우 '내가 필요 없으니 빌려 줄 것'이라고 생각하기 쉽지만, no라고 답한 것을 보면 펜이 필요한지를 묻는 질문에 대한 응답으로 적절하다. 따라서 (C)도 오답이다.

9

Isn't this the last bus going downtown?

(A) A one-way ticket, please.

(B) It lasts about an hour.

(C) No, there are a few more.

이것이 시내로 가는 마지막 버스 아닌가요?

(A) 편도로 부탁해요.

(B) 그것은 약 한 시간 정도 지속돼요.

(C) 아니요, 몇 대 더 있어요.

어휘 one-way 편도의

해설 마지막 버스인지 여부를 묻는 질문에 대해 몇 대 더 있다고 대답하면서 그렇지 않다는 것을 의미하는 (C)가 정답이다. 질문의 bus에서 연상되는 편도(one-way ticket)로 대답한 (A)는 오답이다. 다른 의미로 사용된 last를 이용한 (B) 역시 오답이다. last는 '마지막'이라는 의미 외에도 동사로서 '지속되다'는 의미를 가진다.

10

What was your favorite attraction in Seoul?

(A) The palaces.

(B) Sorry. I lost track of time.

(C) Yes, that's my favorite place.

서울에서 가장 좋은 관광 명소는 무엇이었어요?

(A) 궁전들요.

(B) 미안해요, 시간 가는 줄 몰랐어요.

(C) 네, 그곳은 제가 가장 좋아하는 장소예요.

어휘 attraction (= tourist attraction) 관광 명소 I lost track of time. 시간 가는 줄 몰랐다.

해설 가장 좋았던 관광 명소를 묻는 질문에 대해 궁전이라고 답한 (A)가 정답이다. (C)의 경우 place가 장소이고 favorite이 반복되어 정답처럼 들리지만, 의문사 의문문에 yes로 답했으므로 오답이다. (B)는 attraction과 발음이 유사한 track을 이용한 오답이다.

11

Where are you going tomorrow?

(A) Yes, we are.

(B) To the conference in Canada.

(C) Of course, I will.

내일 어디에 가세요?

(A) 네, 우리는 가요.

(B) 캐나다의 컨퍼런스예요.

(C) 물론이죠, 제가 갈 거예요.

해설 (A)와 (C) 모두 의문사 의문문의 정답이 될 수 없는 yes와 of course로 답하고 있다. 정답은 장소를 언급한 (B)이다.

12

Do you want me to check the printer in the office?

(A) Thanks. That will be helpful.

(B) I printed it yesterday.

(C) No, in the conference room.

제가 사무실에 있는 프린터를 점검해 드릴까요?

(A) 고마워요, 정말 도움이 되겠어요.

(B) 제가 그것을 어제 인쇄했어요.

(C) 아니요, 회의실에요.

해설 프린터를 점검해 주겠다는 제안에 대해 고맙다고 하며 수락하는 (A)가 정답이다. printer와 발음이 비슷한 print를 이용한 (B)는 오답이다. 장소만을 언급하여 수락 여부를 알 수 없는 (C) 역시 오답이다.

13

I'm preparing for Sam's retirement party.

(A) No, he's not tired.

(B) I need to repair that machine.

(C) I can help you with that.

저는 샘의 은퇴 파티를 준비하는 중이에요.

(A) 아니요, 그는 피곤하지 않아요.

(B) 저는 그 기계를 수리해야 해요.

(C) 제가 그것을 도와드릴 수 있어요.

해설 은퇴 파티를 준비한다는 말에 '도와주겠다'는 제안을 한 (C)가 정답이 된다. retire와 tire는 흔하게 등장하는 유사 발음의 오답이므로 (A)는 소거한다. prepare와 repair 또한 자주 등장하는 유사 발음 오답이므로 (B)도 정답이 될 수 없다.

14

Why did you decide to work here?

(A) I walked there for an hour.

(B) Sure, I'll work with you.

(C) I was interested in online marketing.

왜 여기에서 일하기로 결정했나요?

(A) 저는 그곳까지 한 시간 동안 걸었어요.

(B) 물론이죠, 저는 당신과 함께 일하겠어요.

(C) 저는 온라인 마케팅에 관심이 있었어요.

해설 일하게 된 이유를 묻는 질문에 '관심이 있어서'라고 답한 (C)가 정답이다. walk와 work는 대표적인 혼동되는 유사 발음이므로 (A)는 오답이다. 과거의 이유를 묻는 질문에 미래 시제로 답한 (B) 또한 오답이다. (B)는 수락하는 형태의 답변이므로 시제를 고려하지 않더라도 의문사 의문문의 정답이 될 수 없다.

15

Cindy will help you prepare for the conference.

(A) I need to repair this projector.

(B) I have a conference call.

(C) She's out for a meeting.

신디가 회의 준비를 도울 거예요.

(A) 저는 프로젝터를 수리해야 해요.

(B) 저는 전화 회의가 있어요.

(C) 그녀는 회의 때문에 외출했어요.

해설 신디가 도와줄 것이라고 언급하자, 그녀는 회의 때문에 외출했다고 답하면서 도와줄 수 없음을 암시하는 (C)가 정답이다. 파트 2에서 언급된 사람이 부재중이라는 내용의 답변은 자주 출제되는 정답 패턴이다. (B)는 conference라는 단어를 반복한 오답이며, (A)는 prepare와 발음이 유사한 repair를 이용한 오답이다.

16

When will our new application be launched?

(A) Didn't you check the memo?

(B) Lunch sounds good to me.

(C) No, it wasn't postponed.

우리의 새 어플리케이션은 언제 출시되나요?

(A) 메모를 확인하지 않으셨나요?

(B) 저는 점심이 좋을 거 같아요.

(C) 아니요, 그것은 연기되지 않았어요.

해설 새 어플리케이션의 출시 시기를 묻는 질문에 대해 메모를 확인하지 않았는지 되물으면서 메모에 해당 내용이 있었음을 암시하는 (A)가 정답이다. (B)는 launch와 발음이 유사한 lunch를 활용한 오답이며, 의문사로 묻는 질문에 대해 no로 답했을 뿐만 아니라, 미래 시제 질문에 대해 과거 시제로 답한 (C) 또한 정답이 될 수 없다.

17

The meeting is supposed to start at 7:00.

(A) 6:00 will be better.

(B) The memo said it's at 8:00.

(C) To collect more data.

회의는 7시에 시작할 예정이에요.

(A) 6시가 더 좋을 것 같아요.

(B) 메모에는 8시라고 되어 있어요.

(C) 더 많은 자료를 수집하기 위해서요.

어휘 be supposed to ~할 예정이다

해설 회의 시작 시간을 알려주는 평서문에 대해 메모에는 다른 시간으로 작성되어 있다고 말한 (B)가 정답이다. (A)를 정답으로 혼동할 수 있지만, 시간을 결정하려는 것이 아닌 정보를 전달하는 것을 목적으로 하므로 이는 오답이다. 목적을 나타내는 to부정사는 why 의문사 이외의 질문에 대한 정답이 되는 경우는 거의 없다. 따라서, (C)도 오답이다.

18

Why don't you use SNS marketing?

(A) The market is so crowded.

(B) Sure. That's a great idea.

(C) Because I prefer an online shop.

SNS 마케팅을 해보는 게 어때요?

(A) 시장이 매우 혼잡해요.

(B) 물론이죠. 좋은 생각이에요.

(C) 제가 온라인 매장을 더 좋아하기 때문에요.

해설 SNS 마케팅을 제안하는 질문에 대해 좋은 생각이라고 수락하는 (B)가 정답이다. (A)의 market은 자주 등장하는 marketing의 유사 발음 오답이다. why don't you는 why로 시작해서 이유나 목적을 묻는 질문으로 혼동하기 쉬우므로, (C)와 같이 이유에 대한 대답을 정답으로 고르는 실수를 해서는 안 된다.

PART 3

[19-21]

W1	I think **19-1) we need to replace some of the chairs in the office**.
W2	I agree. It's time. **19-2) Many of them make squeaking sounds, and my chair doesn't even go up because the height adjustment lever is broken…**
M	**20) I heard the World Furniture Expo is starting soon. Should we go there?** That would be a good place to compare the quality and prices of chairs.
W1	Perfect. When is it?
W2	Let me check the Web site on my smartphone. **21-1) It's on the 18th of June**.
M	Does it say how many companies will participate?
W2	It says there will be around seventy international and local companies. **21-2) There will also be a special lecture on interior design that night.**

W1 이 사무실의 몇몇 의자들을 교체해야 할 것 같아요.

W2 저도 동의해요. 그럴 때가 됐어요. 많은 의자에서 삐걱거리는 소리가 나고, 높이 조절 레버가 고장 나서 올라가지도 않아요…

M 세계 가구 박람회가 곧 시작한대요. 우리 거기에 가볼까요? 의자들의 품질과 가격을 비교하기 좋은 장소일 거예요.

W1 완벽하군요. 그게 언제인가요?

W2 스마트폰에서 웹사이트를 확인해 볼게요. 1월 18일이네요.

M 얼마나 많은 회사가 참여하는지 언급되어 있나요?

W2 70여개의 해외 및 국내 업체들이 참여할 것이라고 되어있어요. 그날 밤에는 인테리어 디자인에 대한 특별 강연도 있을 거예요.

어휘 squeak 끽하는 소리를 내다 adjustment 조정, 조절 participate 참가하다 lecture 강의

19

여자들이 언급한 문제는 무엇인가?

(A) 직원이 부족하다.

(B) 사무실 가구가 낡았다.

(C) 기계가 제대로 작동하지 않는다.

(D) 회사의 행사가 취소되었다.

해설 문제점을 묻는 문제는 주로 초반부에서 부정적인 표현과 함께 단서가 주어진다. 대화 초반 'we need to replace some of the chairs in the office.'에서 의자를 교체해야 한다고 했고, 이어지는 'Many of them make squeaking sounds, and my chair doesn't even go up because the height adjustment lever is broken…'에서는 의자에서 소리가 나고 높이 조절이 안되는 문제에 대해 언급하고 있다. 따라서 사무실 가구가 낡은 것이 문제이므로 정답은 (B)이다.

20

남자는 여자들에게 무엇을 하자고 권하는가?

(A) 가격을 비교하기

(B) 웹사이트를 확인하기

(C) 업체에 전화하기

(D) 행사에 참여하기

해설 남자의 말 'I heard the World Furniture Expo starts soon. Should we go there?'에서 박람회가 열리는데 같이 가는 것이 어떤 지를 묻고 있으므로 정답은 (D)가 된다.

21

6월 18일 밤에 무슨 일이 일어날 것인가?

(A) 리셉션이 열릴 것이다.

(B) 특별 강연이 제공될 것이다.

(C) 해외 고객들이 참석할 것이다.

(D) 디자인이 공개될 것이다.

해설 문제에 날짜가 언급된 경우, 그 날짜가 언급된 부분에서 정답을 찾아야 한다. 대화 중반에 "1월 18일"이 언급된 후, 대화 후반 'There will also be a special lecture on interior design that night.'에서 그날 디자인에 관한 강연이 있을 것이라고 했으므로 정답은 (B)이다.

[22-24]

W 22) **Please give me an update on our cocoon wool blended coats**.

M I have some good news. Our latest sales are up by nearly fifteen percent in all three colors: tweed, black, and camel.

W That's great. I was wondering how it was going since we fixed the missing sleeve buttons problem.

M Yes, I think promptly addressing the issue by providing customers free pickup and delivery service to repair those missing buttons definitely helped. 23) **We are also receiving positive comments from our customers. You should check them out on the Web site.**

W 24) **Could you prepare a report that I could present at the meeting tomorrow?**

M Of course. I will leave the report on your desk this afternoon.

W 코쿤 울 혼방 코트의 최신 정보를 알려주세요.

M 좋은 소식이 있어요. 우리 최근의 판매가 트위드, 검정, 카멜 세 가지 색상 모두 거의 15퍼센트나 증가했어요.

W 좋은 소식이군요. 저는 우리가 분실된 단추 문제를 해결한 이후 어떻게 진행되고 있는지 궁금했어요.

M 네, 제 생각에는 고객들에게 분실된 단추를 해결하기 위해 무료 픽업 및 배송 서비스를 제공해서 신속하게 문제를 해결했던 것이 많은 도움이 된 것 같아요. 고객들로부터 많은 긍정적인 후기도 들어오고 있어요. 웹사이트를 확인해 보세요.

W 내일 회의에서 보고할 수 있도록 보고서를 준비해 줄래요?

M 물론이죠. 오늘 오후에 보고서를 책상 위에 둘게요.

어휘 cocoon coat 코쿤 코트 (위가 넓고 아래쪽으로 갈수록 좁아지는 형태의 코트) by any chance 혹시 tweed 트위드 (다른 색상의 올이 섞인 천) address 해결하다 definitely 분명히 comment 리뷰, 후기

22

화자들은 어디에서 일하는 것 같은가?

(A) 세탁소에서

(B) 의류회사에서

(C) 화장품 회사에서

(D) 의류 수선점에서

해설 대화의 장소 문제는 주로 초반에 단서가 주어진다. 대화 초반 'Please give me an update on our cocoon wool blended coats.'에서 코트와 관련된 최신 정보를 알려달라고 했으므로 정답은 (B)가 된다. 이어지는 내용에서도 코트의 판매량 및 문제 해결 등과 관련된 내용이 이어지고 있다.

23

남자는 여자에게 무엇을 하라고 제안하는가?

(A) 웹사이트를 업데이트하는 것

(B) 고객들의 피드백을 읽는 것

(C) 무료 배송을 제공하는 것

(D) 몇몇 재료를 가져오는 것

해설 제안의 표현을 잘 듣고 정답을 찾아야 한다. 남자는 'We are also receiving positive comments from our customers. You should check them out on the Web site'라고 하며 고객들의 후기를 읽어보라고 제안하고 있다. 따라서 정답은 (B)이다. 선택지의 feedback은 comment의 동의어이다.

24

여자는 남자에게 무엇을 할 것을 요청하는가?

(A) 회의 일정 변경하기

(B) 몇몇 고객 정보 보내기

(C) **보고서 작성하기**

(D) 섬유 공장에 전화하기

해설 여자의 마지막 말 'Could you prepare a report that I could present at the meeting tomorrow?'에서 보고서를 준비해 달라고 부탁하고 있으므로 정답은 (C)이다.

[25-27]

> W Hey, Kenneth. How are you doing? Have you seen the new play at the Rococo Theater? I thought of you when I read a review about it in the newspaper. 25) **I know how much you enjoy good comedies**.
>
> M Everybody has been telling me about the play. I think I need to see it, 26) **but I was disappointed when I learned that it's completely sold out!** My friend and I tried to buy tickets, but we had no luck.
>
> W Well, the newspaper article said that the play might run longer since it's been so popular. 27) **I bet if you call the theater again, you might be able to find out when the new performances will be.** Maybe the theater can sell you some advance tickets to one of the next shows.
>
> W 안녕하세요, 케네스, 어떻게 지내세요? 로코코 극장에서 하는 새 연극을 보셨나요? 신문에서 그것에 대한 리뷰를 읽을 때, 당신 생각이 났어요. 당신이 좋은 코미디 물을 얼마나 좋아하는지 알고 있거든요.
>
> M 모두가 저에게 그 연극에 대해 얘기하더군요. 그것을 봐야 할 것 같은데, 완전히 매진되어서 매우 실망스러웠어요! 친구와 제가 표를 사려고 했지만 운이 없었어요.
>
> W 음, 신문기사에 따르면 그 연극이 매우 인기가 있어서 더 오래 공연할지도 모른다고 하던데요. 극장에 다시 전화하면, 새 공연이 언제가 될지 알 수 있을 것 같아요. 아마도 극장에서 다음 공연 중의 하나에 대한 표를 사전에 판매할 수도 있어요.

어휘 disappointed 실망한 bet 단언하다 find out 알아내다 performance 공연 advanced 사전의

이달의 새로운 연극 리스트

제목	장르
Father	드라마
Sing	코메디
Sign	스릴러
Rainbow	뮤지컬

25

시각 정보를 보시오. 화자들은 어떤 연극에 대해 이야기하는가?

(A) *Father*

(B) *Sing*

(C) *Sign*

(D) *Rainbow*

해설 시각 정보 문제의 경우 선택지에 있는 단어가 직접 언급되지 않고 그 주변의 정보들이 단서로 언급된다. 대화 초반 'I know how much you enjoy good comedies.'라고 했으므로 화자들은 코메디 연극에 대해 이야기하고 있다는 것을 알 수 있다. 따라서, 정답은 (B)이다.

26

남자는 왜 그 연극을 아직 보지 못했는가?

(A) 극장이 공사 중이다.

(B) 그는 함께 갈 사람을 찾을 수 없었다.

(C) 공연이 취소되었다.

(D) **티켓이 없다.**

해설 이유를 묻는 문제의 경우 질문의 내용이 근거로 사용되는 경우가 많으며, 이유를 언급하는 구문이 정답의 근거가 되는 경우가 많다. 하지만 부정의 구문에 이어서 정답의 단서가 언급되는 경우도 많이 있다. 남자의 말 'but I was disappointed when I learned that it's completely sold out!'에서 모두 매진되어서 실망했다고 했으므로, 남은 티켓이 없다는 의미의 (D)가 정답이다.

27

여자는 남자에게 무엇을 하라고 제안하는가?

(A) 극장에서 자리를 바꾸기

(B) **극장에 전화해 보기**

(C) 줄 서는 것을 피하기 위해서 일찍 도착하기

(D) 연극에 대해 리뷰를 쓰기

해설 대화 마지막 부분의 'I bet if you call the theater again, you might be able to find out when the new performances will be.'에서 극장에 전화해서 다음 공연에 대해 알아보라고 이야기하고 있으므로 정답은 (B)이다.

PART 4

[28-30]

> M Mr. Gables, 28) **this is the supply chain manager at the fulfillment center in Nashville. I want to let you know that the shipping label system is not working due to a server outage, and** 29-1) **it's causing**

significant delays to our delivery schedule. **It turns out that there was a breach in the data center infrastructure that led to this issue.** The engineering team is telling us that the ²⁹⁻²⁾ **issue will not be resolved until the end of the day**. We have many orders that were scheduled to go out for delivery this morning. This is already the third time something like this has happened this quarter. I was told that there are systems we can integrate with that will do real-time monitoring for issues like this, so we can detect them in a more timely manner. ³⁰⁾ **Do you have some time tomorrow to discuss this further?**

M 게이블스 씨, 저는 내슈빌에 있는 풀필먼트 센터의 공급망 관리자입니다. 서버 장애로 인해 배송 라벨 시스템이 작동하지 않고 있으며, 배송 일정에 상당한 지연이 발생하고 있음을 알려드리고자 합니다. 이 문제는 데이터 센터 인프라에 구멍이 있었기 때문입니다. 기술팀에서 문제가 오늘 중으로 해결되지 않을 것이라고 합니다. 오늘 오전에 발송 예정이었던 주문이 많이 있습니다. 이번 분기에 이런 일이 벌써 세 번째 발생했습니다. 이와 같은 문제를 실시간 모니터링으로 통합할 수 있는 시스템이 있어서 이를 보다 적시에 탐지할 수 있다고 들었습니다. 내일 이것에 대해 더 논의할 시간이 있나요?

어휘 fulfillment center 풀필먼트 센터 (물품의 보관, 주문, 배송, CS 관리, 회수 및 반품 등의 모든 업무를 처리하는 물류 센터) turn out 판명되다 breach 구멍, 틈 integrate 통합하다

28
화자는 어디에서 일하는가?
(A) 선적 센터
(B) 소프트웨어 회사
(C) 데이터 분석 회사
(D) 우체국

해설 담화 초반의 'this is the supply chain manager at the fulfillment center in Nashville.'에서 화자는 자신이 풀필먼트 센터의 공급망 관리자라고 했고, 이어서 'I want to let you know that the shipping label system is not working due to a server outage'에서 서버 고장으로 선적 라벨 시스템이 작동하지 않는다고 했으므로, 화자는 선적과 관련된 회사에서 일한다는 것을 알 수 있다. 따라서, 정답은 (A)이다.

29
화자는 왜 "문제는 오늘 안에 해결되지 않을 것입니다"라고 말하는가?
(A) 도움을 요청하기 위해
(B) 과정에 대해 불평하기 위해
(C) 새 소프트웨어를 설치하기 위해
(D) 지연에 대해 설명하기 위해

해설 인용된 문장 앞 'it's causing significant delays to our delivery schedule.'에 배송이 지연되었다는 '문제'를 언급하고 있고,

이어지는 'It turns out that there was a breach in the data center infrastructure that led to this issue.'에서 그 원인을 설명하고 있다. 인용된 부분인 'issue will not be resolved until the end of the day'에서 배송 지연의 원인이 되는 '문제'가 빨리 해결되지 않을 것임을 언급하고 있으므로, '지연에 대해 설명하기 위해서'라는 내용의 (D)가 정답이다.

30
화자는 무엇을 하기를 원하는가?
(A) 장비 변경하기
(B) 회의 준비하기
(C) 공급자에게 연락하기
(D) 디자인 수정하기

해설 화자가 원하는 것을 찾는 문제는 주로 '원하다'라는 표현이나 질문하는 부분에서 정답을 찾을 수 있는 경우가 많다. 담화 마지막의 'Do you have some time tomorrow to discuss this further?'에서 해당 문제에 대해 내일 이야기할 시간이 있는지 묻고 있다. 정답은 (B)이다.

[31-33]

W ³¹⁻¹⁾ **Welcome to the sightseeing bus.** ³¹⁻²⁾ **We're happy to have you join us for this tour of exciting downtown Vancouver,** one of the most beautiful cities in the world. ³²⁾ **It boasts various tourist attractions and famous restaurants.** It's a warm and sunny day, which is perfect for a walking tour. When you get off the bus, you'll have 2 hours of free time. You may want to purchase some souvenirs for your family, and there are plenty of gift shops available. ³³⁾ **Please make sure to keep your return tickets as you will need them to get back on the bus.** Enjoy your trip!

W 관광 버스에 탑승하신 것을 환영합니다. 여러분께서 세계에서 가장 아름다운 도시 중 하나인 벤쿠버의 흥미로운 시내 관광을 저희와 함께 하시게 되어 기쁩니다. 이곳은 다양한 관광 명소와 식당들을 자랑합니다. 오늘은 맑고 따뜻한 날이어서, 걸어서 관광하기에 완벽한 날씨입니다. 버스에서 내리면, 2시간의 자유시간이 주어집니다. 가족들을 위한 기념품을 구매하고 싶으실 텐데, 이곳에는 이용할 수 있는 기념품 판매점이 많습니다. 버스에 다시 탑승할 때 필요하므로 왕복 티켓을 꼭 챙기시기 바랍니다. 즐거운 여행 되세요!

어휘 boast 자랑하다 tourist attraction 관광명소 souvenir 기념품 plenty 많음, 풍부함 available 이용 가능한, 구할 수 있는

31
청자들은 누구인가?
(A) 버스 운전사들
(B) 상점 주인들
(C) 관광객들
(D) 도시 공무원들

담화의 첫 부분에서 관광 버스에 온 것을 환영한다고 말한 다음, 'We're happy to have you join us for this tour of exciting downtown Vancouver'라며 시티 투어를 하게 될 것임을 알리는 것으로 보아, 청자들은 관광 버스에 탑승한 관광객들임을 알 수 있다.

32

투어에 대해 언급된 내용은 무엇인가?
(A) 3시간 이상 걸린다.
(B) 자유 시간이 없다.
(C) 먹을 곳이 많다.
(D) 돌아오는 버스가 없다.

해설 'It boasts various tourist attractions and famous restaurants'에서 관광 명소와 더불어 유명한 식당들이 있다고 언급하고 있으므로 (C)가 정답이다. 버스에서 내린 후 2시간의 자유시간에 대한 언급은 있지만, 투어 전체의 시간은 언급되지 않았으므로 (A)는 오답이다. 'When you get off the bus, you'll have 2 hours of free time.'에서 자유 시간이 주어진다고 했으므로 (B)역시 오답이다. 담화의 마지막 부분에서 왕복 티켓을 잘 챙기라고 했으므로 (D)역시 오답이다.

33

화자가 청자들에게 상기시키는 것은 무엇인가?
(A) 왕복 티켓을 챙기기
(B) 편안한 신발을 신기
(C) 시내 지도를 사용하기
(D) 시간에 맞춰 도착하기

해설 상기시키는 것을 묻는 문제의 경우, 'remember, don't forget, make sure, please' 등이 단서가 되는 구문이다. 담화 마지막의 'Please make sure to keep your return tickets as you will need them to board the bus back.'에서 'please make sure ~' 뒤의 내용이 '티켓을 잘 챙기라'는 것이므로 정답은 (A)이다.

DAY 06 PART 2
고난도 문제 풀이법

📑 실전 문제 연습
p.063

🎧 06-10

1 (B)	2 (B)	3 (A)	4 (B)
5 (B)	6 (C)	7 (B)	8 (B)
9 (A)	10 (C)	11 (B)	12 (A)
13 (A)	14 (C)	15 (C)	16 (B)
17 (C)	18 (A)	19 (A)	20 (D)
21 (C)	22 (A)	23 (A)	24 (A)
25 (C)	26 (C)	27 (B)	28 (B)
29 (C)	30 (A)	31 (C)	32 (D)
33 (B)			

1
(A) A woman is sipping water from a cup.
(B) A woman is sitting at a computer.
(C) A woman is writing something on a notepad.
(D) A woman is seated at an outside café.

(A) 한 여자가 컵에서 물을 조금씩 마시고 있다.
(B) 한 여자가 컴퓨터 앞에 앉아 있다.
(C) 한 여자가 메모장에 무엇인가를 쓰고 있다.
(D) 한 여자가 야외 카페에 앉아 있다.

어휘 sip 홀짝거리다, 조금씩 마시다

해설 사진의 여자는 실내에서 노트북을 사용하고 있으므로 실외 장소를 언급한 (D)는 오답이다. (C)는 notebook과 유사한 단어인 notepad를 이용한 오답이며, (A)의 경우 옆에 컵이 놓여 있기는 하지만, 여자가 무엇인가를 마시고 있지 않으므로 오답이다. 여자가 노트북을 사용하고 있는 동작을 묘사한 (B)가 정답이다.

2
(A) Some customers have lined up at a counter.
(B) A worker is serving food to some customers.
(C) A server is clearing up the table.
(D) Some chairs are being stacked next to a table.

(A) 손님들은 카운터 앞에 줄을 서 있다.
(B) 한 직원이 손님들에게 음식을 서빙하고 있다.
(C) 한 서버가 테이블을 치우고 있다.
(D) 몇몇 의자들이 테이블 옆에 쌓이고 있다.

해설 손님들은 앉아 있고 서버가 음식을 서빙하고 있다. 따라서 손님들이 줄을 서 있다는 내용의 (A)와 테이블을 치우고 있다는 내용의 (C)는 모두 오답이다. 사진 속에 등장하는 인물이 '서버'이기 때문에 server만을 듣고 (C)를 정답으로 고르는 실수를 해서는 안 된다. 의자를 쌓는 동작도 보이지 않으므로 (D)도 오답이다. 직원이 음식을 서빙하고 있다는 내용의 (B)가 정답이다.

3
(A) A mountain is visible in the distance.
(B) Some people are harvesting crops.
(C) A woman is carrying a box with vegetables.
(D) Some boxes are being stocked on a cart.

(A) 멀리 산이 보인다.
(B) 몇몇 사람들이 곡식을 추수하고 있는 중이다.
(C) 한 여자가 채소가 담긴 박스를 나르고 있는 중이다.
(D) 박스 몇 개가 카트에 실리고 있는 중이다.

해설 난이도가 높은 문제의 유형이다. 우선 사진 속에 사람이 한 명뿐이므로 '몇몇 사람들(some people)'의 동작을 묘사한 (B)는 정답이 될 수 없다. 사진에서 눈에 띄는 것은 채소 박스를 만지고 있는 여자의 모습이므로, 채소 박스를 나른다는 내용의 (C)를 정답으로 고르는 실수를 하기 쉽다. 하지만, 여자가 박스를 나르고 있는 것은 아니므로 (C)는 정답이 될 수 없다. 박스들이 카트에 실려 있으므로 (D)를 정답으로 고르는 실수를 하기 쉬운데, being stocked는 '쌓여 있는 상태'를 의미하는 것이 아니라 '쌓이고 있는 동작'을 묘사하는 표현이다. 따라서 (D) 역시 오답이다. 정답은 (A)인데, 이 문제와 같이 중심에 있는 사람이나 사물의 주요 동작이나 상태가 아닌 멀리 있는 배경을 설명하는 유형도 종종 출제된다.

PART 2

4

Where is the marketing seminar scheduled to be held?

(A) You have to be dressed formally.

(B) I haven't been informed yet.

(C) Yes, we should all attend it.

마케팅 세미나는 어디에서 열리나요?
(A) 격식을 갖추어 옷을 입으세요.
(B) 저는 아직 통보 받지 못했어요.
(C) 네, 우리는 모두 거기에 참석해야 해요.

어휘 be held 열리다, 개최되다　be scheduled to ~할 예정이다　be dressed 옷을 입다　formally 격식을 갖추어　be informed 통보 받다, 소식을 듣다

해설 세미나 개최 장소를 묻는 질문에 아직 통보 받지 못했다고 대답한 (B)가 정답이다. (A)는 드레스 코드에 해당하며, (C)는 의문사 의문문에 yes/no로 대답한 전형적인 오답이다.

5

Who do you think will be elected as the new mayor?

(A) The election will be held on Monday.

(B) I couldn't even guess.

(C) I'll change my major.

누가 새로운 시장으로 선출될 것 같나요?
(A) 선거는 월요일에 있을 거예요.
(B) 저는 예측조차 못하겠어요.
(C) 저는 전공을 바꿀 거예요.

어휘 be elected 선출되다　election 선거　mayor 시장　major 전공　guess 추측하다

해설 누가 시장으로 선출될 것 같은지 묻는 질문에 예측도 못하겠다고 답한 (B)가 정답이다. (A)는 elected의 파생어인 election을 이용한 오답이며, (C)는 mayor와 발음이 유사한 major를 이용한 오답이다.

6

Is there a faster way to finish this balance sheet?

(A) The fastest way to get there is by train.

(B) She's been away for a week.

(C) You should ask Paul.

이 대차대조표를 완성할 수 있는 더 빠른 방법이 있을까요?
(A) 그곳에 가는 가장 빠른 방법은 기차예요.
(B) 그녀는 일주일간 떠나 있었어요.
(C) 폴에게 물어보세요.

어휘 balance sheet 대차대조표　be away 자리를 비우다

해설 일을 끝낼 수 있는 더 빠른 방법을 문의했으므로 교통 수단으로 답한 (A)는 오답이다. 질문의 way와 발음이 유사한 away를 사용한 (B)도 오답이다. 다른 사람에게 물어볼 것을 권한 (C)가 정답이다.

7

How many attendees will be at the accounting seminar?

(A) The Accounting Department.

(B) I'll have a look at the list.

(C) The seminar ends at 9:00.

회계 세미나에는 몇 명의 참석자가 있을까요?
(A) 회계 부서요.
(B) 제가 명단을 확인해 볼게요.
(C) 세미나는 9시에 끝나요.

해설 세미나에 몇 명이 올 것인지를 묻는 질문에 명단을 확인하겠다고 대답한 (B)가 정답이다. (A)는 질문의 accounting을 이용한 함정이며, (C)는 when 의문문에 대한 대답이므로 정답이 될 수 없다.

8

Why is the department store closed?

(A) It will open soon.

(B) It didn't pass an inspection.

(C) At the shop downtown.

백화점이 왜 닫혀 있나요?
(A) 곧 문을 열 거예요.
(B) 점검을 통과하지 못했어요.
(C) 시내 상점에요.

어휘 inspection 점검　downtown 중심가

해설 백화점이 닫혀 있는 이유를 묻는 질문에 대해 점검을 통과하지 못했기 때문이라고 이유를 알려주는 (B)가 정답이다. (C)는 질문의 store에서 연상되는 shop을 이용한 오답이다. (A)의 경우 정답처럼 들리지만 백화점이 닫혀 있는 이유를 묻는 질문에 대한 답이 될 수 없다. 또한, 질문의 closed에서 연상되는 open을 이용한 오답이기도 하다.

9

Aren't they opening another branch?

(A) Yes, on Vino Street.

(B) The fallen branches caused the delay.

(C) It will be closed at 9:00.

그들은 다른 지점을 열지 않나요?
(A) 네, 비노 거리에요.
(B) 부러진 가지들이 지연을 발생시켰어요.
(C) 그곳은 9시에 닫을 거예요.

어휘 branch 나뭇가지; 지사, 사무실 지점　cause 원인; 일으키다　delay 연기, 지연

해설 다른 지점을 열 것인지 묻는 질문에 대해 '비노 거리에요'라고 위치를 말한 (A)가 정답이다. (A)는 동사가 생략된 답변으로서, 생략된 동사

는 질문의 동사와 동일하다. (B)의 branch는 '가지'라는 의미로서 질문의 branch(지점)와 다른 뜻이며, (C)는 질문의 open에서 연상되는 close를 이용한 오답이다.

10

What do you think about the new film that started playing yesterday?
(A) You said so.
(B) I have some old movies.
(C) I was fascinated by it.

어제 상영을 시작한 새 연극에 대해 어떻게 생각하세요?
(A) 당신이 그렇게 말했죠.
(B) 저는 몇 편의 옛날 영화를 소장하고 있어요.
(C) 저는 그것에 완전히 매료됐어요.

해설 'What do you think about ~?'은 의견을 묻는 질문이다. 따라서, 자신의 생각을 말한 (C)가 적절한 응답이다. (B)는 film에서 연상되는 movie, new에서 연상되는 old를 이용한 오답이며, (A)는 앞서 말한 것에 동의할 때 사용되는 표현이다.

11

Do you have our fall catalog?
(A) I'll show you in a minute.
(B) No, could I have one?
(C) The leaves have fallen from the trees.

우리의 가을 카탈로그를 가지고 계신가요?
(A) 제가 잠시 후에 보여 드릴게요.
(B) 아니요, 하나 받을 수 있을까요?
(C) 나무에서 잎들이 떨어졌어요.

어휘 catalog 카탈로그, 목록, 일람표   in a minute 잠시 후에

해설 카탈로그를 가지고 있는지 묻는 질문에 대한 부 달라고 답한 (B)가 가장 자연스러운 대답이다. (A)는 '잠시 후에 보여주겠다'는 답변인데, 자신의 회사 카탈로그를 가지고 있는지 묻는 직원에게 그 회사의 카탈로그를 보여 줄 필요는 없다. (C)는 fall과 발음이 비슷한 fallen을 이용한 오답이다.

12

That's not this month's magazine, right?
(A) Actually, it is. It was delivered yesterday.
(B) Last month's issue is better.
(C) Turn to the left.

저것은 이번 달 잡지가 아니에요, 그렇죠?
(A) 사실, 맞아요. 그것은 어제 배송되었어요.
(B) 지난달 호가 더 나았어요.
(C) 왼쪽으로 돌아주세요.

어휘 be delivered 배송 오다, 배송 되다   issue 잡지의 호

해설 잡지가 이번 달 것이 맞는지 묻는 질문에 대해 맞다고 대답한 다음, 어제 배송되었다고 한 (A)가 정답이다. 질문의 month's를 이용한 (B)와, right에서 연상되는 left를 이용한 (C)는 모두 오답이다.

13

What's wrong with the equipment?
(A) We have to replace some parts.
(B) Sorry. Wrong office.
(C) No, it's not that long.

장비에 무슨 문제가 있나요?
(A) 몇 가지 부품을 교체해야 해요.
(B) 미안해요. 사무실을 잘못 찾아왔어요.
(C) 아니요, 그것은 그렇게 길지 않아요.

어휘 equipment 장비   part 부품

해설 장비의 문제가 무엇인지를 묻는 질문에 대해 부품에 문제가 있다는 것을 간접적으로 말한 (A)가 정답이다. (B)는 wrong을 중복 사용한 오답이며, (C)는 의문사 의문문에 no로 답할 수 없으므로 오답이다. 질문의 wrong과 발음이 유사한 long을 이용한 오답이기도 하다.

14

Did you meet the president when you visited headquarters?
(A) Yes, he is the head of the company.
(B) I'll present the idea at the annual conference.
(C) I tried to clear some time in my schedule, but I couldn't.

본사를 방문했을 때 사장님을 만났나요?
(A) 네, 그는 그 회사의 사장이에요.
(B) 저는 연례 컨퍼런스에서 그 아이디어를 발표할 거예요.
(C) 시간을 내보려고 했지만, 그럴 수 없었어요.

어휘 headquarters 본사   clear time 시간을 내다

해설 일반의문문과 의문사가 함께 있는 복합의문문의 경우 의문사에 대한 답을 고르는 것이 대부분이지만, 이는 의문사가 목적어로 쓰이는 경우에만 해당한다. 이 문제는 의문사절이 부사절이므로 의문사에 대한 답을 고르는 문제가 아니다. 질문의 핵심은 사장님을 만났는지 여부를 묻는 것이므로, 시간을 내보려고 했으나 그러지 못했다고 답한 (C)가 정답이다. (A)는 headquarter와 발음이 겹치는 head를 이용한 오답이며, (B)는 president와 발음이 유사한 present를 사용한 오답이다.

15

How long does it take to get to the public library?
(A) It's nearly 10 miles.
(B) It just opened to the public.
(C) Around 10 minutes by taxi.

공공 도서관까지 얼마나 걸릴까요?
(A) 거의 10마일이에요.
(B) 그것은 막 일반인들에게 개관됐어요.
(C) 택시로 10분 정도요.

어휘 public library 공공 도서관   public 대중, 일반인

해설 소요 시간을 묻는 질문에 대해 10마일이라는 거리로 답한 (A)는 오답이다. (B)는 도서관이 개관한 시기를 언급하고 있으므로, 도서관까지 가는 데 걸리는 시간을 묻는 질문에 대한 적절한 답변이 될 수 없다. 택시

로 10분 걸린다는 내용의 (C)가 가장 적절한 대답이다.

16

Where should I send the survey results?

(A) Put them on the table.

(B) Fax them to the president.

(C) To get customers' feedback.

어디에 설문 결과를 보내야 하나요?

(A) 테이블 위에 두세요.

(B) 사장님에게 팩스로 보내세요.

(C) 고객들의 피드백을 받기 위해서요.

어휘 fax 팩스를 보내다 feedback 피드백

해설 where 의문문으로서 설문 결과를 어디로 보내야 하는지 묻는 질문에 대해 사장님께 팩스를 보내라는 (B)가 정답이 된다. (A)의 경우 어디로 보내야 하는지 묻는 질문에 대해서 책상 위에 두라는 것은 동사의 의미가 일치하지 않으므로 오답이다. 간혹, 설문 결과를 어디로 보내야 하는지 묻는 질문에 테이블 위에 잠시 두고 나중에 판단하자는 의미로 (A)가 될 수도 있다고 생각하는 수험자들이 있는데, 질문에서 '어디로 보내야 하는지'를 물었다는 것은 '이미 보내기로 결정된 상황'이라는 것을 염두에 두어야 한다. 파트 2는 '질의-응답'이므로 앞뒤에 '이럴 수도 있겠다'라는 여지가 있는 답변은 정답이 될 수 없다는 것을 꼭 기억하자. (C)와 같은 목적을 의미하는 답변은 why 의문문에 대한 답변이다.

17

Please tell Brian a friend called him.

(A) Please call me back.

(B) Yes, he told me so.

(C) Which friend, specifically?

친구에게서 전화가 왔었다고 브라이언에게 말해주세요.

(A) 저에게 다시 전화해주세요.

(B) 네, 그가 저에게 그렇게 말했어요.

(C) 정확하게 어떤 친구예요?

해설 친구에게서 전화가 왔었다고 전해달라는 부탁에 대해 구체적으로 누구인지를 되물은 (C)가 정답이다. (A)는 call을 중복 사용한 오답이며, (B)는 '그가 그렇게 말했다'는 의미로 질문과 관계없는 내용이다.

18

How is the new art director compared to Mr. Song?

(A) He's quite demanding.

(B) I think I'm qualified.

(C) It was incomparable.

새로운 아트 디렉터는 송 씨에 비교하면 어떤가요?

(A) 그는 꽤 까다로워요.

(B) 제 생각에 저는 자격이 충분한 것 같아요.

(C) 그것은 비할 데가 없었어요.

어휘 compare 비교하다 demanding 까다로운 qualified 자격, 자질이 충분한 incomparable 비할 데 없는

해설 사람의 성격을 물었으므로 까다롭다고 대답한 (A)가 정답이다. (C)는 compared와 발음이 비슷한 incomparable을 이용한 오답이고,

(B)는 새로운 아트 디렉터가 아닌 자신의 이야기를 하고 있으므로 정답이 될 수 없다.

PART 3

[19-21]

W	Good morning. **19) I'm Sally, the new assistant**.
M	Hi, Sally. You'll spend most of this week getting familiar with all the work in the office.
W	**20-1) Would you please tell me what my job involves?**
M	The main duty is to keep the file in order. **20-2) You are also responsible for answering calls and then transferring them or taking messages**.
W	Okay.
M	But first, **21) let me show you around the office and introduce you to your coworkers**.
W	좋은 아침이에요. 저는 새로운 비서 샐리입니다.
M	안녕하세요, 샐리. 이번 주 대부분의 시간은 사무실의 모든 업무에 익숙해지는 데 보내게 될 거예요.
W	제 업무에 무엇이 포함되는지 알려주시겠어요?
M	주 업무는 서류를 순서대로 정리해 두는 거예요. 전화를 받고 나서 연결해 주거나 메시지를 받아 두는 것도 하게 되죠.
W	알겠습니다.
M	하지만 먼저, 사무실을 구경시켜 드리고 동료들에게 소개시켜 드릴게요.

어휘 assistant 비서 be familiar with ~에 익숙하다 coworker 동료

19

여자는 누구인 것 같은가?

(A) 비서

(B) 우체부

(C) 호텔 직원

(D) 콜센터 직원

해설 화자의 직업을 묻는 질문은 주로 대화의 초반에서 정답이 등장한다. 대화의 첫 문장 'I'm Sally, the new assistant.'에서 자신이 새로운 비서인 샐리라고 이야기를 했으므로 정답은 (A)이다.

20

여자는 남자에게 무엇에 관해 묻는가?

(A) 그녀가 어떻게 예약을 해야 하는지

(B) 그녀가 무엇을 타이핑하고 준비해야 하는지

(C) 누가 다른 직원을 지원하는지

(D) 그녀가 무엇을 담당하는지

해설 여자의 대화에서 직접적이거나 간접적으로 질문하는 내용과 이어지는 부분에서 정답을 찾는다. 'Would you please tell me what my job involves?'에서 담당하는 업무에 대해 물었는데, 이에 대해 남자가 'You are also responsible for answering calls and then transferring them or taking messages.'라고 하며 여자가 담당하는 업무에 대해 설명하고 있다. 따라서 정답은 (D)이다.

21
남자는 다음에 무엇을 할 것인가?
(A) 회의에 참여하기
(B) 고객을 만나기
(C) **여자에게 구경 시켜주기**
(D) 전화 받기

해설 마지막 남자의 말 'let me show you around the office and introduce you to your coworkers'에서 사무실을 보여 주겠다고 했으므로 정답은 (C)가 된다. show around와 tour는 동의어이다.

[22-24]

> M Hello. 22) **Welcome to the Grandview Library.** We are waiving all late fees this month in celebration of our 50th anniversary.
>
> W That's great. It's my first time here. 23) **Do you have any guides on using the library's resources?**
>
> M I'm sorry. We just ran out of printed guides due to the high demand this month.
>
> W Well, I'm a bit unsure about how to find books.
>
> M I understand. 24-1) **The information desk is just across the room on the right.**
>
> W Oh, 24-2) **that's good to know. Thanks.**
>
> M 안녕하세요. 그랜드뷰 도서관에 오신 것을 환영합니다. 이번 달에는 저희 도서관의 50주년 기념일을 축하하기 위해 모든 연체료가 면제됩니다.
>
> W 좋네요. 여기는 처음 왔어요. 도서관의 자료를 이용하는 것에 대한 안내서가 있나요?
>
> M 죄송합니다. 이번 달에 수요가 많아서 인쇄된 안내서가 다 떨어졌습니다.
>
> W 음, 저는 책을 어떻게 찾아야 하는지 잘 모르겠어요.
>
> M 알겠습니다. 반대편 오른쪽에 안내 데스크가 있습니다.
>
> W 아, 잘됐네요. 감사합니다.

어휘 waive 면제하다   late fee 연체료   resource 자료   run out of 떨어지다, 소진되다   unsure 확실하지 않은

22
대화는 어디에서 일어나는 것 같은가?
(A) 도서관에서
(B) 주차장에서
(C) 은행에서

(D) 여행사에서

해설 남자의 첫 인사 'Welcome to the Grandview Library.'를 들었다면, 대화의 장소가 도서관임을 알 수 있다. 문제의 난이도가 낮은 편이기는 하지만, 간혹 첫 문장을 놓치면 문제를 틀리는 경우가 있으므로 주의한다. 정답은 (A)이다.

23
여자가 알고 싶어 하는 것은 무엇인가?
(A) **자료 이용 방법**
(B) 가이드 투어 신청 방법
(C) 방 예약 방법
(D) 사본 받는 방법

해설 여자의 첫 질문 'Do you have any guides on using the library's resources?'에서 도서관 자료를 사용하는 안내서가 있는지를 묻고 있으므로, 여자가 알고 싶은 것은 자료 이용 방법이다. 따라서 (A)가 정답이 된다.

24
여자는 다음에 무엇을 할 것 같은가?
(A) 안내 데스크로 가기
(B) 온라인 튜토리얼 찾아보기
(C) 인쇄된 가이드 받기
(D) 다른 업체에 연락하기

해설 대화 마지막 부분의 남자의 말 'The information desk is just across the room on the right.'에서 안내 데스크의 위치를 알려 주고 있고, 이에 대해 여자는 알려 줘서 고맙다고 했다. 따라서 자료 사용 방법을 모르는 여자는 안내 데스크로 갈 가능성이 높다. 따라서 (A)가 정답이 된다.

[25-27]

> W Good afternoon. Grand Wood Hotel. How may I help you?
>
> M Hello. I am Matthew from Gamers United, and 25) **we're trying to find a venue to hold a video game trade show in November this year**.
>
> W Great. We have a lot of experience hosting that type of convention. May I ask how many visitors will be attending the show? We need to know what size event you're planning to have in order to plan the appropriate layout for the show.
>
> M Well, 26-1) **we are hoping to have around 200 visitors. Do you have enough space to accommodate that many people?** However, I don't want it to be too big as that can leave the space looking empty.
>
> W I understand. Lucky for you, 26-2) **we have an assembly hall that can fit between 200 and 250 people.**

M Perfect. There's just one other thing. We need to set up LED wash lights to highlight the show's 50 booths. Do you know any electricians who can do the job?

W Sure. 27) **I will e-mail you the phone number of the company we regularly hire for lighting.**

W 안녕하세요. 그랜드 우드 호텔입니다. 어떻게 도와드릴까요?

M 안녕하세요. 저는 게이머스 유나이티드의 매튜이고, 올해 11월에 비디오 게임 무역 박람회를 열기 위한 장소를 찾고 있어요.

W 잘됐군요. 저희는 그런 종류의 컨벤션을 주최했던 경험이 많습니다. 얼마나 많은 방문객들이 박람회에 참여하는지 알려주실 수 있을까요? 박람회를 위한 적절한 레이아웃을 계획하기 위해 행사의 규모가 어느 정도인지 알아야 합니다.

M 음, 저희는 200명 정도의 방문객이 참석할 것을 기대하고 있어요. 그 정도로 많은 인원을 수용할 수 있는 공간이 있을까요? 하지만, 공간이 너무 커서 빈 공간이 남는 것은 원하지 않아요.

W 알겠습니다. 다행히도 저희는 200명에서 250명 정도에 적합한 회의장이 있습니다.

M 완벽하군요. 한 가지만 더요. 저희는 50개의 행사 부스를 강조하기 위해 LED 워시라이트를 설치해야 해요. 이 작업을 수행할 수 있는 전기 기술자를 아시나요?

W 물론이죠. 저희가 고정적으로 조명을 위해 고용하는 회사의 전화번호를 이메일로 보내드리겠습니다.

어휘 appropriate 적절한 accommodate 수용하다 assembly hall 회의장 wash light 워시 라이트 (무대 등을 골고루 비추기 위해서 사용하는 조명의 종류)

25
남자는 어떤 행사를 계획하고 있는가?
(A) 은퇴 파티
(B) 시상식
(C) **무역 박람회**
(D) 상품 출시

해설 대화 초반 'we're trying to find a venue to hold a video game trade show in November this year.'에서 남자는 무역 박람회를 준비하고 있다고 이야기했다. 따라서 정답은 (C)이다.

그랜드 우드 호텔

위그모어 홀	100–150
메이요 홀	150–200
길드 홀	200–250
쥬빌리 홀	250–400

26
시각 정보를 보시오. 남자는 어떤 홀을 예약할 것 같은가?
(A) 위그모어 홀
(B) 메이요 홀
(C) 길드 홀
(D) 쥬빌 홀

해설 남자의 대화 중 'we are hoping to have around 200 visitors. Do you have enough space to accommodate that many people?'에서 참석자가 200명이라고 했고, 이어서 여자는 'we have an assembly hall that can fit between 200 and 250 people'이라고 했다. 시각 정보에서 200–250명을 수용할 수 있는 홀은 (C)이다.

27
여자는 무엇을 할 것이라고 말하는가?
(A) 계약서 보내기
(B) 전기 기술자에게 전화하기
(C) **정보를 이메일로 보내기**
(D) 사진을 제공하기

해설 대화 마지막 부분의 'I will e-mail you the phone number of the company we regularly hire for lighting.'에서 여자는 남자에게 전화 번호를 제공하겠다고 했으므로 정보를 제공한다는 내용의 (C)가 정답이 된다.

PART 4

[28-30]

W Hello. 28) **The image showing exquisite packaging and the product wrapped in a beautiful gift box caught my attention and made me instantly order the hand cream gift set from your Web site.** But when the package arrived, 29) **I was really disappointed because the product came unwrapped and was without a gift box.** Obviously, this was a mistake, so I'm going to send it back to you now to be exchanged for the product that is properly packaged. But 30) **I want to ask you how long it will take for you to send me a new one.** The previous shipment took about two weeks, and I hope to get the replacement earlier if possible. I was planning on giving it to my mom for Mother's Day next week. I'll leave my number just in case. It's 123-4020. Thanks.

W 안녕하세요. 정교한 패키지와 아름다운 선물 상자에 포장된 상품의 이미지가 제 눈길을 끌어서 당신의 웹사이트에서 핸드 크림 선물 세트를 즉시 주문했었습니다. 그러나, 소포가 도착했을 때 상품이 포장되지도 않았고 선물 박스 상자도 없는 채여서 너무나 실망했습니다. 분명히, 실수인 것 같아서, 저는 제대로 포장된 상품으로 교환하기 위해 물건을 반송할 것입니다. 그런데 저에게 새 상품을 보내 주시는데 얼마의 시간이 더 걸리는지 알고 싶습니다. 이전 배송은 거의 2주 정도 걸렸는데, 가능하다면 교체품을 더 빨리 받고 싶습니다. 그것을 다음 주 어머니의 날에 어머니께 드릴 계획이거든요. 만약을 위해 전화번호를 남깁니다. 제 번호는 123-4020입니다. 감사합니다.

어휘 exquisite 정교한 instantly 즉시 unwrapped 포장되지 않은 exchange 교환하다 shipment 배송

28

화자는 어떤 상품을 주문했는가?

(A) 장갑
(B) 핸드크림
(C) 소독제
(D) 선물 상자

해설 담화의 첫 문장 'The image showing exquisite packaging and the product wrapped in a beautiful gift box caught my attention and made me instantly order the hand cream gift set from your Web site.'에서 핸드크림 선물세트를 구매했다고 했으므로 정답은 (B)가 된다.

29

화자는 어떤 문제에 대해 언급하는가?

(A) 상품이 잘못된 종류였다.
(B) 배송이 지연되고 있다.
(C) 소포가 선물 포장되지 않았다.
(D) 소포가 손상되었다.

해설 문제점은 부정적인 표현과 함께 언급된다. 담화 중반의 'I was really disappointed because the product came unwrapped and was without a gift box.'에서 실망했다는 부정적인 표현 뒤에 포장이 되지 않았고 선물 상자도 없다고 했으므로 정답은 (C)이다.

30

화자는 무엇에 대해 질문하는가?

(A) 배송 날짜
(B) 환불 정책
(C) 선물 영수증
(D) 배송료

해설 담화 마지막 부분의 'I want to ask you how long it will take for you to send me the new one.'에서 새로운 것을 보내는 데 얼마나 오랜 시간이 걸리는지를 묻고 있으므로 정답은 (A)이다.

[31-33]

M **31-1) Welcome to the Pisaro Museum. 32) This building is famous for being Rosy Pisaro's house. She was one of the most influential artists of the 1880s.** This was not only her home but also her workplace. Most of her distinguished paintings are landscapes of places near this house. **31-2) I'm happy to have a chance to tell you about the life of Rosy Pisaro.** She lived and painted in this house her entire life. Today, we will actually get to see the desk she worked at, the rooms she slept in, and even some of her very old paintings. **33) Those objects are fragile, so please don't touch any of them. 31-3) After we finish looking around the house, we will walk over to the memorial center,** which was built right behind the house. There, we can admire some of her known works, including *Sunset*.

M 피사로 박물관에 오신 것을 환영합니다. 이 건물은 로지 피사로의 집으로 유명합니다. 그녀는 1880년대 가장 영향력있는 예술가들 중 한 명이었습니다. 이곳은 단지 그녀의 집이었을 뿐만 아니라 그녀의 작업실이기도 했습니다. 그녀의 가장 뛰어난 작품들 중 대부분은 이 집 근처에 있는 장소들의 풍경입니다. 오늘 여러분들께 로지 피사로의 삶에 대해 알려드릴 수 있는 기회를 가지게 되어 기쁩니다. 그녀는 이 집에서 평생 그림을 그리고 살았습니다. 오늘, 우리는 실제 그녀가 작업했던 책상, 그녀가 잠자던 방, 그리고 심지어 그녀의 예전 그림들까지 볼 수 있을 것입니다. 이 물건들은 부서지기 쉬우므로, 어떤 것도 만지지 말아주세요. 집을 둘러 본 후에 우리는 집 바로 뒤쪽에 있는 기념관으로 갈 것입니다. 그곳에서 *일몰*을 포함한 그녀의 잘 알려진 작품들을 감상할 수 있습니다.

어휘 influential 영향력 있는 distinguished 눈에 띄는 landscape 풍경 entire 전체 admire 감상하다

31

화자는 누구인가?

(A) 역사 교수
(B) 예술가
(C) 투어 가이드
(D) 음악가

해설 담화 초반부에서 박물관에 온 것을 환영한다고 했고, 담화 중반 'I'm happy to have a chance to tell you about the life of Rosy Pisaro'에서 어떤 인물에 대해 안내하고 소개해 준다고 했다. 이어서 청자들이 가 볼 곳들을 설명하고 있으므로, 보기 중에서 화자의 직업으로 가장 적절한 것은 (C)의 투어 가이드이다.

32

로지 피사로는 누구인가?

(A) 건축가
(B) 사진 작가
(C) 큐레이터
(D) 화가

해설 'This building is famous for being Rosy Pisaro's house. She was one of the most influential artists of the 1880s.'에서 로지 피사로가 화가였음을 알 수 있다. 정답은 (D)이다.

33

화자는 왜 "이 물건들은 부서지기 쉽습니다"라고 하는가?

(A) 방문객들이 몇몇 물건들을 볼 수 없는 이유를 설명하기 위해
(B) 방문객들이 물건을 만지는 것이 금지되는 이유를 설명하기 위해
(C) 방문객들이 특정 장소를 방문하는 것을 막기 위해
(D) 방문객들에게 돈을 기부해달라고 요청하기 위해

해설 인용된 문장 뒤에 이어지는 'You're not allowed to touch any of them.'에서 어떤 것도 만지지 말라고 이야기하고 있으므로, 만지면 안 되는 이유를 설명하는 것이 목적임을 알 수 있다. 따라서, 정답은 (B)이다.

실전 문제 연습

p.071

🎧 07-06

1	(A)	2	(D)	3	(A)	4	(A)
5	(B)	6	(C)	7	(B)	8	(A)
9	(A)	10	(B)	11	(B)	12	(C)
13	(B)	14	(B)	15	(B)	16	(B)
17	(A)	18	(A)	19	(D)	20	(B)
21	(A)	22	(A)	23	(C)	24	(A)
25	(D)	26	(D)	27	(A)	28	(A)
29	(D)	30	(A)	31	(D)	32	(D)
33	(A)						

PART 1

1

(A) A window is being installed.
(B) A ladder is being placed against the wall.
(C) The men are putting on overalls.
(D) One of the men is opening the window.

(A) 유리창이 설치되고 있는 중이다.
(B) 사다리가 벽에 기대어지는 중이다.
(C) 남자들이 작업복을 입고 있는 중이다.
(D) 남자들 중 한 명이 창문을 열고 있는 중이다.

어휘 overall 작업복

해설 두 사람이 유리창을 설치하고 있는 모습이므로 (A)가 정답이다. 사다리를 벽에 기대어 놓고 있는 동작을 묘사한 (B)는 정답이 될 수 없다. 작업복을 입고 있는 상태이기 하지만 입고 있는 중이 아니므로, 동작을 묘사하는 putting on으로 표현된 (C) 역시 오답이다. 유리창을 여는 동작을 묘사하고 있는 (D)도 오답이다.

2

(A) Some seats are unoccupied.
(B) They're listening to a lecture.
(C) One of the men is writing something.
(D) They're gathered around the table.

(A) 몇몇 의자들이 비어 있다.
(B) 그들은 강연을 듣는 중이다.
(C) 남자들 중 한 명이 무엇인가를 쓰는 중이다.
(D) 그들은 테이블 주변에 모여 있다.

어휘 gather 모이다

해설 사람들이 테이블 주변에 모여 회의하고 있으므로 (D)가 정답이다. 빈 자리는 없으므로 (A)는 오답이며, 펜을 들고 있거나 쓰고 있는 사람이 없으므로 (C)도 오답이다. 강연하는 상황은 아니므로 (B)도 오답이다.

3

(A) A printer has been placed on the desk.
(B) A monitor has been turned on.
(C) A light fixture is hanging from the ceiling.
(D) A clock is sitting on the chair.

(A) 프린터가 책상위에 놓여있다.
(B) 모니터가 켜져 있다.
(C) 조명 기구가 천장에 걸려 있다.
(D) 시계가 의자 위에 놓여있다.

해설 프린터가 책상위에 놓여있는 모습이므로 (A)가 정답이 된다. 모니터는 꺼져 있으므로 (B)는 오답이며, 조명 기구가 걸기는 하지만 걸려 있지 않고 책상 위에 있으므로 (C)도 오답이다. 시계는 의자가 아닌 책상 위에 있으므로 (D)역시 오답이다.

PART 2

4

Parking is available on Clarkson Avenue.
(A) Is it free?
(B) Anywhere in the park.
(C) Actually, it's out of stock.

클락슨 가에 주차가 가능해요.
(A) 무료인가요?
(B) 공원 내 어디든 가능해요.
(C) 사실, 그것은 재고가 소진됐어요.

어휘 available 이용 가능한   out of stock 재고가 없는

해설 주차가 가능한 곳을 알려준 평서문에 대해 무료인지 여부를 되묻는 (A)가 정답이다. (B)는 park을 반복한 오답이며, (C)는 상품과 관련하여 available의 반대말인 out of stock을 사용한 오답이다.

5

When are you leaving the office today?
(A) It takes about an hour.
(B) As soon as I finish this report.
(C) No, tomorrow.

당신은 오늘 언제 퇴근해요?
(A) 한 시간 정도 걸려요.
(B) 이 보고서를 끝내자마자요.
(C) 아니요, 내일이에요.

어휘 it takes ~만큼 시간이 걸리다   as soon as ~하자마자

해설 때를 묻는 when 의문문이므로, 'as soon as ~'로 답한 (B)가 정답이다. (A)는 기간을 의미하므로 how long에 적절한 대답이며, (C)는 when 의문문에 no라고 답하고 있으므로 오답이다.

6

Why is there such a long line in front of the grocery store?

(A) Sorry. I can't go now.

(B) Okay, I will go there.

(C) There is a discount event.

왜 식료품점 앞에 저렇게 긴 줄이 있는 거예요?

(A) 미안해요. 저는 지금 갈 수 없어요.

(B) 네, 제가 거기에 갈게요.

(C) 할인 행사가 있어요.

어휘 line 줄, 열

해설 길게 줄을 선 이유를 묻는 질문에 할인 행사가 있다는 내용의 문장으로 대답한 (C)가 정답이다. (A), (B)는 갈 것인지를 묻는 질문에 대한 답변이며, why 의문문에 대한 응답이 될 수 없다. 이 문제와 같이 사람이나 차가 많이 모여 있는 이유를 묻는 경우, 행사가 있다는 정답이 자주 출제된다.

7

Don't you want to go out for lunch?

(A) Dinner was great.

(B) I'll be ready in a few minutes.

(C) It will be launched next month.

점심 먹으러 나가는 게 어때요?

(A) 저녁 식사는 훌륭했어요.

(B) 저는 몇 분 후면 준비될 거예요.

(C) 그것은 다음 달에 출시될 거예요.

어휘 launch 출시하다

해설 점심 먹으러 나가는 게 어떠냐는 제안에 대해 몇 분 후면 준비된다며 수락하는 (B)가 정답이다. 질문의 lunch와 함께 자주 출제되는 launch(출시하다)를 이용한 (C)는 유사 발음 단어를 이용한 오답이다. (A)는 lunch에서 연상되는 dinner를 이용한 오답이다.

8

Could you get me the orientation material?

(A) You can download it on our Web site.

(B) He is a new recruit.

(C) The orientation should be delayed.

오리엔테이션 자료를 가져다 주시겠어요?

(A) 웹사이트에서 다운받으시면 돼요.

(B) 그는 신입사원이에요.

(C) 오리엔테이션은 연기되어야 해요.

어휘 get me 가져다 주세요   new recruit 신입사원

해설 자료를 요청하는 표현에 직접 주는 대신에 자료를 구할 수 있는 방법을 알려준 (A)가 정답이다. (B)는 orientation에서 연상되는 신입사원을 이용한 오답이다. (C)는 동일 발음을 반복한 오답이다.

9

Please send me a copy of the financial projections for next year.

(A) They're not ready yet.

(B) The project has already been finished.

(C) Was it rejected?

내년도 재무 계획서 사본을 저에게 보내주세요.

(A) 그것은 아직 준비되지 않았어요.

(B) 그 프로젝트는 이미 끝났어요.

(C) 그것이 거부되었나요?

어휘 projection 예상, 추정, 투사   reject 거절하다, 거부하다

해설 보내달라는 요청에 준비되지 않았다는 이유를 들어 불가능하다고 이야기한 (A)가 정답이다. (B)는 projection - project, (C)는 projection - reject로 발음을 이용한 함정들이다.

10

Would you mind if I put off our meeting to Friday?

(A) No, the meeting wasn't long.

(B) In fact, I prefer Friday, too.

(C) It will be a useful session.

우리의 회의를 금요일로 미뤄도 괜찮으시겠어요?

(A) 아니요, 회의는 오래 걸리지 않았어요.

(B) 사실, 저도 금요일이 더 좋아요.

(C) 그것은 유익한 시간이 될 거예요.

어휘 mind 꺼려하다   put off 미루다, 연기하다   session (특정 활동을 위한) 시간

해설 회의 연기가 가능한지 묻는 질문에 자신도 그렇게 하는 것이 더 좋다고 답한 (B)가 정답이다. meeting을 반복한 (A)와 주어가 일치하지 않는 (C) 모두 오답이다.

11

I want to hire a personal assistant to help me out.

(A) The Personnel Department.

(B) Susan might know someone suitable.

(C) The price is higher this year.

저는 저를 도와줄 개인 비서를 채용하고 싶어요.

(A) 인사부서요.

(B) 수잔이 적합한 누군가를 알 거예요.

(C) 올해는 가격이 더 높아요.

어휘 hire 채용하다   assistant 비서, 보조   suitable 적합한

해설 본인의 바람을 얘기하자, 이를 도와줄 수 있는 사람을 추천한 (B)가 정답이다. (A)는 personal과 발음이 유사한 personnel을 이용한 오답이고, (C)는 hire의 유사 발음 단어인 higher를 이용한 오답이다.

12

Is Mr. Callahan ready to leave, or does he have to stay late?

(A) Stay near the gate.

(B) I called him already.

(C) He hasn't told me.

캘러핸 씨는 갈 준비가 되었나요, 아니면 늦게까지 있어야 하나요?

(A) 문 근처에 계세요.

(B) 저는 이미 그에게 전화했어요.

(C) 그는 저에게 말해주지 않았어요.

[해설] 그가 말해주지 않았기 때문에 모른다는 의미로 대답한 (C)가 정답이다. stay가 반복된 (A)는 발음을 이용한 오답이다. 현재로 묻는 질문에 대해 과거로 대답한 (B) 또한 오답이다.

13

Should we sit in the cafeteria or on the patio outside?

(A) This is very good coffee.

(B) Let's stay indoors.

(C) Pizza and soda, please.

우리 구내 식당 안에 앉을까요, 아니면 외부의 테라스에 앉을까요?

(A) 이것은 매우 훌륭한 커피예요.

(B) 실내에 있도록 해요.

(C) 피자와 탄산 음료를 주세요.

[어휘] patio 야외 테라스 좌석 cafeteria 구내 식당 indoors 실내에

[해설] 구내 식당 안에 앉을 것인지 외부 테라스에 앉을 것인지를 묻는 선택의문문에 대해 실내를 선택하는 대답인 (B)가 정답이다. (A)는 cafeteria와 발음이 유사한 coffee를 이용한 오답이다. (C)의 경우 구내 식당에서 연상되는 상황을 이용한 오답이므로 소거한다.

14

Where can I find the training materials?

(A) Of course. I'll guide the session.

(B) They are stored in the resource storage area.

(C) The train will be here at 9:00 A.M.

어디에서 교육 자료를 찾을 수 있나요?

(A) 물론이죠. 제가 그 과정을 안내할게요.

(B) 그것은 자료 창고에 보관되어 있어요.

(C) 그 기차는 오전 9시에 여기에 올 거예요.

[어휘] guide 인도하다; 지도하다 store 저장하다

[해설] 자료가 있는 곳을 묻는 질문에 대해 위치를 알려주는 (B)가 정답이다. 의문사 의문문에 대해 of course라고 답한 (A)는 오답이며, training의 유사 발음 단어인 train을 이용한 (C) 역시 오답이다.

15

What's the process for returning this book?

(A) You'd better book the room in advance.

(B) You'll need to visit the circulation desk.

(C) Please turn at the next corner.

이 책을 반납하는 과정이 어떻게 되나요?

(A) 객실을 미리 예약하시는 게 좋을 것 같아요.

(B) 도서 대출 반납 창구로 가보세요.

(C) 다음 코너에서 도세요.

[어휘] circulation desk 대출 반납 창구

[해설] 책을 반납하는 방법에 대해 묻는 질문에 대해 도서 반납 창구로 가 보라고 제안하는 (B)가 정답이다. 질문에서의 book은 책이라는 의미지만, (A)의 book은 예약하다라는 의미로 사용되었다. (C)는 return과 음절이 겹치는 발음의 단어인 turn을 이용한 오답 유형이다.

16

The presentation yesterday lasted an hour, right?

(A) Our staff meeting.

(B) Yes, and it was a comprehensive overview.

(C) I left it on my desk.

어제 프레젠테이션은 한 시간 동안 계속됐어요, 그렇죠?

(A) 우리 직원 회의요.

(B) 네, 그리고 그것은 종합적인 개요였어요.

(C) 저는 그것을 책상 위에 두었어요.

[어휘] comprehensive 종합적인, 포괄적인 overview 개요

[해설] 프레젠테이션이 진행된 시간을 재차 확인하는 질문에 대해 'yes'라고 답하며 확인해 준 다음, 추가적인 프레젠테이션에 대한 정보를 제공하는 (B)가 가장 좋은 정답이 된다. hour와 our는 전형적인 발음의 오답으로 (A)는 소거한다. 또한, meeting은 presentation에서 연상되는 단어이기도 하다. (C)는 right을 '오른쪽'이라는 의미로 인식했을 때, 그 반의어인 left를 이용한 오답이다.

17

Who's responsible for authorizing the project budget?

(A) Ask the assistant director.

(B) The cost is truly attractive.

(C) Yes, I need a projector.

프로젝트 예산의 승인 담당자는 누구인가요?

(A) 조감독님께 물어보세요.

(B) 그 가격은 정말 매력적이네요.

(C) 네, 저는 프로젝터가 필요해요.

[어휘] authorize 승인하다

[해설] 승인 담당자를 묻는 질문에 대해 조감독에게 물어보라고 답한 (A)는 조감독이 알 것이며 자신은 모른다는 의미로서 적절한 대답이다. budget이 돈과 관련된 단어이므로, 연상될 수 있는 cost를 이용한 (B)는 오답이다. (C)의 경우 의문사 의문문에 대해 yes나 no로 답할 수 없으며, project의 파생어인 projector를 이용한 오답이다.

18

Do you want me to assist you in arranging the lounge area?

(A) Absolutely. Your help would be appreciated.

(B) I haven't arranged the shelves yet.

(C) Okay, I can help you.

라운지 구역을 정리하는 것을 제가 도와드리는 것을 원하시나요?

(A) 그럼요. 도와주시면 감사하죠.

(B) 저는 아직 선반들을 정리하지 않았어요.

(C) 좋아요, 제가 도와드릴게요.

어휘 assist 돕다 appreciate 감사하다

해설 구역 정리를 도와주는 것을 원하는지 묻는 질문에 대해 도와준다면 너무 고맙겠다고 답한 (A)가 정답이 된다. (C)의 경우 도와주는 것을 원하는지 묻는 질문에 대해 '내가 돕겠다'고 답하는 것은 행동할 사람이 잘못된 오답이다. (B)는 arrange라는 단어를 반복하였고, 질문과 시제가 불일치하는 오답이다.

PART 3

[19-21]

M1   19) **We have almost finished upgrading the Wi-Fi network in your meeting rooms.** From now on, you will get a consistently strong signal.

W   We've been experiencing lags and frozen screens, not to mention having to wait for Web pages and images to load. It has been really frustrating.

M1   Yes, 20) **that happens when there are a ton of devices operating on the same network.** But you no longer need to worry about that. This new device we've set up for you will spread your network to areas of your office that lack great connections to a central router.

W   Thanks.

M1   Arthur, did you finish your work?

M2   Yes

W   That's great news.

M2   By the way, I noticed you use webcams in meeting rooms. We highly recommend a video conferencing camera that allows you to see everyone in the room. 21) **We offer our VIP members a 30% discount on the monthly plan for the newest smart camera. Let me know if you are interested.**

M1   귀사의 회의실들의 와이파이 네트워크 시스템의 업그레이드가 거의 끝났습니다. 지금부터, 지속적으로 강한 전파를 받으시게 될 것입니다.

W   저희는 처리가 지연되고 화면이 정지되는 일을 겪었고, 웹페이지와 이미지 로딩을 기다렸던 것은 말할 것도 없습니다. 정말 당황스러웠죠.

M1   네, 동일한 네트워크에서 너무 많은 기기가 사용되다 보니 발생한 일입니다. 그러나 더 이상은 걱정 안 하셔도 됩니다. 저희가 설치한 새로운 기계는 중앙 라우터에 연결이 잘 되지 않는 사무실의 구역까지 네트워크를 퍼지게 해서, 끊어짐 없는 연결을 보장해 줄 것입니다.

W   감사합니다.

M1   아서, 당신의 일은 끝냈나요?

M2   네.

W   좋은 소식이네요!

M2   그런데, 귀사에서 회의실들에서 웹캠을 사용하시는 것을 봤습니다. 사무실의 모든 사람들을 볼 수 있도록 해주는 화상 회의 카메라를 강력히 추천합니다. 저희 VIP 회원에게는 월정액 요금에서 30% 할인된 가격으로 최신 스마트 카메라를 제공해 드릴 수 있습니다. 관심 있으시면 연락주세요.

어휘 consistently 지속적으로   seamless 끊어짐 없는   ensure 확신하게 하다   excel 뛰어나다

19

남자들은 누구인 것 같은가?
(A) 전기 기사
(B) 정비사
(C) 사진사
(D) IT 지원 기술자

해설 대화 초반부의 'We have almost finished upgrading the Wi-Fi network in your meeting rooms'에서 남자들은 인터넷 시스템을 설치하는 사람들이라는 것을 알 수 있으므로 정답은 (D)가 된다.

20

문제를 일으킨 것은 무엇인가?
(A) 몇몇 직원들이 시간이 없었다.
(B) 너무 많은 기기가 동시에 사용되었다.
(C) 일정의 충돌이 있었다.
(D) 몇몇 기기가 없어졌다.

해설 여자가 웹페이지와 이미지의 로딩을 기다려야 하고, 처리가 지연되는 등의 문제점을 설명하자 남자는 'that happens when there are a ton of devices operating on the same network.'라며 동시에 너무 많은 기기를 사용하기 때문이라고 문제의 원인을 알려주었다. 따라서, 정답은 (B)가 된다.

21

아서는 여자에게 무엇을 제공해 주겠다고 하는가?
(A) 할인
(B) 영화 티켓
(C) 바이러스 퇴치 소프트웨어
(D) 요금제 업그레이드

해설 아서의 이름이 언급된 다음, 대화의 마지막 부분에서 아서는 'We offer our VIP members a 30% discount on the monthly plan for the newest smart camera'라며 요금을 할인을 해 주겠다고 했다. 따라서, 정답은 (A)이다.

[22-24]

M   Hello. This is Jackson Taylor from Greenwood Landscaping. 22-1) **We recently ordered a batch of customized uniforms. Could I speak to someone about our order?**

W Certainly. **22-2) What can I do for you?**

M We received the uniforms today, but 23) **the company name is spelled incorrectly.**

W I'll check your order right now. Oh, I see the issue here. It appears there was a typo in the embroidery. I apologize for this error. I'll inform our team immediately. 24) **We'll send the corrected uniforms by express delivery at no extra cost.**

M 안녕하세요. 저는 그린우드 조경의 잭슨 테일러입니다. 저희가 최근에 맞춤 유니폼을 일괄 주문했는데요. 주문에 대해서 누군가와 이야기를 할 수 있을까요?

W 물론입니다. 무엇을 도와드릴까요?

M 오늘 유니폼을 받았는데, 저희 회사 명칭의 스펠링이 잘못되어 있어요.

W 제가 지금 주문을 확인해 볼게요. 아, 문제가 여기 있었네요. 자수에 오타가 있었던 걸로 보입니다. 실수에 대해 사과를 드립니다. 제가 저희 팀에게 바로 알리도록 할게요. 추가 비용 없이 수정된 유니폼을 특급 배송해 드리겠습니다.

어휘 landscaping 조경 batch 일괄 물건(한번에 제작되는 물건) customized 맞춤의 typo 오타 embroidery 자수

22
여자는 어디에서 일하는 것 같은가?
(A) 의류 회사에서
(B) 원예 용품점에서
(C) 조경 회사에서
(D) 스포츠 용품점에서

해설 화자의 직업을 묻는 문제는 대화의 초반에서 정답을 찾아야 한다. 다만, 남자가 일하는 조경 회사를 고르는 실수를 않도록 어떤 성별의 직업을 묻는지 주의해야 한다. 남자가 주문한 유니폼 주문에 대해 처리하는 것으로 보아 여자는 의류 회사에서 일한다는 것을 알 수 있다. 따라서, 정답은 (A)가 된다.

23
남자는 왜 전화했는가?
(A) 그는 잘못된 사이즈의 물건을 받았다.
(B) 그는 그의 주문을 변경하기를 원한다.
(C) 그의 주문품에 잘못된 점이 있었다.
(D) 그는 배송 시간을 확인하려고 한다.

해설 전화의 목적은 대부분의 자신을 소개한 다음에 언급된다. 남자의 두 번째 말 'the company name is spelled incorrectly.'에서 유니폼에 회사명의 스펠링이 잘못 되었다고 이야기하고 있으므로 주문한 물건에 실수가 있었다는 것을 알 수 있다.

24
여자는 무엇을 해 주겠다고 제안하는가?
(A) 추가 요금 없이 빠르게 아이템을 보내기
(B) 전액 환불해 주기

(C) 문제를 해결하기 위해 사람을 보내기
(D) 남자에게 사과 편지 쓰기

해설 여자가 할 일은 미래 시제의 1인칭 시점으로 언급한 대화를 골라야 한다. 여자의 마지막 말 'We'll send the corrected uniforms by express delivery at no extra cost.'에서 추가 비용 없이 수정된 유니폼을 특급 배송으로 보내 주겠다고 했으므로 물건을 추가 요금 없이 빠르게 보내준다는 내용의 (A)가 정답이 된다.

[25-27]

W Hello. 25) **This is the Queenstown post office.** Can I speak with Mr. Kim, please? We have a package for him to pick up. 26-1) **We sent him a memo about the delivery,** but we haven't gotten a response yet.

M1 Oh, this is Mr. Kim speaking. I just got back from a business trip, and I'd better check with my secretary. Excuse me, Pete. 26-2) **Did you get a memo from the post office?**

M2 Yes, 26-3) **it's in the top drawer of your desk.**

M1 Thanks, Pete. Ah, yeah, now I see it.

W Oh, brilliant. Then 27) **why don't you come to the post office with some photo ID to pick up the package?** The office will close at 6:00 P.M.

W 안녕하세요. 퀸즈타운 우체국입니다. 김 씨와 통화할 수 있을까요? 그가 찾아가야 할 소포를 가지고 있습니다. 배송에 대해 그에게 메모를 남겼지만, 아직 아무런 응답을 받지 못했습니다.

M1 오, 제가 김 씨입니다. 저는 방금 출장에서 돌아왔는데, 제 비서에게 확인해보는 게 좋겠네요. 실례합니다 피트, 우체국에서 온 메모를 받았나요?

M2 네, 그것은 당신의 책상 제일 위쪽 서랍 안에 있습니다.

M1 고마워요, 피트. 아, 네, 이제 보이네요.

W 오, 좋습니다. 그러면, 사진이 있는 신분증을 가지고 저희 우체국으로 오셔서 소포를 찾아가시는 게 어떨까요? 우체국은 저녁 6시에 문을 닫습니다.

어휘 package 소포 pick up 가져가다 response 응답 business trip (업무 상의) 출장 secretary 비서

25
여자는 누구인 것 같은가?
(A) 남자의 비서
(B) 가게 주인
(C) 항공사 직원
(D) 우체국 직원

해설 여자의 첫번째 말 'This is the Queenstown post office.'에서 우체국이라고 했으므로 여자는 우체국 직원일 것이다. 정답은 (D)이다.

26

책상 서랍에 무엇이 있었는가?

(A) 신용카드

(B) 수정된 명세표(송장)

(C) 비행 스케줄

(D) 배송 통지서

해설 여자가 'We sent him a memo about the delivery.'라며 배송과 관련된 메모를 남겼다고 했는데, 김 씨는 자신의 비서에게 'Did you get a memo from the post office?'라고 배송 메모를 받았는지 물었다. 이에 대해 비서는 'it's in the top drawer of your desk.'라고 했으므로 서랍 안에 배송 메모가 있다는 것을 알 수 있다. 정답은 (D)이다.

27

여자는 김 씨에게 무엇을 하라고 제안하는가?

(A) 신분증 양식 가져오기

(B) 계좌 개설하기

(C) 주차 허가증 보여주기

(D) 특급우편으로 소포 보내기

해설 여자가 제안하는 것을 찾는 문제이므로 여자의 말속에서 부탁과 제안의 표현에서 정답을 찾아야 한다. 여자의 마지막 말 'why don't you come to the post office with some photo ID to pick up the package?'에서 신분증을 가지고 오라고 했으므로 정답은 (A)이다.

PART 4

[28-30]

M **28) Today is a very important day for us. I'd like to thank you all for coming in to work early to help prepare for our shoe store's grand opening**. It really shows that we are a team. We will open in an hour, so please double-check there are no empty shelves and make sure to keep the premises clean at all times. Shoes lying on the floor can look very messy. And don't forget to greet every customer, quickly identify their needs, and make suggestions. There's one more thing. **29) A journalist from the local newspaper, David Wilson, will visit our store this afternoon because 30) our store will be the largest shoe store in town. He will write an article about his experience here.** A favorable article from him will definitely be helpful for our business.

M 오늘은 우리에게 매우 중요한 날입니다. 저는 여러분 모두가 우리의 신발 가게 개업 준비를 돕기 위해 일찍 출근해 주셔서 감사합니다. 이것은 정말로 우리가 한 팀이라는 것을 보여줍니다. 우리는 한 시간 뒤에 문을 열 것이므로, 빈 선반이 없는지 다시 확인하시고 건물 내부를 항상 깨끗하게 유지하는 것을 확실하게 해 주세요. 바닥에 놓여있는 신발들은 매우 지저분해 보일 수 있습니다. 그리고 모든 고객들에게 인사하고, 그들의 필요를 파악하고, 추천하는 것을 잊지 마세요. 다른 한가지는, 지역 신문의 기자, 데이비드 윌슨이 우리 가게가 이 마을에서 가장 큰 신발 가게가 될 것이기 때문에 오늘 오후 우리 가게를 방문할 것입니다. 그는 이곳에서의 경험에 대해 기사를 쓸 것입니다. 그의 호의적인 기사는 우리의 사업에 분명한 도움이 될 것입니다.

어휘 double-check 재차 확인하다　premises 지역, 부지, 구내　messy 지저분한　identify 발견하다　definitely 확실하게

28

청자들은 어디에서 일할 것 같은가?

(A) 신발 가게에서

(B) 스포츠 용품점에서

(C) 출판사에서

(D) 식당에서

해설 담화 초반의 'Today is a very important day for us. I'd like to thank you all for coming in to work early to help prepare for our shoe store's grand opening.'에서 직원들이 신발 가게의 개업을 도와주러 일찍 출근했다고 했으므로 정답은 (A)이다.

29

데이비드 윌슨은 누구인가?

(A) 유명한 운동선수

(B) 상점 매니저

(C) 최고 경영자

(D) 기자

해설 사람의 이름이 언급된 문제의 경우, 해당 사람의 이름 바로 앞뒤를 잘 들어야 한다. 데이비드 윌슨이 언급된 바로 앞 'A journalist from the local newspaper, David Wilson, will visit our store this afternoon.'에서 그가 기자라고 했으므로 정답은 (D)이다.

30

가게에 대해서 무엇이 언급되는가?

(A) 그 지역에서 가장 큰 가게가 될 것이다.

(B) 그 지역에서 가장 유명한 가게이다.

(C) 그 가게는 대중교통 근처이다.

(D) 그 가게는 사업을 확장했다.

해설 언급된 것을 찾는 문제의 경우 선택지에 있는 내용을 담화의 정보들과 비교하여 정답을 찾아야 한다. 담화 마지막에 'our store will be the largest shoe store in town. He will write an article about his experience here'에서 마을에서 가장 큰 가게가 될 것이라고 했으므로 정답은 (A)이다.

W	Attention, visitors! **31) Thank you for visiting Wonderland Amusement Park.** Certain attractions can get long lines, especially on weekends. However, this shouldn't be a problem, as with a Wonderland Fast-Track Pass, there is no need to worry about standing in line for hours. For those who are interested in purchasing one, **32) please use the express pass lane located closest to the Wonderland gift shop.** In addition, **33) for items lost on the property, the online lost and found form is the easiest and most efficient way to report lost items.** We hope you have an unforgettable experience here at the Wonderland.
W	방문객 여러분 집중해주세요! 원더랜드 놀이공원을 방문해 주셔서 감사합니다. 특히 주말에는 몇몇 시설들의 줄이 길 수 있습니다. 그러나, 원더랜드 패스트트랙 패스를 가지고 있다면, 이것은 문제가 되지 않으며, 몇 시간 동안 줄을 설 걱정을 하실 필요가 없습니다. 이 티켓을 구매하는 데 관심이 있으신 분들은, 원더랜드 선물 가게에서 가장 가까운 곳에 있는 고속 패스 레인을 이용해 주시기 바랍니다. 또한, 놀이공원 내 분실물에 대해서는, 온라인 분실물 신고 양식이 분실물을 신고하는 가장 쉽고 효과적인 방법입니다. 여러분들이 이곳 원더랜드에서 잊지 못할 경험을 하시기를 바랍니다.

어휘 attractions 시설, 명소, 명물　efficient 효과적인
unforgettable 잊을 수 없는

31
어디에서 공지가 이루어지는가?
(A) 선물가게에서
(B) 워터파크에서
(C) 쇼핑몰에서
(D) 놀이공원에서

해설 담화 초반의 'Thank you for visiting Wonderland Amusement Park.'에서 놀이공원을 방문해 주셔서 감사하다고 했으므로 정답은 (D)이다.

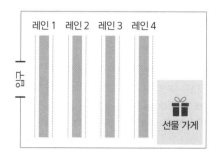

32
시각 정보를 보시오. 어떤 레인이 고속 패스 레인인가?
(A) 레인 1
(B) 레인 2
(C) 레인 3
(D) 레인 4

해설 평면도나 안내도가 나오는 경우, 거리, 좌우, 전치사구 등이 중요한 단서이다. 담화 중반부의 'please use the express pass lane located closest to the Wonderland gift shop.'에서 선물 가게에서 가장 가까운 레인이 고속패스 레인이라고 했으므로 정답은 (D)이다.

33
화자에 따르면, 분실물을 신고하는 가장 효과적인 방법은 무엇인가?
(A) 온라인으로 양식 작성하기
(B) 고속 패스 레인으로부터 도움을 받기
(C) 분실물 부서를 방문하기
(D) 주 출입구 근처의 분실물 박스를 확인하기

해설 분실물에 관련된 질문을 하고 있으므로 분실물이 언급된 부분 주변에서 정답을 찾아야 한다. 담화 마지막의 'for items lost on the property, the online lost and found form is the easiest and most efficient way to report lost items.'에서 온라인 분실물 양식이 분실물을 신고하는 가장 빠르고 효과적인 방법이라고 했으므로 정답은 (A)이다.

DAY **08**	**PARTS 3·4** **초반부 문제 풀이법**

📑 실전 문제 연습　　p.080

🎧 08-05

1	(B)	**2**	(A)	**3**	(A)	**4**	(C)
5	(C)	**6**	(C)	**7**	(B)	**8**	(B)
9	(C)	**10**	(C)	**11**	(A)	**12**	(A)
13	(A)	**14**	(B)	**15**	(B)	**16**	(B)
17	(B)	**18**	(B)	**19**	(C)	**20**	(A)
21	(C)	**22**	(B)	**23**	(C)	**24**	(B)
25	(A)	**26**	(C)	**27**	(A)	**28**	(C)
29	(B)	**30**	(A)	**31**	(A)	**32**	(B)
33	(B)						

PART 1

1
(A) A woman is putting on a lab coat.
(B) A woman is peering into a microscope.
(C) A woman is using a beaker.
(D) A woman is wearing a safety hat.

(A) 한 여자가 실험실 가운을 입는 중이다.
(B) 한 여자가 현미경을 들여다보고 있다.
(C) 한 여자가 비커를 이용하고 있다.
(D) 한 여자가 안전모를 쓰고 있다.

어휘 peer into 자세히 들여다보다 beaker 비커

해설 여자가 현미경을 들여다보고 있는 모습이므로 정답은 (B)이다. 실험실 가운을 입고 있지만 입는 동작이 아니므로 (A)는 오답이 된다. 여자가 비커를 사용하고 있지 않으므로 (C)도 오답이다. 안전모가 보이지 않으므로 (D)는 정답이 될 수 없다.

2

(A) She is trimming a hedge.
(B) She is sitting near the fence.
(C) She is planting trees.
(D) She is entering a building.

(A) 여자가 생울타리를 다듬고 있다.
(B) 여자가 울타리 근처에 앉아 있다.
(C) 여자가 나무를 심고 있다.
(D) 여자가 건물안으로 들어가고 있다.

어휘 hedge 생울타리 trim 다듬다

해설 여자가 나무 울타리를 다듬고 있으므로 정답은 (A)가 된다. 여자는 서 있으므로 (B)는 오답이다. 나무를 심는 중은 아니므로 (C)도 오답이다. 여자가 건물에 들어가고 있지 않으므로 (D) 역시 오답이다.

3

(A) They're staring at the screen.
(B) They're typing on keyboards.
(C) They're facing each other.
(D) They're standing behind the counter.

(A) 그들은 모니터들을 보고 있다.
(B) 그들은 키보드를 치고 있다.
(C) 그들은 서로 마주보고 있다.
(D) 그들은 카운터 뒤에 서 있다.

어휘 face 마주보다

해설 두 사람이 같이 모니터를 보고 있는 모습이므로 정답은 (A)이다. 타이핑하는 사람은 없으므로 (B)는 오답이며, 서로 마주보고 있지 않으므로 (C)도 오답이다. 두 사람은 카운터가 아닌 책상 뒤에 있으므로 (D) 역시 오답이다.

PART 2

4

How often do you visit art museums?
(A) I jog every day.
(B) No, he's not an art director.
(C) I'm not an art lover.

당신은 얼마나 자주 미술관을 방문하나요?
(A) 저는 매일 조깅을 해요.
(B) 아니요, 그는 아트 디렉터가 아니에요.

(C) 저는 예술 애호가가 아니에요.

어휘 ~ lover ~을 좋아하는 사람

해설 빈도수를 묻는 질문의 경우, 주로 횟수로 답변하지만, 이 문제의 경우 '나는 예술을 애호가가 아니다'라고 답하면서 '미술관에 자주 가지 않는다'는 것을 암시한 (C)가 정답이다. 빈도수를 묻는 질문이어서 'every day'라고 답한 (A)를 정답으로 고르기 쉽지만, (A)는 매일 조깅을 한다는 의미이므로 정답이 될 수 없다. (B)의 경우 질문에서 he의 대상이 되는 사람이 언급되지 않았으므로 정답이 될 수 없다.

5

Where are the workshops being held?
(A) You can look around the shops.
(B) To the conference hall.
(C) You can find the list on the Web site.

어디에서 워크숍이 열리고 있나요?
(A) 당신은 주변 상점들을 둘러볼 수 있어요.
(B) 컨퍼런스 홀로요.
(C) 웹사이트에서 목록을 찾으실 수 있어요.

해설 워크숍이 열리는 장소를 묻는 질문인데 where만 듣고 (B)를 정답으로 고르기 쉽다. 하지만, 전치사 to로 답하는 경우 '방향'을 묻는 질문에 대한 대답이므로, '위치'를 묻는 where 의문문에 대한 정답이 될 수 없다. (A)의 경우 workshop과 발음이 겹치는 shop을 이용한 오답이다. 웹사이트에서 목록을 찾을 수 있다는 것은 그 목록에 워크숍의 장소가 있다는 것을 암시하므로 (C)가 정답이다.

6

Half of the documents were misplaced.
(A) Near the exit.
(B) November 5.
(C) I'll handle it. No worries.

서류 중의 절반이 잘못된 곳에 있었어요.
(A) 출구 근처에요.
(B) 11월 5일이에요.
(C) 제가 처리할게요. 걱정 마세요.

어휘 misplace 잘못 놓다 handle 처리하다

해설 서류들이 잘못된 곳에 있었다는 문제점을 언급한 평서문에 대해 자신이 처리하겠다고 해결책을 제시하는 (C)가 정답이다. (A)는 misplace의 place에서 연상되는 exit를 이용한 오답이다. 날짜를 묻는 질문은 아니므로 (B)역시 오답이다.

7

Did you find the new movie enjoyable?
(A) Could you please move it to the right side?
(B) It was too long.
(C) A different director.

새로운 영화는 재미있었나요?
(A) 그것을 오른쪽으로 옮겨 주시겠어요?
(B) 너무 길었어요.
(C) 다른 감독이에요.

어휘 enjoyable 즐거운, 재미있는 director 감독

해설 영화가 재미있었는지를 묻는 질문에 대해 너무 길었다고 대답한 (B)는 영화가 지겨웠다는 의견을 간접적으로 전달하는 정답이다. (A)는 movie와 발음이 비슷한 move를 이용한 오답이다. (C)는 movie에서 연상할 수 있는 director를 이용한 오답이다.

8

They must be excited about the upcoming trip, right?

(A) I visited that place last summer.

(B) Yes, they really are.

(C) I used to travel there often.

그들은 다가오는 여행에 대해 흥분한 상태겠네요, 그렇겠죠?
(A) 저는 지난 여름에 그곳을 방문했어요.
(B) 네, 정말 그래요.
(C) 저는 그곳에 자주 여행을 갔어요.

어휘 upcoming 다가오는

해설 여행 때문에 흥분해 있을 것이라는 말에 대해 정말 그렇다고 맞장구를 치는 (B)가 정답이다. 미래에 있을 여행에 대한 질문에 과거의 방문에 대해 언급하는 (A)는 오답이다. (C)는 trip에서 연상되는 단어인 travel을 이용한 오답이다.

9

Which magazine do you usually read?

(A) Have you checked it out already?

(B) I prefer the red one.

(C) I subscribe to a few different ones.

어떤 잡지를 주로 읽으세요?
(A) 이미 그것을 확인했나요?
(B) 저는 붉은색이 더 마음에 들어요.
(C) 저는 여러 다른 잡지들을 구독해요.

어휘 subscribe 구독하다

해설 어떤 잡지를 주로 읽는지 묻는 질문에 대해 여러 다른 잡지들을 구독한다고 말하며, 주로 읽는 잡지가 하나가 아니라고 답한 (C)가 정답이다. (A)의 경우 어떤 잡지인지를 언급해야 하는데 it이 무엇을 지칭하는지 알 수 없으므로 오답이다. (B)의 경우 read와 red는 자주 출제되는 유사 발음 오답이다.

10

If you purchase it today, you'll receive a special discount.

(A) Especially for you.

(B) I can count it.

(C) It's quite an attractive offer.

만약 오늘 구매하신다면, 특별 할인을 받으실 수 있어요.
(A) 특별히 당신을 위해서요.
(B) 제가 그것을 셀 수 있어요.
(C) 그것은 상당히 매력적인 제안이군요.

어휘 offer 제의, 제안; 할인 attractive 매력적인

해설 할인으로 구매를 유도하려는 제안에 대해 매력적이라고 대답하고 흥미를 보이는 (C)가 정답이다. (B)는 discount와 음절이 겹치는 발음인 count를 이용한 오답이다. (A)는 special과 발음이 유사한 especially가 포함된 오답이다.

11

Is there an additional desk in the storage room?

(A) Yes, there's one more.

(B) I need a chair, too.

(C) Okay, I'll add some colors.

창고에 여유분 책상이 하나 있나요?
(A) 네, 한 개 더 있어요.
(B) 저는 의자도 필요해요.
(C) 좋아요, 제가 몇몇 색상을 추가할게요.

어휘 additional 여유의, 추가의 storage room 창고 add 추가하다

해설 창고에 여유분의 책상이 있는지 묻는 질문에 대해, 한 개 더 있다고 대답한 (A)가 정답이다. desk에서 유추할 수 있는 chair를 이용한 (B)는 오답이며, additional의 파생어인 add를 이용한 (C) 역시 오답이다.

12

What was the reason for changing the meeting time?

(A) Mr. Peterson wasn't available.

(B) A revised agenda.

(C) I think it's 7:00.

회의 시간을 변경한 이유가 무엇이었나요?
(A) 피터슨 씨가 시간이 안 됐어요.
(B) 수정된 안건입니다.
(C) 제 생각에는 7시인 것 같아요.

어휘 available (사람이) 시간이 있는 revised 변경된

해설 시간을 변경한 이유를 묻는 질문에 대해서 피터슨씨가 시간이 없었기 때문에 변경되었다고 답한 (A)가 정답이 된다. 이유를 묻는 질문에 수정된 안건이라고 대답하는 것은 이유를 설명하는 표현이 되지 않는다. why 의문사 문제에서 명사만으로 이루어진 선택지가 정답이 될 수 없는 것과 마찬가지로, what is the reason 역시 이유를 묻는 질문이므로 명사만으로 답한 선택지는 정답이 될 수 없다. 따라서, (B)는 오답이다. meeting time이 질문에 있기는 하지만 회의 시간을 묻는 질문이 아니므로 (C)도 오답이다.

13

You know where the new café is, don't you?

(A) No, I haven't been there.

(B) Why don't we eat in the cafeteria?

(C) Could you guide me, please?

새로운 카페가 어디에 있는지 아시죠, 그렇지 않나요?
(A) 아니요, 저는 그곳에 가 본 적이 없어요.
(B) 우리 구내 식당에서 밥을 먹는 게 어때요?
(C) 저를 안내해 주실 수 있나요?

어휘 cafeteria 구내 식당 guide 안내하다

해설 카페의 위치를 묻는 질문에 대해 가 본 적이 없다고 답하며 모른다고 한 (A)가 정답이 된다. (B)의 경우 café와 발음이 유사한 cafeteria를 활용한 오답이다. 위치를 묻는 질문자에게 안내해 달라고 말하는 것은 어울리지 않는 대답이므로 (C) 역시 오답이다.

14

Do you want a full-time job or a part-time job?
(A) It happened a while ago.
(B) I'm seeking a full-time job.
(C) Ms. Anderson is in charge.

정규직과 비정규직 중에서 어떤 일을 찾고 계신가요?
(A) 그것은 한참 전에 발생했어요.
(B) 저는 정규직을 찾고 있어요.
(C) 앤더슨 씨가 담당자예요.

어휘 seek 찾다

해설 정규직과 비정규직 중에서 선택해야 하는 질문에 대해 정규직이라고 대답한 (B)가 정답이 된다. 언제 발생했는지를 묻는 질문이 아니므로 (A)는 질문과 관계 없는 대답인데, 질문의 time과 관련이 있는 a while ago가 활용된 오답이다. 담당자를 묻는 질문이 아니므로 사람의 이름을 언급한 (C) 역시 질문에 어울리지 않는 답변이다.

15

Can you forward me a duplicate of the financial report?
(A) At the printer, maybe.
(B) Of course. I'll take care of it right away.
(C) About twenty percent less.

재무 보고서의 사본을 저에게 보내 주실래요?
(A) 아마도 프린터에요.
(B) 물론이죠. 제가 바로 처리할게요.
(C) 대략 20퍼센트 적게요.

어휘 duplicate 사본

해설 사본을 보내달라는 질문에 대해 바로 처리하겠다고 답한 (B)가 정답이다. (A)는 사본(duplicate)에서 연상될 수 있는 printer를 이용한 오답이다. (C)의 경우 financial에서 돈이 연상되는데, 돈에서 연상되는 percent를 이용한 오답이다.

16

Is your new smartphone working well?
(A) Yes, the fuel efficiency is better.
(B) It's been okay so far.
(C) No, I didn't walk there.

스마트폰은 잘 작동하나요?
(A) 네, 연비가 더 좋아요.
(B) 지금까지는 괜찮아요.
(C) 아니요, 저는 그곳에 걸어가지 않았어요.

어휘 so far 지금까지

해설 스마트폰 작동이 잘 되는지 묻는 질문에 대해 지금까지 잘 작동한다고 답한 (B)가 정답이다. (A)의 연비(the fuel efficiency)는 자동차와 관련된 내용이므로 오답이다. (C)는 work와 발음이 유사한 walk을 이용한 오답이다.

17

Whose backpack is this?
(A) I didn't pack them yet.
(B) Is there a name on it?
(C) I prefer the gray one.

이것은 누구의 백팩인가요?
(A) 저는 아직 그것들을 싸지 않았어요.
(B) 위에 이름이 없나요?
(C) 저는 회색이 좋아요.

어휘 pack (짐을) 싸다

해설 백팩의 주인을 묻는 질문에 대해 이름이 써 있지 않은지를 묻는 (B)는 자신도 주인을 모르니 확인해 보라는 의미이다. (A)는 backpack에서 pack부분을 이용한 오답이다. 어떤 백팩인지를 선택하는 것이 아니라 누구의 것인지를 묻는 질문이므로 회색을 선택한 (C)도 오답이다.

18

Weren't we supposed to have a team meeting this afternoon?
(A) Three times this week.
(B) I'm sorry, but I need to reschedule it.
(C) Mr. Rodriguez made a reservation.

오늘 오후에 팀 회의를 했어야 하는 것 아니었나요?
(A) 이번 주에 세 번요.
(B) 미안하지만, 날짜를 바꿔야 할 것 같아요.
(C) 로드리게스 씨가 예약했어요.

어휘 reschedule 시간을 변경하다

해설 'weren't supposed to'는 '~을 했어야 하는 것 아닌가요?'라는 의미인데, 이는 했어야 하는 것을 하지 않은 이유를 묻는 표현이다. 따라서, 미안하지만 날짜를 바꾸어야 해서 회의를 하지 못했다고 답한 (B)가 정답이다. 빈도를 묻는 질문이 아니므로 (A)는 오답이고, 예약 여부를 묻는 질문도 아니므로 (C) 역시 오답이다.

PART 3

[19-21]

W   Alex, I didn't see you at our team briefing, but **19-1) there's some exciting news for the department**.

M   Oh? What's the news?

W   **19-2) 20-1) The company is planning to upgrade the computers in the Tech Department to the latest high-performance models.**

M **20-2)** **That's great.** The current ones are really slow, especially with the new software updates. When are we getting the new computers?

W **21)** **There's a delay due to backed-up supply orders,** but we should have them in a couple of weeks.

W 알렉스, 우리 팀 브리핑에서 당신이 보이지 않던데, 우리 부서에 흥미로운 소식이 있어요.

M 오? 무슨 소식인데요?

W 회사에서 기술 부서의 컴퓨터를 최신형 고성능 모델로 업그레이드할 계획이에요.

M 좋네요. 지금 컴퓨터들은 너무 느린데, 특히 새로운 소프트웨어 업데이트를 하고 나서요. 언제 새 컴퓨터를 받게 되나요?

W 공급 주문이 밀려서 지연되고 있지만, 몇 주 안에는 받을 수 있을 거예요.

어휘 briefing 브리핑, 발표 high-performance 고성능 current 현재의 backed-up 정체된, 밀린 update 업데이트, 최신으로 갱신

19
화자들은 어느 부서에서 일하는가?
(A) 마케팅 부서
(B) 인사 부서
(C) 기술 부서
(D) 재무 부서

해설 대화의 첫 부분에서 여자는 '우리 부서를 위한 흥미로운 소식이 있다'고 말한 다음, 'The company is planning to upgrade the computers in the Tech Department'라고 말했다. 즉, 최신형 컴퓨터로 업그레이드해 주는 기술 부서가 두 사람이 일하는 부서임을 알 수 있다. 정답은 (C)이다.

20
남자는 왜 기뻐하는가?
(A) 몇몇 장비가 업그레이드될 것이기 때문에
(B) 팀이 확장될 것이기 때문에
(C) 보너스가 곧 지급될 것이기 때문에
(D) 그가 승진하게 될 것이기 때문에

해설 문제가 감정 표현과 관련된 경우, 해당 감정의 동의어나 명확한 감정의 표현 주변에서 정답의 단서를 찾는다. 대화 중반 남자의 'That's great.'이 기뻐하는 감정을 표현하고 있는데, that에 해당하는 여자의 말, 'The company is planning to upgrade the computers in the Tech Department to the latest high-performance models.'가 남자가 기뻐하는 이유이다. 즉, 컴퓨터의 업그레이드 때문에 기뻐하는 것이므로 computers를 equipment로 바꾸어 표현한 (A)가 정답이다.

21
여자는 무엇 때문에 지연되었다고 말하는가?
(A) 예상치 못한 예산 삭감
(B) IT 보안 문제

(C) 공급 관련 문제
(D) 경영 재편

해설 여자의 마지막 말 'There's a delay due to backed-up supply orders'에서 공급 주문이 밀려서 지연되고 있다고 했으므로 (C)가 정답이 된다.

[22-24]

W **23-1)** **I'd like to talk to you about my vacation, Daniel.**

M **22)** **I'm just going to draw up the holiday rotation this year.** So go ahead and tell me what you want.

W Well, **23-2)** **I'm planning to have three weeks' leave in December, and I want to use my vacation days for this year.**

M Why did you choose December?

W Because **24)** **my father's birthday is December 19. So the entire family is getting together for a party,** and I'm going back to New Zealand.

M All right. I'll do my best to meet your request.

W 다니엘, 제 휴가에 대해서 말씀을 드리고 싶어요.

M 이제 올해의 휴가 일정 조정 계획을 작성할 거예요. 그러니 원하는 것을 말해 주세요.

W 음, 제가 12월에 3주 간의 휴가를 계획하고 있어서, 올해의 휴가를 사용하고 싶어요.

M 왜 12월을 고르셨어요?

W 아버지 생신이 12월 19일이에요. 그래서 모든 가족들이 파티를 하려고 모일 것이어서 제가 뉴질랜드로 가려고요.

M 알겠어요. 요청을 들어줄 수 있도록 최선을 다할게요.

어휘 draw up (계획 등을) 세우다, 작성하다 leave 휴가 do one's best 최선을 다하다

22
남자는 아마도 어느 부서에서 일하는가?
(A) 연구 및 개발
(B) 인사 관리
(C) 생산
(D) 회계 및 재무

해설 대화 초반의 'I'm just going to draw up the holiday rotation this year.'에서 남자가 사람들의 휴가를 일정을 조정하는 역할을 담당하고 있다는 것을 알 수 있다. 따라서 정답은 (B)이다.

23
대화는 주로 무엇에 대한 것인가?
(A) 직원의 사직
(B) 월별 판매 자료
(C) 휴가 요청
(D) 상품 출시

해설 여자는 첫 대화에서 'I'd like to talk to you about my vacation, Daniel.'이라고 했고, 이어서 'I'm planning to have three weeks' leave in December, and I want to use my vacation days for this year.'라고 했다. 이 내용을 통해 휴가 신청에 대한 대화라는 것을 알 수 있다. 따라서, 정답은 (C)이다.

24

12월에는 무슨 일이 일어날 것인가?

(A) 관광 박람회
(B) 생일 파티
(C) 비즈니스 컨벤션
(D) 지점 개업

해설 시간이 언급된 문제의 경우, 해당 시간 주변에서 정답을 찾아야 한다. 여자는 'my father's birthday is December 19'라고 하며 12월에 아버지 생신이 있다고 했고, 'So the entire family is getting together for the party'라고 하며 가족들이 모여서 파티를 한다고 했으므로 정답은 (B)이다.

[25-27]

W	Hello. Silverdale Community Recreation Center.
M	Hi. 25) 26) **I will be attending the class on Wednesdays, and I wonder if I need to bring my own racket**. Details weren't listed in the class description.
W	We apologize for the confusion. For those who don't have their own racket, we do provide one to use during the class. Just remember to bring a pair of comfortable shoes.
M	Okay.
W	27) **Please note that your class won't start until next week because the instructor has a personal issue to deal with.**
M	Oh, really? I didn't know that. I almost made a trip for nothing.
W	여보세요, 실버데일 커뮤니티 레크리에이션 센터입니다.
M	안녕하세요, 저는 수요일마다 열리는 수업에 참여할 예정인데, 제가 개인 라켓을 가지고 와야 하는지 궁금해서요. 수업 안내에는 자세한 정보가 나와 있지 않아서요.
W	혼동을 드려 죄송합니다. 개인 라켓이 없으신 분들을 위해, 수업 시간에 사용할 라켓을 제공해드립니다. 편안한 신발을 가지고 오시는 것만 잊지 않으시면 됩니다.
M	알겠습니다.
W	강사에게 해결해야 할 개인적인 이유가 있어서 회원님의 강좌가 다음 주부터 시작한다는 것을 확인해 주세요.
M	아 정말인가요? 모르고 있었어요. 헛걸음할 뻔했네요.

어휘 bring 가져오다 description 설명, 정보 trip 여행, 이동 particular 특정한

25

남자는 왜 전화했는가?

(A) 수업 준비물에 대해 문의하기 위해
(B) 결석을 알리기 위해서
(C) 강사에 대해 불만을 제기하기 위해
(D) 수업 비용에 대해 문의하기 위해

해설 남자의 첫 번째 대화 'I will be attending the class on Wednesdays, and I wonder if I need to bring my own racket.'에서 개인 라켓이 필요한지 궁금해서 전화를 걸었다고 했으므로 정답은 (A)이다.

실버데일 커뮤니티 레크리에이션 센터 수업 스케줄

월요일	화요일	수요일	목요일	금요일
요가	탁구	테니스	무술	배드민턴

26

시각 정보를 보시오. 화자들은 어떤 수업에 대해 이야기하고 있는가?

(A) 요가
(B) 탁구
(C) 테니스
(D) 배드민턴

해설 대화 초반에서 남자는 'I will be attending the class on Wednesdays'라고 했으므로, 시각 정보에서 수요일에 있는 수업인 테니스가 정답이 된다. 정답은 (C)이다.

27

남자의 강좌는 왜 다음 주에 시작하는가?

(A) 강사의 부재 때문에
(B) 낮은 등록률 때문에
(C) 공휴일 때문에
(D) 보수 공사의 연기 때문에

해설 대화 마지막 부분의 'Please note that your class won't start until next week because the instructor has a personal issue to deal with.'에서 강사의 개인적인 사정 때문에 수업이 다음 주부터 시작한다고 했으므로 정답은 (A)이다.

PART 4

[28-30]

| M | Good morning, team. 28-1) 29) **Dr. Phillips just called off the seminar in Green Hall. The exact reasons weren't given**. However, we were expecting 40 participants for the workshop, and most of the materials are already set up. 28-2) **Let's repurpose those materials for a hands-on training session this afternoon.** We can use the now available Green Hall to accommodate more staffers. There's a backup list of employees |

who requested additional training sessions, and **28-3) they should be informed as soon as possible.** Tina, you know where that list is stored. **30) I'll go and rearrange the setup in Green Hall.**

M 여러분, 좋은 아침입니다. 필립스 박사가 그린 홀에서의 세미나를 취소했어요. 정확한 이유는 알려지지 않았어요. 하지만, 우리는 워크샵에 40명의 참가자가 올 것으로 예상했고, 대부분의 자료들은 이미 준비되어 있어요. 그 자료들을 오늘 오후에 있을 실습 교육 세션으로 용도를 변경하도록 해요. 이제 그린 홀을 사용할 수 있어서 더 많은 직원들을 수용할 수 있어요. 추가 교육 세션을 요청한 직원들의 대기 목록이 있고, 그들에게 가능한 한 빨리 알려야 해요. 티나, 당신은 그 목록이 어디에 있는지 알고 있을 거예요. 저는 그린 홀의 세팅을 다시 정리하러 갈게요.

어휘 call off 취소하다 repurpose 다른 목적에 맞게 용도를 변경하다 hands-on 실제로 참가하는 accommodate 수용하다 store 저장하다

28
발표의 목적은 무엇인가?
(A) 직원들을 교육하기 위해
(B) 세미나 장소를 찾기 위해
(C) 일정 변경을 알리기 위해
(D) 참가 인원을 확인하기 위해

해설 담화 초반 'Dr. Phillips just called off the seminar in Green Hall. The exact reasons weren't given'에서 필립스 박사의 세미나가 취소되었다고 말한 다음, 담화 중반 이후에 자료와 트레이닝의 변경에 대해 이야기하고 있으므로 정답은 (C)가 된다.

29
화자는 필립스 박사에 대해 무엇이라고 말하는가?
(A) 그는 오늘 워크샵에 참석할 것이다.
(B) 그는 세미나를 취소했다.
(C) 그는 팀 리더이다.
(D) 그는 교육 자료를 배부할 것이다.

해설 담화 초반 'Dr. Phillips just called off the seminar in Green Hall. The exact reasons weren't given'에서 필립스 박사가 세미나를 취소했다고 말했으므로 정답은 (B)가 된다.

30
남자는 무엇을 하겠다고 제안하는가?
(A) 장소 준비하기
(B) 목록 확인하기
(C) 교육 세션 참석하기
(D) 자료 찾기

해설 담화 마지막 부분에서 남자가 'I'll go and rearrange the setup in Green Hall.'이라고 했으므로, 남자는 그린 홀의 세팅을 다시 정리하러 갈 것이다. 그린 홀이 행사의 장소이므로 정답은 (A)이다.

[31-33]

W Are you tired of crowded movie theaters and missing show times? Exciting news awaits movie enthusiasts! **31) Cinemagic Plus now provides a movie streaming service across various regions. 32) What sets us apart from other streaming services is our monthly subscription model, which includes exclusive early access to new releases.** Still not convinced? **33) Sign up through our Web site and enjoy a 20% discount on your first month's subscription.** Cinemagic Plus. Watch what you love anytime you want.

W 혼잡한 영화관과 상영 시간을 놓치는 것에 지치셨나요? 영화 팬 여러분을 위한 흥미로운 소식이 기다리고 있습니다! 시네매직 플러스는 이제 다양한 지역에서 영화 스트리밍 서비스를 제공합니다. 다른 스트리밍 서비스와 다른 점은 당사의 월 구독 상품인데, 여기에는 새롭게 출시된 영화들을 독점적으로 빠르게 접할 수 있는 것을 포함됩니다. 아직 확신이 서지 않으신가요? 저희 웹사이트를 통해 가입하고 첫 달 구독에 대해 20%의 할인을 받아보세요. 시네매직 플러스: 원하시는 때에 원하시는 것을 시청하세요.

어휘 await ~을 기다리다 enthusiast 열성 팬 region 지역 subscription 구독 exclusive 독점적인

31
무엇이 광고되는가?
(A) 스트리밍 서비스
(B) 온라인 잡지
(C) 신문 구독
(D) 새로운 영화관

해설 질문으로 흥미를 유발한 다음, 'Cinemagic Plus now provides a movie streaming service across various regions.'에서 광고의 대상이 되는 상품명과 함께, 해당 상품이 스트리밍 서비스라는 것을 이야기하고 있다. 정답은 (A)이다.

32
이 업체에 대해 언급된 것은 무엇인가?
(A) 무료 배송 서비스를 제공한다.
(B) 구독 플랜을 포함한다.
(C) 생방송 스포츠 스트리밍을 제공한다.
(D) 추천을 위한 고급 알고리즘을 사용한다.

해설 담화 중반 'What sets us apart from other streaming services is our monthly subscription model, which includes exclusive early access to new releases.'에서 다른 회사와 다르게 월 구독을 통해 독점적으로 새로 출시된 영화를 접할 수 있게 해 준다고 했다. 따라서 (B)가 정답이다.

33
왜 청자들은 웹사이트를 통해 가입해야 하는가?

(A) 할인 쿠폰을 받기 위해서

(B) 프로모션 혜택을 받기 위해서

(C) 무료 구독을 받기 위해서

(D) 무료 샘플을 받기 위해서

해설 'Why should ~'로 시작되는 문제의 경우 뒤에 나온 내용이 언급된 부분에서 정답을 찾아야 한다. 담화 마지막 부분의 'Sign up through our Web site and enjoy a 20% discount on your first month's subscription.'에서 웹사이트를 통해 가입하면, 할인을 받을 수 있다고 했으므로 (B)가 정답이다. 할인 쿠폰을 다운받거나 제공하는 것이 아니라, 가입시 할인을 해 주는 것이므로 (A)를 정답으로 고르지 않도록 주의한다.

DAY 09 PARTS 3·4
후반부 문제 풀이법

📝 실전 문제 연습
p.088

🎧 09-04

1	(A)	2	(C)	3	(C)	4	(A)
5	(B)	6	(C)	7	(A)	8	(A)
9	(B)	10	(B)	11	(B)	12	(C)
13	(A)	14	(B)	15	(C)	16	(A)
17	(B)	18	(B)	19	(A)	20	(B)
21	(A)	22	(D)	23	(B)	24	(B)
25	(A)	26	(C)	27	(D)	28	(B)
29	(C)	30	(D)	31	(D)	32	(A)
33	(C)						

PART 1

1

(A) The man is standing while using a computer.

(B) The man is using a printer.

(C) The man is carrying some folders.

(D) The man is stocking shelves.

(A) 남자가 컴퓨터를 사용하며 서 있다.

(B) 남자가 프린터를 사용하는 중이다.

(C) 남자가 폴더들을 옮기고 있는 중이다.

(D) 남자가 선반을 채우고 있는 중이다.

어휘 stock 채우다

해설 남자가 서서 컴퓨터를 사용하고 있으므로 (A)가 정답이다. 프린터가 사용되고 있는지는 알 수 없으므로 (B)는 정답이 될 수 없다. 폴더들은 정리되어 있고 옮겨지고 있지 않으므로 (C)도 오답이다. 선반이 있기는 하지만 남자가 선반에 사물을 채우고 있지 않으므로 (D)도 오답이다.

2

(A) Some people are resting on the chairs.

(B) Some lights are being installed.

(C) Potted plants are decorating a seating area.

(D) Some cushions are piled on the floor.

(A) 몇몇 사람들이 의자에 앉아 쉬고 있다.

(B) 몇몇 전등이 설치 되고 있다.

(C) 화분에 심은 식물들이 좌석 구역을 장식하고 있다.

(D) 쿠션들이 바닥에 쌓여 있다.

어휘 decorate 장식하다   rest 쉬다

해설 사진에 사람이나 사람의 동작이 보이지 않으므로 움직임을 묘사하는 being이 포함된 (B)와 사람이 언급된 (A)는 오답이다. 쿠션들이 있기는 하지만 바닥에 쌓여 있지 않으므로 (D) 역시 오답이다. 따라서, 식물들이 좌석 구역에 놓여 있는 모습을 묘사한 (C)가 정답이다.

3

(A) Workers are entering the building.

(B) A worker is ascending a ladder.

(C) Some construction work is being undergone.

(D) They are holding hardhats.

(A) 작업자들이 건물 안으로 들어가고 있다.

(B) 한 작업자가 사다리를 오르고 있다.

(C) 건설 작업이 진행되고 있다.

(D) 그들이 헬멧을 들고 있다.

어휘 ascend 오르다   undergo 겪다; 진행하다   hardhat 헬멧

해설 건설 현장에서 건물을 바라보고 있는 두 남자의 모습이다. 남자들이 건물 안으로 들어가고 있지 않으므로 (A)는 오답이다. 사다리는 보이지 않고 올라가는 사람도 없으므로 (B) 역시 오답이다. 헬멧을 쓰고 있기는 하지만 들고 있지는 않으므로 (D)도 정답이 아니다. 건설이 진행되고 있는 상황을 묘사한 (C)가 정답이다.

PART 2

4

Who is the keynote speaker for today's presentation?

(A) I think Julio from Accounting.

(B) Yes, the speaker keeps making a buzzing sound.

(C) No, I spoke yesterday.

오늘 프레젠테이션의 기조 연설자는 누구인가요?

(A) 회계 부서의 훌리오일 거예요.

(B) 네, 그 스피커는 계속 윙윙거리는 소리가 나요.

(C) 아니요, 저는 어제 연설을 했어요.

해설 who 의문에 대해 정확하게 이름으로 대답한 (A)가 정답이다. (B), (C)는 의문사 의문문에 yes/no로 대답했으므로 모두 오답이다. 뿐만 아니라, (B)는 질문의 speaker를 반복했고, (C)는 speaker의 파생어인 spoke를 이용하여 혼동을 유발하고 있다.

5

What bakery do you usually go to?

(A) I eat raisin toast.

(B) The one with the yellow signboard.

(C) I'm going there on foot.

당신은 어떤 빵집에 주로 가나요?

(A) 저는 건포도 토스트를 먹어요.

(B) 노란 간판이 있는 곳이에요.

(C) 저는 거기에 걸어서 가요.

어휘 bakery 베이커리, 빵집   raisin toast 건포도 토스트 (빵)
signboard 간판   on foot 걸어서

해설 어떤 빵집인지 묻는 질문에 노란 간판이 달린 가게임을 알려준
(B)가 정답이다. (A)는 bakery와 관련된 어휘인 toast를 이용한
오답이며, (C)는 방법을 묻는 how 의문문에 대한 대답이다.

6

When is the flight from Prague arriving?

(A) From the Internet shopping mall.

(B) I'm flying to Hong Kong.

(C) You can check on the monitor near the exit.

프라하에서 오는 비행기는 언제 도착하나요?

(A) 인터넷 쇼핑몰에서요.

(B) 저는 홍콩으로 가요.

(C) 출구 근처에 있는 모니터에서 확인하실 수 있어요.

어휘 be arriving 도착할 예정이다   fly 날아가다 (비행기를 타고
가다)   exit 출구

해설 언제 비행기가 도착할 것인지를 묻는 질문이다. (A)는 비행기에
대한 질문이 아닌 출처를 묻는 질문에 적절한 대답이다. (B)는 프라하가
언급되자 다른 지역 언급하여 혼동을 유발한 오답이다. 모니터를 확인하
면 정보를 찾을 수 있다고 간접적인 답변을 한 (C)가 정답이다.

7

Which bag do you want to buy?

(A) I love the one with the red chains.

(B) It's a hundred and fifty dollars.

(C) I like it so much.

어떤 가방을 사고 싶어요?

(A) 이 빨간색 체인이 있는 게 좋아요.

(B) 150불이에요.

(C) 그게 매우 마음에 들어요.

해설 어떤 가방을 사고 싶은지 묻는 질문에 (C)와 같이 '이게 매우
마음에 든다'는 답변이 '눈에 보이는 것이 좋다'라는 의미의 적절한 답변
이라고 착각하기 쉽다. 그러나, 마음에 드는 가방이 무엇인지 선택하는
답변은 아니므로 이는 정답이 되지 않는다. 가격을 묻는 질문이 아니라
가방의 종류를 이야기하는 것이므로 (B)역시 오답이다. 정답은 (A)인데,
which 의문문의 답변으로 많이 출제되는 'the one'이 포함되어 있다.

8

Why is the fashion show delayed?

(A) One of the main models hasn't arrived yet.

(B) It has been delayed about an hour.

(C) Yes, in a fashion magazine.

왜 패션쇼가 지연되었나요?

(A) 메인 모델 중 한 명이 아직 도착하지 않아서요.

(B) 거의 한 시간 정도 지연되었어요.

(C) 네, 패션 잡지에요.

어휘 delay 연기하다, 미루다

해설 패션쇼가 지연된 이유를 묻는 질문에 대해 모델 한 명이 도착하지
않았다며 이유를 언급한 (A)가 정답이다. delay를 반복한 (B)는 대표적인
발음 오답으로서, 지연된 시간을 묻는 질문이 아니므로 소거해야 한다.
의문사 문제에 yes/no로 답할 수 없으므로 (C) 역시 정답이 될 수 없다.

9

Are there any tickets available for the evening show?

(A) Keep your valuables in the locker.

(B) Sorry. It's already sold out.

(C) Present your tickets.

저녁 공연을 위한 티켓이 있나요?

(A) 보관함에 당신의 귀중품들을 두세요.

(B) 죄송해요. 이미 매진됐어요.

(C) 티켓을 보여주세요.

어휘 valuables 귀중품   locker 보관함, 락커   present 보여주다

해설 티켓이 남아있는지 묻는 질문에 대해 이미 다 팔렸기 때문에 없다
고 답한 (B)가 정답이다. available과 발음이 비슷한 valuables을 이용
한 (A)와 ticket을 반복한 (C)는 모두 오답이다.

10

Daniel will be transferred to the Tokyo office, won't
he?

(A) Japan is warm at this time of the year.

(B) I don't really know.

(C) No, I prefer using public transportation.

대니얼은 도쿄 지사로 전근 가게 될 거예요, 그렇지 않나요?

(A) 일본은 연중 이맘 때 따뜻해요.

(B) 저는 잘 몰라요.

(C) 아니요, 저는 대중 교통을 이용하는 것을 선호해요.

어휘 be transferred to ～로 전근 보내지다   this time of the
year 연중 이맘 때

해설 전근 여부에 대해 묻는 질문에 잘 모른다고 답한 (B)가 정답이
된다. 도쿄가 언급된 질문에서 Japan을 연상할 수 있는데, 이를 함정으
로 이용한 (A)는 오답이다. transfer와 transportation은 일부 음절이
겹치는 단어인데, 이를 이용한 (C) 또한 오답이다.

11

Who is attending the meeting today?
(A) The company picnic is next week.
(B) Mr. Jackson is scheduled to join us shortly.
(C) A new software update.

오늘 회의에 누가 참석하나요?
(A) 회사 야유회는 다음 주예요.
(B) 잭슨 씨가 곧 합류하기로 되어 있어요.
(C) 새로운 소프트웨어 업데이트요.

어휘 company picnic 회사 야유회

해설 회의에 참석할 사람을 묻는 질문에 대해 잭슨 씨가 곧 참여할 것이라는 내용의 (B)가 가장 적절한 대답이다. 문제에서 시간을 의미하는 today가 언급되었기 때문에 'next week'이라는 시간이 언급된 (A)를 정답으로 고르는 실수를 해서는 안 된다. 사람을 묻는 질문에 대해 소프트웨어 업데이트라고 답한 (C)는 질문과 무관한 내용으로서, 'what ~ about'과 같이 주제를 묻는 질문에 어울리는 답변이다.

12

Does the ceiling in the lobby need repairing?
(A) I need a pair of shoes.
(B) The lamp should be replaced.
(C) Yes, it is planned for autumn.

로비 천장을 수리해야 하나요?
(A) 저는 신발 한 켤레가 필요해요.
(B) 램프는 교체되어야 해요.
(C) 네, 그것은 가을에 계획되어 있어요.

어휘 ceiling 천장   replace 교체하다

해설 로비 천장이 수리가 필요한지 여부를 묻는 질문에 가을에 계획되어 있다고 답한 (C)가 정답이다. (A)의 경우 repair와 발음이 유사한 pair를 이용한 오답이다. '천장 수리'에서 연상될 수 있는 '램프 교체'를 언급한 (B)는 연상되는 단어를 이용한 오답 유형이다.

13

Where can I find the agenda for the team meeting?
(A) It's usually e-mailed to everyone.
(B) It will be held on Friday.
(C) No, I'll meet her tomorrow.

팀 회의 안건은 어디에서 찾을 수 있나요?
(A) 그것은 주로 모든 사람에게 이메일로 발송돼요.
(B) 그것은 금요일에 열릴 거예요.
(C) 아니요, 저는 그녀를 내일 만날 거예요.

어휘 agenda 의제   cafeteria 구내식당

해설 팀 회의 안건을 어디에서 찾을 수 있는지를 묻는 질문에 대해, 그것들이 이메일로 발송된다고 하며 이메일에 안건이 있을 것이라고 간접적으로 답한 (A)가 정답이다. where 의문문에 시간으로 답한 (B)는 전형적인 의문사 불일치 오답이다. (C)는 meeting과 meet의 유사 발음을 이용한 오답이다.

14

What's the best way to reach the event venue?
(A) The event will be held in the auditorium.
(B) Taking the metro is recommended.
(C) I'll call you tomorrow.

행사 장소로 가는 가장 좋은 방법은 무엇인가요?
(A) 그 행사는 강당에서 열릴 거예요.
(B) 지하철을 타는 것을 추천해요.
(C) 제가 내일 전화할게요.

어휘 reach ~에 이르다   metro 지하철

해설 행사 장소까지 가는 방법을 묻는 질문에 대해 지하철을 추천하는 (B)가 정답이다. 가는 방법을 묻는 질문에 대해 행사 장소로 답한 (A)는 event를 반복한 오답이다. 질문의 reach에는 '연락하다'라는 의미도 있는데, (C)의 경우 여기에서 연상되는 call을 이용한 오답이다.

15

Have you made all the travel arrangements?
(A) At the Kingston Hotel.
(B) I'll arrange the projector.
(C) I only booked the flights.

여행 준비는 모두 끝내셨나요?
(A) 킹스턴 호텔에서요.
(B) 제가 프로젝터를 준비할게요.
(C) 비행기만 예약했어요.

어휘 travel arrangement 여행 준비 (주로 여행관련 예약들)

해설 여행 준비를 모두 끝냈는지를 묻는 질문에 대해 비행기만 예약했다고 답하며, 아직 준비할 것들이 남았다는 의미로 대답한 (C)가 정답이다. (A)는 여행에서 연상되는 호텔을 이용한 오답이다. (B)는 arrangement와 파생어 관계인 arrange를 이용한 오답이다.

16

I can assist with arranging the computers for the workshop.
(A) Tablets will be provided to attendees.
(B) Is there a store near here?
(C) A seminar about managing your schedule.

워크숍을 위한 컴퓨터 배치를 도와드릴게요.
(A) 참가자들에게는 태블릿이 제공될 거예요.
(B) 근처에 가게가 있나요?
(C) 일정 관리에 대한 세미나예요.

어휘 assist 돕다   attendee 참가자

해설 '도와줄 수 있다'고 말하는 것은 '도와드릴까요?'라고 묻는 것과 의미가 같다. 따라서, 이 문제의 경우 컴퓨터 배치를 도와주겠다고 제안하는 것인데, 이에 대해 참가자들에게 태블릿이 제공된다고 답하면서 도움이 필요없다며 제안을 간접적으로 거절한 (A)가 정답이다. (B)는 workshop의 shop에서 연상되는 store를 이용한 오답이며, (C)는 세미나의 주제를 물을 때 적합한 내용의 대답이다. 평서문 유형의 경우 명사나 명사구가 정답이 되는 경우는 거의 없다.

17

Is the company implementing a new recycling program?

(A) The bicycle should be adjusted.

(B) Yes, it will start on Wednesday.

(C) This bag is made of recycled paper.

회사가 새로운 재활용 프로그램을 시행하고 있나요?

(A) 그 자전거는 조정되어야 해요.

(B) 네, 그것은 수요일에 시작할 거예요.

(C) 이 가방은 재활용 종이로 만들어졌어요.

어휘 implement 시행하다 adjust 조정하다, 조절하다 recycle 재활용하다

해설 새로운 프로그램의 시행 여부를 묻는 질문에 대해 수요일부터 시작한다고 대답한 (B)가 정답이다. 늘 질문에서 가장 중요한 부분은 동사이므로, 재활용(recycle)이 반복된 (C)를 정답으로 고르지 않도록 주의한다. (A)는 recycle과 발음이 유사한 bicycle을 이용한 오답이다.

18

How many people will be at the upcoming tech event?

(A) Not really. It wasn't that hard.

(B) I'll contact the event planners.

(C) In the conference room.

다가오는 기술 행사에 얼마나 많은 사람들이 참석하나요?

(A) 별로요. 그렇게 힘들지 않았어요.

(B) 제가 행사 기획자에게 연락해 볼게요.

(C) 컨퍼런스 룸 안에요.

어휘 upcoming 다가오는 lead 인도하다, 지도하다

해설 사람의 숫자를 묻는 질문에 대해 직접적으로 숫자를 말하는 대신 행사 기획자에게 연락해 보겠다며 우회적으로 모른다고 답변한 (B)가 정답이다. 의문사 의문문의 경우 yes/no로 답할 수 없으므로 (A)는 오답이다. (C)는 event에서 연상되는 conference room을 사용했고, 의문사 where의 정답인 장소로 답하고 있으므로 오답이다.

PART 3

[19-21]

M Welcome to Greenway Botanical Gardens. What brings you here today?

W 19) **I teach biology at a school in this area**, and I'm planning a field trip for my class. I'd like to discuss some educational programs you offer.

M 20) **For organized visits, you'll need to fill out a reservation form**. We organize these events carefully to protect the plant habitats.

W I understand. When can we schedule our visit?

M We usually schedule school visits at least three weeks in advance. For more information about our educational programs and to download the reservation form, 21) **please check our Web site at www. Greenwaygardens.com.**

M 그린웨이 식물원에 오신 것을 환영합니다. 어떻게 오셨나요?

W 저는 이 지역의 학교에서 생물을 가르치고 있고, 학생들을 위한 현장 학습을 계획하고 있어요. 이곳에서 제공하는 교육 프로그램에 대해 논의하고 싶어요.

M 방문을 준비하시려면, 예약 양식을 작성해야 합니다. 저희는 식물 서식지를 보호하기 위해 이러한 행사들을 신중하게 준비하고 있습니다.

W 알겠습니다. 우리는 언제 방문을 예약할 수 있나요?

M 일반적으로 학교 방문은 최소한 3주 전에 예약합니다. 교육 프로그램에 대한 더 많은 정보를 원하시거나 예약 양식을 다운받으시려면, 저희 웹사이트 www.Greenwaygardens.com을 확인해 주시기 바랍니다.

어휘 biology 생물학 field trip 현장 학습 organize 조직하다, 준비하다 habitat 서식처 in advance 미리

19

여자의 직업은 무엇인가?

(A) 생물 교사

(B) 접수원

(C) 행사 조정자

(D) 투어 가이드

해설 대화의 첫 부분에서 여자는 'I teach biology at a school in this area'라고 하며 자신이 학교에서 생물을 가르치고 있다고 했다. 따라서 정답은 (A)이다.

20

여자는 어떻게 현장 학습을 준비할 수 있는가?

(A) 식물원에 직접 전화함으로써

(B) 양식을 작성함으로써

(C) 수수료를 지불함으로써

(D) 직접 방문함으로써

해설 여자가 현장 학습을 계획하고 있다고 하자, 남자는 'For organized visits, you'll need to fill out a reservation form.'이라고 말했다. 즉, 현장 학습을 위해서는 예약 양식을 작성해야 하므로 서류를 작성한다는 내용의 (B)가 정답이다.

21

남자는 여자에게 무엇을 하라고 제안하는가?

(A) 식물원의 웹사이트를 방문하기

(B) 예약하기

(C) 교통편을 준비하기

(D) 수업 계획을 제출하기

해설 남자의 마지막 말 'please check our Web site at www. Greenwaygardens.com'에서 정보를 원한다면 웹사이트를 방문하라고 했으므로 남자가 제안하는 것은 (A)이다.

[22-24]

W	**22) Thanks for coming for an interview today, Tony**. My name is Anita. I was really impressed by your application. You have a lot of experience, but most importantly, after reading your résumé, I think you are highly dedicated and passionate about your work. Our advertising agency needs someone like you who is an expert in the fields of design and copywriting.
M	Yes. I've been copywriting at a top advertising agency for more than 10 years.
W	**23-1) Why do you want to leave your current company?**
M	**23-2) Oh, I moved recently, and it takes me an hour and a half to get there**.
W	I see. Let me have a look at your portfolio. Then, **24) I will show you around the office.**
W	오늘 면접에 와 주셔서 감사합니다, 토니 씨. 제 이름은 아니타예요. 저는 당신의 지원서에 매우 감명을 받았어요. 당신은 많은 경험을 가지고 있지만, 무엇보다도 당신의 이력서를 읽은 후에, 당신이 정말 업무에 헌신적이고 열정적이라고 생각했어요. 저희 광고 대행사는 디자인과 카피라이터 분야의 전문가인 당신과 같은 사람이 필요해요.
M	네, 저는 최고의 광고회사에서 10년 이상 카피라이터 업무를 해왔어요.
W	지금 회사를 왜 그만두려고 하나요?
M	음, 저는 최근에 이사를 했는데, 그곳에 가는 데 한 시간 반이나 걸려요.
W	그렇군요. 당신의 포트폴리오를 볼게요. 그런 다음, 사무실을 보여 드리죠.

어휘 interview 면접 impressed 감명을 받은 application 지원서 résumé 이력서 dedicated 헌신적인 passionate 열정적인 agency 대행사

22
남자는 왜 여자를 만나는가?
(A) 프로그램에 등록하기 위해
(B) 업체를 평가하기 위해
(C) 여행 예약을 하기 위해
(D) 면접을 하기 위해

해설 대화의 목적을 묻는 문제이므로 초반부에서 근거를 찾아야 한다. 'Thanks for coming for an interview today,'에서 면접에 와 주셔서 감사하다고 했으므로 정답은 (D)이다.

23
남자는 왜 변화를 주기로 결정했는가?
(A) 남자는 그 지역을 잘 모른다.
(B) 출퇴근이 불편하다.
(C) 그의 업무에 너무 많은 출장이 필요하다.
(D) 그는 임금 인상을 원한다.

해설 남자가 변화를 원하는 이유를 묻고 있으므로, '변화'가 먼저 언급이 되어야 한다. 여자가 'Why do you want to leave your current company?'라고 하며 왜 회사를 그만두는지 물었고, 남자는 'Oh, I moved recently, and it takes me an hour and a half to get there.'라며 출퇴근에 한 시간 반이나 걸린다고 했다. 즉, 출퇴근이 불편해서 이직하려는 것임을 알 수 있으므로 정답은 (B)이다.

24
여자가 제안한 것은 무엇인가?
(A) 남자에게 포트폴리오를 설명할 시간을 주기
(B) 구경시켜 주기
(C) 남자를 그녀의 직원들에게 소개시켜 주기
(D) 임금 협상하기

해설 대화의 마지막 여자의 말 'I will show you around the office.'에서 여자는 남자에게 사무실을 보여 주겠다고 했으므로 구경시켜 준다는 의미의 (B)가 정답이다.

[25-27]

M	In today's meeting, I have to express my concern for the drop in sales for our new product. In my opinion, the main problem is that it is not advertised enough. What I mean is that it is not advertised in the right places. We need to boost awareness of our product. Any ideas?
W	I did some research. Look at this graph. It shows where people most frequently visit online.
M	Hmm… **25) Remember that our target group is females aged between 20 and 30 who are searching for a signature scent. Did you consider this?**
W	Yes, I did. **26) This graph shows forty percent use social media sites, so it's great that we already advertise our perfume on them. However, look at the next highest category. At thirty percent, it'd be worth investing in.**
M	That's a good catch. This means we need to increase our advertising budget.
W	Actually, **27) I'm meeting with the accounting and finance teams tomorrow. I'll mention our need for extra funds.**

M 오늘 회의에서는 우리 신제품의 판매가 감소한 것에 대한 우려를 말씀드려야 할 것 같군요. 제 의견으로는, 중요한 문제는 충분한 광고가 이루어지지 않는다는 거예요. 제 말의 의미는, 광고가 적절한 곳에 이루어지지 않는다는 것이죠. 우리는 우리 상품에 대한 인지도를 올려야 해요. 아이디어 있나요?	**해설** 시각 정보 문제의 경우, 선택지에 나와있는 단어가 직접 언급되는 경우 이는 오답일 가능성이 높다. 'This graph shows forty percent use social media sites, 부분의 social media'를 듣고 (A)를 정답으로 고르는 실수를 하지 않도록 주의해야 한다. 이어지는 'so it's great that we already advertise our perfume on them. However, look at the next highest category.'에서 두 번째로 높은 범주라고 한 후 'At thirty percent, it'd be worth investing in.'에서 30퍼센트를 직접 언급했으므로, 두 조건에 일치하는 (C)가 정답이 된다.

M 오늘 회의에서는 우리 신제품의 판매가 감소한 것에 대한 우려를 말씀드려야 할 것 같군요. 제 의견으로는, 중요한 문제는 충분한 광고가 이루어지지 않는다는 거예요. 제 말의 의미는, 광고가 적절한 곳에 이루어지지 않는다는 것이죠. 우리는 우리 상품에 대한 인지도를 올려야 해요. 아이디어 있나요?

W 제가 조사를 해봤는데요. 이 그래프를 봐 주세요. 이것은 사람들이 온라인에서 가장 많이 방문하는 곳을 보여주고 있어요.

M 흠… 우리의 대상이 되는 집단은 자신들만의 특별한 향을 찾는 20~30세의 여성들이라는 것을 기억하세요. 이것을 고려했나요?

W 네, 했어요. 이 그래프를 보시면 40퍼센트의 사람들이 소셜미디어를 사용하고 있어서, 우리가 이미 이곳에서 향수를 광고하고 있는 것은 좋은 상황이에요. 하지만, 여기 다음으로 높은 범주를 보세요. 30퍼센트로서, 여기에 투자할 가치가 있어요.

M 잘 찾아냈군요. 이는 우리가 광고 예산을 늘려야 한다는 것을 의미해요.

W 사실, 제가 내일 회계 및 재무 팀을 만날 거예요. 저희에게 추가 자금이 필요하다는 것을 언급할 거예요.

어휘 concern 걱정 boost 신장시키다 awareness 인식, 관심 signature 특징 scent 향기 budget 예산

25
화자들은 어디에서 일하는 것 같은가?
(A) 향수 회사에서
(B) 제약 회사에서
(C) 광고 회사에서
(D) 백화점에서

해설 화자의 직업을 묻는 문제는 대화의 초반에서 단서를 찾을 수 있는 경우가 많지만, 초반에서 찾지 못하면 끝까지 듣고 해결한다. 대화 중반 'Remember that our target group is females aged between 20 and 30 who are searching for a signature scent. Did you consider this?'에서 20~30세 여성들이 고객층인 향이라고 말했으므로, 향기와 관련된 제품을 판매하는 곳임을 알 수 있다. 따라서, 정답은 (A)가 된다.

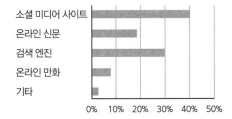
사람들이 가장 자주 방문하는 온라인

26
시각 정보를 보시오. 화자들은 어디에 그들의 상품 광고를 시작할 계획인가?
(A) 소셜 미디어 사이트
(B) 온라인 신문
(C) 검색 엔진
(D) 온라인 만화

27
여자는 내일 무엇을 할 것이라고 말하는가?
(A) 분야 연구를 수행하기
(B) 신상품 테스트하기
(C) 워크샵에 참여하기
(D) 예산 조정을 제안하기

해설 여자의 마지막 말 'I'm meeting with the accounting and finance teams tomorrow. I'll mention our need for extra funds'에서 내일 재정 미팅에 참여해 추가 예산을 요구한다고 했으므로 정답은 (D)가 된다.

PART 4

[28-30]

W 29) **If you are becoming more environmentally conscious when shopping but are having trouble finding stores that sell eco-products, then there's no better place to shop than at All Natural!** 28) **At our shop, everything from fruit to dairy products is sold in bulk, and no plastic packaging is allowed.** Shoppers bring their own reusable cloth or glass containers to shop at the store, and after purchasing them, take them home in paper bags. We guarantee that at our store, we only stock certified organic food. 30) **And we have a limited-time offer for you. If you visit our store by this Friday, you will get a 30% discount on all your purchases.**

W 쇼핑할 때 환경에 더 특별한 관심을 갖고 있지만 친환경 제품을 판매하는 상점을 찾는 데 어려움이 있다면, 올 내츄럴보다 더 좋은 곳은 없습니다! 저희 점포에서, 과일부터 유제품까지 모든 상품들은 대용량으로 판매되며, 플라스틱 포장은 허용되지 않습니다. 상점에서 물건을 살 때 소비자들은 재사용이 가능한 천이나 유리 용기를 가지고 오셔야 하며, 구매한 후 종이 봉투에 담아서 집으로 가지고 가셔야 합니다. 저희는 인증된 유기농 식품만을 갖춰두고 있다는 것을 보장합니다. 그리고 여러분들께 한정된 시간 동안 특별 할인을 제공합니다. 이번 주 금요일에 저희 가게를 방문하신다면, 모든 구매에 대해 30퍼센트 할인을 받게 될 것입니다.

어휘 environmentally 환경적으로 conscious 의식이 있는 eco-product 친환경 제품 dairy 유제품의 in bulk 대량으로 reusable 재활용 가능한 certified 인증된

28

상점은 무엇을 판매하는가?

(A) 의류
(B) 식료품
(C) 유리 제품
(D) 화장품

해설 업종을 묻는 문제의 단서는 주로 담화 초반에 등장한다. 'At our shop, everything from fruit to dairy products is sold in bulk, and no plastic packaging is allowed.'에서 과일과 유제품을 판매한다고 했으므로 정답은 (B)이다.

29

화자는 상품들에 대해 무엇을 강조하는가?

(A) 그것들은 신선하다.
(B) 그것들은 특별 할인 중이다.
(C) 그것들은 환경에 해가 되지 않는다.
(D) 그것들은 거의 재고가 없다.

해설 광고의 경우 해당 상품의 종류나 특성이 시작 부분에서 언급되므로 초반부터 잘 들어야 한다. 'If you are becoming more environmentally conscious when shopping but are having trouble finding stores that sell eco-products, then there's no better place to shop than at All Natural!'에서 환경을 걱정하는 사람들이 찾기에 좋은 상점임을 강조하고 있으므로 정답은 (C)이다.

30

금요일에 무엇이 끝나는가?

(A) 무료 종이 봉투
(B) 과일류 할인
(C) 무료 배송
(D) 할인

해설 요일이 언급된 문제의 경우 해당 요일이 언급된 부분에서 정답을 찾아야 한다. 'And we have a limited-time offer for you. If you visit our store by this Friday, you will get a 30% discount on all your purchases.'에서 한정된 시간 동안만 할인을 제공한다고 했고, 금요일까지 구매하면 할인을 해준다고 했으므로 정답은 (D)이다.

[31-33]

> M Hello. ³¹⁾ **This is John Kim, reporting live from Albert Park, located in the heart of the city.** ³²⁾ **Starting next month, the park will be building a new facility.** That's good news for dog owners! With acres to run and play on, the off-leash dog park at Albert Park will be a great spot for your pups to exercise and socialize. It will feature separate large and small dog areas and will have a large

lake where your dog can swim and play. There will also be a dog-washing area and water fountains only for dogs! ³³⁻¹⁾ **Amanda Simms, the supervisor of Albert Park, asks that all visitors leash their dogs until they are safely inside. ³³⁻²⁾ The rules and regulations will be listed at the entry point of the dog park** once it opens. Now, back to the studio.

> M 안녕하세요. 저는 도시 중심에 위치한 알버트 공원에서 실시간으로 보도 중인 존 킴입니다. 다음 달부터, 공원은 새로운 시설을 건설하는 공사를 시작할 것입니다. 강아지 주인들에게 좋은 소식입니다! 달리면서 놀 수 있는 넓은 공간과 함께, 알버트 공원에 있는 목줄을 풀어 놓을 수 있는 강아지 공원은 여러분의 강아지들이 운동을 하고 다른 개들과 어울릴 수 있는 멋진 공간이 될 것입니다. 이곳에는 분리되어 있는 큰 강아지와 작은 강아지 구역과 강아지들이 수영하고 놀 수 있는 큰 호수가 있습니다. 강아지들만 이용할 수 있는 음수대와 씻길 수 있는 구역도 있습니다. 알버트 공원의 관리자인 아만다 심즈는 모든 방문객들에게 강아지들이 안전하게 안으로 들어갈 때까지 목줄을 채워줄 것을 요청했습니다. 규칙과 규정은 강아지 공원이 개장하면 입장하는 곳에 작성되어 있을 것입니다. 이제 다시 스튜디오로 돌아가겠습니다.

어휘 undergoing 진행 중인 leash 목줄 socialize 사귀다, 어울리다 feature 특징으로 하다

31

화자는 어디에 있는가?

(A) 놀이공원에
(B) 호수에
(C) 동물원에
(D) 공원에

해설 담화 초반의 'This is John Kim, reporting live from Albert Park, located in the heart of the city.'에서 화자는 공원에서 실시간으로 보도하고 있다고 했으므로 정답은 (D)이다.

32

다음 달에 무슨 일이 있을 것인가?

(A) 건설 공사가 시작될 것이다.
(B) 공원이 개장할 것이다.
(C) 새로운 전시가 준비될 것이다.
(D) 공연이 열릴 것이다.

해설 시간이 언급된 문제의 단서는 시간 주변에서 언급되므로 'Starting next month, the park will be building a new facility'에서 정답의 단서를 찾는다. 다음 달부터 새로운 시설의 건설을 시작한다는 내용이므로 정답은 (A)이다.

33

화자는 왜 "규칙과 규정은 강아지 공원이 개장하면 입장하는 곳에 작성되어 있을 것입니다"라고 하는가?

(A) 사람들이 공원을 이용하도록 요청하기 위해

(B) 그 장소를 항상 청결하게 유지하기 위해

(C) 사람들에게 목록을 읽도록 요청하기 위해

(D) 사람들에게 돈을 기부하도록 권장하기 위해

해설 해당 문장 앞의 'Amanda Simms, the supervisor of Albert Park, asks that all visitors leash their dogs until they are safely inside.'에서 규칙과 규정의 내용이 언급되었다. 이어서 해당 문장이 이어지고 있으므로, 규칙과 규정을 읽고 숙지하라는 의미임을 알 수 있다. 정답은 (C)이다.

DAY 10 PARTS 3·4 키워드 문제 풀이법

📑 실전 문제 연습

p.096

🎧 10-11

1 (C)	2 (D)	3 (B)	4 (A)
5 (B)	6 (B)	7 (C)	8 (C)
9 (A)	10 (C)	11 (B)	12 (B)
13 (C)	14 (B)	15 (B)	16 (B)
17 (B)	18 (B)	19 (C)	20 (C)
21 (A)	22 (A)	23 (B)	24 (A)
25 (A)	26 (B)	27 (D)	28 (B)
29 (C)	30 (A)	31 (B)	32 (B)
33 (D)			

PART 1

1

(A) He's parking his car.

(B) He's opening a car door.

(C) He's working on a car.

(D) He's driving a car.

(A) 그는 차를 주차하고 있다.

(B) 그는 차 문을 열고 있다.

(C) 그는 차를 수리하고 있다.

(D) 그는 차를 운전하고 있다.

어휘 work on 작업하다, 수리하다

해설 남자가 차에 타고 있지 않으므로 운전하거나 주차하는 내용의 선택지인 (A)와 (D)는 정답에서 제외된다. 차 문을 여는 모습도 아니므로 (B) 역시 오답이다. 차량의 후드를 열고 내부를 수리하는 모습이므로 정답은 (C)이다. work on은 '작업하다'라는 의미 외에 '수리하다'라는 의미로도 사용된다.

2

(A) A woman is typing on a keyboard.

(B) A woman is purchasing a shirt.

(C) A woman is standing at a desk.

(D) A woman is taking some notes.

(A) 한 여자가 키보드를 치고 있다.

(B) 한 여자가 셔츠를 구매하는 중이다.

(C) 한 여자가 책상 앞에 서 있다.

(D) 한 여자가 무엇인가를 작성하고 있다.

해설 한 여자가 책상에 앉아서 무엇인가를 작성하는 모습이므로 정답은 (D)이다. 컴퓨터 앞에 있지만 키보드를 치고 있지는 않으므로 (A)는 오답이다. 여자가 셔츠를 구매하고 있다는 내용의 (B)도 오답이다. 책상 앞에 앉아 있는지 서 있는지 알 수 없으므로 (C)도 정답이 될 수 없다.

3

(A) A woman is reviewing some reading material.

(B) Items have been spread out on the desk.

(C) A pencil is being used.

(D) Glasses have been placed on the chair.

(A) 한 여자가 읽기 자료를 검토하고 있다.

(B) 물건들이 책상 위에 펼쳐져 있다.

(C) 연필이 사용되고 있다.

(D) 안경이 의자에 놓여 있다.

어휘 spread 펼쳐지다 glasses 안경

해설 사람이나 동작이 보이지 않으므로 사람이 언급된 (A)와 being으로 동작을 묘사한 (C)는 오답이다. 안경이 보이기는 하지만, 의자에 놓여 있지 않으므로 (D) 역시 오답이다. item은 다양한 물건을 모두 지칭할 수 있으므로 물건들이 책상 위에 있는 모습을 묘사한 (B)가 정답이다.

PART 2

4

Isn't the flight departing at 8:00?

(A) No, it has been delayed.

(B) No, I'll take the subway.

(C) 7 days a week.

비행기가 8시에 출발하지 않아요?

(A) 아니에요, 그것은 지연되었어요.

(B) 아니요, 저는 기차를 탈 거예요.

(C) 일주일에 7일요.

해설 비행기의 출발 시간이 8시인지를 묻는 부정의문문이다. 이에 대해 지연되었다고 답한 (A)가 정답이다. 비행기에서 연상되는 다른 교통 수단인 subway를 이용한 (B)와 질문에 숫자가 언급된 것을 이용하여 숫자로 답한 (C)는 모두 오답이다. 이와 같이 연속된 숫자를 오답으로 이용하는 경우가 많으므로 주의해야 한다.

5

The vendor said we would get the delivery by 3:00, didn't he?

(A) There is a vending machine near the library.

(B) Actually, it has been delayed due to heavy rain.

(C) I think we need more than 3.

판매자는 우리가 3시까지 배송을 받을 거라고 했어요, 그렇지 않았나요?
(A) 도서관 근처에 자판기가 있어요.
(B) 사실, 그것은 폭우로 인해 지연되었어요.
(C) 제 생각에는 3개 이상 필요할 것 같아요.

해설 배송이 3시까지 오는지를 묻는 질문에 대해 폭우 때문에 지연된다고 말한 (B)가 정답이다. actually는 질문자가 기대하지 않은 답변을 말할 때 사용되는 부정적인 단어이다. (A)는 vendor와 발음이 유사한 vending을 이용한 오답이며, (C)는 숫자 3을 반복한 오답이다.

6

Do you want me to get you a copy of our newsletter?
(A) I'm feeling excellent.
(B) I'd appreciate that.
(C) In the morning news.

우리 소식지의 사본을 당신께 가져다 드릴까요?
(A) 저는 기분이 좋아요.
(B) 그러면 감사하겠어요.
(C) 아침 뉴스에 있어요.

어휘 excellent 끝내주는, 훌륭한, 탁월한 appreciate 고마워하다, 알아주다, 진가를 인정하다, 감사하다

해설 소식지를 갖다 주겠다는 제안에 대해 감사하다며 받아들인 (B)가 정답이다. 기분을 묻는 질문이 아니므로 기분이 좋다고 답한 (A)는 오답이다. (C)는 news를 반복한 오답이다.

7

Do you mind taking my early morning shift tomorrow?
(A) Okay, I'll go there with you.
(B) I took a night shift.
(C) No problem.

내일 저의 이른 아침의 근무를 대신해 주실 수 있나요?
(A) 네, 제가 그곳에 당신과 함께 갈게요.
(B) 저는 야간 근무를 했어요.
(C) 문제 없어요.

어휘 mind 상관하다, 꺼려하다 shift 교대 근무 시간, 교대 근무, 근무조

해설 'Do you mind ～?'는 '～하는 것을 꺼리시나요?'라는 의미로서, 내일 아침 근무를 대신 해달라고 부탁하는 질문이다. 이에 대해 문제 없다고 답하며 수락하는 (C)가 정답이다. (B)의 경우 밤 근무를 했으니 아침 근무를 못한다는 거절의 답변이라고 착각하기 쉽다. 하지만, 부탁하는 근무 시간은 '미래'인 내일인데 밤 근무를 했다는 것은 시제는 '과거'이므로, (B)는 질문과 답변의 시제가 다른 오답이다. 같이 가자는 부탁이 아니므로 (A) 역시 오답이다.

8

Why don't you ask Kate to complete the research?
(A) I'm searching for him.
(B) I don't know when I should complete it.
(C) Why not? I'll call her right now.

케이트에게 연구를 완료하라고 요청하는 게 어때요?
(A) 저는 그를 찾고 있어요.
(B) 그것을 언제 완료해야 할지 모르겠어요.
(C) 좋아요, 제가 그녀에게 지금 전화할게요.

어휘 complete 완성하다, 끝내다 research 연구 search 찾다

해설 케이트에게 요청하라는 제안을 받아들인 (C)가 가장 적절한 대답이 된다. 'why not?'은 전형적 수락의 표현으로 '그 제안이 좋으므로 받아들이겠다'는 의미로 파악하면 된다. research와 search의 발음이 유사한 것을 이용한 (A)와 complete을 반복한 (B) 둘 다 오답이다. (B)의 경우 '모른다'는 표현 때문에 답으로 고르기 쉽지만, 이어지는 내용이 질문과 관련이 없다.

9

Please send me a text message when you get home.
(A) I'll be sure to do that.
(B) It was a long message.
(C) We should meet up soon.

집에 도착하면 문자 메시지를 보내주세요.
(A) 꼭 그렇게 할게요.
(B) 그것은 긴 메시지였어요.
(C) 우리는 곧 만나야 해요.

해설 문자 메시지를 보내달라는 요청에 대해 그렇게 하겠다고 수락하는 (A)가 정답이 된다. message를 반복한 (B)는 동일한 단어를 반복한 오답이다. 질문의 내용을 보면 만났다가 헤어지는 상황인 것으로 보이므로, '곧 만나야 한다'는 내용의 (C)는 어색한 대답이다.

10

You should type this letter by tomorrow.
(A) Sorry. The ladder is broken.
(B) There are some typos in your report.
(C) Wasn't Katherine supposed to do it?

내일까지 이 편지를 타이핑해 주셔야 해요.
(A) 죄송해요. 사다리가 망가졌어요.
(B) 당신의 보고서에 몇몇 오타들이 있어요.
(C) 캐서린이 해야 하는 것 아니었나요?

어휘 letter 편지 ladder 사다리 be broken 망가진 typo 오타

해설 'you should ～'는 '～해야 해'라는 강한 제안으로 해석하면 된다. 제안에 대해 수락하거나 거절하는 답변이 정답인 경우가 많지만, 이 문제의 경우 제 3자의 이름을 언급하면서 자신이 아닌 다른 사람이 해야 하는 일이라고 답한 (C)가 정답이다. (A)는 letter와 발음이 유사한 ladder를, (B)는 type과 발음이 유사한 typo를 이용한 오답이다.

11

Can you finish typing it yourself, or do you need some help?
(A) He's not selfish.
(B) I'm going to be done soon.
(C) Not completely.

이것을 스스로 타이핑할 수 있나요, 아니면 도움이 필요한가요?
(A) 그는 이기적이지 않아요.
(B) 곧 끝날 것 같아요.
(C) 완전히는 아니에요.

어휘 selfish 이기적인   completely 완전히

해설 혼자 할 수 있는지 아닌지를 물어본 것에 대해 이미 거의 다 끝나간다고 하며 혼자 처리할 수 있다고 대답한 (B)가 정답이다. (A)는 yourself와 selfish의 발음이 유사한 점을 이용한 오답이다. (C)의 경우 no에 가까운 의미로서 '작업을 마무리했어요?'라고 물어봤을 경우 가능한 대답이다.

12

Where did you buy that nice shirt?
(A) T-shirts and pants.
(B) It was a gift from my father.
(C) Yes, he is nice.

어디에서 그 멋진 셔츠를 샀어요?
(A) 티셔츠와 바지예요.
(B) 아버지께서 주신 선물이에요.
(C) 네, 그는 멋져요.

해설 셔츠를 어디에서 샀는지 묻는 질문에 대해 아버지의 선물이라고 대답한 (B)가 정답이다. where 의문문의 경우 묻는 것이 위치, 출처, 방향 중 어디인지를 구분해야 한다. (A)는 shirt를 반복한 오답이며, (C)는 nice를 반복한 오답이다. 특히, (C)는 의문사 의문문에 yes로 답했으므로, 오답임을 바로 알 수 있다.

13

The deadline for reimbursing this month's spending is tomorrow.
(A) It hasn't been decided.
(B) I should try to spend less.
(C) I almost forgot about that.

이번 달 지출에 대한 상환의 마감일은 내일이에요.
(A) 그것은 결정되지 않았어요.
(B) 지출을 줄이도록 해봐야 하겠어요.
(C) 거의 잊고 있었어요.

어휘 reimburse 상환하다 (공적으로 쓴 돈을 돌려받는 것)
spending 소비

해설 회사에 상환 신청 마감일을 알려 주는 것에 대해 '거의 잊고 있었다'고 말한 (C)가 정답이다. 정해진 마감일을 알려 주고 있으므로 '결정되지 않았다'라는 내용의 (A)는 정답이 될 수 없다. (B)는 spend를 반복한 오답이다.

14

When is the marketing team meeting scheduled for?
(A) The meeting room is booked.
(B) It's set for next Monday at 10:00 A.M.
(C) I have a project deadline.

마케팅 팀 회의는 언제로 예정되어 있나요?
(A) 회의실이 예약되었어요.
(B) 다음 주 월요일 오전 10시로 준비되어 있어요.
(C) 저는 프로젝트 마감 기한이 있어요.

어휘 be scheduled for 예정되어 있다   set for ~할 준비가 되어 있는

해설 회의 시간을 묻는 질문에 대해 날짜와 시간을 알려 주는 (B)가 정답이 된다. meeting을 반복한 (A)는 오답이며, schedule에서 연상될 수 있는 deadline(마감 기한)을 언급한 (C) 역시 오답이다.

15

Are you attending the conference in New York next month?
(A) I didn't book a conference room.
(B) No, I have a prior commitment.
(C) The weather was unpredictable last month.

다음 달 뉴욕에서 열리는 컨퍼런스에 참석하실 건가요?
(A) 저는 회의실을 예약하지 않았어요.
(B) 아니요, 선약이 있어요.
(C) 지난달의 날씨는 예측이 불가능했어요.

어휘 prior 앞선   commitment 약속   unpredictable 예측할 수 없는

해설 컨퍼런스 참여 여부를 묻는 질문에 대해 선약이 있어서 참석할 수 없다고 답한 (B)가 정답이다. 회의실을 예약하지 않았다고 답한 (A)는 질문에서 언급된 conference를 반복한 오답이다. 질문의 next month에서 연상되는 last month를 이용한 (C) 역시 오답이다.

16

Did you manage to finish the financial report last night?
(A) I need more coffee.
(B) Yes, I got some help.
(C) He didn't report the problem.

어젯밤에 재무 보고서를 끝낼 수 있었나요?
(A) 저는 커피가 더 필요해요.
(B) 네, 저는 도움을 받았어요.
(C) 그는 문제를 보고하지 않았어요.

어휘 manage to 성공하다, 해내다   financial 재정적인

해설 'manage to'는 하기 힘든 일을 해낼 때 사용되는 표현이다. 질문자는 어젯밤에 보고서를 끝내는 것이 힘들었을 텐데 해냈는지 여부를 묻고 있는데, 누군가에게 도움을 받았다고 답한 (B)가 가장 적절한 대답이다. 일을 끝내기 힘들다는 의미의 질문에서 연상되는 '커피가 필요하다'라는 의미인 (A)는 업무의 마무리 여부와 상관없는 답변이다. 질문에서 사람이 언급되지 않았으므로 he가 주어인 (C)는 정답이 될 수 없다. 이는 report를 반복한 오답이기도 하다.

17

Have you heard about the new software update?
(A) The IT Department is swamped.

(B) Yes, it was just released yesterday.

(C) The manuals are outdated.

새로운 소프트웨어 업데이트에 대해서 들었어요?

(A) IT 부서는 눈코 뜰 새 없이 바빠요.

(B) 네, 그것은 어제 막 출시되었어요.

(C) 그 매뉴얼은 오래되었어요.

어휘 swamped 눈코 뜰 새 없이 바쁜 release 출시하다

해설 새로운 소프트웨어 업데이트에 대해 들었는지 묻는 질문에 대해 어제 출시되었다고 대답하면서 알고 있다는 의미로 답한 (B)가 정답이다. 소프트웨어를 다루는 부서인 IT 부서를 언급한 (A)는 질문과 관계 없는 내용이다. update와 date의 발음이 겹치는 것을 이용한 (C) 역시 전형적인 오답 유형이다.

18

Do you have any plans for the long weekend?

(A) I forgot to check my calendar.

(B) Yes, I'm going camping with some friends.

(C) The traffic during holidays is always terrible.

긴 주말 동안 어떤 계획이 있나요?

(A) 일정표를 확인하는 것을 잊고 있었어요.

(B) 네, 친구들과 캠핑을 갈 거예요.

(C) 휴일 동안의 교통은 늘 끔찍해요.

어휘 long weekend 연휴 calendar 달력; 일정표

해설 긴 주말 동안 무엇을 할 것인지를 묻는 질문에 대해 친구들과 캠핑을 간다는 계획을 알려 주는 (B)가 정답이다. (A)는 plan에서 연상되는 calendar를 이용한 오답이다. 일정표를 확인하는 것을 잊어서 계획을 세우지 못했다는 의미로 추론할 수도 있지만, 파트 2에서는 이와 같이 추론하는 답변은 정답이 될 수 없다. 'long weekend'에서 연상되는 holidays(휴일)를 이용한 (C)역시 정답이 아니다.

PART 3

[19-21]

> W **20-1) I have one follow-up question before we finish this interview.** Can you please tell me how **19-1) you would contribute to our school community** if you took a position in our program?
>
> M Well, I believe that my unique experience of working in the nonprofit sector gives me a very different perspective on the education business from others. My five years of work experience have taught me the importance of giving back to society and sustainability, even in business. I think I can help add value in the classroom.
>
> W **20-2) You seem to be the exact job candidate that we've been looking for.**
>
> We are always looking for diverse groups of people with different perspectives to enrich our discussions in class. So unless you have any questions for me, **19-2) 21) why don't I show you around the campus?**

> W 우리가 이 면접을 마치기 전에 한 가지 추가 질문이 있어요. 만약 당신이 저희 프로그램에서 직책을 맡게 된다면, 우리 학교 공동체에 어떻게 기여할지 말씀해 주시겠어요?
>
> M 비영리 부문에서 일한 저의 특별한 경험은 저에게 교육 사업에 대하여 다른 이들과는 매우 다른 시각을 주었다고 생각합니다. 5년간의 제 경험은, 심지어 사업이라는 분야에서도, 사회에 환원하는 것과 지속 가능성의 중요함에 대해 가르쳐 주었습니다. 저는 수업에서도 제가 훌륭한 가치를 더할 수 있으리라 생각합니다.
>
> W 당신은 우리가 찾던 이 직책에 안성맞춤인 지원자인 것 같아요. 우리는 수업에서 토론의 질을 높이기 위해 항상 다른 시각을 가진 다양한 그룹의 사람들을 찾고 있어요. 질문이 없다면, 캠퍼스를 안내해 드려도 될까요?

어휘 follow-up 후속, 덧붙이는 take a position 직책을 맡다 contribute to ~에 기여하는 community 지역사회, 공동체 accept 수락하다 unique 독특한 experience 경험 nonprofit 비영리의 sector 부문 perspective 시각, 관점 sustainability 지속 가능성 add 더하다 value 가치, 미덕 diverse 다양한 enrich 풍성하게 하다, 질을 높이다

19

대화는 어디에서 이루어지는가?

(A) 회사 파티에서

(B) 식료품점에서

(C) 학교 캠퍼스에서

(D) 공항에서

해설 대화 초반의 'you would contribute to our school community'에서 대화의 장소가 학교와 관련이 있다는 것을 알 수 있다. 또한, 마지막 부분의 'why don't I show you around the campus?'에서 대화의 장소가 캠퍼스임을 알 수 있으므로 정답은 (C)이다.

20

대화는 왜 이루어지고 있는가?

(A) 회사의 새로운 정책 발표를 위해

(B) 광고 캠페인에 대해 이야기하기 위해

(C) 취업 기회에 관한 논의를 하기 위해

(D) 새로운 교육 프로그램을 개설하기 위해

해설 대화의 첫 부분에서 'I have one follow-up question before we finish this interview.'라고 했으므로 현재 면접을 보고 있는 상황임을 알 수 있다. 그리고 대화 중반부의 'You seem to be the exact job candidate that we've been looking for'에서 남자가 지원자임을 알 수 있으므로, 대화가 일자리와 관련되었음을 알 수 있다. 정답은 (C)이다.

21

여자는 무엇을 해 주겠다고 하는가?

(A) 구경을 시켜주기

(B) 면접을 시작하기
(C) 최신 설비를 보여주기
(D) 보고서 작업을 하기

해설 여자의 마지막 말 'why don't I show you around the campus?'에서 여자는 남자에게 캠퍼스 구경을 시켜주겠다고 했다. 따라서 정답은 (A)이다.

[22-24]

W	Paul, 22) **I'm having trouble using the new copy machine**. The red button on the side keeps blinking, but I don't know what to do. I already checked the toner, and there is no jammed paper inside. Do you know what to do?
M	Oh, the red light warns you that the machine is overheated. This new machine has a specific feature to prevent fires. So we can't use it until it cools down. The copier also requires regular ventilation.
W	Now I know what the problem is. I was using it for over an hour. 23) **Maybe I have to take a break and then start again**. By the way, 24) **do you have a manual for this machine? If you have one, please make a copy for me. I think I have to look it over.**
M	John in the Technical Department has one. I'll ask him to copy it for you.
W	폴, 제가 새로운 복사기를 사용하는 데 문제가 있어요. 옆쪽에 있는 빨간 버튼이 계속 깜박이는데 어떻게 해야 할지 모르겠어요. 토너도 확인했고 걸려 있는 종이도 없어요. 어떻게 해야 할까요?
M	아, 그 빨간색 빛은 기기가 과열되었다고 경고하는 거예요. 이 새 기기는 화재를 예방하는 특별한 기능이 있어요. 그래서 그것이 식을 때까지는 사용할 수 없어요. 복사기는 정기적인 환기도 필요해요.
W	이제 뭐가 문제인지 알겠네요. 제가 한 시간이 넘게 기기를 사용하고 있었거든요. 쉬고 나서 다시 시작해야 할 것 같아요. 그런데, 혹시 이 기기의 설명서를 가지고 있나요? 만약 있다면 복사본을 하나만 만들어 주세요. 한 번 살펴봐야 할 것 같아요.
M	기술 지원부의 존이 하나 가지고 있어요. 그에게 복사해 달라고 부탁할게요.

어휘 blink 깜박거리다 jammed 끼어 있는, 막혀 있는
warn 경고하다 ventilation 환기

22

여자는 왜 도움이 필요한가?
(A) 기기가 제대로 작동하지 않는다.
(B) 여자는 복사를 할 시간이 없다.
(C) 여자는 제시간에 자신의 일을 끝내지 못했다.
(D) 복사기에 종이가 떨어졌다.

해설 문제에 'need help'가 있는 유형은 문제점이 무엇인지를 묻는 문제이므로 여자가 가지고 있는 문제점을 찾아야 한다. 여자는 대화 초반부에서 'I'm having trouble using the new copy machine.'이라고 하며 새로운 복사기에 문제가 있다고 했다. 따라서 기기가 제대로 작동하지 않는다는 내용의 (A)가 정답이다.

23

여자는 무엇을 하겠다고 말하는가?
(A) 수리 기사에게 전화하기
(B) 휴식을 취하기
(C) 기기를 즉시 가동하기
(D) 빨간 버튼을 누르기

해설 미래 시제가 언급되는 문제의 경우 주로 대화의 중후반부에서 단서가 주어진다. 마지막 여자의 말 'Maybe I have to take a break and then start again.'에서 여자는 잠시 쉬었다가 다시 기기를 가동하겠다고 했다. 따라서 여자가 할 일은 '쉬는 것'이므로 정답은 (B)이다.

24

남자가 해 줄 것을 부탁 받은 것은 무엇인가?
(A) 여자에게 설명서를 주기
(B) 다른 복사기 제공하기
(C) 기기를 끄기
(D) 휴식을 취하기

해설 수동의 형태로 남자가 부탁 받은 내용을 묻고 있으므로, 정답의 단서는 여자가 제안하거나 부탁하는 부분에서 찾을 수 있다. 제안이나 부탁은 의문문, if, 또는 명령문으로 표현할 수 있다. 대화 후반부의 'do you have a manual for this machine? If you have one, please make a copy for me. I think I have to look it over.'에서 여자는 설명서를 복사해달라고 했으므로 정답은 (A)이다.

[25-27]

M	25) **We gave the test group of 20 people our new twin bell alarm clock prior to launching**. Today, I would like to share with you their opinions on how the product worked, what they thought of the design, and their other feelings about the product. 26) **The one negative review that came up over and over again was about the alarm clock making a loud noise when it ticks**.
W	Okay. The design team will think of a way to muffle the sound of ticking.
M	If it's impossible to silence the noise completely, then make it quieter than now at least.
W	We will try our best. By the way, did any of them mention anything about our company logo?
M	What about it?

W　Well, **27-1) many of us thought it looked better placed above the number 6. At the moment, it's engraved on the left twin bell.**

M　Hmm, I see your point. **27-2) Let's change that.**

M　우리는 출시에 앞서 20명의 테스트 그룹에게 새로운 트윈 벨 알람 시계를 제공했습니다. 오늘, 제품이 어떻게 작동되는지에 대한 그들의 의견, 디자인에 대한 그들의 생각, 그리고 제품에 대한 그들의 여러 다른 느낌들을 여러분과 공유하고자 합니다. 지속적으로 언급된 한 가지 부정적인 반응은 알람 시계가 째깍째깍할 때 큰 소리를 낸다는 것이었습니다.

W　좋아요. 디자인 팀에서 째깍거리는 소리를 약하게 할 방법을 찾을 거예요.

M　만약 소리를 완전히 없애는 것이 불가능 하다면, 적어도 지금 보다 조용하게 만들어 주세요.

W　최선을 다할게요. 그런데, 그들이 회사 로고에 대해서는 아무런 언급이 없었나요?

M　무엇에 대해서요?

W　음, 우리들 중 많은 사람들이 숫자 6위에 로고를 넣는 것이 더 나아 보인다고 생각했거든요. 지금은 왼쪽 트윈벨에 새겨져 있고요.

M　흠… 무슨 이야기인지 알겠어요. 변경할게요.

어휘 launch 출시하다　come up with 제안하다, 제시하다　tick 째깍거리다　muffle (소리를) 죽이다, 약하게 하다　engrave 새기다

25
화자들은 어떤 종류의 회사에 근무하는가?
(A) 제조 회사
(B) 디자인 회사
(C) 취업 알선 회사
(D) 기술 회사

해설 대화 첫 문장의 'We gave the test group of 20 people our new twin bell alarm clock prior to launching.'에서 제품을 출시하기 전에 테스트를 진행했다고 했으므로, 화자들은 제품을 제조하는 회사에 근무하고 있을 것이다. 따라서 정답은 (A)이다.

26
남자는 제품의 어떤 문제에 대해 언급하는가?
(A) 안전성
(B) 소음
(C) 가격
(D) 크기

해설 문제점을 이야기하는 문제의 단서는 부정적인 의미의 문장에서 찾아야 한다. 'The one negative review that came up over and over again was about the alarm clock making a loud noise when it ticks.'에서 계속 언급되는 부정적인 의견은 알람 시계의 째깍거리는 소리가 너무 크다는 것임을 알 수 있다. 그러므로 정답은 (B)이다.

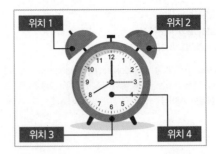

27
시각 정보를 보시오. 회사 로고는 어디에 위치하게 될 것인가?
(A) 위치 1
(B) 위치 2
(C) 위치 3
(D) 위치 4

해설 대화의 마지막 부분 'many of us thought it looked better placed above the number 6. At the moment, it's engraved on the left twin bell'에서 여자는 숫자 6 위에 로고가 위치하는 것이 좋겠다는 의견을 제시했고, 남자는 'Let's change that.'이라고 말하며 여자의 의견에 동의했다. 따라서, 정답은 (D)이다.

PART 4
[28-30]

W　I am thrilled to have the opportunity to speak to all of you today. **28) Your dedication and innovation have been crucial to our success. 29) Our cloud service solutions are now powering businesses across the globe, and we expect the usage of our services to continue to rise.** This growth has led us to develop a new data center in Maple Grove. The construction team is scheduled to begin their work in the coming weeks. **30) Please visit our Web site to view the site plans and virtual models of the new facility.**

W　오늘 여러분 모두와 이야기를 나눌 수 있어 기쁩니다. 여러분의 헌신과 혁신은 우리 회사의 성공에 매우 중요했습니다. 우리의 클라우드 서비스 솔루션은 이제 전 세계 기업들을 지원하고 있으며, 우리 서비스의 사용량이 계속해서 증가할 것으로 예상됩니다. 이러한 성장으로 우리는 메이플 그로브에 새 데이터 센터를 개발하게 되었습니다. 건설 팀이 몇 주 후에 작업을 시작할 예정입니다. 새로운 시설의 단지 계획도와 가상 모델을 보시려면 우리 웹사이트를 방문해 주시기 바랍니다.

어휘 thrilled 아주 흥분한, 기쁜　dedication 헌신　innovation 혁신　crucial 중요한　power 동력을 공급하다, 힘이 되다　virtual 가상의

28

청자들은 누구일 것 같은가?
(A) 주주들
(B) 직원들
(C) 회의 참석자들
(D) 경쟁사들

해설 담화 초반의 'Your dedication and innovation have been crucial to our success.'에서 헌신과 혁신으로 회사의 성공을 이끈 사람들은 직원들을 의미할 것이므로 (B)가 정답이 된다.

29

화자는 어떤 종류의 회사에서 일하는가?
(A) 소프트웨어 개발 회사
(B) 컴퓨터 제조 회사
(C) 클라우드 서비스 제공 회사
(D) 인터넷 서비스 제공 회사

해설 'Our cloud service solutions are now powering businesses across the globe, and we expect the usage of our services to continue to rise.'에서 화자가 근무하는 회사는 클라우드 서비스 회사임을 알 수 있으므로 (C)가 정답이다.

30

청자들은 프로젝트의 세부 사항을 어떻게 볼 수 있는가?
(A) 웹사이트를 방문함으로써
(B) 소프트웨어를 사용함으로써
(C) 교육에 참석함으로써
(D) 브로셔를 검토함으로써

해설 담화 마지막 부분의 'Please visit our Web site to view the site plans and virtual models of the new facility.'에서 프로젝트의 세부사항에 해당하는 단지 계획도와 가상 모델을 보고 싶으면 웹사이트를 방문하라고 했으므로 정답은 (A)가 된다. 'site plans'과 'virtual models'가 상위어인 details로 패러프레이징되었다.

[31-33]

M 31) **Good afternoon, shoppers. We are very glad you visited our shopping plaza**. At Furniture Land, we are proud to announce an upcoming furniture sale at our store. The sale will begin this Friday with up to 70% discounts on each product. Grab the items of your choice and make the best deal with us for sofas, chairs, and other furniture. 32) **A live furniture auction on Sunday will provide you with the opportunity to discover amazing products at incredible prices**. 33) **Don't miss out on this special offer to pick up the best products at desirable prices. The event will last for only one day!** Thank you for shopping at Shopping Plaza and have a wonderful day.

M 안녕하세요, 쇼핑객 여러분. 저희 쇼핑 플라자를 방문해 주셔서 감사합니다. 퍼니처 랜드에서는, 저희 매장에서 곧 있을 가구 할인 행사를 알려드리게 되어 기쁩니다. 이번 주 금요일부터 제품별로 최대 70%의 할인 행사를 시작합니다. 여러분의 물건을 선택하시고 소파, 의자, 그리고 다른 가구들에 대한 가장 좋은 거래를 저희와 함께 하세요. 일요일에 열리는 가구 경매는 여러분에게 놀라운 가격으로 멋진 상품을 발견할 수 있는 기회를 제공할 것입니다. 이 특별 행사를 놓치지 마시고 원하는 가격에 최고의 제품을 고르세요. 행사는 단 하루 동안만 진행됩니다! 쇼핑 플라자에서 쇼핑해 주셔서 감사드리며 즐거운 하루 보내세요.

어휘 upcoming 다가오는 auction 경매 desirable 원하는

31

화자는 어디에서 일하는 것 같은가?
(A) 미디어 매체에서
(B) 쇼핑몰에서
(C) 컨벤션 센터에서
(D) 호텔에서

해설 담화 초반의 'Good afternoon, shoppers. We are very glad you visited our shopping plaza.'에서 쇼핑객들에게 인사하고 환영하고 있으므로 정답은 (B)이다.

32

일요일에는 무슨 일이 있을 것인가?
(A) 상점 개업
(B) 라이브 가구 경매
(C) 무역 박람회
(D) 자선 행사

해설 문제에 일요일이 언급되어 있으므로 일요일이 포함된 내용을 잘 들어야 한다. 담화 중후반부의 'A live furniture auction on Sunday will provide you with the opportunity to discover amazing products at incredible prices.'에서 일요일에 라이브 가구 경매가 진행된다고 했으므로 정답은 (B)이다.

33

화자는 왜 "그 행사는 하루만 지속됩니다"라고 말하는가?
(A) 청자들에게 도움을 요청하려고
(B) 청자들에게 날짜를 알려주려고
(C) 상점을 홍보하려고
(D) 청자들에게 행사 참여를 독려하려고

해설 담화 마지막의 'Don't miss out on this special offer to pick up the best products at desirable prices. The event will last for only one day!'에서 단 하루만 열리는 행사를 놓치지 말라고 했다. 따라서 행사 참여를 유도하기 위한 의도임을 알 수 있으므로 정답은 (D)이다.

📝 실전 문제 연습
p.105

🎧 11-06

1	(A)	**2**	(C)	**3**	(A)	**4**	(A)
5	(A)	**6**	(C)	**7**	(B)	**8**	(B)
9	(A)	**10**	(B)	**11**	(B)	**12**	(C)
13	(B)	**14**	(A)	**15**	(A)	**16**	(A)
17	(C)	**18**	(A)	**19**	(A)	**20**	(D)
21	(B)	**22**	(B)	**23**	(D)	**24**	(A)
25	(B)	**26**	(B)	**27**	(B)	**28**	(B)
29	(D)	**30**	(B)	**31**	(D)	**32**	(B)
33	(C)						

PART 1

1
(A) They are carrying suitcases.
(B) The cars are parked on one side of the road.
(C) They are leaning against a car.
(D) They are shopping for some bags.

(A) 그들은 여행 가방을 옮기고 있는 중이다.
(B) 자동차들은 길 한쪽에 주차 되어 있다.
(C) 그들은 자동차에 기대어 있다.
(D) 그들은 가방을 쇼핑하고 있는 중이다.

어휘 carry 옮기다   suitcase 여행 가방

해설 두 사람이 여행 가방을 끌고 주차장에서 걸어가고 있으므로 여행 가방을 옮기고 있는 중이라는 내용의 (A)가 정답이다. 차들이 세워져 있는 모습은 맞지만 도로가 아닌 실내에 주차되어 있으므로 (B)는 정답이 될 수 없다. 파트 1 문제는 끝까지 잘 듣고 전치사구의 내용이 사진과 일치하는지를 판단하는 것이 중요하다. 두 사람은 차에 기대어 있지 않고 걷고 있으므로 (C) 역시 오답이다. 가방이 보이기는 하지만 가방을 쇼핑하고 있지 않으므로 (D)도 정답이 될 수 없다.

2
(A) They are putting down their poles.
(B) They are packing their backpacks.
(C) They are hiking outdoors.
(D) They are crossing a river.

(A) 그들은 그들의 막대를 내려놓는 중이다.
(B) 그들은 배낭을 싸고 있다.
(C) 그들은 야외를 걷고 있다.
(D) 그들은 강을 건너고 있다.

해설 hiking은 흔히 생각하는 것처럼 자전거를 타는 것이 아니라 야외를 걸으면서 여행하는 것이다. 야외를 걸으며 도보 여행을 하고 있는

사진이므로 정답은 (C)이다. 등산용 스틱을 들고 있기는 하지만 내려 놓고 있지는 않으므로 (A)는 오답이다. 배낭을 메고 있기는 하지만 배낭을 싸고 있지는 아니므로 (B) 역시 오답이다. 사진에서 강은 보이지 않으므로 (D)도 정답이 될 수 없다.

3
(A) An umbrella has been unfolded.
(B) Some seats are being arranged under an umbrella.
(C) Some plants are placed on the chairs.
(D) Some people are swimming in the pool.

(A) 파라솔이 펼쳐진 상태이다.
(B) 의자들이 파라솔 아래 놓이고 있다.
(C) 식물들이 의자들 위에 놓여 있다.
(D) 몇몇 사람들이 수영장에서 수영하고 있다.

어휘 unfolded 펼쳐진   umbrella 우산, 파라솔

해설 un은 부정의 의미로 사용되는 접두어이므로 unfold를 접혀 있는 상태로 착각하기 쉽지만, folded가 접힌 상태를 의미하므로 unfolded는 펼쳐진 상태를 의미한다. 파라솔이 펼쳐진 상태를 가장 적절하게 묘사한 (A)가 정답이다. 의자를 놓고 있는 사람들은 보이지 않으므로 (B)는 오답이다. 식물은 의자가 아닌 테이블 위에 놓여 있으므로 위치를 잘못 설명한 (C)는 정답이 될 수 없다. 사진에서 사람은 보이지 않으므로 (D) 또한 오답이다.

PART 2

4
What time is the marketing presentation?
(A) At 2:00 P.M. in the boardroom.
(B) Let's visit the market near the train station.
(C) I don't have a watch.

마케팅 프레젠테이션은 몇 시인가요?
(A) 이사회실에서 오후 2시에요.
(B) 기차역 근처에 있는 시장에 방문하도록 해요.
(C) 저는 시계가 없어요.

어휘 boardroom 이사회실

해설 프레젠테이션의 시각을 묻는 질문에 오후 2시에 열린다는 시간을 언급한 (A)가 정답이다. (B)는 marketing과 발음이 유사한 market을 이용한 오답이다. (C)는 질문의 time에서 연상되는 단어인 watch를 이용한 오답이다.

5
Which train are you planning to take?
(A) The usual one.
(B) It's raining.
(C) Yes, it departs at 8:00.

어떤 기차를 탈 계획이에요?
(A) 늘 타던 거요.
(B) 비가 와요.
(C) 네, 그것은 8시에 출발해요.

어휘 **usual** 일상적인 **depart** 출발하다

해설 어떤 기차를 탈 것인지를 묻는 which 의문문이다. 8시에 출발한다고 대답하는 (C)를 정답으로 고르는 실수를 하기 쉬운데, 의문사 의문문에 대해 yes로 대답할 수 없으므로 이는 오답이다. (B)는 train과 발음이 유사한 rain을 이용한 오답이다. (A)의 one은 기차를 지칭하는 대명사로서 늘 타던 기차라고 답한 (A)가 정답이다.

6

When is the deadline for submitting the project proposal?

(A) Let's meet in the cafeteria.

(B) The line is busy.

(C) It's due next Friday.

프로젝트 제안서를 제출해야 하는 마감일이 언제인가요?

(A) 구내 식당에서 만나요.

(B) 지금은 통화 중이에요.

(C) 다음 주 금요일까지예요.

어휘 **submit** 제출하다 **proposal** 제안, 제안서 **cafeteria** 구내 식당

해설 마감일을 묻는 질문에 대해 다음 주 금요일이라는 시간으로 대답한 (C)가 정답이다. 시간을 묻는 질문에 장소로 답한 (A)는 정답이 될 수 없다. deadline과 음절이 겹치는 line을 이용한 (B)도 오답이다.

7

Are you attending the training session tomorrow?

(A) The training room is on the fifth floor.

(B) Yes, I've already registered.

(C) Can you pass me the stapler, please?

내일 있을 교육 세션에 참석하나요?

(A) 교육실은 5층에 있어요.

(B) 네, 저는 이미 등록했어요.

(C) 저에게 스테이플러를 건네 주시겠어요?

어휘 **training session** 교육 세션 **register** 등록하다

해설 교육 세션 참여 여부를 묻는 질문에 대해 이미 등록했다고 답한 (B)는 참여하겠다는 것을 간접적으로 언급한 정답이다. (A)는 training을 반복한 오답으로서, 참석 여부를 알 수 없는 내용이다. 교육 세션과 스테이플러는 상관없는 내용이므로 (C)도 오답이다.

8

How many vacation days do employees get in their first year?

(A) I don't know where to go.

(B) It's typically two weeks.

(C) The rooms are vacated.

입사 첫해에 직원들은 며칠의 휴가를 받게 되나요?

(A) 저는 어디로 갈지 몰라요.

(B) 보통 2주예요.

(C) 그 방들은 비워져 있어요.

어휘 **typically** 전형적으로, 일반적으로 **vacate** 비우다

해설 휴가가 며칠 주어지는지 묻는 질문에 대해 2주라고 답한 (B)가 정답이다. 'I don't know'만 듣고 모른다는 대답으로 착각해 (A)를 정답으로 고르지 않도록 주의한다. 'I don't know'가 나오는 경우 항상 끝까지 잘 듣고 질문에서 묻는 것과 일치하는 내용인지를 확인해야 한다. (C)는 vacation과 유사한 발음의 vacate를 이용한 오답이다.

9

Is there a dress code for the upcoming team-building event?

(A) Yes, it's casual attire.

(B) I need to buy new shoes.

(C) The event starts at 9:00 A.M.

다가오는 팀 빌딩 행사에 복장 규정이 있나요?

(A) 네, 캐주얼한 복장이에요.

(B) 저는 새 신발을 사야 해요.

(C) 행사는 9시에 시작해요.

어휘 **dress code** 복장 규정 **upcoming** 다가오는 **attire** 복장

해설 행사의 복장 규정이 있는지 묻는 질문에 대해 캐주얼한 복장이라고 알려 주는 (A)가 가장 좋은 대답이다. 복장 규정에서 연상되는 신발(shoes)을 언급한 (B)는 질문에 대한 답변으로 적절하지 않은 내용이다. 행사의 시간을 묻는 질문이 아니므로 (C)는 또한 정답이 될 수 없다.

10

How did you resolve the technical issue?

(A) I didn't understand the problem.

(B) We had to consult the IT Department.

(C) This month's issue was released yesterday.

기술적인 문제를 어떻게 해결했나요?

(A) 저는 그 문제를 이해하지 못했어요.

(B) 우리는 IT 부서에 상의해야 했어요.

(C) 이번 달 호는 어제 출간되었어요.

어휘 **resolve** 해결하다 **consult** 상담하다, 상의하다 **issue** 문제, (잡지 등의) 호

해설 기술적인 문제를 해결한 방법을 묻는 질문에 대해 IT 부서에 상의해야 했다며 도움을 받았음을 암시하는 (B)가 가장 좋은 대답이다. (A)는 '문제'라는 의미의 issue와 동의어인 problem을 이용해 혼동을 주는 오답이다. 의미상으로도, 문제를 해결한 방법을 묻는 질문에 대해 문제를 이해하지 못했다고 답하는 것은 부자연스럽다. (C)는 issue를 반복한 오답인데, (C)의 issue는 '(잡지 등의) 호'라는 의미로 사용되었다.

11

Can you review the slides for the staff meeting?

(A) We plan to have an interview tomorrow.

(B) I have a meeting with a client this afternoon.

(C) We're still understaffed.

직원 회의를 위한 슬라이드를 검토해 주시겠어요?

(A) 우리는 내일 인터뷰를 계획하고 있어요.

(B) 저는 오후에 고객과 미팅이 있어요.

(C) 우리는 여전히 직원이 부족해요.

어휘 understaffed 인력이 부족한

해설 슬라이드를 검토해 줄 수 있는지 묻는 질문에 대해 오후에 고객을 만나야 한다고 답하며 간접적으로 부탁을 거절하는 (B)가 정답이다. (A)는 review와 발음이 일부 겹치는 interview를 이용한 오답이다. 문제에 언급된 staff와 발음이 일부 겹치는 understaffed를 이용하여 혼동을 유발한 (C) 역시 오답이다.

12

Why hasn't the elevator been fixed yet?
(A) Fax me the estimate.
(B) To get better results.
(C) A replacement part hasn't arrived yet.

엘리베이터는 왜 아직 고쳐지지 않았나요?
(A) 저에게 견적을 팩스로 보내주세요.
(B) 더 나은 결과를 얻기 위해서요.
(C) 교체 부품이 아직 도착하지 않았어요.

어휘 fix 고치다 estimate 견적 replacement 교체

해설 엘리베이터가 아직 수리되지 않은 이유를 묻는 질문에 대해 교체 부품이 도착하지 않았다며 이유를 설명한 (C)가 정답이다. 더 나은 결과를 위해 수리를 연기했다는 내용이 자연스럽다고 생각하기 쉽지만, 이유를 묻는 질문일 뿐 목적을 묻는 질문이 아니므로 (B)를 정답으로 골라서는 안된다. (A)의 경우 발음이 비슷한 fix와 fax를 이용한 오답이다.

13

Let's make a new logo for our fall catalogue.
(A) I think I can't go.
(B) I can do that.
(C) Spring is better.

가을 카탈로그를 위한 새로운 로고를 만들도록 해요.
(A) 저는 갈 수 없을 것 같아요.
(B) 제가 할 수 있어요.
(C) 봄이 더 좋아요.

해설 새로운 로고를 만들자는 제안에 대해 자신이 하겠다고 답한 (B)가 정답이다. logo와 go의 음절이 겹치는 것을 이용한 (A)는 질문의 응답으로 적절한 내용이 아니다. fall에서 연상되는 spring을 이용한 (C) 또한 연상되는 단어를 이용한 오답이다.

14

Who is in charge of installing the new software?
(A) Noah in tech support.
(B) No, it's free of charge.
(C) The warehouse is full of boxes.

새 소프트웨어 설치를 담당하는 사람은 누구인가요?
(A) 기술지원팀의 노아요.
(B) 아니요, 그것은 무료예요.
(C) 창고는 상자로 가득해요.

어휘 install 설치하다 free of charge 무료의 warehouse 창고

해설 'who is in charge of ~'는 담당자를 묻는 질문이므로, 사람 이름을 언급한 (A)가 정답이다. who 의문문의 경우 뒤에 나오는 동사를 듣고 선택지에 언급된 사람이 답변으로 어울리는지를 분별하는 것이 중요하다. charge라는 단어가 질문과 다른 의미로 사용된 (B)는 발음을 이용한 오답이다. software의 뒷부분 ware와 발음이 겹치는 warehouse를 이용한 (C) 또한 오답이다. hardware, warehouse, kitchenware 등의 단어들도 활용될 수 있다.

15

Which seminar do you want to attend, the one on the 15th or the 16th?
(A) Why don't we ask Sam first?
(B) I don't like it either.
(C) How much is the admission fee?

15일과 16일 중 어떤 세미나에 참여하는 것을 원하나요?
(A) 샘에게 먼저 물어보는 게 어떨까요?
(B) 저도 역시 좋아하지 않아요.
(C) 입장료는 얼마인가요?

어휘 admission fee 입장료

해설 두 날짜 중의 하나를 골라야 하는 질문에서 제 3자에게 먼저 물어보자고 답하는 것은 결정할 수 없다는 의미의 대답이다. 따라서 정답은 (A)이다. either는 선택의문문에 대해 '둘 다 좋다'라는 의미로 자주 사용되어 정답이라고 생각하기 쉽지만, (B)의 경우 '나도 역시 싫어한다'라는 의미이므로, 질문에 대한 대답으로 적절하지 않다. 입장료를 물어보는 (C) 또한 한 쪽을 선택하는 대답이 될 수 없다.

16

Which company should we use to make promotional materials?
(A) The cheaper one.
(B) Yes, I was promoted last week.
(C) I'll accompany you.

판촉물을 만들기 위해 어떤 회사를 이용해야 할까요?
(A) 더 저렴한 곳요.
(B) 네, 저는 지난주에 승진했어요.
(C) 제가 함께 갈게요.

어휘 promotional 판촉의 promote 판촉하다, 승진하다 accompany 동행하다

해설 어떤 회사를 선택할 것인지를 물었으므로 '회사'로 대답해야 한다. (A)의 'one'은 회사를 대신할 수 있는 대명사이므로, (A)는 '더 저렴한 회사'라고 답한 정답이다. which 의문에 대한 정답으로 'the one'이 자주 사용된다. (B)의 promote는 질문의 '판촉하다'라는 의미가 아닌 '승진하다'라는 의미로 사용되었다. (C)는 company와 음절이 겹치는 accompany를 이용한 오답이다.

17

The floor plan for our new office space has been changed.

(A) The special offer will be finished tonight.

(B) Yes, we're going to plant some flowers.

(C) Some more employees will join this office.

새로운 사무 공간의 평면도가 변경되었네요.

(A) 특가 판매는 오늘 밤에 끝나요.

(B) 네, 저희는 약간의 꽃을 심을 계획이에요.

(C) 더 많은 직원들이 사무실에 합류할 거예요.

어휘 floor plan 평면도　special offer 특가 판매

해설 평면도가 변경되었다는 정보에 대해 더 많은 직원들이 합류할 것이라며 변경된 이유를 말한 (C)가 정답이다. (B)의 경우 plan과 plant의 발음이 유사한 것을 이용한 오답 유형이다. (A)의 경우 offer와 office의 발음이 유사한 점을 이용한 오답으로서, 우리가 듣기에는 두 단어가 전혀 비슷하지 않은 것 같지만, 이 단어들은 토익에 자주 출제되는 발음 오답 유형이다.

18

We should leave for the company retreat, shouldn't we?

(A) We still have another hour.

(B) It will be held at Fisher Park.

(C) I left it on my desk.

회사 야유회를 위해서 떠나야 해요, 그렇지 않아요?

(A) 아직 한 시간 더 남았어요.

(B) 그것은 피셔 공원에서 열릴 거예요.

(C) 저는 그것을 책상 위에 두었어요.

어휘 company retreat 회사 야유회

해설 야유회를 위해 떠나야 한다고 말하는 것은 출발하자고 제안하는 것인데, 아직 한 시간 더 남았다는 것은 벌써 출발할 필요가 없다는 의미의 적절한 대답이다. 따라서 정답은 (A)이다. 야유회의 장소를 언급하는 (B)는 지금 떠날 것인지 아닌지를 알려줄 수 없는 대답이다. 질문의 leave는 '떠나다'의 의미로 사용되었는데 (C)의 left는 '두다'라는 의미로 사용되었다.

PART 3

[19-21]

> W　Hey, Jason. ¹⁹⁾ **The pictures you took at my wedding are amazing!** I love all the pictures, but do you remember the one of the bride and groom's first dance? That is my favorite. ²⁰⁾ **I would love to have it framed so that we can display it in our living room.**
>
> M　Of course. All you need to do is tell me what size and what type of frame you would like on our Web site. Then, I can prepare the picture the way you want it.

> W　That's great to hear! Once I send you the information, how long will it take for the picture to be ready? I actually have a plan to be in your neighborhood next Thursday, so I was wondering if I could pick it up then.
>
> M　²¹⁾ **We provide free delivery for our customers.** So why don't I just ship it to your place to save you a trip? Simply give me your address with the rest of the information, and I'll ship it to you as soon as the picture is ready.

> W　안녕하세요, 제이슨. 당신이 나의 결혼식에서 찍어 준 사진들은 정말 놀라워요! 모든 사진들이 마음에 들지만, 신랑 신부의 첫 춤 사진 기억 나시죠? 그게 제가 가장 좋아하는 거예요. 거실에 진열할 수 있도록 그 사진을 액자에 넣고 싶어요.
>
> M　물론이죠. 우리 웹사이트에 있는 액자들 중에서 원하시는 크기와 액자의 종류를 골라주시기만 하면 돼요. 그리고 나면, 당신이 원하는 방식으로 사진을 준비할 수 있어요.
>
> W　정말 좋네요! 제가 정보를 드리고 나면, 사진이 준비되는 데 얼마나 걸릴까요? 사실은 당신 동네로 다음 주 목요일에 방문할 계획이 있어서, 혹시 그때 그것을 찾을 수 있을까 해서요.
>
> M　우리는 고객들께 무료 배송을 제공하고 있어요. 그러니 굳이 오시지 않도록 그냥 당신에게 배송하는 것은 어때요? 나머지 정보와 함께 주소만 주시면, 사진이 완성되자마자 바로 보내도록 할게요.

어휘 wedding 결혼, 결혼식　amazing (감탄할 정도로) 놀라운　bride and groom 신랑 신부　favorite 가장 좋아하는　frame 액자, 틀; 틀(액자)에 넣다, 테를 두르다　neighborhood 동네　simply 그냥, 그저

19

남자의 직업은 무엇인 것 같은가?

(A) 사진사

(B) 웨딩 플래너

(C) 댄서

(D) 인테리어 디자이너

해설 대화 첫 부분의 'The pictures you took at my wedding are amazing!'이라는 표현에서 정답은 (A)임을 알 수 있다.

20

여자는 무엇을 하기를 원하는가?

(A) 행사 일정 잡기

(B) 프로젝트에 대한 피드백 제공하기

(C) 무료 선물 받기

(D) 추가 서비스 받기

해설 여자의 첫 번째 대화의 'I would love to have it framed so that we can display it in our living room.'에서 여자는 사진을 액자에 끼워 전시하고 싶다고 했으므로, 액자를 끼우는 추가 서비스를 받고 싶어 한다는 것을 알 수 있다. 따라서, 정답은 (D)가 된다.

21

남자는 무엇을 하겠다고 말하는가?

(A) 몇 장의 사진을 찍기
(B) 무료 배송 제공하기
(C) 스튜디오에 들르기
(D) 액자 고르기

해설 남자의 말 'We provide free delivery for our customers.'에서 남자는 여자에게 무료로 배송을 해주겠다고 말했다. 따라서, 정답은 (B)가 된다.

[22-24]

M1 Jake, **22-1) are you looking forward to the new gym opening next month?**

M2 Of course. **22-2) It's about time we opened a second location.**

W I visited the place this morning to let the painters in. By the way, **23) I think we should hire two more trainers and order one more treadmill.**

M2 But I'm hesitant about placing the order right away. We had to pay our employees yesterday, so **24) I'm worried that we don't have enough funds to cover the costs.**

W I checked the account balance half an hour ago.

M2 Okay then. I'll place the order right now.

M1 제이크, 다음 달에 새로운 체육관 개장이 기대되지 않아요?

M2 물론이죠. 우리가 두 번째 체육관을 열 때가 왔군요.

W 제가 오늘 아침에 그곳에 방문해서 페인트 업자들을 들여보냈어요. 그건 그렇고, 제 생각에는 두 명의 트레이너를 고용하고 러닝머신을 하나 더 주문해야 할 것 같아요.

M2 사실 저는 지금 주문하는 것이 조금 망설여져요. 어제 직원들에게 임금을 지불했는데, 비용을 지불할 만큼 충분한 잔액이 있는지 걱정이네요.

W 제가 30분 전에 계좌 잔고를 확인했어요.

M2 그럼 좋아요. 지금 즉시 주문할게요.

어휘 look forward to ~을 고대하다 location 지역 treadmill 트레드밀, 러닝머신 account 계좌 balance 잔고, 잔액

22

화자들은 무엇에 대해 이야기하는가?

(A) 사업체를 이전하는 것
(B) 신규 지점을 개업하는 것
(C) 새로운 집을 페인트칠하는 것
(D) 대회를 위해 훈련하는 것

해설 대화 초반 'are you looking forward to the new gym opening next month?'라고 묻는 질문에 대해 'It's about time we opened a second location.'이라고 대답했다. 따라서 새로운 체육관

이 개관할 예정이며, 그 체육관이 두 번째 지점이라는 것을 알 수 있다. 정답은 (B)이다.

23

여자는 무엇을 사고 싶어 하는가?

(A) 페인트
(B) 가구
(C) 사무용품
(D) 운동 기구

해설 여자가 사고 싶어 하는 것을 묻고 있으므로 여자의 말에서 정답을 찾아야 한다. 여자의 말 'I think we should hire two more trainers and order one more treadmill.'에서 트레이너를 고용하고 러닝머신을 주문해야 한다고 했으므로, 보기 중에서 운동 기구를 사려고 한다는 내용의 (D)가 정답이다. order는 buy와 동의어이다.

24

여자는 왜 "제가 30분 전에 계좌 잔고를 확인했어요"라고 하는가?

(A) 안심하도록 하기 위해
(B) 상황의 긴급함을 강조하기 위해
(C) 놀라움을 표시하기 위해
(D) 변명을 하기 위해

해설 인용된 문장 바로 앞에서 남자 중 한 명이 돈에 대해 걱정하자, 여자가 잔고를 확인했다고 말했다. 이어서 남자는 그렇다면 주문을 하겠다고 했으므로, 여자의 말은 잔고를 걱정하는 남자를 안심시키기 위해 해당 문장을 이야기했다는 것을 알 수 있다. 따라서, 정답은 (A)이다. 참고로, reassurance라는 표현이 정답이 되려면, 앞에 걱정하는 내용, 문제, 혹은 어려운 일 등이 언급되어야 한다.

[25-27]

M Good morning. My name is Adam Jackson. **25) I am here to see Ms. Parker, the Human Resources manager**. I will be working here starting today, and I was instructed to report to her for a building tour. Can you help me find her?

W1 Oh, she's right here. Jane, Adam Jackson is here to meet you.

W2 Hello. I'm Jane Parker. It's a pleasure to finally meet you, Adam. Before I walk you around the building, I'll take you to your desk. Do you know your access code yet? **27-1) You should have received it from the technical support team this morning. 26-1) Without the access code, there is not much work you can do here at the office**, so you must get your code as soon as possible.

M Nope. What's it for? To enter the building?

W2 No. **26-2) It's your password to log on to our computer system. 27-2) Someone from**

technical support is on the way here right now. He should be here any minute now.

M   안녕하세요? 제 이름은 아담 잭슨입니다. 인사 담당자인 파커 씨를 만나러 왔습니다. 오늘부터 이곳에서 근무를 시작하기로 했는데, 파커 씨에게 건물 안내를 받으라고 지시를 받았거든요. 그분이 어디에 있는지 알려 주실 수 있나요?

W1   오, 그녀는 바로 여기 있어요. 제인, 아담 잭슨이 당신을 만나러 왔어요.

W2   안녕하세요. 제가 제인 파커예요. 드디어 만나게 되어 반가워요. 건물을 안내하기 전에, 먼저 당신의 자리로 안내할게요. 보안 코드를 알고 있나요? 오늘 오전에 기술 지원팀으로부터 받았어야 할 텐데. 보안 코드가 없다면, 아무 일도 할 수 없어서, 최대한 빨리 당신의 코드를 받아야 해요.

M   아니요. 그것은 무엇을 위한 거예요? 건물에 들어올 때 필요한 건가요?

W2   아니요. 그건 우리 컴퓨터 시스템에 접속하기 위해 필요한 당신의 개인 비밀번호예요. 기술 지원팀에서 누군가가 지금 오고 있어요. 여기에 금방 올 거예요.

어휘 be instructed to ~하도록 지시를 받다   crucial 중대한, 결정적인   on the way 가는 (오는) 중인   any minute now 곧, 머지않아

25
제인 파커는 누구인가?
(A) 기술지원부 직원
(B) 인사부 관리자
(C) 유지보수 직원
(D) 신입 직원

해설 사람의 이름이 언급된 질문의 경우, 이름의 바로 앞뒤에서 정답을 찾으면 된다. 남자의 첫 대화 'I am here to see Ms. Parker, the Human Resources manager.'에서 남자는 파커 씨가 'Human Resources manager'라고 했으므로 정답은 (B)이다.

26
왜 남자는 보안 코드가 필요한가?
(A) 개인 정보를 검색하기 위해서
(B) 컴퓨터 시스템에 로그인하기 위해서
(C) 새로운 소프트웨어를 설치하기 위해서
(D) 시스템에 근무 시간을 입력하기 위해서

해설 access code라는 명사가 언급된 부분의 주변에서 정답의 단서를 찾아야 한다. 'Without the access code, there is not much work you can do here at the office'에서 access code가 언급되었고, 이어서 여자는 'It's your password to log on to our computer system.'라고 했다. 즉, access code는 시스템 로그인에 필요하다는 의미이므로 정답은 (B)이다.

27
남자는 다음에 무엇을 할 것 같은가?
(A) 회사 주변을 산책한다
(B) 기술 지원팀이 올 때까지 기다린다

(C) 컴퓨터 시스템을 설치한다
(D) 책상으로 간다

해설 대화 중반부의 여자의 말 'You should have received it from the technical support team this morning.'에서 기술 지원부에서 access code를 받을 수 있다고 이야기했고, 마지막 여자의 말 'Someone from technical support is on the way here right now.'에서 지금 기술 지원팀이 오고 있다고 했으므로, 남자는 다음에 기술 지원팀을 기다려야 한다는 것을 알 수 있다.

PART 4

[28-30]

W   Hello and 28) **welcome to this online tutorial, where I will show you how to set up your new home office desk, the DX200.** It's straightforward and can be completed in about 15 minutes. 29) **You'll find all the necessary screws and a screwdriver included in the package.** Before you start setting it up, ensure that you have all these items. First, unfold the desk frame and secure the legs in place. Next, 30-1) **align the desktop with the frame, ensuring that the screw holes match up.** 30-2) **It's quite big, so consider getting someone to help you with this part.**

W   안녕하세요, 새로운 홈 오피스 책상 DX200의 설치 방법을 보여드리는 온라인 사용 지침서에 오신 것을 환영합니다. 이것은 매우 간단하며 대략 15분이면 끝낼 수 있습니다. 필요한 모든 나사와 드라이버가 포장된 상자에 포함되어 있습니다. 설치를 시작하기 전에, 이 모든 물품들이 있는지 확인하세요. 첫 번째로, 책상 프레임을 펼치고 다리를 제자리에 고정하세요. 그 다음, 책상판을 프레임에 맞추고, 나사 구멍이 일치하도록 놓으세요. 상판이 꽤 크기 때문에, 이 부분은 누군가에게 도움을 받으시는 것도 고려해 보세요.

어휘 tutorial 사용 지침서   set up 설치하다   straightforward 간단한   screw 나사   ensure 확실히 하다   unfold 펼치다   secure 고정하다   in place 제자리에   align 정렬하다

28
이 설명은 무엇에 관한 것인가?
(A) 자전거 설치 방법
(B) 책상 조립 방법
(C) 책장 설치 방법
(D) 정원 가꾸는 방법

해설 담화 시작 부분의 'welcome to this online tutorial, where I will show you how to set up your new home office desk, the DX200.'에서 책상을 조립하기 위한 온라인 사용 지침서라고 이야기를 했으므로 (B)가 정답이다.

29

청자들은 어떻게 필요한 도구들을 구할 수 있는가?

(A) 근처 가게를 방문하면 된다.

(B) 어느 슈퍼마켓에서나 구매할 수 있다.

(C) 온라인으로 구매할 수 있다.

(D) 포장된 상자 안에서 찾을 수 있다.

해설 담화 중반부 'You'll find all the necessary screws and a screwdriver included in the package.'에서 필요한 나사와 드라이버는 패키지에 포함되어 있다고 했으므로 (D)가 정답이다.

30

어떤 활동에 도움이 필요할 수 있는가?

(A) 높이 조정하기

(B) 부품 정렬하기

(C) 케이블 부착하기

(D) 프레임 놓기

해설 질문 속 help가 키워드이므로 도움을 요청하는 부분에서 정답을 찾아야 한다. 담화 마지막 부분의 'It's quite big, so consider getting someone to help you with this part.'에서 그것이 크기 때문에 도움을 받을 것을 고려해 보라고 했으므로, 바로 앞 문장에서 무엇이 큰지를 확인해야 한다. 바로 앞 문장 'align the desktop with the frame'에서 상판을 프레임에 맞추라고 했고, 그것이 크다고 했으므로 (B)가 정답이된다.

[31-33]

M Hello, Debbie. 31) **This is Sam Bean from Bean's Coffee Shop**. I am truly sorry, but one of our trainees made a mistake on the order form she faxed to you this afternoon. 32) **We actually need thirty cheese scones** since tomorrow is Saturday. Hopefully, you get this message before you send us our order tomorrow. Another thing. 33) **I'm sure I ordered five pieces of chocolate fudge yesterday, but we didn't get any when I checked the delivery this morning. Please check the purchase order and call me. Thanks.**

M 안녕하세요, 데비. 저는 빈스 커피숍의 샘 빈입니다. 정말 죄송합니다만, 저희 수습 직원들 중 한 명이 오늘 오후 귀하께 팩스로 보내 드린 주문서에 실수를 범했습니다. 내일은 토요일이기 때문에 저희는 사실 30개의 치즈 스콘이 필요합니다. 내일 주문품을 보내시기 전에 이 메시지를 받으셨으면 좋겠습니다. 다른 하나는, 어제 분명히 초콜릿 퍼지 다섯 조각을 주문했는데, 오늘 아침에 배달을 확인했을 때 하나도 받지 못했습니다. 구매 주문을 확인해 주시고 전화해 주세요. 감사합니다.

어휘 trainee 수습 직원 fudge 퍼지(설탕, 버터, 우유로 만든 캔디) delivery 배송

31

화자는 어디에서 일하는 것 같은가?

(A) 제과점에서

(B) 식당에서

(C) 구내 식당에서

(D) 카페에서

해설 담화 초반 'This is Sam Bean from Bean's Coffee Shop.'에서 커피숍에서 전화를 걸었다고 했으므로 정답은 (D)이다.

주문 양식

음식 아이템	수량
초콜릿 퍼지	5
치즈 스콘	10
베이글	30
블루베리 머핀	20

32

시각 정보를 보시오. 화자는 어떤 숫자를 변경하고 싶어 하는가?

(A) 5

(B) 10

(C) 30

(D) 20

해설 담화 중반 'We actually need thirty cheese scones.'에서 치즈 스콘의 숫자가 잘못 되었다고 했으므로 정답은 (B)이다.

33

화자는 왜 여자에게 전화를 걸어 달라고 요청하는가?

(A) 다음 주를 위한 주문을 미리 하기 위해

(B) 개인적으로 사과하기 위해

(C) 다른 주문을 확인하기 위해

(D) 새로운 식품을 요청하기 위해

해설 담화 후반부의 'I'm sure I ordered five pieces of chocolate fudge yesterday, but we didn't get any when I checked the delivery this morning. Please check the purchase order and call me.'에서 배송이 오지 않은 주문에 대해 질문한 다음, 구매 주문을 확인하고 나서 연락을 달라고 했으므로 정답은 (C)이다.

DAY 12 **PARTS 3·4 의도 파악 문제 풀이법**

🔖 실전 문제 연습
p.114

🎧 12-05

1 (C)	2 (A)	3 (B)	4 (A)
5 (C)	6 (A)	7 (B)	8 (B)
9 (C)	10 (A)	11 (B)	12 (A)

13 (B)	14 (A)	15 (A)	16 (C)
17 (A)	18 (A)	19 (A)	20 (B)
21 (A)	22 (C)	23 (A)	24 (B)
25 (B)	26 (C)	27 (B)	28 (A)
29 (C)	30 (B)	31 (D)	32 (B)
33 (B)			

PART 1

1

(A) A lamp is being turned on.

(B) A bed is being made.

(C) A box of tissues is on the table.

(D) A plant is on the ledge.

(A) 램프가 켜지고 있는 중이다.
(B) 침대가 정리되고 있는 중이다.
(C) 티슈 한 상자가 테이블 위에 있다.
(D) 식물이 창틀에 놓여있다.

어휘 make a bed 침대를 정리하다   ledge 창틀

해설 사진에 사람의 모습이나 동작은 보이지 않는다. (A)는 being이 포함된 동작을 묘사하는 문장이므로 오답이다. (B) 역시 침대를 정리하는 모습이 아니라 이미 정리되어 있으므로 소거한다. 식물이 놓여 있는 곳은 창틀이 아니라 침대의 헤드보드 위이므로 (D)도 오답이다. 따라서, 테이블 위에 티슈가 놓여 있는 모습을 정확하게 묘사한 (C)가 정답이 된다.

2

(A) The woman is resting her arm on the desk.

(B) The woman is drinking some coffee.

(C) The shelves are full of books.

(D) The woman is writing something on a notepad.

(A) 여자는 책상 위에 팔을 놓아두었다.
(B) 여자는 커피를 마시는 중이다.
(C) 선반들은 책들로 가득 하다.
(D) 여자는 메모장에 무엇인가를 쓰고 있는 중이다.

어휘 rest 쉬다; 놓아두다; 놓여있다   be full of 가득하다

해설 컴퓨터 앞에 앉아 한 손은 올리고 한 손은 책상 위에 올려둔 모습이다. 따라서, 한 팔을 책상 위에 둔 모습을 묘사한 (A)가 정답이다. 커피가 옆에 놓여 있기는 하지만 마시고 있지는 않으므로 (B)는 오답이다. 책장에 책이 있기는 하지만 가득하지는 않으므로 (C) 역시 오답이다. 여자 옆에 메모장이 있기는 하지만 필기를 하거나 사용하고 있지는 않으므로 (D)역시 정답이 될 수 없다.

3

(A) Cars are moving in both directions.

(B) The road has some painted lines.

(C) Some people are standing near the curb.

(D) Vehicles are parked next to the sidewalk.

(A) 차들이 양방향으로 움직이고 있다.
(B) 길에 페인트칠이 된 선들이 있다.
(C) 사람들이 연석 근처에 서있다.
(D) 탈것들이 인도 옆에 세워져 있다.

어휘 curb 연석   sidewalk 인도

해설 사람들이 길을 건너고 차들은 횡단보도 앞에 멈춰 있는 모습이다. 차들은 한 방향으로 서 있고 움직이는 모습도 아니므로 (A)는 정답이 아니다. 도로에 횡단보도가 페인트칠 된 선으로 구성되어 있으므로 (B)가 그림을 정확하게 묘사한 보기이다. 사람들은 길을 건너고 있고 서있는 사람들이 보이지 않으므로 (C)도 오답이다. 차들이 잠시 횡단보도 앞에 서 있기는 하지만, 인도 옆에 주차한 모습은 아니기 때문에 (D) 역시 정답이 될 수 없다.

PART 2

4

Haven't the cartridges arrived yet?

(A) We just ordered them this morning.

(B) We need one more printer.

(C) Through the Internet.

카트리지는 아직 도착하지 않았나요?
(A) 우리는 그것을 오늘 아침에 막 주문했어요.
(B) 우리는 프린터가 한 대 더 필요해요.
(C) 인터넷으로요.

어휘 cartridge 카트리지

해설 카트리지의 도착 여부를 묻는 질문에 대해 오늘 아침에 주문했다고 말하는 것은 주문한지 얼마 되지 않았으므로 도착하지 않는 것이 당연하다는 의미이다. 따라서, (A)가 정답이다. 카트리지에서 연상되는 프린터를 언급한 (B)는 오답이다. (C) 역시 도착 여부를 판단할 수는 없는 오답 유형이다. 이는 물건의 도착 여부를 묻는 질문을 듣고 어디에서 구입했는지를 연상하도록 한 오답이다.

5

Do you think this pink shirt looks good on me?

(A) Pink, red, and yellow.

(B) I think he is.

(C) Why don't you try on the green one?

당신이 생각하기에 이 분홍 셔츠가 저에게 어울리나요?
(A) 분홍, 빨강, 그리고 노랑요.
(B) 제 생각에는 그가 그래요.
(C) 저 초록색을 입어 보시는 게 어때요?

어휘 look good on 어울리다

해설 색깔이 어울리는지 묻는 질문에 대해 초록색을 입어 보는 게 어떤지 제안하는 (C)는 잘 어울리지 않는다는 것을 간접적으로 표현한 정답이다. 색상만 나열한 (A)는 어울리는지 여부를 알려 주지 못하는 오답이다. (B)와 같이 he로 대답하기 위해서는 질문에 he가 가리키는 사람이 있어야만 한다.

6

This coat is expensive.
(A) It is made of good fabric.
(B) Yes, we have to expand it.
(C) At the store downtown.

이 코트는 비싸요.
(A) 이것은 좋은 천으로 만들어졌어요.
(B) 네, 우리는 그것을 확장해야 해요.
(C) 시내에 있는 상점에서요.

어휘 made of ~로 만들어지다   expand 확장하다

해설 코트의 가격이 비싸다는 의견에 대해 좋은 천으로 만들어졌기 때문이라고 이유를 설명하는 (A)가 적절한 정답이 된다. (B)는 expensive와 발음이 비슷한 expand를 이용한 오답이다. 코트를 구입한 장소를 언급한 (C) 역시 오답이다.

7

Would you like to enter the art competition?
(A) It's compatible with this computer.
(B) Do you think I have a chance to win?
(C) He is a renowned artist.

당신은 미술 대회에 지원하기를 원하나요?
(A) 그것은 이 컴퓨터와 호환돼요.
(B) 제가 수상할 가능성이 있다고 생각하세요?
(C) 그는 유명한 예술가예요.

어휘 competition 대회   compatible 호환 가능한

해설 미술 대회 참가를 원하는지 묻는 질문에 대해 (B)와 같이 상을 받을 가능성이 있는지 묻는 것은 참가해도 될지 가능성을 묻는 대답이다. (A)의 compatible은 competition과 음절이 겹치는 발음을 이용한 오답이다. (C)의 artist는 질문의 art를 반복한 오답 유형이다.

8

You still have last month's sales report, right?
(A) The sale will end this weekend.
(B) Oh, Abigail was in charge of it.
(C) It lasts for an hour.

지난달의 판매 보고서를 아직 가지고 계시죠, 그렇죠?
(A) 그 할인은 이번 주말에 끝날 거예요.
(B) 오, 아비가일이 그것을 담당했어요.
(C) 그것은 한 시간 동안 지속돼요.

어휘 sales report 판매 보고서   last 지속되다

해설 판매 보고서를 가지고 있는지 묻는 질문에 대해 아비가일이 담당자였다고 말하면서 그녀에게 물어볼 것을 의미하는 (B)가 정답이다. (A)는 판매라는 의미인 sales와 발음이 유사한 할인이라는 의미인 sale을 이용한 오답이다. (C)는 문제의 last와 발음이 동일한 동사 last를 이용한 오답이다.

9

How did the interview for your new job go?
(A) I love the view.
(B) As an accountant.
(C) I got an offer.

새로운 일자리를 위한 면접은 어떻게 되었어요?
(A) 저는 그 뷰가 좋아요.
(B) 회계사로요.
(C) 저는 그 일을 제안받았어요.

해설 go는 뒤에 장소가 오는 경우 '가다'라는 의미이지만, 사물 주어와 함께 사용되어 뒤에 장소가 없으면 '되다'라는 의미이다. 따라서, 질문은 면접에 어떻게 갔는지를 묻는 질문이 아니라 면접은 어떻게 됐는지를 묻는 질문이다. (C)의 '내가 제안을 받았다'는 것은 면접을 통과했음을 의미하는 것이므로 가장 좋은 대답이다. (A)의 view는 interview와 음절이 겹치는 것을 이용한 오답이다. 질문의 interview에서 연상되는 직업을 언급한 (B) 역시 정답이 될 수 없다.

10

Clients from Italy are coming this afternoon.
(A) Do you have time to pick them up?
(B) I've never been to Rome.
(C) Yes, I signed the contract.

이탈리아에서 오는 고객들은 오늘 오후에 오실 거예요.
(A) 그분들을 태우고 올 시간이 있으세요?
(B) 저는 로마에 한 번도 가보지 못했어요.
(C) 네, 저는 계약서에 사인을 했어요.

어휘 pick up (사람을) 태워 오다   contract 계약서

해설 손님들이 온다는 정보에 대해 그들을 태워 올 수 있는 시간이 있는지 여부를 묻는 (A)가 정답이 된다. 이탈리아에서 연상되는 로마가 언급된 (B)는 연상의 오답이며, 시제도 일치하지 않는다. 고객과 주로 하는 업무가 계약을 하는 일이므로, (C)는 contract를 이용한 오답이다. 의미상으로도 고객이 오는 것과 전혀 상관이 없는 내용이다.

11

Let's have a conference call after lunch.
(A) Call him whenever you have time.
(B) I'm flying to New York this afternoon.
(C) Dinner will be served.

점심 시간 이후 전화 회의를 진행해요.
(A) 시간 있을 때 언제든지 그에게 전화하세요.
(B) 저는 오늘 오후에 뉴욕으로 비행기를 타고 가요.
(C) 저녁 식사가 제공될 거예요.

어휘 conference call 전화 회의   fly 날다; 비행기를 타고 가다

해설 회의를 진행하자는 제안에 대해 오후에 시간이 없어서 참여할 수 없다는 것을 간접적으로 전달하는 (B)가 정답이다. 질문의 conference call을 듣고 '전화를 하라'는 내용의 (A)를 정답으로 고르는 실수를 해서는 안 된다. (C)는 lunch에서 연상되는 단어인 dinner를 이용한 오답이다.

12

Should I go to the print shop now, or can I wait until tomorrow?

(A) It's already closed.

(B) Some brochures.

(C) I always shop there.

지금 인쇄소에 가야 할까요, 아니면 내일까지 기다려도 될까요?

(A) 그곳은 이미 영업이 끝났어요.

(B) 소책자들요.

(C) 저는 항상 그곳에서 쇼핑을 해요.

어휘 print shop 인쇄소   brochure 소책자

해설 인쇄소에 지금 가야 하는지 여부를 묻는 질문에 대해 이미 문을 닫았으므로 지금 갈 수 없다는 의미의 답변인 (A)가 정답이다. 인쇄소에서 연상되는 '소책자(brochure)'가 언급된 (B)는 오답이며, (C)는 print shop에서 shop이라는 단어만 반복한 오답이다.

13

Is there a list of attendees who sent responses?

(A) There is a great pond next to the library.

(B) The planner has all the necessary information.

(C) A grand ballroom at the Cima Hotel.

답신을 보낸 참석자들의 명단이 있나요?

(A) 도서관 옆에 멋진 연못이 있어요.

(B) 계획자가 모든 필요한 정보를 가지고 있어요.

(C) 시마 호텔의 그랜드 볼룸요.

어휘 attendee 참석자   pond 연못

해설 참석자의 명단이 있는지를 묻는 질문에 대해 계획자가 모든 정보를 가지고 있다고 대답하면서 그 사람에게 물어보라는 의미의 (B)가 가장 적절한 대답이다. (A)는 response와 음절이 겹치는 pond를 이용한 오답이다. 행사가 자주 열리는 장소인 볼룸을 언급한 (C) 또한 오답이다. 참석자 명단이 호텔의 그랜드 볼룸에 있다고 착각할 수도 있지만 그랜드 볼룸은 행사가 열리는 장소이지 명단이 있는 장소라고 보기 어렵다. 뿐만 아니라 전치사 없이 '그랜드 볼룸(a grand ballroom)'이라는 명사만 주어져 있으므로 문법적으로도 정답이 될 수 없다.

14

Why don't you use overnight delivery?

(A) Overnight delivery is more expensive.

(B) Because we didn't get the delivery yet.

(C) I'll send it to you.

익일 배송을 이용하는 게 어때요?

(A) 익일 배송은 더 비싸요.

(B) 우리는 그 배송을 아직 받지 못했기 때문이에요.

(C) 제가 그것을 당신에게 보낼게요.

어휘 overnight delivery 익일 배송

해설 익일 배송을 이용하라는 제안에 대해 그것이 더 비싸다고 답한 것은 사용하지 않겠다는 의미일 것이므로 (A)는 적절한 대답이다. 'Why don't you ~'는 대부분의 경우 제안하는 의미이므로 (B)와 같이 because로 답한 선택지는 정답이 될 가능성이 매우 낮다. 내가 보내겠다고 답한 (C)는 익일 배송을 이용할 것인지에 대한 답변이 될 수 없다.

15

How do I turn on the heater?

(A) The temperature is automatically controlled.

(B) Turn right at the corner.

(C) No, I didn't turn on the heater.

히터를 어떻게 켜야 하나요?

(A) 온도가 자동으로 조절돼요.

(B) 코너에서 오른쪽으로 도세요.

(C) 아니요, 저는 히터를 틀지 않았어요.

어휘 heater 히터   automatically 자동으로

해설 히터를 트는 방법을 묻는다는 것은 춥다는 것을 간접적으로 의미한다. 따라서, 온도가 자동으로 조절이 되므로 히터를 틀 필요가 없다는 의미의 (A)가 가장 적절한 대답이다. 질문의 'turn on'에서 turn을 반복하여 혼동을 유발한 (B)는 오답이다. 의문사 의문문에 yes와 no로 답할 수 없으므로 (C) 또한 오답이다.

16

Can you tell me how to use the new time-reporting software?

(A) I can't tell you why.

(B) Yes, I bought some new kitchenware.

(C) Sorry. I couldn't attend the training session.

새로운 근무 시간 보고 소프트웨어를 어떻게 사용하는지 알려 줄 수 있나요?

(A) 저는 이유를 말할 수 없어요.

(B) 네, 저는 새로운 식기를 구입했어요.

(C) 죄송해요. 저는 교육에 참여하지 않았어요.

어휘 time-reporting 시간 보고 (근무 시간에 대한 보고) kitchenware 식기

해설 소프트웨어 사용법을 알려달라는 요청에 대해 교육을 받지 않아서 잘 모른다는 의미로 답한 (C)가 가장 적절한 대답이다. (A)의 경우 방법을 묻는 질문에 이유를 말할 수 없다는 답변은 어울리지 않는다. software와 kitchenware는 ware 부분이 겹치는데, 이 부분의 발음이 같다는 점을 이용한 (B) 역시 오답이다.

17

We're meeting at 2:00 to negotiate the contract.

(A) Yes, I noted it on the schedule.

(B) Contact him at his e-mail address.

(C) No, he's a lawyer.

우리는 계약을 협상하기 위해 2시에 만날 거예요.

(A) 네, 일정표에 그렇게 적어 두었어요.

(B) 그의 이메일 주소로 연락해보세요.

(C) 아니요, 그는 변호사예요.

어휘 negotiate 협상하다   note 적다

회의 시간을 알려주자 '일정표에 기록해 두었다'고 말하며 '이미 알고 있다'는 의미로 답한 (A)가 정답이다. (B)의 contact는 contract와 발음이 유사한 오답으로 많이 출제된다. 또한, 질문에서 사람이 언급되지 않았으므로 his e-mail address와 같이 답할 수 없다. (C) 또한 (B)와 마찬가지로 질문에서 지칭하는 사람이 없는데 he로 답했으므로 정답이 될 수 없다. (C)는 contract(계약서)에서 연상되는 lawyer(변호사)를 이용한 오답이기도 하다.

18

The design team needs more workers.

(A) They've worked overtime since last month.

(B) Yes, he resigned last year.

(C) We have a team meeting this afternoon.

디자인 팀에는 직원이 더 필요해요.

(A) 그들은 지난달부터 계속 초과 근무 중이에요.

(B) 네, 그는 작년에 사임했어요.

(C) 우리는 오늘 오후에 팀 회의를 해요.

어휘 work overtime 초과 근무하다　resign 사임하다

해설 디자인 팀에 직원이 더 필요하다고 언급하자 그들이 계속해서 초과 근무를 하고 있다고 말하며 직원이 더 필요하다는 의견에 동의하는 (A)가 가장 적절한 대답이다. (B)는 design과 발음이 유사한 resign을 이용한 오답이다. sign도 design과 resign의 유사 발음 오답으로 많이 사용된다. (C)는 team을 반복한 오답인데, '오늘 오후에 회의를 해서 결정하겠구나'라고 확대 해석을 해서는 안 된다. (C)는 팀 회의가 있다는 사실만을 전달하는 문장이다.

PART 3

[19-21]

> M　Hello, Michelle. 19) **We're making a video manual about operating cutting machines** this coming weekend to show them to our new staff. 20) **You're the most experienced supervisor, so I'd like you to play a main role in this video.**
>
> W　Of course. I'd be glad to help you. But I wonder if you can give me any directions or materials to refer to.
>
> M　Don't worry. This is a written manual that you can use. You can just explain all the details here.
> 21) **You'd better review it and give me feedback tomorrow.**
>
> M　안녕하세요, 미셸. 우리가 이번 주말에 새로운 직원들에게 보여주기 위해 새 절단 기계의 사용법에 대한 비디오 매뉴얼을 제작하려고 해요. 당신이 가장 경험이 많은 관리자이므로 당신이 이 비디오에서 중요한 역할을 담당했으면 좋겠어요.
>
> W　물론이죠. 제가 도움이 된다면 좋겠네요. 그런데 혹시 참고할 만한 지시 사항이나 자료를 받을 수 있을지 궁금하네요.

> M　걱정 마세요. 여기 당신이 사용할 문서 매뉴얼이 있어요. 거기에 있는 모든 세부 사항들을 설명해 주시기만 하면 돼요. 한번 훑어보고 내일 저한테 피드백을 주세요.

어휘 play a role in ~에서 역할을 하다　refer 참고하다　details 세부사항　feedback 피드백

19

남자는 무엇을 준비하는가?

(A) 비디오 매뉴얼

(B) 기기 배송

(C) 새로운 영화

(D) 텔레비전 쇼

해설 대화 초반부의 'We're making a video manual about operating cutting machines'에서 기계 사용법에 관한 비디오 매뉴얼을 제작한다고 했으므로 정답은 (A)이다.

20

남자는 왜 "당신이 가장 경험이 많은 관리자이다"라고 말하는가?

(A) 실수를 수정하기 위해

(B) 도움을 요청하기 위해

(C) 승진시키기 위해

(D) 여자의 의견을 지지하기 위해

해설 대화에서 당신이 가장 경험 많은 관리자이므로 비디오에서 중요한 역할을 맡아 달라는 부탁을 하고 있으므로, 여자에게 도움을 요청한다는 (B)가 정답이다. (A)가 정답이 되기 위해서는 앞이나 뒤에 실수에 대한 내용이 있어야 하고, (C)가 정답이 되려면 되기 위해서는 승진(promotion)에 대한 대화가 이어져야 한다. 또한, (D)가 정답이 되기 위해서는 인용된 대화 앞에 여자의 의견이 언급되어야 한다.

21

남자는 여자에게 내일 무엇을 하라고 요청하는가?

(A) 의견을 제시하기

(B) 새 매뉴얼을 작성하기

(C) 회신 전화하기

(D) 남자의 사무실에 방문하기

해설 남자의 마지막 말 'You'd better review it and give me feedback tomorrow.'에서 남자는 여자에게 검토한 다음 내일 피드백을 달라고 했다. 따라서 feedback을 opinion으로 바꾼 (A)가 정답이다.

[22-24]

> W　22-1) **Did you see the *Boston Daily* this morning? 23) Our restaurant got a five-star rating in the local restaurant section!**
>
> M　What? That's excellent news. 22-2) **Did the food critic comment on any of the dishes in particular? What was his favorite dish?**

W Let me think… I think the writer recommended every entrée on our menu, but he especially praised our steak and shrimp scampi. I'm going out to grab some more copies of the paper.

M You probably have to wait until this afternoon. People will be here for lunch any moment now. 24) **And I bet we'll have a lot more people in today because of this amazing review.** This is very exciting news for our business!

W 오늘 아침 *보스턴 데일리* 보셨어요? 우리 식당이 지역 레스토랑 섹션에서 별 5개를 받았어요!

M 뭐라고요? 멋진 소식이네요. 음식 평론가가 특정 요리에 대해 언급했어요? 제일 마음에 들었던 음식은 뭐였대요?

W 잠깐 생각해볼게요… 아, 평론가는 우리 메뉴에 있는 모든 메인 요리를 추천한다고 했지만, 특히 우리 연어 스테이크와 새우 튀김에 대해 극찬했어요. 나가서 신문을 더 사 올게요.

M 아마도 오늘 오후까지 기다려야 할 거예요. 언제든지 점심을 먹으러 사람들이 올 거예요. 그리고 좋은 평가 덕분에 아마 오늘은 더 많은 사람들이 오겠군요. 우리 영업을 위해서 정말 흥미로운 소식이네요!

어휘 food critic 음식 평론가 entrée 앙뜨레, 메인 요리 scampi 새우튀김

22

대화의 주제는 무엇인가?
(A) 점심 메뉴
(B) 새로운 편집자
(C) 신문 기사
(D) 유명 작가

해설 대화의 첫 부분에서 여자는 'Did you see the *Boston Daily* this morning?'이라고 언급해서 신문 기사에 대해 언급했고, 남자 또한 'Did the food critic comment on any of the dishes in particular? What was his favorite dish?'라며 신문 기사에 대해 이야기하고 있다. 따라서, 정답은 (C)이다.

23

화자들은 어떤 종류의 업체에서 일하는가?
(A) 음식점
(B) 식료품점
(C) 신문사
(D) 도서관

해설 업종을 묻는 문제의 단서는 대화 초반에서 찾아야 한다. 여자의 대화 'Our restaurant got a five-star rating in the local restaurant section!'에서 화자들이 식당에서 일한다는 것을 알 수 있다. 따라서, 정답은 (A)이다.

24

남자에 의하면, 오늘 어떤 일이 있을 것인가?
(A) 더 많은 의자를 주문할 것이다.
(B) 평소보다 더 많은 손님이 올 것이다.
(C) 식당에 좋은 소식이 있을 것이다.
(D) 기념 행사가 있을 것이다.

해설 일어날 일을 묻는 문제이므로 대화의 마지막 부분에 집중한다. 남자의 마지막 대화 'And I bet we'll have a lot more people in today because of this amazing review.'에서 좋은 평가 덕분에 훨씬 더 많은 사람들이 올 것이라고 했으므로 정답은 (B)이다.

[25-27]

W Hi. 25) **I'm calling to inquire about the annual street cleaning schedule.** 26) **My shop is on Folsom Avenue, and I was wondering when the work for my street is scheduled.**

M Let me check on that for you…. Folsom Avenue is scheduled for cleaning next Friday. 27) **The work will likely start at 9:00 A.M. and end by 5:00 P.M**. It lasts about 8 hours. However, we will be closing the street only to vehicles.

W That's a relief! Then people can walk on the road.

M Of course. You don't need to worry about opening the store.

W 안녕하세요. 저는 연례 거리 청소 일정에 대해서 문의하려고 전화했어요. 저희 가게는 폴섬 가에 있는데, 언제 저희 거리에서의 작업은 언제로 예정되어 있는지 궁금해서요.

M 확인해 볼게요… 폴섬 가는 다음 주 금요일에 청소가 계획되어 있습니다. 작업은 9시에 시작해서 5시에 끝날 것입니다. 8시간 동안 지속될 것입니다. 하지만, 차량들만 통제할 예정입니다.

W 다행이군요! 그러면 사람들은 그 길을 걸어 다닐 수 있겠군요.

M 물론입니다. 가게 문을 여는 것에 대해 고민하지 않으셔도 됩니다.

어휘 inquire 문의하다 annual 해마다의 relief 안도, 안심

25

여자는 왜 전화를 걸었는가?
(A) 약속을 변경하기 위해
(B) 일정을 확인하기 위해
(C) 요청서를 제출하기 위해
(D) 길 안내를 제공하기 위해

해설 여자의 첫 번째 대화 'I'm calling to inquire about the annual street cleaning schedule.'에서 여자는 청소 작업 일정을 확인하기 위해 전화했다는 것을 알 수 있다. 따라서, 정답은 (B)이다.

26

시각 정보를 보시오. 여자는 어떤 업체에서 전화를 걸고 있는가?

(A) ABC 마켓
(B) 뷰 살롱
(C) 바질 가든
(D) 팀스 커피

해설 여자가 어떤 업체에서 전화를 걸고 있는지 묻고 있으므로, 여자의 직업을 묻는 질문과 동일한 문제이다. 지도가 주어지는 경우에는 도로명에 집중하며 들어야 하는데, 'My shop is on Folsom Avenue, and I was wondering when the work for my street is scheduled.'에서 여자의 가게가 폴섬 가에 있다고 했으므로 (C)가 정답이 된다.

27

언제 작업이 시작될 것인가?

(A) 오전 9시 30분에
(B) 오전 9시에
(C) 오후 5시에
(D) 오후 7시에

해설 'The work will likely start at 9:00 A.M. and end by 5:00 P.M.'에서 오전 9시에 작업이 시작되고 오후 5시에 끝난다고 했으므로 정답은 (B)이다.

PART 4

[28-30]

W   **28) In today's news, the city nature preservation committee is finally reopening the newly renovated wildlife preservation center this Friday.** The center was first opened to protect and assist endangered species in Wellington City during the late 1980s. When it opened, there were only 20 species protected, but **29-1) now there are over 100 species in the center.** **29-2) The 50-year-old building has been entirely renovated to accommodate more wildlife species and to provide them with the best conditions.** **30) Beginning at 5:00 P.M. on Friday, a free guided tour will be given for everyone who visits the new center.** Anyone interested is more than welcome to attend the event.

W   오늘 뉴스에 따르면, 이번 주 금요일에 시립 자연 보호 위원회에서 마침내 새롭게 건설된 야생동물 보호 센터를 재개장합니다. 이 센터는 웰링턴 시에서 1980년대 후반에 멸종 위기의 종들을 돕고 보호하기 위해 처음으로 개관했습니다. 처음 개관했을 때, 보호되는 종은 단지 20종이었습니다만, 현재 센터에는 100종 이상이 있습니다. 이 50년 된 건물은 더 많은 동물을 수용하고 그들에게 최고의 환경을 제공하기 위해 완전히 개보수되었습니다. 금요일 오후 5시부터, 새로운 센터를 방문하는 모든 분들에게 무료 가이드 투어가 제공됩니다. 관심 있는 모든 분들께서 이 이벤트에 함께 하실 것을 환영합니다.

어휘 reopen 재재장하다   wildlife 야생동물   preservation 보존   protect 보호하다   assist 돕다   endangered 멸종위기의   species 종

28

화자는 무엇에 대해 이야기하는가?

(A) 새롭게 재개장된 건물
(B) 신임 이사
(C) 새로운 도시 계획
(D) 새로운 연구 결과

해설 주제를 묻는 문제는 담화의 초반에 단서가 주어지는데, 특히 뉴스의 경우 첫 번째 문장을 잘 들어야 한다. 첫 문장 'In today's news, the city nature preservation committee is finally reopening the newly renovated wildlife preservation center this Friday.'에서 건물의 재개장을 이야기하고 있으므로 정답은 (A)이다.

29

화자가 "현재 센터에는 100종 이상이 있습니다"라고 말할 때 여자는 무엇을 암시하는가?

(A) 시스템이 구식이었다.
(B) 사무실에 인력이 더 필요하다.
(C) 공간이 충분히 넓지 않았다.
(D) 예산이 증가되어야 한다.

해설 인용된 문장 바로 앞에서 이전에는 20종이었던 것이 100종 이상으로 늘었다고 하면서, 'The 50-year-old building has been entirely renovated to accommodate more wildlife species and to provide them with the best conditions.'라고 했다. 따라서 더 큰 공간을 확보하기 위해 개보수 공사를 진행했다고 했으므로, 공간이 부족했다는 것을 알 수 있다. 정답은 (C)이다.

30

화자에 따르면, 금요일에는 무엇이 제공될 것인가?

(A) 연회
(B) 무료 가이드 투어
(C) 컴퓨터 워크숍
(D) 무료 콘서트 티켓

해설 금요일이 언급된 'Beginning at 5:00 P.M. on Friday, a free guided tour will be given for everyone who visits the new center.'에서 금요일부터 무료 가이드 투어를 제공한다고 했으므로 정답은 (B)이다.

M Attention, team members! You've already seen last quarter's sales data. Sales have been excellent this quarter, and customers seem very happy with our line of cellular phones. **31) In addition, the survey we did last week shows** that **32) they're pleased with our 2-year warranty promotion, so sales were double that particular month compared to the previous month.** As you all know, we launched our first foldable smartphone, the Xee 7, which is selling well, but our competitor KN Mobile also introduced a similar model, so we have to put more effort into advertising. **33) Let's discuss some effective ways to market this product.**

M 팀원 여러분, 주목하세요! 이미 지난 분기의 매출 자료를 보셨습니다. 이번 분기 매출이 매우 좋았고, 고객들은 우리의 휴대폰 제품군에 매우 만족하는 것 같습니다. 또한, 지난주에 실시한 설문 조사에서 우리의 2년 보증 프로모션에 만족하는 것으로 나타났기 때문에, 해당 달의 매출이 전월에 비해 두 배로 증가했습니다. 여러분들도 아시다시피, 우리는 첫 번째 폴더블 스마트폰인 Xee 7을 출시했고, 이는 매우 잘 팔리고 있습니다만 경쟁사인 KN모바일도 비슷한 모델을 출시했으므로, 홍보에 더 힘써야 할 것 같습니다. 이 제품을 효과적으로 마케팅하는 방법에 대해 논의해 봅시다.

어휘 quarter 분기 survey 설문 조사 warranty 보증 launch 출시하다 competitor 경쟁자 effective 효과적인

31

지난주에는 무슨 일이 있었는가?
(A) 업체는 할인을 제공했다.
(B) 업체는 무료 선물을 주었다.
(C) 업체는 새로운 핸드폰을 출시했다.
(D) 업체는 설문 조사를 했다.

해설 시간이 언급된 문제의 경우 시간 표현이 들린 부분에서 정답을 찾아야한다. 'the survey we did last week shows'에서 지난주에 진행한 설문 조사에 대해 이야기하고 있으므로 정답은 (D)이다.

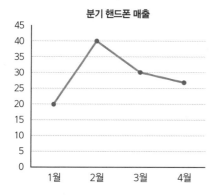

분기 핸드폰 매출

32

시각 정보를 보시오. 할인은 언제 있었는가?
(A) 1월
(B) 2월
(C) 3월
(D) 4월

해설 'they're pleased with our 2-year warranty promotion, so sales were double that particular month compared to the previous month'에서 보증 기간을 늘려주는 판촉 행사 기간에 그 전달보다 2배의 판매 증가가 있었다고 했다. 따라서 정답은 2배로 상승한 달인 (B)의 2월이다.

33

청자들은 다음에 무엇을 논의할 것인가?
(A) 프로젝트의 스케줄
(B) 마케팅 계획
(C) 상품 디자인
(D) 고객 설문

해설 다음에 이야기할 내용은 주로 담화 마지막 부분에서 등장한다. 담화 마지막 'Let's discuss some effective ways to market this product.'에서 상품을 마케팅할 방법을 이야기하자고 했으므로 정답은 (B)이다.

Reading
Comprehension

DAY 01 동사와 문장의 구조

PRACTICE
pp.120-123

1 My new computer is very expensive, but its performance is great.

2 There is a high demand for electric cars nowadays because the price of gas has been increasing continuously.

3 3형식	4 3형식	5 5형식
6 risen	7 addition	8 address
9 join		

1 나의 새로운 컴퓨터가 비싸기는 하지만, 성능은 만족스럽다.

2 휘발유 가격이 계속해서 상승하고 있기 때문에 요즘은 전기차에 대한 수요가 높다.

3 우리 호텔은 현재 접수 담당자를 고용 중입니다.

4 이 쿠폰은 샐러드바 무료 이용권을 포함하고 있습니다.

5 그레이 씨는 수정된 재무 보고서가 훨씬 상세하다는 것을 알게 되었다.

6 KMC 보험의 주식은 꾸준히 상승했다.

7 클라인 씨는 경영팀에 소중한 신입이 될 것이다.

8 기술자들이 고장을 처리할 것으로 기대된다.

9 오늘 멤버십 클럽에 등록하면, 10% 할인을 받을 수 있습니다.

실전 문제 연습
p.125

1 (B)	2 (C)	3 (A)	4 (B)
5 (B)	6 (D)	7 (D)	8 (A)
9 (B)	10 (B)	11 (C)	12 (C)
13 (D)	14 (D)	15 (A)	16 (C)
17 (B)	18 (D)	19 (C)	20 (B)
21 (D)	22 (C)	23 (D)	24 (B)
25 (D)	26 (D)	27 (C)	28 (D)
29 (B)	30 (C)		

PART 5

1

강연장에 입장할 때 참석자들은 유효한 신분증을 소지하고 있어야 한다.

어휘 attendee 참석자 valid 근거가 확실한; 유효한 identification 신분 증명, 신원 확인; 신분증 lecture 강의, 강연

해설 빈칸은 동사 should have앞의 주어 자리이다. 주어 자리에 올 수 있는 것은 명사, 명사구, 명사절 등이므로 정답은 명사인 (B) Attendees(참석자들)이다. 동명사인 (A) Attending은 주어 자리에 올 수 있지만 뒤에 동명사의 목적어가 필요하므로 이는 오답이다.

2

고객 불만 사항을 효과적으로 해결하는 것은 우리 사업의 성공에 있어 결정적이다.

어휘 address 연설; 연설하다; 해결하다 consumer 소비자 critical 결정적인, 중대한

해설 동사 is 앞의 '------- customer complaints(고객 불만들)'이 문장의 주어 역할을 한다. 주어 자리에는 명사, 명사구, 명사절 등이 위치해야 하므로 보기 중 명사인 address(주소)나 addresses와 동명사인 addressing(해결하는 것)이 정답 후보가 된다. 하지만 명사인 address나 addresses는 빈칸 뒤 명사인 customer complaints와 연결되기 위해서는 전치사가 필요하므로 모두 오답이다. 동명사인 addressing은 customer complaints를 목적어로 취하여 '고객의 불만사항을 해결하는 것'이라고 해석되므로 정답은 (C) addressing이다.

3

새로운 마케팅 이사의 임명은 지난 월요일에 회사 소식지에 발표되었다.

어휘 appointment 약속, 임명

해설 문장의 주어는 'The appointment of the new marketing director'이며 문장에 동사가 보이지 않으므로 빈칸에는 동사가 와야 한다. 따라서 보기 중 유일한 동사인 (A) was announced가 정답이다. 동명사인 (B) having announced와 to부정사인 (C) to be announced는 동사 역할을 할 수 없다. 보기가 동사와 동사가 아닌 성분들로 구성되어 있다면 빈칸이 동사 자리인지 먼저 확인해야 한다. 모든 문장에는 꼭 동사가 필요하다는 것을 기억해 두자.

4

다음 주부터, 모든 사람들은 연구실에 접근하기 위해 새로운 보안카드를 사용해야 한다.

어휘 security 보안, 경비 laboratory 실험실

해설 문장에 동사 must be used가 이미 있고 접속사는 보이지 않으므로 빈칸에는 동사가 올 수 없다. 따라서 보기 중 동사인 (A) has gained, (C) was gained (D) is gaining은 모두 오답이다. 정답은 to부정사인 (B) to gain인데, 'to gain access'는 to부정사의 부사적 용법으로서 '접근하기 위해서'로 해석된다.

5

주간 현장 실습에 참여하기를 원하는 직원은 반드시 인사부장에게 신청서를 제출해야 한다.

어휘 join 참가하다 submit 제출하다 application 지원(서), 신청(서) Human Resources manager 인사부장

해설 문장의 주어는 any employee이고 동사는 must submit인데, 문장에 접속사가 없기 때문에 추가적인 동사는 필요하지 않다. 보기 중에서 (B) wishing을 제외한 모든 보기는 동사이므로 정답은 (B)이다. wishing은 앞에 있는 any employee를 수식하는 형용사 역할을 하는 현재분사로서 'any employee wishing to join'은 '참여하기를 바라는 모든 직원들'로 해석된다.

6

바튼 연구소에 따르면, 설문 조사는 이번 달 말까지 완료될 것으로 예상된다.

어휘 conclude 결론을 내리다; 끝나다

해설 주절 앞 명사구인 'the Barton Research Center'를 연결하기 위해서는 전치사가 필요하다. 보기 중에서 전치사는 (A) In case of(만일 ~한다면), (C) Prior to(~에 앞서), (D) According to(~에 따르면)인데 해석 상 가장 어울리는 전치사는 (D)이다.

7

그 회사는 시장에서의 입지를 강화하기 위해 공격적인 마케팅 캠페인을 펼치고 있다.

어휘 carry out 수행하다 aggressive 공격적인 presence 존재(함), 참석 reinforcement 강화 reinforce 강화하다, 보강하다

해설 문장에 동사인 is carrying이 있고 접속사는 보이지 않으므로 추가적인 동사는 필요하지 않다. 따라서 보기 중 동사인 (B) is reinforcing과 (C) has reinforced는 오답이다. 완전한 절 뒤에서 수식하는 역할을 하는 부사적 용법의 to부정사인 (D) to reinforce가 정답이다. 명사인 (A) reinforcement는 빈칸 앞뒤의 명사들과 전치사 없이 연결될 수 없으므로 정답이 될 수 없다.

8

클레이 브라운 감독이 영화 개봉일을 연말로 연기해 달라고 요청했다.

어휘 release date 출시일 postpone 연기하다, 미루다

해설 빈칸은 that절의 동사 자리이므로 보기 중 동사인 (A) postpone, (C) were postponing, (D) have postponed가 정답 후보이다. 정답은 (A) postpone인데, 동사 request(요청하다) 뒤 that절에서의 동사는 주어와 상관없이 동사 원형이어야 한다는 것을 꼭 기억해 두자.

9

직원들은 출장에서 돌아온 후 숙박비와 교통비 등의 영수증 원본을 제출해야 한다.

어휘 original 최초의, 근원의, 원래의 receipt 영수증 accommodations 숙박 시설 transportation 교통 수단 assignment 과제, 임무 booking 예약

해설 출장 후에 숙박 및 교통비 등의 '비용'에 대한 영수증을 제출해야 한다는 내용의 문장이므로 정답은 (B) expenses이다. (C) estimates (견적서)는 어떠한 활동을 하거나 서비스를 받기 전에 지불 금액을 산정하는 것이므로 출장 후에 제출하는 것으로는 적절하지 않다.

10

알비노 스토어즈 사는 시장 확장을 위한 투자로 성장 전략을 가속화하려고 한다.

어휘 reach (세력, 영향력 등의) 범위[권한]

해설 (B) accelerate는 속도나 비율을 가속화한다는 것을 의미하며, 문장의 의미는 시장 확장을 위한 투자를 통해 회사의 성장 전략을 더 빠르게 하려고 계획한다는 것이다. 따라서 (B)가 정답이다. (A) alleviate는 교통 체증과 같은 문제들을 완화할 때 사용되며, (C) anticipate는 예상하거나 기대한다는 의미이므로 문맥에 맞지 않다. (D) accumulate는 시간이 지나면서 무언가를 모은다는 의미이므로 역시 적절하지 않다.

11

새로운 규정은 글로벌 금융 시장의 특히 복잡한 도전 과제를 해결하기 위해 설계되었다.

어휘 regulation 규정, 규제 challenge 도전, 시험대

해설 (C) particularly는 '특별히' 또는 '구체적으로'라는 뜻의 부사로, 문제에서는 글로벌 금융 시장이 직면한 도전 과제가 '특별히' 복잡하다는 것을 강조하기 위해 사용되었다. (A) precisely(정확하게), (B) assertively(단호하게), (D) immediately(즉시) 모두 형용사 complex를 수식하기에는 의미상 어색하다.

12

재무부장인 브라이언 크로스는 다음 주 월요일에 자동 급여 시스템에 대한 교육 세미나 일정을 잡았다.

어휘 automated 자동화된 payroll 급여 대상자 명단; 급여 지불 총액

해설 다음 주 월요일에 교육 세미나 일정을 잡았다는 의미가 되어야 하므로 정답은 (C) scheduled(일정을 잡다)이다. 참고로 invited의 목적어는 초대의 대상(누구를)이 되어야 하므로 (A)는 오답이다.

13

기계 작동에 대한 지시 사항이 너무 복잡해서 경험이 많은 기술자조차 이해하는 데 어려움이 있었다.

어휘 instruction 설명, 지시 complicated 복잡한

해설 기계 작동 지침서를 이해하기 어려워서, 경험이 있는 기술자들조차도 어려움을 겪고 있다는 내용이다. even이 기계에 익숙할 것으로 예상되는 기술자들조차도 어려움을 겪고 있다는 것을 강조하고 있으므로 정답은 (D) experienced(경험이 많은)이다. (A) considerate(사려 깊은, 배려하는)는 복잡한 지시 사항을 이해하는 능력과 관련이 없으며, (B) demanding(요구가 많은)은 작업을 완료하는 데 많은 노력이나 기술이 필요하다는 것을 의미할 뿐이다. (C) preventable(예방 가능한) 또한 피할 수 있거나 일어나는 것을 막을 수 있는 것을 의미하므로 technicians를 수식하기에는 적절하지 않다.

14

아담 라인스는 내일 수업에서 새로운 장비의 적절한 사용법을 보여줄 것이다.

어휘 proper 적절한 equipment 장비, 용품

해설 아담 라인스가 내일 수업 중에 새로운 장비의 적절한 사용법을 보여주거나 설명할 것이라는 의미가 되어야 자연스러우므로 (D) demonstrate(보여주다, 설명하다)가 정답이다. 장비 사용법을 감독하는 것은 어색하므로 (A) supervise(감독하다)는 오답이며, (B) customize(맞춤화 하다)는 무엇인가를 개인이나 목적에 맞게 변경하는 것을 의미하므로 문장의 맥락과 어울리지 않는다. (C) accomplish(성취하다) 또한 장비 사용법을 가르치거나 설명하는 것과는 관련이 없다.

15

수익이 10개월 연속 상승하여, 회사는 이제 해외 시장으로 확장하는 것을 고려하고 있다.

어휘 in a row 잇달아   expand into ~로 확대하다   overseas 해외로, 해외의

해설 빈칸은 절과 절을 연결하는 접속사 자리이므로, 연결하는 역할을 할 수 없는 접속부사 (C) therefore는 오답이다. 수익이 계속 증가하고 있고, 그래서 회사가 해외 시장으로 확장하는 것을 고려 중이므로 문맥상 가장 어울리는 것은 (A) so이다.

PART 6

[16-19]

> 직원 여러분께,
>
> 이 공지는 즉시 시행되며, 회사를 대신한 구매와 경비에 대한 모든 요청에 대해 반드시 관리자나 매니저의 승인이 필요함을 알려드리기 위한 것입니다. **승인된 경비에 한하여 비용이 지급됩니다.** 미리 승인되지 않은 경비나 구매에 대해서는 지급이 이루어지지 않으니 참고해 주시기 바랍니다.
>
> 모든 경비가 적절히 승인되었는지 확인하는 데 협조해 주셔서 감사합니다.
>
> 진심을 담아,
>
> 라야 개빈
> 경리부장

어휘 effective 효과적인; 시행되는   on behalf of ~을 대신하여   supervisor 감독관, 관리자   prior 사전의   approval 승인   reimburse 배상하다, 상환하다   expenditure 지출, 비용, 경비   authorize 재가하다, 권한을 부여하다

16

해설 회사의 경비나 구매에 관한 정책 변화를 알리고, 이것이 '즉시' 시행된다는 의미가 되어야 자연스러우므로 정답은 (C) immediately(즉시)이다. (A) markedly(현저히)와 (D) substantially(상당히, 많이)는 어떠한 차이나 증감의 폭이 클 때 사용되며, (B) potentially(잠재적으로)는 일어날 가능성이 있는 일에 사용된다.

17

(A) 회사 정책이 변경되어야 합니다.
(B) **승인된 경비에 한하여 비용이 지급됩니다.**
(C) 귀하의 환불 요청이 처리될 것입니다.
(D) 올해의 경비가 상당히 증가하였습니다.

어휘 reimbursement 상환, 변제   significantly 상당히, 크게

해설 빈칸 앞에는 직원들이 회사를 대신해서 구매한 것이나 경비를 청구하는 것에 대한 모든 요청은 승인이 필요하다는 내용의 문장이 있는데, 이는 회사가 승인된 경비만 환급한다는 것을 의미한다. 따라서 '승인된 경비만 환급된다'는 의미인 (B)가 정답이다.

18

해설 빈칸이 포함된 문장은 회사의 사전 승인 없이 발생하는 모든 지출이나 구매는 환급되지 않을 것이라는 의미이다. 따라서 '~ 없이'라는 의미의 전치사인 (D) without이 정답이다.

19

해설 이 문장은 모든 경비가 적절히 승인되었는지 확인하는 데 협조해 주어서 감사한다는 내용이다. (C) ensuring(확실하게 하다, 보장하다)은 어떤 일이나 사실이 올바르게 처리되도록 확실히 한다는 의미로서, 지출이 승인된 후에 지급되었는지 확실하게 한다는 의미를 만들기에 적절하다. (B) imposing은 새로운 법률을 도입하거나 세금 등을 부과할 때 사용되므로 의미상 정답이 될 수 없다.

[20-23]

> 현재, 선버스트 호텔은 우리 직원들에게 독점적인 특별한 기회를 제공하고 있습니다. 각 직원은 최소 2주 전에 예약을 하면 50% 할인된 가격으로 객실을 예약할 수 있습니다. **예약한 방에는 반드시 직원 본인이 머물러야 합니다.** 이는 그 방을 다른 사람을 위해 예약할 수 없다는 것을 의미합니다. 우리는 열심히 일하는 직원들에게 감사의 표시로 이 혜택을 제공하는 것에 자부심을 느끼고 있습니다. 일을 위한 것이든 여가를 위한 것이든, 호텔은 직원들에게 보상하고 감사의 마음을 전하기 위한 최고의 방법을 찾고 있습니다.

어휘 currently 현재, 지금   opportunity 기회   exclusively 독점적으로, 전용으로   rate 요금   in advance 미리   take pride in 자부심을 느끼다   hardworking 근면한, 열심히 일하는   as a token of appreciation 감사의 표시로   reward 보상하다   gratitude 고마움, 감사

20

해설 문장의 주어인 the Sunburst Hotel 뒤에 위치한 빈칸은 동사 자리이므로, 보기 중 동사인 (B) is offering과 (C) was offering이 정답 후보이다. 다음 문장에서 현재 모든 직원이 50% 할인된 요금으로 방을 예약할 수 있다고 했으므로, 기회를 제공하고 있는 것이 '현재'임을 알 수 있다. 따라서 정답은 현재진행형 시제 동사인 (B) is offering이다.

21

(A) 지금 전화해서 더 많은 비용을 절감할 수 있는 방법을 찾아보세요.
(B) 우리는 현재 손님들에게 할인된 요금을 제공하고 있습니다.
(C) 결과적으로, 많은 근로자들이 그것을 이용했습니다.
(D) **예약한 방에는 반드시 직원 본인이 머물러야 합니다.**

어휘 rate 요금   as a result 결과적으로   take advantage of 이용하다

해설 바로 뒤에 이어지는 문장에서 빈칸의 문장을 this로 표현하고 있고, 이는 그 방을 다른 사람을 위해 예약할 수 없다는 것을 의미한다고 했다. 그러므로 빈칸에는 직원 본인이 예약한 방에 꼭 머물러야 한다는 내용의 문장이 오는 것이 자연스럽다. 따라서 정답은 (D)이다.

22

어휘 salary 급여   vision 시각, 통찰력

해설 지문의 첫 부분에서 호텔이 직원들에게 매우 특별한 기회를 제공하고 있고, 이제 모든 직원이 50% 할인된 요금으로 방을 예약할 수 있다는 내용이 이어지고 있다. 이는 호텔이 직원들에게 제공하는 혜택이므로 정답은 (C) benefit이다.

23

[해설] 빈칸은 두 절을 연결하는 접속사 자리이다. 특히 'it is for business or leisure'는 주절 앞에서 주절을 수식하는 부사절이므로 빈칸에는 부사절 접속사가 와야 한다. 따라서 보기 중 부사절 접속사로 사용 가능한 (B), (C), (D) 중에 정답을 골라야 한다. 이 중 빈칸 뒤의 or leisure를 근거로 하여 빈칸에 가장 어울리는 접속사는 whether라는 것을 유추할 수 있다. whether가 부사절 접속사로 쓰일 경우 or과 함께 사용된다는 것을 참고하자. 따라서 정답은 (D) Whether이다.

PART 7

[24-25]

공지

오늘부터, 베드포드 역의 승차권 자동발매기에서 예약되지 않은 티켓을 구매할 수 없게 되었습니다. **24) 현재 자동발매기는 더욱 빠르고 편리한 서비스를 제공하기 위해 업그레이드 작업이 진행 중입니다.** 작업은 3월 21일 금요일까지 완료될 예정입니다. 그 동안, 승객들께서는 열차 승차권을 온라인으로 예약하시거나 역 내에 위치한 매표소에서 구매하시기 바랍니다. 이로 인해 발생할 수 있는 불편함에 대해 사과드립니다. 승객들께서는 www.easytrip.com에서 **25) 온라인으로 표를 구입하시면 5% 할인을 받으실 수 있고 줄을 서서 기다리지 않으셔도 된다는 것을 알려드립니다.**

[어휘] unreserved 예약되어 있지 않은   currently 현재   undergo 겪다   inconvenience 불편, 애로사항

24

왜 승차권 자동발매기를 사용할 수 없는가?
(A) 그것들은 역에서 철거되었다.
(B) 그것들은 지금 더 나은 서비스를 위해 개선되고 있다.
(C) 그것들은 정전으로 인해 작동이 중단되었다.
(D) 그것들은 너무 구식이어서 교체가 필요하다.

[어휘] remove 치우다, 제거하다   improve 개선하다, 향상시키다   power outage 정전   outdated 구식인

[해설] 지문의 전반부에 승차권 자동발매기가 현재 더 빠르고 편리한 서비스를 위해 업그레이드되고 있다고 언급되어 있으므로 정답은 (B)이다. 지문에서 승차권 자동발매기가 업그레이드되는 중이라고 했을 뿐, 철거되거나 구식이어서 교체가 필요하다는 내용은 없으므로 (A)와 (D)는 오답이며, 승차권 자동발매기가 정전 때문이 아닌 업그레이드 중이라서 사용 할 수 없을 뿐이므로 (C) 또한 오답이다.

25

승객들은 어떻게 할인된 표를 살 수 있는가?
(A) 역의 매표소를 방문함으로써
(B) 온라인 멤버십에 가입함으로써
(C) 월 정기권을 구입함으로써
(D) 인터넷으로 표를 예매함으로써

[해설] 지문 후반부에서 온라인으로 티켓을 구입하면 5%를 절약할 수 있다고 했는데, 이는 승객들이 5%의 할인을 받을 수 있다는 의미이다. 따라서 정답은 (D)이다.

[26-30]

11월 10일

지나 켄트
선셋 대로 51번지
볼티모어 21202

켄트 씨께,

리먼 어패럴에 대한 고객님의 사랑에 감사드립니다. **28) 최근에 저희 상점에서 구매하신 청바지와 스웨터에 대해서도 감사드립니다. 26) 저희는 고객 여러분의 쇼핑 경험을 더욱 27) 개선하기 위해 간단한 설문조사를 진행하고 있으며, 고객님의 참여를 정중하게 부탁드립니다.** 편의를 위해, 사전에 주소와 우편요금이 미리 지불된 봉투를 첨부하였습니다. 이 봉투를 사용하여 설문 조사를 회신해 주시기 바랍니다.

감사의 표시로, **29-1) 11월 21일 이전에 완료된 설문 조사를 제출한 고객분들께는 유명한 화가인 라라 콜버트가 특별 제작한 한정판 스카프를 드립니다.** 이 기한 이후에 제출하는 고객들께는 다음 구매시 5% 할인 쿠폰을 제공합니다.

고객님의 시간과 의견에 감사드리며, 저희 제품과 서비스를 지속적으로 개선할 수 있도록 도와주셔서 감사합니다. 리먼 어패럴의 소중한 고객이 되어 주셔서 감사드립니다.

진심을 담아,

안젤라 웨버
고객 서비스 매니저

[어휘] enhance (좋은 점·가치·지위를) 높이다[향상시키다]   convenience 편의, 편리   enclosed 동봉된; 에워싸인   completed 작성한   limited 제한된, 한정된   voucher 상품권, 할인권, 쿠폰

리먼 어패럴

고객 여러분의 참여는 고객님들께 최상의 쇼핑 경험을 제공하는 데 도움이 됩니다.

이름: *지나 켄트*
29-2) 날짜: *11월 27일*

A. 의류를 얼마나 자주 구매하십니까?
☐ 일주일에 한 번   ☑ 한 달에 한 번
☐ 몇 개월에 한 번   ☐ 일 년에 한 번 이하

B. 일반적으로 새로운 의류 브랜드나 제품을 어떻게 알게 되십니까?
☑ 소셜 미디어   ☐ 친구/가족
☐ 광고 (TV, 인쇄물, 온라인)
☐ 매장 디스플레이
☐ 기타 (자세히 기재): _____

C. 제품을 일반적으로 어떻게 구매하십니까?

☑ 리먼 어패럴 매장 중 한 곳에서 직접 구매

☑ 웹사이트에서 온라인으로 구매

자세한 내용을 기재해주세요: *온라인 구매 전 제품을 직접 보기 위해 가장 가까운 리먼 어패럴 매장 중 한 곳에 방문하는 것을 선호합니다.*

D. 리먼 어페럴에 최근에 방문하셨을 때, 원하는 제품을 찾으셨습니까?

☐ 예   ☑ 아니요

자세한 내용을 기재해주세요: ***30) 제품의 다양성, 특히 스웨터에 감명을 받았지만,*** *원하는 색상을 찾지 못했습니다. 하지만, 판매원은 매우 친절하게 원하는 제품을 창고에서 바로 배송하겠다고 제안해주었습니다.*

어휘 typically 일반적으로, 전형적으로   specify (구체적으로) 명시하다   in person 직접, 몸소   impressed 인상 깊게 생각하는, 감명을 받은   desired 바랐던, 희망했던   end up 결국 (어떤 처지에) 처하게 되다   available 구할 수 있는, 이용할 수 있는

26

위버 씨의 편지의 목적은 무엇인가?

(A) 켄트 씨에게 조사 결과를 알리기 위해

(B) 켄트 씨에게 환불 양식 작성을 요청하기 위해

(C) 켄트 씨가 제기한 불만에 대처하기 위해

(D) 켄트 씨로부터 의견을 요청하기 위해

어휘 finding (조사·연구 등의) 결과[결론]   address (문제·상황 등에 대해) 고심하다, 다루다   complaint 불평, 항의

해설 편지 첫 문단의 'we are conducting a brief survey and kindly ask for your participation'에서 간단한 설문조사를 진행하고 있으며, 이에 참여를 부탁한다고 했다. 따라서 편지의 목적은 켄트 씨에게 의견을 요청하기 위해서이므로 정답은 (D)이다.

27

편지의 첫 번째 문단 세 번째 줄의 "enhance"와 그 의미가 가장 가까운 단어는?

(A) 겪다

(B) 평가하다

(C) 향상시키다

(D) 동기를 부여하다

해설 'To further enhance our customers' shopping experiences'는 '고객의 쇼핑 경험을 더 개선하기 위해서'라고 해석되므로 enhance와 문맥상 가장 가까운 의미의 동사는 (C) improve이다.

28

켄트 씨에 대해 추론할 수 있는 것은 무엇인가?

(A) 그녀는 옷을 사기 위해 보통 온라인 상점을 둘러본다.

(B) 그녀는 지인들로부터 상품 정보를 얻는다.

(C) 그녀는 월 1회 리먼 어패럴을 방문한다.

(D) 그녀는 최근에 옷을 구매했다.

어휘 browse 둘러보다   obtain (특히 노력 끝에) 얻다

해설 편지의 첫 문단에서 최근에 가게에서 구매한 청바지와 스웨터에 대해서도 감사한다고 했으므로 켄트 씨가 최근에 옷을 구매한 사실을 알 수 있다. 따라서 정답은 (D)이다.

29

켄트 씨는 리먼 어패럴로부터 무엇을 받을 것 같은가?

(A) 특별히 디자인된 스카프

(B) 할인을 제공하는 쿠폰

(C) 유명 작가의 그림

(D) 그녀가 찾던 스웨터

해설 편지의 두 번째 문단에서 11월 21일 이전에 완료된 설문조사를 제출한 고객들은 유명한 화가인 라라 콜버트가 특별 제작한 한정판 스카프를, 이 기한 이후에 제출하는 고객들은 다음 구매시 5% 할인 쿠폰을 제공한다고 했다. 그런데 두 번째 지문인 설문지에서 작성 날짜가 11월 27일임을 확인할 수 있으므로, 켄트 씨가 리먼 어패럴로부터 받을 수 있는 것은 할인 쿠폰임을 알 수 있다. 따라서 정답은 (B)이다.

30

켄트 씨가 리먼 어패럴에 대해 언급한 것은?

(A) 효과적으로 소셜 미디어를 사용한다.

(B) 판매원들은 친절하지 않다.

(C) 다양한 제품을 보유하고 있다.

(D) 종종 제품 부족을 겪는다.

어휘 friendly 친절한, 우호적인   a range of 다양한   shortage 부족

해설 설문지의 D 항목에 대한 답변에서 켄트 씨가 제품의 다양성에 감명을 받았다고 했으므로 정답은 (C)이다.

DAY 02 동사의 종류

PRACTICE

pp.133-135

1 show	2 offering
3 inform	4 assure
5 allows	6 flourish
7 keeping	

1 당신의 주장을 뒷받침할 문서화된 증거를 보여주시기 바랍니다.

2 패롯 항공사는 이제 모든 항공편에서 채식주의자를 위한 기내식 선택권을 제공합니다.

3 리즈 씨에게 최근 영화 산업에서 소비자 관심사의 변화에 대한 발표를 준비해야 한다는 것을 알려주세요.

4 귀하의 우려 사항을 해결하고 문제를 신속하게 해결하기 위해 모든 노력을 다할 것을 보장합니다.

5 매니저는 직원들이 오후 3시 이후 30분의 휴식을 취할 수 있도록 허용합니다.

6 환경 전문가들에 따르면, 이번 봄의 좋은 날씨가 식물들이 번성할 수 있도록 도와줄 것입니다.

7 소기업 사장들은 지역 경제의 생산성을 유지하는 데 중요한 역할을 하는 다양한 집단을 대표한다.

📋 실전 문제 연습

1 (D)	2 (C)	3 (A)	4 (D)
5 (A)	6 (D)	7 (B)	8 (B)
9 (C)	10 (C)	11 (B)	12 (D)
13 (B)	14 (C)	15 (D)	16 (B)
17 (D)	18 (B)	19 (D)	20 (A)
21 (C)	22 (C)	23 (D)	24 (A)
25 (B)	26 (D)	27 (C)	28 (A)
29 (A)	30 (D)	31 (B)	

PART 5

1
이사회는 지난달에 제출된 모든 비용 견적을 검토했으며 다음 주 월요일에 최종 결정을 발표할 것이다.

어휘 board 이사회   cost 비용   estimate 견적(서)   final 마지막의, 최종적인   examine 조사하다, 검토하다

해설 등위 접속사 and 앞 절에 동사가 필요하므로 동사인 (B) will be examined와 (D) has examined가 정답 후보이다. 이사회가 비용 견적을 검토하는 능동의 의미이므로, 둘 중 능동태 동사인 (D) has examined가 정답이다.

2
일요일 오후 2시에 출국하는 비행 스케줄을 확인하기 위해, 렌즈 씨는 퍼시픽 항공에 전화를 걸었다.

어휘 consent 동의하다; 허락하다   confirm 확인해 주다, 확정하다   proceed 진행하다, 나아가다

해설 빈칸 뒤에 to부정사의 목적어인 his flight이 있으므로 빈칸에는 타동사가 필요하다. 따라서 자동사인 (A) consent와 (D) proceed는 오답이며, 타동사인 (B) remind와 (C) confirm 중에서 정답을 골라야 한다. 그런데 빈칸 뒤의 목적어는 직접목적어이므로, 간접목적어를 필요로 하는 (B) remind는 오답이다. 정답은 3형식 동사인 (C) confirm이다.

3
그들이 일반적인 비즈니스 관행을 준수하는지 확인하기 위해서 계약 조항을 철저히 검토하는 것이 중요하다.

어휘 thoroughly 완전히, 철저히   terms 조건   standard 기준; 일반적인   practice 관행, 실습

해설 빈칸 앞의 comply(준수하다)는 자동사로서, 명사인 standard business practices를 목적어로 취하려면 전치사가 필요하다. 정답은 (A) with이며, comply with를 하나의 단어처럼 외워 두어야 한다.

4
볼 투자에서 떠나기로 결정하기 전에 홍보부장은 그라프 씨에게 그의 직책을 제안했다.

어휘 colleague 동료   depart 떠나다, 출발하다

해설 빈칸 뒤에 간접목적어인 Mr. Graff와 직접목적어인 his position 이 있으므로 4형식 동사를 정답으로 골라야 한다. 보기 중 4형식 동사로 사용 가능한 것은 (D) offered이다.

5
회사의 경영진은 주요 산업 행사와 일정을 맞추기 위해 제품 출시를 의도적으로 지연시켰다.

어휘 launch 출시, 개시   coincide 동시에 일어나다, 일치하다   intentionally 의도적으로

해설 빈칸은 주어와 동사 사이에서 동사를 수식하는 부사 자리이다. 따라서 정답은 부사인 (A) intentionally이다.

6
이사회는 켄트 씨가 작성한 재무 보고서가 포괄적이고 잘 구성되었다고 생각했다.

어휘 the board of directors 이사회   financial 금융의, 재정의   well structured 잘 구성된   comprehend (충분히) 이해하다   comprehensive 포괄적인, 종합적인

해설 문장의 동사인 found가 '~라고 여기다, 생각하다'라는 의미로 사용될 때, 이는 5형식 동사로서 목적어와 목적격 보어를 취한다. '------- and well structured'가 found의 목적격 보어인데, and 뒤의 well structured가 형용사이므로 빈칸에도 형용사가 와야 한다. 따라서 정답은 형용사인 (D) comprehensive이다.

7
아코스타 파이낸스는 중요한 구매를 할 때 자산관리사의 안내를 청할 것을 고객들에게 조언한다.

어휘 guidance 지도, 안내   significant 중요한, 커다란

해설 빈칸 뒤에 목적어인 clients가 있고, 그 뒤에 목적격 보어로서 to부정사인 to seek이 있다. 그러므로 빈칸에는 to부정사를 목적격 보어로 취하는 5형식 동사가 필요하다. 정답은 5형식 동사로 사용될 수 있는 (B) advises이다.

8
토마스 슈퍼마켓은 과일, 채소, 허브를 포함한 다양한 신선한 농산물을 제공한다.

어휘 produce 농작물   including ~을 포함하여

해설 a wide variety of는 '아주 다양한'이라는 의미의 관용 표현이다. 정답은 (B) wide이다.

9
회의를 연기하는 대신, 예정대로 회의가 진행되도록 최선을 다해 노력해야 한다.

해설 빈칸은 명사구인 'postponing the meeting' 앞에 사용되는 전치사 자리이다. 따라서 전치사인 (A) Except for(~을 제외하고)와 (C) Instead of(~ 대신에) 중에서 정답을 골라야 한다. 회의를 연기하는

87

대신 예정대로 회의가 진행되도록 최선을 다해 노력해야 한다는 해석이
자연스러우므로 정답은 (C)이다.

10

우리는 주주들에 대한 의무를 충실히 이행하고 장기적으로 지속 가능한
성장을 보장하기 위해 전념하고 있다.

어휘 committed to ~에 전념하는 obligation 의무
sustainable 지속 가능한, 오랫동안 유지 가능한 in the long term
장기적으로

해설 문장은 주주들에 대한 의무를 충실히 이행하는 데 전념하고
있다고 해석되므로 빈칸에 가장 어울리는 동사는 (C) fulfilling이다.
(A) altering(변경하다), (B) settling(해결하다), (D) obtaining(획득하다)
는 모두 문맥과 어울리지 않는다.

11

그 회사의 프리미엄 멤버십 제도에는 무료 배송 및 모든 구매에 대한
연장된 품질 보증 기간 등 다양한 혜택이 포함되어 있다.

어휘 premium 아주 높은, 고급의 such as 예를 들어 (~와 같은)

해설 문맥상 자연스럽고 형용사인 extended(연장된)의 수식을 받
기에 적절한 것은 (B) warranty(보증)이다. 'an extended warranty
on all purchases'는 모든 구매에 대한 연장된 보증을 의미한다. (A)
operation(운영)은 회사의 프리미엄 멤버십이 제공하는 혜택으로 알맞
지 않고, (C) expense(비용)와 (D) inventory(재고)는 빈칸의 명사를
수식하는 extended와 어울리지 않는다.

12

IT 부서는 민감한 회사 정보가 안전하게 유지되도록 새로운 보안 조치를
시행하고 있다.

어휘 implement 시행하다 security 보안 measure 조치, 정책
critical 비판적인; 대단히 중요한

해설 IT 부서가 새로운 보안 조치를 시행하는 이유로 회사의 민감한
정보가 '안전하게' 유지되도록 하기 위해서라는 의미가 되어야 자연스러
우므로 정답은 (D) secure(안전한)이다.

13

저희 제품이 엄격한 품질 관리 절차를 거쳐 최고의 성능 기준을 충족한다
는 것에 대해 안심하셔도 좋습니다.

어휘 undergo 겪다 rigorous 철저한, 엄격한 measures 방안,
방법, 조치 standard 수준

해설 빈칸에 들어갈 과거분사는 be동사와 결합하여 수동태 문장을
만든다. 따라서 주어인 you가 능동태 문장에서 빈칸에 들어갈 동사의
목적어였다는 점을 생각하면 문제를 쉽게 풀 수 있다. 보기 중 assure는
간접목적어(~에게) 뒤에 명사절인 that절을 연결하여 '~에게 ~을 확언
하다, 확약하다'를 의미하므로 (B) assured가 정답이다. (A) insisted
(강조된), (C) checked(확인된), (D) expressed(표현된)는 모두 문맥상
어울리지 않는다.

14

새로운 레스토랑은 엇갈리는 평가를 받았지만, 매일 꾸준한 수의 손님들
을 유치하고 있다.

어휘 mixed 뒤섞인, 엇갈리는 review 검토, 논평 a steady
stream of 끊임없이 이어지는

해설 'the new restaurant has received mixed reviews'가 완전한
절이므로 빈칸에는 절과 절을 연결하는 접속사가 와야 한다. 보기 중에서
접속사는 (C) Although뿐이다. (A) In spite of(~에도 불구하고)와 (D)
Apart from(~ 외에는, ~을 제외하고)는 전치사로 명사나 동명사 앞에
사용될 수 있으며, (B) However(하지만)는 접속부사로 절과 절을 연결
할 수 없다.

15

앨런 김 교수는 환경 단체에서 일한 후에 재생 에너지 개발에 대한 열정
이 강해졌다고 학생들에게 설명했다.

어휘 renewable 재생 가능한 intensify 심해지다, 강화하다
environmental 환경의 organization 조직, 단체

해설 (A) informed, (B) allowed, (C) convinced 뒤에는 전치사 없이
간접목적어가 바로 와야 하므로, to his students 앞에 사용되기에 적절
하지 않다. 따라서 명사절인 that절을 목적어로 삼을 수 있는 3형식
동사인 (D) explained가 정답이다.

PART 6
[16-19]

> #### 웨스트코트 파이낸셜의 우려 해소 및 신뢰
> #### 재구축에 대한 약속
>
> 웨스트코트 파이낸셜 사는 걱정을 해소시키고 주주들의 신뢰를
> 회복하기 위해 즉각적인 조치를 취하고 있다. 투명성과 책임감을
> 통해, 회사는 문제 해결과 신뢰 회복에 전념하고 있다. 전담 인력이
> 철저히 조사하고 효과적인 해결책을 실행한다. **또한 주주들은 정기
> 적인 소식을 받을 수 있다.** 이는 그들에게 정확하고 시기 적절한
> 정보를 제공할 것으로 예상된다. 회사는 이 상황을 성장과 개선의
> 기회로 여기며, 투명하고 빠르게 우려를 해결하여 향후 사건을 방지
> 하는 것을 목표로 하고 있다.

어휘 immediate 즉각적인 regain 되찾다, 회복하다
confidence 신뢰, 자신감 transparency 투명도, 투명성
accountability 책임 rebuild 재건하다, 새로 세우다 dedicated
전념하는, 헌신적인 task force 대책 위원회, 프로젝트 팀
investigate 조사하다, 살피다 implement 시행하다 timely
시기 적절한, 때맞춘 transparently 분명하게, 투명하게

16

해설 웨스트코트 파이낸셜 사는 걱정을 해소하고 주주들의 신뢰를 회
복하기 위해 즉각적인 조치를 '취하고 있다'라는 의미가 되는 것이 자연
스럽다. 따라서 정답은 (B) taking(취하다)이다. 'take action'은 '~에 대
해 조치를 취하다, 행동에 옮기다'라는 의미이다.

17

해설 전문적인 해법을 구하기 위해 전담 인력이 '철저하게' 조사 중이라
는 의미가 되어야 자연스러우므로 (D) thoroughly(철저하게)가 정답이
다. (A) incidentally(부수적으로, 우연히)와 (C) creatively(창조적으로,
독창적으로)는 동사 investigates(조사하다)를 수식하기에 어울리지 않
으며, (B) previously(이전에)는 과거의 일과 어울리므로 모두 오답이다.

18

(A) 당신의 지속적인 헌신에 감사하고 있다.

(B) 또한 주주들은 정기적인 소식을 받을 수 있다.

(C) 광범위한 연구 끝에, 우리는 마침내 그것을 찾았다.

(D) 새로운 제품에 대한 문의가 접수되고 있다.

어휘 regular 규칙적인, 정기적인   extensive 아주 넓은, 광범위한
inquiry 조사, 문의

해설 지문의 전체적인 내용은 웨스트코트 파이낸셜 사가 주주들의 걱정을 해소시키고 그들의 신뢰를 회복하기 위해 조치를 취하고 있다는 것이다. 따라서 이러한 조치의 일환으로 주주들이 정기적인 소식을 받을 수 있게 한다는 내용의 (B)가 문맥상 가장 어울린다. 또한 빈칸 뒤의 문장에서 그들(주주들)에게 정확하고 시기 적절한 정보를 제공할 것으로 예상된다고 했으므로, 주주들이 정기적인 소식을 받아 볼 수 있다는 문장이 빈칸에 가장 적절하다는 것을 다시 한 번 확인할 수 있다.

19

어휘 aim 목표로 하다

해설 문장에 동사 views가 있고 접속사는 보이지 않으므로, 문장에 더 이상 동사가 포함될 수 없다. 따라서 동사인 (A) has aimed, (B) is aimed, (C) will aim은 모두 오답이다. 정답은 (D) aiming이다.

[20-23]

> 수신: nelsen@webconstructor.com
> 발신: beth_rider@mycutecloset.com
> 날짜: 9월 19일
> 제목: 도움 요청
>
> 친애하는 넬슨 씨께,
>
> 최근에 저희 웹사이트의 제품 페이지에 몇 가지 변경을 했습니다. **그 과정에서 실수로 몇몇 사진들을 삭제하였습니다.** 최선을 다 했지만, 삭제된 내용을 복구하지 못했습니다. 삭제된 사진들을 검색하여 웹사이트에 복원하는 데 도움을 주실 수 있을지 궁금합니다. 또한, 제가 웹사이트에 직접 간단한 업데이트를 할 수 있도록 지도를 받을 수 있다면 정말 감사하겠습니다. 저는 열심히 배우고자 하며 간단한 수정이 필요할 때마다 매번 다른 사람의 도움을 받지 않는 쪽이 좋을 것 같습니다.
>
> 시간 내주시고 도움 주셔서 감사합니다.
>
> 안부를 전하며,
>
> 베스 라이더

어휘 missing 없어진, 실종된   retrieve (특히 제자리가 아닌 곳에 있는 것을) 되찾아오다[회수하다]   be eager to do ~을 하고 싶어 하다

20

(A) 그 과정에서 실수로 몇몇 사진들을 삭제하였습니다.

(B) 그러나, 이 프로젝트에는 어떤 문제도 없습니다.

(C) 제 의견으로는, 상황이 나아졌습니다.

(D) 어떻게 작동하는지 확인하기 위해 몇 가지 조정을 해봤습니다.

어휘 accidentally 우연히, 뜻하지 않게, 잘못하여   circumstance
(일·사건 등을 둘러싼) 환경, 상황, 정황   adjustment 수정, 조정

해설 빈칸 뒤 문장에서 최선을 다했지만, 삭제된 내용을 복구하지 못했다고 언급하고 있으므로 빈칸에는 무엇을 삭제했는지에 대한 설명이 필요하다. 따라서 정답은 (A)이다.

21

어휘 restore 회복시키다, 복원하다

해설 등위 접속사 and는 같은 성분끼리 연결할 수 있다. 빈칸 앞 and가 'retrieving the deleted photos'와 '------- them to my Web site'를 연결하고 있으므로 빈칸에는 retrieving과 같은 형태인 동명사가 와야 한다. 따라서 정답은 (C) restoring이다.

22

어휘 unfortunately 불행하게도, 유감스럽게도   specifically
분명히, 명확하게

해설 빈칸 앞에서는 삭제된 사진을 복구해 달라는 부탁을, 빈칸 뒤에서는 간단한 편집을 스스로 할 수 있도록 지도해 달라는 부탁을 하고 있다. 즉, 추가적인 부탁을 하고 있으므로 빈칸에 어울리는 부사는 (C) Additionally(게다가, 또)이다. 참고로, consequently(그 결과)는 원인과 결과를 연결할 때 사용되는데, 빈칸의 앞과 뒤의 내용은 원인과 결과라고 볼 수 없다.

23

어휘 account for 설명하다, (부분, 비율)을 차지하다   carry out
수행하다   subscribe to ~을 구독하다

해설 웹사이트에 스스로 간단한 업데이트를 할 수 있도록 지도를 부탁하면서 열심히 배우고 싶다고 언급하는 것은, 간단한 수정이 필요할 때마다 매번 다른 사람에게 의존하지 않기 위해서이다. 따라서 (D) depend on(의존하다)가 정답이다.

PART 7

[24-26]

> 스콧 브라이언트 씨가 약 10년간 회사를 위해 근무한 후 은퇴 예정이어서, 플린트 기술은 현재 홍보부장 자리를 충원하기 위해 구인 중입니다. 그의 마지막 근무일은 4월 30일입니다.
>
> **25-1) 플린트 기술의 홍보 부서 책임자로서, 홍보부장은 부사장에게 직접 보고하며** 회사의 목표를 지원하는 다양한 홍보 전략을 개발하고 실행하는 역할을 담당합니다. 이 역할은 미디어 관계, 위기 대응, 그리고 평판 관리를 포함한 회사의 홍보 활동을 관리할 수 있는 능력도 필요로 합니다.
>
> **25-2) 부사장 로건 홀은 이 직책이 상당한 책임을 수반한다고 강조하며, 24) "우리는 회사나 기관을 위해 브랜드 정체성을 개발 및 유지하고 모든 홍보 채널에 걸쳐 메시지를 전달하는 데 폭넓은 경험이 있는 지원자를 찾고 있습니다."라고 했습니다.**
>
> 회사는 홍보부장 직책에 대한 면접 일정을 2월 초부터 시작하는 것으로 잡았습니다. **26) 2월 5일 이후 제출된 지원서는 고려되지 않을 예정입니다.** 목표는 3월 말까지 새로운 홍보부장을 선임하는 것입니다.

24

홍보부장 직책에 요구되는 것은?

(A) 브랜드 이미지 창출 경험

(B) 인사 관리 전문 지식

(C) 마케팅 관련 고급 학위

(D) 다국어 구사 능력

어휘 expertise 전문 지식 fluency 유창성, 능숙도

해설 지문 중반의 로건 홀 부사장의 인터뷰에 따르면, 브랜드 정체성을 개발 및 유지하는 데 폭넓은 경험이 있는 지원자를 찾고 있다고 했으므로 정답은 (A)이다.

25

브라이언트 씨에 대해 암시된 것은?

(A) 그는 지원자들을 면접 볼 것이다.

(B) 그의 상사는 홀 씨이다.

(C) 그는 10년간 홍보부장이었다.

(D) 그는 부사장으로 승진할 것이다.

어휘 supervisor 감독관, 관리자 decade 10년 be promoted to ~로 승진하다

해설 지문 초반부에 플린트 기술의 홍보 부서의 책임자로서, 홍보부장은 부사장에게 직접 보고한다는 내용이 있다. 그런데 세 번째 문단에서 로건 홀 씨가 회사의 부사장이라는 것을 알 수 있으므로, 로건 홀씨가 홍보부장인 브라이언트 씨의 상관이라는 사실을 유추할 수 있다. 따라서 정답은 (B)이다.

26

[1], [2], [3], [4] 중에서 다음 문장이 위치하기에 가장 적절한 곳은?

"2월 5일 이후 제출된 지원서는 고려되지 않을 예정입니다."

(A) [1]

(B) [2]

(C) [3]

(D) [4]

해설 주어진 문장이 지원서 제출 일정에 대한 것임을 단서로 하여 정답을 고를 수 있다. 마지막 문단에서 면접 일정이 2월 초라고 언급하고 있으므로, 지원서는 그 전에 제출되어야 한다는 것을 알 수 있다. 따라서 주어진 문장이 가장 잘 어울리는 자리는 [4]이다.

[27-31]

흥미진진한 소식!

저희 전담 팀에서 환상적인 소식을 전하게 되어 매우 기쁩니다. *세이보리 스푼 매거진*에서 샌프란시스코 최고의 레스토랑을 집중 조명하는 기사에 저희 레스토랑을 소개할 예정입니다! 저희의 대표적인 요리인 클램 차우더를 우리 시 최고의 요리로 선보일 예정입니다.

그들은 또한 친절한 직원들이 만들어내는 따뜻하고 반갑게 맞이하는 분위기를 담고자 합니다. 우리 팀이 귀한 손님들을 모시는 모습과 모든 직원들의 단체 사진을 촬영할 것입니다.

31-1) 6월 8일 금요일 오전 9시 30분에 촬영이 예정되어 있습니다. **28)** 모든 직원들이 단체 사진을 찍을 예정이니, 금요일 오전에 유니폼을 입고 조금 더 일찍 도착해 주시기 바랍니다.

27-1) 29-1) 제가 작년에 이 식당을 개업했을 때만 해도, 저희의 놀라운 성공을 예상하지 못했습니다. 이 성과는 여러분 한 분 한 분의 덕택이며, 여러분 모두가 마땅히 받아야 할 인정에 자부심을 가져야 할 것입니다.

수신: 브렌다 올리베리아 〈chefbrenda@seaharvestkitchen.com〉
발신: 마크 존슨 〈mark77@savoryspoon.com〉
제목: 금요일 약속
날짜: 6월 7일 목요일

올리베리아 씨께,

29-2) 우리가 통화로 논의한 것처럼, 내일 오전 9시 30분에 있을 예정인 사진 촬영 일정을 확인하기 위해 메일을 보냅니다. 사진 촬영은 고객님의 식당에서 진행될 예정이며, 그곳에서 메뉴와 직원들의 모습을 촬영할 것입니다.

우선, 고객님의 가장 유명한 요리들 중 하나인 클램 차우더를 촬영할 예정이오니, 이 시간을 위한 준비를 해주시면 감사하겠습니다. 이어서, 직원들이 메인 식당에 모이는 모습을 촬영하겠습니다. 고객님의 직원들은 오전 10시 30분까지 준비를 완료해야 한다고 말씀해 주셨는데, 이는 문제가 되지 않을 것입니다. 단체 사진 세션은 오전 10시까지 끝날 것으로 예상됩니다. **31-2)** 또한, 사진 촬영이 끝난 후에는 캐시 월 기자가 귀하와 귀하의 일부 고객들을 대상으로 간단한 인터뷰를 진행할 예정입니다.

일정과 관련하여 궁금한 점이나 고민이 있으시면, 언제든지 연락주시기 바랍니다. 그렇지 않다면, 내일 뵙기를 고대하겠습니다.

안부를 전하며,

마크 존슨
세이보리 스푼 매거진

씨 하베스트 키친

이 인기 있는 씨 하베스트 키친은 자리를 잡기 위해서 문을 열기 최대 30분 전에 도착하는 손님들과, 칠판에 정확한 도착 시간을 기록하는 손님들로 사람들을 일찍 끌어 모았다. 이 북적대는 대기자 명단은 사워 도우와 함께 제공되는 클래식하고, 순하며, 크림이 풍부한 차우더를 포함하여, 신선하고 유쾌하게 복잡하지 않은 요리의 매력을 강조하고 있다.

29-3) 작년에 막 문을 열었음에도 불구하고, **27-2)** 이 식당은 주인이자 요리사인 브렌다 올리베리아 씨에 의해 만들어진 전통적인 아일랜드 요리 메뉴로 유명해지면서, 빠르게 지역의 명소로 자리 잡았다.

30) 올리베리아 씨는 "우리는 각 계절의 가장 좋을 때에 재료를 선택하는데, 이것이 우리의 메뉴에 반영됩니다."라고 강조한다.

31-3) 최근 금요일 오후 방문에서, 단골 손님인 캐롤 린은 그녀의 열정을 공유했다: "빵으로 만든 용기에 담긴 유명한 클램 차우더 외에도, 디저트를 위한 공간을 남겨두는 것을 잊지 마세요; 사워도우 애플 파이는 꼭 먹어야 합니다!"

맛있는 음식 이상으로, 씨 하베스트 키친의 매력은 따뜻하고 친절한 직원들에게 있는데, 이것이 식당의 폭넓은 인기에 기여하는 매력적인 분위기를 만들고 있다.

캐시 윌
사진: 마크 존슨

어휘 secure 확보하다 precise 정확한 chalkboard 칠판 bustling 북적거리는 underscore 밑줄을 긋다; 강조하다 delightfully 유쾌하게 cuisine 요리 chowder 차우더(수프의 일종) bread bowl 빵으로 만든 그릇 fame 명성 emphasize 강조하다 delectable 맛있는 fare 음식; 요금 accommodating 잘 협조하는

27

누가 공지를 게시했는가?
(A) 마크 존슨
(B) 캐시 윌
(C) 브렌다 올리베리아
(D) 캐롤 린

해설 공지의 마지막 문단에 '제가 작년에 이 식당을 개업했을 때만 해도 저희의 놀라운 성공을 예상하지 못했다'는 내용이 있는데, 공지를 게시한 사람은 식당 주인이라는 것을 알 수 있다. 기사 지문의 두 번째 문단에서 브렌다 올리베리아 씨가 식당의 주인이자 요리사라고 했으므로 정답은 (C)이다.

28

직원들은 6월 8일에 무엇을 하라고 요청 받는가?
(A) 평소보다 일찍 도착하는 것
(B) 시상식에 참석하는 것
(C) 신문 기사를 위한 인터뷰에 응하는 것
(D) 그들의 새로운 메뉴 사진을 찍는 것

어휘 than usual 평소보다 awards ceremony 시상식 photograph 사진, ~의 사진을 찍다

해설 공지의 두 번째 문단에서 모든 직원들이 단체 사진을 찍을 예정이니, 금요일 오전에 유니폼을 입고 조금 더 일찍 도착해 주기 바란다는 내용이 있으므로 정답은 (A)이다.

29

올리베리아 씨에 대해서 언급되지 않은 것은?
(A) 그녀는 샌프란시스코에 몇 개의 식당을 가지고 있다.
(B) 그녀는 씨 하베스트 키친의 요리사이다.
(C) 그녀는 작년에 식당을 열었다.

(D) 그녀는 촬영 전에 존슨 씨와 대화를 나눴다.

해설 기사 지문 두 번째 문단에서 올리베리아 씨가 주인이자 요리사라고 했으므로 (B)는 언급된 내용이다. 공지의 세 번째 문단에서 작년에 이 식당을 열었을 때만 해도 이렇게 단기간에 성공할 줄은 몰랐다고 했고, 기사 지문 두 번째 문단에서 씨 하베스트 키친은 작년에 막 문을 연 식당이라고 소개하고 있으므로 (C)도 언급되었다. 이메일 첫 문단에서 우리가 통화로 논의한 대로 사진 촬영 일정을 확인하기 위해 메일을 보낸다고 했으므로, 촬영 전에 존슨 씨와 전화로 논의를 했다는 사실을 알 수 있다. 따라서 (D) 역시 언급된 내용이다. 정답은 (A)이다.

30

씨 하베스트 키친에 대한 것 중 사실인 것은?
(A) 매일 점심에 영업을 한다.
(B) 최근에 이전했다.
(C) 작년에는 별로 인기가 없었다.
(D) 계절에 따라 메뉴를 바꾼다.

어휘 recently 최근에 relocate 이동하다, 이전하다 seasonally 계절에 따라

해설 기사 지문 두 번째 문단에서 각 계절의 가장 좋은 시기에 재료를 선택하여 이를 메뉴에 반영한다고 했으므로, 이 식당에서는 계절마다 메뉴를 바꾼다는 것을 알 수 있다. 따라서 정답은 (D)이다.

31

린 씨에 대해 추론할 수 있는 것은?
(A) 그녀는 식당의 분위기에 감명받았다.
(B) 그녀는 6월 8일에 씨 하베스트 키친에서 점심을 먹었다.
(C) 그녀는 인터뷰 전에 그 식당을 방문한 적이 없다.
(D) 그녀는 그 식당이 인기가 많을 것이라고 생각하지 않았다.

어휘 impressed 감명받은 atmosphere 분위기

해설 공지의 두 번째 문단에서 6월 8일에 사진 촬영이 있을 것임을 알 수 있다. 그리고, 이메일 두 번째 문단에서 사진 촬영이 끝난 후에는 캐시 윌 기자가 일부 고객들을 대상으로 간단한 인터뷰를 진행할 예정이라고 했고, 기사 지문 세 번째 문단에서 최근 금요일 오후 방문에서, 단골 손님인 캐롤 린과 그녀의 열정을 공유했다는 내용이 있다. 따라서 린 씨가 촬영일이었던 6월 8일 금요일에 씨 하베스트 키친에서 점심 식사를 했다는 것을 유추할 수 있으므로 정답은 (B)이다.

DAY 03 동사의 형태 (수 / 태 / 시제)

PRACTICE

pp.144-148

1	purchases	2	operates
3	receive	4	be paid
5	were released	6	to wear
7	dedicated	8	goes

9	As long as	10	joined
11	since	12	has added
13	applied	14	will have worked

1 사무실의 관리자는 주로 피크 사무용품점의 온라인 상점을 통해 물품을 구매한다.

2 블루스카이 에어라인은 동북아시아 노선에 매일 4대의 항공기를 운영한다.

3 로스 씨는 늦어도 내일까지는 수정된 견적서를 받기를 원했다.

4 미결제 잔액은 월말까지 납부되어야 한다.

5 합병과 관련된 모든 세부 사항이 오늘 오전에 공개되었다.

6 방문객들은 연구실에 출입할 때 항상 이름표를 착용해야 한다.

7 업사이드 파이낸셜스는 고객들에게 정확한 정보를 제공하는 데 전념하고 있다.

8 벤슨 씨가 다음 주에 싱가포르에 가면, 공장을 방문할 것이다.

9 케이브 씨가 우리의 제안을 수락하는 한, 우리는 그 프로젝트를 다음 달에 진행할 수 있을 것이다.

10 그가 KLM 부동산에 합류한 지 단지 2개월이 되었지만, 그는 이미 주목할 만한 성과를 내고 있다.

11 복사기가 오늘 아침부터 제대로 작동하지 않았다.

12 *프라임 데일리 뉴스*는 최근 웹사이트에 몇 가지 새로운 기능을 추가했다.

13 엘리스 씨는 인턴십에 지원했을 때 약 3년간 마케팅 공부를 하고 있었다.

14 프로젝트가 완료될 때쯤이면, 그들은 거의 3년 동안 그 업무를 하게 되는 것이다.

📝 실전 문제 연습   p.150

1	(B)	2	(D)	3	(C)	4	(B)
5	(C)	6	(D)	7	(A)	8	(D)
9	(D)	10	(B)	11	(A)	12	(A)
13	(C)	14	(D)	15	(C)	16	(C)
17	(D)	18	(B)	19	(B)	20	(B)
21	(D)	22	(B)	23	(A)	24	(C)
25	(D)	26	(C)	27	(C)	28	(D)
29	(D)	30	(A)	31	(B)		

PART 5

1

웰차트 리테일의 회장인 론 주버는 올해 매출액의 상당한 증가를 보고할 것으로 예상된다.

어휘 significant 중요한

해설 expect는 to부정사를 목적격 보어로 사용하는 5형식 동사이므로 수동태 동사 be expected로 바뀌면 be expected 뒤에 목적격 보어인 to부정사가 남게 된다. 따라서 빈칸에는 to부정사인 (B) to report가 와야 한다. 'be expected to do(~하기로 예상되다)'는 관용 표현으로 외워 두자.

2

낮은 지역에 거주하는 주민들에게 접근 중인 폭풍우를 대비하여 대피할 것을 권고하는 경고 공지가 발표되었다.

어휘 resident 거주자 low-lying 평평하게 낮은 evacuate 대피시키다, 대피하다 ahead of ~ 앞에, ~보다 빨리 approaching 다가오는 issue 발표하다; 발부하다

해설 빈칸 뒤에 수식어구는 있지만 목적어는 보이지 않으므로 수동태 동사를 정답으로 고른다. 의미상으로도 주어인 '경고 공지'는 '발표되는' 것이므로 수동태 문장이 되어야 한다. 따라서 정답은 (D)이다.

3

정보에 근거한 결정을 내리고 위험을 효과적으로 관리하기 위해, 투자하기 전에 재무 전문가와 상담하는 것이 바람직하다.

어휘 financial 금융의, 재정의 professional 전문적인; 전문직 종사자 informed 잘 아는; 정보에 근거한 effectively 효과적으로; 실질적으로

해설 빈칸이 be동사 뒤에 있으므로, 수동태를 만들 수 있는 과거분사 (A) advised와 be동사의 보어가 될 수 있는 형용사 (B) advisory(자문의)와 (C) advisable(바람직한) 중에서 정답을 고른다. 동사 advise의 목적어는 '조언을 받는 대상'인데, 수동태 문장이 되면 주어가 조언을 받는 대상이 되어야 한다. 문장의 주어인 consulting(상담 하는 것)은 조언을 받는 대상이 될 수 없으므로 (A)는 오답이다. (B)와 (C)는 모두 형용사이므로 해석상 더 자연스러운 보기를 정답으로 골라야 하는데, '바람직한'이라는 의미인 (C) advisable이 적절하다.

4

유명한 카피라이터인 조앤 파이크의 강연들은 참석한 이들에게 유익하고 매력적이라고 여겨진다.

어휘 renowned 유명한, 명성 있는 informative 유용한 정보를 주는, 유익한 engaging 호감이 가는, 매력 있는

해설 빈칸 뒤에 타동사인 consider의 목적어가 보이지 않으므로 수동태 동사인 (B) are considered가 정답이다. 5형식 동사 consider가 수동태 동사가 되면서 목적격 보어였던 형용사구 informative and engaging이 동사 are considered 뒤에 남아 있는 형태이다.

5

작년에 개장한 이후, 새로운 쇼핑몰은 쇼핑객들의 인기 명소가 되고 있다.

어휘 destination 목적지, 도착지

해설 주절의 동사가 현재완료 시제이므로 빈칸은 '과거의 특정한 시점 이래로 (현재까지)'를 의미하는 전치사 (C) Since가 정답이다. (A) Before는 쇼핑몰의 개장 이전을 의미하게 되므로 주절에 과거 시제 동사가 와야 하고, (D) Until 또한 작년에 쇼핑몰이 개장한 시점까지만을 의미하므로 주절에 과거 시제 동사가 필요하다. (B) When은 접속사이므로 정답이 될 수 없다.

6

원활한 업무 운영을 위해서, 우리의 자원을 언제나 접근하기 쉽게 유지하는 것이 중요하다.

어휘 operation 사업, 운영 imperative 반드시 해야 하는, 긴요한 resource 자원, 재원 at all times 항상

해설 that절의 동사 keep은 5형식으로 사용되는 경우 목적격 보어 자리에 형용사를 취하여 '목적어를 ~하게 유지하다'라는 의미가 된다. 그러므로 형용사인 (D) more accessible이 정답이다.

7

필요한 자금을 받지 못하면, 연구 프로젝트를 진행할 수 없을 것이다.

어휘 funding 자금, 자금 제공 proceed with ~을 계속하다 whereas ~에 반하여

해설 필요한 자금을 받지 못하면 연구 프로젝트를 진행할 수 없을 것이라는 의미이므로 정답은 (A) Unless(~하지 않는 한)이다. 주절의 동사는 미래 시제이지만, 시간 및 조건의 부사절에서는 현재 시제가 미래 시제를 대신한다는 사실을 기억하자.

8

회사는 모든 문제에 대해 시기 적절하고 만족스러운 해결책을 보장하기 위해 24시간 이내에 고객 문의에 응답할 것이다.

어휘 inquiry 조사, 질문 timely 시기 적절한, 때맞춘 satisfactory 만족스러운 resolution 해결, 결의안

해설 빈칸 뒤에 수식어구만 있고 목적어가 보이지 않으므로 완전자동사를 정답으로 고른다. 따라서 보기 중 완전자동사인 (D) respond(응답하다)가 정답이다. (A) explain(설명하다), (B) promise(약속하다), (C) request(요청하다)는 모두 타동사이므로 목적어가 필요하다.

9

새로운 파트너쉽은 새로운 시장으로의 확장 및 우리의 세계적인 존재감을 제고하는 특별한 기회를 제공할 것이다.

어휘 presence 있음, 존재(함) personality 성격 assurance 확언, 자신감 relationship 관계

해설 '새로운 파트너쉽이 새로운 시장으로의 확장과 세계적인 존재감을 높이는 특별한 ------ 을 제공할 것'이라는 의미인데, 문맥상 (D) opportunity(기회)이 가장 적절하다.

10

비용 절감과 향상된 효율성을 개요로 서술한 상세한 제안서는 고객이 우리 회사의 서비스로 전환하는 것을 고려하도록 했다.

어휘 detailed 상세한 savings 절약된 금액 efficiency 효율성, 능률

해설 동사 어휘 문제는 빈칸 뒤의 문장 성분을 파악하여 정답을 찾을 수 있다. 빈칸 뒤에 목적어인 the client가 있고 그 뒤에 동사 원형인 consider가 있으므로, 빈칸에는 목적격 보어로 동사 원형을 취하는 5형식 동사인 사역동사나 지각동사가 필요하다. 그러므로 사역동사로 사용 가능한 (B) made가 정답이다.

11

이익도 중요하지만, 회사는 윤리적인 사업 실천과 사회적 책임도 높이 평가한다.

어휘 ethical 윤리적인 practice 관행, 업무, 영업 responsibility 책임, 책무

해설 '------ profits are important'는 주절을 수식하는 부사절이므로, 빈칸은 부사절 접속사 자리이다. 보기에서 부사절 접속사는 (A) While(~ 동안에, ~이기는 하지만)뿐이다. (B) Despite는 전치사, (C) However는 접속부사이므로 오답이다. 상관접속사인 (D) Not only 또한 정답이 될 수 없다.

12

주최측은 내년에 개최될 예정인 회의에 참석할 저명한 연사들에게 이미 초청장을 발송하기 시작했다.

어휘 organizer 조직자, 주최측 prominent 중요한, 유명한

해설 동사 have begun을 수식하기에 적절한 의미의 부사를 골라야 한다. (A) already(이미, 벌써), (B) politely(공손하게), (C) briefly(잠시), (D) closely(면밀히) 중 동사 have begun과 가장 어울리는 부사는 already이므로 (A)가 정답이다. already는 주로 현재완료 시제와 어울리는 부사라는 점을 참고하자.

13

도시 중심부에 위치한 새로운 박물관은 전 세계에서 온 방문객들에게 인기 있는 관광 명소가 되었다.

어휘 registration 등록 transition 이행, 변화

해설 새로운 박물관이 인기 있는 관광 명소가 되었다는 의미의 문장이므로 정답은 (C) attraction이다. tourist attraction은 복합명사로 관광 명소라는 의미이다.

14

유전학 분야에서의 획기적인 연구로 털리 박사는 권위있는 상을 받을 후보자로 지명되었다.

어휘 nominate 지명하다, 추천하다 recognition 인식, 인정 groundbreaking 신기원을 이룬, 획기적인 genetics 유전학

해설 award(상)를 수식하기에 적절한 형용사를 골라야 한다. (A) repetitive(반복적인), (B) deliberate(고의의, 신중한), (C) meticulous(꼼꼼한, 세심한), (D) prestigious(명망 있는) 중 award를 수식하는 데 가장 어울리는 형용사는 (D) prestigious이다. 상을 누구에게 수여할 것인지 신중하게 고려할 수는 있으나 상 자체가 신중할 수는 없으므로 (B) deliberate은 오답이다.

15

최근 좋지 않은 사건들을 고려하여, 회사는 기밀 자료를 보호하기 위해 보다 엄격한 보안 조치를 시행하기로 결정했다.

어휘 unfortunate 불운한, 나쁜 implement 실행하다 security measures 경계 대책, 보안 대책 confidential 비밀의, 기밀의 in spite of ~에도 불구하고 apart from ~을 제외하고, ~ 외에도 according to ~에 따르면, ~에 의하면

해설 회사가 기밀 자료를 보호하기 위해 보다 엄격한 보안 조치를 시행하기로 한 것은 최근의 좋지 않은 사건들을 '고려하여' 내린 결정이므로 정답은 (C) In light of(~을 고려하여, ~에 비추어)이다.

PART 6

[16-19]

자신의 창의적인 잠재력을 발휘하고 싶어요? 세러소타 대학교 연장 교육 프로그램이 글쓰기 기술을 향상시키고자 하는 지역사회 구성원들을 위한 다양한 프로그램을 제공합니다. 우리의 전문가 팀은 시, 소설, 문학 번역, 그리고 각본 작성을 포함한 다양한 매체를 전문으로 합니다.

우리의 프로그램을 통해, 당신은 단순히 글쓰기 능력을 발전시키는 것뿐만 아니라, 자신의 작품을 선보일 기회를 갖게 됩니다. 엄선된 작품은 우리 웹사이트에 게재되어, 당신의 노력을 인정받을 수 있는 기회를 드립니다. 강좌 등록은 우리 웹사이트 www. stetsonextension.org.에서 가능합니다. **프로그램의 상세 일정 또한 온라인에서 확인하실 수 있습니다.**

어휘 unlock (열쇠로) 열다, (비밀 등을) 드러내다 potential 가능성 있는, 잠재적인, 잠재력 specialize 전문적으로 다루다 fiction 소설 literary 문학의, 문학적인 translation 번역, 통역 medium 매체, 수단 poetry 시 showcase 공개 행사; 전시하다

16

해설 빈칸 뒤에 명사구인 writing skills가 있으므로, 보기 중에서 대명사의 소유격인 (C)의 their를 정답으로 고른다.

17

해설 빈칸 뒤의 'poetry, fiction, literary translation, and screenwriting'은 빈칸 앞에 언급된 various mediums에 속하는 것들이므로 정답은 (D) including(~을 포함하여)이다. 문장에 동사 specialize가 있으므로 빈칸에는 동사인 (A) includes가 올 수 없다. 빈칸에 들어갈 단어가 빈칸 앞의 명사와 빈칸 뒤의 명사들을 연결해 주어야 하므로, 형용사인 (B) inclusive(가격에 일체의 경비가 포함된)도 오답이다. (C) included를 과거분사로 볼 경우 이는 명사를 수식할 수는 있지만 목적어를 가질 수는 없으므로 명사와 명사 사이에는 위치할 수 없다. 따라서 (C) 또한 오답이다.

18

어휘 feature 특색을 이루다, 특종(특집)으로 하다

해설 빈칸 뒤에 수식어구만 있고 목적어는 없으므로 수동태 동사를 정답으로 고른다. 앞 문장에서 작품을 선보일 수 있는 기회를 갖는 것이 미래 시제이므로, 해당 문장 또한 미래 시제여야 한다. 따라서 미래 시제 수동태인 (B) will be featured가 정답이다.

19

(A) 많은 분들이 책 사인회에 관심을 보였습니다.
(B) 프로그램의 상세 일정 또한 온라인에서 확인하실 수 있습니다.
(C) 수업이 끝나면 당신의 글이 출판될 것입니다.
(D) 교육 과정은 이번 달 말까지 제출되어야 합니다.

어휘 detailed 상세한 curriculum 교육과정

해설 앞 문장에서 등록은 웹사이트에서 가능하다고 했으므로, 웹사이트에서 구체적인 일정도 확인할 수 있다는 내용이 이어지는 것이 자연스럽다. 따라서 정답은 (B)이다.

[20-23]

수신: 크로스드 팜스 주택 판매팀
발신: 칼 툰버그, 판매 매니저
날짜: 4월 13일 수요일
제목: 카멜백 콘도미니엄의 예정된 투어

잠재적 구매자들 사이에서 진행되고 있는 주택 개발 프로젝트인 카멜백 콘도미니엄에 대한 엄청난 관심을 보게 되어 매우 기쁩니다. 이번 주말 주택 투어가 가능한 모든 시간대가 예약이 완료되었다는 소식을 전해드립니다. **이는 사람들이 이곳에 집을 소유하기를 간절히 원한다는 것을 확인해 줍니다.** 그러나, 거래를 마무리하는 책임은 여러분에게 있습니다. 저희는 견본 주택을 세 개만 완성했기 때문에, 잠재적 구매자들이 카멜백 콘도미니엄에서 생활하는 것을 상상할 수 있도록 도와주셔야 합니다. 방문객들이 모델 하우스를 관람할 때, 여러분은 개발 지역이 고급 상점, 레스토랑 및 편리한 대중교통에 가까운 곳에 위치해 있다는 것을 강조해야 합니다.

어휘 thrilled 아주 흥분한(신이 난) immense 엄청난, 어마어마한 ongoing 계속 진행 중인 potential 가능성이 있는, 잠재적인 responsibility 책무, 책임 prospective 장래의, 곧 있을 visualize 상상하다, 마음속에 그려 보다 proximity 가까움, 근접

20

해설 진행 중인 주택 개발 프로젝트인 카멜백 콘도미니엄에 대한 엄청난 관심이 잠재적 구매자들 사이에 있었던 것이므로 빈칸의 정답은 (B) among(~의 가운데에, ~ 사이에)이다.

21

(A) 초대장이 있는 사람만 견본 주택을 방문할 수 있습니다.
(B) 견본 주택까지의 길 안내는 우리 웹사이트에서 찾을 수 있습니다.
(C) 우리는 현재 고객과 계약 협상 중입니다.
(D) 이는 사람들이 이곳에 집을 소유하기를 간절히 원한다는 것을 확인해 줍니다.

어휘 direction 방향, 위치 eager 간절히 ~하고 싶은, ~을 열망하는

해설 빈칸 앞의 내용은 잠재적 구매자들 사이에서 진행 중인 주택 개발 프로젝트인 카멜백 콘도미니엄에 대한 엄청난 관심을 보게 되었고, 이번 주말 주택 투어가 가능한 모든 시간대가 예약 완료되었다는 것이다. 이는 사람들이 이곳에서 주택을 소유하고자 한다는 근거가 되므로 빈칸에 가장 어울리는 문장은 (D)이다.

22

해설 빈칸 뒤에 목적어가 있으므로 능동태인 (B)와 (C) 중에서 정답을 골라야 한다. 빈칸이 포함된 부분은 현재까지 견본 주택을 단지 세 개만 완성했다는 의미이므로, 능동태 현재완료 시제 동사인 (B) have competed가 가장 적절하다.

23

어휘 accelerate 가속화하다 accompany 동반하다 encounter 맞닥뜨리다, 부딪히다

해설 개발 지역이 고급 상점, 레스토랑 및 편리한 대중교통에 가깝다는 것은 방문객들이 모델 하우스를 관람할 때 판매자들이 강조해야 할 장점이므로, 정답은 (A) emphasize(강조하다)이다.

[24-26]

http://www.morrishotel.com

모리스 호텔

| 호텔 소개 | 여행 정보 | 리뷰 | 연락처 | **예약** |

모리스 호텔을 선택해 주셔서 감사합니다. 다음과 같이 예약이 확정되었습니다.

예약 상세 정보

예약 번호: MSF#231021
객실 유형: 트윈룸 1
투숙 인원: 성인 2명
체크인 날짜: 4월 13일
체크아웃 날짜: 4월 16일 (3박)

게스트 정보

이름: 존 구딩
이메일: gooding78@ohyesmail.com
휴대폰: (480) 708-2021

요금 정보

1박 요금: 120달러
3박 요금: 360달러
25) 단골 고객 10% 할인: -36달러
총 숙박 비용: 324달러
결제 수단: 민트 카드 (815-****-****-5340)

*** 24-1) 요금에는 2인 무료 아침 식사, 무료 Wi-Fi 인터넷 접속, 무료 주차가 포함됩니다. 도착일로부터 15일 전까지는 무료로 취소할 수 있습니다. 도착일로부터 7일 전까지 취소 요청을 하시면 50% 환불이 이루어집니다. 그 이후에는 환불이 불가능합니다.

24-2) 5층에 위치한 24시간 운영되는 헬스장을 이용하시려면, 도착 시 접수 데스크 직원에게 객실 카드키에 무료 이용 권한을 추가해 달라고 요청해 주세요. 또한, 26) 객실 카드키로 호텔 로비에 위치한 식당과 카페에서 15% 할인 혜택을 받으실 수 있습니다.

2시간 이내에 저희로부터 공식적인 환영 이메일을 받으실 것입니다. 모리스 호텔을 예약해 주셔서 다시 한번 감사드립니다. 곧 만나뵙기를 기대합니다.

어휘 issue 발급하다, 지급하다 thereafter 그 후에 attendant 종업원, 안내원 complimentary 무료의 additionally 게다가

24

구딩 씨의 예약에 포함되지 않은 것은?
(A) 인터넷 이용
(B) 체육관 사용
(C) 무료 셔틀 버스 서비스
(D) 무료 아침 식사

해설 지문 후반에 요금에는 무료 아침 식사, 무료 Wi-Fi 인터넷 접속이 포함된다고 했으므로 (A)와 (D)는 오답이다. 도착 시 접수 데스크 직원에게 말하면 5층에 위치한 헬스장 이용이 가능하다고 했으므로 (B)도 구딩 씨의 예약에 포함된 서비스이다. (C) Free shuttle bus service(무료 셔틀 버스 서비스)는 언급되지 않았다.

25

구딩 씨에 대해 추론할 수 있는 것은?
(A) 그는 그의 이름으로 두 개의 방을 예약했다.
(B) 그는 언제든지 무료로 취소할 수 있다.
(C) 그는 숙박비를 현금으로 지불할 것이다.
(D) 그는 이 호텔에서 예전에 묵은 적이 있다.

어휘 previously 이전에

해설 지문의 요금 정보에서 자주 이용하는 고객에게 주어지는 10% 할인을 받았으므로 그가 이 호텔에서 묵은 적이 있다는 것을 알 수 있다. 따라서 정답은 (D)이다. 하나의 트윈룸이 예약되었다고 표시되어 있으므로 (A)는 틀린 내용이다. 도착일로부터 15일 전까지는 무료로 취소가 가능하지만, 도착일로부터 7일 전까지 취소 요청 시 50% 환불이 이루어지고 그 이후에는 환불이 불가능하다고 했으므로 (B)도 잘못된 정보이다. 지불 방법에서 카드를 사용했음을 알 수 있으므로 (C) 또한 오답이다.

26

호텔 식당에서 할인을 받기 위해 제시해야 하는 것은 무엇인가?
(A) 확정 편지
(B) 식사 쿠폰
(C) 객실 카드키
(D) 신분증

해설 지문 후반부에서 객실 카드키로 호텔 로비에 위치한 식당과 카페에서 15% 할인 혜택을 받을 수 있다고 했으므로 정답은 (C)이다.

[27-31]

젤코바 주식회사

9월 15일 – 50년 이상의 견고한 기반을 바탕으로, 젤코바 주식회사는 종합적인 엔지니어링, 기술, 물류, 그리고 관리 서비스를 제공합니다. 우리는 개인과 파트너로 구성된 탁월한 팀을 구성하여 항상 우수한 성과를 거두며 고객을 섬기고 있습니다.

현재, 우리는 상업 고객뿐만 아니라 정부 기관을 포함하여 사업을 확장하고 있습니다. 그 결과, 우리는 고객에게 우수한 서비스와 가치를 제공하는 데 열정을 공유하는 재능 있는 인재를 찾고 있습니다.

현재 다음 분야에서 채용을 진행하고 있습니다:

입문자 직책:	관리 직책:
• 데이터 입력 • 생산 라인 운영 담당자: 타미 코헨 이메일: tamie@zelkova.com	31-1) • 엔지니어링 • 마케팅 담당자: 수잔 트래버스 이메일: susan@zelkova.com
입문자 직책:	관리 직책:
• 고객 서비스 • 영업 담당자: 제프 필즈 이메일: jeff@zelkova.com	• 회계 • 컴퓨터 프로그래밍 담당자: 러스 라이언 이메일: russ@zelkova.com

열거된 직책에 관심이 있는 지원자는 원하는 부서의 채용 담당자에게 이메일로 신청서와 추천서 세 부를 제출해야 합니다. **²⁷⁾ 9월 20일 이후에 제출된 신청서는 고려되지 않습니다. ²⁸⁾ 선정된 지원자들에게만 이메일로 면접 일정을 통지하며, 이는 9월 30일까지 발송될 것입니다.** 자세한 정보를 위해, 위에 열거된 담당자들 중 누구에게든 문의하시면 됩니다.

어휘 based on ~에 근거하여 foundation 토대, 기초 establish 설립하다 comprehensive 포괄적인, 종합적인 engineering 공학 기술 logistics 실행 계획 exemplary 모범적인 performance 공연, 성과 commercial 상업의, 민간의 governmental 정부의 as a result 그 결과, 따라서 talented 재능이 있는 individual 개인 passion 열정 candidate 입후보자 along with ~과 함께 via ~을 경유하여, 통하여 respective 각자의, 각각의 recruiter 모집자 reference 추천서 no later than 늦어도 ~까지는

수신: 수잔 트래버스 〈susan@zelkova.com〉
발신: 알렉스 하우 〈alexhowe@ourspace.com〉
제목: 지원
날짜: 9월 17일

트래버스 씨께,

저는 채용 사이트인 www.wanted.com에서 귀사의 채용 공고를 우연히 발견했으며, 젤코바 주식회사에 입사하는 것에 상당한 관심을 가지고 있습니다.

저는 귀사에서 요구하는 자격을 충분히 갖추고 있다고 자신합니다. **³⁰⁻¹⁾ 소더비 그룹에서 회계사 역할을 담당하는 것으로 전직하기 전에 다양한 광고 회사에서 10년 이상의 경력을 ²⁹⁾ 쌓았습니다. ³⁰⁻²⁾ ³¹⁻²⁾ 브랜딩 및 홍보 분야에서의 광범위한 저의 경험이 귀사에 중요한 자산이 될 것입니다.** 게다가, 저는 애리조나주 템피 대학교에서 경영학사 학위를 취득하였으며 회계학을 부전공했습니다. 첨부한 이력서에서도 알 수 있듯이, 저는 직책에 이상적인 후보자입니다.

귀하의 응답을 기다리고 있겠습니다.

진심으로,

알렉스 하우

어휘 come across ~을 우연히 발견하다 possess 소유하다 qualification 자격 transition 이행, 이행하다 accountant 회계사 extensive 아주 넓은, 폭넓은 asset 자산 degree 학위 business administration 경영학 accounting 회계 (업무) evident 분명한 candidate 후보자, 지원자 await ~을 기다리다

27
지원서는 언제까지 제출되어야 하는가?
(A) 9월 15일
(B) 9월 17일
(C) 9월 20일
(D) 9월 30일

해설 광고 지문 마지막 문단의 'Applications received after September 20 will not be considered.'에서 9월 20일 이후에 제출된 지원서는 검토되지 않을 것이라고 했으므로 지원서는 적어도 9월 20일까지는 제출되어야 한다. 따라서 정답은 (C)이다.

28
트래버스 씨는 하우 씨에게 어떻게 연락할 것 같은가?
(A) 그에게 전화해서
(B) 그에게 서류를 보내서
(C) 웹사이트에 공지사항을 게시해서
(D) 그에게 이메일을 보내서

어휘 mail 우편물을 발송하다 document 서류, 문서 post 게시하다, 공고하다

해설 광고 지문 마지막 문단의 'Only selected candidates will be contacted via e-mail for interviews with notifications sent no later than September 30.'에서 면접을 위해 선발된 지원자에게만 늦어도 9월 30일까지 이메일로 연락이 갈 것이라고 했으므로 정답은 (D)이다.

29
이메일에서 두 번째 문단 첫 번째 줄의 "accumulated"와 의미상 가장 가까운 어휘는?
(A) 실행하다
(B) 남다
(C) 연장하다
(D) 모으다, 쌓다

해설 '소더비 그룹에서 회계사 역할을 하는 것으로 전직하기 전에 다양한 마케팅 회사에서 10년 이상의 경력을 쌓았다'라는 의미이므로, accumulated는 '축적하다, 쌓다'의 뜻으로 사용되었다. 이와 비슷한 의미의 동사는 (D) gained이다.

30
하우 씨가 이메일에 기재하지 않은 자격 요건은 무엇인가?
(A) 그는 영업사원을 관리한 경험이 있다.
(B) 그는 대학에서 회계학을 공부했다.
(C) 그는 이전에 광고 회사에서 일한 적이 있다.
(D) 그는 10년 이상의 경력을 가지고 있다.

어휘 qualification 자격 supervise 감독하다 accounting 회계(업무) business administration 경영학

해설 이메일에서 그는 애리조나에 있는 템피 대학교에서 경영학을 전공했고 부전공으로 회계학을 공부했다고 했으므로 (B)는 언급된 내용이다. 또한 이메일 두 번째 문단에서 그는 10년 넘게 여러 광고 회사에서 일했다고 했으므로 (C)와 (D) 역시 언급된 내용이다. 따라서 정답은 (A)이다.

31
하우 씨는 어느 부서에 지원할 것 같은가?
(A) 고객 서비스
(B) 마케팅
(C) 회계
(D) 컴퓨터 프로그래밍

DAY 04 명사

PRACTICE
pp.158-161

1 The company's profits have increased by 20% compared to last year.

2 The conference will be held at the Garwood Hotel on Friday, October 12.

3 Our new product line has received positive feedback from customers.

4 The shipment of goods has been delayed due to unforeseen circumstances.

5 Please submit your résumé and cover letter to the HR Department by the end of this week.

6 The members of the sales team achieved their monthly targets ahead of schedule.

7 The company is considering expanding its operations to international markets.

8 As a responsible employer, we always consider the work-life balance of our employees our highest priority.

9 The training session will take place in the conference room on the second floor.

10 The deadline for submitting the monthly sales report is next Monday.

11 facility		12 competition	
13 Purchases		14 performance	
15 survey		16 complaint	
17 consideration		18 carefully	
19 planning		20 opening	

1 회사의 이익은 작년 대비 20% 증가했다.
2 회의는 10월 12일 금요일에 가우드 호텔에서 개최될 예정이다.
3 우리의 신제품 라인은 고객들로부터 긍정적인 피드백을 받았다.
4 상품의 발송이 예기치 않은 사정으로 지연되었다.

5 이력서와 자기소개서를 인사부로 이번 주 안에 제출하세요.

6 영업 팀원들은 월간 목표를 일정보다 빠르게 달성했다.

7 회사는 국제 시장으로 사업을 확장하는 것을 고려하고 있다.

8 책임 있는 고용주로서, 우리는 항상 직원들의 워라밸을 최우선 과제로 고려한다.

9 교육 세션은 2층 회의실에서 진행될 예정이다.

10 월간 판매 보고서의 제출 마감일은 다음 주 월요일이다.

11 신규 제조 시설은 생산 능력을 크게 향상시켰다.

12 시장에서의 이 치열한 경쟁은 우리가 지속적으로 전략을 조정하고 개선할 것을 요구한다.

13 두 개의 매장이 동일한 기업에 속해 있더라도, 한 매장에서 구매한 것들에 대한 환불은 다른 매장에서 받을 수 없습니다.

14 바이올리니스트가 *파르티타 No. 1* 연주에 대해 기립 박수를 받았다.

15 우리는 청소년들이 매일 얼마나 많은 시간을 인터넷에 소비하는지 알아보기 위해 설문조사를 실시했다.

16 고객 만족을 유지하기 위해서, 모든 고객 불만들을 신속하게 처리해야 한다.

17 이 문제들은 최종 결정을 내리기 전에 고려되어야 한다.

18 이사회는 출품작을 주의깊게 검토한 후 만장일치로 결정했다.

19 뛰어난 계획 덕분에, 건설사는 쇼핑 센터를 예상보다 일찍 완공했다.

20 캐서린은 스타은행 홍보부서의 공석에 상당히 관심이 있다.

📝 실전 문제 연습
p.163

1 (D)	2 (B)	3 (B)	4 (C)
5 (B)	6 (C)	7 (C)	8 (B)
9 (A)	10 (A)	11 (C)	12 (C)
13 (A)	14 (A)	15 (B)	16 (A)
17 (B)	18 (B)	19 (D)	20 (C)
21 (A)	22 (D)	23 (C)	24 (B)
25 (D)	26 (B)	27 (A)	28 (B)
29 (C)	30 (D)		

PART 5

1
판테온 인베스트먼트는 소중한 직원들을 효과적으로 계속 유지하기 위해 우수한 혜택을 제공한다.

어휘 in order to ~하기 위해 retain (계속) 유지하다, 보유하다
valued 평가된, 귀중한, 소중한 beneficial 유익한, 이로운
benefit 혜택, 이득; 유익하다

해설 빈칸은 동사 offers의 목적어 자리로 형용사 excellent의 수식을 받는 명사가 와야 한다. 따라서 정답은 (D)이다. 동명사는 형용사의 수식을 받을 수 없으므로 (A)는 정답이 될 수 없다.

2
월간 직원 교육을 실시함으로써, 오로라 일렉트로닉스는 영업 사원들이 제품 개발 상황에 대해 계속 정보를 얻을 수 있도록 보장한다.

어휘 conduct (특정한 활동을) 하다, 지휘하다   session 시간, 기간, 세션   sales staff 판매 사원, 영업 사원   inform 알리다, 통지하다   development 발달, 성장, 개발

해설 빈칸은 2형식 동사 remains의 주격 보어 자리이므로 형용사인 (B)가 정답이다. 문장에 동사 remains가 있으므로 동사인 (A)와 (D)는 오답이며, 주격 보어 자리에 명사가 오면 이 명사는 주어와 동격이 되어야 하는데, (C)의 information은 that절의 주어인 its sales staff와 동격이 될 수 없다.

3

신규 지점의 장비 및 용품 주문과 관련된 모든 요청은 지원 서비스 부서의 노블 씨에게 직접 문의해 주세요.

어휘 request 요청, 요구; 요청하다   equipment 장비, 설비   supply 공급; 비품; 공급하다   direct ~로 향하다; ~로 보내다   support 지지; 지원하다   division (조직의) 분과, 부서

해설 빈칸은 동사 direct의 목적어 자리이므로 명사가 와야 하는데 빈칸 앞에 한정사 all이 있다. all 뒤에는 복수 가산 명사나 불가산 명사가 와야 하므로 정답은 (B)이다.

4

현금 창출을 위한 다양한 옵션이 있지만, 회사채를 다시 발행하는 것이 가장 현명한 방법으로 보인다.

어휘 generate 발생시키다   corporate bond 회사채   prudent 신중한, 조심성 있는; 현명한   issue 발행, 발행하다

해설 '------- another series of corporate bonds'는 동사 appears의 주어이므로, (A), (C), (D)가 정답 후보이다. 빈칸 뒤의 another series of corporate bonds를 목적어로 취할 수 있어야 하므로 동명사인 (C)가 정답이다. 과거분사인 (B)의 issued가 명사를 수식할 수는 있지만, 이는 한정사 another 앞에 올 수 없다.

5

제품에 대한 상세한 설명과 더 많은 정보를 위해서, 당사 웹사이트 www.bellappliance.com을 방문해 주세요.

어휘 detailed 상세한   description 서술, 묘사   faculty 능력, 학부   resolution 해결; 결의안; 결단력   installment 할부금

해설 제품에 대한 상세한 설명과 더 많은 정보를 위해서 웹사이트를 방문하라는 내용이 되어야 자연스러우므로 '설명'을 의미하는 명사인 (B) descriptions가 정답이다.

6

공인중개사가 새로운 세입자를 구하면, 집주인은 당신의 보증금을 돌려줄 수 있을 것이다.

어휘 realtor 부동산업자, 공인중개사   tenant 세입자, 임차인   landlord 주인, 임대주   deposit 보증금, 착수금

해설 시간·조건의 부사절에서는 현재 시제가 미래 시제를 대신하므로 빈칸에는 현재 시제 동사가 와야 한다. 빈칸 앞의 주어는 3인칭 단수이므로 단수 동사인 (C) finds가 정답이다.

7

세이무어 건설이 리모델링 프로젝트의 예산 제약을 어떻게 극복할 것인지를 설명하는 제안서를 제출했다.

어휘 submit 제출하다; 항복하다   proposal 제안, 제의   overcome 극복하다   budget 예산   constraint 제약, 통제   outline 개요를 서술하다, 윤곽을 보여주다

해설 문장에 동사 has submitted가 있으므로 동사인 (A)와 (B)는 정답이 될 수 없다. (A)와 (B)를 명사로 보더라도 'proposal outline'이라는 복합명사는 존재하지 않는다. 빈칸 뒤의 how로 시작하는 명사절을 목적어로 취할 수 있는 현재분사인 (C)가 정답이다.

8

시장에서의 경쟁 증가로 인해, 셔먼 보험은 올해 수익 감소를 겪고 있다.

어휘 due to ~ 때문에   increasing 커지는, 증가하는   competition 경쟁   suffer 겪다, 고통받다   revenue 수익

해설 문장은 시장에서의 경쟁 증가로 인해 셔먼 보험의 수익이 감소했다는 내용이 되어야 자연스럽다. 따라서 (B) losses(손실)이 정답이다. revenue loss는 '수입 감소'를 의미하는 복합 명사이다.

9

부서 간 소통을 원활하게 하기 위해, 경영진은 매주 월요일에 전체 직원 회의를 개최하기로 결정했다.

어휘 in an effort to ~해보려는 노력으로   interaction 상호 작용, 소통   department 부서   management 경영, 경영진   general staff meeting 전체 직원 회의   indicate 나타내다, 가리키다   appraise 감정하다, 평가하다   dominate 지배하다, 우위를 차지하다

해설 이 문장은 부서간 소통을 원활하게 하기 위해 경영진이 매주 월요일에 전체 직원 회의를 개최하기로 결정했다는 의미가 되어야 자연스러우므로, 정답은 (A) facilitate(촉진하다, 용이하게 하다)이다. facilitate은 어떤 일을 원활하게 이루어지도록 돕거나 장려하는 것을 의미하므로 interaction(상호 작용, 소통)을 목적어로 취하는 동사로 어울린다.

10

썬시티 출판사는 디지털 배부를 기반으로 출판되는 모든 콘텐츠에 독자들이 쉽게 접근할 수 있도록 하는 것을 목표로 한다.

어휘 based on ~에 근거하여   distribution 분배 (방식), 배급, 배부   distributor 배급 업자(회사), 유통 업자(회사)   distribute 나누어 주다, 분배하다, 배부하다

해설 빈칸은 전치사 based on 뒤에 있으므로 명사구 자리이다. 보기 중 명사인 (A) distribution과 (C) distributors가 정답 후보인데, 고객이 출판사에서 출판하는 컨텐츠에 더 쉽게 접근할 수 있도록 디지털 배부를 기반으로 출판한다는 내용이 되어야 자연스러우므로 정답은 (A) distribution이다.

11

우리는 새로운 화장품 라인의 판매 촉진 캠페인에 대한 창의적인 아이디어를 공유하는 데 모든 직원들이 솔선수범하기를 권장한다.

어휘 encourage 격려하다, 권장하다   creative 창조적인, 창의적인   sales promotion 판촉 행사   cosmetic 화장품   appraisal 평가, 판단   precaution 예방책, 예방 조치   initiative 진취성, 주도(권)   directory (이름·주소 등의 관련 정보를 보통 알파벳순으로 나열한) 안내 책자

해설 모든 직원들이 새로운 화장품 라인의 판매 촉진 캠페인에 대한 자신들의 창의적인 아이디어를 솔선하여 적극적으로 공유해야 한다는 내용의 문장이므로 정답은 (C) initiative이다. 'take initiative'는 '솔선수

범하다' 혹은 '주도권을 잡다'라는 의미이다.

12

스완 부동산은 환경을 고려한 주거용 건물을 원하는 사람들에게 합리적인 대안을 제공한다.

어휘 reasonable 타당한, 합리적인 seek 찾다, 추구하다 environmentally 환경적으로, 환경 보호적으로 conscious 의식하는, 의식이 있는 residential 주택지의, 거주하기 좋은 construction 건설, 공사; 건축물 alternate 번갈아 생기는, 번갈아 나오는, 번갈아 나오게 만들다 alternation 교대, 교체 alternative 대안; 대체 가능한 alternatively 그 대신에, 그렇지 않으면

해설 빈칸은 동사 offers의 목적어로서 형용사 reasonable의 수식을 받는 명사 자리이므로, 명사인 (A)와 (C) 중에서 정답을 골라야 한다. alternative는 선택지 또는 대안을 의미하며 alternation은 시간, 순서, 또는 패턴의 변화 등 두 가지 이상의 대상 또는 요소가 번갈아 발생하는 것을 의미한다. '합리적인 대안'을 제공한다는 내용이 되는 것이 자연스러우므로 정답은 (C)이다.

13

의료 서비스 제공 업체로서, 우리는 건강에 대한 우리의 헌신을 보여주는 최고 품질의 건강 보조 식품만을 생산한다.

어휘 nutritional supplement 영양(보조)제 wellness 건강(함) commitment 약속; 전념, 헌신 measurement 측정, 측량 employment 직장; 고용 arrangement 준비, 마련

해설 의료 서비스 제공 업체가 최고의 건강 보조 식품만을 생산한다는 것은 건강에 대한 그들의 '헌신'을 보여 주는 것이므로 정답은 (A) commitment이다. 참고로 'commitment to ~'는 '~에 대한 전념, 헌신'이며, 이때의 to는 전치사이므로 명사나 동명사가 연결된다.

14

이 웹사이트의 목표는 소비자들에게 그들의 생활비를 줄이는 데 도움을 줄 수 있는 실용적인 팁을 제공하는 것이다.

어휘 practical 실용적인, 현실적인 tip 팁, 정보 lower 줄이다, 낮추다 living expenses 생활비 repetitive 반복되는 comparable 비교할 만한 knowledgeable 아는 것이 많은

해설 '소비자들이 생활비를 줄이는 데 도움이 되는 팁'을 수식하기에 의미상 적절한 형용사를 골라야 한다. repetitive(반복되는)와 comparable(비교할 만한)은 의미상 어색하므로 (B)와 (C)는 오답이다. knowledgeable(아는 것이 많은)은 사람만 수식할 수 있으므로 이 또한 오답이다. '실용적인 팁'이 해석상 가장 자연스러우므로 (A)가 정답이다.

15

다음 달부터, 영업팀의 모든 직원은 매주 중간 경과 보고서를 제출해야 한다.

어휘 submit 제출하다; 항복하다 weekly 매주의 progress 진전, 진행, 진척 report 기록; 보고서; 알리다

해설 member는 단수 가산 명사이므로, 단수 가산 명사 앞에 사용되는 한정사인 (B)가 정답이다. 참고로 one another(서로)는 명사 앞에 사용될 수 없고, other와 most는 복수 명사나 불가산 명사 앞에 사용되는 한정사이므로 (A), (C), (D)는 모두 오답이다.

PART 6

[16-19]

> 제 10회 연례 프레즈노 카운티 리더스가 9월 10일에 열릴 예정입니다. 그것의 엄청난 인기 때문에, 이번 독서 축제는 새로운 장소인 역사적인 프레스코 극장에서 열릴 예정입니다. 이 장소는 최대 500명의 참석자를 수용할 것으로 예상됩니다. 더 큰 시설은 지역 사회의 더 많은 구성원들이 참여할 수 있도록 할 것입니다. 올해의 특별 작가는 이 지역 출신의 저명한 환경운동가인 조지 로튼 씨입니다. 그는 자신의 최신 책인 *침묵의 신호*에 사인해 줄 것입니다. 관심 있는 사람들은 이번 행사를 위해 로튼 씨의 작품 한 권을 가져오실 것을 권장합니다. **이 책은 현재 지역의 몇몇 서점에서 판매되고 있습니다.** 이번 축제와 다가오는 행사 목록에 대한 자세한 정보는 www.fresnos.com에서 확인하실 수 있습니다.

어휘 be set to do ~하도록 예정되어 있다 take place 개최되다, 일어나다 immense 엄청난, 어마어마한 historical 역사적, 역사상의 venue 장소 accommodate 공간을 제공하다, 수용하다 featured ~을 특색으로 한; 주연의 prominent 중요한; 유명한 environmentalist 환경 운동가 occasion 때, 기회

16

해설 이번 해의 독서 축제는 더 큰 장소에서 열린다고 했고 이는 '축제'의 엄청난 인기 때문이므로, 빈칸에는 '축제'를 지칭하는 대명사인 its(그것의)가 와야 한다.

17

어휘 situation 상황

해설 지문의 전반부에서 엄청난 인기로 축제가 새로운 장소인 역사적인 프레스코 극장에서 열릴 것이며, 이 장소는 최대 500명의 참석자를 수용할 것으로 예상된다고 했으므로 빈칸에는 '장소'를 의미하는 단어가 와야 한다는 것을 유추할 수 있다. 따라서 빈칸은 '시설'을 뜻하는 (B) facility가 정답이다.

18

해설 빈칸은 앞과 뒤의 두 절을 연결하는 연결어 자리이다. 빈칸 뒤의 절에 주어가 없으므로 빈칸에는 주격 관계대명사가 필요한데, 보기 중에서 주격 관계대명사는 (B) who뿐이다. (A) as to(~에 관해)와 (D) among(~중에)은 전치사로서 명사 앞에 위치할 수 있으며, (C) in order는 to부정사 앞에 붙는 수식어구 혹은 전명구로서 절과 절을 연결할 수 없다.

19

(A) 올해의 행사 또한 매우 성공적이었습니다.
(B) 그는 지금 그 시리즈의 새 책을 계획하고 있습니다.
(C) 그 축제는 올해 공원에서 열릴 것입니다.
(D) 이 책은 현재 지역의 몇몇 서점에서 판매되고 있습니다.

해설 빈칸 앞 문장에서 관심 있는 사람들은 이번 행사를 위해 로튼 씨의 작품 한 권을 가져오는 것이 권장된다고 했으므로, 이 책을 어디에서 구할 수 있는지 설명해주는 내용인 (D)가 빈칸에 가장 어울린다.

[20-23]

> 유명 요리사 도나 홈즈의 오랜 꿈인 정통 남부 스타일 레스토랑을 브루클린에 개장하는 것이 거의 20여년을 5성급 호텔의 요리사로 보낸 후에 드디어 이루어졌습니다. 브루클린의 유티카 애비뉴 1343번지에 위치한 도나스 테이블에서 5월 15일 금요일 오전 10시부터 오후 9시까지 열리는 그랜드 오프닝 행사에 여러분을 초대합니다. **리본 커팅식은 오전 11시에 시작됩니다.** 존경받는 지역 사회의 지도자들이 행사에 참석할 예정입니다. 우리의 고전적인 남부 요리를 맛보고 요리사 도나 홈즈의 요리 열정을 만끽하세요. 참석자들은 그들에게만 제공되는 할인과 쿠폰 혜택을 누릴 수 있습니다. 자세한 정보는 donnastable.com을 방문하거나 (212) 310-2525로 문의해주세요.

어휘 lifelong 평생 동안의　authentic 진품인, 진짜인, 정확한　southern 남부에 위치한　celebrate 기념하다, 축하하다　opening 시작 부분, 개막식　invite 초대하다, 요청하다　participate 참가하다　ceremony 식, 의식　indulge 마음껏 하다, 충족시키다　classic 일류의, 대표적인, 고전적인　dish 접시, 요리　savor 맛, 풍미　opportunity 기회　exclusive 독점적인, 전용의

20

어휘 while ~하는 동안에　prior to ~에 앞서　only if ~해야만

해설 빈칸은 빈칸 뒤 명사구 almost 20 years를 연결하는 전치사 자리이므로 부사절 접속사인 (A)와 (D)는 오답이다. 해석상 20년 동안 5성급 호텔의 레스토랑에서 요리사로 지낸 '후에' 그의 꿈인 자신의 레스토랑을 여는 것이 마침내 실현되었다는 의미의 문장이 되어야 하므로 정답은 (C)이다.

21

해설 '------- at 1343 Utica Ave., Brooklyn'은 'Donna's table'을 수식하는 형용사구이다. 따라서 명사를 수식할 수 있는 과거분사 (A), 현재분사 (C), 그리고 형용사적 용법의 to부정사인 (D)가 정답 후보이다. 그런데 뒤에 목적어가 보이지 않으므로 과거분사 located가 정답이 된다. Donna's table과 located 사이에 주격 관계 대명사 which와 is가 생략된 형태이다.

22

(A) 예상보다 더 많은 사람들이 이 행사에 모여들었습니다.
(B) 그것은 이 동네에서 두 번째 지점의 개장을 기념합니다.
(C) 이 식당은 매주 일요일과 월요일에 문을 닫습니다.
(D) 리본 커팅식은 오전 11시에 시작됩니다.

어휘 anticipated 예상되는　assemble 모이다　mark 표시하다, 기념하다　branch 지사, 지점　ribbon-cutting 개관식, 개통식, 준공식　commence 시작되다

해설 빈칸 앞 문장에서 개업식의 일정이 언급되었으므로, 연결되는 문장 또한 개업식 행사 일정에 관련된 내용이어야 한다. 또한 빈칸 뒤 문장에서 존경받는 지역 사회의 지도자들이 행사에 참석할 예정이라고 했으므로, 이에 앞서 리본 커팅식이 언급되는 것이 자연스럽다. 정답은 (D)이다.

23

해설 빈칸 뒤에 할인과 쿠폰 혜택을 누릴 수 있다는 내용이 이어지고 있으므로, 주어는 행사나 이벤트에 참석하는 사람들을 의미하는 명사가 되어야 한다. 따라서 정답은 (C) Attendees(참석자들)인데, attendants는 주로 종업원이나 도우미를 가리키는 명사이다.

PART 7

[24-25]

조쉬 가드너	오후 2시 21분

안녕, 안젤라. 25-1) **비벌리 로드의 오픈 하우스에서 사무실로 돌아가는 길이에요.** 오늘 집을 보러 온 방문객들이 많았어요.

안젤라 코드	오후 2시 23분

잘됐네요. 그건 그렇고, 여기 회의 시간에 맞춰 올 수 있나요? 3시에 하는 것 맞죠?

조쉬 가드너	오후 2시 24분

네, 맞아요. 사실, 오후 3시에 겨우 도착할 것 같아요. 말 나온 김에, 24) **저를 도와줄 수 있나요?**

안젤라 코드	오후 2시 25분

물론이죠. 제가 뭘 하면 될까요?

조쉬 가드너	오후 2시 26분

25-2) **제 책상 위에 우리가 고객들에게 추천하는 플랫부쉬의 상업용 부동산에 대한 자세한 정보가 담긴 파일이 있을 거예요.** 그것을 두 부 복사해 주실 수 있나요?

안젤라 코드	오후 2시 27분

알겠어요. 걱정하지 마세요. 도착하자마자 회의에 참석하실 수 있도록 회의실 책상 위에 올려 놓을게요.

조쉬 가드너	오후 2시 27분

정말 감사해요!

어휘 by the way 그런데　make it to ~에 이르다, 도착하다　on time 정각에, 시간을 어기지 않고　actually 사실은, 실제로　speaking of ~에 관해서 말한다면　absolutely 전적으로, 틀림없이　contain ~이 들어있다　detail 세부 사항　commercial 상업의, 상업적인　property 재산, 부동산　place 놓다　as soon as ~하자마자, ~하자 곧

24

오후 2시 25분에 코드 씨가 "물론이죠"라고 쓴 것은 무슨 의미인가?
(A) 그녀는 가드너 씨가 그녀에게 연락해서 기쁘다.
(B) 그녀는 가드너 씨를 도울 준비가 되었다.
(C) 그녀는 가드너 씨의 성공을 확신한다.
(D) 그녀는 지금 회의에 참석하기 위해 가고 있다.

어휘 pleasure 기쁨, 만족　assistance 도움　confidence 확신, 자신감　on one's(the) way to ~로 가는 중에

해설 'Absolutely'는 가드너 씨가 도와줄 수 있는지를 물은 것에 대한 답변이다. 이는 가드너 씨를 돕겠다는 표현이므로 정답은 (B)이다.

25

가드너 씨는 어떤 종류의 사업에 종사할 것 같은가?
(A) 조경 회사
(B) 출판사

(C) 광고 회사

(D) 부동산 회사

해설 오후 2시 21분 가드너 씨가 'I'm returning to the office from the open house on Beverly Road.'라고 했을 때 비벌리 가의 오픈 하우스에서 일을 했다는 단서를 얻을 수 있다. 그리고, 오후 2시 26분에 그가 'There should be a file on my desk containing details of the commercial properties in Flatbush that we recommend to clients.'라고 한 것에서 고객들에게 추천하는 플랫부쉬의 상업용 부동산에 대한 정보가 담긴 파일이 그의 책상 위에 있다는 것도 정답의 단서이다. 가드너 씨는 오픈 하우스에서 일하고 고객에게 부동산을 소개하는 직업을 갖고 있으므로 정답은 (D)이다.

[26-30]

http://www.magnoliamoving.com

| 소개 | 문의처 | 배송 추적 | 이사 서비스 | 견적 보기 |

매그놀리아 무빙: 완벽한 이사 해법

매그놀리아 무빙은 고객의 26) **요구에 맞춰 맞춤형 이사 서비스를 제공합니다.** 현지 이전이든 전국 이동이든, 당사의 경험 많은 팀은 규모에 상관없이 고객을 지원할 준비가 되어 있습니다. 거의 20년 동안 업계를 선도해 온 당사는 고객 만족도를 높이기 위해 최신 이사 기술에 대한 정보를 지속적으로 업데이트하는 것에 최선을 다하고 있습니다. 당사의 직원들은 효율적이고, 정중하며, 세부 사항에 주의를 기울여 이삿짐의 안전을 보장합니다.

가격은 심플합니다: 직원 1명당 1시간에 50달러입니다. 전문 작업을 위해 트럭이나 가구용 짐수레가 필요한 경우 추가 요금이 부과될 수 있습니다. 정확한 견적을 받으려면, 신속한 작업 주문 양식을 작성하세요.

아래는 당사의 표준 요금입니다.

이삿짐 직원	시간당 임금
1명	50달러
2명	100달러
28-1) 3명	150달러
4명 이상	200 – 300달러

여러분께 매끄러운 이사 경험을 제공하는 매그놀리아 무빙의 편리함을 경험해 보세요. 당신의 이삿짐에 대해 안심할 수 있습니다.

어휘 shipment 배송, 수송 track 추적하다 estimate 추정; 견적서 an array of 다수의 customizable 주문에 따라 만들 수 있는 latest 최근의; 최신의 소식 mover 움직이는 사람, 물건을 옮기는 사람 efficient 효율적인, 능률적인 courteous 공손한, 정중한 attentive 신경을 쓰는, 주의를 기울이는 seamless 아주 매끄러운 belonging 재산, 소지품 in capable hands (맡겨서) 안심할 수 있는, 잘 관리되는

	매그놀리아 무빙 작업 주문서 양식
오늘 날짜	10월 28일 목요일
성명	라라 스미스
이메일 주소	lalasmith@worldnet.com
전화번호	602-811-1165
이사 나가는 곳	애리조나주 스코츠데일 카멜백 로드 6993번지, D300호, 85552
이사 들어가는 곳	애리조나주 메사 페코스 로드 8773번지, 스위트 355호, 85212
이사 예정일	30-1) 11월 20일
이사할 물건	27) 12개의 나무 선반: 그 중 5개는 폭 3.5 피트 길이 6피트, 3개는 폭 3피트 길이 5피트, 나머지는 폭 2피트 길이 5피트
의견	저는 제조업체에서 곧 개업할 신발 가게까지 나무 선반 12개를 운반하는 데 도움이 필요합니다. 그 가게는 메사 쇼핑 센터의 3층에 위치해 있습니다. 29) 지난달 비슷한 양의 물건을 옮기고 귀사의 서비스를 강력히 추천했던 동료는 제가 설명한 물건을 옮기는 데 적어도 두 명이 필요할 것 같다고 말했습니다. 30-2) 11월 20일을 원하는 이사 날짜로 표시했지만, 11월 20일이 불가능하다면 같은 주 내에 다른 날도 가능합니다.

어휘 wooden 목재의, 나무로 된 shelf 선반, 책꽂이 wide 폭이 ~인 long 길이가 ~인 rest 나머지 manufacturer 제조자, 생산 회사 situated 위치해 있는 comparable 비슷한, 비교할 만한 volume 용량, 용적 describe 말하다, 묘사하다 indicate 나타내다

수신: 라라 스미스 〈lalasmith@worldnet.com〉
발신: 브랜든 존슨 〈branden77@magnoliamoving.com〉
제목: 견적서
날짜: 10월 28일
첨부파일: 견적_R1028_M1120.pdf

배송이 필요하여 매그놀리아 무빙을 선택해 주셔서 감사합니다. 저희 경험상, 물품의 크기와 28-2) **3층 위치 때문에, 전문 직원 3명으로 구성된 그룹을 추천합니다.** 저희는 램프와 보호 커버가 완비된 트럭과 함께 서비스를 제공하는 견적서를 첨부했습니다. 조립 서비스는 포함되어 있지 않으므로 주의하시기 바랍니다. 30-3) **안타깝게도, 11월 20일은 불가능하지만 다음 날 배송이 가능합니다.** 문의 사항이 있거나 자세한 내용을 확인하고 싶다면 480-225-2757로 연락해 주시거나 제공된 주소로 이메일을 보내 주시기 바랍니다.

진심으로,

브랜든 존슨
매그놀리아 이사

어휘 attached 부착된, 첨부된 crew 팀, 무리, 승무원 equipped 장비를 갖춘 ramp 램프(화물 적재 등을 위한 경사 계단) protective 보호용의 assembly 조립, 의회 via ~을 통하여, 경유하여

26

웹페이지에서 첫 번째 문단의 첫 번째 줄 단어 "cater to"와 의미상 가장 가까운 것은?

(A) 재건하다

(B) (요구에) 부응하다

(C) 변형시키다

(D) 강하게 하다

해설 매그놀리아 무빙은 맞춤형 이사 서비스를 제공하여, 현지 이전이든 전국 이동이든, 규모에 상관없이 고객을 지원할 준비가 되어 있다고 했으므로 'cater to your needs'는 '당신의 요구에 맞춘다'는 의미이다. 따라서 'cater to(~을 충족시키다)'와 가장 가까운 의미의 동사는 (B) accommodate이다.

27

스미스 씨가 그녀의 이사에 대해 언급한 것은?

(A) 각각 다른 사이즈의 물품을 포함할 것이다.

(B) 이미 예정보다 훨씬 늦었다.

(C) 특수한 장비가 필요할 것이다.

(D) 다른 주로 이사할 것이다.

어휘 far 훨씬, 아주 behind schedule 예정(정시)보다 늦게 equipment 장비, 설비 involve 수반하다, 포함하다, 관련시키다

해설 양식의 'Items to be moved' 항목에서 그녀가 옮겨야 하는 12개의 나무 선반 크기의 설명을 보면, 그녀가 여러 가지 크기의 선반을 옮겨야 한다는 것을 알 수 있다. 따라서 정답은 (A)이다.

28

스미스 씨가 매그놀리아 무빙을 이용할 경우 가장 지불할 가능성이 높은 시간당 임금은?

(A) 100달러

(B) 150달러

(C) 200달러

(D) 300달러

해설 이메일의 'we recommend a crew of three professional movers'에서, 스미스 씨의 짐을 옮기기 위해서는 3명의 전문 이삿짐 직원이 필요하다는 것을 알 수 있다. 웹페이지의 표에서 3명의 이삿짐 직원에 대해 시간당 150달러가 청구된다는 것을 알 수 있으므로 정답은 (B)이다.

29

스미스 씨에 대해 암시되는 것은?

(A) 그녀는 지난달 매그놀리아 이사의 서비스를 이용했다.

(B) 그녀는 11월에 그녀의 신발 매장을 닫을 계획이다.

(C) 그녀는 그녀의 친구가 추천해 준 사업체에 연락했다.

(D) 그녀는 가구 제조 공장을 운영하고 있다.

어휘 run (사업체 등을) 운영하다, 관리하다 a manufacturing plant 제조 공장

해설 양식의 'Comments' 항목에서 스미스 씨는 자신에게 매그놀리아 무빙을 추천한 친구 중 하나가 지난달에 그녀와 비슷한 물량의 물품을 옮겼다고 언급하고 있으므로 정답은 (C)이다.

30

존슨 씨에 따르면, 그의 회사가 할 수 있는 것은?

(A) 지역 내에서 가장 저렴한 가격을 제공해 준다.

(B) 이전 고객들의 추천서를 제공해 준다.

(C) 배송 시 무료로 가구를 조립해 준다.

(D) 제안된 것보다 늦게 이삿짐을 옮겨 준다.

어휘 affordable 알맞은, 줄 수 있는 reference 추천서; 언급; 참고 assemble 조립하다 make the move 옮기다, 이사하다

해설 양식의 'Move date' 항목에 11월 20일이라고 기재되어 있지만, 이메일에서 11월 20일은 예약이 꽉 차 있기 때문에 그 다음 날 배송이 가능하다고 언급하고 있다. 즉, 회사는 스미스 씨가 제안한 날짜보다 늦게 이삿짐을 옮겨 줄 수 있다는 것을 알 수 있으므로 정답은 (D)이다.

DAY 05 대명사

PRACTICE

1 yours	2 ours	3 their
4 themselves	5 herself	6 himself
7 Those	8 those	9 It
10 those	11 the other	12 another
13 others	14 Much	15 have

1 틸러 씨의 제안은 당신의 제안과 매우 유사하다.

2 헤펀 사는 작년 대비 수익이 17% 증가한 반면, 우리의 수익은 지속적으로 감소하고 있다.

3 경제 전망에서 대다수의 기업들이 그들의 인건비를 줄이고 있을 것이라고 예측했다.

4 학생들은 그들의 주도권과 리더십을 보여주면서, 그 행사를 직접 준비했다.

5 펙 씨가 고객과 회의를 하는 동안 글렌 씨는 혼자서 프로젝트를 진행했다.

6 로빈 씨는 탁월한 실적을 통해 자신이 회사에 소중한 자산임을 입증했다.

7 이례적인 헌신을 보여주는 사람들은 그들의 노력에 성공할 가능성이 더 높다.

8 부서장의 승인을 얻은 사람들만 본사의 공석에 지원할 수 있다.

9 교육 과정에 참여하는 직원들은 생산성 향상을 경험할 것으로 예상된다.

10 재료비가 올랐음에도 불구하고, 우리의 가격은 경쟁사들의 가격보다 상당히 낮은 상태를 유지하고 있다.

11 한 지원자는 경험이 풍부한 반면, 다른 지원자는 문제 해결 능력이 뛰어나다.

12 신입사원들은 하나의 교육을 마치고 현재 다른 교육에 참여하고 있다.

13 어떤 직원들은 팀을 이루어 일하는 것을 선호하는 반면, 다른 직원들은 개별 업무에 뛰어나다.

14 보고서에 제공된 대부분의 정보는 오래되어서 더 이상 적절하지 않다.

15 연구에 참여한 대부분의 참가자들은 경쟁사들보다 신제품에 대한 강한 선호도를 나타냈다.

📝 실전 문제 연습
p.176

1 (B)	**2** (B)	**3** (B)	**4** (C)
5 (C)	**6** (A)	**7** (B)	**8** (D)
9 (D)	**10** (A)	**11** (D)	**12** (C)
13 (D)	**14** (B)	**15** (A)	**16** (D)
17 (A)	**18** (B)	**19** (C)	**20** (B)
21 (D)	**22** (A)	**23** (C)	**24** (A)
25 (A)	**26** (B)	**27** (B)	**28** (D)
29 (B)	**30** (C)	**31** (D)	**32** (C)

PART 5

1
마케팅 이사인 크리스 하비 씨는 자기의 사업을 시작하기 위해서 곧 현재의 직책에서 사퇴할 예정이다.

어휘 stepping down 내려가다, 퇴진하다   position 위치, 직위, 처지   venture into ~을 감행하다   one's own 자기의

해설 'one's own'은 '자기의, 자신의'를 의미하는 관용 표현이다. 빈칸에는 소유격 대명사인 (B)가 와야 한다.

2
프랫 씨는 커밍스 그룹 내 그의 새로운 직책에서 대처해야 할 여러가지 흥미로운 도전에 이미 직면했다고 말했다.

어휘 encounter 직면하다   challenge 도전, 도전하다   deal with ~을 다루다, 처리하다

해설 빈칸은 동사 has encountered의 목적어 자리이므로 명사인 (A)와 (B)가 정답 후보이다. 그런데 수량 형용사인 several은 복수 가산 명사만 수식하므로 복수 명사인 (B)가 정답이다.

3
저명한 소설가 오드리 쇼는 까다로운 태도의 작가들 중 한 명으로 악명이 높다.

어휘 renowned 유명한, 명성 있는   novelist 소설가   notoriety 악명   author 작가, 저자   possess 소유하다   demanding 요구가 많은, 쉽게 만족하지 않는   demeanor 처신

해설 빈칸은 명사 authors를 한정하는 한정사 자리이므로 지시 형용사인 (A)와 (B)가 정답 후보이다. 둘 중 복수 명사를 한정하는 지시 형용사는 those이므로 정답은 (B)이다.

4
알트만 건축은 마켓 지구의 쇼핑 센터를 위한 최종 계획안이 이번 주말까지 전달될 것을 보장했다.

어휘 architecture 건축학   ensure 보장하다   finalize 마무리하다, 완결하다

해설 빈칸 앞에 조동사 will이 있으므로, 보기 중 유일한 동사 원형인 (C)가 정답이다. (A) delivers는 3인칭 단수 동사이며 (B) delivered는 과거 시제 동사이다.

5
팀원들 중 어느 한 사람도 그보다 더 정보를 알지 못해서, 토레스 씨는 촉박한 마감 기한을 지키기 위해 자신이 직접 판매 보고서를 작성했다.

어휘 informed 잘 아는, 정보통인   complete 완료하다; 작성하다   sales report 판매 보고서   meet (기한 등을) 지키다   tight 빠듯한, 빡빡한   deadline 기한, 마감 시간

해설 빈칸이 없어도 완전한 문장이 되므로, 빈칸에는 재귀대명사가 와야 한다. 따라서 재귀대명사인 (C)가 정답이다.

6
우리는 새로운 채식주의자 메뉴를 위한 재료를 공급하는 괜찮은 식품 공급업체들의 목록을 만들었다.

어휘 compile 엮다   acceptable 훌륭한, 괜찮은; 수용 가능한   supplier 공급업자, 공급 회사   ingredient 재료, 구성 요소   vegetarian 채식주의자   accepting 받아들이는, 수락하는

해설 빈칸은 명사 food suppliers를 수식하는 형용사 자리이다. 보기 중 형용사는 acceptable뿐이므로 (A)가 정답이다. 현재분사인 (B) accepting이 명사를 수식할 수는 있지만, '수락하는'은 의미상 빈칸에 어울리지 않는다.

7
매년 주요 기부자 전원은 감사장과 함께 기부된 돈의 배분을 설명하는 책자를 받는다.

어휘 major 주요한, 중대한   donor 기부자, 기증자   booklet 작은 책자   detail 상세히 알리다, 열거하다   allocate 할당하다   along with ~와 함께   appreciation 감탄, 감사

해설 빈칸은 문장의 주어 자리이므로 한정사 역할만 가능한 (C)는 오답이다. 문장의 동사 are sent가 복수 동사이므로 빈칸의 주어 또한 복수가 되어야 한다. 따라서 정답은 (B)이다. much는 불가산 명사를 대신할 수 있으므로 가산 명사인 donors를 대신할 수 없다.

8
예상치 못한 기상 상황으로 인해 공사 프로젝트 완료가 더 오래 걸리면서, 결국 회사가 계획했던 것보다 많은 비용이 들었다.

어휘 construction 건설, 공사   unexpected 예기치 않은   end up 결국 (어떤 처지에) 처하게 되다   firm 회사   cost (값·비용이) 들다

해설 예상하지 못한 기상 상황으로 공사의 완료가 늦어지면서 결국에는 당초 계획보다 더 많은 비용이 들었다는 의미인데, '계획한 행위'는 건설 프로젝트가 마무리되고 비용이 더 많이 들기 전에 일어난 일이다. 따라서 과거보다 이전에 일어난 일을 표현하는 시제인 과거완료 시제 (D) had planned가 정답이다.

9

홀트 일렉트로닉스의 새로운 스마트폰의 가격은 주요 경쟁사들이 판매하는 제품들보다 상대적으로 더 높다.

어휘 comparatively 상대적으로, 비교적으로 primary 주된, 기본적인 competitor 경쟁자, 경쟁 상대

해설 빈칸은 '주요 경쟁사 제품들의 가격'을 대신하는 대명사 자리이므로, 실체가 서로 다르지만 반복되는 명사를 대신하는 대명사인 that과 those가 정답 후보이다. 그런데, 반복되는 명사인 the prices가 복수 명사이므로 정답은 복수 명사를 대신하는 (D)이다.

10

도시 중심가 가까이에 위치한 이 신축 상업 복합 시설은 기업들이 자신의 존재를 확고히 하기에 최적의 위치를 제공한다.

어휘 commercial 상업의 complex 복합 건물 establish 설립하다, 수립하다 presence (특정한 곳에) 있음, 존재(함), 참석 proximity 가까움, 근접 durability 내구성 alignment 가지런함 designation 지정, 지명

해설 주절의 내용은 '신축 상업 복합 시설은 기업들이 자신의 존재를 확고히 하기에 최적의 위치를 제공한다'는 것이다. 따라서 빈칸에는 도시 중심가와 가깝다는 의미의 (A) proximity가 가장 어울린다.

11

세계적으로 유명한 광고 회사인 쾌틀러 광고사는 뛰어난 업적으로 여러 상을 받았다.

어휘 globally 세계적으로 renowned 유명한 achievement 업적 considerate 사려 깊은 compatible 호환이 되는, 화합할 수 있는 experienced 경험 있는 outstanding 뛰어난, 두드러진

해설 세계적으로 유명한 광고 회사인 쾌틀러 광고사가 그들의 업적으로 여러 상을 받았다고 언급하고 있다. 그들의 업적이 상을 받을 정도로 뛰어나거나 주목할 만한 것이라는 의미를 전달하기 위해 가장 적합한 단어는 (D) outstanding이다. (A) considerate(사려 깊은)이나 (C) experienced(경험 있는)은 사람을 수식하는 형용사이다.

12

제프 힐과 리사 브래들리는 프로젝트를 위해 협력할 것이고, 그래서 그들이 서로에게 상호간의 도움을 제공할 것으로 기대된다.

어휘 collaborate 협력하다 mutual 상호간의, 서로의 assistance 도움, 원조

해설 문장은 제프 힐과 리사 브래들리가 프로젝트를 위해 협력할 것이고, 그래서 그들이 서로에게 상호간의 도움을 제공할 것으로 기대된다고 해석된다. 따라서 '서로'를 의미하는 (C)가 정답이다. 문장이나 절에서 목적어 자리에 목적격 대명사가 위치하려면 주어와 목적어가 서로 다른 인물이어야 하므로 (B)는 오답이다. 또한 제공하는 것이 '상호간의 도움(mutual assistance)'이므로 해석상 (A) anyone(누구나)이나 (D) others(다른 사람들)은 오답이다.

13

회사는 다양한 부서를 통합하여 운영을 원활하게 하고 전반적인 효율성을 향상시키는 것을 목표로 한다.

어휘 aim 목표로 하다 integrate 통합시키다 operation 사업,

운용 improve 개선되다, 향상시키다 identify 확인하다, 발견하다 distribute 유통시키다, 나누어 주다 cooperate 협력하다

해설 streamline은 어떤 작업이나 프로세스를 간소화하고 효율적으로 만드는 것을 의미하는데, 이 문장에서는 다양한 부서를 통합하여 운영을 간소화하고 전체적인 효율성을 향상시키는 것을 목표로 하고 있다고 해석되므로 문맥상 빈칸에 (D) streamline이 가장 적절하다. (C) cooperate은 완전자동사이므로 목적어를 취할 수 없다.

14

회사의 프리미엄 멤버십 요금제에는 모든 구매에 대해 무료 배송 및 연장된 보증 기간과 같은 많은 혜택이 포함되어 있다.

어휘 premium 아주 높은, 고급의 extended 연장된 advantage 유리한 점, 이점 inventory 물품 목록, 재고

해설 빈칸의 명사는 프리미엄 멤버십에 가입하면 받을 수 있는 구매에 대한 혜택이 되어야 한다. 보기 중 고객이 받을 수 있는 혜택으로 가장 어울리는 것은 연장된 보증 기간이므로 정답은 (B) warranty이다.

15

브루크 풋웨어는 개장일에 고객들로 가득 찼지만, 실제로 구매를 한 사람은 거의 없었다.

어휘 filled 가득 찬, 가득 든 actually 사실은, 실제로 purchase 구입, 구매; 구입하다 whoever 누구든 ~하는 사람 few 소수, 약간의 수(복수 명사 및 복수 동사와 함께 쓰임) little (불가산 명사와 함께 쓰여) 약간의, 거의 없는

해설 빈칸은 접속사 but 뒤에 이어지는 절의 주어 자리로, 복합 관계사인 (A)는 '복합관계사 + of them'의 형태가 될 수 없으므로 오답이다. 해석상 빈칸은 앞에서 언급된 customers를 대신하는 대명사가 위치해야 하므로 불가산 명사를 대신하는 (C) 또한 오답이다. 브루크 풋웨어의 개장일에 고객들로 가득 찼지만 실제로 구매를 한 사람이 거의 없다는 내용이 되어야 자연스러우므로 해석상 정답은 (B)이다.

PART 6

[16-19]

> 전 직원 여러분께,
>
> 저희는 6월 30일, 젤코 리테일링에서 의무적인 응급 절차 테스트를 실시할 예정임을 알려드립니다. 이는 응급 상황 발생시 여러분의 안전을 보장하기 위해 법적으로 요구되는 저희의 장비 및 절차에 대해 주기적으로 실시되는 테스트입니다.
>
> 비상 경보음이 울리면, 즉시 여러분의 장비를 끄고 질서 정연하게 사무실을 떠나시기 바랍니다. 지정된 야외 모임 장소로 이동하여 추가 지시 사항을 기다려 주세요. **여러분이 업무 장소로 돌아가야 할 때 저희가 안내해 드리겠습니다.**
>
> 저희의 응급 절차가 효과적이고 최신 상태임을 보장하기 위한 이번 테스트에 여러분의 협조와 참여에 대해 감사드립니다. 항상 그렇듯이, 여러분의 안전이 최우선입니다.

어휘 conduct (특정한 활동을) 하다 procedure 절차(방법) testing 테스트[실험/시험/검사](하기) routine 일상적인, 보통의 in case of ~이 발생할 시에는 immediately 즉시, 즉각

proceed to ~으로 나아가다 designated 지정된, 관선의
instruction 설명, 지시 up to date 현대식의, 최신 유행의

16

어휘 unexpected 예기치 않은, 예상 밖의, 뜻밖의 industrious
근면한, 부지런한 prolonged 오래 계속되는, 장기적인

해설 이어지는 문장에서 응급 절차 테스트가 법적으로 요구되는 것
이라고 설명하고 있으므로 문맥상 빈칸에 가장 어울리는 형용사는 (D)
mandatory(법에 정해진, 의무적인)이다.

17

해설 문맥상 비상 경보음이 울리면, 즉시 장비를 종료하고 질서 정연하
게 업무 장소를 떠나서 지정된 야외 모임 장소로 이동하라는 의미의 문
장이 되어야 하므로 정답은 (A) orderly이다. 'in an orderly manner'는
'질서 정연하게'를 뜻하는 관용 표현이다.

18

(A) 행사는 해당 장소에서 예정되어 있습니다.
(B) 여러분이 업무 장소로 돌아가야 할 때 저희가 안내해 드리겠습니다.
(C) 회의는 다음 주로 연기되었습니다.
(D) 설명서의 지시 사항을 주의 깊게 읽어 보세요.

어휘 manual 설명서

해설 앞 문장에서 지정된 야외 모임 장소로 이동하여 추가 지시 사항을
기다리라고 했으므로, 이어지는 문장은 업무 장소로 돌아가야 할 때를 안
내하겠다는 내용이 가장 자연스럽다. 따라서 정답은 (B)이다.

19

어휘 posting 인터넷에 올리는 글 ranking 순위

해설 앞 문장에서 이번 테스트가 우리의 응급 절차가 효과적이고 최신
상태임을 보장하기 위한 것이라고 했으므로 직원들의 안전이 항상 '최우
선 사항'이라는 문장이 이어지는 것이 자연스럽다. 따라서 정답은
(C) priority(우선 사항)이다.

[20-23]

발신: customersupport@petswellness.com
수신: Kevinweil@globalnet.com
날짜: 11월 3일
회신: 구독

월간지 *펫츠 웰니스*의 소중한 구독자가 되신 것을 축하합니다. 선택
하신 구독 요금제는 온라인 콘텐츠를 무제한으로 이용할 수 있는 권
한을 부여합니다. **또한 매달 인쇄본을 받아 보시게 됩니다.** 구독 설
정을 변경하시려면 주저하지 말고 515-323-2800으로 전화하여
전담 고객 서비스 팀에 문의하세요. 그렇지 않으면, 가입자는 당사
웹사이트 www.petswellness.com에서 계정 세부 정보를 직접 업
데이트할 수 있습니다.

우리는 귀하께서 우리의 프로모션 기간 동안 구독한 결과로서 우리
의 11월호를 무료로 받으실 것임을 알려드리게 되어 기쁩니다. 따
라서, 구독료는 12월부터 부과될 것입니다.

귀하의 거래와 지속적인 성원에 매우 감사드립니다.

어휘 subscription 구독, 구독료 subscriber 구독자, 이용자
entitle 자격을 주다 unlimited 무제한의, 무한의 receive 받다,
받아들이다 preference 선호, 선도 dedicated 전념하는,
헌신적인 account 이용 계정 note ~에 주목(주의)하다 issue
(잡지나 신문 등의 정기 간행물의) 호 promotional 홍보의, 판촉의

20

(A) 이번 달에 구독을 갱신해야 합니다.
(B) 또한 매달 인쇄본을 받아 보시게 됩니다.
(C) 매일 온라인에서 보내는 시간을 줄일 수 있습니다.
(D) 우리의 독자층은 전 세계 10개국 이상에 있습니다.

어휘 renew 갱신하다 readership 독자 수, 독자 층 span
(넓은 범위 많은 것에[을]) 걸치다

해설 앞 문장에서 선택한 구독 요금제가 온라인 콘텐츠를 무제한으로
이용할 수 있는 권한을 부여한다고 설명하고 있으므로, 선택한 구독
요금제로 받을 수 있는 또 다른 혜택으로서 매달 잡지의 인쇄본을 받아
볼 수 있다는 의미의 문장이 이어지는 것이 자연스럽다. 따라서 정답은
(B)이다.

21

해설 빈칸을 제외해도 완전한 문장이므로, 빈칸에는 강조의 역할을 하
는 재귀대명사 (D)가 와야 한다. 해석상으로도 구독자들은 '그들이 직접'
계정을 업데이트할 수 있다는 의미가 되므로 재귀대명사 themselves가
정답이다.

22

어휘 as a result of ~의 결과로 in advance of ~보다 앞서
in charge of ~을 맡아서, 담당해서 on behalf of ~을 대신하여,
~을 대표하여

해설 11월호를 무료로 받을 수 있는 것은 프로모션 기간 동안 구독한
결과이므로 빈칸 뒤 of와 결합하여 '~의 결과로'의 뜻이 되는 (A) as a
result가 정답이다.

23

어휘 similarly 비슷하게, 유사하게 accordingly (상황에)
부응해서, 그에 맞춰 otherwise 그렇지 않으면

해설 앞서 프로모션 기간 동안 구독하여 11월호를 무료로 받을 것이라
고 했고, 따라서 12월부터 구독료가 부과된다고 했으므로 해석상 빈칸은
(C) accordingly가 가장 어울린다. 빈칸은 완전한 문장을 수식하는 부사
자리이므로 복합관계사인 (A) whenever는 오답이다.

PART 7
[24-27]

발신: Bradley Joe ⟨bradley77@crowderengineering.com⟩
수신: 신입사원 명단
제목: 환영합니다
날짜: 2월 18일

크라우더 엔지니어링 팀은 재능 있는 신입 사원들이 우리 연구개발
부에 온 것을 기쁘게 생각합니다. **24) 아래의 회사 정책을 검토하고
우리 시설 내의 중요한 위치들을 숙지하기 바랍니다.**

여러분의 업무 연관된 작업과 관련하여, 개인용 컴퓨터 사용을 자제해 주시기 바랍니다. 26) 외부 업무에 보안이 가능한 승인된 노트북이 필요하시면, 건물 7층에 있는 저희 IT 부서를 방문해 주시기 바랍니다.

건물 내에서는 언제나 신분증을 착용해주세요. 이 신분증은 제한 구역을 제외한 건물의 모든 곳에 접근할 수 있게 해줍니다. 25) 배지는 다음 주에 배포될 예정입니다.

11층에 위치한 저희 도서관은 월요일부터 목요일까지 오후 2시 30분까지 이용 가능합니다. 자료 대출을 원하시는 분들은, 도서관 운영 시간을 참고하시기 바랍니다.

마지막으로, 17층 옥상 카페테리아는 평일 오전 8시부터 오후 5시까지 운영됩니다. 27) 1층 라운지는 매일 오후 5시 30분까지 커피, 차, 주스, 가벼운 간식을 무료로 제공하는 휴식공간입니다.

따뜻한 안부를 전하며,

브래들리 조
인사 담당 대리

어휘 thrilled 아주 흥분한, 신이 난 acquaint 익히다, 숙지하다 refrain from ~을 삼가다 security-enabled 보안 기능이 있는 offsite (어느 특정한 장소에서) 떨어진 identification badge 신분 확인 명찰 at all times 항상, 언제나 excluding ~을 제외하고 restricted 제한된 promptly 지체 없이 extension 내선, 구내전화 accessible 접근 가능한 material 직물, 재료, 자료 refer 참고하다, 알아보도록 하다 rooftop 옥상 complimentary 무료의, 칭찬하는

24

이메일의 목적은 무엇인가?
(A) 새롭게 고용된 직원들에게 자세한 정보를 제공하기 위해
(B) 회사 복리후생 패키지를 설명하기 위해
(C) 시설 견학에 대한 안내를 제공하기 위해
(D) 직원에게 작업 공간을 할당하기 위해

어휘 detail 세부 사항 benefits package 복리 후생 제도 guidance 지도, 안내 assign 맡기다, 배치하다

해설 첫 문단에서 아래의 회사 정책을 검토하고 시설 내의 중요한 위치들을 숙지하라고 했으므로, 최근 고용된 신입 사원들에게 정보를 제공하기 위한 글이라는 것을 알 수 있다. 따라서 정답은 (A)이다.

25

신입 사원에 대해 암시된 것은 무엇인가?
(A) 그들은 다음 주에 보안 배지를 발급 받을 것이다.
(B) 그들은 인사 부서에서 근무할 것이다.
(C) 그들은 출입 금지 구역에 접근할 수 있을 것이다.
(D) 그들은 도서관을 매일 사용할 수 있을 것이다.

어휘 issue 발표하다, 발부하다 Personnel Department 인사 담당 부서

해설 세 번째 문단에 건물 내에서 제한 구역을 제외한 모든 구역에 출입할 수 있는 신분증을 착용하라는 내용이 있는데, 신분증이 다음 주에 배포될 것이라고 했으므로 정답은 (A)이다.

26

보안 기능이 있는 노트북을 어디서 구할 수 있는가?
(A) 1층에서
(B) 7층에서
(C) 11층에서
(D) 17층에서

해설 두 번째 문단에서 외부 업무에 보안 기능이 있는 컴퓨터가 필요할 경우 IT 부서에 방문하여 요청하라고 했고, 해당 부서는 7층에 있다고 했다. 따라서 정답은 (B)이다.

27

이메일에 따르면, 모든 직원에게 제공되는 것은 무엇인가?
(A) 우편함
(B) 승인된 노트북
(C) 간식과 음료
(D) 도서관 카드

해설 마지막 문단에서 라운지에 매일 오후 5시 30분까지 무료 커피, 차, 주스, 가벼운 스낵이 준비되어 있다고 했으므로 정답은 (C)이다.

[28-32]

수신: 에리카 로메인 〈romain92@penguinretail.com〉
발신: 제임스 다빈 〈Jdavin@penguinretail.com〉
제목: 조언 요청
날짜: 6월 5일

친애하는 로메인 씨께,

31-1) 저는 휴스턴 사무실에서 당신에게 연락하는 제임스 다빈입니다. 28) 저는 다음 주에 런던 출장이 있는데, 당신이 지난달에 런던으로 출장을 갔었다는 것을 최근에 알았습니다. 제가 당신의 조언을 구하기 위해 연락을 드려도 괜찮으시기를 바랍니다. 29) 저는 지난달에 해외 영업부에 입사했는데, 국제적인 사업 수행에 대해 배울 점이 아직 많이 남아 있다고 생각합니다. 해외 여러 국가에서의 광범위한 경험이 있는 당신은 가치 있는 팁을 줄 수 있는 이상적인 분일 겁니다. 조언을 해주시면 대단히 감사하겠습니다. 이번 출장은 대리로서 첫 출장이 될 것이기에 좋은 인상을 남기는 것에 대해 열망하고 있습니다.

당신의 답변을 간절히 기다리겠습니다.

따뜻한 안부를 전하며,

제임스 다빈

어휘 upcoming 다가오는, 곧 있을 discover 발견하다 reach ~에 이르다(닿다/도달하다) overseas 해외의 conduct (특정한 활동을) 하다 foreign 외국의 impression 인상, 감동 internationally 국제적으로 extensive 넓은, 광대한 enthusiastic 열렬한, 열광적인 positive 긍정적인, 명확한 impression 인상, 감명

친애하는 다빈 씨께,

제가 할 수 있는 어떤 방법으로든 기꺼이 도와드리겠습니다. 출발 전에 당신이 참고할 수 있는 런던에 대한 정보를 모아 보겠습니다. 30-1) 타워 브릿지와 내셔널 갤러리같은 랜드마크를 둘러보는 것도 좋지만, 32-1) 도착하면 동네 카페와 상점들을 둘러보는 것을 추천합니다. 32-2) 잠재 고객들과 재미있는 대화 주제를 제공할 수 있는 30-2) 유명 셰프들이 운영하는 레스토랑도 추천합니다. 저는 이 시설들의 목록을 첨부했습니다.

또한, 32-3) 회의나 약속에 도착하기에 충분한 시간을 할당해야 합니다. 30-3) 특히 아침의 교통 체증은 상당히 심할 수 있고 예상보다 긴 이동 시간을 야기할 수 있습니다. 더 궁금한 점이 있으면 알려주시기 바랍니다. 31-2) 저는 다음 달에 회의를 위해 당신의 사무실을 방문할 예정이며 그때 뵙기를 희망합니다.

출장 잘 다녀 오시고 즐거운 시간 보내세요.

에리카 로메인

어휘 gather 모으다, 수집하다 refer to (정보를 알아내기 위해) ~을 보다 departure 출발 landmark 주요 지형지물 explore 탐험하다, 답사하다 renowned 유명한, 명성 있는 potential 잠재적인 establishment 기관, 시설 additionally 게다가 sufficient 충분한 appointment 약속 especially 특히 anticipate 예상하다

28

다빈 씨는 왜 이메일을 보냈는가?
(A) 해외 영업부에 대한 정보를 요청하기 위해서
(B) 발표 준비에 도움을 요청하기 위해서
(C) 런던에서 방문할 수 있는 인기 있는 명소에 대해 문의하기 위해서
(D) 다가오는 출장과 관련하여 조언을 구하기 위해서

어휘 assistance 도움 overseas 해외의, 국외의 inquire 묻다, 알아보다 attraction 명소 solicit 간청하다 regarding ~에 관하여 upcoming 다가오는, 곧 있을

해설 다빈 씨의 이메일 전반부에서 그가 다음 주에 런던 출장이 있는데, 로메인 씨가 지난달에 런던으로 출장을 갔다는 것을 최근에 알게 되어 조언을 구하기 위해 연락을 했다고 했으므로 정답은 (D)이다.

29

다빈 씨에 대해 암시된 것은?
(A) 그는 가까운 미래에 런던으로 이사할 것이다.
(B) 그는 최근에 새로운 직책에서 일하기 시작했다.
(C) 그는 지난달에 런던으로 출장을 갔다.
(D) 그는 사업 목적으로 해외여행을 자주 간다.

어휘 relocate 이전하다, 이동하다 recently 최근에 frequently 자주, 흔히

해설 다빈 씨의 이메일 중반부의 'Having joined the overseas sales division just last month, I believe there is still much for me to learn'에서, 다빈 씨는 지난달에 해외 영업부에 합류했다고 했으므로 정답은 (B)이다.

30

런던에 대해 언급되지 않은 것은?
(A) 방문할 가치가 있는 몇몇 유명한 명소를 자랑한다.
(B) 아침에 교통 체증이 심하다.
(C) 국가의 중심적인 비즈니스 중심지 역할을 한다.
(D) 유명한 요리사들이 운영하는 식당이 몇 군데 있다.

어휘 celebrated 유명한 significant 중요한, 커다란 congestion 혼잡 central 중심이 되는, 가장 중요한 well-known 유명한, 잘 알려진

해설 로메인 씨의 이메일 첫 문단에서 타워 브릿지나 내셔널 갤러리같은 랜드마크를 둘러보는 것도 좋고, 유명 셰프들이 운영하는 레스토랑도 추천한다고 했으므로 (A)와 (D)는 언급된 내용이다. 또한, 아침의 교통 체증은 상당히 심할 수 있다고 했으므로 (B)도 언급된 내용이다. 따라서 언급되지 않은 내용은 (C)이다.

31

로메인 씨에 대해 가장 옳은 것은?
(A) 그녀는 수년간 런던에서 일해 왔다.
(B) 그녀는 해외 영업부에서 근무한 경험이 있다.
(C) 그녀는 외국에서 자신의 사업을 운영해 왔다.
(D) 그녀는 다음 달에 휴스턴으로 갈 계획이다.

어휘 prior 이전의, 앞의 run 운영하다

해설 다빈 씨의 이메일 첫 단락에서 그는 휴스턴 사무실에서 연락한다고 했고, 로메인 씨의 이메일 마지막 문단에서 그녀는 다음 달에 회의를 위해 다빈 씨의 사무실에 방문한다고 했다. 따라서, 다음 달에 그녀가 휴스턴을 방문할 예정인 것을 알 수 있으므로 정답은 (D)이다.

32

로메인 씨의 제안이 아닌 것은 무엇인가?
(A) 지역 상점과 커피숍을 찾아보는 것
(B) 회의 시간을 엄수하는 것
(C) 식당에서 회의를 준비하는 것
(D) 토론 주제를 미리 작성하는 것

어휘 discover 발견하다 punctuality 시간 엄수, 정확함 arrange 정돈하다, 준비하다 in advance 사전에

해설 이메일 첫 문단에서 로메인 씨는 동네 카페와 상점들을 둘러보는 것을 추천하고 있고, 고객과의 대화 주제를 제공할 수 있는 유명 셰프들이 운영하는 레스토랑도 추천한다고 했으므로 (A)와 (D)는 그녀가 추천한 내용이다. 또한, 두 번째 문단에서 어떤 회의나 약속에 가기 위해서 충분한 시간을 감안하라고 했으므로 (B)도 추천한 내용이다. 식당에서 회의를 하는 것을 추천하는 내용은 찾을 수 없으므로 정답은 (C)이다.

DAY 06 형용사와 부사

PRACTICE
pp.185-186

1 ideal
2 aware
3 other
4 considerate
5 surrounding
6 conveniently
7 closely

1 존의 뛰어난 의사소통 능력은 그를 지도자 자리에 이상적으로 만들었다.
2 롱 씨는 오늘 아침에 동료가 알려줄 때까지 새로운 정책에 대해 알지 못했다.
3 그 외에 해당 주제에 대한 정보를 제공해 주시면 감사하겠습니다.
4 도서관에서 다른 사람들을 배려하고 소음의 수준을 낮추세요.
5 호텔은 주변 지역의 멋진 전망을 제공한다.
6 그것은 대중교통 이용이 편리하게 위치해 있다.
7 보안팀은 모든 탑승자의 안전을 보장하기 위해 건물을 면밀히 감시할 것이다.

📑 실전 문제 연습
p.189

1 (C)	2 (B)	3 (B)	4 (A)
5 (B)	6 (B)	7 (C)	8 (A)
9 (A)	10 (A)	11 (A)	12 (B)
13 (A)	14 (B)	15 (A)	16 (D)
17 (C)	18 (A)	19 (C)	20 (A)
21 (D)	22 (D)	23 (A)	24 (D)
25 (D)	26 (C)	27 (C)	28 (C)
29 (D)	30 (C)	31 (C)	32 (D)

PART 5

1
샘스 오가닉 푸드는 요리할 시간이 없는 고객에게 적합한 편리하고 건강한 다양한 편의 식품을 제공한다.

어휘 organic 유기농의　prepared 준비가 된, 미리 준비된　suited 적합한, 어울리는　widen 넓히다, 넓어지다　width 폭, 너비　wide 넓은, 다양한　widely 널리, 폭넓게

해설 빈칸은 한정사인 a와 명사인 range 사이에서 명사를 수식하는 형용사 자리이므로 정답은 형용사인 (C)이다. 'a wide range of'는 '광범위한, 다양한'을 뜻하는 관용 표현이다.

2
다양한 그룹의 사람들 중, 어떤 사람들은 하이킹과 같은 야외 활동을 즐기는 반면, 다른 사람들은 온라인 게임과 같은 실내 활동에서 즐거움을 찾는다.

어휘 diverse 다양한　pursuit 추구, 취미

해설 주절의 주어인 some(일부)은 야외 활동을 즐긴다고 했으므로, 이들을 제외한 실내 활동을 좋아하는 다른 사람들은 others로 표현하는 것이 적합하다. 따라서 정답은 (B)이다.

3
연구팀은 멸종 위기에 처한 종의 개체수가 지난 10년 동안 약 30% 감소했다고 결론을 내렸다.

어휘 conclude 결론을 내리다　population 인구; 개체수　endangered 멸종 위기에 처한　decade 10년　approximate 거의 정확한, 근사치인; 근사치를 내다

해설 빈칸은 30%를 수식하는 성분이 필요하므로 수사를 수식하는 부사인 (B) approximately(대략)가 정답이다. 수량 표현은 부사가 수식한다는 것을 기억해 두자.

4
영업 사원은 고객과의 계약 전반에 걸쳐 모범적인 전문성과 전문 지식을 보여 주었다.

어휘 demonstrate 증거[실례]를 들어가며 보여 주다　exemplary 모범적인　professionalism 전문성　expertise 전문 지식　engagement 약속; 업무　representative 대표(자), 대리인　representation 묘사, 표현

해설 빈칸은 동사 demonstrated(보여 주다)의 주어 자리이다. 따라서 sales와 결합하여 영업 사원의 의미가 되는 (A) representative(대표, 대리인)가 정답이다.

5
에릭 아담스는 그의 인상적인 기고문을 인정받아 롱아일랜드 프레스 클럽으로부터 명망 있는 올해의 기자상을 받았다.

어휘 prestigious 명망 있는　journalist 기자, 저널리스트　contribution 기여; 기고문　impress 감명을 주다, 깊은 인상을 주다　impressively 감명 깊게, 인상적으로

해설 빈칸이 한정사인 his와 명사 contributions 사이에 있으므로, 빈칸은 명사를 수식하는 형용사 자리이다. 따라서 정답은 형용사인 (B) impressive(인상적인, 감명 깊은)이다. (D) impressed(감명을 받은, 인상 깊게 생각하는) 또한 형용사이지만, 이는 사람을 주어로 하거나 사람을 수식하기에 적절하다.

6
주목받는 아티스트 프레드 웨스터가 디자인한 한정판 운동화는 아이언 우드 거리에 위치한 에이스 기어에서만 구입할 수 있다.

어휘 notable 주목할 만한, 유명한　available 구할(이용할) 수 있는　exclusive 독점적인, 특권층의　exclusively 배타적으로, 독점적으로　exclusion 제외, 배제　exclude 제외하다, 거부하다

해설 빈칸은 완전한 절에 연결된 전명구인 'at the ACE Gear'를 수식하는 부사 자리이므로 정답은 (B)이다.

7

스트러스 펀딩이 정부 지원에 따라 수익성이 높아졌다는 주장에도 불구하고, 투자자들은 여전히 손실을 겪고 있다.

어휘 claim 주장, 주장하다 following ~ 후에 government 정부, 통치 체제 assistance 도움, 지원 investor 투자자 profit 이익, 이득, 이익을 얻다 profitable 수익성이 있는 profitably 유익하게

해설 빈칸은 that절의 동사인 has become 뒤 주격 보어 자리이므로 명사나 형용사가 와야 한다. 하지만 주격 보어 자리의 명사는 주어와 동격이 되어야 하므로 (A) profits(이윤)는 정답이 될 수 없고, 형용사인 (C) profitable이 정답이다. 참고로 profit이 '~으로부터 이익을 얻다'라는 의미의 동사로 사용되는 경우 이는 자동사이므로 수동태 동사가 될 수 없다. 그러므로 (B) 역시 오답이다.

8

클레어필드 리테일과의 계약 만료일은 10월 31일로 정해져 있으며, 이 시점에서 더 이상 유효하지 않다.

어휘 valid 유효한 expiration 만료 appointment 약속 specification 설명서, 사양 requirement 필요, 요건

해설 계약은 정해진 날짜인 10월 31일의 시점에서 더 이상 유효하지 않다고 했으므로 'the ------- date'는 계약의 '만료일'이 되어야 한다. 따라서 빈칸에 어울리는 보기는 (A) expiration(만료, 만기)이다. expiration date는 유효 기간 혹은 만기일을 뜻하는 복합 명사이다.

9

인쇄된 티셔츠뿐만 아니라, 행사 주최자들은 참석자들에게 다른 홍보 물품들도 나눠 주었다.

어휘 in addition to ~에 더하여, ~일 뿐 아니라 promotional 홍보의 distribute 나누어 주다, 분배[배부]하다 attendee 참석자

해설 빈칸은 명사구인 promotional items 앞의 한정사 자리이므로 명사 자리에 사용되는 (C)는 오답이다. 또한 promotional items가 복수형이므로 단수 명사 앞에 사용되는 한정사인 (B)와 (D) 또한 오답이다. 따라서 정답은 (A)인데, other는 복수 가산 명사나 불가산 명사를 한정할 수 있다.

10

업그레이드된 퀵 택스 프로를 설치하기 전에, 어떤 소프트웨어 패키지가 그것과 호환되는지 확인하고 그것들의 특징을 숙지하세요.

어휘 install 설치하다 informed 잘 아는, 정보통인 feature 특징, 특색 compatible 호환이 되는, 양립할 수 있는 qualified 자격이 있는 supportive 지원하는, 도와주는 comparable 비슷한, 비교할 만한

해설 문맥상 업그레이드된 프로그램이 어떤 소프트웨어 패키지와 '호환되는지'를 확인하라는 내용이 되어야 자연스러우므로 정답은 (A)이다. 'compatible with'는 '~와 호환되는'이라는 의미이다.

11

재생 가능한 에너지원의 채택으로 도시의 산업 부문의 탄소 발자국이 상당히 감소했다.

어휘 adoption 채택, 차용 carbon 탄소 footprint 발자국 industrial 산업의 sector 부문, 분야 elaborately 공들여

해설 동사 has reduced를 수식하기에 가장 어울리는 부사는 (A) markedly(뚜렷하게, 현저하게)이다. 재생 에너지원의 도입이 도시의 산업 부문의 탄소 발자국을 '현저하게' 줄였다고 해석되는 것이 의미상으로도 자연스럽다.

12

펠레 스포츠는 최근 새로운 자전거 장비 제품의 야심찬 출시를 위해 새로운 마케팅 전략을 시행했다.

어휘 implement 시행하다 strategy 계획, 전략 gear 장비, 복장 launch 시작하다, 출시하다 ambitious 야심찬 conveniently 편리하게 recently 최근에 extremely 극도로 securely 단단히, 안전하게

해설 문맥상 펠레 스포츠가 '최근에' 새로운 마케팅 전략을 시행했다는 의미가 되어야 자연스러우므로 정답은 (B)이다. recently는 의미상 과거 시제 동사나 현재 완료 시제 동사와 어울린다는 점도 기억하자.

13

도리아 화장품은 모든 제품이 시장에 출시되기 전에 지속적으로 광범위한 안전성 테스트를 실시하고 있다.

어휘 perform 수행하다, 실시하다 prior to ~ 전에 extensive 광범위한, 아주 넓은 competitive 경쟁을 하는, 경쟁력 있는 respective 각자의, 각각의 tentative 잠정적인, 자신 없는

해설 제품을 출시하기 전에 항상 광범위한 안전성 테스트를 한다는 해석이 자연스러우므로, 보기 중 'safety testing(안전성 검사)'를 수식하기에 자연스러운 형용사는 (A) extensive이다.

14

순조로운 경제 상황으로 인해, 주택 시장은 집값이 꾸준히 상승하는 등 상승세를 타고 있다.

어휘 favorable 호의적인, 유리한, 순조로운 economic 경제상의 condition 상태, 조건 steadily 꾸준히 pending 미결의 reverse 반대의

해설 경기 호조로 인해 주택 가격이 지속적으로 상승하고 있다고 했으므로 주택 시장이 상승세에 있다는 내용이 되어야 자연스럽다. 따라서 정답은 (B) upward(향상하는, 올라가는)이다.

15

플레이 조이의 새로운 게임 콘솔은 최근 출시되었음에도 불구하고 벌써 전 세계의 열광적인 게이머들 사이에서 인기가 있다.

어휘 despite ~에도 불구하고 release 발표, 공개 enthusiastic 열렬한, 열광적인 worldwide 전 세계적인, 전 세계적으로 seldom 거의 ~ 않는 elsewhere (어딘가) 다른 곳에서, 다른 곳으로

해설 문장은 새로운 게임 콘솔이 최근에 출시되었음에도 불구하고 이미 전 세계에서 열광적인 게이머들 사이에서 인기를 끌고 있다고 해석되므로 정답은 (A) already(이미, 벌써)이다. already는 현재의 시간과 과거를 연결하여 어떤 행동이 이미 일어났음을 나타낸다. enough는 부사로서 형용사를 수식할 때 형용사 뒤에 위치한다.

[16-19]

파월 호텔에 오신 것을 환영하며, 이곳은 개와 고양이를 따뜻하게 환영합니다! 저희는 전국의 거의 모든 파월 호텔에서 애완동물 친화적인 다양한 객실을 제공하는 것을 자랑스럽게 생각합니다. 1박에 10달러의 추가 요금으로 애완동물 친화적인 객실을 제공하여, 투숙하시는 동안 사랑하는 애완동물이 여러분과 함께 할 수 있게 하여 기쁩니다.

그러나, 안내견과 동행하시는 경우, 해당 안내견은 추가 요금 없이 여러분의 객실에 함께 머무를 수 있습니다. **이 경우, 우리는 관련 서류를 요청합니다.** 우리가 여러분의 털복숭이 동료를 제대로 수용할 수 있도록, 예약하시기 전에 우리의 웹사이트나 애플리케이션을 통해 연락해주세요.

우리는 여러분과 여러분의 네 발 달린 친구가 파월 호텔에서 즐거운 경험을 할 수 있기를 고대합니다!

어휘 take pride in ~을 자랑하다 a selection of 엄선된, 다양한 pet-friendly 반려동물 친화적인 nationwide 전국에, 전국적인 accompany 동반하다, 동행하다 guide dog 안내견 at no additional cost 추가 요금 없이 accommodate 공간을 제공하다, 수용하다 furry 털로 덮인 companion 동반자

16

어휘 audibly 들리도록, 들을 수 있게 already 이미, 벌써 around 약; 사방에서, 주위에

해설 문맥상 전국의 거의 모든 파월 호텔에 다수의 반려동물 친화적인 객실이 있다는 내용이 되어야 자연스러우므로 정답은 (D) almost(거의)이다. almost는 수사나 all, every, no 등과 같은 수량 표현을 수식하기에 적절한 부사이다. (C) around 또한 숫자를 수식하는 데 사용되지만, all, every, no와 같은 수량 표현을 수식하기에는 어색하다.

17

어휘 in spite of ~에도 불구하고 whereas 그러나 afterward 나중에, 그 뒤에

해설 빈칸은 완전한 절 앞에 위치하고 있고 뒤에 쉼표가 있으므로, 완전한 절을 수식하는 부사 자리이다. 따라서 전치사인 (A)와 부사절 접속사인 (B)는 오답이며, 접속부사인 (C)와 (D) 중에서 정답을 골라야 한다. 빈칸 앞 문장은 1박에 10달러의 저렴한 요금으로 애완동물 친화적인 객실을 제공한다는 내용이며, 빈칸 뒤 문장은 안내견과 동행하는 경우 추가 비용이 없다는 내용이다. 이 두 문장은 서로 상반되는 의미이므로 빈칸에 어울리는 접속부사는 (C) However이다.

18

(A) 이 경우, 우리는 관련 서류를 요청합니다.
(B) 빠른 체크인에 대한 추가 요금이 적용되었습니다.
(C) 호텔 수영장은 17층에 있습니다.
(D) 개나 고양이와 함께 지내는 것은 정신적인 행복에 도움이 됩니다.

해설 빈칸 앞에서 1박에 10달러의 요금으로 애완동물 친화적인 객실을 제공하지만, 안내견과 동행하는 경우 추가 요금이 없다고 했다. 따라서, 동반하는 애완동물이 안내견임을 증명하는 서류를 요청한다는 내용의 문장인 (A)가 이어지는 것이 자연스럽다.

19

어휘 on account of ~ 때문에 aside from ~ 외에는, ~을 제외하고

해설 빈칸은 빈칸 뒤의 명사를 연결하는 전치사 자리이므로 to부정사인 (A)는 오답이다. 보기의 전치사구들 중에서 예약하기 '전에' 웹사이트나 애플리케이션을 통해 연락해달라는 해석이 가장 자연스러우므로 정답은 (C) prior to(~ 전에)이다.

[20-23]

오늘, 오클라호마 시의 시장실은 오랫동안 기대되었던 역사적인 다리 건설 프로젝트에 3,500만 달러 이상이 배정되었다고 발표했다. **이 자금은 노후화된 다리를 복구하는 데 사용될 것이다.** 데이비드 홀트 시장에 따르면, "불행히도, 오클라호마 시의 많은 다리들은 수리가 절실히 필요합니다."라고 한 다음, "우리는 미래 세대를 위해 도시의 기반 시설을 현대화하기 위해 필수적인 자금을 공급하는 데 전념하고 있습니다."라고 덧붙였다. 오클라호마 시의 많은 지역 주민들은 이것을 오클라호마 시의 오래된 물리적 인프라를 재건하기 위해 절실히 필요한 재정적 지원의 원천으로 인식하며 따뜻하게 환영하고 있다.

어휘 long-anticipated 오래 기다린 unfortunately 불행하게도, 유감스럽게도 desperate 필사적인, 간절히 필요로 하는 funding 자금, 재정 지원 modernize 현대화하다 infrastructure 사회 기반시설 generation 세대 resident 주민, 거주자, 투숙객 rebuild 재건하다, 다시 세우다 physical 육체의, 물리적인

20

어휘 designate 지정하다; 지적하다

해설 문장의 동사가 과거 시제인 made이므로 미래 시제인 (C)는 정답에서 제외한다. 빈칸에 들어갈 동사인 designate와 that절의 주어인 'over $35 million'은 수동의 관계이므로, 능동 형태인 (B)와 (D)도 정답이 될 수 없다. 따라서 정답은 (A)이다.

21

(A) 이 도시에서 가장 오래된 다리는 더 이상 운전자들이 접근할 수 없게 될 것이다.
(B) 관계자들은 공사가 연기되었다고 확인해 주었다.
(C) 그 도시의 새 다리는 다음 달에 개통될 예정이다.
(D) 이 자금은 노후화된 다리를 복구하는 데 사용될 것이다.

어휘 accessible 접근 가능한, 이용 가능한 motorist 운전자 official 공무원; 공무상의, 공식적인 confirm 확인해 주다, 사실임을 보여주다 postpone 미루다, 연기하다 utilize 활용하다 restore 회복시키다, 복구하다

해설 지문은 도시의 오래된 교량을 수리하고 재건하기 위한 자금에 관련된 내용이므로 앞에서 언급된 3천 5백만 달러 이상의 자금이 오래된 다리를 복구하는 데 사용될 것이라는 문장이 빈칸에 가장 어울린다. 따라서 정답은 (D)이다.

22

어휘 decisive 결정적인, 결단력 있는

해설 앞서 오클라호마 시의 많은 다리들은 수리가 간절히 필요하다고 했으므로, 미래 세대를 위한 오클라호마 시의 사회 기반시설을 현대화하는 데 전념하고 있다는 해석이 자연스럽다. 따라서 정답은 (D) committed(전념하는)이다. be committed to는 "~에 전념하다"를 의미하는 관용 표현인데, 여기에서 to는 전치사로서 뒤에 동명사가 와야 한다. 지문에서도 to 뒤에 동명사인 supplying이 있는 것을 확인할 수 있다."

23

어휘 recognize 인정하다, 알아보다   acquire 습득하다 speculate 추측하다   transform 변형시키다

해설 오클라호마 시의 많은 지역 주민들이 따뜻하게 환영하고 있다고 했으므로 오클라호마 시의 오래된 물리적 인프라를 재건하기 위해 절실히 필요한 재정적 지원의 원천으로 '인식하고 있다'는 내용이 되어야 자연스럽다. 따라서 정답은 (A) recognizing이다.

PART 7

[24-27]

대담한 발걸음을 내딛는 데이비드 릴로
25-1) 에리카 뎀마, *아울 디스패치*

산호세 (2월 21일) – 비평가들로부터 극찬을 받아 그에게 **27-1) 명망 있는** *아메리칸 무비 어워드 베스트 오리지널 뮤직* 상을 안겨준 *시애틀의 비 내리는 날*을 포함하여, **27-2) 최근 몇 편의 영화에 탁월한 음악적 기여를 한** 것으로 유명한 전도유망한 작곡가 데이비드 릴로가 최근 인터넷 게임 분야에 진출했다. 릴로는 지난 8년간 쌍방향 엔터테인먼트의 노련한 제작자인 게임 엠파이어가 개발한 온라인 게임 영웅과 승리에 자신의 놀라운 작곡 기술을 빌려주었다.

24) 27-3) 데이비드 릴로와 게임 엠파이어의 협업은 이전에 릴로 씨와 여러 영화 음악을 작곡한 적이 있는 알렉스 포워드가 주최한 사회 행사에서 게임 엠파이어의 아트 디렉터 켄 모건을 소개받으면서 시작되었다. 모건 씨가 그에게 영웅과 승리를 위한 음악을 만들 것을 요청한 것은 이 행사 동안이었다.

인터뷰 동안, 릴로는 영웅과 승리에 등장하는 매혹적인 그래픽과 애니메이션에 대한 깊은 감탄을 표현했다. 그는 게임을 하는 경험을 영화를 보는 것에 비유했는데, 이것이 그가 즉시 협업을 수용하도록 했다. 릴로는 또한 인터넷 게임을 위한 음악을 작곡하는 과정이 영화 음악에 대한 그의 작업과 매우 유사하다고 언급했다. "제가 해야 할 일은 게임에 묘사된 다양한 장면의 분위기에 맞는 음악을 만드는 것이었습니다"라고 릴로가 덧붙였다.

25-2) 같은 인터뷰에서, 모건 씨는 영웅과 승리가 이미 5만 건의 놀라운 사전 주문을 받았다고 자신 있게 말했다. 26) 5월 10일로 예정된 이 게임의 공식 출시와 함께, 그는 그들의 최신 제품이 성공할 것이라고 굳게 믿고 있다.

어휘 daring 대담한, 용감한   promising 장래성 있는, 전도유망한 composer 작곡가, 작자   compose 구성하다, 작문하다, 작곡하다 exceptional 예외적인, 뛰어난   acclaim 환호하다   venture into ~을 감행하다   realm 영역, 왕국   remarkable 놀랄 만한, 주목할 만한 seasoned 경험 많은, 노련한   film score 영화 음악   admiration 감탄, 존경   captivate ~의 마음을 사로잡다   feature 특징을 포함하다, 중요한 역할을 하다   liken 비유하다   resemble 닮다,

비슷하다   atmosphere 대기, 분위기   depict (그림으로) 그리다 destine 예정해 두다, 정해지다

24

포워드 씨는 누구일 것 같은가?
(A) 텔레비전 쇼의 진행자
(B) 인터넷 게임 개발자
(C) 영화감독
(D) 작곡가

해설 두 번째 문단에서 데이비드 릴로와 게임 엠파이어의 협업은 이전에 릴로 씨와 여러 영화 음악을 작곡한 적이 있는 알렉스 포워드가 주최한 사회 행사에서 게임 엠파이어의 아트 디렉터 켄 모건을 소개받으면서 시작되었다고 했으므로, 포워드 씨는 작곡가라는 사실을 알 수 있다. 따라서 정답은 (D)이다.

25

모건 씨에 대해 암시된 것은?
(A) 그는 최근에 게임 엠파이어의 아트 디렉터가 되었다.
(B) 그는 몇몇 사교 행사를 조직하는 데 참여했다.
(C) 그는 과거에 릴로 씨와 협력한 적이 있다.
(D) 그는 최근에 뎀마 씨와 대화를 나눴다.

어휘 organize 준비하다, 조직하다   collaborate 협력하다

해설 마지막 문단에서 그가 인터뷰한 것을 알 수 있는데, 기사문을 작성한 기자의 이름이 에리카 뎀마이다. 따라서, 그가 최근에 뎀마 씨와 인터뷰를 했다는 것을 유추할 수 있으므로 정답은 (D)이다.

26

영웅과 승리에 대하여 암시된 것은?
(A) 출시될 때까지 개발하는 데 몇 년이 걸렸다.
(B) 50,000명의 사용자만이 사용할 수 있다.
(C) 그것은 5월에 출시될 것으로 예상된다.
(D) 그것은 영화 *시애틀의 비 내리는 날*에서 영감을 받았다.

어휘 exclusively 독점적으로, 전용으로   inspire 고무하다, 영감을 주다

해설 마지막 문단에서 5월 10일로 게임의 공식 출시가 예정되어 있다고 했으므로 정답은 (C)이다. 사전 주문량이 50,000 건이라고 했으므로, '50,000명의 사용자만이 게임을 사용할 수 있다'는 내용의 (B)는 잘못된 정보이다.

27

릴로 씨에 대해 언급된 것이 아닌 것은?
(A) 그는 뛰어난 작품으로 상을 받았다.
(B) 그는 이전에 포워드 씨가 주최한 행사에 초대됐었다.
(C) 그는 여가 시간에 인터넷 게임을 즐겨왔다.
(D) 그는 여러 영화에서 음악 제작에 참여했다.

어휘 honor ~에게 영광을 베풀다, 수여하다   exceptional 예외적인, 뛰어난   be involved in ~에 개입되다, 관련되다

해설 첫 번째 문단에서 그가 *시애틀의 비 내리는 날*로 명망 있는 *아메리칸 무비 어워드 베스트 오리지널 뮤직* 상을 받았다고 했으므로 (A)는 언급된 내용이다. 두 번째 문단에서 데이비드 릴로와 게임 엠파이어의 협업은 이전에 알렉스 포워드가 주최한 사회 행사에서 시작되었다고 했으

으로 (B) 또한 언급된 내용이다. 첫 번째 문단에서 데이비드 릴로가 최근 몇 편의 영화에 탁월한 음악적 기여를 한 것으로 유명하다고 했으므로 (D)도 언급된 내용이다. 따라서 지문에서 언급되지 않은 사실은 (C)이다.

[28-32]

발신: 크레이그 넬슨 〈customerservice@bryanthotels.com〉
수신: 제니퍼 길슨 〈gilson77@networld.com〉
날짜: 10월 12일
첨부파일: 브라이언트_호텔_멤버십_프로그램

친애하는 길슨 씨께,

저희의 기록에 따르면, 귀하의 브라이언트 호텔 멤버십 프로그램 회원 자격은 올해 11월 30일에 만료될 예정입니다. **28) 지난 3년 동안 누려 오신 것처럼, 저희가 제공하는 혜택에 대해 중단 없는 접근 권한을 보장하기 위해 만료일 전에 회원 자격을 갱신해 주시기 바랍니다.** **30-1) 추가 인센티브로, 10월 31일까지 갱신하시면 연회비를 15% 할인 받으실 수 있습니다.**

또한, 회원제 프로그램을 업데이트했음을 알려드립니다. 이 새로운 프로그램들은 내년 초에 시행될 것이고 연장된 체크아웃 시간, 무료 룸 업그레이드, 그리고 신속한 포인트 적립을 포함한 다양한 유리한 정책들을 포함합니다. 자세한 내용은 본 메일에 첨부된 파일을 참조하시기 바랍니다.

따뜻한 안부를 전하며,

크레이그 넬슨
브라이언트 호텔 고객 서비스

어휘 expire 만료되다, 만기가 되다 renew 갱신하다 uninterrupted 중단되지 않는, 연속된 come into effect 시행되다 encompass 포함하다, 아우르다 advantageous 이로운, 유리한 complimentary 무료의 expedite 더 신속히 처리하다 accumulation 축적

새로운 브라이언트 호텔 멤버십 정책 업데이트

29) 1월 1일부터, 우리는 존경하는 브라이언트 호텔 회원들을 위한 향상된 혜택을 소개하게 되어 기쁩니다. 다음과 같은 추가 권한을 사용할 수 있습니다:

✓ 체크아웃 시간 연장: 다이아몬드 프레스티지 회원의 경우, 체크아웃 시간이 오후 3시 30분까지 연장되며, **31-1) 루비 엘리트 회원은 오후 2시 30분의 체크아웃 시간을 즐길 수 있는데**, 두 경우 모두 정규 체크아웃 시간인 오전 11시를 초과하는 것입니다. 크리스탈 티어 회원들은 오후 1시 30분의 체크아웃 시간을 가질 수 있습니다.

✓ 무료 객실 업그레이드: 다이아몬드 프레스티지와 루비 엘리트 회원들은 호텔에서 연속 2박 이상 투숙 시 객실 업그레이드를 무료로 받을 수 있습니다. 이 특전을 받기 위해, 회원님의 이름으로 객실을 예약해야 합니다.

✓ 보너스 포인트: 다이아몬드 프레스티지 회원들은 그들이 호텔에서 쓰는 모든 달러의 20%에 해당하는 포인트를 얻게 될 것입니다. 또한, 다이아몬드 프레스티지 회원에게는 매 숙박마다 1,000점의

보너스 포인트가 추가로 부여됩니다. 루비 엘리트와 크리스탈 티어 회원은 매 숙박마다 각각 500점과 300점의 보너스 포인트를 획득할 수 있습니다.

우리는 우리의 소중한 회원들에게 이러한 추가적인 이점을 제공하게 되어 기쁘고, 브라이언트 호텔에서의 경험을 지속적으로 향상시킬 수 있기를 기대합니다.

안부를 전하며,

브라이언트 호텔 멤버십 서비스

어휘 commence 개시하다, 시작하다 enhance 강화하다 esteemed 존중받는, 존경받는 privilege 특권 extend 연장하다 surpass 능가하다, 넘다 eligible for ~에 대한 자격이 있는 consecutive 연속적인 qualify ~에게 자격을 주다 respectively 각각

---

https://www.bryanthotels.com/membership/renewal

브라이언트 호텔 멤버십 프로그램 갱신 양식

30-2) 신청 날짜: 11월 8일

회원 이름	제니퍼 길슨
전화	(510) 913-8582
이메일 주소	gilson77@networld.com
거주지 주소	반 네스 가 1688번지, 샌프란시스코, 캘리포니아, 94103
멤버십 유형	**31-2) 루비 엘리트**
신용카드 번호	1001 5382 2021 1819

☑ 수정된 멤버십 프로그램 약관에 동의함을 확인합니다.

☐ **32) 회원 자격 업그레이드를 고려해 보시겠습니까?** 관심이 있으시다면, 24시간 이내에 고객 서비스 담당자 중 한 명이 연락을 드릴 것입니다.

제출

어휘 residential 거주의, 주거의 hereby 이에 의하여, 이로써 acceptance 동의, 승인, 수락 terms (합의·계약 등의) 조건 associate (사업, 직장) 동료

28

이메일에 언급된 내용은 무엇인가?
(A) 브라이언트 호텔은 현재 할인 요금을 제공하고 있다.
(B) 업그레이드된 멤버십 프로그램이 즉시 적용된다.
(C) 길슨 씨는 지난 몇 년 동안 회원이었다.
(D) 길슨 씨는 12월에 누적 점수를 잃게 된다.

어휘 take effect 효력을 발휘하기 시작하다, 시행되다 immediately 즉각적으로 accumulate 모으다, 축적하다

해설 이메일의 첫 문단에 지난 3년 동안 해온 것처럼 다양한 혜택을 중단 없이 계속 누릴 수 있도록 만료일 전에 회원 자격을 갱신해 달라는 내용이 있으므로, 길슨 씨는 지난 몇 년간 호텔의 회원이었다는 사실을 알 수 있다. 따라서 정답은 (C)이다.

29

공지의 목적은 무엇인가?

(A) 호텔 투숙객에게 회원 자격을 갱신하라고 요청하기 위해

(B) 회원들에게 객실 요금 조정을 알리기 위해

(C) 호텔 직원들에게 휴가 정책에 대한 세부 사항을 제공하기 위해

(D) 멤버십 정책에 대한 업데이트를 전달하기 위해

어휘 adjustment (약간의) 수정, 조정   communicate 전하다, 알리다, 의사소통을 하다

해설 공지의 첫 문단에서, 1월 1일부터 브라이언트 호텔 회원들을 위한 향상된 혜택을 소개하게 되어 기쁘다고 언급하고 있으므로, 공지의 목적은 멤버십 프로그램의 변화된 정책을 알리기 위한 것임을 알 수 있다. 따라서 정답은 (D)이다.

30

길슨 씨에 대해 암시된 것은?

(A) 그녀는 자신의 회원 자격을 업그레이드하는 데 관심이 있다.

(B) 그녀는 이미 회원 자격이 만료된 후에 회원 자격을 갱신했다.

(C) 그녀는 연회비 15% 할인을 받을 수 없었다.

(D) 그녀의 회원 자격은 10월에 만료될 예정이었다.

해설 이메일 첫 문단에서 10월 31일까지 갱신하시면 연회비 15% 할인을 받을 수 있다고 했다. 그런데 온라인 양식에서 신청일이 11월 8일임을 알 수 있으므로, 길슨 씨는 할인을 받지 못했을 것이다. 따라서 정답은 (C)이다.

31

길슨 씨가 호텔에서 체크아웃 할 수 있는 가장 늦은 시간은 언제인가?

(A) 오전 11시

(B) 오후 1시 30분

(C) 오후 2시 30분

(D) 오후 3시 30분

해설 온라인 양식에 따르면 길슨 씨의 멤버십 종류는 루비 엘리트이다. 그런데 공지의 두 번째 문단에서 루비 엘리트 회원은 오후 2시 30분의 체크아웃 시간을 즐길 수 있다고 언급되어 있으므로 정답은 (C)이다.

32

온라인 양식에 언급된 것은?

(A) 고객 서비스 담당자가 길슨 씨와 연락을 취할 것이다.

(B) 길슨 씨의 회원 자격은 11월 8일에 만료될 예정이다.

(C) 작년에 비해 회비가 더 적다.

(D) 길슨 씨의 회원 유형은 변경되지 않을 것이다.

어휘 compared to ~와 비교하여   alteration 변화, 개조

해설 온라인 양식 마지막 부분의 회원 자격 업그레이드를 고려할 것인지를 묻는 항목에 체크되어 있지 않으므로, 길슨 씨는 현재의 멤버십 유형을 그대로 신청했다는 것을 알 수 있다. 따라서 정답은 (D)이다.

PRACTICE

pp.197-199

1	to improve	2	to travel
3	In order for	4	To be
5	afford	6	likely
7	scheduled	8	makes
9	improving		

1 그녀는 장학금을 받을 기회를 늘리기 위해 열심히 공부했다.

2 나는 해외 여행을 하고 다른 문화를 경험할 수 있는 기회를 갖게 되어 감격했다.

3 그들이 목표를 달성하기 위해서, 그들은 집중하고 그들의 일에 전념해야 한다.

4 장학금의 대상으로 고려되기 위해서는, 지원자가 자격 기준을 충족해야 한다.

5 그녀는 하루 더 일을 쉴 여유가 없어서, 몸이 불편함에도 불구하고 사무실로 갔다.

6 신제품 출시는 상당한 관심을 불러일으키고 매출을 견인할 것으로 보인다.

7 회의는 내일 오후 2시에 회의실에서 열릴 예정이다.

8 젊은 고객들을 끌어들이는 것은 그것의 제품과 서비스를 시장에서 더욱 트렌디하고 적절하게 만든다.

9 디자이너들은 신제품 디자인을 개선하는 데 한 달 이상을 보냈다.

📑 실전 문제 연습

p.201

1	(C)	2	(C)	3	(D)	4	(C)
5	(B)	6	(B)	7	(B)	8	(B)
9	(C)	10	(D)	11	(A)	12	(A)
13	(D)	14	(D)	15	(B)	16	(A)
17	(D)	18	(B)	19	(C)	20	(C)
21	(B)	22	(A)	23	(D)	24	(C)
25	(D)	26	(D)	27	(B)	28	(B)
29	(A)	30	(C)	31	(B)	32	(B)

PART 5

1

직원들은 새로운 일을 시작하기 전에 의무적인 안전 교육 수업에 참석해야 한다.

어휘 mandatory 법에 정해진, 의무적인

해설 주어인 직원들이 의무 안전 교육 수업에 참석하도록 요구받는 입장이므로, 빈칸에는 수동태 동사인 are required가 와야 한다. 따라서 정답은 (C)이다. 'be required to'는 '~해야 한다, ~하도록 요구받다'라는 의미이다.

2

예산 제약으로 인해 맥헤일 메디컬 센터는 새로운 침대나 다른 비기술 장비의 구입을 연기해야 했다.

어휘 postpone 미루다, 연기하다 equipment 장비, 설비 purchase 구입, 구매; 구입(구매)하다 due to ~ 때문에 budget 예산 constraint 제약

해설 빈칸은 동명사를 목적어로 취하는 동사인 postpone의 목적어 자리이므로, 정답은 동명사인 (C)이다. 명사도 postpone의 목적어가 될 수는 있지만, 빈칸 뒤에 동명사의 목적어인 'new beds and other nontechnical equipment'가 있으므로 명사인 (A)와 (B)는 정답이 될 수 없다.

3

우리 회사는 시장에서 상당한 발전을 이루었지만, 우리는 경쟁사의 서비스를 능가하기 위해 지속적으로 서비스를 향상시키기 위해 노력하고 있다.

어휘 significant 중요한, 의미 있는 progress 전진, 진보 continuously 끊임없이 strive 노력하다 exceed (수, 양, 정도를) 넘다 competitor 경쟁자

해설 빈칸에는 경쟁사의 'services'를 대신하는 대명사가 와야 한다. 서로 실체는 다르지만 명사가 반복될 때 사용하는 대명사는 that과 those인데, services는 복수 명사이므로 빈칸에 어울리는 대명사는 (D) those이다.

4

연구팀은 조사를 마무리하는 것과 동료의 심사를 받는 저널에 결과를 발표하는 것을 아직 하지 않았다.

어휘 conclude 끝내다, 결론을 내다 investigation 조사 findings 연구 결과

해설 빈칸 앞에 has가 있고 빈칸 뒤에 to부정사가 있으므로, 빈칸에 어울리는 부사는 yet이다. '아직 ~하지 않았다'를 의미하는 관용 표현인 'have yet to'를 외워 두어야 한다.

5

어려운 상황에도 불구하고, 팀은 예산 범위 내에서 프로젝트를 제때에 수행할 수 있었는데, 이는 그들의 헌신을 돋보이게 했다.

어휘 challenging 도전적인, 힘이 드는 circumstance 환경, 상황 showcase 전시하다; ~을 돋보이게 하다 regulate 규제하다, 조절하다 achieve 달성하다, 성취하다 undertake 착수하다; 약속하다 manage to do 간신히 ~을 해내다

해설 빈칸 뒤에 to deliver가 있으므로 빈칸에는 to부정사를 목적어로 취하는 동사가 필요하다. 따라서 정답은 (B)이다. 'manage to 동사'는 '겨우 해내다'라는 의미이다.

6

그 기관은 교육 및 권한 부여 계획을 통해 지역 사회의 긍정적인 변화를 촉진하는 데 전념하고 있다.

어휘 through ~을 통해 empowerment 권한 부여 initiative 계획; 진취성; 주도권 facilitate 가능하게 하다 facilitation 편리화, 용이하게 함

해설 'devoted to'는 '~에 헌신하는'이라는 의미의 관용구인데, to는 전치사이므로 뒤에 명사나 동명사가 와야 한다. 그런데 빈칸 뒤에 동명사의 목적어인 positive changes가 있으므로 정답은 동명사인 (B) facilitating이다.

7

그의 최근 제안이 승인된 후에, 랭킨 씨는 그가 담당하던 다른 프로젝트를 보류해야 했다.

어휘 following ~ 후에 proposal 제안, 제의 in charge of ~을 맡아서, 담당해서 on hold 보류된, 연기된

해설 빈칸 앞 전치사 following(~ 후에)과 빈칸 뒤 전명구인 'of his latest proposal(그의 최근 제안의)'와 자연스럽게 연결되는 명사를 골라야 한다. (A) capacity(역량), (B) approval(승인), (C) allowance (수당), (D) flexibility(유연성) 중 해석 상 가장 어울리는 어휘는 (B) approval이다.

8

각 참가자는 컨퍼런스 중에 각자에게 맞는 의미 있는 경험을 할 수 있도록 사전 이벤트 설문 조사를 완료해야 한다.

어휘 participant 참가자 tailored 맞춤의 meaningful 의미 있는, 중요한

해설 빈칸 뒤 participant가 단수 명사이므로 정답은 단수 명사 앞에 붙는 한정사인 (B) Each이다. 수량 형용사인 several은 복수 명사를 수식하므로 (A)는 오답이며, single은 단순한 형용사로 single participant 앞에 한정사가 필요하므로 (C) 또한 오답이다. all이 가산 명사를 수식하는 경우 그 명사는 복수형이어야 하므로 (D)도 오답이다.

9

우리 회사는 5년 연속 기록적인 매출을 달성했는데, 이는 우리의 꾸준한 성장을 보여준다.

어휘 achieve 이루다, 성취하다 record-breaking 기록적인 demonstrate 입증하다, 보여주다 consistent 일관된 repetitive 반복적인 thorough 빈틈없는, 철두철미한 profitable 유익한; 수익성이 있는

해설 꾸준한 성장을 보이고 있다고 했으므로, 우리 회사가 5년 연속으로 기록적인 매출을 달성했다는 의미가 되어야 자연스럽다. 따라서 정답은 (C) consecutive(연이은)이다. (A) repetitive는 수식 받는 명사인 year(해)가 반복된다는 의미이므로 의미상 어색하다.

10

뛰어난 업적과 함께, 그녀는 뛰어난 지도력을 가지고 있는데, 이것이 그녀를 그 직책에 이상적인 후보자로 만든다.

어휘 outstanding 눈에 띄는, 우수한 achievement 성취, 업적 exceptional 예외적인, 뛰어난

해설 빈칸은 명사구인 her outstanding achievements 앞에 있으므로 전치사가 필요한 자리이다. 보기 중에서 전치사는 (D) Along with (~와 함께, ~에 덧붙여)뿐이다. (A)와 (B)는 절을 연결하는 접속사이고, (C) In order to뒤에는 동사 원형이 필요하므로 모두 오답이다.

11

그 역할은 고객의 까다로운 기대를 충족시키기 위해 높은 수준의 전문 지식과 강한 직업 윤리를 필요로 한다.

어휘 expertise 전문 지식 work ethic 직업 윤리 demanding 힘든, 요구가 많은 accountable 책임이 있는 collective 집단의, 공동의

해설 그 역할이 높은 수준의 전문 지식과 강력한 직업 의식을 필요로 한다는 것은 고객의 '까다로운' 기대를 충족시키기 위해서라는 내용이 되어야 자연스러우므로 정답은 (A) demanding이다.

12

우리가 필요한 수리를 위해 열심히 노력하고 있기 때문에, 추후 통지가 있을 때까지 시설은 일시적으로 폐쇄될 것이다.

어휘 facility 설비, 시설 until further notice 추후 통지가 있을 때까지 diligently 부지런히, 열심히 temporarily 일시적으로 uncertainly 자신 없게, 머뭇거리며 substantially 상당히

해설 필요한 수리를 하고 있다고 했으므로, 시설이 추후 통지가 있을 때까지 시설이 일시적으로 폐쇄될 것이라는 내용이 되어야 자연스럽다. 따라서 정답은 (A) temporarily이다.

13

워크숍에서는 생산성을 높이기 위해 새로운 소프트웨어 시스템을 효과적으로 활용하는 방법에 대한 포괄적인 가이드를 제공할 것이다.

어휘 comprehensive 포괄적인 utilize 이용하다 enhance 높이다, 강화하다 productivity 생산성

해설 워크숍은 생산성을 높이기 위해 새로운 소프트웨어 시스템을 효과적으로 활용하는 '방법'에 대한 포괄적인 가이드를 제공할 것이라는 내용이 되어야 자연스러우므로 정답은 (D) how이다. 참고로 「의문사 + to부정사」는 '～할지, ～해야 할지'로 해석되며, 의문사 중 why는 to부정사 앞에 사용되지 않는다.

14

회사는 타겟 마케팅 캠페인을 통해 향후 3년 내에 시장 점유율을 25%까지 확대한다는 목표를 세웠다.

어휘 targeted 목표가 된 above ～보다 위에 behind ～ 뒤에

해설 빈칸 뒤의 the next three years는 다음 3년간의 기간을 의미하는데, 숫자 기간 명사 앞에 사용되는 전치사인 (D) within(～ 이내에)이 정답이다.

15

프로젝트 일정 및 예산 내역에 관한 추가 정보는 첨부 문서를 참조해 주세요.

어휘 regarding ～에 관하여 breakdown 고장; 명세서 arbitrary 임의적인, 제멋대로인 superfluous 필요치 않은, 불필요한

해설 명사 information(정보)을 수식하기에 알맞은 형용사를 골라야 한다. 프로젝트 일정 및 예산 내역에 관한 '추가적인' 정보는 첨부 문서를 참조하라는 내용이 되어야 자연스러우므로 정답은 (B) supplemental(보충의, 추가의)이다.

PART 6

[16-19]

친애하는 챈 씨께,

귀하의 프리티 트립을 통한 마이애미행 항공권 구매가 다음과 같은 이유로 취소되었음을 알려 드리게 되어 유감입니다. 이번 구매에 사용하신 쿠폰은 블루밍 카드 소지자가 해당 카드로 거래하는 것을 목적으로 발행된 것입니다. 그러나, 이 쿠폰이 블루밍 카드 소지자가 아닌 분들께 잘못 배포되어, 블루밍 카드 이외의 다른 카드로 구매하여 부적절하게 사용된 것으로 확인되었습니다. 또한, 쿠폰의 약관에는 추가적인 제한 사항도 포함되어 있습니다. **계정당 쿠폰을 두 개 이상 사용하는 것은 금지되어 있습니다.** 참고로, 사용하신 쿠폰의 사본을 첨부하였습니다.

불편을 끼쳐드린 점 사과드립니다.

진심으로,

고객 서비스
프리티 트립

어휘 specifically 명확하게, 특별히 issue 발표하다; 발행하다 cardholder 카드 소지자 transaction 거래, 매매 improper 부적절한 other than ～ 외에, ～와 다른 terms and conditions (계약이나 지불 등의) 조건 restriction 제한, 규제 reference 참고, 참조

16

어휘 equivalent 동등한 specialized 전문적인 favorable 호의적인

해설 다음 문장에서 이번 구매에 사용한 쿠폰은 블루밍 카드 소지자에게 발행된 것으로서, 블루밍 카드로 거래할 때 사용할 수 있다고 구매가 취소된 이유를 설명하고 있다. 따라서, 빈칸에 어울리는 형용사는 (A) following(다음의)이다.

17

해설 빈칸은 their Blooming card 앞에 위치한 전치사 자리이다. 블루밍 카드'로' 이루어진 거래를 위한 쿠폰이라는 내용이 되어야 하므로 정답은 (D) with이다. with는 '～와 함께'라는 의미 외에도 '～으로, ～로'와 같은 '수단'을 의미하기도 한다. 문장에 동사인 was issued가 있으므로 빈칸 앞의 made는 동사가 아닌 앞의 명사 transactions를 수식하는 과거분사이다. 과거분사인 made 뒤에는 목적어가 올 수 없으므로 대명사인 (A) it은 정답이 될 수 없다.

18

어휘 therefore 그러니, 그러므로 to that end 그러기 위해서 nevertheless 그렇기는 하지만, 그럼에도 불구하고

해설 빈칸 앞에서 프리티 트립을 통한 마이애미행 항공권 구매가 취소된 이유를 설명하고, 빈칸 뒤 문장에서도 항공권 구매가 취소된 추가적인 이유를 설명하고 있으므로 빈칸에 어울리는 접속부사는 (B) Furthermore(뿐만 아니라, 더욱이)이다.

19

(A) 블루밍 카드를 이용해 주셔서 대단히 감사합니다.
(B) 우리는 당신의 마이애미 여행이 편안하기를 바랍니다.

(C) 계정당 쿠폰을 두 개 이상 사용하는 것은 금지되어 있습니다.

(D) 카드를 사용하기 전에 동봉된 전단지를 읽어 보시기 바랍니다.

어휘 journey 여행, 여정 comfortable 편안한, 쾌적한 prohibit 금지하다 enclosed 동봉된, 에워싸인 leaflet 전단

해설 빈칸 앞 문장에서 쿠폰의 약관에는 추가적인 제한 사항도 포함되어 있다고 했으므로, 그 제한 사항이 무엇인지를 구체적으로 설명하는 문장인 (C)가 빈칸에 가장 어울리는 문장이다.

[20-23]

> 당신이 카마스 리테일 스프링데일의 지역 영업 부장 직책을 수락하게 되어 기쁩니다. 인사부의 짐 피셔가 당신의 교육 담당자가 될 것입니다. **그는 당신의 책무에 대한 세부 내용을 제공할 것입니다.** 이전에 논의한 바와 같이, 당신은 회사의 급여 정책에 따라 2주마다 급여를 받게 될 것입니다. 또한, 포괄적인 의료보험 적용과 함께 성과에 따른 보상이 매년 주어질 것입니다. 추가 질문이나 우려 사항이 있으면, randall84@camas.com으로 닉 랜달에게 문의하십시오. 우리는 당신과 함께 일하는 것을 굉장히 기대 중입니다.

어휘 regional 지방의, 지역의 Human Resources 인사부 specific 명확한, 구체적인 previously 이전에 paycheck 급료 payroll 급여 지불 총액 performance-based compensation 성과급 grant 수여하다, 승인하다 comprehensive 포괄적인, 종합적인 insurance coverage 보험 범위

20

어휘 accept 수락하다

해설 이어지는 문장에서 인사부의 짐 피셔가 당신의 교육 담당자가 될 것이라고 했으므로 편지를 받는 사람이 지역 영업 부장 직책을 수락했음을 알 수 있다. 따라서 현재 수락한 상태임을 의미하는 현재완료 시제 동사인 (C) have accepted가 정답이다. 빈칸 뒤에 목적어인 the position이 있으므로 수동태 동사인 (D) were accepted는 정답이 될 수 없다.

21

(A) 상사에게 허가를 받으십시오.

(B) 그는 당신의 책무에 대한 세부 내용을 제공할 것입니다.

(C) 당신은 세 부의 추천서를 제출해야 합니다.

(D) 포상금으로 현금 보너스가 지급됩니다.

어휘 obtain 얻다 permission 허락, 허가 supervisor 감독자, 상급자 reference 참조; 추천서 reward 보상하다

해설 빈칸 앞 문장에서 인사부의 짐 피셔가 당신의 트레이너가 될 것이라고 했으므로, '그가 당신의 책임에 대한 세부 사항을 제공할 것'이라는 내용이 이어지는 것이 가장 자연스럽다. 따라서 정답은 (B)이다.

22

어휘 consequently 그 결과, 따라서 in other words 달리 말하면, 다시 말해서 otherwise 그 외에는, 그렇지 않으면

해설 빈칸 앞의 문장에서 급여에 대해 설명했고, 빈칸 뒤 문장에서는 급여 외에 추가적으로 제공되는 매년 연말 지급될 성과급과 의료 보험에 대해 설명했으므로, 빈칸에 가장 어울리는 접속 부사는 (A) Additionally (게다가)이다.

23

어휘 reliable 믿을 수 있는 valued 귀중한, 소중한

해설 지문 전반적으로 카마스 리테일 스프링데일의 지역 영업 부장으로 일하게 될 상대방에게 직책에 관련된 혜택 등을 설명하고 있으므로, 마지막에 '우리가 당신과 함께 일하는 것을 굉장히 기대 중'이라는 의미의 문장이 이어지는 것이 자연스럽다. 따라서 빈칸에 가장 어울리는 형용사는 (D)이다. be eager to do는 '~을 하고 싶어 하다, 열망하다'라는 의미이다.

PART 7

[24-27]

> 노드스톰 패션
> 6월 6일–12일 주간 진행 상황 보고서
> 프로젝트 관리자 토드 와일리가 준비
>
> 이번 주 성과:
>
> - 25) 수영복 생산 전문성을 보유한 중국 광저우 소재 제조업체 세 곳과 접촉 시작. 24) 우리의 새로운 수영복 디자인 사양을 그들과 공유하고 최소 주문 수량, 생산 및 배송 비용, 소요 시간에 대해 문의했습니다.
>
> - 27) 초기 대응 검토 결과, 치야 인더스트리가 우리의 요구 사항을 충족시키기에 가장 적합한 제조사인 것 같습니다. 다른 두 회사에 비해 상대적으로 규모는 작지만, 그곳은 우리의 주문 요구 사항을 충족하기 위해 인력을 늘릴 준비가 되어 있습니다. 26) 게다가, 해외 영업 담당자인 알렌 펑은 즉시 저에게 연락하여 전문성과 친근함을 보여주었습니다. 그는 저의 모든 질문에 명확하고 솔직한 답변을 해주었습니다. 저는 그와 상호 이익이 되는 비즈니스 관계를 구축할 수 있기를 기대합니다.
>
> - 연락한 나머지 두 회사는 우리의 일정을 수용할 수 없거나 우리의 가격 기준을 충족하지 못했습니다. 결과적으로, 그들은 더 이상의 고려 대상에서 제외되었습니다.
>
> 6월 13일부터 19일까지 일주일 동안 계획된 활동:
>
> - 치야 인더스트리와 프로젝트 요구 사항 및 지불 조건에 대해 지속적으로 논의합니다.
>
> - 설계팀에 최종 치수, 직물, 그리고 색상을 문서화하고 생산 공정 단계를 대략적으로 설명하도록 지시합니다. 그런 다음, 샘플 제작을 용이하게 하기 위해 이 정보를 치야 인더스트리에 제출합니다.

어휘 initiate 게시되게 하다; 착수시키다 expertise 전문 지식 specification (자세한) 설명서, 사양 minimum 최저의, 최소한의 quantity 양, 수량 turnaround 작업을 완료해서 회송하는 데 걸리는 시간 promptly 신속하게, 즉시 cordiality 따뜻한 우정 cultivate 경작하다; 구축하다 mutually 상호간에 association 연계, 유대 accommodate (의견 등을) 수용하다 criteria criterion의 복수형, (판단이나 결정을 위한) 기준 exclude 제외하다, 배제하다 measurement 측정, 측량; 치수 subsequently 그 뒤에, 나중에 facilitate 가능하게 하다, 용이하게 하다

24

노드스톰 패션에 대해 유추할 수 있는 것은?
(A) 중국 광저우로의 이전을 고려하고 있다.
(B) 현재 해외 영업 담당자를 모집 중이다.
(C) 신제품 개발에 관여하고 있다.
(D) 다른 회사와의 합병에 관련되어 있다.

어휘 recruit 모집하다   be engaged in ~에 종사하고 있다
be involved in ~에 개입되다   merger 합병

해설 첫 번째 문단에서 새로운 수영복 디자인 사양을 그들과 공유하고 최소 주문 수량, 생산 및 배송 비용, 소요 시간에 대해 문의했다고 했으므로, 현재 새로운 수영복을 개발 중임을 유추할 수 있다. 따라서 정답은 (C)이다.

25

보고서에 따르면, 와일리 씨는 6월 6일 주에 무엇을 했는가?
(A) 그는 선적 일정을 진행했다.
(B) 그는 건축 허가를 받았다.
(C) 그는 공장 직원들에게 교육을 제공했다.
(D) 그는 잠재적인 사업 파트너를 평가했다.

어휘 obtain 얻다, 구하다   assess 평가하다

해설 첫 문단에서 수영복 생산 전문성을 보유한 중국 광저우 소재 3개의 제조업체와 접촉하여 새로운 수영복 디자인 사양을 그들과 공유하고 최소 주문 수량, 생산 및 배송 비용, 소요 시간에 대해 문의했다고 했다. 그러므로 그는 새로운 수영복 생산을 맡길 잠재적인 사업 파트너들을 평가했다는 것을 알 수 있다. 따라서 정답은 (D)이다.

26

펑 씨에 대해 어떤 정보가 제공되었는가?
(A) 그는 와일리 씨와 직접 이야기를 나눴다.
(B) 그는 디자인 부서에서 일하고 있다.
(C) 그는 그 프로젝트에 대해 몇 가지 문의를 받았다.
(D) 그는 능숙하고 협력적이었다.

어휘 proficient 능숙한   cooperative 협력하는, 협동하는

해설 두 번째 문단에서 해외 영업 담당자인 알렌 펑은 즉시 자신에게 연락하여 전문성과 친근함을 보여주었고, 모든 질문에 명확하고 솔직한 답변을 해주었다고 했다. 따라서 정답은 (D)이다. 그는 와일리 씨를 직접 만난 것이 아니며, 디자인 부서에서 일하고 있는 것도 아니다. 또한 그가 프로젝트에 관한 질문을 했다는 내용은 없으므로 (A), (B), (C)는 모두 오답이다

27

다음 문장은 [1], [2], [3], [4]의 어느 위치에 오는 것이 가장 적절한가?
"다른 두 회사에 비해 상대적으로 규모는 작지만, 그곳은 우리의 주문 요구 사항을 충족하기 위해 인력을 늘릴 준비가 되어 있습니다."
(A) [1]
(B) [2]
(C) [3]
(D) [4]

어휘 relatively 비교적   workforce 노동자, 직원

해설 주어진 문장에서 이곳이 다른 두 회사에 비해 상대적으로 규모는 작지만 요구 사항을 충족하기 위해 인력을 늘릴 준비가 되어 있다고 설명하고 있다. 특정한 회사가 언급된 부분은 [2]번 앞 문장으로, 초기 대응을 검토해 본 결과, 치야 인더스트리가 우리의 요구 사항을 충족시키기에 가장 적합한 제조사인 것 같다고 설명하고 있다. 따라서 정답은 (B)이다.

[28-32]

수신: 브루노 발디니 〈baldini80@bigcircle.net〉
발신: 메리 펜튼 〈maryfenton@citylight.com〉
날짜: 8월 3일
첨부: 바우처

발디니 씨께,

28) 29-1) 7월 23일에 밴쿠버 시티 라이트 호텔에 머무르는 동안 당신이 최근에 직면한 문제에 대해 듣게 유감스럽게 생각합니다. 30) 예약이 확정되었음에도 불구하고, 예약하신 특정 객실을 이용할 수 없으셨다는 사실을 알게 되었습니다. 29-2) 그럼에도 불구하고, 우리의 전담 프런트 직원이 당신을 위해 대체 숙소를 마련해 주어서 기쁩니다.

조사 결과, 우리는 컴퓨터 프로그램의 오작동으로 인해 이미 예약이 되어 있음에도 불구하고 특정 객실이 이용 가능한 것으로 잘못 기재된 것을 발견했습니다. 유감스럽게도, 귀하의 밴쿠버 방문은 저희 호텔 근처에서 열린 국제 회의와 겹쳐서, 예상 외로 많은 손님들이 방문하게 되었습니다. 이로 인해 의도치 않게 오버부킹이 발생했습니다.

시티 라이트 호텔을 대표하여 불편을 끼쳐드린 점 진심으로 사과드립니다. 호의의 표시로, 저희 시티 라이트 호텔의 숙박 시설(밴쿠버, 토론토, 몬트리올, 캘거리) 중 어느 곳이든 1박을 무료로 제공해 드리고 싶습니다. 자세한 내용은 첨부된 바우처를 참조하시기 바랍니다.

안부를 전하며,

32-1) 메리 펜튼
고객 서비스 책임자
시티 라이트 호텔

어휘 encounter 맞닥뜨리다, 접하다   specific 구체적인, 특정한   nevertheless 그렇기는 하지만   alternative 대체 가능한, 대안이 되는   accommodations 숙소, 시설   investigation 수사, 조사   malfunction 고장; 제대로 작동하지 않다   coincide 동시에 일어나다   in the vicinity of ~의 부근에   unintentionally 무심코, 의도 없이   as a gesture of goodwill 호의의 표시로써   complimentary 무료의

시티 라이트 호텔 바우처

이 바우처는 다음의 시티 라이트 호텔의 일반 객실에서 1박 무료 숙박권을 제공합니다: 게스트 스위트 시티 라이트 밴쿠버, 오션뷰 시티 라이트 몬트리올, 하이 스퀘어 시티 라이트 토론토, 또는 포레스트 시티 라이트 캘거리.

31) 객실 예약은 반드시 사전에 해야 한다는 점을 참고하시기 바랍니다. 식사는 포함되지 않습니다.

손님 서명: _____

날짜: _____

32-2) 문의 사항이 있으면 고객 서비스 팀에 문의하십시오:
이메일: customerservices@citylight.com
전화: 604-665-5111
32-3) 우편: 워터 스트리트 53번지, 토론토, 온타리오 M6B 2A5, 캐나다

어휘 entitle 자격을 주다 inquiry 질문, 조사

28

펜튼 씨는 왜 이메일을 보냈는가?
(A) 발디니 씨의 예약을 확인하려고
(B) 발디니 씨의 불만 사항을 해결하려고
(C) 발디니 씨의 예약을 도우려고
(D) 발디니 씨의 여행 일정에 대해 물어보려고

해설 이메일에서 7월 23일에 밴쿠버 시티 라이트 호텔에 머무르는 동안 당신이 최근에 직면한 문제에 대해 듣게 유감스럽게 생각한다고 했으므로, 발디니 씨가 예약했던 방을 이용할 수 없었던 사실을 알렸고, 이에 대한 응답으로 펜튼 씨가 이메일을 보낸 것을 유추할 수 있다. 따라서 정답은 (B)이다.

29

펜튼 씨에 따르면 7월 23일에 무슨 일이 있었는가?
(A) 호텔 직원들이 문제를 해결했다.
(B) 호텔이 새로운 예약 시스템을 시행했다.
(C) 발디니 씨는 무료 숙박권을 받았다.
(D) 호텔에서 국제 대회가 열리고 있었다.

어휘 resolve (문제를) 풀다, 해결하다

해설 이메일의 첫 번째 문단에 따르면 발디니씨가 7월 23일에 밴쿠버 시티 라이트 호텔에 머무를 때 예약한 방에 문제가 있었지만, 전담 프런트 직원이 대체 숙소를 마련해 주었다고 했으므로 정답은 (A)이다.

30

발디니 씨에 대해 암시된 것은?
(A) 그는 회의에 참석하기 위해 밴쿠버로 여행을 갔다.
(B) 그는 도착하자마자 방 변경 요청을 했다.
(C) 그는 방을 미리 예약했다.
(D) 그는 정기적으로 시티 라이트 호텔에 머물렀다.

어휘 upon arrival 도착하자마자 regularly 정기적으로

해설 이메일 첫 번째 문단에서 발디니 씨가 예약했던 방이 예약이 확정되었음에도 불구하고 이용할 수 없었다고 했으므로, 발디니 씨가 미리 예약을 하고 호텔에 방문한 것을 알 수 있다. 따라서 정답은 (C)이다.

31

발디니 씨가 바우처를 사용하려면 어떻게 해야 하는가?
(A) 호텔 멤버십에 등록한다.
(B) 미리 예약한다.
(C) 고객 서비스 센터에 문의한다.
(D) 그의 이전 체류에 대한 증거를 제공한다.

어휘 enroll in ~에 등록하다 beforehand 사전에, 미리 previous 이전의

해설 바우처 네 번째 줄에서 객실 예약은 반드시 사전에 해야 한다는 점을 참고하라고 했으므로 정답은 (B)이다.

32

펜튼 씨의 사무실이 있을 가능성이 가장 높은 곳은 어디인가?
(A) 밴쿠버
(B) 토론토
(C) 몬트리올
(D) 캘거리

해설 이메일의 발신자 정보 "Director of Customer Service"에서 메리 펜튼 씨가 고객 서비스 책임자라는 것을 알 수 있다. 바우처 마지막 문단에서 문의 사항이 있으면 고객 서비스 팀에 문의하라는 내용이 있는데, 그 주소가 토론토라는 것을 확인할 수 있다. 따라서 펜튼 씨의 사무실이 있는 곳은 토론토일 것이다.

DAY 08

준동사 II (분사)

PRACTICE

pp.208-211

1 staying	**2** revised
3 which is	**4** working
5 seeking	**6** promising
7 satisfied	

1 302호 투숙객이 에어컨에 사소한 문제가 있다고 신고했다.

2 수정된 기사는 편집자로부터 긍정적인 피드백을 받았다.

3 운영 효율화를 위해 설계된 새로운 시스템이 성공적으로 구현되었다.

4 전문 개발 워크숍은 교육 분야에서 일하는 사람들에게 귀중한 자원을 제공한다.

5 인사 부서는 적격 비용에 대한 보상을 요구하는 직원들에게 지침을 제공한다.

6 연구의 예비 결과는 유망한 결과를 보여주며, 이 분야의 잠재적인 발전을 나타낸다.

7 우리 회사는 고객의 만족과 충성도를 유지하기 위해 서비스를 제공하려는 노력을 하고 있다.

1	(B)	**2**	(D)	**3**	(B)	**4**	(C)
5	(C)	**6**	(A)	**7**	(B)	**8**	(D)
9	(D)	**10**	(C)	**11**	(B)	**12**	(C)
13	(D)	**14**	(C)	**15**	(B)	**16**	(D)
17	(B)	**18**	(C)	**19**	(A)	**20**	(A)
21	(C)	**22**	(D)	**23**	(A)	**24**	(B)
25	(D)	**26**	(C)	**27**	(D)	**28**	(C)
29	(B)	**30**	(C)	**31**	(A)		

PART 5

1

판매 직원은 고객과 적극적으로 접촉하고 맞춤형 지원을 제공하여 쇼핑 환경을 개선하도록 장려되었다.

어휘 actively 적극적으로   engage 관여하다   personalize 개인화하다   enhance 강화하다

해설 동사 encourage는 목적격 보어로 to부정사를 취하는 동사인데, 빈칸 뒤에 to부정사인 to actively engage가 있고 목적어는 없으므로 encourage가 수동태 동사가 되었다는 것을 알 수 있다. 따라서 정답은 (B) was encouraged이다.

2

마케팅 캠페인의 성공은 효과적인 대상 설정과 참여형 컨텐츠에 달려 있다.

어휘 target 대상으로 삼다   engage (주의·관심을) 사로잡다 reliable 믿을 수 있는   reliant 의존하는

해설 빈칸은 be동사 뒤 주격 보어 자리이므로 동사인 (B)는 정답이 될 수 없다. 나머지 보기 중 빈칸 뒤 on과 결합하여 '~에 의존적인'을 뜻하는 형용사 reliant가 정답이다. 참고로 rely는 자동사로서 수동태 형태가 될 수 없으므로 (A)는 오답이다.

3

다양한 화학물질을 관리하는 실험실 기술자는 안전하고 효율적으로 다룰 수 있도록 교육을 잘 받아야 한다.

어휘 chemical 화학적인, 화학물질   manageable 관리할 수 있는

해설 문장에 동사 should be가 있으므로 빈칸에는 동사가 올 수 없다. 따라서 동사인 (A)는 오답이다. 빈칸 앞과 뒤에 명사가 있으므로 빈칸에는 현재분사가 와야 한다. 따라서 정답은 (B) managing이다. managing은 the laboratory technician을 수식하며, 빈칸 뒤의 various chemicals는 managing의 의미상의 목적어이다.

4

프로젝트 관리 경험이 있는 사람들은 종종 조직 내에서 리더십 역할에 대한 요구를 받는다.

해설 문장의 동사가 복수형인 are 이므로 주어 자리에도 복수 명사가 필요하다. 따라서 보기 중 유일한 복수 대명사인 (C) Those가 정답이다. those와 with experience 사이에 「주격 관계대명사 + be동사」가 생략된 형태로서, those는 '사람들'을 뜻한다.

5

새로 임명된 의장은 새로운 전략을 시행하고 조직을 더 높은 곳으로 이끌기를 열망한다.

어휘 chairperson 의장   be eager to ~을 하고 싶어 하다 appointment 약속; 임명   appoint 임명하다

해설 빈칸은 한정사와 명사 사이에 있으므로 명사를 수식하는 형용사 자리이다. 따라서, 형용사 역할이 가능한 현재분사 (B) appointing과 과거분사 (C) appointed 중에서 정답을 고른다. 그런데 빈칸 뒤의 명사인 chairperson과 appoint가 수동의 관계이므로 정답은 과거분사인 (C)이다. 참고로 to부정사가 형용사적 용법으로 사용될 때는 수식을 받는 명사 뒤에 위치한다.

6

회의에 참석할 예정인 사람들은 자리를 확보할 수 있을 만큼 일찍 등록하는 것이 좋다.

어휘 conference 회의, 학회   register 등록하다   secure 확보하다   spot 자리, 곳

해설 문장에 이미 동사인 are advised가 있으므로 동사인 (D) are planning은 정답이 될 수 없다. 또한 those는 컨퍼런스에 참석하는 것을 계획하는 '사람들'을 뜻하므로 사물을 수식하는 관계대명사 which가 포함된 (B) which plan도 오답이다. 남은 보기들은 모두 분사로서 those를 수식할 수 있지만 빈칸 뒤에 의미상의 목적어인 to부정사 to attend가 있으므로 현재분사인 (A) planning이 정답이다.

7

휴잇 법률 회사는 그들의 존경받는 팀에 합류하기를 열망하는 많은 유망한 변호사들로부터 수많은 지원서를 받았다.

어휘 esteemed 존중받는, 존경받는   challenging 도전적인 promising 유망한, 촉망되는   rewarding 보람 있는, 수익이 많이 나는   experiencing 경험하는

해설 빈칸 뒤의 명사인 lawyer를 수식하기에 의미상 적절한 형용사를 골라야 한다. 보기 중 사람인 lawyers를 수식하기에 가장 적절한 형용사는 (B) promising(유망한)이다. promising은 -ing형 형용사로 목적어를 필요로 하지 않는다는 점을 기억해 두어야 한다.

8

유니온 광장에서 행사를 개최하는 행사 주최자는 인근 사업장의 혼잡을 최소화하기 위해 교통 통제 인력을 고용해야 한다.

어휘 minimize 최소화하다   nearby 인근의, 가까운 곳의 organizer 조직자, 주최자   traffic 차량들, 교통(량)   movement 움직임, 운동   convenience 편리, 편의   infection 감염 disruption 혼란, 중단

해설 행사 주최자들이 교통 통제 인력을 고용하는 목적은 행사 개최 장소 주변에 차량으로 인한 혼잡이 예상되고, 이로 인한 인근 사업장에 혼잡을 최소화하기 위한 것이므로 정답은 (D) disruption이다.

9

프로젝트에 대한 특정 자원의 이용 가능성이 제한되어 있어서, 그것의 완료가 지연되었다.

어휘 availability 이용 가능성   completion 완료, 완성   cause 야기하다, 초래하다

119

해설 문장에 동사 has been limited가 있으므로 동사인 (A) has caused와 (C) will cause는 모두 오답이다. '------- delays in its completion'은 완전한 절 뒤에 있으므로 이것을 분사구문으로 볼 수 있는데, 빈칸 뒤에 목적어인 delays가 있으므로 현재분사인 (D) causing이 정답이다.

10

팀 회의 동안 논의된 대로 변경 사항을 반영하도록 건설 프로젝트 일정이 업데이트되었다.

어휘 timeline 연대표, 시각표

해설 as는 접속사 혹은 전치사로 모두 사용될 수 있다. 문장의 as가 전치사일 경우 '~로써'라는 의미이며 뒤에 명사나 동명사가 올 수 있는데, 명사인 (A) discussion은 '팀 회의 동안 논의로써의 변화'라는 어색한 의미가 된다. 빈칸 뒤에 목적어가 없으므로 동명사인 (D) discussing도 정답이 될 수 없다. as를 접속사로 볼 경우 동사인 (B) discuss는 주어 없이 단독으로 사용될 수 없다. 정답은 (C) discussed로서, as 뒤에 it is가 생략된 형태이다.

11

그 식당은 식사를 더욱 즐겁게 즐길 수 있게 하기 위해 메인 코스 외에도 다양한 전채 요리와 디저트를 제공한다.

어휘 appetizer 전채   enhance 높이다, 향상시키다   owing to ~ 때문에   on account of ~ 때문에, ~으로

해설 콤마 뒤의 내용은 식사 경험을 향상시키기 위해서(식사를 더욱 즐겁게 즐길 수 있도록), 다양한 전채 요리와 디저트도 제공한다는 내용이다. 그러므로 빈칸 뒤의 the main course 앞에는 '~ 외에도'를 뜻하는 전치사 (B) Apart from이 의미상 가장 어울린다. (A) Among(~ 사이에, 중에서)은 복수 명사를 목적어로 취하므로 정답에서 제외된다.

12

명시된 기간 내에 장비를 반환하지 않는 고객은 임대 계약서에 명시된 대로 추가 요금을 지불하게 될 것이다.

어휘 specify 명시하다   timeframe 기간   alternate 번갈아 나오다   coincide 동시에 일어나다   inspire 고무하다, 격려하다

해설 문맥상 명시된 기간 내에 장비를 반환하지 않은 고객은 계약서에 명시된 대로 추가 요금이 '발생할 것이다'(추가 요금을 지불하게 될 것이다)라는 의미이므로 정답은 (C) incur(초래하다, 발생시키다)이다.

13

그 회사의 수익이 지난 1년 동안 꾸준히 증가한 반면, 시장 점유율은 상대적으로 정체되어 있다.

어휘 relatively 비교적   stagnant 침체된

해설 주절에서 회사의 수익이 꾸준히 증가해 왔다고 했지만, 빈칸 뒤의 종속절에서 시장 점유율이 상대적으로 정체되어 있다는 주절과 상반된 내용이 이어지고 있다. 따라서 빈칸에 알맞은 부사절 접속사는 (D) whereas(~에 반해서)이다.

14

CEO는 특히 프로젝트 전반에 걸친 그들의 탁월한 헌신을 강조하며 팀에 감사를 표했다.

어휘 gratitude 고마움, 감사   highlight 강조하다   exceptional 우수한, 특출한   dedication 전념, 헌신   throughout ~ 동안 쭉, 내내   originally 원래, 본래   shortly 곧   ambiguously 애매모호하게

해설 빈칸에 들어가기에 의미상 가장 어울리는 부사를 골라야 한다. CEO가 팀에게 감사를 표했고, 특히나 프로젝트 전반에 걸친 그들의 탁월한 헌신을 강조했다는 내용이 되어야 자연스러우므로 정답은 (C) particularly(특히, 특별히)이다.

15

우리는 광범위한 시장 분석을 실시하여, 우리의 확장에 가장 적합한 파트너가 어떤 회사인지에 대한 데이터를 수집하고 통찰력을 얻었다.

어휘 extensive 광범위한   insight 통찰력, 이해   expansion 확대, 확장

해설 빈칸 뒤로 절이 이어지고 있기 때문에 접속사인 (B) which와 (D) that이 정답 후보이다. (D) that은 전치사 뒤에 사용하지 않으므로 오답이며, 관계형용사로서 명사인 company를 수식하고 절과 절을 연결하는 (B) which가 정답이다.

PART 6

[16-19]

> 6월 15일에, 보니 프리미엄 푸드의 마케팅 이사인 제니스 리는 버뱅크에서 일리노이주 윌로우브룩으로 사업을 확장하고 이전하는 데 300만 달러를 투자할 계획이라고 발표했다. 이 전략적인 움직임은 회사의 성장을 지원하는 것을 목표로 한다. **그것은 또한 증가하는 수요를 충족시킬 것이다.** 윌로우브룩 75번가에 위치한 신규 지점은 8월 말 전에 운영될 것으로 예상된다. 1969년 시카고에 설립된 이래로, 이 회사는 지속적으로 레스토랑 포트폴리오를 확장하고, 15개 주에 서비스를 제공하는 5개 이상의 창고를 포함하는 프리미엄 식품 서비스 고객 유통망을 구축했다.

어휘 expand 확대되다, 확장시키다   relocate 이전하다   operation 기업, 사업체   strategic 전략상 중요한, 전략적인   be projected to ~할 것으로 예상되다, 추정되다   operational 사용(가동)할 준비가 갖춰진   consistently 지속적으로   portfolio (특정 회사·기관의) 상품 혹은 서비스 목록   distribution network 유통망   warehouse 창고

16

어휘 with all 무엇보다도   according to ~에 의하면   in order that ~하기 위하여

해설 보니 프리미엄 푸드의 마케팅 이사인 제니스 리가 회사의 '계획에 대한' 발표를 했다는 내용이 되어야 자연스러우므로 (D) regarding(~에 관하여)이 정답이다.

17

(A) 그들은 뛰어난 이전 서비스를 제공해 왔다.
(B) 그것은 또한 증가하는 수요를 충족시킬 것이다.
(C) 식품 산업에서 주목할 만한 성장이 있었다.
(D) 새 공장 부지를 검토 중이다.

어휘 outstanding 눈에 띄는, 우수한 notable 주목할 만한, 뛰어난
under consideration 고려 중인

해설 빈칸 앞 문장은 이 전략적인 움직임이 회사의 성장을 지원하는 것을 목표로 한다는 의미이다. '이 움직임이 증가하는 수요 또한 충족시킬 수 있을 것'이라는 또 다른 이전 및 확장의 이유를 의미하는 문장이 이어지는 것이 자연스럽다. 따라서 정답은 (B)이다.

18

어휘 situate (어떤 위치에) 짓다, 위치시키다

해설 문장에 동사 is projected to become이 있으므로 동사인 (B) is situating과 (D) has situated는 오답이다. 빈칸은 명사인 the new location을 수식하는 분사 자리인데 뒤에 목적어가 존재하지 않으므로 과거분사인 (C) situated가 정답이다.

19

해설 빈칸은 more than five warehouses를 수식하는 현재분사 자리이다. '15개 주에 서비스를 제공하는 창고들'이라는 내용이 되어야 자연스러우므로 정답은 (A) serving이다. remaining은 자동사에서 파생된 현재분사이기 때문에 목적어를 취할 수 없다.

[20-23]

> 퀸 비 스테이크하우스는 현재 헌신적인 사람들로 구성된 팀과 함께 우리 식당의 전반적인 관리를 감독할 책임을 담당할 리더를 찾고 있습니다. 합격자들은 외식 산업에 대한 진정한 열정을 가지고 있어야 합니다. 우리의 성과 중심적인 환경은 당신이 이 분야에서 보람 있는 경력을 쌓을 수 있는 토대를 마련해 줄 것입니다.
>
> 새로 채용된 관리자로서, 당신의 최우선 과제는 고객과 직원 모두의 만족도 향상이 될 것입니다. 여기에는 향상된 결과를 이끌어내기 위한 팀의 개발과 훈련을 이끄는 것이 포함됩니다. **또한, 그것은 우리의 높은 기준을 유지하는 것을 수반합니다.** 이 직책에 대한 자세한 내용을 위해, 당사 웹사이트 queenbee.com을 방문하세요. 경쟁력 있는 급여뿐만 아니라, 유급 휴가, 종합 의료 보험 등의 혜택을 제공합니다.

어휘 alongside ~ 곁에, ~와 함께 possess 소유하다, 가지다
genuine 진짜의, 진품인 passion 열정 performance 성과, 실적
-driven ~ 주도의, ~ 중심의 environment 환경 prepare
준비하다, 마련하다 primary 주된, 주요한 enhance 높이다,
향상시키다 satisfaction 만족, 충족 outcome 결과
paid vacation 유급 휴가 comprehensive 포괄적인, 종합적인
medical plan 의료 보험

20

어휘 assume (역할·임무 등을) 맡다 withstand 견디다

해설 빈칸 뒤의 목적어 responsibility와 의미상 어울리는 동사를 골라야 한다. 식당의 전반적인 관리를 감독할 책임을 맡을 지도자를 찾고 있다는 해석이 자연스러우므로 정답은 (A) assume이다.

21

어휘 reward 보상하다, 보답하다

해설 빈칸은 명사인 career를 수식하는 분사 자리이다. 보람 있는 경력을 쌓을 수 있도록 준비시켜 줄 것이라는 내용이 되어야 자연스러우므로

(C) rewarding(보람있는)이 정답이다.

22

(A) 따라서, 경력 발전의 가능성이 있습니다.
(B) 이를 위해, 그들은 영업 직원들과 협업할 것입니다.
(C) 저희 주방 매니저들은 모두 요리에 대한 전문 지식을 가지고 있습니다.
(D) 또한, 그것은 우리의 높은 기준을 유지하는 것을 수반합니다.

어휘 potential 가능성이 있는, 잠재력 to that end 그 목적을
달성하기 위해서 culinary 요리의, 음식의 expertise 전문 지식
entail 수반하다 uphold 유지시키다

해설 빈칸 앞에서 채용된 관리자로서 할 일을 설명하고 있으므로, 관리자로서의 책임에 식당의 높은 기준을 유지하는 일도 수반한다고 설명하는 (D)가 문맥상 빈칸에 가장 어울리는 문장이다.

23

어휘 by means of ~에 의하여, ~의 도움으로 in an effort to
do ~을 하려는 노력으로 in advance of ~보다 앞에

해설 경쟁력 있는 급여와 유급 휴가, 종합 의료 보험 등의 혜택은 모두 회사에서 합격자에게 제공하는 혜택의 예시이므로, 빈칸에 가장 어울리는 전치사구는 (A) In addition to(~에 더하여)이다.

PART 7

[24-26]

> #### 올랜도 골든로드 호텔 방문을 환영합니다!
>
> 올랜도를 업무차 방문하시든 관광차 방문하시든, 탁월한 편의 시설과 최상급 서비스를 마음껏 즐기시기 바랍니다. 골든로드 호텔에서, 우리는 올랜도 스카이라인의 숨이 멎는 듯한 전망을 제공하는 넓고 매력적인 객실과 스위트룸을 투숙객에게 제공합니다.
>
> 인터넷 접속이나 생산적인 업무 공간이 필요하다면, **24-1) 25-1) 26-1) "오피스 인 골든로드"라고 알려진 저희 2층 비즈니스 센터를 마음껏 사용하시면 됩니다.** 컴퓨터, 프린터, 팩스, 그리고 기타 필수 장비를 갖추고 있어서, 연구 및 문서 작성에 최적의 장소입니다. **25-2) "오피스 인 골든로드" 옆에는 24-2) "코지 라운지"**가 있는데, 이곳에서 긴장을 풀면서 합리적인 가격의 다과와 간식을 맛볼 수 있습니다.
>
> 출장이나 휴가 기간 동안 운동 루틴을 유지하는 것이 우선이라면, 저희가 도와드립니다. 최근 7층에 새롭게 단장한 **24-3) 26-2) 피트니스 센터인 "피트니스 스튜디오"**가 당신의 방문을 기다리고 있습니다. 최첨단 체육관 시설을 갖춘 이곳은, 여러분의 즐거움을 위해 따뜻한 실내 수영장 또한 자랑합니다.
>
> 올랜도의 경치를 탐험하며 북적거리는 하루를 보낸 후, 당신의 식욕을 손쉽게 만족시키세요. 다양한 맛있는 옵션을 원하시면, 안내서의 20페이지부터 시작하는 다이닝 섹션에 위치한 룸 서비스 메뉴를 참조하세요. 또는, **24-4) 26-3) 호평을 받고 있는 "홀리데이 인 올랜도"** 레스토랑의 요리의 즐거움에 흠뻑 빠져보세요. 신중하게 엄선된 현지 와인과 혁신적인 간식을 즐기고, 전통적인 지역 음식을 맛보세요. 레스토랑은 아침, 점심, 저녁 식사로 손님을 맞이합니다.
>
> 올랜도에서의 경험을 위해 골든로드 호텔을 선택해 주셔서 감사합니다. 편안함과 즐거움으로 가득 찬 멋진 숙박을 하실 수 있으리라 믿습니다.

어휘 whether ~인지 아니면 ~인지, ~이든 아니면 ~이든
leisure 여가   indulge 마음껏 즐기다   amenity 생활 편의 시설
top-tier 일류의   spacious 널찍한   breathtaking 숨이 막히는
reasonably 상당히, 합리적으로   priced 값이 붙은   unwind
긴장을 풀다   revamp 개조하다, 수리하다   equipped with
~을 갖춘   state-of-the-art 최신식의, 최첨단의   heated 열띤;
난방을 한   bustling 부산한, 북적거리는   directory 안내 책자
alternatively 그 대신에, 그렇지 않으면   immerse 담그다, 몰두하다
culinary 요리의   curated 전문적인 식견으로 엄선한   innovative
획기적인, 혁신적인   savor 맛, 맛이 있다   remarkable 두드러진,
괄목할 만한

24

호텔에 대해 서술된 것은?

(A) 큰 공원 근처에 위치해 있다.
(B) 고객들을 위한 다양한 서비스를 제공한다.
(C) 출장 여행자에게 인기가 있다.
(D) 단골 고객들에게 할인 혜택을 제공한다.

어휘 discount 할인   frequent 잦은, 빈번한

해설 지문 전반에 걸쳐 고객들이 이용할 수 있는 비즈니스 센터, 피트니스 센터, 식당 등의 시설들을 설명하고 있으므로 정답은 (B)이다.

25

코지 라운지에 대해 언급된 것은?

(A) 컴퓨터를 갖추고 있다.
(B) 최근에 보수되었다.
(C) 무료 커피와 스낵을 제공한다.
(D) 2층에 위치해 있다.

어휘 equip 장비를 갖추다, 준비를 갖춰 주다

해설 두 번째 단락에서 비즈니스 센터가 2층에 위치해 있고, 코지 라운지는 그 옆에 있다고 했으므로 코지 라운지 또한 2층에 있다는 것을 유추할 수 있다. 따라서 정답은 (D)이다. 코지 라운지에서 합리적인 가격의 다과와 간식을 맛볼 수 있다고 했으므로, 무료 커피와 스낵을 제공한다는 내용의 (C)는 오답이다.

26

호텔의 특징으로 언급되지 않은 것은?

(A) 운동 시설
(B) 유명한 식당
(C) 넓은 주차장
(D) 비즈니스 시설

어휘 exercise 운동, 연습   renowned 유명한, 명성 있는
parking lot 주차장, 주차 지역

해설 세 번째 문단에서 7층에 새로 보수된 피트니스 센터인 피트니스 스튜디오가 있다고 했고, 네 번째 문단에서 호평을 받는 식당인 홀리데이인 올란도를 소개하고 있으므로 (A)와 (B)는 모두 언급된 내용이다. 또한 두 번째 단락에서 2층에 위치한 비즈니스 센터 오피스 인 골든로드에 대해 설명하고 있으므로 (D) 또한 언급된 시설이다. 지문에 언급되지 않은 보기는 (C)이다.

[27-31]

애저 스카이 투어
뉴욕

새해를 기념하여, 애저 스카이 투어는 작년 요금 대비 15% 할인된 단독 패키지를 선보입니다. **30-1) 이 특별 할인은 1월 15일 이전에 예약한 경우에 적용됩니다.** 우리의 **27) 호주 투어는 매주 이용할 수 있지만, 놓치지 않도록 우리는 여러분의 자리를 일찍 확보하는 것을 추천합니다.** 아래에서, 우리의 기본 상품들에 대한 미리보기를 확인하실 수 있을 것입니다:

브리즈번 & 골드 코스트 여행: 도시의 모험과 해안의 매력
이 7일간의 여행은 퀸즐랜드의 화창한 수도 브리즈번에서 시작하며, 이곳에서 야외 식사, 강변 피크닉을 즐기고, 인근 해안의 섬을 방문할 수 있습니다. 그런 다음, 아름다운 레저 여행지인 골드 코스트로 계속 이동합니다. 그곳의 황금빛 해변과 광대한 국립 공원을 탐험하십시오.

29-1) 시드니 스플렌더스: 호주 최고의 항구 도시를 탐험하세요!
시드니 오페라 하우스와 시드니 하버 브리지와 같은 유명한 장소들이 멋진 경치를 만들어내는 시드니의 마법을 발견하세요.
29-2) 5일이나 7일의 여행 동안, 여러분을 매료시키고 더 많은 경험을 하고 싶게 만드는 활기찬 문화, 아름다운 해변, 그리고 맛있는 음식을 경험하세요.

30-2) 베일 벗은 퍼스: 호주 서해안의 보물을 발견하세요
아름다운 해변과 신나는 도시 생활이 만나는 퍼스에서의 모험을 준비하세요. 스카버러 해변의 맑은 물은 휴식을 취하고 즐기기에 좋습니다. 여러분은 돌고래 디스커버리 센터에서 돌고래들이 노는 것을 보고 **30-3) 바닷가의 도시 역사에 대해 배울 수 있습니다. 30-4) 이 7일간의 여행은 모두가 즐기고 기억할 수 있는 놀라운 여행을 제공할 것입니다.**

28) * 우리는 특정 그룹을 위한 맞춤형 투어를 만들 수 있으며, 투어 기간과 포함된 명소의 종류를 조정할 수 있습니다.**

어휘 in celebration of ~을 축하하여   exclusive 독점적인, 특권층의   applicable 해당되는, 적용되는   exquisite 매우 아름다운, 정교한   vast 어마어마한, 방대한   splendor 훌륭함, 화려함   stunning 굉장히 아름다운   fascinated 매료된   tailor 맞추다, 조정하다   adjust 조정하다, 조절하다   duration 지속, 기간   attraction 명소

발신: tours@azuresky.com
수신: annamay77@gouniverse.net
30-5) 날짜: 1월 10일
제목: 예약 확인

친애하는 메이 씨께,

애저 스카이 투어를 선택해 주셔서 감사합니다. 두 분의 예약을 확인하게 되어 기쁩니다.

30-6) 31-1) 여행 상품명: 베일 벗은 퍼스: 호주 서해안의 보물을 발견하세요

뉴욕 출발: 3월 10일 토요일 오전 9시 30분
뉴욕 도착: 3월 18일 일요일 오후 8시
총 카드 청구 금액: 3,600달러

여행일 전에 궁금한 점이 있으시면 언제든지 저희 고객 상담실 담당자에게 문의하시기 바랍니다. 문의 사항은 tours@azuresy.com으로 이메일을 보내거나 (212) 245-9090으로 전화주시기 바랍니다.

어휘 departure 출발 customer relations 고객 상담실 inquiry 문의

여행자의 피드백

애저 스카이 투어의 프로모션을 우연히 발견한 후, 우리는 결혼 10주년을 기념하여 호주로 여행을 떠나기로 한 신나는 결정을 내렸습니다. 이 회사는 뛰어난 고객 경험을 제공하는 방법을 정확히 이해하고 있으며, 그들과 함께하는 더 많은 모험을 간절히 기대하고 있습니다. **31-2) 우리의 가이드였던 마커스 도노반은 그의 열정과 풍부한 지식으로 우리에게 깊은 인상을 주었습니다. 우리가 탐험한 도시의 현지인으로서,** 그는 그 도시의 전통과 문화에 대한 매혹적인 통찰력을 공유했습니다.

공유자: 안나 메이

어휘 come across ~을 우연히 발견하다 in honor of ~을 기념하여, ~을 축하하여 exceptional 우수한, 특출한 eagerly 간절하게 enthusiasm 열광, 열정 captivating 매혹적인 insight 통찰력, 이해

27

애저 스카이 투어에 대해 암시된 것은 무엇인가?
(A) 본사는 호주에 위치해 있다.
(B) 매년 할인된 상품을 제공한다.
(C) 수요를 충족시키기 위해 새로운 투어를 개발했다.
(D) 한 달에 여러 번 투어를 마련한다.

어휘 headquarters 본사, 본부 multiple 다수의

해설 광고 지문의 첫 문단에서 호주 투어는 매주 이용할 수 있지만 놓치지 않도록 자리를 일찍 확보하는 것을 추천한다고 했으므로, 한 달에 여러 번 투어를 마련한다는 것을 알 수 있다. 따라서 정답은 (D)이다. 회사가 위치한 곳은 뉴욕이며, 작년 요금 대비 15% 할인된 가격의 상품을 선보인다고 했을 뿐 매년 할인된 상품을 제공하는지는 알 수 없다.

28

광고에 따르면 애저 스카이 투어는 고객에게 무엇을 제공할 수 있는가?
(A) 유명 공연 무료 입장
(B) 단골 고객의 가격 인하
(C) 특별한 단체를 위한 맞춤형 투어
(D) 특정한 수를 기준으로 한 단체 할인

어휘 admission 입장 clientele 의뢰인들, 고객들 customized 개개인의 요구에 맞춘 specified 명시된

해설 광고 지문의 마지막 문단에서 특정 그룹을 위한 맞춤형 투어를 만들 수 있고, 투어 기간과 포함된 명소의 종류를 조정할 수 있다고 언급하고 있으므로 정답은 (C)이다.

29

시드니 스플렌더스에 대해 언급된 것은?
(A) 무료 극장 티켓을 제공한다.
(B) 기간을 선택할 수 있는 옵션을 제공한다.
(C) 야생동물을 관찰할 수 있는 기회를 제공한다.
(D) 근처 섬으로의 배 여행을 포함한다.

어휘 complimentary 무료의 duration 지속, 기간

해설 광고 지문의 세 번째 문단에서 5일이나 7일의 동안의 여행이라고 언급되어 있으므로 시드니 스플렌더스 상품은 여행 기간을 선택할 수 있는 옵션이 제공된다는 것을 알 수 있다. 따라서 정답은 (B)이다.

30

메이 씨의 투어에 대해 사실이 아닌 것은?
(A) 일주일 동안 계속될 것이다.
(B) 할인된 가격으로 구입되었다.
(C) 국립 공원 방문을 포함한다.
(D) 역사에 대해 배울 수 있는 기회를 제공할 것이다.

어휘 completion 완료, 완성 acquire 습득하다, 얻다

해설 이메일에서 메이 씨가 선택한 여행 상품이 '베일 벗은 퍼스: 호주 서해안의 보물을 발견하세요'라는 것을 알 수 있고, 광고 지문의 네 번째 문단에서 이 상품에 관한 설명을 확인할 수 있다. 광고 지문에 따르면, 여행은 7일간 진행되고, 도시의 역사에 대해서 배울 수 있다고 했으므로 (A)와 (D)는 모두 언급된 사실이다. 또한 광고 지문의 첫 문단에서 특별 할인은 1월 15일 이전에 예약한 경우에 적용된다고 했는데, 이메일에서 메이 씨가 예약 확인 메일을 받은 날짜가 1월 10일이라는 것을 확인할 수 있다. 그러므로 그녀가 할인된 가격에 여행을 예약했다는 내용의 (B) 또한 언급된 사실이다. 광고 지문의 '베일 벗은 퍼스'에 대한 설명에 국립 공원 방문에 관한 내용은 없으므로 정답은 (C)이다.

31

도노반 씨에 대해 언급된 것은?
(A) 그는 퍼스의 주민이다.
(B) 그는 더 많은 여행을 위해 돌아오기를 희망한다.
(C) 그는 기념일을 축하하기 위해 여행을 했다.
(D) 그는 대학에서 역사를 가르친다.

어휘 resident 거주자

해설 여행자의 피드백 지문에서 마커스 도노반 씨가 여행의 가이드라는 것을 확인할 수 있고, 같은 지문의 마지막 부분에서 그가 현지인으로서 도시의 전통과 문화에 대한 매혹적인 통찰력을 공유했다는 내용이 있다. 여행자의 피드백은 안나 메이 씨에 의해 공유되었는데, 이메일에서 메이 씨가 선택한 여행은 '베일 벗은 퍼스'라는 것을 확인할 수 있다. 따라서, 도노반 씨는 퍼스의 현지인이므로 그가 퍼스에서 거주한다는 사실을 알 수 있다. 정답은 (A)이다.

PRACTICE

pp.221-224

1 Although	2 While
3 whether	4 or
5 through	6 under
7 By	8 opposite

1 날씨가 추웠지만, 그 행사는 야외에서 열렸다.
2 그녀가 시험 공부를 하는 동안, 그는 같은 방에서 TV를 시청했다.
3 우리는 그들이 회의에 시간 내에 도착할지 아닐지 모른다.
4 그녀는 휴가를 해변에서 보낼지 산에서 보낼지를 결정할 수 없었다.
5 그 회사는 정교하게 계획된 전략을 통해 시장 확장을 달성했다.
6 그 프로젝트는 경험 많은 프로젝트 매니저의 지도 하에 성공적으로 완료되었다.
7 연말까지, 우리는 사무실 공간 개보수를 완료할 것을 목표로 한다.
8 그 식당은 시청 맞은편에 위치하여 편리한 만남의 장소가 되고 있다.

📑 실전 문제 연습

p.226

1 (A)	**2** (B)	**3** (A)	**4** (D)
5 (B)	**6** (C)	**7** (C)	**8** (D)
9 (C)	**10** (C)	**11** (D)	**12** (C)
13 (B)	**14** (C)	**15** (D)	**16** (A)
17 (C)	**18** (C)	**19** (C)	**20** (B)
21 (B)	**22** (D)	**23** (D)	**24** (B)
25 (C)	**26** (C)	**27** (A)	**28** (B)
29 (D)	**30** (B)	**31** (A)	**32** (D)

PART 5

1
월쉬 씨는 금요일 아침 로스앤젤레스행 좌석이 있는지 여부와 항공료를 둘 다 알고 싶어 한다.

어휘 availability 유효성, 유용성   airfare 항공 요금

해설 빈칸 뒤에 명사인 availability of seats와 airfare가 등위 접속사인 and로 연결되어 있으므로, and와 결합하여 등위 상관 접속사를 만드는 (A) both가 정답이다.

2
던랩 모터스가 충분한 정보를 바탕으로 한 해외 진출 전략을 수립하기 위해서는 철두철미한 시장 조사가 필요하다.

어휘 thorough 빈틈없는, 철두철미한   well-informed 사정에 밝은   expansion 확대, 확장   necessitate ~을 필요하게 만들다

해설 빈칸은 be동사인 is 뒤 주격 보어 자리이므로 명사나 형용사가 필요하다. 주격 보어 자리의 명사는 주어와 동격이 되어야 하는데, (A) necessity(필요성, 필수품)가 주어인 thorough market research와 동격이 될 수 없으므로 정답에서 제외된다. 정답은 형용사인 (B) necessary(필요한, 불가피한)이다.

3
일단 완공되면, 새로운 고속도로는 통근 시간을 크게 줄이고 도시의 교통 혼잡을 완화할 것이다.

어휘 significantly 상당히, 의미가 있게   congestion 혼잡   alleviate 완화하다

해설 빈칸 앞 등위 접속사 and는 단어와 단어, 구와 구, 절과 절 등 모든 성분을 연결할 수 있는데, 연결되는 성분의 성격은 같아야 한다. 새로운 고속도로가 통근 시간을 크게 줄이고 도시의 교통 혼잡을 완화할 것이라는 내용의 문장이므로, 등위 접속사 and로 연결된 동사 reduce와 성분이 같은 (A) alleviate이 정답이다.

4
그 인턴들은 프로젝트 내내 탁월한 헌신과 숙련도를 보여주어, 프로젝트의 성공적인 완료에 기여했다.

어휘 demonstrate 보여주다, 입증하다   exceptional 우수한, 특출한   dedication 전념, 헌신   proficiency 숙달, 능숙

해설 빈칸은 복수 명사 interns를 수식하는 형용사 자리이다. 보기 중 명사를 수식할 수 있는 것은 지시형용사인 those뿐이므로 정답은 (D)이다. 지시형용사 this와 that은 단수 명사를, these와 those는 복수 명사를 수식한다. (B)의 every(모든)는 단수 명사를 한정한다.

5
경쟁이 치열했음에도 불구하고, 우리 팀은 여전히 업계 1위 자리를 지키고 있다.

어휘 fierce 격렬한, 극심한   secure 확보하다; 고정시키다   nevertheless 그렇기는 하지만, 그럼에도 불구하고

해설 빈칸이 포함된 절이 주절 앞에 위치하고 있으므로, 빈칸은 부사절 접속사 자리이다. 따라서, 접속 부사인 (A)의 nevertheless와 명사절 접속사인 (C)의 whether는 오답이다. whether는 부사절 접속사로도 사용될 수 있지만, 이 경우 or과 함께 사용되어야 한다. 빈칸 뒤의 절은 '경쟁이 치열하다'는 의미이고, 주절은 '팀이 계속해서 업계 1위를 차지하고 있다'는 내용으로서, 두 절은 대비되는 의미이다. 따라서 정답은 (B) Even though이다.

6
아트 웰치 재단은 봉사자들에게 이 모금 행사 준비를 위한 그들의 기여에 대해서 깊은 감사를 표하고자 한다.

어휘 extend appreciation 감사를 표하다   volunteer 자원 봉사자   fundraising event 모금 행사   profession 직업, 직종   instruction 설명, 지시   contribution 기여, 이바지, 기부금   occupation 직업, 점령(기간)

해설 봉사자들이 모금 행사를 준비하는 데 '기여한 것'에 대해서 감사를 표하고 싶다는 의미가 되어야 자연스러우므로 정답은 (C) contributions이다.

7

프라임 버거의 배달 서비스는 효율적이고 빠른 반면, 다른 지역 식당들보다 가격이 높다.

어휘 surpass 능가하다, 뛰어넘다 eatery 음식점, 식당

해설 빈칸이 포함된 절이 주절 앞에 위치하고 있으므로 부사절 접속사를 정답으로 골라야 한다. 보기 중에서 부사절 접속사는 (C) While뿐이다. 부사절 접속사 while은 '~ 동안에'라는 의미 이외에도 '~이기는 하지만, ~ 반면에'라는 의미로도 사용된다.

8

최근 발표된 재무제표에 따르면, 회사의 매출은 지난 분기에 15% 증가한 것으로 보고되었다.

어휘 revenue 수익 statement 성명, 진술, 성명서, 진술서 conventionally 인습적으로, 진부하게 domestically 가정적으로; 국내에서 thoughtfully 사려 깊게

해설 지난 분기에 회사의 매출이 15% 오른 것이 최근 발표된 재무제표에 따른 것이므로, 의미상 부사는 (D) reportedly(전하는 바에 따르면)이다.

9

그 예술가는 버려진 재료들로 걸작을 만들어서 자신의 탁월한 창의력과 자원 활용 능력을 증명했다.

어휘 masterpiece 걸작, 명작 discard 버리다, 폐기하다 resourcefulness 자원이 풍부함, 기발함

해설 예술가가 걸작을 만들었고, 그 걸작은 버려진 재료들로부터 만들어졌다는 해석이 자연스러우므로 정답은 (C) from이다.

10

해리 씨가 내놓은 제안이 조금 놀라웠는데, 그는 최근에 팀의 일원이 되었다.

어휘 put forward 제안하다

해설 it은 가주어이며 '------- the proposal put forward by Mr. Harry, who recently became a member of the team'이 진주어이다. 진주어는 명사적 용법의 to부정사나 명사절인 that절의 형태인데, 빈칸 뒤에 절이 이어지고 있으므로 정답은 (C) that이다. (D) whether도 명사절 접속사이기는 하지만, whether는 '~인지 아닌지'라는 의미이므로 정답이 될 수 없다.

11

요청된 문서들은 수령 후 2주 이내에 검토된 후 답변이 제공되어야 한다.

어휘 receipt 영수증; 수령

해설 빈칸 뒤에 기간을 표현하는 명사구인 two weeks가 있으므로 (B) throughout(~ 동안 내내)과 (D) within(~ 이내에)이 정답 후보이다. 수령일로부터 2주 동안 내내 응답이 제공될 수는 없으므로 (B)는 오답이며, 정해진 범위 내에서 완료되는 일에 자주 사용되는 전치사인 (D) within이 정답이다. (A) by는 기간이 아닌 시점을 표현하는 명사 앞에 사용된다.

12

고객과 사전 약속이 있는 라슨 씨를 제외한 모든 팀원들이 회의에 참석했다.

어휘 engagement 약속, 업무 whereas ~에 반하여 likewise 똑같이, 비슷하게

해설 빈칸은 명사 Mr. Larsen 앞에 사용되기에 적절한 전치사 자리이므로 (C) except for(~이 없으면, ~을 제외하고)와 (D) along with (~와 함께)가 정답 후보이다. 모든 팀 구성원이 참석했지만, 라슨 씨는 고객과의 선약이 있어서 참석하지 못한 상황임을 알 수 있다. 따라서 '~을 제외하고'를 의미하는 (C)가 정답이다.

13

현재의 시장 동향에 근거하여, 그 회사의 이익은 다음 분기에 긍정적인 상승을 경험할 것으로 보인다.

어휘 based on ~에 근거하여 upturn 호전, 상승 haltingly 머뭇거리며

해설 (B) likely를 제외한 모든 보기가 동사 experience(경험하다)를 수식하기 어색하고 문맥상으로도 어울리지 않는다. likely는 형용사로서 '~할 것 같은, ~할 것으로 예상되는'을 의미하며, 부사로서 '아마, 어쩌면'을 뜻한다.

14

세계적인 불황으로 인한 어려움에도 불구하고, 회사는 성공적으로 신제품 라인을 출시하고 시장 점유율을 유지했다.

어휘 pose (위험이나 문제 등을) 제기하다 recession 불경기, 불황

해설 빈칸은 명사구구 the challenges posed by the global recession 앞에 있으므로 전치사를 정답으로 골라야 한다. 보기 중 전치사는 (C) Notwithstanding(~에도 불구하고)과 (D) Aside from(~ 외에는, ~을 제외하고)인데, 세계적인 불황으로 인한 어려움에도 불구하고, 회사가 신제품 라인을 출시하고 시장 점유율도 유지했다고 해석되는 것이 자연스러우므로 정답은 (C)이다.

15

대학에서 학업을 마친 후, 에커트는 다른 곳에서 그의 경력 기회를 추구하기로 결정하고, 결국 뉴욕으로 이사했다.

어휘 pursue 추구하다 ultimately 궁극적으로 marginally 아주 조금, 미미하게 evidently 분명히, 눈에 띄게

해설 에커트가 대학에서의 공부를 마친 후 그의 경력 기회를 다른 곳에서 찾으려고 한다는 해석이 자연스러우므로 정답은 (D) elsewhere(다른 곳으로)이다. 이 문장은 에커트가 자신의 직장을 다른 지역으로 옮기기로 결정해서, 결국 뉴욕 시로 이사 간 사실을 설명하고 있다.

PART 6

[16-19]

환경에 대한 인식을 고취시키는 미술 전시회

최근 수십 년 동안, 예술가들은 기후 위기를 해결하는 것의 긴급함을 강조하기 위해 점점 더 그들의 작품을 이용해 왔다. 올해, 유럽 전역의 전시회는 어떻게 예술이 기후 변화와 환경을 중심에 둘 수 있는지를 계속해서 보여주고 있다.

환경을 의식하는 전시회들 중에는 "Back to Earth"라고 불리는 중요한 전시회가 있다. **이것은 현재 런던의 몬트로즈 갤러리에서 열리고 있다.** 5월 10일부터 6월 13일까지 열리는 이 행사는 인간이

자연과 교감하는 방법을 탐구하고 우리가 직면하는 도전에 대처하기 위해 선도적인 현대 예술가들을 모으고 있다.

몬트로즈 갤러리의 큐레이터인 스테이시 크롤락은 "예술과 환경 보호주의가 어떻게 협력하는지 다시 생각하기 위해 합류하세요."라고 말한다.

어휘 exhibition 전시회　awareness 의식, 관심　decade 10년　highlight 강조하다　urgency 긴급, 위급　address 다루다, 고심하다　climate 기후　crisis 위기　environmentally conscious 환경에 특별한 관심이 있는　contemporary 동시대의　tackle (힘든 상황과) 씨름하다　encounter 맞닥뜨리다, 부딪히다　environmentalism 환경 결정론, 환경 보호주의

16

어휘 sequentially 순차적으로　expectedly 예상한 바와 같이, 역시나　regrettably 유감스럽게, 애석하게

해설 빈칸에 어울리는 부사를 찾아야 하는 문제인데, (A) increasingly를 제외한 모든 보기가 동사 used를 수식하기 어색하다. increasingly(점점 더, 갈수록 더)는 예술가들이 기후 위기를 해결하는 것의 긴급함을 강조하기 위해 점점 더 그들의 작품을 활용하고 있다는 의미로 문맥상 자연스럽다.

17

어휘 apart from ~ 외에는, ~ 외에도　among ~ 중에서　across ~ 건너편에; ~을 가로질러; ~ 전체에 걸쳐　along ~을 따라

해설 'exhibitions ------- Europe'은 '유럽 전역에서 열리는 전시회'로 해석되므로 정답은 (C)이다.

18

(A) 자연 환경의 손실은 우리에게 가장 큰 위협이다.
(B) 미술관은 모든 사람들이 예술을 탐험하고 경험하는 것을 환영한다.
(C) 이것은 현재 런던의 몬트로즈 갤러리에서 열리고 있다.
(D) 우리는 흥미로운 문화 행사를 많이 하고 있다.

어휘 loss 손실, 상실　threat 협박, 위협　plenty of 많은

해설 빈칸 앞 문장에서 "Back to Earth"라고 불리는 중요한 전시회가 있다고 했으므로 이 전시회가 현재 런던의 몬트로즈 갤러리에서 열리고 있다는 문장이 빈칸에 오기에 자연스럽다. 또한 뒤에 이어지는 문장에서 전시회가 5월 10일부터 6월 13일까지 열린다는 내용과도 자연스럽게 이어진다. 따라서 정답은 (C)이다.

19

어휘 collaboratively 협력적으로

해설 'how art and environmentalism -------'는 to부정사인 to rethink의 목적어 역할을 하는 명사절이므로 빈칸에는 동사가 필요하다. 따라서 정답은 동사인 (C)이다. how는 명사절 접속사로서, 완전한 절을 연결하거나 to부정사 앞에 온다는 점을 기억해두자.

[20-23]

쉐나 콘
카멜백로 1880번지
스위트 310호실, 애리조나 주 스코츠데일
84522

친애하는 Korn 씨께,

스마트 웨이 온라인 스토어에서 신형 4문형 냉장고를 구입해 주셔서 감사합니다. 스마트 웨이에서, 우리는 고객 만족을 보장하기 위해 최선을 다하고 있으며, 이것이 모든 고객에게 포괄적인 제품 보증을 제공하는 이유입니다. 우리는 우리의 품질 보증이 다른 가전 제품 상점에서 제공하는 것보다 훨씬 우수한 보상 범위를 제공한다고 확신합니다. **품질 보증은 구매일로부터 2년 후에 만료됩니다.** 이 기간 동안, 보증 하에 무상 수리 서비스를 받으실 수 있습니다. 문의 사항이 있으시면, 망설이지 말고 고객지원팀 202-555-2323으로 연락해 주세요.

안부를 전하며,

제이슨 버튼
고객 지원

어휘 refrigerator 냉장고　fully 완전히, 충분히　commit 약속하다　ensure 반드시 ~하게 하다　satisfaction 만족, 흡족　warranty 품질 보증　confident 자신감 있는　coverage 보도; 범위　superior 우수한, 상급의　appliance (가정용) 기기　eligible ~을 가질(할) 수 있는

20

해설 스마트 웨이에서는 고객 만족을 보장하기 위해 최선을 다하고 있다고 해석되므로 정답은 장소 명사 앞에 사용되어 '~에, 에서'를 의미하는 (B) At이다.

21

어휘 subsequent 다음의, 차후의　comprehensive 포괄적인, 종합적인　incompatible 양립할 수 없는, 공존할 수 없는　successive 연이은, 연속적인

해설 빈칸 뒤 명사구 'product warranty(제품 보증)'를 수식하기에 적절한 형용사를 보기 중에 골라야 한다. 문맥상 회사가 포괄적인 제품 보증을 제공한다는 내용이 되어야 자연스러우므로 정답은 (B)이다.

22

해설 해당 문장은 당사의 품질 보증이 '다른' 어떤 가전 제품 상점에서 제공하는 것보다 훨씬 우수한 보상 범위를 제공한다는 것을 확신한다고 해석되므로 정답은 (D) other이다. their이나 these로 지칭하기 위해서는 앞서 특정한 상점들이 언급되어 있어야 한다. each는 단수 가산 명사 앞에 붙는 한정사이다.

23

(A) 영업일 기준 5일 이내에 냉장고를 받으실 수 있습니다.
(B) 품질 보증 카드와 제품 번호를 준비해 주세요.
(C) 요청하시면 신제품 안내 책자를 보내 드리겠습니다.
(D) 품질 보증은 구매일로부터 2년 후에 만료됩니다.

어휘 business day 영업일 unit number 제품 번호 brochure 책자 expire 만료되다

해설 빈칸 뒤 문장에서 이 기간 동안 보증 하에 무상 수리 서비스를 받을 수 있다고 설명하고 있으므로, 빈칸에는 특정한 기간이 언급된 문장이 필요하다. 따라서 빈칸에 가장 어울리는 문장은 (D)이다.

PART 7

[24-27]

캐리	오전 10시

좋은 아침이군요. 팀 여러분의 관심이 필요해요. 제가 여러분 모두와 논의하고 싶었던 중요한 회의가 다가오고 있어요.

토드	오전 10시 1분

좋은 아침이에요, 캐리. 무슨 회의예요?

캐리	오전 10시 1분

안녕하세요, 토드. 이번 주 금요일에 콜드웰 에너지 솔루션 고객과 미팅이 예정되어 있어요. 24) **그들은 우리의 최신 광고 제안에 대해 논의하는 것에 관심을 표명했어요.**

아리언	오전 10시 2분

정말 좋은 소식이네요! 우리는 그 제안서를 열심히 준비해 왔잖아요.

토드	오전 10시 2분

그러면, 우리는 그들에게 캠페인 전략, 광고 대상자 분석, 그리고 예상되는 결과를 보여줄 준비를 해야 해요.

로라	오전 10시 3분

아리언, 우리의 제안을 뒷받침할 모든 필요한 자료와 통계를 우리가 보유하고 있나요?

아리언	오전 10시 4분

물론이죠, 로라. 우리의 전략을 뒷받침할 모든 숫자와 통계가 준비되어 있어요. 참고하시도록 회의 후에 파일을 보낼게요.

토드	오전 10시 5분

27-1) **회의 중에 특별히 해결해야 할 문제나 과제가 있을까요?**

캐리	오전 10시 6분

27-2) **좋은 질문이군요, 토드.** 25) **우리는 잠재적인 예산 제약을 해결하고 제안된 투자에 대한 정당성을 제시할 준비가 되어 있어야 해요.**

로라	오전 10시 7분

추가적으로, 우리는 고객이 캠페인의 일정과 예상되는 결과와 관련하여 가질 수 있는 질문이나 우려 사항을 해결할 준비가 되어 있어야 해요.

캐리	오전 10시 8분

26) **정장을 입고 시간을 엄수해야 하는 것을 기억하세요. 우리가 결속력 있고 자신감 있는 팀이라는 것을 보여주도록 해요.**

아리언	오전 10시 9분

좋아요.

어휘 analysis 분석 연구 projected 예상된 outcome 결과 statistic 통계 reference 참고, 참조 particular 특정한 constraint 제약 justification 타당한 이유 regarding ~에 관하여 timeline 시각표 punctual 시간을 지키는 cohesive 화합하는, 결합하는

24

캐리는 어느 회사에서 일할 것 같은가?
(A) 웹 디자인 회사
(B) 광고 대행사
(C) 회계 사무소
(D) 투자 회사

해설 오전 10시 1분에 캐리가 고객이 그들의 광고 제안에 관심을 표했다고 했으므로, 캐리와 그의 동료 모두 광고 대행사 직원이라는 것을 알 수 있다. 따라서 정답은 (B)이다.

25

그들은 금요일까지 무엇을 준비해야 하는가?
(A) 그들은 광고를 제작해야 한다.
(B) 그들은 어디에 투자할지 결정해야 한다.
(C) 그들은 예산 제약 문제를 다뤄야 한다.
D) 그들은 기존의 전략을 수정해야 한다.

어휘 tackle (문제 등을) 다루다, 부딪히다 limitation 제한, 한정

해설 오전 10시 6분에 캐리가 우리는 잠재적인 예산 제약을 해결하고 제안된 투자에 대한 정당성을 제공할 준비가 되어 있어야 한다고 했으므로 정답은 (C)이다.

26

캐리가 팀원들에게 요청한 것이 아닌 것은?
(A) 적절한 옷을 입는 것
(B) 고객에게 자신감을 보여주는 것
(C) 그녀에게 서류를 전달하는 것
(D) 회의 시간을 지키는 것

어휘 appropriate 적절한 demonstrate 보여주다, 입증하다 forward 보내다, 전달하다

해설 오전 10시 8분에 캐리가 정장을 입고 시간을 엄수하는 것을 기억하라고 했으므로 (A)와 (D)는 캐리가 팀원들에게 요청한 사항이다. 또한 결속력 있고 자신감 있는 팀이라는 것을 보여주자고 했으므로 (B)도 요청한 사항이다. 서류를 전달하는 것은 캐리가 요청한 사항이 아니므로 정답은 (C)이다.

27

오전 10시 6분에 캐리가 "좋은 질문이군요, 토드"라고 쓸 때, 그녀가 의도한 바는 무엇인가?
(A) 그녀는 잠재적인 어려움을 다루고 싶어 한다.
(B) 그녀는 고객 불만에 대응하고 싶어 한다.
(C) 그녀는 토드가 금요일 회의를 이끌기를 원한다.
(D) 그녀는 광고의 결과를 검토하고자 한다.

해설 토드가 회의 중에 특별히 해결해야 할 문제나 과제가 있는지 묻는 질문에 대해 캐리가 좋은 질문이라고 말한 후, 잠재적인 예산 제약을 해결하고 제안된 투자에 대한 정당성을 제공할 준비가 되어 있어야 한다

고 했다. 따라서 그녀가 잠재적인 문제들을 다루고자 한다는 것을 알 수 있으므로 정답은 (A)이다.

[28-32]

채용 공고

애플비 스테이크하우스, 보델 에버렛 하이웨이 22906번지, 보델, 워싱턴 98021

고메 로드 매거진의 올해의 최고 식당으로 선정된 애플비 스테이크하우스는 우리 직원들이 진정한 차이를 만든다는 것을 알고 있습니다. 우리는 우리 팀에 합류할 열정적이고 노력하는 개인들을 찾고 있습니다.

호스트	서버
이 직책은 탁월한 소통 기술과 활발한 성격을 가진 사람에게 이상적입니다. 합격자는 식당 예약을 관리하고, 손님을 환영하고 테이블까지 안내하며, 좌석 배치를 관리할 것입니다. **28-1) 31-1) 이 역할은 금요일부터 일요일까지의 저녁 근무를 포함합니다.**	합격자는 음식과 음료를 제공하며, 고객의 요청에 계속 응대함으로써 손님의 만족도를 관리할 것입니다. 이전의 경력은 선호되지만 필수는 아닙니다. **28-3) 이 직책은 수요일부터 토요일 오전 10시부터 오후 5시까지의 시간에 근무가 가능해야 합니다.**
출납원	보조 요리사
합격자는 **29) 결제 거래를 처리**하고, 영수증을 발행하며, 고객의 수표의 정확성을 확인하고, 매일 밤 식당의 수입을 계산할 것입니다. **28-2) 이 직책은 금요일과 토요일 저녁 5시부터 9시까지 근무가 가능해야 합니다.**	이 역할에서, 우리의 조리팀은 다양한 지역에서 가져온 제철 식재료와 현대적인 기법을 결합하는 것에 초점을 둡니다. 이 직책에는 음식 준비에 대한 기본 지식이 필요합니다. **28-4) 근무 시간은 월요일부터 목요일까지 주당 25시간입니다.**

애플비 스테이크하우스는 우리 직원들의 노고를 인정하기 위해 경쟁력 있는 보상을 제공합니다. 높은 시급 외에도, **30) 직원들은 분기별 성과 보너스를 받을 자격을 가집니다.** 직원들은 또한 모든 메뉴에 대해 30% 할인 혜택을 받습니다. 관심 있는 분들은 3월 31일까지 레스토랑 매니저인 수잔 레이놀즈에게 susanreynolds@applebees.com으로 연락해 주시기 바랍니다.

어휘 enthusiastic 열정적인 ideal 이상적인 outgoing 외향적인, 사교적인 personality 성격, 인격 oversee 감독하다 greet 맞다, 환영하다 accompany 동반하다, 동행하다 monitor 감시하다, 추적 관찰하다 flow 흐름 involve 수반하다 responsible 책임지고 있는 satisfaction 만족 continuously 지속적으로 previous 이전의 preferred 우선의 availability 이용 가능성 transaction 거래, 매매 verify 확인하다 accuracy 정확, 정확도 revenue 수익 culinary 요리의, 음식의 combine 결합하다 technique 기법 seasonal 계절에 따라 다른 ingredient 재료 source 얻다 competitive 경쟁력 있는 compensation 보상금 acknowledge 인정하다 eligible ~을 할 수 있는, 가질 수 있는 quarterly 분기별의 performance 공연, 성과

수신: 수잔 레이놀즈 〈susanreynolds@applebees.com〉
발신: 앨런 그레이 〈allen89@worldnet.com〉
날짜: 3월 17일
제목: 지원서
첨부: 이력서

친애하는 레이놀즈 씨,

31-2) 저는 호스트나 서버로 귀사의 레스토랑에 합류하는 데 관심을 표현하려고 메일을 쓰게 되었습니다. 두 역할 모두 관련 경력을 가지고 있으며, 귀사에 가치를 제공할 수 있다고 생각합니다. 참고하시도록 이력서를 첨부하였습니다.

31-3) 저는 현재 월요일부터 수요일까지 수업을 듣고 있다는 사실을 알려드리고 싶습니다만, 그 외의 시간에는 레스토랑에 시간을 할애할 수 있습니다. 또한, **32) 두 직책의 시간당 임금에 대한 정보를 알려주시면 감사하겠습니다.** 저의 지원서에 관심을 가져 주셔서 감사합니다. 곧 회신을 받게 되기를 바랍니다.

감사합니다.

앨런 그레이

어휘 interest 관심, 흥미 relevant 관련 있는 establishment 기관, 시설 reference 언급, 참고 dedicate (시간·노력)을 ~에 바치다 available 이용할 수 있는, 시간이 있는 furthermore 뿐만 아니라, 더욱이 regarding ~에 관하여 wage 임금, 급료 look forward to ~을 고대하다

28

광고된 직책들에 대해 추론할 수 있는 것은?
(A) 여러 지점에서의 근무가 요구된다.
(B) 다양한 근무 시간을 가지고 있다.
(C) 해당 분야에서 관련 경험이 요구된다.
(D) 음식 준비에 대한 지식이 필요하다.

어휘 branch 지사, 분점 relevant 관련 있는 experience 경험 expertise 전문 지식 preparation 준비

해설 광고 지문의 모든 직책들의 근무 시간을 보면 일주일 중 특정 시간 동안만 근무를 요구하고 있다. 즉, 모든 직책이 다양한 시간제임을 알 수 있으므로 정답은 (B)이다.

29

광고에 따르면, 출납원의 역할로 언급되지 않은 것은 무엇인가?
(A) 결제 거래를 처리하는 것
(B) 수표의 유효성을 확인하는 것
(C) 식당의 매상을 확인하는 것
(D) 좌석 배치를 관리하는 것

어휘 transaction 거래, 매매 examine 조사하다, 검토하다 validity 유효함, 타당성 revenue 수입 arrangement 배치, 배열

해설 광고 지문에서 출납원의 역할로 언급된 것은 결제 거래의 처리, 영수증 발행, 수표의 정확성 확인, 그리고 매일 밤 식당의 수입을 계산하는 것이다. 보기 중에서 이에 해당하지 않는 것은 (D)이다.

30

광고에서 합격자들을 위해 언급된 혜택은 무엇인가?

(A) 의료보험

(B) 분기별 성과 장려금

(C) 근무 시간 동안 무료 식사

(D) 유급휴가

어휘 insurance coverage 보험 보장　performance 공연, 성과
incentive 장려책, 우대책

해설 광고 지문 마지막 문단의 'In addition to a high hourly wage,
our employees are eligible for quarterly performance bonuses'
에서 직원들은 분기별 성과급을 받는다고 했으므로 정답은 (B)이다. 직원
들은 또한 모든 메뉴 항목에 대해 30% 할인을 받는다고 했을 뿐 무료로
식사가 제공된다는 언급은 없으므로 (C)는 오답이다.

31

그레이 씨는 어떤 직책에 고용될 가능성이 가장 높은가?

(A) **호스트**

(B) 서버

(C) 출납원

(D) 요리사

해설 이메일에서 그레이 씨는 호스트나 서버 직책에 관심이 있다는
것을 알 수 있다. 그런데, 'I am currently attending classes from
Monday through Wednesday'에서 그가 월요일부터 수요일까지
수업을 듣고 있다고 했으므로, 이 시간에는 근무를 할 수 없음을 유추할
수 있다. 광고 지문에서 호스트와 서버 중 월요일부터 수요일 근무를
요구하지 않는 직책은 호스트이므로 정답은 (A)이다.

32

이메일에서 그레이 씨가 문의한 것은 무엇인가?

(A) 식당의 개점 및 폐점 시간

(B) 면접을 위해 언제 연락 받을 수 있는지

(C) 교육 수업을 제공하는지

(D) **두 직책의 급여가 얼마인지**

어휘 salary 급여

해설 이메일 두 번째 문단의 'if you could provide information
regarding the hourly wages for both positions'에서 두 직책의
시간당 임금이 얼마인지 궁금하다고 했으므로 정답은 (D)이다.

DAY 10 명사절과 형용사절

PRACTICE
pp.234-236

1 That he was able to complete the marathon
despite the challenging weather conditions
was truly impressive.

2 The job that she applied for required extensive
experience in project management.

3 whether　　4 when

5 how　　6 whose

7 that

1 힘든 날씨에도 불구하고 그가 마라톤을 완주할 수 있었다는 것은
정말 인상적이었다.

2 그녀가 지원한 일자리는 프로젝트 관리에 대한 풍부한 경험을
요구했다.

3 그녀는 폭우로 인해 회의 일정이 변경되었는지 여부를 물었다.

4 존은 언제 면접 일정을 잡을지 결정할 필요가 있었다.

5 완성된 작품을 보고, 그녀는 그의 재능이 얼마나 인상적인지 감탄하
지 않을 수 없었다.

6 폭풍으로 유리창이 깨진 그 집은 대대적인 수리가 필요했다.

7 지난 여름에 잠들지 않는 도시를 방문했는데, 잊지 못할 경험이었다.

📝 실전 문제 연습
p.239

1	(D)	2	(C)	3	(B)	4	(B)
5	(B)	6	(B)	7	(B)	8	(D)
9	(B)	10	(D)	11	(C)	12	(A)
13	(D)	14	(C)	15	(C)	16	(C)
17	(B)	18	(C)	19	(A)	20	(B)
21	(D)	22	(D)	23	(C)	24	(B)
25	(D)	26	(A)	27	(D)	28	(A)
29	(B)	30	(C)	31	(D)		

PART 5

1

조지 그린 건설의 건축가들은 현대적인 건축 트렌드를 오래된 스타일의
건물에 능숙하게 접목시키는 것으로 유명하다.

어휘 architect 건축가, 설계자　be known for ~로 알려져 있다
skillfully 솜씨있게　incorporate 포함하다, 통합하다　modern
현대의, 현대적인　architectural 건축학의　trend 동향, 추세
incorporation 결합, 혼합, 법인

해설 빈칸은 전치사 for의 목적어 자리이므로 명사인 (C)와 동명
사인 (D) 중에서 정답을 고른다. 빈칸 뒤에 명사구 'the modern
architectural trends'가 있으므로, 명사구를 목적어로 취할 수 있는 동
명사 (D)가 정답이다. 전치사 없이 명사와 명사를 연결할 수는 없으므로
명사 (C)는 오답이다.

2

제 10회 뉴올리언스 재즈 페스티벌에서는 전국의 뛰어난 음악가들이
다수 출연할 것이다.

어휘 feature 특별히 포함하다, 특징으로 삼다　accomplished
기량이 뛰어난, 재주가 많은　across ~ 전체에 걸쳐; 가로질러; 건너편에
accomplish 완수하다, 성취하다　accomplishment 업적; 기량;
완수

해설 빈칸은 빈칸 뒤 명사인 musicians를 수식하는 형용사 자리다. accomplished는 '기량이 뛰어난, 재주가 많은'이라는 의미의 형용사로서 musicians를 수식하기에 적절하다. 따라서 정답은 (C)이다.

3

페이튼 엔지니어링의 경영진은 현재 연구 개발에 더 많은 자원을 투자할지 여부에 대해 결정하지 못하고 있다.

어휘 management 경영; 경영진 undecided 결정하지 못하는 as to ~에 관해 resource 자원, 재원

해설 '------- or not to invest more resources in research and development currently'는 전치사인 as to의 목적어이므로 명사구가 되어야 한다. 따라서 to부정사 앞에 위치하면서 명사구를 만드는 (B)와 (C)가 정답 후보이다. 'whether or not'은 '~할지 말지', '~인지 아닌지'를 의미하는 관용 표현이므로 빈칸에 들어가기에 의미상 적절하다. 따라서 정답은 (B)이다.

4

휴가 신청은 최소 2주 전에 승인을 받아야 한다는 것이 이나바 은행의 방침이다.

어휘 policy 정책, 방침 approve 찬성하다, 승인하다 in advance 미리, 전부터

해설 문장에 동사가 is와 should be approved 두 개이므로, 빈칸에는 접속사가 필요하다. 따라서 보기 중 유일한 접속사인 (B)가 정답이다. it은 문장의 가주어이며 명사절인 that절이 진주어이다.

5

어니스트 미래 에너지 재단이 초청한 모든 초청 연사들은 샌디에이고행 항공편과 2박의 숙박을 제공받을 것이다.

어휘 accommodation 숙소, 숙박 시설

해설 빈칸 뒤에 연결된 절은 동사 invites의 목적어가 생략된 불완전한 절이므로, 빈칸에는 목적격 관계대명사가 와야 한다. 따라서 정답은 (B)이다.

6

당사의 제품에 관심이 있으신 분은 웹사이트 www.baldinijewelry.com에서 보다 자세한 정보를 얻을 수 있습니다.

어휘 obtain 얻다 detailed 상세한

해설 문장에 동사가 있고 접속사는 존재하지 않으므로 동사인 (A)와 (D)는 모두 오답이다. (C)의 경우 주격관계대명사인 who뒤에 동사인 interested가 있는데, 빈칸 뒤에 interested의 목적어가 없으므로 (C)도 정답이 될 수 없다. 빈칸 앞의 those를 수식하는 과거분사인 (B)가 빈칸에 가장 알맞다.

7

미치 라이스가 회사를 매각할 생각이 있느냐는 질문을 받았을 때, 그는 기자들에게 말을 아꼈다.

어휘 decline 감소하다; 거절하다 comment 논평하다

해설 빈칸 뒤에 절이 연결되어 있으므로 빈칸에는 접속사가 필요하다. 따라서 접속사인 (B)와 (D) 중에서 정답을 고른다. 빈칸 뒤에 이어지는 절은 완전한 절이므로, 불완전한 절 앞에 사용되는 (D)는 정답이 될 수 없다. 완전한 절 앞에 사용되는 명사절 접속사인 (B)가 정답이다.

8

밀러 모터스의 신형 소형 전기차는 독특한 디자인으로 올해의 디자인 혁신상을 받았다.

어휘 electric 전기의, 전기를 이용하는 unique 독특한, 고유의 uneasy 불안한, 우려되는 rigorous 철저한, 엄격한 temporary 임시의, 일시적인

해설 명사 design을 수식하기에 적절한 형용사를 고르는 문제이다. '불안한 디자인', '엄격한 디자인', '일시적인 디자인'은 모두 디자인 혁신상을 받을 근거로 어울리지 않으므로 (A), (B), (C)는 모두 오답이다. 정답은 '독특한'이라는 의미의 형용사인 (D)이다.

9

이제, 보다 빠른 배송을 위해서 케덴 가구 제품을 창고에서 고객에게 바로 배송할 수 있다.

어휘 ship 실어 나르다, 수송하다 directly 곧장, 똑바로 warehouse 창고 thoroughly 대단히, 철저히 evidently 분명히, 눈에 띄게 rarely 드물게, 좀처럼 ~하지 않는

해설 케덴 가구 제품이 창고에서 고객에게 '곧장' 배송될 수 있어서 더 빠르게 주문한 상품을 받을 수 있다는 내용이 되어야 자연스러우므로, '곧장, 바로'를 의미하는 부사인 (B)가 정답이다.

10

차먼 물류 회사는 최근 틈새 시장을 선점하기 위해서 획기적인 접근 방식을 시행했다.

어휘 recently 최근에 implement 시행하다 innovative 획기적인 approach 접근법 dominate 지배하다 niche 틈새 estimate 추산하다, 추정하다 compromise 타협하다 preside 주재하다, 주도하다

해설 빈칸 뒤 목적어인 'innovative approaches(획기적인 접근 방식)'와 어울리는 동사를 골라야 한다. 최근 틈새 시장을 선점하기 위해서 획기적인 접근 방식을 '시행했다'는 해석이 자연스러우므로 정답은 (D)이다.

11

매출 실적이 전월 대비 15% 이상 증가한 직원은 성과급을 받을 수 있다.

어휘 compared to ~와 비교하여 previous 이전의 eligible ~을 가질 수 있는, ~할 수 있는

해설 빈칸 뒤의 절은 주어와 목적어가 모두 포함된 완전한 절이므로 소유격 관계대명사인 (C)가 정답이다. that은 소유격 관계대명사를 대신할 수 없다는 것을 알아 두자.

12

피아노 독주회에서 그녀의 연주는 정말 뛰어났고, 청중들은 모두 그녀의 기교가 얼마나 인상적이었는지에 대해 언급하지 않을 수 없었다.

어휘 truly 정말로, 진심으로 outstanding 뛰어난 cannot help but ~하지 않을 수 없다

해설 빈칸 뒤 문장의 어순(주어 + 동사)을 보면, how 뒤에 형용사나 부사가 와야 한다는 것을 알 수 있다. 보기 중에서 형용사는 (A)와 (B), 부사는 (C)인데, 그녀의 기교가 '인상적이었다'는 내용이 되어야 자연스러우므로 정답은 (A) impressive(인상깊은)이다. impressed(감동받은)는 사람의 감정을 표현하는 형용사이며, 부사는 be동사의 보어가

될 수 없으므로 (B)와 (C)는 모두 오답이다.

13

그는 고려해야 할 흥미로운 여행 옵션이 너무 많아서, 언제 휴가를 낼지 결정할 수 없었다.

어휘 affordable (가격 등이) 알맞은, 감당할 수 있는

해설 빈칸 뒤에 to부정사가 있으므로 의문사인 (A)와 (D)가 정답 후보가 되며, to부정사 앞에 위치할 수 없는 (B) through와 (C) ifs는 오답이다. 빈칸 뒤 to부정사구에는 to take의 목적어인 her vacation이 있으므로 정답은 (D) when이다. what이 절이나 to부정사구 앞에 올 경우에는, 절이나 to부정사구에서 what이 대신하는 명사 하나가 생략된다.

14

빅토리아 키친웨어는 연말까지 워싱턴과 오리건에 최소 5개의 소매점을 추가로 개장할 계획이다.

어휘 retail 소매; 소매의   location 장소, 위치   appliance (가정용) 기기   vacancy 공석, 결원; 빈 방   design 설계, 디자인

해설 빈칸은 to open의 목적어로 어울리는 명사로 채워야 한다. 보기 중 to open의 목적어로 가장 어울리는 명사는 (C)이다. retail location은 '소매점'을 의미하는 복합 명사이다.

15

다음 주 금요일 회사 행사 준비 비용은 약 8,500달러이며, 케이터링 비용은 3,500달러다.

어휘 arrange 마련하다, 준비하다   function 기능; 행사   approximately 거의, 대략   plus ~뿐만 아니라, ~ 외에도   catering 음식 공급   charge 요금, 비용   whatever ~한 모든, ~한 무엇이든   in addition 게다가, 덧붙여   how much 얼마, 어느 정도

해설 빈칸은 명사구인 'a catering charge of $3,500'를 주절에 연결하는 전치사 자리이다. 따라서 보기 중 유일하게 전치사로 활용 가능한 (C)가 정답이다. plus는 전치사로서 '~뿐만 아니라, ~ 외에도'를 의미한다.

PART 6

[16-19]

친애하는 맥린 씨께,

지난 목요일에 있었던 유니온 채용박람회에서 채용을 제안해 주신 것에 대해 진심으로 감사드립니다. 심사숙고 끝에, 귀하의 관대한 제안을 거절해야 한다는 말씀을 드리게 되어 유감입니다. 귀사가 제공하는 직책과 혜택에 대해 설명해 주신 내용은 매우 인상적이었습니다. **하지만, 저는 다른 기회를 쫓기로 결정하였습니다.** 그 직무가 기술적인 측면보다는 고객 서비스 관리에 초점을 맞추어 저의 경력에 대한 열망에 더 밀접하게 부합합니다.

뵙게 되어 진심으로 기뻤으며, 앞으로도 다른 상황에서 다시 만날 수 있기를 바랍니다. 앞으로도 계속해서 성공하시기를 기원합니다.

안부를 전하며,

다니엘 플로레스

어휘 gratitude 고마움, 감사   regret 후회하다, 유감스럽게 생각하다   decline 감소하다, 거절하다   align 나란히 만들다, 나란하다   aspiration 열망, 포부   circumstance 환경, 상황   endeavor 노력, 시도

16

해설 빈칸은 동사 자리이므로 빈칸 앞 that은 주격 관계대명사이다. 주격 관계대명사가 연결하는 절의 동사는 선행사와 수가 일치해야 하므로, 단수 명사인 a job offer에 일치하는 단수 동사가 필요하다. 또한 빈칸 뒤에 동사의 목적어가 존재하지 않으므로 동사는 수동태 형태여야 한다. 따라서 수동태 단수 동사인 (C)가 정답이다.

17

해설 '------- you explained about the role of the position and the benefits your company is offering'이 동사 was 앞에서 문장의 주어 역할을 하므로 명사절이 되어야 한다. 또한 빈칸 뒤의 절은 동사 explained의 목적어가 생략된 불완전한 절이므로, 불완전한 절을 연결하는 명사절 접속사인 (B) What이 정답이다. 명사절 접속사 that은 완전한 절 앞에 사용된다.

18

(A) 저는 그 일에 대한 추가적인 정보를 요구합니다.
(B) 이메일에 첨부된 이력서를 검토해 주시기 바랍니다.
(C) 하지만, 저는 다른 기회를 쫓기로 결정하였습니다.
(D) 의료 및 치과 의료 혜택이 특히 매력적입니다.

어휘 regarding ~에 관하여   pursue 추구하다   exceptionally 유난히, 특별히   appealing 매력적인

해설 지문 초반부에서 채용 제안을 거절한다고 했고 빈칸 뒤 문장에서 다른 일자리에 대해 설명하고 있으므로, 다른 일자리 제안을 수락하기로 했다는 내용인 (C)가 정답이다.

19

해설 빈칸 앞의 'I hope our paths cross again'은 다시 만나기를 바란다는 의미이며, 빈칸 뒤의 'different circumstances'는 '다른 상황'을 의미한다. '다른 상황에서'라는 의미가 되어야 자연스러우므로 (A)의 under가 정답이다.

[20-23]

소중한 고객 여러분께,

4월 27일 금요일부로, 머피 가구 제조사 위스콘신 지점이 스티븐스 포인트 빌딩 내에 있는 54481 위스콘신 주 스티븐스 포인트 처치 스트리트 2725번지의 넓은 새로운 시설로 이전할 예정입니다. 저희의 새로운 전화번호 (715) 555-7500을 기억해 주시기 바랍니다.

이 흥미진진한 이전을 기념하기 위해, 당사의 전 제품군에 대한 독점적인 할인을 제공하게 되어 기쁩니다. **이 특별 행사는 이달 말까지 유효합니다.** 당사의 정교한 제품에 대한 보다 자세한 내용은 동봉된 브로셔를 통해 확인하실 수 있습니다. 또한 당사 제품의 종합적인 모습과 지속적인 프로모션에 대한 자세한 내용은 당사 웹사이트 www.murphyfurniture.com을 방문해 주십시오.

지속적인 지원에 진심으로 감사드리며, 새로운 위치에서 보다 나은 서비스를 제공하기를 기대합니다.

어휘 relocate 이전하다, 이동시키다 exquisite 정교한 offering 매물, 상품 enclose 동봉하다 promotion 승진, 홍보 (활동)

20

어휘 as of ~일자로 prior 이전의

해설 문장은 4월 27일 금요일부로 머피 가구 제조사 위스콘신 지점이 이전할 예정이라고 해석되므로 정답은 (B)이다. for는 시점 명사 앞에 사용될 수 없고 when은 명사절 접속사 혹은 부사절 접속사로서 완전한 절 앞에 와야 한다. prior는 형용사이므로 정답이 될 수 없다.

21

해설 보기 중 빈칸 뒤 to부정사구 앞에 올 수 있는 (A), (B), (D)가 모두 정답 후보이다. whether to do와 how to do는 명사구가 되어 빈칸에 오기에 적절하지 않으므로 (A)와 (B)는 모두 오답이다. to부정사 앞에 사용되어 '~하기 위하여'를 뜻하는 (D)가 정답이다.

22

(A) 우리는 당신에게 할인된 배송료를 제공하게 되어 기쁩니다.
(B) 안내 책자는 프런트 데스크에 진열되어 있습니다.
(C) 우리는 개장 행사에 초대하는 바입니다.
(D) 이 특별 행사는 이달 말까지 유효합니다.

어휘 shipping rate 운송료 brochure 안내 책자 valid 유효한

해설 빈칸 앞 문장에서 이전을 축하하기 위해 모든 상품을 할인해 주고 있다고 했으므로, 빈칸에도 할인 행사에 관한 설명이 이어지는 것이 자연스럽다. 따라서 정답은 (D)이다.

23

어휘 subsequently 그 뒤에 accordingly (상황에) 부응해서, 그에 맞춰 in other words 다시 말해서

해설 빈칸 앞 문장에서 브로셔에 대한 자세한 내용을 설명하고 있고, 그 이후에 웹사이트 방문을 권장하는 내용이 이어지고 있다.
(C) Additionally가 이런 상황에서 사용하기에 적절한데, 이는 '게다가', '또한', '더불어' 등의 의미로서, 이어지는 내용이 이전 문장에 덧붙여질 때 사용된다.

PART 7

[24-26]

슈루즈버리 웰빙 센터 (SWBC)

브리스틀 시내에서 자동차로 15분 거리에 위치하고 벅아이 호수의 그림 같은 경치를 볼 수 있는 SWBC는 지역 사회의 여가, 운동, 그리고 휴식을 위한 인기 있는 행선지가 되었습니다. 24) 저희 센터는 요가, 명상, 피트니스 및 사이클링 수업, 모던 스파에서 원하는 대로 받을 수 있는 마사지 등 다양한 종류의 원기 회복 체험을 제공합니다.

우리는 일과 가족과의 약속이 종종 자기 관리를 위한 시간을 거의 남기지 않는 바쁜 일상의 부담들을 이해합니다. 그것이 SWBC가 도와드리기 위해 존재하는 이유입니다. 이곳은 여러분의 웰빙을 우선시하고 앞으로 나아갈 에너지를 되찾기에 완벽한 장소입니다. 26) 당사의 전담 코디네이터가 당신의 요구에 맞춘 개인 맞춤형 계획을 수립하는 데 도움을 드릴 수 있습니다. 25) 또한, 추가 요금으로 목욕 용품 패키지 옵션을 제공합니다.

우리의 멤버십 코디네이터에게 연락하려면 (480) 543-7070으로 전화하거나 customerservice@swbc.org로 이메일을 보내 주세요. 더 자세한 정보를 원하시면, 저희 웹사이트 www.swbc.org를 방문해 주세요.

어휘 conveniently 편리하게, 안성맞춤으로 picturesque 그림 같은 destination 목적지, 도착지 leisure 여가 exercise 운동 rejuvenate 활기를 되찾게 하다 indulgent (자기) 하고 싶은 대로 다 하게 놔두는 commitment 약속, 전념, 헌신 prioritize 우선적으로 처리하다 regain 되찾다, 회복하다 move forward 전진하다 personalize (개인의 필요에) 맞추다 tailor 맞추다, 조정하다 additionally 게다가 optional 선택적인 coordinator 조정하는 사람, 진행자 extra charge 추가 요금

24

슈루즈버리 웰빙 센터에 대해 알 수 있는 것은?
(A) 브리스틀 시내 중심에 위치해 있다.
(B) 명상 수업은 제공되는 것의 일부로 이용할 수 있다.
(C) 모임과 행사를 주최할 수 있는 공간을 제공한다.
(D) 구내 식당은 건물 내에서 편리하게 위치해 있다.

어휘 situated (특정한 장소에) 위치해 있는 in the heart of ~의 한 가운데에 meditation 명상, 묵상 offering 제공된 것, 내놓는 것 gathering 모임

해설 첫 번째 문단에서 SWBC는 요가, 명상, 피트니스 및 사이클링 수업을 제공한다고 했으므로 정답은 (B)이다. 브리스틀 시내에서 차로 15분 떨어진 곳에 위치했다고 했으므로 (A)는 정답이 될 수 없다.

25

추가 요금으로 무엇을 할 수 있는가?
(A) 요가 수업 한 세트
(B) 식당에서 식사
(C) 운동 시설에 대한 접근 권한
(D) 욕실 용품

어휘 exercise 운동 facility 시설 supplies 용품

해설 두 번째 문단의 'Additionally, we offer an optional bath accessory package for an extra charge.'에서 추가 요금을 지불하시면 목욕 용품 패키지를 제공한다고 했으므로 정답은 (D)이다.

26

광고에 따르면, 코디네이터들은 어떤 서비스를 제공하는가?
(A) 계획 수립을 돕는 것
(B) 긴장을 푸는 법을 알려주는 것
(C) 개인 파티를 준비하는 것
(D) 객실 사용 가능 여부를 확인하는 것

어휘 relaxation 휴식 technique 기법 organize 준비하다, 조직하다 verify (진실인지, 또는 정확한지) 확인하다 availability 유효성, 이용할 수 있음

해설 두 번째 문단 후반부에서 코디네이터가 고객의 요구에 맞는 맞춤형 계획을 수립하는 데 도움을 줄 수 있다고 했으므로 정답은 (A)이다.

[27-31]

브라운 온라인 비즈니스 트레이닝 연구소

내년을 여러분 스스로에게 투자함으로써 마침내 사업을 시작하거나 성장하는 해로 만들어 보세요. **27)** 브라운 온라인 비즈니스 트레이닝 연구소에서, 우리는 바쁜 기업가, 사업주, 창업을 고려 중인 사람들에게 다양한 맞춤형 온라인 트레이닝 세션을 제공합니다. **28-1)** 저명한 비즈니스 전문가들이 이끄는 온라인 세미나와 세션에 여러분의 집, 사무실, 업무 공간에서 편하게 참여하세요. 다가오는 교육 세션은 여러분의 사업을 성공으로 이끌기 위해 고안되었습니다! **28-2)** 각 세미나의 참가자가 100명으로 제한되므로 지금 바로 온라인 등록을 통해 여러분의 자리를 확보하세요. 교육 세션에 대한 보다 자세한 정보는 www.browninstitute.org를 방문하거나 (415) 940-2911로 닉 쿠퍼에게 문의하세요.

어휘 institute 기관 a range of 다양한 tailor 맞추다, 조정하다 entrepreneur 사업가, 기업가 contemplate 고려하다, 생각하다 distinguished 유명한, 성공한 propel 나아가게 하다 secure 얻어내다, 획득하다

---

http://www.browninstitute.org/business_training

브라운 온라인 비즈니스 트레이닝 연구소에 오신 것을 환영합니다!

잠시 시간을 내어 아래 세션 일정을 검토하시고 오늘 자리를 확보해 주시기 바랍니다. 자리가 한정되어 있으니 서둘러 주시기 바랍니다.

1월 3일 ~ 5일 **시간:** 오후 7시 ~ 9시 **세션:** 성공적인 협상: 필수 전략 및 스킬 **강사:** 케빈 린, 털사 대학교	**29-1)** **1월 10일 ~ 12일** **시간:** 오후 6시 30분 ~ 8시 **29-2)** **세션:** 효과적인 리더십: 개인에게 영감을 주고 동기 부여하기 **강사:** 로버트 버튼, 위스콘신 리더십 그룹
1월 17일 ~ 19일 **시간:** 오후 6시 30분 ~ 8시 **세션:** 비즈니스를 위한 주요 기술 **강사:** 캐리 비 굿맨, 브랜슨 기술 연구소	**1월 24일 ~ 26일** **시간:** 오후 7시 30분 ~ 9시 30분 **31-1)** **세션: 프로젝트 기획 및 경영의 기본** **강사:** 트레이시 브로드먼, 맨하탄 마케팅 컨설팅

*** 등록 절차가 완료되면 등록금은 지정된 날짜에 납부해야 합니다.
- 12월 10일까지 등록시 200달러
- 12월 15일까지 등록시 220달러
- 12월 20일까지 등록시 240달러
- **30-1)** 12월 25일까지 등록시 260달러
- 1월 2일까지 등록시 300달러 (가능 여부에 따라 다름)

어휘 institute 기관 upcoming 다가오는, 곧 있을 session (특정한 활동을 위한) 시간 schedule 일정, 일정을 잡다 below 아래에 limited 제한된, 한정된 negotiation 협상, 교섭 essential 필수적인 strategy 계획, 전략 effective 효과적인 inspire 고무하다, 격려하다 motivate 동기를 부여하다

---

fundamental 기본 원칙 tuition 수업료 registration process 등록 절차 complete 완료하다, 기입하다 available 구할 수 있는, 이용할 수 있는

---

www.browninstitute.org/business_training/registration

30-2) 등록일: 12월 21일

브라운 온라인 비즈니스 트레이닝 연구소 등록 양식

이름	수잔 휴이트
전화	(513) 407-8340
이메일	susanhewitt@widenet.com
주소	드레이크스 랜딩 가 500번지, 그린브레, 캘리포니아, 94904
등록 세션	**31-2) 프로젝트 기획 및 경영의 기본**

등록해 주셔서 감사하며, 앞으로 24시간 이내에 확인 메일을 받으실 수 있습니다.

어휘 fundamental 기본 원칙 management 경영, 경영진 confirmation 확인

27

누구를 위한 광고인 것 같은가?
(A) 컴퓨터 엔지니어
(B) 대학교수
(C) 언어 강사
(D) 사업주

어휘 engineer 기사, 기술자 professor 교수 instructor 강사 owner 주인, 소유주

해설 광고 지문에서 브라운 온라인 비즈니스 트레이닝 연구소에서는 바쁜 기업가, 사업주, 창업을 고려 중인 사람들에게 다양한 맞춤형 온라인 트레이닝 세션을 제공한다고 했으므로 정답은 (D)이다.

28

세션에 대해 암시되지 않은 것은?
(A) 12월에 시작할 것이다.
(B) 유명한 인물들이 이끌고 있다.
(C) 수용 인원이 제한되어 있다.
(D) 모두 온라인으로 진행될 것이다.

어휘 well-known 유명한, 잘 알려진 figure 수치, 인물 limited 제한된, 한정된 seating 좌석, 자리 capacity 용량, 수용력

해설 광고 지문에서 저명한 비즈니스 전문가들이 이끄는 온라인 세미나와 세션에 참여하라고 하고 있으므로 (B)와 (D)는 언급된 내용이다. 웹페이지에서 자리가 한정되어 있으니 서두르라고 하고 있으므로 (C) 또한 언급된 내용이다. 웹페이지에서 모든 수업이 1월에 진행된다는 것을 확인할 수 있으므로 (A)는 잘못된 내용이다.

29

팀을 이끄는 효과적인 방법은 언제 다루어질 것인가?
(A) 1월 3일

(B) 1월 12일

(C) 1월 18일

(D) 1월 24일

해설 웹페이지 'Effective Leadership: Inspiring and Motivating Individuals'에서 사람들에게 영감을 주고 동기를 부여하는 효과적인 리더십을 다루는 수업이 진행된다는 것을 알 수 있는데, 이 수업은 1월 10일부터 12일까지 진행되므로 정답은 (B)이다.

30

휴이트 씨는 세미나 비용을 얼마나 낼 것인가?

(A) 220달러

(B) 240달러

(C) 260달러

(D) 300달러

해설 양식의 'Date of Registration: December 21'에서 등록 날짜가 12월 21일인 것을 확인할 수 있다. 웹페이지 마지막 단락에서 12월 25일까지 등록하면 260달러라고 했으므로 정답은 (C)이다.

31

휴이트 씨는 누구의 수업에 등록하는가?

(A) 케빈 린

(B) 로버트 버튼

(C) 캐리 비 굿맨

(D) 트레이시 브로드먼

해설 양식에서 휴이트 씨가 'Fundamentals of Project Planning and Management(프로젝트 기획 및 경영의 기본)'에 등록한 것을 확인할 수 있는데, 웹페이지에서 해당 수업의 강사는 트레이시 브로드먼 씨라는 것을 확인할 수 있으므로 정답은 (D)이다.

DAY 11 부사절

PRACTICE
pp.247-249

1	Although	2	Because
3	Because of	4	has increased
5	complete	6	although
7	completed	8	When
9	Otherwise	10	so

1 비록 비가 많이 내렸지만, 그들은 산으로 하이킹을 가기로 결정했다.

2 그 식당은 예약이 다 찼기 때문에, 우리는 다른 식사 장소를 찾아야 했다.

3 교통체증 때문에, 우리는 파티에 예상보다 훨씬 늦게 도착했다.

4 그녀가 재택근무를 시작한 이후로, 그녀의 생산성이 향상되었다.

5 등록 절차를 완료하면, 모든 기능을 이용할 수 있다.

6 비록 그것이 새로운 도시로 이전하는 것을 의미했지만, 그녀는 그 일자리 제안을 받아들이기로 결정했다.

7 이 새로운 고속도로가 완공되면, 두 도시 사이의 이동 시간이 크게 단축될 것이다.

8 프로젝트를 관리할 책임이 있을 때, 그녀는 모든 작업이 예산 내에서 완료되도록 보장했다.

9 그는 마감일까지 과제를 완료해야 했다. 그렇지 않으면 늦게 제출하여 불이익을 받게 되었을 것이다.

10 공사 때문에 도로가 폐쇄되어서, 우리는 우회해서 목적지에 도착해야 했다.

실전 문제 연습
p.251

1	(B)	**2**	(D)	**3**	(C)	**4**	(B)
5	(A)	**6**	(B)	**7**	(B)	**8**	(D)
9	(B)	**10**	(A)	**11**	(C)	**12**	(A)
13	(D)	**14**	(C)	**15**	(C)	**16**	(C)
17	(B)	**18**	(C)	**19**	(D)	**20**	(C)
21	(D)	**22**	(A)	**23**	(B)	**24**	(B)
25	(D)	**26**	(C)	**27**	(B)	**28**	(A)
29	(D)	**30**	(B)	**31**	(D)		

PART 5

1

본 출판물의 내용이 반드시 파이낸셜 투데이의 견해나 정책과 꼭 일치하는 것은 아니다.

어휘 content 내용, 내용물　publication 출판, 출판물　necessarily 반드시, 필연적으로　align with ~에 맞추어 조정하다　publishing 출판업　publisher 출판인, 출판사

해설 빈칸은 동사 'may not align with'의 주어 자리이므로 명사인 (A), (B), (C)가 정답 후보이다. 보기 중 '출판물'이 잡지사의 견해를 꼭 반영하고 있는 것은 아니라는 의미가 되어야 자연스러우므로 정답은 (B)이다.

2

랭포드 인베스트먼트의 직원 교육 설명서는 직원 성장을 미션의 핵심에 두도록 의도적으로 설계되었다.

어휘 manual 설명서　deliberately 의도적으로, 신중하게　mission 임무, 사명　deliberate 고의의, 의도적인; 신중히 생각하다　deliberation 숙고, 신중함

해설 빈칸은 be동사 is와 수동태를 완성하는 과거분사 designed 사이의 부사 자리이므로 부사인 (D)가 정답이다. 수동태 동사의 be동사와 과거분사 사이 빈칸은 부사 자리임을 꼭 기억해 두자.

3

추가 장학금 기회에 대해 문의하시려면 귀하의 대학, 학생 단체, 그리고 기타 캠퍼스 프로그램에 연락하시기 바랍니다.

어휘 organization 조직, 단체　inquire 알아보다, 질문을 하다　scholarship 장학금

해설 해석상 추가 장학금 기회에 대해서 문의하기 위해서는 대학, 학생

단체 및 기타 캠퍼스 프로그램에 연락하라는 문장이므로 정답은 (C)이다. to부정사가 완전한 절을 수식하는 부사적 용법으로 사용되면 '~하기 위해서'로 해석될 수 있다. 현재분사인 (B) inquiring도 명사인 programs 를 수식할 수 있지만, 이 경우 '프로그램이 문의한다'는 의미가 되므로 (B)는 정답이 될 수 없다.

4

이사회에서, 생산성을 극대화하기 위해 무엇에 집중할지에 대해 현재 논의가 진행 중이다.

어휘 maximize 극대화하다　productivity 생산성
in progress 진행 중인

해설 모든 의문사는 to부정사구 앞에 붙을 수 있지만, 빈칸 뒤 to부정사구에서 전치사 on의 목적어가 생략되었으므로, 생략된 명사를 대신할 수 있는 (B) what이 정답이다.

5

폴 워린의 3개월 수습 기간은 이달 말에 종료되며, 그는 다음 달부터 정규직으로 근무하게 된다.

어휘 probationary period 수습 기간　permanent employee 정규직 사원

해설 빈칸은 명사구인 a permanent employee 앞에 위치한 전치사 자리이다. 폴 워린이 다음 달부터 정규직 직원으로서 근무할 예정이라고 해석되므로 '~로서'를 의미하는 전치사인 (A)가 정답이다.

6

올해 스웻랜드 파크에서 열리는 재즈 콘서트는 완전히 무료이지만, 어떤 액수라도 기부해 주시면 감사하겠습니다.

어휘 appreciate 고마워하다, 환영하다　contribution 기부금, 기여

해설 빈칸은 부사절 앞의 접속사 자리이므로 보기 중 유일한 부사절 접속사인 (B)가 정답이다.

7

새로운 다리가 개통되면 몬태노 대교의 교통은 지금보다 훨씬 원활해질 것이다.

어휘 flow 흐르다　smoothly 부드럽게, 순조롭게　as though 마치 ~인 것처럼

해설 빈칸은 부사절 앞의 접속사 자리이므로 보기 중 부사절 접속사인 (B)와 (D)가 정답 후보이다. 새로운 다리가 개통되면 몬태노 대교의 교통이 지금보다 훨씬 원활해질 것이라고 해석되므로 정답은 (B)이다.

8

저가 항공사들은 일반적으로 평균 180달러의 비용으로 유럽의 주요 도시들 간의 항공편을 제공한다.

어휘 budget 저렴한, 저가의　typically 보통, 일반적으로
sensitive 세심한, 예민한　expense 비용　pending 미정인, 곧 있을

해설 보기 중 명사인 airlines를 수식하기에 적절한 형용사를 골라야 한다. budget은 명사로도 사용되지만, 형용사로 '저렴한, 저가의'의 의미로도 사용된다. 따라서 airlines를 수식하여 '저가 항공사'라는 의미를 만드는 (D)가 정답이다.

9

세계적으로 유명한 스타 폴라 로즈는 연기뿐만 아니라 음악에도 뛰어 들었고, 그녀의 첫 싱글은 다음 주에 발매될 예정이다.

어휘 in addition to ~에 더하여　venture into ~을 감행하다
release 발매하다, 출시하다　by the time ~할 때까지는　as far as ~하는 한　in the event of ~할 경우에는

해설 빈칸은 her acting career 앞의 전치사 자리이다. 따라서 접속사인 (A)와 (C)는 오답이다. 폴라 로즈가 연기는 물론 음악에도 뛰어 들어 다음 주에 첫 싱글이 발표될 예정이라는 의미의 문장이므로 정답은 (B)의 in addition to이다.

10

각각의 예약에 대해 체크인할 때 헬스 카드 제출을 요청 드리므로, 그것이 유효한지와 만료되지 않았는지를 확인해 주세요.

어휘 present 제출하다　valid 유효한　expire 만료되다

해설 부사절 접속사인 when은 완전한 절을 연결하므로 주어 없이 동사 앞에 사용될 수 없다. 따라서 동사인 (B)와 (C)는 오답이다. 부사절에서 주어를 생략한 다음 동사를 분사로 바꿔 분사 구문으로 만들 수 있으므로, 정답은 현재분사인 (A) checking이다.

11

반갑지 않은 전화나 메시지를 받을 경우, 전화기에 내장된 통화 거부 기능으로 발신자 번호를 차단할 수 있다.

어휘 unwelcome 반갑지 않은　block 차단하다　rejection 거절, 거부　feature 기능, 특징　outstanding 뛰어난, 중요한
interactive 상호적인

해설 전화기에 내장된 통화 거부 기능으로 발신자 번호를 차단한다는 것은 원치 않는 전화나 메시지를 받는 경우이므로 정답은 (C)이다.

12

어니 마틴은 자료를 기록 및 분석하고 고객 서비스 절차를 개선함으로써 지난 분기의 영업 목표를 달성할 수 있었다.

어휘 procedure 절차; 방법

해설 어니 마틴이 자료를 기록 및 분석하고 고객 서비스 절차를 개선한 것은 지난 분기의 영업 목표를 달성한 '방법', '수단'이라고 볼 수 있다. 따라서 정답은 (A)이다. 'by + 동명사'는 '~함으로써'로 해석된다.

13

예산의 제약으로 인해, 펜은 프로젝트 매니저에게 원래의 마케팅 캠페인 계획에 대한 수정을 요청해야 했다.

어휘 budget constraint 예산 제약　modification 수정
original 원래의　inevitable 불가피한, 피할 수 없는　occasional 가끔의, 때때로의　upcoming 곧 있을, 다가오는

해설 빈칸은 plans를 수식하기에 적절한 의미의 형용사를 골라야 한다. '원래의 계획을 수정하는 것'이 자연스러우므로 (D)가 정답이다. 나머지는 모두 의미상 어색하다.

14

새보리어 비스트로의 총괄 셰프인 미치 라이스는 주방 운영을 총괄하고 감독하는 것을 주로 책임지고 있다.

어휘 executive 간부, 경영의 **primarily** 주된, 주요한; 최초의 **responsible** 책임지고 있는 **oversee** 감독하다 **direct** 총괄하다, 감독하다 **operation** 사업, 운영 **gradually** 서서히 **admiringly** 감탄하여 **hastily** 급히

해설 빈칸 뒤 responsible을 수식하기에 가장 적절한 부사를 골라야 한다. '주로 책임이 있는'을 의미하는 (C)가 해석상 가장 자연스러우므로 정답이다. 나머지는 모두 의미상 어색하다.

15

예상치 못한 예산 삭감을 고려하여, 이사회는 다가오는 회계 연도의 재정적 우선 순위를 평가하기로 결정했다.

어휘 unexpected 예기치 않은, 예상 밖의 **evaluate** 평가하다, 감정하다 **priority** 우선 사항 **fiscal year** 회계 연도 **in lieu of** ~ 대신에

해설 빈칸이 포함된 부분의 내용은 '예산 삭감'이며, 이어지는 내용은 이와 관련된 결정에 대한 것이다. (C)의 in light of는 '~을 고려하여', 또는 '~을 바탕으로'라는 의미로서, 빈칸에 오기에 의미상 가장 적절하다.

PART 6

[16-19]

발디니 씨께,

웨스트브룩 가구를 대표하여 제작해 주신 웹사이트 디자인의 탁월함에 진심으로 감사드립니다. 웹사이트의 변화는 우리의 예상을 뛰어넘었고, 고객들의 긍정적인 반응은 압도적이었습니다. **이는 또한 우리 사업에 새로운 고객들을 많이 끌어들였습니다.**

저희는 귀사의 작업에 깊은 감명을 받았으며 저희의 다른 가족 사이트, 특히 웨스트브룩 인테리어와 웨스트브룩 키친을 설계하는 데 전문적인 기술을 요청하고 싶습니다. 이 문제에 대해 더 논의하기 위해, 저는 가급적 귀하의 사무실에서 편한 시간에 회의를 준비하고 싶습니다. 이 회의를 위해 귀하께서 원하는 시간을 알려주시기 바랍니다. 512-5800번으로 연락주시면 됩니다.

감사와 안부를 전하며,

마이클 영
웨스트브룩 가구

어휘 heartfelt 진심 어린 **gratitude** 고마움, 감사 **transformation** 변화, 탈바꿈, 변신 **exceed** 넘다, 초월하다 **overwhelming** 압도적인 **expertise** 전문 지식, 전문 기술 **preferably** 되도록이면

16

어휘 in case of 만일 ~한다면, ~의 경우에는 **in regard to** ~에 관해서는 **on behalf of** ~을 대신하여, ~을 대표하여 **as a result of** ~의 결과로서

해설 빈칸 뒤에 회사명이 있고, 편지의 작성자인 마이클 영 씨는 발디니 씨가 훌륭하게 웹사이트를 디자인해 준 것에 대한 감사 인사를 하고 있다. 따라서, 마이클 영 씨가 웨스트 브룩 가구를 대표하여 감사 인사를 전한다는 것을 알 수 있으므로 정답은 (C)이다.

17

(A) 제 동료 중 한 명이 당신의 서비스를 높이 평가했습니다.
(B) 이는 또한 우리 사업에 새로운 고객들을 많이 끌어들였습니다.
(C) 사무실 인테리어를 바꾸는 것이 필수적입니다.
(D) 우리의 이전 디자인은 대중들로부터 큰 호평을 받았습니다.

어휘 praise 칭찬하다 **imperative** 반드시 해야 하는 **acclaim** 칭찬, 찬사

해설 빈칸 앞 문장에서 웹사이트의 변화는 예상을 뛰어넘었고 고객들의 긍정적인 반응은 압도적이었다고 했으므로, 그로 인한 긍정적인 결과로써 많은 새로운 고객을 유치했다는 내용이 어울린다. 따라서 빈칸에 가장 어울리는 문장은 (B)이다.

18

어휘 urgently 급하게 **recklessly** 무모하게 **periodically** 주기적으로

해설 빈칸에 오기에 가장 자연스러운 부사 어휘를 골라야 한다. 설계를 요청하는 사이트로 웨스트브룩의 가족 사이트들 중에서도 웨스트브룩 인테리어와 웨스트브룩 키친을 구체적으로 언급하고 있으므로, 빈칸에 (C) specifically(특별히, 구체적으로 말하면)가 오는 것이 가장 적절하다.

19

어휘 prefer 선호하다, ~을 (더) 좋아하다 **preference** 선호, 선호되는 것

해설 소유격 대명사 your와 명사인 time 사이에 빈칸이 있으므로 time을 수식하는 형용사가 와야 한다. 보기 중 형용사 역할이 가능한 것은 현재분사인 (A)와 과거분사인 (D)이다. 해석상 '선호되는' 시간이 되어야 하므로 정답은 과거분사인 (D)이다.

[20-23]

현재 프랭클린 홀과 노스 메릭 홀에서 콘크리트 작업이 진행 중이며, 봄 내내 계속될 예정입니다. 이 건물들은 공과대학과 엘몬트 폴리테크닉 연구소에 사용될 것인데, 디자인 스튜디오, 교육 구역, 협업 공간, 그리고 행정실을 위한 시설을 제공합니다. **게다가, 그것들은 새로운 캠퍼스 관문 역할을 할 것입니다.**

웨스트베리 로와 유니언데이 가 근처에서는 진행 중인 공사로 인해 트럭 운행이 증가할 것으로 예상하시기 바라며, 이는 여름까지 이어질 것입니다. 따라서, 보행자, 자전거 이용자, 그리고 운전자들은 해당 지역에서 주의를 기울이시고 게시된 모든 표지판을 준수하실 것을 촉구합니다. 문의를 위해서, 프로젝트 매니저인 매트 풀러에게 mattfuller@elmont.edu로 연락하세요.

어휘 concrete 콘크리트; 콘크리트로 된; 구체적인 **underway** 진행 중인 **throughout** 도처에; 내내 **college of engineering** 공과대학 **instructional** 교육용의 **administrative** 관리상의, 행정상의 **in the vicinity of** ~의 부근에 **pedestrian** 보행자 **bicyclist** 자전거 타는 사람 **motorist** 승용차 운전자 **cautious** 조심스러운, 신중한 **adhere to** ~을 고수하다 **signage** 신호들

20

해설 문장에 동사 is가 있고 접속사는 보이지 않으므로 동사인 (A)와 (B)는 오답이다. schedule을 명사로 보더라도 앞의 명사와 동격이 아닌 경우 전치사로 연결되어야 하므로 (A)와 (B)는 여전히 오답이다.

(C) scheduled와 (D) scheduling은 각각 과거분사와 현재분사로 빈칸에 올 수 있는데, 콘크리트 작업은 일정이 '잡히는' 수동의 의미이므로 과거분사인 (C) scheduled가 정답이다.

21

(A) 수업 공간을 강화하는 것이 필수적입니다.
(B) 행정실이 메리디안 홀로 이전합니다.
(C) 새 사무실들은 현재 공사 단계에 있습니다.
(D) 게다가, 그것들은 새로운 캠퍼스 관문 역할을 할 것입니다.

어휘 instructional 교육용의 imperative 반드시 해야 하는
administrative 관리상의, 행정상의 phase 단계 gateway 입구,
관문

해설 빈칸 앞 문장에서 새로운 시설에는 디자인 스튜디오, 교육 공간, 협업 공간, 그리고 행정실이 들어설 것이라고 설명했으므로, 이어지는 문장에서도 새로운 시설의 용도에 대한 설명이 이어지는 것이 자연스럽다. 따라서, 새로운 시설이 새로운 캠퍼스 관문 역할을 수행할 것이라는 내용의 (D)가 정답이다.

22

어휘 duration 기간 fraction 일부 aspect 측면

해설 해석상 웨스트베리 로와 유니언데일 가 근처에서 공사가 진행 중이라는 의미가 되어야 하므로, (A) vicinity(인근, 부근)가 정답이다. in the vicinity of는 '~의 부근에'를 뜻하는 전치사구이다.

23

어휘 preside 주재하다

해설 보행자, 자전거 타는 사람, 그리고 운전자들에게 주의를 촉구하는 문장이다. (B) exercise는 '행동을 취하다', 또는 '실천하다'라는 뜻으로, 주의나 조심하는 '행동을 취하라'는 의미로 빈칸에 가장 어울리는 동사다. 'exercise caution'이라는 관용구는 주어진 상황에서 주의나 조심을 기울인다는 의미를 가지고 있다.

PART 7

[24-26]

은퇴 발표 – 컬렉션 수석 큐레이터 패트릭 애덤스

우리는 괴로우면서도 즐거운 소식을 나눌 것이 있습니다. NNHM(내슈빌 자연사 박물관)과의 놀라운 40년간의 여정을 마치고, 존경하는 컬렉션 수석 큐레이터 패트릭 애덤스가 은퇴합니다. **24) 인턴으로 근무했던 초기부터 수석 큐레이터로서의 놀라운 6년간의 역할에 이르기까지, 애덤스 씨는 내슈빌의 역사를 가능한 모든 방법으로 보존하는 데 헌신해 왔습니다.** **25) 그는 전시회를 개발하고, 가치 있는 물건들을 보존하고, 견학과 강의를 통해 학생들과 방문객들을 교육함으로써 NNHM을 형성하는 데 중추적인 역할을 했습니다.** 그가 최근에 출판한 책 *역사로 가득 찬 내슈빌*은 그의 40년간의 연구에 대한 증거입니다.

NNHM 이사회는 그의 탁월한 경력을 인정하여, **26-1) 애덤스 씨에게 평생 공로상을 수여하기로 결정했습니다. 26-2) 이번 주 금요일 송년회에서 애덤스 씨에게 기념패를 수여하면서 그에게 존경을 표할 것입니다.** NNHM의 모든 직원들이 애덤스 씨와 그의 공헌을 축하하기

위한 기념식에 이어 진행되는 리셉션에 참석할 수 있도록 초대합니다. **26-3) 작별 인사를 남기고 싶다면, 테리 왓슨의 사무실에 들러 그를 위한 사진 앨범에 사인해주세요.**

애덤스 씨의 은퇴는 한 시대의 끝을 의미하며, 우리는 그에게 작별을 고하기도 하지만, 그의 유산을 기리고자 합니다. 그의 열정, 지식, 헌신은 그리울 것이지만, 그것들이 우리에게 계속해서 영감을 줄 것입니다.

패트릭, 당신의 훌륭한 봉사에 감사드립니다. 당신이 마땅히 받아야 할 행복한 은퇴가 되기를 기원합니다.

어휘 bittersweet 씁쓸하면서도 달콤한, 괴로우면서도 즐거운
incredible 믿기 힘든 esteemed 존중받는, 존경받는
remarkable 놀라운, 주목할 만한 preserve 지키다, 보존하다
object 물건, 물체 pivotal 중심이 되는 testament (존재·사실의)
증거 commemorative 기념하는 plaque 명판, 상패 signify
의미하다, 나타내다 legacy (과거의) 유산 well-deserved 충분한
자격이 있는

24

애덤스 씨는 어떤 분야에서 일하는가?
(A) 기업 교육
(B) 역사적 기록 보관
(C) 야생 동물 보호
(D) 도시 개발

어휘 corporate 기업의, 법인의 archiving 파일 보관
wildlife 야생 동물 conservation 보호, 보존 urban 도시의

해설 첫 문단에서 애덤스 씨가 내슈빌의 역사를 가능한 모든 방법으로 보존하는 데 헌신해 왔다고 했으므로, 그가 역사적인 자료를 기록하고 보관하는 일에 종사했다는 것을 알 수 있다. 따라서 정답은 (B)이다.

25

애덤스 씨에 대한 설명으로 옳은 것은?
(A) 그는 6년 전에 NNHM에 입사했다.
(B) 그는 대학에서 학생들을 가르친다.
(C) 그는 역사에 관한 몇 권의 책을 썼다.
(D) 그는 수많은 유물을 목록으로 만들었다.

어휘 artifact 인공물, 공예품

해설 첫 문단에 그는 전시회를 개발하고, 가치 있는 물건들을 보존하고, 견학과 강의를 통해 학생들과 방문객들을 교육함으로써 NNHM을 형성하는 데 중추적인 역할을 했다는 내용이 있는데, 가치있는 물건을 보존하는 것과 관련이 있는 (D)가 정답이다.

26

애덤스 씨를 기리기 위해 주어지는 것이 아닌 것은?
(A) 명패
(B) 상
(C) 전기
(D) 사진첩

해설 두 번째 문단에서 이사회는 그에게 평생 공로상을 수여하기로 의결했으며, 금요일 박물관 송년회에서 기념패로 수여할 예정이라고 했으므로 (A)와 (B)는 애덤스 씨에게 수여되는 것들이다. 또한 애덤스 씨

에게 작별 편지를 쓰고 싶으면 테리 왓슨의 사무실에 들러 파티에서 수여될 사진첩에 서명해 달라고 했으므로 (D)도 정답이 될 수 없다. 전기 (biography)는 언급되지 않았다.

[27-31]

http://www.sweetbeans.com/custserv/shippinginfo

구매	회사 소개	제품 소개	고객 서비스	배송 정책

스위트빈즈 로스터리 앤드 카페
열정으로 가공된 신선한 원두,
진짜 커피의 향과 맛을 위한 선택

무료 배송을 즐기세요!

27) 캘리포니아 내 주문의 경우, $60 이상 구매 시 무료 배송이 가능합니다. 캘리포니아 외 주문의 경우, $75 이상 구매 시 무료 배송이 가능합니다.
*** 30-1) 표준 배송 요금은 캘리포니아 내에서는 $8이며, 캘리포니아 외 주문의 경우 $15입니다.

저희 커피의 원두는 전문적으로 로스팅되며, 콜드 브루는 월요일부터 금요일까지 매주 5일 동안 신중하게 병에 담깁니다. 30-2) 캘리포니아 내 주문의 경우 주문을 28) **처리하고 배송하기 위해 최대 영업일로 3일이 소요될 수 있으며, 캘리포니아 외 주문의 경우 최대 5일이 소요될 수 있습니다.** 주문이 준비되는 대로, 이메일 확인서와 추적 정보를 보내드립니다. 휴일과 주말에는 지연이 있을 수도 있다는 사실에 유의해 주세요.

주문 배송에 관한 질문이 있으시면 언제든지 service@sweetbeans.com으로 연락주세요.

어휘 cultivate 경작하다 dedication 기부, 헌신 exceptional 비범한, 뛰어난 complimentary 무료의 expertly 노련하게, 전문적으로 track 추적하다 potential 가능성이 있는 hesitate 주저하다, 망설이다

수신: service@sweetbeans.com
발신: elisefay@widespace.net
날짜: 8월 15일
제목: 주문 번호 91783

일주일 전에 친구들에게 선물용으로 귀사의 훌륭한 콜드 브루 커피를 세 병 주문했으며, 30-3) **총 금액은 $45입니다.** 배송 정책에 따르면, 주문은 구매 후 3일 이내에 도착해야 합니다. 하지만, 아직 받지 못했습니다.

이번 주말에 친구들에게 선물을 줄 수 있도록, 제품들이 아무리 늦어도 금요일까지는 배송될 수 있도록 해 주세요. 31) **만약 그때까지 제품을 배송될 수 없다면, 주문을 취소하고 환불해주시면 감사하겠습니다.**

29) **주문 상태에 대한 최신 정보를 제공해 주시겠어요?** 응답을 빨리 해주시면 감사하겠습니다.

안부를 전하며,

엘리즈 페이

어휘 total 총계가 ~이 되다   be supposed to ~하기로 되어 있다 present 주다, 수여하다   no later than 아무리 늦어도   prompt 즉각적인, 신속한

27

웹페이지에서, 스위트빈즈 로스터리 앤드 카페에 대해 언급된 것은?
(A) 일주일 내내 영업한다.
(B) 다양한 배송 요금을 제공한다.
(C) 전국에 여러 지점이 있다.
(D) 최근에 캘리포니아에 지점을 열었다.

어휘 a wide range of 광범위한, 다양한   multiple 많은, 다수의

해설 웹페이지의 첫 단락에 배송비에 관한 설명을 보면 캘리포니아 내에서의 배송비와 캘리포니아 이외 지역으로의 배송비가 다르며, 구매액에 따라 배송비가 다르다는 것을 알 수 있다. 따라서 정답은 (B)이다.

28

웹페이지에서 두 번째 문단 두 번째 줄의 "process"와 의미상 가장 가까운 것은?
(A) 처리하다
(B) 개발하다
(C) 촉진시키다
(D) 상담하다

해설 지문에서 process는 주문을 "처리하다"는 뜻으로 사용되었다. 따라서 "처리하다"라는 의미로 쓰이는 (A) handle이 정답이다.

29

이메일의 목적은 무엇인가?
(A) 구매를 위한 주문을 하기 위해서
(B) 제품의 종류에 대해 문의하기 위해서
(C) 잘못된 배송을 알리기 위해서
(D) 현재 배송 상태 확인하기 위해서

어휘 inquire ~을 묻다, 알아보다   status (진행 과정의) 상황

해설 이메일 마지막 문단에서 주문 상태에 대한 최신 정보를 제공해 줄 수 있는지 묻고 있으므로 정답은 (D)이다.

30

페이 씨의 주문에 대한 배송비는 얼마인가?
(A) 무료
(B) 8달러
(C) 15달러
(D) 45달러

해설 이메일에 따르면, 페이 씨의 총 주문 금액이 45달러인데, 웹페이지의 첫 문단의 정보에 따르면 이 주문은 무료 배송에 해당되지 않는다. 따라서 표준 배송비인 8달러(캘리포니아 내)나 15달러(캘리포니아 외) 중에서 정답을 골라야 한다. 이메일의 첫 번째 문단에서 페이 씨의 주문은 구매 후 3일 이내에 도착해야 한다는 내용이 있고, 웹페이지에서 캘리포니아 내에서의 주문이 최대 3일까지 소요된다는 내용을 찾을 수 있으므로, 페이 씨에게는 캘리포니아 내 배송비가 적용될 것이다. 따라서 정답은 (B)이다.

31

이메일에서, 페이 씨에 대해 암시된 것은?

(A) 그녀는 카페의 단골 고객이다.

(B) 그녀는 이번 금요일에 친구들을 만날 예정이다.

(C) 그녀는 배송비에 관한 문의 사항이 있다.

(D) 그녀는 필요한 경우 환불 받고 싶어 한다.

어휘 regular 잦은, 주기적인   regarding ~에 관하여
necessary 필요한, 불가피한

해설 이메일의 두 번째 문단에서 만약 금요일까지 제품을 배송할 수 없다면 주문을 취소하고 환불을 받고 싶다고 했으므로 정답은 (D)이다.

DAY 12 가정법과 비교구문

PRACTICE
pp.259-262

1 were	2 have caught
3 Should	4 have gotten
5 try	6 attend
7 significantly	

1 만약 그녀가 자신의 능력에 더 자신이 있다면, 직장에서 훨씬 더 큰 성공을 거둘 수 있을 텐데.

2 만약 내가 공항에 더 일찍 도착했더라면, 나는 어젯밤 비행기를 탑승했을 텐데.

3 질문이나 우려 사항이 있으면, 언제든지 고객 지원 팀에 문의하여 지원을 받으세요.

4 그녀가 더 일찍 길을 물었더라면, 낯선 도시에서 길을 잃지 않았을 것이다.

5 그에게 시내에 새로 생긴 식당을 꼭 한 번 가 볼 것을 권했는데, 음식이 정말 훌륭하다.

6 모든 직원은 매년 안전 교육에 참석해야 한다.

7 새 스마트폰은 전작에 비해 훨씬 더 많은 저장 공간을 제공한다.

실전 문제 연습
p.264

1 (D)	2 (C)	3 (D)	4 (A)
5 (A)	6 (A)	7 (C)	8 (D)
9 (C)	10 (D)	11 (B)	12 (C)
13 (D)	14 (B)	15 (C)	16 (C)
17 (D)	18 (A)	19 (B)	20 (D)
21 (D)	22 (D)	23 (C)	24 (D)
25 (A)	26 (B)	27 (B)	28 (C)
29 (B)	30 (C)	31 (C)	32 (D)

PART 5

1

토드 와일리는 프로 데뷔 이후 지난 10년 동안 혁신적인 예술성으로 수많은 상을 수상했다.

어휘 innovative 획기적인   artistry 예술성, 예술적 재능
professional 직업의, 전문적인

해설 'over the past ten years(지난 10년 동안)'을 통해 토드 와일리가 수많은 상을 받아온 기간이 과거부터 현재까지 이어지는 것을 알 수 있으므로 빈칸에 가장 어울리는 시제는 현재완료 시제이다. 정답은 (D)이다.

2

쇼 씨는 다음 주 밴쿠버에서 열리는 회의에 참석할 때, 행사가 열리고 있는 페어뷰 호텔에 머물 것이다.

어휘 be held 개최되다

해설 빈칸은 부사절의 동사 자리이므로 동사인 (C)와 (D)가 정답 후보이다. 시간의 부사절에서는 현재 시제가 미래 시제를 대신하므로 정답은 현재 시제 동사인 (C)이다.

3

코헨 개발이 제시한 뉴버그의 부동산에 대한 제안은 다른 제안들보다 훨씬 합리적인 것 같다.

어휘 property 재산, 부동산   reasonable 합리적인

해설 빈칸은 형용사의 비교급인 more reasonable을 수식하는 부사 자리이다. 따라서 비교급 강조 부사 중 하나인 (D)가 정답이다.

4

왓츠 그룹은 올 시즌 경쟁사들의 제품의 인기가 어느 정도인지를 확인한 이후에 캠핑 용품을 생산하기로 결정했다.

어휘 gear 장비   competitor 경쟁자

해설 빈칸에는 의문사 how의 수식을 받을 형용사나 부사가 필요하다. 빈칸 뒤의 절에서 be동사인 were 뒤에 주격 보어가 없으므로, 주격 보어인 형용사가 빈칸으로 이동했다는 것을 알 수 있다. 따라서 형용사인 (A)가 정답이다.

5

만약 팀원 중 한 명이 새로운 기계를 어떻게 작동하는지 안다면, 외부 엔지니어를 고용하는 것은 불필요할 것이다.

어휘 operate 작동되다, 가동하다   external 외부의
unnecessary 불필요한

해설 주절의 동사 시제로 미루어 보았을 때, 문장은 가정법 과거라는 것을 알 수 있다. 따라서 과거 시제인 (A)가 정답이다.

6

온라인 상에서 탄탄한 존재감을 유지하는 것은 잠재적인 고객, 특히 젊은 전문가들과의 연결을 위한 효과적인 전략이다.

어휘 robust 원기 왕성한, 탄탄한   presence 참석, 존재(함)
strategy 계획, 전략   professional 전문직 종사자   potential
잠재적인, (~이 될) 가능성이 있는   artificial 인공의, 인위적인
partial 부분적인   optional 선택적인

해설 온라인 상에서 탄탄한 존재감을 유지하는 것은 특히 젊은 전문가들과 같은 잠재 고객들과 접촉하는 좋은 전략이 될 수 있다고 해석되므로, '잠재적인'을 뜻하는 형용사인 (A)가 정답이다. 나머지 보기는 모두 빈칸에 오기에 의미상 어색하다.

7

스피넬라 기술은 최근 근무 환경 개선을 목표로 직원 복리 후생 제도를 대폭 변경했다.

어휘 employee benefits package 복리 후생 제도　aim to ~하는 것을 목표로 하다　enhance 높이다, 향상시키다 environment 환경　soon 곧, 머지않아　shortly 곧, 얼마 안 되어 recently 최근에　currently 현재, 지금

해설 동사의 시제가 현재완료 시제이므로 미래 시제와 어울리는 부사인 (A)와 (B), 그리고 현재 시제와 어울리는 (D)는 모두 오답이다. 과거 시제나 현재완료 시제 동사와 어울리는 부사인 (C)가 정답이다.

8

만약 발로그 씨가 다른 일자리 제안을 받을 것이라는 것을 알았다면, 그는 지난주 코어 밸류스 투자회사의 제안을 받아들이지 않았을 것이다.

어휘 accept 받아들이다, 수락하다

해설 if절의 동사인 had known이 과거완료 시제이므로, 가정법 과거완료 시제 문장을 완성하는 동사를 정답으로 골라야 한다. 가정법 과거완료 문장은 주절에 'would have p.p.' 형태의 동사가 필요하므로 정답은 (D)이다.

9

올해 자선 경매는 지난번만큼 모금을 했고, 수익금은 지역 재단에 기부될 예정이다.

어휘 charity 자선, 자선 단체　auction 경매　raise money 자금을 모으다　proceeds 수익금　foundation 재단

해설 빈칸 뒤 as와 함께 원급 비교 구문을 만드는 as가 필요하다. 그런데 money는 불가산 명사이므로 불가산 명사를 수식하는 형용사인 much가 money를 수식해야 한다. 따라서 정답은 (C)이다.

10

프로스페리티 캐피탈 그룹에서 오는 손님들이 늦게 도착할 경우, 회의가 두세 시간 정도 연기될 것이다.

어휘 conference 회의, 학회　postpone 미루다, 연기하다

해설 부사절의 주어와 동사가 도치된 것을 미루어 보아, 부사절의 접속사인 if가 생략되었음을 알 수 있다. 부사절이 조동사 should로 시작하므로 이는 가정법 미래 문장이다. 따라서 정답은 (D)이다. 참고로 빈칸 뒤에 동사의 목적어가 존재하지 않으므로 빈칸에는 수동태 동사가 필요하다.

11

가장 최근의 조사에 따르면, 내츄럴리 프레시 마켓의 고급 유기농 제품은 작년에 비해 두 배나 많은 쇼핑객들을 끌어 모았다.

어휘 according to ~에 따르면　premium 고급의　compared to ~와 비교하여　in addition to ~에 덧붙여, 게다가　to that end 그 목적을 달성하기 위해　provided that ~을 조건으로

해설 빈칸은 명사 the latest survey 앞에 위치한 전치사 자리이므로, 전치사인 (A)와 (B)가 정답의 후보이다. 최근의 조사에 '따르면', 내츄럴리 프레시 마켓의 고품질 유기농 제품이 지난해 대비 2배 가까이의 고객을 끌어들이고 있다는 의미가 되어야 자연스러우므로 정답은 (B)이다.

12

예상하지 못한 기상 조건으로 인해 건설 프로젝트가 지연되었고, 결국 회사의 예산 초과를 야기했다.

어휘 unexpected 예기치 않은　result in ~을 야기하다　exceed 넘다, 넘어서다　urgently 급히　densely 빽빽하게　eventually 결국　occasionally 가끔

해설 예상치 못한 기상 상황으로 공사의 완료가 늦어지면서, '결국에는' 당초 예산보다 더 많은 비용이 들었다는 의미이므로 (C)가 문맥상 가장 자연스럽다.

13

트레일러에 효율적으로 적재하기 위해, 표준화된 운송 컨테이너가 필요하며, 이를 통해 균일하고 호환성 있는 솔루션을 제공해야 한다.

어휘 standardize 표준화하다　container 용기, 컨테이너　load 짐을 싣다　uniform 균일한, 획일적인　compatible 호환이 되는

해설 빈칸은 빈칸 뒤 명사인 shipping containers를 수식할 형용사 자리이므로, 형용사 역할이 가능한 현재분사 (A)와 과거분사 (D)가 정답 후보이다. 운송 컨테이너는 규격화되는 '대상'이므로 과거분사인 (D)가 정답이다. (A)를 동명사로 본다고 하더라도 동사와의 수 일치가 되지 않으므로 (A)는 정답이 될 수 없다.

14

엘리자베스 시티로 통근하는 사람들의 수가 많을수록, 도시의 공기를 가득 채우는 스모그는 더 심해졌다.

어휘 commuter 통근자

해설 쉼표 뒤에 the heavier가 있으므로 'the 비교급 ~, the 비교급 (~하면 할수록 더욱 더 ~하다)' 관용 표현이 사용되었다는 것을 파악해야 한다. 따라서 형용사의 비교급인 (B)가 정답이다.

15

에코파워 이노베이션은 에너지 절약 정책을 촉진하기 위해 그들의 사무실 건물에 태양열 전지판을 설치했고 다른 업체들도 똑같이 하기를 바란다.

어휘 install 설치하다　solar panel 태양 전지판　promote 촉진하다, 홍보하다　energy-saving 에너지를 절약하는　measures 방안, 방법, 정책　likewise 똑같이　apparently 겉으로는, 보아 하니　furthermore 더욱이, 뿐만 아니라　consistently 지속적으로

해설 에코파워 이노베이션이 에너지 절약 정책을 촉진하기 위해 그들의 사무실 건물에 태양열 전지판을 설치했고 다른 사업체들도 그들과 똑같이 하기를 바란다는 의미가 되어야 자연스럽다. 따라서 '똑같이'라는 의미의 부사인 (C)가 정답이다.

[16-19]

트랭퀼 세레니티 스파 – 일시 폐쇄

7월 13일 수요일, 최근 발생한 심한 폭풍우로 인한 피해로 인해 저희는 트랭퀼 세레니티 스파를 일시적으로 폐쇄하기로 결정하였습니다. 하지만, 이번 일시적인 폐쇄를 통해 시설 복구뿐만 아니라 일부 노후화된 장비를 업그레이드하고 교체할 수 있는 기회가 마련되었습니다. 저희는 이로써 더욱 우수한 시설과 다시 새로워진 스파 체험을 제공할 수 있게 될 것으로 믿고 있습니다.

고객님의 만족은 항상 저희의 최우선 과제였으며, 저희는 여러분 한 분 한 분을 진심으로 아끼고 있습니다. 이 결정에 대해 양해해 주셔서 감사합니다. **저희는 가능한 한 빨리 재개장할 것입니다.** 이 기간 동안, 저희의 진행 상황과 계획에 대해 계속 알려드리겠습니다. 가까운 시일 내에 더욱 활기찬 트랭퀼 세레니티 스파에서 여러분을 다시 환영할 수 있게 되기를 바랍니다.

어휘 temporarily 일시적으로 restore 복구하다 rejuvenate 다시 젊어지게 하다 revitalize 새로운 활력을 주다

16

어휘 otherwise 그렇지 않으면 for instance 예를 들어 in other words 다시 말해서

해설 빈칸 앞에서는 스파를 잠정 폐쇄하기로 한 이유를 설명하고 있고, 빈칸 뒤에서는 반대로 그것에 대한 긍정적인 면을 언급하고 있다. 따라서 정답은 (C) However이다. however는 앞 문장과 그 다음 문장의 대비를 나타내는 데 사용된다.

17

해설 트랭퀼 세레니티 스파가 일시적인 폐쇄를 결정하고 이를 통해 시설 복구와 일부 노후된 장비를 업그레이드하고 교체하는 것은 앞으로 있을 일이므로, 미래 시제 동사인 (D) will create이 정답이다.

18

어휘 regarding ~에 관하여 despite ~에도 불구하고 instead of ~ 대신에 up to ~까지

해설 지점을 일시적으로 폐쇄하고 수리하는 동안, 자신들의 계획에 대해서 고객에게 계속 알려주겠다는 내용이다. 그러므로 '~에 관하여'라는 의미의 전치사 regarding이 빈칸에 가장 어울린다.

19

(A) 새로운 시설을 짓는 데 예상보다 많은 비용이 들었습니다.
(B) **저희는 가능한 한 빨리 재개장할 것입니다.**
(C) 새로 오픈하는 지점의 개점 행사에 참석해 주시기 바랍니다.
(D) 우리는 현재 이전할 장소를 찾고 있습니다.

어휘 than expected 예상보다 opening ceremony 개업식

해설 지문에 새로운 시설을 짓는다거나 이전을 한다는 내용은 없으므로 (A), (C), (D)는 모두 오답이다. 정답은 가능한 한 빨리 재개장할 것이라는 내용의 (B)이다.

[20-23]

리사 홀먼
길버트 가 5700번지
일리노이 주 웨스턴 스프링스
60438

친애하는 홀먼 씨께,

20년이 넘는 기간 동안, 커밍스 연구센터는 시카고에서 가장 혁신적인 연구 재단 중 하나였습니다. 창립 20주년을 기념하여, 12월 15일 저녁 7시부터 클라렌던 호텔에서 개최되는 감사 연회에 귀하를 초대하게 되어 기쁩니다. 이 행사는 귀하를 포함한 우리의 아낌없는 후원자와 기부자들을 기리기 위한 것입니다. **귀하께서 참석해 주시면 대단히 감사하겠습니다.**

저희는 귀하께서 지속적인 성공에 기여하신 바가 매우 크다는 것을 잘 알고 있으며, 여러 해 동안 변함없는 성원을 보내주신 데 대해 감사를 표합니다. 참석 여부 확인을 위해, 최대한 빠른 시일 내에 535−1311로 연락을 주시거나 mikecave@cummingsresearch.org로 이메일을 보내주시기 바랍니다. 연회에 참석해 주시기를 진심으로 바랍니다.

따뜻한 안부와 함께,

마이크 케이브
홍보 관리자
커밍스 연구소

어휘 decade 10년 foundation 재단 in celebration of ~을 기념하여 appreciation 감사, 감상 banquet 연회 generous 후한, 너그러운 gratitude 고마움, 감사 steadfast 변함없는 earnestly 진지하게, 진정으로

20

어휘 innovative 획기적인, 혁신적인

해설 빈칸은 명사인 research foundations를 수식하는 형용사 자리이므로, 형용사인 (B)와 (D)가 정답 후보이다. 커밍스 연구소와 비교될 다른 연구소가 언급되지 않았고, 이 연구소가 시카고에서 가장 혁신적인 연구 재단이라는 의미가 되어야 자연스러우므로 정답은 최상급 표현인 (D)이다.

21

(A) 그 신약은 우리의 오랜 노력의 결과입니다.
(B) 그 연구에 대한 당신의 헌신은 놀라웠습니다.
(C) 이번 행사 개최에 도움을 주셔서 감사합니다.
(D) **귀하께서 참석해 주시면 대단히 감사하겠습니다.**

어휘 lengthy 너무 긴 dedication 전념 remarkable 놀라운, 주목할 만한 presence 존재, 참석 exceptional 특출한, 예외적인

해설 빈칸 앞 문장에서 이 행사가 귀하와 같은 후원자와 기부자들을 위해 준비된 것이라고 했으므로, 귀하가 행사에 참석해 준다면 감사하겠다는 의미의 문장이 이어지는 것이 자연스럽다. 따라서 정답은 (D)이다.

22

해설 이 행사는 후원자와 기부자들을 기리기 위한 것이라고 했으므로, 홀먼 씨가 과거부터 현재까지 커밍스 연구소에 공헌해 왔음을 알 수

있다. 따라서 정답은 현재완료 시제 동사인 (D) have made이다. (C) should have made는 과거에 했어야 하는데 하지 못했던 일에 대한 후회를 나타낼 때 사용된다.

23

어휘 feasibility 타당성

해설 참석을 확인하기 위해서는 최대한 빠른 시일 내에 연락을 달라는 내용이므로 정답은 (C) convenience이다. 'at one's convenience'는 '가급적 빨리'라는 의미의 관용 표현이다.

PART 7

[24-27]

워드스미스 출판사
뉴욕주 뉴욕시 1번가 350번지, 10019
웹사이트: www.wordsmithpublishers.com

하퍼 싱
워싱턴주 시애틀시 배터리가 599번지, 95213

9월 13일

싱 씨께,

워드스미스 출판사는 귀하의 책인 *리빙 위드 스타일: 당신의 이상적인 라이프스타일 만들기 가이드*의 최신판에 대한 협력을 계속하게 되어 매우 기쁩니다. 업계의 변화하는 추세에 따라, 당사는 접근성을 강화하고 귀하의 소중한 컨텐츠를 25) **더 많은 독자들이 쉽게 이용할 수 있도록 전자 유통을 채택했습니다.**

24) 26) **지난번 뉴욕 사무실의 회의에서 논의했듯이, 인세를 다소 조정한 것을 제외하면 이전 계약 조건은 변경되지 않습니다.** 27) **귀하의 검토 및 서명을 위해 갱신 계약서를 동봉합니다.** 만약 이전에 저의 비서가 보낸 저자 정보 양식을 아직 보내지 않으셨다면, 서명된 계약서와 함께 포함시켜 주십시오.

워드스미스 출판사에 대한 귀하의 공헌에 깊이 감사드립니다. 제안된 조건에 동의하신다면, 9월 25일까지 서명된 계약서를 다시 보내주십시오. 귀하의 작품을 계속 라이선스 계약하고 다양한 형식으로 출판할 수 있게 되어 영광입니다.

궁금한 점이나 고민이 있으시면, 언제든지 편한 시간에 연락주시기 바랍니다.

진심을 담아,

프랭크 놀란
워드스미스 출판사 편집장

어휘 evolving 발전하는 enhance (좋은 점·가치·지위를) 높이다 accessibility 접근 가능성, 접근하기 쉬움 modest 그다지 대단하지는 않은, 보통의 adjustment 수정, 조정 license ~에 면허 인가를 주다

24

놀란 씨는 왜 싱 씨에게 편지를 보냈는가?
(A) 그녀가 책을 검토하도록 요청하기 위해서
(B) 인터뷰 일정을 조정하기 위해서
(C) 그녀에게 책 사인회에 참석해 달라고 부탁하기 위해서

(D) 계약의 수정 사항을 설명하기 위해서

어휘 arrange 마련하다; 처리하다 schedule 일정; 일정을 잡다 modification 수정, 변경 agreement 합의, 동의

해설 두 번째 문단에서 이전 회의에서 논의했던 것처럼 인세를 다소 조정한 것을 제외하면 이전 계약 조건은 변경되지 않는다고 했으므로 정답은 (D)이다.

25

첫 번째 문단 네 번째 줄의 "easily"와 의미상 가장 가까운 것은?
(A) 쉽게, 순조롭게
(B) 기꺼이
(C) 잠시
(D) 또렷하게, 분명히

해설 전자 유통을 채택함으로써 컨텐츠를 쉽게 이용 가능하게 하고, 그래서 더 넓은 층의 독자들에게 잘 제공되도록 하겠다는 의미의 문장이다. 따라서 'easily'는 컨텐츠가 노력이나 어려움 없이 '쉽게' 사용 가능하다는 의미로, (A) readily(손쉽게, 순조롭게)와 가장 유사하다.

26

싱 씨에 대해 암시된 것은?
(A) 그녀는 현재 뉴욕에 거주하고 있다.
(B) 그녀는 놀란 씨를 직접 만난 적이 있다.
(C) 그녀는 최근에 놀란 씨와 책을 함께 썼다.
(D) 그녀의 첫 번째 책이 곧 출판될 예정이다.

해설 두 번째 문단 'As we discussed during our previous meeting at our New York office (지난번 뉴욕 사무소 회의에서 논의했던 것처럼)'에서 놀란 씨와 싱 씨가 뉴욕 사무실에서 회의차 만난 사실을 알 수 있으므로 정답은 (B)이다.

27

[1], [2], [3], [4]로 표시된 위치 중 다음 문장이 가장 어울리는 곳은?
"귀하의 검토 및 서명을 위해 갱신 계약서를 동봉합니다."
(A) [1]
(B) [2]
(C) [3]
(D) [4]

어휘 enclosed 동봉된 signature 서명

해설 두 번째 문단에서 계약에 대해 설명을 시작하고 있고, [2]번 뒤 문장에서 만약에 이전에 비서가 보낸 저자 정보 양식을 아직 보내지 않았다면 그것을 서명된 계약서와 함께 보내 달라고 언급하고 있다. 그러므로 동봉된 계약서를 확인하라는 내용의 주어진 문장의 위치는 [2]가 가장 적절하다.

[28-32]

로라 브라이언트 다큐멘터리 우수상 수상

다큐멘터리 영화 협회는 로라 브라이언트에게 올해 최고의 다큐멘터리에 수여하는 권위 있는 상을 곧 발표하게 되어 기쁩니다. 이 충분한 자격이 있는 시상은 12월 21일에 할 예정이며, *십자포화 속에서의 꿈: 아이들과 내전*을 제작한 그녀의 놀라운 업적을 기념합니다.

이 놀라운 영화를 통해, 브라이언트 씨는 위기에 처한 어린이들을 위한 운동을 열정적으로 지지하며, 전국적으로 자선 활동에 대한 인식을 높였습니다. 개봉 이후, 이 영화는 전 세계적으로 내전의 참혹한 영향으로 인해 고통받는 집을 잃은 어린이와 고아원을 지원하기 위한 기부가 10%가 넘을 정도로 믿을 수 없이 급증하는 상황을 촉발시켰습니다.

로라 브라이언트는 아이들이 분쟁의 영향을 받는 지역에서 성장할 때 직면하는 어려움을 밝히는 데 항상 헌신해 왔습니다. 그녀의 초기 다큐멘터리인 *침묵당한 목소리*에서, 그녀는 이 어린 아이들의 어려운 삶을 보여주었습니다. **28-1) 브라이언트 씨는 또한 전쟁의 피해를 입은 아이들을 돕는 비영리 단체들을 강조했습니다.** 이는 이러한 단체들에 거의 두 배에 달하는 자금 지원으로 이어졌고, 단체들이 아이들에게 더 중요한 도움을 제공하고 위험한 지역에서 아이들을 구출할 수 있게 해주었습니다.

이 중요한 행사에 참여하고 싶은 분들을 위해, 시상식 티켓은 다큐멘터리 영화 협회의 공식 웹사이트인 www.dfa.org/awards에서 구입할 수 있습니다. **28-2) 행사의 29) 수익금 전액은 브라이언트 씨의 진심 어린 요청에 따라 자선 단체에 기부될 것입니다.**

12월 21일에 로라 브라이언트의 놀라운 작품 *십자포화 속에서의 꿈: 아이들과 내전*을 축하하는 자리에 함께 해 주시기 바랍니다.

어휘 prestigious 명망 있는, 일류의 well-deserved 충분한 자격이 있는 commemorate (중요 인물 및 사건을) 기념하다 achievement 업적, 성취한 것 extraordinary 보기 드문, 비범한; 대단한 passionately 열렬히 advocate 옹호하다 cause 주의, 주장; 운동 endeavor 노력, 애씀 surge 급증, 급등 raise awareness 의식을 높이다 orphanage 고아원 devastating 엄청나게 충격적인 proceeds 수익금 heartfelt 진심에서 우러난

---

http://www.sunsethaven.com/events

흥미로운 12월 특별 행사가 여러분을 기다립니다!

12월 1일 ~ 15일: 우아한 스위트룸의 호화로움을 만끽하며 숙박을 즐기세요! 2박 이상 연속 예약하시면, 25% 전용 할인 혜택을 누릴 수 있습니다. **30-1) 여러분의 기분 좋은 패키지에는 이틀간의 숙박과 1층에 위치한 이탈리안 레스토랑의 아주 맛있는 아침 식사가 포함되어 있습니다.** 이 상품은 우리의 소중한 선셋 헤이븐 호텔 단골 회원들을 위한 특별 혜택입니다.

12월 19일 ~ 23일: 인근 메트로폴리탄 아트 플라자에서 주최하는 권위 있는 다큐멘터리 영화 협회(DFA) 시상을 축하하는 자리에 참석하여 주시기 바랍니다. **31-1) 31-2) 이 주목할 만한 행사에 참석하신 고객분들께는 숙박비의 30%를 할인해 드립니다. 30-2) 또한, 저희 5성급 레스토랑에서 무료 조식 뷔페 이용권을 즐기시기 바랍니다.** 이뿐만이 아니라, 이 놀라운 할인은 행사 이틀 전과 이틀 후까지 진행되어, 방문 기간을 최대한 활용하실 수 있습니다.

32-2) 할인을 받으시려면, 체크인할 때 프런트 데스크에서 DFA 이벤트 티켓을 제시해주시기만 하면 요금을 조정해 드립니다. 이 특별 요금은 지정된 5일 동안 적용되며, 특별한 언급이 없는 한 추가적인 숙박 기간에 대해서는 표준 요금이 부과됩니다. 이 놀라운 12월 할인 혜택을 놓치지 마세요!

어휘 indulge 마음껏 하다 consecutive 연이은 exclusive 독점적인, 전용의 scrumptious 아주 맛있는 cherish 소중히 아끼다 esteemed 존중받는, 존경받는, 호평받는. adjust 조정하다 accordingly 부응해서, 그에 맞춰 applicable 해당되는 specify 명시하다 unless ~하지 않는 한 otherwise 그렇지 않으면, 달리

선셋 헤이븐 호텔
발보아 대로 3606번지, 로스앤젤레스, 캘리포니아 90022
(310) 725-5000

31-2) 고객명: 로버트 스튜어트
주소: 59번가 1085번지, 오클랜드, 캘리포니아 94508
31-3) 32-3) 체크인 날짜: 12월 20일
체크아웃 날짜: 12월 22일
객실 번호: 1008 (퀸사이즈 침대 2개가 있는 디럭스 퀸 룸)
객실 요금: 150달러 (조식 포함) / 2박

31-4) 32-4) 총계: 210달러 (조정: 할인 적용)
결제 신용카드 번호: 3002-XXXX-XXXX-0815

28

로라 브라이언트 씨에 대해 언급된 것은?

(A) 그녀는 최근에 영화 감독으로 데뷔했다.

(B) 그녀는 비영리 단체에서 일한다.

(C) 그녀는 어린이들을 위한 자선 단체를 지원하고 있다.

(D) 그녀는 그녀의 영화로 여러 번 상을 받았다.

어휘 recently 최근에 nonprofit organization 비영리 기관 support 지지, 지원하다 charity 자선, 자선단체 award 상, 수여하다

해설 기사 지문의 두 번째 문단에 브라이언트 씨는 전쟁의 피해를 입은 아이들을 돕는 비영리 단체들을 강조했다는 내용이 있으며, 마지막 문단에서 행사의 수익금 전액은 브라이언트 씨의 진심 어린 요청에 따라 자선 단체에 기부될 것이라고 했다. 즉, 그녀가 어린이들을 위한 자선 단체를 지원한다는 것을 알 수 있으므로 정답은 (C)이다.

29

기사에서, 세 번째 문단 여섯 번째 줄의 단어 "proceeds"와 의미상 가장 가까운 어휘는?

(A) 진보

(B) 수익

(C) 주도권

(D) 예측

해설 해당 문장은 브라이언트 씨의 요청에 따라 행사의 모든 수익금이 자선 단체에 기부될 것이라고 해석되므로, proceeds(수익금)와 가장 유사한 의미의 단어는 (B) profits이다.

30

웹페이지에서, 특별 할인에 대해 암시된 것은 무엇인가?

(A) 12월 내내 제공된다.

(B) 선셋 헤이븐 호텔 단골 회원 전용이다.

(C) 호텔 레스토랑에서의 무료 아침 식사를 포함한다.

(D) 3박 이상 숙박 시에만 적용된다.

어휘 **throughout** ~ 도처에, ~ 동안 쭉   **apply** 신청하다, 적용하다

해설 웹페이지 첫 문단에서 12월 1일부터 15일까지의 특별 행사에는 2박의 숙박과 1층 이탈리안 레스토랑의 아주 맛있는 아침 식사가 패키지에 포함되어 있다고 했다. 또한, 두 번째 문단의 12월 19일부터 23일까지의 특별 행사에는 5성급 레스토랑에서 무료 조식 뷔페 이용권을 즐기기 바란다고 했다. 그러므로 두 특별 할인 모두 무료 아침 식사가 포함되어 있다는 것을 알 수 있다. 따라서 정답은 (C)이다.

31

스튜어트 씨는 호텔 투숙 기간 동안 무엇을 받을 자격이 있었는가?
(A) 무료 1박 숙박
(B) 호텔 멤버십 자격
(C) 호텔 숙박료 30% 할인
(D) 시상식 티켓

어휘 **accommodations** 숙소, 숙박 시설   **qualification** 자격
award ceremony 시상식

해설 영수증에서 스튜어트 씨의 체크인 날짜와 체크아웃 날짜가 각각 12월 20일과 12월 22일이라는 것을 확인할 수 있다. 그런데, 웹페이지의 12월 19일부터 23일까지의 할인 행사 정보에 따르면, 다큐멘터리 영화 협회 시상식에 참석하는 투숙객에게는 숙박료 30% 할인 혜택과 5성급 레스토랑의 무료 조식 뷔페 이용권이 제공된다. 영수증의 'Total $210 (Adjusted: Discount Applied)'에서, 총 금액 210달러는 할인이 적용된 조정된 금액임을 알 수 있으므로, 그가 호텔 숙박료의 30%를 할인 받았다는 것을 알 수 있다. 따라서 정답은 (C)이다.

32

스튜어트 씨에 대해 암시된 것은?
(A) 그는 선셋 헤이븐 호텔 단골 회원이다.
(B) 그는 객실 요금을 현금으로 지불했다.
(C) 그는 가족과 함께 호텔에 머물렀다.
(D) 그는 행사에 참석한다는 증거를 보여주었다.

어휘 **proof** 증거, 증명서   **attendance** 출석, 참석

해설 위 31번 문제의 해설에서 설명된 바와 같이, 스튜어트 씨는 다큐멘터리 영화 시상식에 참여하여 30%의 숙박료 할인을 받았다. 그런데, 웹페이지 세 번째 문단에 이와 같은 할인을 받으려면 체크인 시에 DFA 행사 티켓을 프런트에 제시해야 한다는 내용이 있다. 따라서 정답은 (D)이다.

참 토익
COMPLETE
800+
LC+RC

빠르게 점수를 올려주는 효율적인 **토익 실전서!**

- LC와 RC 각각 12회분의 미니 테스트를 풀어 보면서 단기간에 실전에 대비할 수 있습니다.

- 파트별 문제 풀이법과 토익에 꼭 필요한 문법 사항들이 꼼꼼하게 정리되어 있어, 토익의 실력을 다질 수 있습니다.

- 파트별 빈출 어휘들이 수록되어 있어, 중요 표현 및 필수 어휘를 정리할 수 있습니다.

- 교재에 수록된 QR 코드를 스캔하여 음원을 바로 들을 수 있습니다.